MISSISSIPPIAN

SHATTER ZONE

Mapping the Mississippian Shatter Zone

The Colonial Indian Slave Trade and
Regional Instability in the American South

Edited by Robbie Ethridge and Sheri M. Shuck-Hall

UNIVERSITY OF NEBRASKA PRESS | LINCOLN & LONDON

Library of Congress Cataloging-in-Publication Data
Mapping the Mississippian shatter zone : the colonial
Indian slave trade and regional instability in the
American South / edited by Robbie Ethridge and
Sheri M. Shuck-Hall.
p. cm.
Includes bibliographical references and index.
ISBN 978-0-8032-1759-1 (paper : alk. paper)
1. Mississippian culture – Southern States. 2. Indian
slaves – Southern States – History. 3. Slave trade –
Southern States – History. 4. Regionalism – Southern
States – History. 5. Social change – Southern States
– History. 6. Europeans – Southern States – History.
7. Colonists – Southern States – History. 8. North
America – Colonization. 9. North America – Ethnic
relations. I. Ethridge, Robbie Franklyn, 1955– II.
Shuck-Hall, Sheri Marie, 1972–
E99.M6815M36 2009   976.2 – dc22

Set in Minion Pro by Kim Essman.
Designed by Nathan Putens.

Contents

Illustrations

Acknowledgments

We would like to thank all of the contributors to this volume for the work and thought that went into their chapters and for their considered engagement with the shatter zone concept in relation to their own areas of expertise. We would also like to thank all of the original participants in the two symposia from which these papers were drawn as well as all of the attendees who contributed much to conversation and discussion during and afterward. We are especially grateful to the discussants at these symposia, Charles Hudson, Daniel Usner, Alan Gallay, and Helen Tanner for their comments, critiques, and suggestions on the papers.

Others have also taken an interest in this volume and the conceptual groundwork we are attempting to lay with it. We would like to thank Jay Johnson, James Brooks, Claudio Saunt, Joel Martin, Jason Jackson, Joshua Piker, Brett Rushforth, Ned Blackhawk, Max Carocci, Stephanie Pratt, Shepard Krech, Ray Fogelson, Robin Fable, John Cottier, Dave Moore, Chris Rodning, Greg Waselkov, Greg O'Brien, Christina Snyder, Steven Pincus, Paige West, J. C. Saylor, and Gary Dunham. We also extend thanks to the two readers of the volume, Marvin Smith and Jamey Carson, for critiquing such a long volume and especially for their careful readings and for the generous spirit in which their comments were given. Charles Hudson also read a draft and offered his insights and comments, and we are especially grateful to him. We would also like to thank Jeff Jackson, Ned Blackhawk, Alice Kehoe, and David Anderson for reading and commenting on a draft of the introduction. We also acknowledge and thank Pat Galloway for the language of "mapping" in the title.

As with any long-term project such as this, family and friends have been the foundation on which we stand. We would like to extend our grateful appreciation for all of their support to Denton Marcotte, Tom Hall, Nonie and Rusty Dunn, Ryan Duncan, Kirsten Dellinger, Jeff Jackson, Minjoo Oh, and Laurie Cozad.

Abbreviations

AC   Archives des Colonies
AGI   Archivo General de las Indias
AGN   Archivo General de la Nación México
AM   Archives de la Marine
ASH   Archives du Service Hydrographique
BNF   Bibliothèque National de France
CAH   Center for American History
CJC   Collège des Jésuites de Clermont
HL   Hargrett Library
HNO   Historic New Orleans Collection
LC   Library of Congress
NAUK   National Archives of the United Kingdom
PKY   P. K. Yonge Library of Florida History
SCDAH   South Carolina Department of Archives and History
SI   Smithsonian Institution
SPG   Society for the Propagation of the Gospel

1 | *Introduction*

MAPPING THE MISSISSIPPIAN SHATTER ZONE

ROBBIE ETHRIDGE

Two hundred years after Europeans invaded what is now the American South, the Mississippian world of the Native peoples was in collapse. This collapse was not sudden. It took almost two centuries to run its course. This collapse was not caused by a mere exercise of European military might; indeed, Natives participated in and in some cases precipitated it. Nor did the collapse extinguish Native peoples. Although thousands of Indians died and were enslaved and although virtually all Native polities were destroyed, there were survivors who regrouped and reformed new kinds of polities, and they reorganized and restructured their lives for living in the new geopolitical landscape that was securely in place by 1730. The goal of this book is to begin to reconstruct and explain the collapse of the Mississippian world and the transformation of Southern Native societies that occurred between roughly 1540 and 1730.

Scholars have identified some of the forces that caused this collapse and transformation: military losses at the hands of early explorers and destabilization of Native chiefdoms; the introduction of Old World diseases; and political and economic incorporation into the Atlantic World economic circuit, a subsection of the modern world-system and world economy.[1] However, scholars have not integrated all of these phenomena into a coherent account. Further, they have not identified the full sweep of internal and external forces at work, fully evaluated the reorganization of Native societies that followed, or securely connected this reorganization to widespread colonial disturbances.

The disturbances in the early South between 1540 and 1730 have not been difficult to identify. The archeological and documentary evidence attests to the disappearance of Native polities, movements of people into tightly compacted and heavily fortified towns, a dramatic loss of life, multiple migrations and splintering of groups, the coalescence of some groups, the disappearance of many, and an overall decline in artistic life. Additionally, scholars are beginning to understand that the collapse and transformation of Southern Native societies were not uniform across space and time. If we are to comprehensively understand the full transformation of the Mississippian world, we need an interpretive framework against which each instance of collapse and reformation can be placed.[2]

This volume offers such a framework, one that has come to be known as the "Mississippian shatter zone."[3] The Mississippian shatter zone, as I have defined it elsewhere, was a large region of instability in eastern North America that existed from the late sixteenth through the early eighteenth centuries and was created by the combined conditions of the structural instability of the Mississippian world and the inability of Native polities to withstand the full force of colonialism; the introduction of Old World pathogens and the subsequent serial disease episodes and loss of life; the inauguration of a nascent capitalist economic system by Europeans through a commercial trade in animal skins and especially in Indian slaves, whom other Indians procured and sold to European buyers; and the intensification and spread of violence and warfare through the Indian slave trade and particularly through the emergence of militaristic Native slaving societies who held control of the European trade.[4] The Mississippian shatter zone is intended as a kind of big picture framework for conceptualizing and explaining the destabilization and reformation of Southern Native societies by offering a regional framework for integrating events and people from the Mississippi Valley to those in the Atlantic region into a single interactive world.

The goal of this volume is to begin mapping the Mississippian shatter zone spatially, temporally, and conceptually. With contributions from anthropologists, historians, and archaeologists, this book begins to define the scope of the historical forces at work, to map out the range of regional connections and regional instability, to identify Native societies caught up in the shatter zone, and to outline the collapse of the Mississippian world and also the new social landscape that emerged out of it. The contributors to this volume frame their chapters around the shatter zone framework, if applicable, and use it as an initial explanatory tool for understanding the late sixteenth-, seventeenth-, and early eighteenth-century South. The authors are mindful of not exceeding the model's explanatory reach and of not allowing the concept to drive their arguments. In their chapters each author uses the shatter zone as a beginning point from which to formulate her or his own analyses and conclusions, thus refining the framework. In some cases authors use the framework as a counterpoint to their own arguments, opening new questions and directions for testing it and its applications.

By necessity some peoples and places in the South have been omitted from this volume, but this omission is not to say that these peoples or places were absent from the shatter zone or unaffected by it. The reader will find many Indian societies not examined here such as the Chickasaws, the Cherokees, and the Yuchis, among others. European colonists, undoubtedly affected by living in the shatter zone, are not represented here except for a handful of Virginia and Carolina traders who were instrumental in forging trade relations with specific Native groups. Africans caught in the shatter zone, likewise, are not dealt with here. There are also gaps in the temporal coverage, especially the period from 1600 to 1650, yet those are the very decades of intensive interior slaving campaigns by the Iroquois, Occaneechis, and perhaps others. Large geographic gaps also exist; present-day Tennessee is only marginally covered, as is western Arkansas, most of Louisiana, and eastern Texas. Despite these gaps, the differing points of view, and the diverse disciplinary backgrounds of the authors, the chapters herein are both coherent and integrated, and a nascent narrative begins to emerge from them. It is the story of the earliest sustained contact between the Old and New Worlds as it unfolded in the American South and of its consequences for the Southern Indians.

The Mississippian World

"Mississippian" is the name archaeologists use to designate the time period between roughly 900 CE and 1700 CE, during which Southern peoples were organized into a particular kind of political organization termed the "chiefdom."[5] The chiefdom is a political order with basically two ranks:

ruling elite lineages and nonelite lineages. It was during the Mississippian Period that people of the chiefdoms built the flat-topped, pyramidal
earthen temple mounds that one finds throughout the South.[6]

The members of the chiefly lineage were believed to be related to
supernatural beings, which gave them religious sanction for their status, prestige, and political authority. The political and religious center of
a chiefdom was a relatively large town with an earthen temple mound
fronted by a large plaza and often surrounded by other mounds. Neighborhoods of the common people typically surrounded the town center.
The *mico* (or chief) lived atop the temple mound and lesser people of
the chiefly lineage resided on the lesser mounds.[7] Archaeologists are
uncertain as to the extent and nature of a *mico*'s authority and power.
They generally agree that the chiefly elite constituted a centralized political body and that those members held permanent offices of high rank
and authority, with the *mico* holding the highest office. The *mico* had the
authority to settle disputes, punish wrongdoers, make judgments, and
command tribute, usually in the form of surplus production and labor. But
it appears that an elite's consolidation of power varied from one chiefdom
to another. In some cases the *mico* held coercive if not autocratic power
and consulted only with leaders from the elite lineage, but in other cases
the *mico* exerted influence and authority but not real power, and he or
she deliberated with local town councils as well as with the elite lineage
when making decisions.[8]

Commoners lived in neighborhoods situated around the mounds and
public plaza and also in farming villages strung up and down a river valley
that constituted the heart of the chiefdom's territory. These farming villages provided the foundation of the Mississippian economy, which was
based on intensive corn agriculture. The common folks farmed, fished,
hunted, and gathered wild plant stuffs for food and other materials necessary for daily life.

A chiefdom was largely self-sufficient economically in that the population could feed, house, cloth, and defend themselves using resources
available within their boundaries. The exceptions to this were salt and
hoes made out of particularly good stone. These items were necessary
to daily life, and they were found in only a few places and then traded

throughout the South. Prestige goods made out of hard-to-get materials such as shell and fine stone likewise circulated widely. Thus the chiefly elite or their sponsored traders maintained a far-flung trade in exotic goods and materials that constituted the emblems of power, prestige, and religious authority. Although the circulation of salt, hoes, and prestige goods were a vital part of the Mississippian world, it is unlikely that their exchanges served to integrate the Mississippian chiefdoms into a single economy.[9]

Within the chiefdom the economy was one of household or community-level self-sufficiency in that people made their living from farming, fishing, hunting, gathering of wild plant foods, and using local resources such as wood, cane, and other raw goods for buildings and clothing. And although these communities were oftentimes engaged in trade, they were not dependent on it. In the more autocratic polities the chiefly elites were exempt from mundane activities such as farming, and they received tribute from the citizens in the form of surplus foodstuffs, animal skins, stone, and other raw and finished materials. In the less-centralized chiefdoms elites engaged in subsistence activities such as farming and hunting, but they still received tribute from the non-elites. In both cases the *micos* used tribute goods for themselves and their families as well as to mediate arguments, garner allies, give succor to villages who found themselves low on resources, and otherwise maintain control and order over the towns and villages in the chiefdom.[10]

Archaeologists divide the Mississippian Period into the Early Mississippian (900 CE–1200 CE), the Middle Mississippian (1200 CE–1500 CE), and the Late Mississippian (1500 CE–1700 CE). The largest of all Mississippian mound complexes, Cahokia, was occupied during the Early Mississippian. At its height around 1050–1200 CE, Cahokia was a sprawling center covering six square miles, with a population of around twenty thousand and over a hundred mounds of various sizes. Cahokia dominated the Early Mississippian landscape, and by the Middle Mississippian era the Mississippian way of life was firmly in place across most of the South.[11] The most famous Middle Mississippian sites are Moundville and Etowah, in western Alabama and northwestern Georgia, respectively, but there are also impressive Middle Mississippian mound complexes throughout the central Mississippi River Valley, the lower Ohio River Valley, and most of the mid-South area, including western and central Kentucky, western Tennessee, and northern Alabama and Mississippi. This region appears to have been the core of the classic Mississippian culture area, although other chiefdoms of various sizes existed on the margins.[12]

The ritual and political gear of the Mississippian people constitutes some of the most important prehistoric works of art from North America. Part-time craftspeople used an assortment of stone, clay, mica, copper, shell, feathers, and fabric to fashion an amazing array of functional and ceremonial items such as headdresses, beads, cups, masks, statues, cave art, ceramic wares, ceremonial weaponry, necklaces and earrings, and figurines. Many of these ritual items are decorated with a specific repertoire of motifs such as the hand-and-eye motif, the falcon warrior, bi-lobed arrows, severed heads, spiders, rattlesnakes, and mythical beings.[13] War iconography, in particular, is prevalent on much Mississippian artwork, indicating that warfare was important and "touched all aspects of daily life."[14] The palisaded towns that typically lay on a chiefdom's borders and the large buffer zones, or uninhabited regions between chiefdoms, indicate that warfare was not just important but probably endemic.

Chiefdoms were not uniformly alike across space and time. Archaeologists understand the classic Mississippian chiefdoms such as Cahokia and Moundville to have been quite large, complex chiefdoms. A "complex chiefdom" is a political designation for chiefdoms in which one large chiefdom exercised some sort of control or influence over smaller chiefdoms within a defined area. Archaeologists call the smaller chiefdoms, "simple chiefdoms," in that they were polities in which the elite only controlled the towns connected to that chiefdom. Simple chiefdoms were clusters of about four to seven towns, with one or two of these having a mound and serving as the center of the chiefdom. These towns were small, with an average population of 350 to 650 people, and simple chiefdoms, as a whole, had an average population between 2,800 to 5,400 people. The average diameter of a simple chiefdom was about 20 km (12.43 mi), while the average distance between simple chiefdoms was 30 km (18.64 mi).[15]

In the Late Mississippian complex and simple chiefdoms existed side by side, and in a few cases single and especially charismatic leaders forged an alliance of several complex and simple chiefdoms into "paramount chiefdoms." Archaeologists are not in agreement as to the specific organizational mechanisms that held a paramount chiefdom together. Whereas one can think of a simple chiefdom as a "hands-on, workaday administrative unit under the aegis of a particular chief, the paramount chiefdom may have been little more than a kind of non-aggression pact, and the power of a paramount chief may have been little more than that of first among equals." Charles Hudson understands paramount chiefdoms to have been political entities that could have ranged from strongly to weakly integrated and paramount chiefs as possessing power *or* influence. The concept of the paramount chiefdom then implies a less centralized administration than larger statelike organizations but possessing a larger area of geographic influence than that of simple chiefdoms, sometimes spanning several hundred miles.[16]

Archaeological evidence indicates the occurrence of a pattern of cycling in complex and simple chiefdoms — a seeming endemic rise and fall of chiefdoms through time. For example, in the Savannah River area in present-day Georgia and South Carolina, there were a number of chiefdoms that rose and fell between 1100 and 1450 CE, after which the area was abandoned until around 1660 CE. How and why Mississippian chiefdoms rose and fell is still poorly understood. Certain stresses such as soil exhaustion, drought, depletion of core resources, military defeats, and contested claims to the chieftainship may constitute proximate causes for collapse. However, archaeologists generally agree that within the structure of a chiefdom, there also were structural instabilities, most likely those associated with chiefly power and authority.[17] Chiefdoms then apparently could not withstand serious and prolonged stresses (either external or internal).

When a chiefdom fell, other chiefdoms around it did not necessarily fall. Archaeologists are beginning to understand that despite the cycling of chiefdoms, there was an overall regional stability to the Mississippian world. As David J. Hally demonstrates for present-day north Georgia, the chiefdoms in this area were integrated into a regional system of "interaction, interdependence, and the movement of energy, material, and information among polities." When a chiefdom fell, there was a regional adjustment as people joined other existing chiefdoms, and new areas opened for the settlement and development of new chiefdoms. Ecological parameters also shifted to accommodate the new settlement layout. Hally proposes that the interplay between cycling chiefdoms and the interactions between extant chiefdoms sponsored a sustained regional stability.[18]

When Europeans came into the American South, they penetrated the Mississippian world. In the late fifteenth and early sixteenth centuries, European sailors explored portions of the Atlantic coastline, but European colonization of North America did not begin until the early 1500s. Spanish conquistadors such as Juan Ponce de Leon and Lucas Vazquez de Ayllón made contact with Native Southerners, and their expeditions — although ending in failure — provided invaluable information for Hernando de Soto, who launched his expedition in 1539. Landing in present-day Tampa, Florida, and moving north, Soto's expedition explored the Southern heartland but failed in its objective of establishing a colony in North America. The records from the expedition are the first written records describing the interior South, and over the past few decades scholars have combined the records from the Soto and the later Tristán de Luna and Juan Pardo expeditions with archaeology to reconstruct the lay of the land in the Native South at the time of contact.[19]

At the time of European contact there were dozens of chiefdoms in the South, many of which Soto and his army encountered.[20] As mentioned earlier, simple and complex chiefdoms existed side by side, and in at least one case in northwest Georgia, Soto encountered a powerful chief named Coosa who had built an alliance of several chiefdoms into a paramount chiefdom that spanned from present-day east Tennessee into northern Georgia and eastern Alabama.[21] When Soto and his army of six hundred plus men trekked through the Southern interior, they depended on the food stores of the Native people. They also came as a conquering army, and in the cases of those chiefdoms that saw intense action, the direct military assault of the Spanish may have precipitated their collapse. This was probably the case at the chiefdoms of Napituca in northern Florida, Chicaza in Mississippi, Anlico in Arkansas, and most particularly Tascalusa in Alabama where the Indians took heavy losses in the battle of Mabila on October 18, 1540.[22]

It is also likely that Soto's presence upset the balance of power in some complex and paramount chiefdoms. Records from the expedition describe several instances in which *micos* of simple chiefdoms challenged and defied the authority of a chief under whose power they had fallen. In these political struggles the more powerful *mico* often enlisted Soto's influence and military aid to prevail against the rebellion. In some cases a savvy lesser *mico* used Soto to bolster his authority in challenging the overarching *mico*. In either case, given the fragile nature of the ties binding complex and paramount chiefdoms, the presence of a new and powerful ally could have easily upset the balance of power resulting in a reshuffling of authority among these chiefdoms. This may have been the case at Cofitachequi in South Carolina, Coosa in north Georgia, and Guachoya in Arkansas.[23]

Such political ups and downs were not unusual in the Mississippian world, and with each rise and fall of a chiefdom, there were regional readjustments. But the Soto expedition cut a swath through the entire Mississippian world, destabilizing many chiefdoms and thus making regional readjustments and recovery difficult. As several chapters in this volume show, the Mississippian world was in the process of recovery from the Soto expedition when it was assaulted again by the introduction of Old World diseases and Indian slave raiders. Chiefdoms then began to collapse in quick succession, interrupting the processes that regulated regional stability. The Mississippian world could neither withstand nor recover from the regionwide and unprecedented succession of chiefdom failures, attacks, epidemics, and economic upheavals in the first one hundred and ninety years of contact.

Because the fall of the Mississippian world is at the core of the shatter zone, the history of its collapse sets the chronological parameters of this volume from 1540 to 1730. Some chiefdoms such as Apalachee, Natchez, and Caddo functioned into the eighteenth century, although as we will see, how closely these chiefdoms resembled Mississippian chiefdoms is in question. Others, such as the paramount chiefdom of Coosa, fell by 1600. Such a broad temporal parameter is necessary to cover the complete collapse of the Mississippian world and the full reorganization of the geopolitical landscape that followed. The shatter zone then is defined here by the chronological and spatial parameters of the Mississippian world, distinguishing it as a particular historical case.[24]

When Hernando de Soto entered the South, he passed through a heterogeneous world composed of dozens of polities, albeit with many cultural, social, and economic traits in common. Although his army came to conquer, subdue, and take, Soto saw this world at work. He and his army passed through large and small polities and engaged with powerful *micos* and not-so-powerful *micos*, both of whom alternately accommodated, defied, or used Soto to their own ends. The relations between chiefdoms were oftentimes hostile, but Soto saw on more than one occasion the military and political power a *mico* could gather when he or she united two or more chiefdoms. Although each chiefdom had its own history and its own cast of actors, great and small, none existed in isolation. The chiefdoms in a region were tied together in myriad ways — ecologically, politically, socially, economically, and religiously. Although the exact nature of these ties has yet to be fully explained, they undoubtedly served to integrate these ancient chiefdoms of the South into a single world.

The Demography of Diseases and Slaving

In addition to the instabilities created by the Spanish *entrada*, disease and slaving were two other principal forces that created the Mississippian shatter zone. Thus as we begin to map the shatter zone, the question of the impact of introduced diseases arises. Most scholars of Southern Indians agree that the introduction of Old World diseases into virgin soil populations of North America resulted in a demographic collapse on the order of ninety percent. However, there is still considerable debate on the timing of this collapse, the diseases that were introduced and their specific pathologies, and for the South the consequences for the Mississippian chiefdoms. Paul Kelton argues in this volume and elsewhere that the first widespread episode of Old World disease in the South occurred in 1696 in what he has dubbed the Great Southeastern Smallpox Epidemic. Kelton's first pandemic, not coincidentally, correlates with the first ample written documentation for disease in the interior South, but what about the century and a half before 1696, before good written evidence?[25]

There is only scant documentary evidence that disease had traveled into the interior South during the sixteenth or seventeenth centuries, but this lack of evidence may simply be a function of the paucity of documentary records for this time. To assess the impact of disease during the late sixteenth and early seventeenth century, scholars have to rely on archaeological evidence. Direct archaeological evidence for Old World diseases must come from burial remains, but diseases such as measles and smallpox typically do not leave skeletal traces.

Archaeologists mostly depend on indirect evidence for disease, particularly settlement pattern data that would indicate some demographic shift and depopulation, aberrant mortuary patterns such as mass graves, and evidence for poor health in general among a population. In the first attempts to reconstruct the population decline in the South, archaeologists used settlement pattern data to document both abandonment of towns and movement of people as well as amalgamations of dispersed populations into larger towns. Despite the lack of direct evidence, they posited disease as being responsible for these changing settlement patterns after contact.[26] Archaeologists Ann Ramenofsky, working in the lower Mississippi Valley; Marvin Smith, working in northwest Georgia and Alabama; and Timothy Perttula, working in western Louisiana and eastern Texas, proposed independently that disease was introduced into the South in the sixteenth century and that a demographic collapse that resulted in the fall of the Mississippian chiefdoms occurred well before sustained European colonization.[27]

These scholars represent one side of a debate that occurred in the 1990s about the effects of disease and the scope of Native population decline. On the other side of the debate, scholars questioned the archaeological and documentary evidence for demographic collapse as well as whether or not such a collapse could have occurred so quickly and before sustained European contact.[28] Both sides acknowledged that a demographic collapse occurred, but their main point of disagreement was over the timing. There was also general agreement that disease was but one factor in the collapse, and all pointed to contributing factors such as slaving, internecine warfare, dropping fertility rates, violent colonial strategies such as genocide, and general cultural and social malaise from colonial oppression.[29]

Today, scholars agree that examining the dramatic loss of Native life after European contact calls for a multicausal model. However, that model has yet to be adequately developed, and most scholars still use catastrophic demographic collapse resulting from Old World disease to explain the demise of the Mississippian world.[30] The Mississippian shatter zone framework aids in building such a multicausal model because it insists that one must examine forces other than disease — in particular the commercial trade in Indian slaves — and it argues that one must also consider the interplay between trade, disease, warfare, and slavery.[31]

The Mississippian shatter zone framework can be used to reinterpret some of the early demographic work on the South. For example, Perttula and Ramenofsky document the complete depopulation of the Red River and lower Mississippi valleys, respectively, and they argue for a sixteenth-century collapse. In both cases, however, their sixteenth centuries run long — roughly from 1565 to 1680. Given these chronological parameters, the effects of slaving could be plugged easily into their studies and used to reinterpret some of their data and conclusions. And as we will see in this volume, recent archaeological and ethnohistorical evidence is beginning to suggest that these regions were not depopulated solely because of death resulting from disease but also because of emigration as people fled areas affected by slave raids, war, and political collapse.

Marvin Smith's work on the late Mississippian paramount chiefdom of Coosa has much finer chronological control than those of Perttula and Ramenofsky because of his use of the archaeological recovery of European artifacts that can be used as time markers. Pairing settlement pattern data with his chronological parameters, Smith tracks the changes in Coosa through which Soto passed in the 1540s. Sixty years later, by 1600, the people of Coosa had quit building mounds, moved away from their mound centers, and began a migration south into present-day Alabama where they eventually coalesced with the Creek Confederacy. Smith proposes that the Coosa example was typical of Southern chiefdoms in its fall within a few decades after European contact. Although he suggests that other factors may have been involved, he posits demographic collapse due to disease as the prime mover.[32]

I would argue, however, that the decline of Coosa does not necessarily typify the history of other Southern chiefdoms. Rather, the fall of Coosa was a particular historic event that undoubtedly had regionwide repercussions, but it did not signal the collapse of the Mississippian world. Perhaps what Smith's data reveal for the first decades after Soto is the collapse of the paramount chiefdom of Coosa, but not because of catastrophic population loss due to disease. Coosa as a paramount chiefdom would have been one of the most unstable political structures in the Mississippian world and it could have fallen for any number of reasons, including the instability brought on by Soto's march through the entire province.[33]

In other areas new evidence suggests that disease did not necessarily entail demographic collapse or the fall of Mississippian chiefdoms. The Indians of Spanish Florida, more than any other Southern group, had the most prolonged and direct contact with Europeans from about 1550 to 1700. Although there is much documentary evidence for epidemic disease episodes in Spanish Florida, there is no evidence for a catastrophic loss of life across the region. In fact, recent investigations show epidemics to have been localized occurrences, albeit with high mortality rates.[34] There also was no sweeping cultural upheaval between 1550 and 1700 in La Florida. The chiefdoms continued to function into the eighteenth century and adjusted to the presence of the Spanish in various ways. As we will see in this volume, the Guale, Apalachee, and Timucuan chiefdoms fell not because of disease or because of the Spanish presence but because of the late seventeenth-and early eighteenth-century slaving campaigns of the Yamasees, Creeks, Alabamas, and others.

The demographic effects of slaving and disease were undoubtedly complex and profound. The evidence is extremely sketchy, but the demographic profile of the slave trade bears scrutinizing in this regard. We have only a few accounts from the South about commercial slaving expeditions, but they give us an outline of how these expeditions worked. During the colonial era commercial slaving was conducted as a part of warfare; therefore slave raids resembled warfare and were conducted by male warriors. In some cases small groups of about a dozen men would conceal themselves in the woods around vulnerable towns and snatch people as opportunity allowed. Another tactic was a full-scale surprise raid on a town by a group of warriors. In the attack the warriors of the town would marshal a defense. If the raiders managed to break the town's defense, they besieged the town, taking captives and killing any who could not escape. The records indicate that those captured were mostly women and children. The elderly and the very young were killed in the melee. There were also associated high death tolls of adult men on both sides.[35]

After the raid captives not designated for adoption or exchange by their Indian slavers were kept in holding pens before being taken to the European port towns. The infrastructure in the South at this time consisted mostly of overland trails, so all captives had to be capable of walking very long distances. This could help account for the killing of the very young and the very old — neither could make the journey and neither would fetch a good price in the slave markets. Once in the port towns, slaves were shipped to the West Indies and South America to work on the plantations and in the mines, as well as to New England, French Canada, and French Louisiana where they were used as domestic servants, concubines, urban laborers, and small-scale agricultural laborers. Some undoubtedly were sold to planters and others in Jamestown and Charleston.[36]

We do not have a good reckoning of the number of Southern Native peoples who were enslaved. The few known accounts of slave raids describe hundreds of women and children taken at a time in a raiding expedition. In the famous slave raids of Spanish Florida of 1704–7, Native slavers captured an estimated ten thousand to twelve thousand women and children.[37]

Alan Gallay recently calculated that between 1685 and 1715, the English enslaved twenty-four thousand to fifty-one thousand Indians, although he thinks these numbers are low.[38] The Canadians, English in New England, and Louisiana French were also engaged in the slave trade, but the number of Southern Indians taken by these traders remains untabulated.[39] The exact number of Indians living in the South in 1685 is not firmly known, but Peter Wood estimates there were around 199,400 people at that time. Thirty years later, in 1715, the population dropped to 90,100, a fifty-four percent loss of population.[40] Combining Wood's and Gallay's figures, slaving could account for as many as half of this population loss during these thirty years. Disease and deaths in warfare most likely account for most of the other half.

Taking Gallay's higher figure of fifty-one thousand and breaking it down over thirty years, on average about seventeen hundred Indians a year were taken by English-sponsored slave raiders. This number may seem low, but considering that the population of a simple chiefdom was around two to five thousand, slave raiders, taking only children and women and killing the rest or forcing them to flee, could decimate a simple chiefdom by netting only two hundred to five hundred captives to sell as slaves. Even though some captives were kept within Indian societies through adoption, marriage, exchange, or indigenous slavery, these additions to a group could not stem the steep losses from both disease and the selling of slaves. It follows that population recovery would have been almost impossible, not only because the young were killed or enslaved but also because fertility rates undoubtedly bottomed out with the loss of so many women of childbearing age.[41] In other words, the number of people enslaved, as calculated here and elsewhere in this volume, indicates that slaving was more than sufficient to stress a simple chiefdom beyond its breaking point, especially if one combines slaving with population losses from disease episodes.

Paul Kelton in his chapter for this volume presents a provocative case study of the spread of disease during the slave trade era. He shows that once the Mississippian shatter zone had widened to include the interior groups after about 1690, disease moved swiftly throughout the region following the trade paths that Indian slavers used. Kelton's argument that depopulation from disease and slaving was the root cause of the Yamasee War, a theme echoed in John Worth's treatment of La Florida, strips bare the banal practicalities of capitalism and the supply and demand mechanism of the market. With the indigenous peoples of the South either enslaved or killed by disease and with the survivors living close to or among Europeans or grouped into formidable coalescent societies such as the Creeks, Cherokees, Chickasaws, and Choctaws, the supply of Indian slaves dwindled and the trade in Indian slaves faltered. Three final conflagrations — the Tuscarora War of 1712, the Yamasee War of 1715 and, as George Milne convincingly argues in this volume, the Natchez Revolt of 1729 — signal not only the end of the slave trade era but also the collapse of the last chiefdom that retained resemblance to its Mississippian roots.

Certainly disease epidemics and cultural exchanges with Europeans had profound effects on Native life during this time. But these epidemics and exchanges in and of themselves were not transforming. Not until Native peoples became engaged in the world economy through contact with the English, French, and Dutch did they revamp their social, political, and economic orders to adapt to this system. Economic incorporation into the world capitalist economic system through the trade in furs and Indian slaves was one of the fundamental causes for the collapse and transformation of the Mississippian world and for the shape of the new geopolitical landscape that emerged.[42]

Because capitalist incorporation is fundamental to the Mississippian shatter zone, some definitions are in order. I use the term "capitalism" as delineated by Immanuel Wallerstein in his modern world-systems paradigm. Wallerstein understands capitalism to be a world economic system that emerged in the sixteenth and seventeenth centuries with the failure of European feudalism and the massive importation of raw goods and precious metals that resulted from European profits from expansion into first Eurasia and Africa and then into the New World. As argued by Wallerstein, at the time of its emergence capitalism operated by fundamental principles that are still in play today — namely the large-scale extraction of raw materials, the production and distribution of commodities, the endless accumulation of capital, the supply-demand-pricing mechanism of the market, economies of scale, the appropriation of human labor in service to capitalist production, and means of production controlled by and profits accruing to a few.[43]

Wallerstein's main contribution is in reconstructing the history of capitalism and in envisaging it as an interconnected world economy. In conceptualizing this world economy, Wallerstein divides the world into core, periphery, and semiperiphery regions depending on what function a region plays in the larger system at a particular time. The core provides the center of banking, commerce, and manufacturing. A periphery is characterized by extractive economies and coercive labor practices and is under the political and economic control of the core. The semiperiphery has some independent access to banking, commerce, and manufacturing but in a limited way because the core has some control over this access. These partitions are also quite dynamic, changing throughout the last five centuries. A brief summary for our purposes is that Spain and Portugal were core areas during the late fifteenth and early to mid-sixteenth centuries, but their prominence in the global economy was eclipsed by the Netherlands in the late sixteenth century. However, Dutch interests lay in India and Asia rather than in the Atlantic, and by the time Dutch interests turned to North America in the early seventeenth century, they had to vie with England and France for economic hegemony.[44] As we will see, the Spanish presence in the American South during the seventeenth century occurred at the nadir of Spanish colonial power. Hence during the mid-seventeenth century France and England were in a contest for the Atlantic arena, with England finally emerging as the core area by the early eighteenth century. In the imperial contest over North America, the American South was a periphery.[45]

Among other things, world-systems theory has been criticized for being too reductionist in that Wallerstein proposes that the world economic system underlies much about global and local politics, social systems, and even some cultural traits. Others have criticized world-systems theory for overemphasizing the power and domination of the core and hence deemphasizing the agency of people in the periphery.[46] Since Wallerstein's first enunciation of world-systems theory in the 1970s and 1980s, many world-systems analysts have addressed these criticisms and refined the concept.[47] I use the contemporary version of world-systems theory as formulated from the decades of research since Wallerstein's *The Modern World-System* was first published, and like these scholars, I am duly cautious of being reductionist and deterministic.

I understand the world-system as but one of several long-term global structures that integrated with other long-term structural elements of Southern Native life. The task at hand then is to examine both Native and European social structures and their points of articulation in order to present a well-balanced picture of Indian life in the new global context that came about with contact. In other words, incorporation into the world-system was a transforming event in Native life, but the specifics of this incorporation played out in dialectical fashion with Native social orders, Native participation, Native people's perceptions of their options, and as Galloway demonstrates in this volume, Native economic categories.

The chronological parameters of capitalism follow those set by Wallerstein, namely that the system emerged in Europe and developed during the early years of European expansion in what Wallerstein dubs the long sixteenth century (1450–1620). The system has gone through its own historical changes from mercantile capital to industrial capital to post-industrial globalization, but through all of these forms it operated (and continues to operate) with the same fundamental principles of capitalism listed earlier. By using Wallerstein's history of capitalism, I place the Mississippian shatter zone outside of the debates in American colonial history about whether and when European colonies were precapitalist and capitalist.[48] According to world-systems theory, the Dutch, French, and English were involved in the world capitalist economy when they first anchored off the Atlantic coast in the early seventeenth century, at which time they also brought the first sustained ties to the world economy for Native peoples in eastern North America.[49]

Who were these Europeans and what sorts of ties to their homelands did they bring with them? This has been a central question to American colonial history almost from its inception. In the context of world-systems analysis, during the seventeenth century key European core countries (primarily the Netherlands and England in competition with declining Spain and Portugal) were knitting together a global economy by articulating economic circuits such as the Atlantic trade circuit with the Asian trade circuit. And although the American colonies were in the Atlantic circuit, they were still a subset of the larger global economy.[50] In this light the American colonies by the seventeenth century were strategic commercial outposts situated in a global periphery through which European core countries extracted labor and resources.

The North American overseas ventures then were largely one set of commercial endeavors among a host of many others that crisscrossed the globe. And the North American settlements served mostly as extractive trade factories, at least in the first hundred years or so. These settlements may have been small and overwhelmed by Indian populations, but they were one conduit through which the economic power of the core countries flowed. Hence one should not look on the American colonies and colonists themselves as wielding extraordinary transforming power over Native life, but rather it was the system in which they served that was so transformative. It was not Quebec, New Amsterdam, Jamestown, or Charles Town that created the shatter zone; it was the global commercial power of the Netherlands, England, and France as funneled through these settlements.[51]

Many of the European men and women who first came to eastern North America came as business people and they understood themselves to be embarking on commercial enterprises through which they hoped to gain wealth and prestige. Most of them had much prior experience working for European trade companies in other areas of the world, and they brought these experiences to North America. They accepted that this business was not for the faint of heart, and they knew that real dangers awaited them. Nor were they all novices in dealing with people different from themselves, and the most enterprising, such as John Smith of Virginia and the South Carolina slaver Henry Woodward, had experience in other cultures and good linguistic and negotiating skills. They also had some ideas about how to engage the locals in trade, especially through the sale of armaments, and they had a good sense for commodities, in this case animal skins and Indian slaves.[52]

These early venture capitalists were experienced, skilled, commercially savvy immigrants to North America who were instrumental in expanding and consolidating the nascent global economy. But like the Indians with whom they traded, these immigrants too lived in a periphery of the modern world-system, at least for a while. Like the Indians, they lived on the edge of this world-system, and hence were also subject to the structures of inequality, uneven development, and violence characteristic of peripheries. Although we will not treat much with Europeans living in the Mississippian shatter zone in this volume, it is safe to say that their lives and the options open to them were also shaped by it.

Incorporation of indigenous people into the modern world-system has almost always been a violent process. For the American South historians and anthropologists have acknowledged the turmoil in which Native peoples found themselves during the early years of colonialism, and Southern colonial historians have long discussed the various colonial Indian wars. Likewise, for at least a decade Southeastern archaeologists investigating this era have been piecing together a confusing array of movements and amalgamations of Native peoples after the collapse of the Mississippian chiefdoms.[53] Much of mainstream American colonial history couches this violence in terms of European struggles over land and sovereignty, and indigenous people are usually portrayed as minor participants, usually as allies in European military encounters. Intra-Indian conflicts receive little attention, and few notice the effects of colonialism on indigenous patterns of warfare.

Anthropologists likewise have underestimated the effects of colonialism on indigenous intra-Native conflict. They usually look for the causes of intra-Native conflicts in long-lived cultural attributes such as ancient animosities, status and prestige seeking, fierceness and bravery, or functionalist explanations such as competition over natural resources.[54] These works not only fail to associate violence with imperialism but also fail to associate colonial violence and other changes in indigenous life with the rise of the nation state and the incorporation of indigenous peoples into the world economy. In short, they fail to place indigenous people into the rough and tumble of history.

Eric Wolf in *Europe and the People without History* first showed us that once we understand that indigenous people, like Westerners, are products of history, then one can see that imperialism and the inauguration of capitalism has almost always been attended by political turmoil, cultural upheaval, dislocation, and social transformation of Native societies and that much of this resulted in or was the result of war and other kinds of colonial violence. More recently, historian Irene Silverblatt, in an investigation of the Spanish Inquisition in Peru, brings the violence of Western imperialism to center stage and argues that the very emergence of the modern nation state was underlain by violence and cruelty, much of it aimed at indigenous peoples. Ned Blackhawk in *Violence over the Land* makes the same point for North America when he states that "violence and American nationhood, in short, progressed hand in hand." Silver-blatt and Blackhawk castigate earlier scholars for obscuring this violence and thus casting the history of the modern world as a narrative of moral success.[55]

Still, we have neither securely connected the turmoil of seventeenth-century America and the reorganization of Native societies with the painful birth of the modern era in America, nor have we recognized — beyond particular instances — that this turmoil, as well as the system that generated it, was an interconnected force for change in Native life.[56] The framework of the Mississippian shatter zone links the inauguration of the modern world-system to deep, integrated, and widespread regional instability that began with first contact and continued into the early eighteenth century

Following Wolf, Silverblatt, and Blackhawk, I understand the Mississippian shatter zone, as the name implies, to take violence as attendant to imperialism and the birth of the early modern world. It also takes violence to be part and parcel of capitalist incorporation as theorized in *War in the Tribal Zone*, edited by Brian Ferguson and Neil Whitehead. Ferguson and Whitehead have begun to devise a theoretical framework for understanding the historical context of indigenous violence. They argue that one general result of state expansion and capitalist incorporation is the militarization of indigenous peoples through an increase, intensification, and transformation of indigenous warfare on the edges of empire, or the "tribal zone." Ferguson and Whitehead, however, do not understand indigenous people to be victims of expanding states. They insist that in addition to the colonizers' violence, indigenous people who lived and participated in the colonial world also contributed to and sometimes created colonial violence. They point out that this is especially true when indigenous people became involved in commercial slave trading.[57]

Slavery was not completely new to North American Indians at contact as most Native groups practiced an indigenous form of slavery in which war captives sometimes were put into bondage. Large-scale captive taking as occurred during the seventeenth and early eighteenth centuries was most likely not conducted during the Mississippian Period but came about with the colonial commercial slave trade. Hence the forms of indigenous bondage during the Historic Period that Europeans observed may not have existed in the Mississippian Period.[58] Archaeologists are only now beginning to piece together the full scope of precontact forms of bondage and the fates of war captives.[59] For now, they interpret the biological evidence for death and dying during the Mississippian Period as indicative that women and children were not spared in combat. In precontact warfare Mississippian warriors took human body parts as war trophies, and because male status was largely based on exploits in war, an attack usually resulted in "relatively indiscriminate slaughter" as warriors would kill or maim anyone in order to obtain a war trophy.[60] If any captives were taken, they were most likely young women. We are not certain about the fate of these captive women except to say that there is some archaeological evidence for them being unwilling immigrants to new locales and in some cases of the use of physical coercion against them.[61]

The best examples of physical coercion during the Mississippian are the famous retainer burials: when a chief died, men and women were often killed and buried with him or her. The most famous case of retainer burial is Mound 72 at Cahokia in which 272 people were interred. Of these, many were sacrificial burials interred with elites at various funeral episodes. In one stupendous elite burial at Mound 72, fifty-three young women (aged 15 to 30) and four men with their heads and hands cut off were sacrificed. At their deaths these women were undernourished and hence probably of a lower status than the elite. Bioarchaeologists also believe that most of these women were from populations outside of Cahokia proper, suggesting that they most likely were war captives.[62]

From the Historic Period we know a little more about war captives since Europeans sometimes recorded their observations of them. Examining the documentary record, archaeologist David Dye found that male captives were usually killed as in precontact times but that there was an increase in the taking of women and children during the late seventeenth and early eighteenth centuries. Dye argues that this change in the patterns of war occurred because women and children "became valued replacements for productive members of the polity who had died in epidemics or been taken as slaves."[63]

The fate of war captives during the Historic Period varied. Captors sometimes used them as forced labor with no social rights. Captors sometimes adopted captives into a kin group, used them in prisoner exchanges with their foes, married them, gave them as gifts of alliance, obtained ransoms for them, or used them to forge trade alignments.[64] Southern Indians also engaged in the buying and selling of Indian slaves on a commercial scale once Europeans introduced commercial slaving in the mid-seventeenth century.

Almon Wheeler Lauber as early as 1913 wrote extensively on the widespread buying and selling and use of Indian slaves by Europeans and Natives in the early colonial era in eastern North America. Yet with a few exceptions, scholars only gave the Indian enslavement and sale into slavery cursory attention until the past few years.[65] In 2002 two seminal works were published simultaneously — Alan Gallay's *The Indian Slave Trade* and James Brooks's *Captives and Cousins*. Both received numerous prestigious awards in history and are widely read today. It is not an exaggeration to say that the publication of these two books charted a new field of inquiry in American history and anthropology, and we are beginning to see the results of some of this work.

Both Gallay and Brooks document the intra-Indian violence and disruptions that accompanied the Indian slave trade as Europeans enlisted Indians to capture prisoners for later exchange and sale. Gallay examines how the English used the Indian slave trade to build their empire in the American South. He gives much attention to the effects of Native participation in slaving. Although he opens his book with a portrait of the Mississippian world, pointing out that it was transformed with the slave trade, generally his treatment of Native affairs is secondary in his inquiry.[66] Brooks, on the other hand, frames the colonial slave system of the American Southwest not so much as empire building but as creating new social landscapes through the exchange, adoption, genetic mixing, and flow of captives between and through various Native and Spanish communities that made up the region. He also gives much attention to intra-Indian affairs as well as Indian-European affairs. In both books the brutality of the slave trade is understood but not highlighted. Brooks, for example, downplays the dark side of the slave system he reconstructs, arguing that the slave system of the Southwest was based on ancient forms of indigenous captive taking that during the colonial era served to weave together a multifaceted world.[67]

The works generated since Brooks's and Gallay's publications also tend to downplay the brutality and violence of the colonial Indian slave trade and to emphasize the indigenous (usually presumed as precontact) aspects of captive taking such as adoption, exchange, alliance building, sexual unions, ritual killings, laborers, and the creation of connections across groups fostered by such practices.[68] As Ned Blackhawk states, "such tendency to minimize the violence of captivity and to naturalize its presence among precontact Indian populations ultimately serves to diminish the deforming effects of colonialism."[69] Furthermore, except in the case of Eric Bowne's *Westo Indians*, the new scholarship on Indian slaving also downplays the fact that Indians were preying on other Indians in order to acquire captives with whom they could purchase guns, ammunition, metal tools, and other items available through the European trade system.[70]

Of all the types of colonial commerce, the commercial trade in captive laborers requires a high level of force against other humans as a necessary accompaniment to trade.[71] In other words, whereas trading in furs or deerskins does not necessarily involve warfare, trading in slaves does because it requires force. Certainly warfare penetrated Mississippian life, so much so that war, not peace, may have been the accepted state of affairs. Once Europeans arrived, one can see that Native war efforts became entwined with market interests and international commerce.[72] As warfare became tied to commercial interests, the Mississippian chiefdoms' mechanisms for mitigating war and brokering peace broke down, meaning that as Indian commercial interests intensified, so did warfare and the militarization of those Native groups who sought to control the trade.[73]

The trade in Indian slaves then intensified warfare and folded precontact motivations for war such as revenge and retaliation into burgeoning commercial interests. The result in some cases was the emergence of what I have termed "militaristic slaving societies." These were Indian societies that gained control of the trade and "through their slave raiding, spread internecine warfare and created widespread dislocation, migration, amalgamation, and, in some cases, extinction of Native peoples."[74] Most of these militaristic slaving societies were short lived, existing for only about a hundred years — from 1620 to 1720. During this brief window of time, they were key agents in the creation and expansion of the Mississippian shatter zone through a relentless raiding of their Indian neighbors for slaves.

As we will see, not all militaristic slaving societies were the same, nor were all of their motives for slaving and warfare the same. In the case of the Iroquois, for example, their widespread slaving, although entwined with their trade interests, was to replace their dwindling population. The Westos, on the other hand, first took up slaving as a defense against Iroquois predations, but within a few decades they were nothing less than market predators, controlling the trade and conducting destructive raids throughout much of the South.

A few decades into the slave trade, some newly formed coalescent groups such as the Creeks were responding to a powerful dynamic by which the commercial trade in Indian slaves worked. In this dynamic Indian men incurred debts when they accepted guns, ammunition, metal tools, and other items from European traders. European traders in turn requested that the debt be paid in slaves and furs and skins. Armed with European-manufactured weapons, Indian groups raided rival groups for slaves. Members of the unarmed group would then have to acquire guns with which to defend themselves, and they in turn would become slave raiders. The result was a vicious cycle of slaving, trading, and weapons escalation. As we will see, the process snowballed creating several militaristic slaving societies throughout the South by 1700.[75]

As several chapters in this volume document, the Indian slave trade overlay some precontact patterns of Indian life. Warfare, for instance, although intensified, was nothing new to Southern Indians, and Indian men were well-trained warriors when the trade opened. Given the intra-chiefdom hostility evident in the Mississippian world, one can assume that people of a chiefdom had a ready supply of enemies that they could target in their raiding. Likewise, the long-distance travel and migrations that were attendant to the slave trade were not new phenomena: Mississippian people had been doing these things for centuries. However, the Mississippian shatter zone takes the Indian slave trade to be primarily a commercial venture with violence and internecine warfare as part and parcel of the slaving business. In other words, in the Mississippian shatter zone the commercial trade in Indian slaves was not a continuation and adaptation of preexisting captivity patterns; it was a new kind of slaving, requiring a new kind of occupation created on the edge of the modern world-system — that of organized militaristic slavers. The capture and sale of Indian slaves did not serve to weld a world together; rather, Indian slaving was one of the hammers that shattered the world in which they themselves existed.

A Preface to the Mississippian Shatter Zone

By the late seventeenth century England, France, Spain, and the Netherlands had established "beachheads of empire" along the Atlantic seaboard and into the Gulf of Mexico (table 1).[76] These four European colonizers struggled to establish empires in North America, and each employed different strategies to engage and incorporate Native allies into their imperial designs.

Table 1. A colonial time line for North America

DATE	EUROPEAN COLONY
1565	St. Augustine settled by Spanish and Spanish mission system established
1584	Roanoke settled by English, abandoned by 1587
1604	Acadia (Nova Scotia) settled by French
1607	Jamestown settled by English
1608	Quebec City settled by French
1620	Puritan Separatists land at Cape Cod
1624	New Amsterdam settled by Dutch
1670	Charleston settled by English
1702	Mobile settled by French

After a series of colonial failures in the South, such as that of Soto, Spanish officials settled on maintaining a small garrison on the Atlantic side of the peninsula of present-day Florida from where they could police the shipping lanes from New Spain and ward off English, Dutch, and

French pirates raiding in the seas and along the coast lines. This outpost was St. Augustine, and the fort and town housed a small number of military personnel and their families. Instead of conquest, the Spanish sought to colonize this part of North America through the mission system, a colonial strategy wherein Catholic missionaries worked to convert Native inhabitants to become Catholic, Spanish peasants. In addition, unlike other Europeans, the Spanish in the South prohibited large-scale trade with the Indians and they prohibited the sale of guns to Indians altogether.[77]

In present-day Florida and south Georgia, between 1565 and 1704, a handful of Jesuit and then Franciscan missionaries labored to convert thousands of Indians into Catholic peasants.[78] They established dozens of missions, proselytizing to the Guale and Mocama chiefdoms on the Georgia coast, the Apalachee chiefdom in northwest Florida, and thirty-five or so Timucuan-speaking simple chiefdoms spread across north Florida and south Georgia. The friars did not attempt to revamp all of Indian life; they focused mostly on those things that conflicted with Catholicism such as polygamy, religious beliefs, and anything they considered idolatrous behavior such as playing the ball games. They also sought to eventually pull them into the Spanish regime.

Because the mission strategy was devised for using Native inhabitants as colonists, the Spanish hoped to assimilate the Indians, not annihilate them. The friars and Spanish military officials worked through the chiefdom political order, which most likely accounts for why the chiefdoms in La Florida persisted into the eighteenth century. The friars' method was to first convert a *mico*, and then with his permission to establish a mission in the central town of the chiefdom. Here he would work to convert others. The friars, however, also worked through the *mico*'s authority to conscript Indian labor for growing corn, building facilities, operating ferries, maintaining the new roadways, and doing other work for the friars, Spanish military, and colonists in St. Augustine and elsewhere. In addition, the friars and Spanish personnel imported fruits, vegetables, cattle, horses, pigs, iron tools, and many other things typical of Spanish life in the New World, and Indian people soon incorporated some of these things into their lives as well. The Spanish also brought European diseases, and throughout the next two centuries, the Native populations of La Florida suffered repeated deadly disease episodes.[79] Thus Indian life in Spanish Florida became "a curious blend of old and new."[80] For instance, even though the chiefdom political orders survived, they most likely came to only vaguely resemble their Mississippian antecedents. During the Spanish years chiefdom leadership saw much interference from the friars and military officials who continually sought to place pro-Spanish *micos* in office. These machinations inevitably led to suspicions, power struggles within the elite lineages, and general political unrest throughout the chiefdoms. Furthermore, the Native population of La Florida began to drain away as early as 1590 and continued to fall throughout the next one hundred and thirty years, putting a strain on all of the chiefdoms. Introduced diseases certainly took their toll on mission Indians, but the conscripted labor system was equally as stressful and detrimental to Indian health. Recent bioarchaeological studies are showing that the Indian populations across La Florida suffered from malnutrition, severe and physically damaging labor practices, and other associated health risks from displacement into work camps. La Florida may not have been a shatter zone at this time, but Native life was not a picture of rosy health and stable political and social institutions. In fact, violent Native revolts punctuated the entire mission period, telling evidence for the unrest and discontent of a large number of mission Indians.[81]

Because the colony did not engage in commercial trade with local Indians it is tempting to mark Spanish Florida as the southern edge of the Mississippian shatter zone. However, that mission Indians took the brunt of slaving places in Spanish Florida well within the shatter zone by the eighteenth century. The coastal mission chiefdoms of Guale and Mocama were the first to suffer from Indian slaving and pirate slave traders.[82] As early as 1661 the Westos (called Chichimecos by the Spanish) and perhaps others were raiding the Georgia coast for Indian slaves to sell to Jamestown traders. This raiding also marked the beginning of an almost twenty-five-year retreat into Spanish Florida for the Guales and Mocamas. By 1684 all of the Guales and Mocamas who had not been enslaved or who had not joined other groups had moved south, away from the Georgia coast leaving the entire coastline void of people. Afterward, the new coalescent society known as the Yamasees would colonize this area and begin slaving campaigns sponsored by the English into Spanish Florida.[83] As John Worth documents in this volume, the mission system, weak and flawed, could not withstand the onslaught of armed slave raiders. The results were calamitous and left La Florida virtually depopulated of Indians on the eve of the Yamasee War in 1715.

The shock waves that penetrated into La Florida during the mid-seventeenth century originated in the first blows creating the shatter zone. These arose far away in the present-day northeastern United States, where European commercial interests first developed. Like the Spanish, the English, Dutch, and French colonial projects in North America had political, religious, and military dimensions. However, by the seventeenth century Spain was in decline as a world and commercial power. At this time it was the Dutch, French, and English colonial projects that carried significant commercial dimensions — they came to make money. As soon as English, French, and Dutch settlers landed on North American shores, they set about this business, and they brought with them strong commercial connections to the nascent global economy. By the early 1620s the Dutch, English, and French had established colonies and trade interests in the St. Lawrence, Chesapeake, Susquehanna, and Hudson river corridors, and each lost no time in recruiting Native allies and traders. Some scholars maintain that Northern businessmen prized furs (beaver and other furs) and not Indian slaves as their most valuable commodity and that in the Northeast the intra-Indian competition for access to the fur trade lay at the root of intra-Indian conflict and hostility.[84]

Out of this intra-Indian hostility was generated the first militaristic slaving society — the Five Nations Iroquois of present-day upstate New York. The repercussions of Iroquois warfare and raiding in the seventeenth century were felt as far south as Spanish Florida and as far west as the Mississippi River. Hence, as we will see, the geographic scope of the Mississippian shatter zone extends into the Northeast to include groups such as the Iroquois, Erie, Susquehannock, and Shawnee. At some time just prior to European contact, the Mohawks, Onondagas, Oneidas, Senecas, and Cayugas, who were situated between the Mohawk and Genesee river valleys in present-day New York, joined in The Great League of Peace and

Power. The Great League was an alliance that guaranteed peace among its members and mutual aid against outside aggressors. At the time of contact many other groups surrounded the Iroquois: Algonquin-speakers to the north, who united into a confederacy soon after contact; the Hurons; the Petuns; the Neutrals; the Wenros; the Mahicans; and the Susquehannocks. The relationships among these groups were intensely hostile as evidenced by the fact that all of their villages were heavily fortified and palisaded.[85] Much of this hostility had resulted from animosities generated by Iroquois raiding for war captives. Iroquois wars were usually mourning wars, the objective of which was to take captives who were then used to replace the deceased through a ceremony known as requickening. The mourning wars created low-level, perhaps chronic violence. However, Europeans introduced two factors that powerfully reshaped the mourning wars — disease and trade.[86]

The first recorded instance of Old World disease among the Iroquois appeared in the 1630s and was followed by successive waves of disease epidemics in 1647, 1656, 1661, 1668, 1673, and 1676, so that by end of the seventeenth century they had suffered an estimated ninety-five percent population loss. With this kind of population loss the mourning wars took on vastly increased significance: they were necessary to keep Iroquois numbers up.[87] Although scholars do not think that the Iroquois were selling war captives to European buyers, the Iroquois mourning wars became folded into their trade interests, which included the acquisition of hunting lands. The Iroquois first directed their mourning wars against those groups blocking their way to the European trade centers. The Mahicans took the first blow and were eliminated by 1628. By 1649 the Hurons and their allies the Petuns, Neutrals, Wenros, and Eries began to break apart, and by 1650 groups in the Algonquian Confederacy to the northeast were dispatched.[88] Many of these Northeastern groups fled to the Great Lakes region where they formed new groups such as the Wyandots and forced local groups such as the Sioux to flee onto the Plains; some moved south into the present-day Mid-Atlantic States.[89] After emptying the surrounding areas of people, the Iroquois turned their attention to distant northern and western groups — the Abenakis, Ojibwa, Ottawas,

Wyandots, Crees, Illinois, Miamis, and Chipewyans, who were located about sixteen hundred miles northwest of Iroquoia.[90]

Iroquois slaving campaigns also had serious repercussions in the South. By the mid-1600s Iroquois raiders were moving into the lower midwest by way of the Ohio and Mississippi river valleys. Archaeologists believe that the eastern Ohio Valley (Kentucky and West Virginia) was largely depopulated in the mid-1600s, although they are not in agreement as to whether or not this was due primarily to Iroquois depredations.[91] Archaeologists also suspect that many refugees from Iroquois raiding migrated west into present-day Michigan, Ohio, and Illinois where they settled in unpopulated areas or joined or displaced local populations.[92] Some may have moved into the lower South. Marvin Jeter in this volume argues that the Quapaws, who lived at the mouth of the Arkansas River in 1690 and who have puzzled archaeologists and others for many years, may have been relative newcomers to the area. They probably originated in the eastern Ohio River Valley and were displaced by Iroquois raiding at some time in the mid-to late-seventeenth century.[93]

It is also quite possible that through the turmoil, dislocation, and depopulation in the Ohio River Valley, we have the formation of some new groups, in particular the Shawnees. We know very little about early Shawnee history except to say it was one of several extraordinarily complex movements between Pennsylvania, the Savannah River, the Great Lakes, and Maryland. Stephen Warren in this volume understands the Shawnees to have formed in response to Iroquois predations and conflicts with Europeans, and that they adjusted to the tumultuous times by adopting a very fluid social structure and becoming highly mobile mercenaries.[94]

Iroquois and other Northern raiders also filtered down the Atlantic seaboard. In at least one early document the Senecas are mentioned by name as harassing the Delaware Bay Indians.[95] By the mid-seventeenth century, as William Fox and Maureen Meyers in this volume demonstrate, Susquehannocks and other Northern groups, who were forced south by the Iroquois, displaced and raided the Chesapeake Bay Indians as well other Virginia and Maryland groups.[96]

By around 1640 new trade opportunities opened in Jamestown, and other militaristic slaving societies emerged. Unlike the Iroquois, however, these militaristic slaving societies were engaged in commercial slaving in order to acquire guns and ammunition, not just to replace their dead. One of the earliest examples of such a commercial slaving society in the South may be the Occaneechis. The first documentary reference to them is in 1650 by a Virginia English trader who encountered them on the Roanoke River. Not much is known about their early encounters with the Virginians, but by 1670 the Occaneechis had moved to the crossing point of the Trade Path on the Roanoke and acted as middle men for the Virginia traders, reportedly controlling the English southern trade for a distance of five hundred miles.[97] Furthermore, the Occaneechis were coalescing with surrounding smaller groups, in particular the Tutelos and Saponis and later some Susquehannocks.[98] Joining the raiders was one method of coping, and the Occaneechis may be an early example of a confederation that, if nothing else, required mutual agreements that those in the alliance would not conduct slave raids against each other.

The Occaneechis are not covered in this volume, but the effects of their slaving and that of the Iroquois in the mid-Atlantic and southern Piedmont regions are covered in the chapters by Robin Beck and by Mary Beth Fitts and Charles Heath. As these and other scholars show, the archaeology and ethnohistory from the lower Piedmont are beginning to reveal a picture of intense turmoil, multiple movements, and instability as the numerous simple chiefdoms and Woodland villages that character-ized this area broke apart. People abandoned and relocated their towns, and some groups merged to form new groups. Some simply disappeared, most likely slaved out or decimated by migration and disease.[99] Some southern Piedmont groups such as the Yuchis, Chiahas, Coosas, and perhaps others fled south to the lower Coosa and Chattahoochee river valleys where they began to coalesce along with others into the Creek Confederacy.[100] The Cherokees also moved their towns from the northeast toward the southwest between 1600 and 1700 and were actively taking in refugees.[101] There is increasing evidence that the Powhatan chiefdom of Pocahontas fame — which appears to have been a relatively stable politi-cal unit on the eastern edge of the Mississippian shatter zone — also took in refugees and may have congealed politically in response to the social turmoil on all sides.[102]

Yet another militaristic slaving society that may have formed out of the crucible of the slave trade was the perplexing Chisca, which was a chiefdom somewhere in present southwestern Virginia and eastern Tennessee at the time of the Pardo and Soto expeditions. As early as 1620 Spanish authorities were reporting that Chiscas were raiding mission Indians. Then in 1624 they suddenly appeared in Spanish Florida, perhaps because of the Iroquois-based disruptions in Virginia. In their raids Chiscas would kill many men and carry off women and children. There is no evidence that the Chiscas were selling these Indians to European slavers, and the fact that they only had two guns in a 1677 battle with the Apalachee and the Spanish also suggests that Chisca captives were not sold directly to Europeans. In the 1677 battle a combined Apalachee and Spanish force ran the Chiscas out. After this, they retreated into the historical shadows. Some appeared in Illinois, and others moved to the Tallapoosa River in present-day Alabama where they slaved the groups who were beginning to form the Creeks, particularly the Apalachicola.[103]

Another early example of a militaristic slaving society is that of the Westos. The Westos figure prominently in this volume and emerge as one of the preeminent militaristic slaving societies in the South. Eric Bowne's recent book on the Westos opens our eyes to their predatory strategies, their early incorporation into the commercial slave trade system through their partnership with English traders, and their monopoly of the Southern trade for almost two decades. The Westos were originally a group of Eries who, fleeing Iroquois predations, moved to the Ohio River where they formed a partnership with the Susquahannocks in the fur and perhaps the slave trade. Around 1640 five to six hundred of them moved to the James River in Virginia where they became known as Richahecrians and began slaving for Jamestown slavers.[104] Meyers in this volume, through some historical sleuthing, suggests that they may have received the name Westo while in Virginia. By the early 1660s the Westos were raiding for slaves in present-day Georgia and Florida. Sometime in the 1660s they moved to the Savannah River in present-day Georgia to be closer to vulnerable bow-and-arrow Indians of the lower South. The location also proved a good one for trade with Carolina once the colony was founded in 1670. In the following decade the Westos, armed with European guns and deploying a by now well-honed predatory strategy conducted slave raids for their English partners against many of the Native polities in present-day Georgia, North Carolina, South Carolina, Florida, and perhaps as far west as present-day central Alabama.[105]

Bowne presents a summary of his book on the Westos for this volume, and William Fox and Maureen Meyers cover the Westos' early years in New York and Virginia, respectively. Almost every contributor to this volume documents the depopulation of and multiple migrations by various Native groups in Alabama, Georgia, and South Carolina that resulted from Westo predations between 1660 and 1682. As shown by Robin Beck in this volume, Westo (and perhaps Occaneechi) aggressions can also account for the disappearance of Cofitachequi and other Piedmont chiefdoms visited by Soto and Pardo in the sixteenth century.[106] The coalescences of the Creek Confederacy, the Alabamas and Coushattas, and the Catawbas, covered here by Ned Jenkins, Sheri Shuck-Hall, and Mary Beth Fitts and Charles Heath, respectively, are perhaps the most profound consequences of the Westo presence in the South.

Eric Bowne argues in this volume that Westo raiding also generated the so-called settlement Indians in and around Charles Town. These were small Native groups who took up a migratory existence in the Carolina low country and developed close relationships with Europeans and Africans. These groups chose to stay in this region despite Carolinian animosities that forced them to cede choice agricultural lands. Yet they had no other option because the Westos restricted their movement toward the west and south, and the Occaneechis and later the Tuscaroras blocked their movement to the north. All of this left the settlement Indians with little recourse except to forge some kind of détente with Carolina, even if such agreements weighed more in Carolina's favor.[107]

The first signs that militaristic slaving societies had outlived their usefulness to English trade interests occurred by around 1680, and a series of European and Indian wars ensued. The Occaneechis were diminished in 1676 during Bacon's Rebellion, after which the survivors moved further south. The Westos were destroyed in 1682 by a group of Shawnee mercenaries in the pay of Carolina traders. In 1686 the Chiscas on the Tallapoosa River were dispatched by the Apalachicola, who armed with English guns, turned on these raiders who had been terrorizing them for years. The Iroquois were seriously reduced by their wars with Europeans and Indians, and by 1686 they began their long retreat into New York and Canada.[108]

With the monopolies of these militaristic slaving societies broken, the interior Natives whom the monopolies had blocked from the trade for decades joined with European traders, especially the group from South Carolina known as the Goose Creek Men, and we see the emergence of a second generation of militaristic Indian slaving societies. After the Occaneechis were dislodged, the Tuscaroras became the prevailing middlemen in the southern Piedmont.[109] The Cherokees also began slaving throughout the southwestern Appalachians and Piedmont.[110] Brett Riggs in another volume uses the Mississippian shatter zone framework to characterize the early colonial Yuchis, and he understands them to have been mobile militaristic slavers by the early eighteenth century.[111] As documented here by Matthew Jennings, John Worth, and Paul Kelton, the Yamasees of the South Carolina and Georgia coasts soon stepped into the breach created with the destruction of the Westos. Furthermore, between 1685 and 1698 the Abhikas, Alabamas, Tallapoosas, Apalachicolas, Cussetas, and Cowetas (those groups that would later form the core of the Creek Confederacy in Georgia and Alabama) began intense slaving campaigns. The result was a "frenzy of slaving" in the lower South.[112]

The Chickasaws, situated at the terminus of the Upper and Lower Trade Paths, were the westernmost militaristic slaving society in the shatter zone.[113] The Chickasaws lived in present-day north Mississippi and had become involved in the slave trade perhaps as early as 1680. By 1700 they controlled the trade from the Tombigbee to the lower Mississippi River Valley, and perhaps beyond. The impact of Chickasaw slaving was dramatic: many were forced to abandon the Lower Mississippi Valley.[114] Although the refugees' movements have yet to be worked out in detail, some of these groups — probably the Yazoos, the Chakchiumas, the Ibitoupas, and the Taposas — joined the Chickasaws. Peoples such as the Grigras, the Kororas, and Kious may have joined the Natchez. Others may have moved west, either into Arkansas or western Louisiana. Some undoubtedly joined the Caddo along the Red River, who took in refugees by this time. Some groups became extinct or were absorbed into other groups as they disappear from the documentary and archaeological record, while others coalesced with refugees from Creek raiding into the Choctaw Confederacy around the Pearl River in present-day Mississippi.[115] Many moved south, in and around the French Gulf colonies where they formed the *petites nations,* or "small nations," the Gulf equivalent of the Atlantic settlement Indians.[116]

The Chickasaws' success as militaristic slavers was because of the monopoly they held on the English slave trade between the Tombigbee and Mississippi rivers; this monopoly also inhibited English trade relations from developing with the Choctaws, Natchez, and other Natives. Why English trade relations did not fully develop this far west was also a matter of geography. The distance between Native groups west of the Tombigbee River and the English seaports and commercial centers on the Atlantic was simply too far for sustained, direct involvement in the English trade system. Such involvement would have been necessary in order to break the Chickasaw monopoly.[117] This monopoly meant, of course, that other Indians in the area looked to the French for their commercial ties. The French had a presence in this area, but France's North American commercial interests were focused around the Great Lakes. Their southern colony at Mobile was an understaffed, underfunded colonial outpost, and their trade system was, likewise, underdeveloped. The contributors to this volume studying the lower Mississippi Valley—Patricia Galloway, Marvin Jeter, and George Milne—all agree that because of these underdeveloped commercial interests, the western edge of the Mississippian shatter zone was the lower Mississippi Valley.

The Meaning of Transformation

As slaving and disease spread, the entire geopolitical landscape in the Mississippian shatter zone was transformed. This is not to say that Native Southerners had not gone through other transformations, historical changes, and large and small events before Europeans came on the scene. For example, they endured the transformation that led to the spread of the

Mississippian organization throughout most of the South. They survived and reorganized after the collapse of Cahokia. Nor is it to say that nothing of their previous lives remained in the eighteenth century.[118] Precontact Mississippian history, like postcontact history, undoubtedly was full of political intrigue, diplomacy, warfare, peace, love, and periods of change and upheaval as well as periods of stability. I subscribe to Charles Hudson's statement that there are structural continuities to Southern history that reach back to the Mississippian era and perhaps beyond.[119] In these years Southern Indian history was marked by monumental, transformative world-shaping events. But one can argue still that contact between the Old and New Worlds was one such monumental event and "foundational experience" in Southern Indian history.[120]

We are only just beginning to understand precisely what happened when a chiefdom fell; it most likely broke apart, although the lines of breakage are unclear. Splinter groups must have migrated short and long distances and joined other splinter groups as they reorganized themselves into altogether new social types.[121] The *petites nations* and settlement Indians, for example, represent new social types. In the case of the settlement Indians, these groups did not coalesce but remained small independent groups. The settlement Indians stayed in the Carolina low country until the Yamasee War, after which many moved north to join the Catawbas or west to join the Creeks.[122] Like the settlement Indians, the *petites nations* of the Louisiana Gulf did not coalesce but remained as small and independent groups. Unlike the settlement Indians, however, they stayed in and around New Orleans and Mobile throughout the Historic Period, and some are still there today. Here they joined their lives with Africans, Europeans, and other Native refugees to develop a unique economy and Creole culture.[123]

John Worth in another publication identifies a social type born out of the geopolitical instability of the contact era that he calls aggregation, wherein immigrant communities attached themselves to functioning chiefdoms, presumably in a subordinate position. This process was especially prevalent in Spanish Florida, and many refugees from Westo and later Yamasee slaving fled to Florida where they joined the Apalachee or Timucuan chiefdoms. Aggregation may also have been taking place among the Natchez and perhaps even the Powhatans, both of which were functioning chiefdoms in the seventeenth and eighteenth centuries and are known to have taken in refugees.[124]

Yet all of the chiefdoms that served as nodes of aggregation could not withstand the sustained instability in the Mississippian shatter zone. Powhatan was destroyed by 1650 after a series of wars with the English in Virginia. The chiefdoms of Spanish Florida were destroyed by 1710. The Caddo chiefdoms began to break up around the same time with the survivors reconfiguring themselves into so-called confederacies.[125] The Natchez chiefdom broke apart after its disastrous revolt against the French in 1729, with splinter groups joining the Chickasaws, Creeks, Caddos, and others.[126]

Another response to living in the shatter zone was coalescence, in which two or more relocated chiefdoms or splinter groups joined together into a new social formation that did not necessarily resemble preexisting chiefdoms.[127] Although we have yet to pinpoint all of the colonial coalescent societies, for now we can say that in the new social landscape of the eighteenth century, the Yamasees, Creeks, Catawbas, Chickasaws, Choctaws, Caddo confederacies, Alabama-Coushattas, and perhaps the Cherokees were coalescent societies. However, as is becoming clear, these groups represent various types of political and social orders, and as this research progresses, we may need to further differentiate between them. For instance, the Yamasee coalescence certainly was not identical to that of the Creeks and may more closely have resembled that of the Catawbas.[128] The Caddo coalescence appears to have been a singular case, perhaps because of interactions with their western neighbors and the Mexican Spanish.[129] As Jenkins, Shuck-Hall, and Fitts and Heath show in this volume, the particular form a coalescence took and the people who coalesced were contingent on a variety of factors, one being a complex interplay between old lines of chiefdom alliance and animosity, new alliances and animosities, and the shifting nature of both in such uncertain times.[130]

The mechanisms of coalescence, likewise, are only now coming to light. As authors in this volume demonstrate, marriage, adoption, linguistic affiliations, and former chiefdom alliances were all used to glue disparate groups together. In some cases the mechanism may have determined whether or not a group was absorbed or retained some sort of separate identity. In the case of the Natchez and Alabamas, for instance, Milne and Shuck-Hall in this volume propose that marriage was used as one way to weave newcomers into extant social orders, but in the case of the Natchez, the newly married entered on the lower rung of the social order, whereas among the Alabamas newcomers who married in entered as full-fledged members of the group. On the other hand, Jenkins, in delineating the origins of the Creek Confederacy, shows that migration and coalescence into plural societies were common mechanisms for dealing with political upheavals. These mechanisms were most likely put to a new use in the Mississippian shatter zone in order to merge the polities in central Alabama into the Creek Confederacy and to take in refugee groups. In the case of the Creeks all of the various groups retained their political and social identities. The Chickasaws too put an old social institution to a new use in the Mississippian shatter zone but with different results. The Chickasaws absorbed people through the *fanimingo* institution wherein an outside group was ritually adopted. The Chakchiumas and others were completely absorbed in the Chickasaw order, and, as far as we can tell, they became Chickasaws.[131] These are just some of the processes identified so far.

As these examples show, although monumental and transformative, contact with Europeans did not leave Native lives absolutely destroyed. The Mississippian world may have collapsed, but in the reformation that followed, people rebuilt their communities and constructed new social and political organizations using some social institutions that resembled those of their former chiefdoms. The new societies maintained institutions and practices such as town councils, blood revenge, reciprocity, clan organization, corn agriculture, hunting and gathering, and a matrilineal kin system, all of which had their roots in the Mississippian Period and perhaps even in prior times. These institutions and practices proved to be highly adaptable and could be integrated into the new global economic situation. For example, the Southern Native domestic economy and division of labor was flexible enough to form linkages to the capitalist system. The broad structural patterns of Southern Native households show much continuity from the Mississippian Period until the early nineteenth century.[132]

Other institutions, however, were transformed. The hierarchal political institutions of the old chiefdoms, for instance, simply did not work in the new geopolitical landscape and capitalist economy. The European trade system worked to transform indigenous leadership institutions by promoting internal factionalism and by redefining the basis of power and authority from one of succession through kinship and religious sanction to one of economic prowess and international diplomatic skills.[133] After all, English traders did not have to persuade an anti-English, hereditary *mico* to their side. They could and did simply ally with another person in that society. Given the disunity of the coalescent societies, usually several men could claim influence over any particular faction. The English chose to deal with whoever seemed most inclined to listen to their overtures, and given the new opportunities for self-gain, this could be any number of people. An Indian man who had a modicum of influence over a particular faction could broker good trade deals and rise in prestige and authority. An Indian man's position became tied to his access to European trade goods and his political, business, and diplomatic acumen. The overall effect was at once a leveling of political power and a check on the rise of any one person to political prominence. With the chiefdom political order revamped, we also see the disappearance of those emblems of power and authority associated with the hierarchy. People quit building platform mounds; craftspeople quit producing elaborate religious and political paraphernalia; the priestly cult used to buttress the elite was transformed into a cadre of prophets administering to the common person; and chiefs were no longer considered divine but mortal men and women. All was replaced by town councils of warriors and elders wherein every man was given equal opportunity to participate in decision making.

Indeed, by 1730 a new South was emerging. Gone were all the many polities that Soto saw, replaced by large Indian nations such as the Creek Confederacy, the Cherokee, the Choctaw, the Chickasaw, the Catawba, and the Caddo confederacies. Each of these nations claimed huge tracts of the interior lands, so much so that the European colonies were still mostly confined to small slivers along the coast. Even here various settlement

Indians and *petites nations* held onto small land holdings. The colonies though soon began to exercise their growing economic strength and launched an era of expansion in population, territory, and ambition.

The Europeans divvied the South amongst themselves, with slices for Spain, France, and England. Over the next decades the Indian coalescent societies would take full advantage of this tripartite division. The Creeks, for example, managed to garner especially favorable trade agreements for most of the eighteenth century by playing the international game better — at least in the short run — than the Europeans did. The Creeks used their own internal disunity and decentralized political order to play one European power against another, thus brokering especially good trade and military agreements.

This new South also included thousands of Africans imported through the African slave trade, which replaced the Indian slave trade. Although their lives were consigned mostly to European settlements and plantations, many Africans made their way to Indian country where they joined the coalescent societies and built homes and families there. A small number of European traders also cast their lot in Indian country where they married Indian women and moved back and forth between their European and Indian circles. An even smaller number of European women, too, opted to marry, raise families, and live among the Indians rather than among their countrymen. The children from these mixed marriages, through their contacts and comfort in both European and Indian societies, would eventually take the reins of leadership in the coalescent societies.[134]

In this new South Indians were fully engaged in the global trade system. Cloth, guns, metal tools, and other items were as common and necessary to Indians as they were to Europeans. Only now, the Indian trade was not in slaves but in deerskins, and instead of slave raiders, most of the men became commercial hunters, harvesting millions of deerskins over the eighteenth century until deer came close to extinction in the South. Southern Indian men and women assuredly still farmed, fished, hunted for wild meats, and gathered wild plant foods, but they also entered into a series of new part-time occupations — guide, translator, mercenary, postal rider, horse thief, slave catcher, prostitute, and so on.

The new South of 1730 was born out of the Mississippian shatter zone.

The Mississippian chiefdoms, with their long histories of rising and fall-ing, fell spectacularly with European contact, and they failed to rise again because of the turmoil and wide regional instability created by the intro-duction of Old World diseases and the increased violence and disruptions of the commercial trade in Indian slaves. Faced with the collapse of many of their chiefdoms, people invented new ways of putting their social lives back together, ways that sought to adapt to a field of play with nation states and a global capitalist economy.

Notes

1. Charles Hudson enumerates these in his Introduction to *Transformation*.

2. For some of the Southern protohistoric and contact archaeology and ethno-historical studies, see Brose, Cowan, and Mainfort, *Societies in Eclipse*; Ethridge and Hudson, *Transformation*; Galloway, *Choctaw Genesis*; Hudson, *Knights of Spain*; Hudson and Tesser, *Forgotten Centuries*; McEwan, *Indians of the Greater Southeast*; Milanich and Hudson, *Hernando de Soto and the Indians of Florida*; Milanich, *Florida Indians*; Moore, *Catawba Valley Mississippian*; Perttula, *Caddo Nation*; Ramenofsky, *Vectors of Death*; Smith, *Archaeology of Aboriginal Culture Change*; Smith, *Coosa*; Thomas, *Columbian Consequences*; Wesson and Rees, *Between Contact and Colonies*; Williams and Shapiro, *Lamar Archaeology*; and Worth, *Timucuan Chiefdoms*.

3. The term "shatter zone" is not a new coinage. Others in this volume (Marvin Jeter, Mary Beth Fitts, and Charles Heath) discuss the history of the term from its academic inception in geography to its application to early twentieth-century disturbances and its subsequent incorporation into studies of the demographics of the African slave trade. I will not repeat that here. I initially took the term from Eric Wolf's *Europe and the People Without History*, 231, in which the term is used descriptively in discussing West Africa during the slave trade, and from Richard White who also uses the term in discussing the Iroquoian role in the creation of the middle ground (White, *Middle Ground*, 14). Influenced by Ferguson's and Whitehead's "tribal zone," I broaden the term in a conceptual way as a process of capitalist development, but I tailor it to the history of contact in the South (Ferguson and Whitehead, "Violent Edge of Empire").

I began presenting papers on the shatter zone framework at academic con-ferences five years ago. Admittedly, in those first few presentations, I was not sensitive to the implications of my language for reproducing "the trope of the declining Indian," as Jamey Carson later put it and as Shepard Krech generously pointed out at one of my talks. I have subsequently taken care to clarify the term more precisely and to divest it of any such implications. Readers should not take the term "shatter zone" to mean that Native peoples disappeared with European contact, and let me emphasize here that although the Mississippian shatter zone was characterized by violence and disruption, the result was not full destruction of Native peoples. As many of the chapters in this volume stress, the violence and disruption in the Mississippian shatter zone was also regenerative and productive of new social and cultural forms. In short, Mississippian Native life may have been "shattered," but it was not obliterated.

4. First set forth in Ethridge, "Creating the Shatter Zone."

5. The term "chiefdom" is used to designate a social type. Other social types are sociopolitical entities such as state, nation, kingdom, band, and tribe. The term "chiefdom" entered anthropological circles in the 1960s and 1970s with the publication of Elman R. Service's *Primitive Social Organization* and Morton Herbert Fried's *Evolution of Political Society*. Fried and Service used the term to indicate a particular stage of human development in the social evolutionary spectrum from band to state. In recent years some archaeologists have begun to question the utility of using the term chiefdom because of its evolutionary implications. Kehoe in *Land of Prehistory*, for example, understands that the neoevolutionists of the mid-twentieth century such as Service and Fried harkened back to earlier nineteenth-century racist ideas. She takes American archaeologists to task for keeping these old evolutionary schemes in theoretical play through the use of terms such as "band," "tribe," "chiefdom," and "state." See also Kehoe, "Why Anthropologists Should Abandon the Term 'Chiefdom,'" 10. Sturtevant in "Turpinambá Chiefdoms?" also questions the political reality of the chiefdom concept. Pauketat in *Chiefdoms and Other Archaeological Delusions* makes perhaps the final statement in divesting the concept of chiefdom of its evolutionary baggage.

Although scholars such as Kehoe and Pauketat call for abandoning the concept altogether, their proposed replacement terms such as "kingdom," "civilization," and "nation" are likewise problematic. Instead, I agree with archaeologist Patrick Livingood when he states in "Recent Discussions in Lake Prehistoric Southern Archaeology" that the term "has become a useful shorthand for the type of hierarchical, kin-based, hereditary, territorial polities that are so common throughout the South between the ninth and thirteenth centuries AD" (5). In addition, the concept of the chiefdom has been extremely productive in interpreting the Mississippian world because it has provided a unit of social analysis through which archaeologists have been able to reconstruct not only the structures of Mississippian political organization but also the variability between and across them. See Livingood, "Recent Discussions in Lake Prehistoric Southern Archaeology"; and Hudson et al., "On Cofitachequi," 467.

Although one can still find vestiges of evolutionary language in the literature on Mississippian chiefdoms, in its modern usage the evolutionary aspects are being excised. In the Mississippian South chiefdoms as a social type were widespread, and they existed alongside other nonchiefdom societies such as the Calusa, the eastern Plains villagers, and the northeast Woodland villagers. It should be understood then that Southern chiefdoms were not "more evolved" or "higher" social or cultural orders than these other societies nor that complex and paramount chiefdoms were more developed than simple chiefdoms. Rather, the various social types coexisting at the same time reflect geopolitical complexity across a wide region of the South.

6. Earthen mounds have a long history in the South beginning with those found at the Watson Brake site (5400–5000 BCE)and the Poverty Point site (1650–700 BCE).

7. The literature on the Mississippian Period is quite extensive. Some book-length treatments are Anderson, *Savannah River Chiefdoms*; Blitz and Lorenz, *Chattahoochee Chiefdoms*; Dye and Cox, *Towns and Temples*; King, *Etowah*; Knight and Steponaitis, *Archaeology of the Moundville Chiefdom*; Lewis and Stout, *Mississippian Towns and Sacred Spaces*; and Pauketat, *Ancient Cahokia*.

8. For the most recent statements on differing Mississippian leadership patterns, see the essays in Butler and Welch, *Leadership and Polity*. Also see Beck, "Consolidation and Hierarchy"; Blitz, "Mississippian Chiefdoms"; Emerson, *Cahokia and the Archaeology of Power*; King, "Historic Period Transformation"; King, *Etowah*; Knight, "Social Organization"; Pauketat, *Ascent of Chiefs*; Pauketat and Barker, *Lords of the Southeast*; Pollack, *Caborn-Welborn*; and Scarry and Maxham, "Elite Actors."

9. On the stone-hoe production and trade, see Cobb, *From Quarry to Cornfield*. On salt production, see Muller, "Mississippian Specialization and Salt"; Muller, *Mississippian Political Economy*; and Early, *Caddoan Saltmakers*.

10. On Mississippian economies, see Lapham, *Hunting for Hides*; Welch, *Moundville's Economy*; Blitz, *Ancient Chiefdoms of the Tombigbee*; Muller, *Mississippian Political Economy*; Cobb, "Mississippian Chiefdoms"; and Pauketat and Emerson, *Cahokia*.

11. Recent overviews of the archaeology and reconstruction of Cahokia his-

tory are Milner, *Cahokia Chiefdom*, and Pauketat, *Ancient Cahokia*. For the most recent archaeological investigations at Cahokia, see Emerson, "Contributions of Transportation Archaeology." One can visit the center of Cahokia, which is now a state historic site just east of present-day St. Louis, Missouri.

12. The full regional range of the Mississippian culture was established in the essays collected by Bruce Smith in *Mississippian Settlement Patterns*. Also see Payne and Scarry, "Town Structure at the Edge," figure 2.1; Knight and Steponaitis, *Moundville Chiefdom*; King, *Etowah;* Dye and Cox, *Towns and Temples*; and Lewis and Stout, *Mississippian Towns and Sacred Spaces*. Although this area is considered the center of the Mississippian world, archaeologists understand that societies along the borders were also a part of it. For the frontiers, see Payne and Scary, "Town Structure at the Edge"; King and Meyers, "Frontiers, Backwaters, and Peripheries"; and Clay, "Interpreting the Mississippian Hinterlands."

13. For an impressive catalog of Mississippian Period art as well as excellent overviews of Southern Native prehistory, see Townsend, *Hero, Hawk, and Open Hand*. For detailed treatments of Southern Mississippian art, see Galloway, *Southeastern Ceremonial Complex* and Power, *Early Art*. The volume by Reilly and Garber, *Ancient Objects*, offers the most recent and thorough analysis of the iconography and meaning of art in Mississippian life.

14. Dye, "Art, Ritual, and Chiefly Warfare," 193.

15. For the definitions of complex and simple chiefdoms as applied in the South, see Steponaitis, "Location Theory"; and Anderson, *Savannah River Chiefdoms*, 4–9. On the size and population of simple chiefdoms, see Hally, Smith, and Langford, "Archaeological Reality."

16. Quote is from Hudson et al., "On Cofitachequi," 467. On the political workings of paramount chiefdoms see Hally, Smith, and Langford, "Archaeological Reality"; Hally, "Nature of Mississippian Regional Systems," 30–39; and Beck, "Consolidation and Hierarchy."

17. Anderson, *Savannah River Chiefdoms*, 1–52; Blitz, "Mississippian Chiefdoms," 583–90; Beck, "Consolidation and Hierarchy"; Hally, "Nature of Mississippian Regional Systems," 33–37; and Pollack, *Caborn-Welborn*, 19–24. Also see the essays in Scarry, *Political Structure and Change*. Anderson (personal communication, July 2008) understands cycling to be a useful mode for describing the general rise and fall of Mississippian chiefdoms and the regionwide repercussions of such. However, he also points out that one must use the model generally and then move to the particular history of a chiefdom. For a good discussion on chiefdom cycling, see Jenkins, this volume.

18. Hally in "Nature of Mississippian Regional Systems," 26, 30–32; Blitz in "Mississippian Chiefdoms." Pollack in *Caborn-Welborn*, 179–82, 192–99, 199–206, also documents regional readjustments after the fall of the Angel chiefdom during the Middle Mississippi on the lower Ohio River. Here people reestablished their hierarchies but with a dispersal of hierarchical duties from a temple mound center to several large, non-mound towns. Pollack says that archaeologically these resembled Historic Period polities more than chiefdoms. He also notes that this new configuration may have been influenced by the proximity of the Angel people to the nonhierarchical Oneota people to the Northeast.

19. Charles Hudson and his colleagues conducted this research over the past three decades, and it continues today; the amount of scholarship generated from the Soto project is enormous. Charles Hudson synthesizes much of this research in *Knights of Spain*. Also see the second edition of Hudson, *Juan Pardo Expeditions*. The most spectacular recent find related to the Pardo and Soto expeditions is the identification of Pardo's Fort San Juan; Beck, Moore, and Rodning, "Identifying Fort San Juan." For an essay describing the impact of Hudson's scholarship and the Soto project on Southern Indian studies, see Pluckhahn, Ethridge, Milanich, and Smith, Introduction.

20. Hudson in *Knights of Spain* reconstructs the geopolitical landscape of the Mississippian South at the time Soto came through the region. I refer readers to this work for a good understanding of the Mississippian world at the time of contact.

21. Marvin Smith in *Coosa* documents the rise and fall of this paramount chiefdom. Combining archaeological and documentary evidence, *Coosa* is one of the best histories to date of a Late Mississippian chiefdom.

22. Hudson, *Knights of Spain*, 110–15, 238–49, 266–74, 336–38.

23. Hudson, *Knights of Spain*, 179–80, 228–29.

24. This is not to say that the Mississippian shatter zone was the only shatter zone created in the early years of colonialism. Rather, I am attempting to distinguish this as one particular case of instability. And although I do not suggest here that the shatter zone concept is more general, future comparative work with other places of colonial instability may find some similarities between them and the Mississippian shatter zone.

25. Kelton, "Great Southeastern Smallpox Epidemic" and *Epidemics and Enslavement*. It should be noted that Kelton does not examine the possibility of disease moving from New Spain into the southern Plains and hence entering the South from the west. Susan C. Vehik documents possible and probable disease episodes

in the southern Plains as early as 1535 and into the mid-seventeenth century; Vehik, "Problems and Potential"; and Vehik, "Cultural Continuity and Discontinuity," 259. Nor does Kelton examine the possibility of epidemics moving from north to south. Betts in "Pots and Pox" understands early seventeenth-century disease episodes to be responsible for population decline in the upper Mississippi River Valley. Disease then could have entered the South via the Mississippi River Valley well before 1696. Still, Kelton's understanding of the scope of the 1696 outbreak holds.

26. For a good discussion on the problems in determining the occurrence of Old World disease in archaeology, see Baker and Kealhofer, "Assessing the Impact of European-Contact"; and Milner, "Prospects and Problems." On changing mortuary patterns and a discussion of Tatham Mound in Florida, the best-documented case of a mass burial in the South, see Hutchinson and Mitchem, "Correlates of Contact"; and Hutchinson, *Tatham Mound*.

27. Smith, *Archaeology of Aboriginal Culture Change*; Perttula, *Caddo Nation*; and Ramenofsky, *Vectors of Death*. These scholars build on the work of Dobyns (see especially *Their Number Become Thinned*), who was one of the first to suggest for the South that a demographic collapse occurred in the sixteenth century. Dobyns, however, used mostly archival and ecological evidence and little archeological evidence.

28. Other notable works in this debate are the essays in Baker and Kealhofer, *Bioarchaeology*; Henige, "Primary Source by Primary Source"; Henige, *Numbers from Nowhere*; Milner, "Epidemic Disease"; Snow and Lamphear, "European Contact and Indian Depopulation"; Stannard, "Consequences of Contact"; and Thornton, *American Indian Holocaust*. Daniels in "Indian Population of North America" and Dobyns in "Disease Transfer at Contact" offer detailed summaries of the debates at the time. Daniels closes by suggesting that the best approach would be a group-by-group analysis "taking all direct evidence seriously and using simple inference only when absolutely essential" (320). Alchon in the appendix to *Pest in the Land* has a superb summary of the debate with detailed compilations of the various population figures that have been put forward.

29. One should note that all of the proponents of the Southern "sixteenth-century collapse" suggested at the time of their first analyses that disease was probably only one factor. They were some of the first scholars to point to the Indian slave trade as a contributing factor; Smith, *Archaeology of Aboriginal Culture Change*, 129–47; Pertulla, *Caddo Nation*, 148–82; and Ramenofsky, *Vectors of Death*, 174–76. Dobyns too noted colonial effects as contributing factors to

the population decline, although he does not single out slaving; Dobyns, *Their Number Become Thinned*, 275–90, 304–6. Soon after the population debate began, scholars noted the need for a multicausal model. Thornton in *Indian Holocaust* especially stresses factors other than disease. Also see Milner, "Epidemic Disease"; Snow and Lamphear, "European Contact and Indian Depopulation"; and Stannard, "Consequences of Contact"; Stannard, *American Holocaust*; Thornton, Miller, and Warren, "American Indian Population Recovery"; and Ward and Davis, "Impact of Old World Diseases." Smith, Perttula, and Ramenofsky later refined their initial statements; Smith, *Coosa*, 112–22 and "Aboriginal Population Movements in the Postcontact Southeast"; Perttula, "Social Changes among the Caddo"; Ramenofsky and Galloway, "Disease and the Soto Entrada"; and Ramenofsky, "Historical Science." Alchon in *Pest in the Land* confronts this question head on in a hemisphere-wide perspective. Jones in "Virgin Soils Revisited," 716–20, examines the hypothesis of virgin soil populations, which underlies most discussions of catastrophic demographic collapse due to disease, and he too calls for new examinations using multicausal models. Today, Southern Indian scholars are beginning to formulate multicausal models; Dye, "Warfare in the Protohistoric Southeast," 137–38; Galloway, *Choctaw Genesis*, 134–41, 159–63; Worth, *Timucuan Chiefdoms*, 2:1–37; Kelton, "Great Southeastern Smallpox Epidemic"; and Kelton, "Avoiding the Smallpox Spirits." Bioarchaeologists are making tremendous strides toward developing a multicausal model; for example Hutchinson, *Tatham Mound*; the essays in Baker and Kealhofer, *Bioarchaeology*; and Larsen, *Bioarchaeology of Spanish Florida*. For the effects of migration on population profiles in Spanish Florida, see Stojanowski, *Biocultural Histories*; Stojanowski, "Population History"; and Stojanowski, "Bioarchaeology." Although most of these scholars recognize the importance of slave raiding on Indian demography, they do not emphasize it.

30. Ewen in "Continuity and Change," 42, points out that most scholars working on the early Historic Period in the South still take demographic collapse due to epidemic disease as their starting point and that they usually understand this to have occurred in the sixteenth century before sustained European contact. The idea also has gained currency in popular conceptions of the consequences of European contact, and popular media usually presents disease as the primary reason for the colonial demise of Indians in the Americas. Native scholars have disputed this idea since it was first introduced, insisting that colonial oppression combined with disease accounts for their domination by Euro-Americans. Jones argues in *Rationalizing Epidemics*, 19, that the real reasons for health disparities between American Indians and Euro-Americans is not because of an inherent susceptibil-

ity of American Indian populations to Old World diseases but to the interplay between disease and the disparities in wealth and power that have existed since colonization. Taking a cue from Jones, one can also see that the popular notions today about the contact-era demographic collapse are contemporary expressions of a long-term trend among Euro-Americans to rationalize the health disparities and inequalities between themselves and American Indians.

31. Kelton makes the same point; Kelton, this volume, and *Epidemics and Enslavement.*

32. Smith, *Coosa*, 96–121.

33. In this scenario the paramountcy of Coosa fell, and it did so along the time line set by Smith in *Coosa*, 96–121. The difference is that I propose the reasons for the fall were not primarily disease episodes and that this occurrence should not be projected across the South as the total collapse of the Mississippian. This conclusion is in contrast to Paul Hoffman, who, by examining the documentary evidence, challenges whether or not Coosa fell in the first place. Hoffman, however, did not reexamine the archaeological evidence for the decline of Coosa that Smith used in his reconstruction; Hoffman, "Did Coosa Decline?"

34. There has been much research on the bioarcheology of Spanish Florida. A comprehensive look at health in Spanish Florida is provided in the essays in Larsen, *Bioarchaeology of Spanish Florida.* Also see Ewen, "Continuity and Change"; Hutchinson, *Tatham Mound;* Hutchinson and Mitchem, "Correlates of Contact"; Larsen et al., "Frontiers of Contact"; Milanich, *Florida Indians,* 99–231; Saunders, "Guale Indians"; and Saunders, "Seasonality, Sedentism, Subsistence, and Disease." Stojanowski in "Population History" and *Biocultural Histories* details other factors for the overall decline in Native health in the Spanish missions. He understands poor health to work in conjunction with epidemic diseases to strain the fertility and fecundity of the population and to contribute to an overall steep mortality rate.

35. Dye, "Warfare in the Protohistoric Southeast," 137–38; Nairne, *Nairne's Muskhogean Journals,* 43; Boyd, Smith, and Griffin, *Here They Once Stood,* 15, 37, 50, 53, 90, 92; and Worth, *Struggle for the Georgia Coast,* 15. There are numerous references to the Indian slave trade in McDowell, *Journals of the Commissioners.* See also Le Page du Pratz, *History of Louisiana,* 297; Iberville, *Gulf Journals,* 171–75; and Tonti, "Extract." The use of both guerilla tactics and full-scale military movements was also typical of Mississippian warfare; Dye, "Warfare in the Protohistoric Southeast," 131–35. For a discussion on the demographics of Indian slaves, see Ramsey, "'All and Singular the Slaves.'"

36. Alchon, *Pest in the Land*, 138–39; Usner, "American Indians"; Lauber, *Indian Slavery*, 55–57, 82–86, 242–49; and Gallay, *Indian Slave Trade*, 288–314. On South Carolina Indian slavery, see Ramsey, "'All and Singular the Slaves,'" and on Virginia slavery, see Everett, "'They Shalbe Slaves for Their Lives.'" There are numerous references in colonial documents to the kinds of labor for which Carolinians and Louisiana French used Indian slaves. These uses are quite variable and include labor in agriculture, business ventures, domestic uses, and manufacturing; McDowell, *Journals of the Commissioners*; and Rowland and Sanders, *Mississippi Provincial Archives*, vols. 2 and 3. Other primary sources regarding the fate of Indian slaves are Nairne, Nairne's *Muskhogean Journals*, 43; Le Page Du Pratz, *History of Louisiana*, 297; Iberville, *Gulf Journals*, 171–75; Tonti, "Extract," 159.

37. Boyd, Smith, and Griffin, *Here They Once Stood*, 90. See also Worth, this volume; and Kelton, this volume. By way of comparison historic demographers estimate the number of South American Indians enslaved in the late sixteenth century to have been over half a million; Alchon, *Pest in the Land*, 136–38.

38. Gallay, *Indian Slave Trade*, 298–99.

39. Lauber, *Indian Slavery*, 63–118; and Alchon, *Pest in the Land*, 138–39. In addition, French traders sold many midwestern Indians to Carolina traders; Rushforth, "Little Flesh We Offer You."

40. Wood, "Changing Population," 38–39.

41. For discussions on fertility rates and disease and the implications for population recovery, see Stannard, "Disease and Infertility"; and Thornton, Miller, and Warren, "American Indian Population Recovery."

42. Certainly Indian participants sold other items to Europeans such as skins and furs; however, the argument here is that the trade in Indian slaves was especially pernicious and violent, resulting in much regional instability. Hollis in "Contact, Incorporation, and the North American Southeast" argues that the Spanish explorers brought the first contacts to the global economy into the South through their capture and exchange of Indian slaves and that these expeditions to the South constituted the "emergence of the Atlantic circuit of trade" (121). I agree with Hollis here and take up the story during the later era of capitalist expansion, especially with the Dutch and English hegemonies of the seventeenth and early eighteenth centuries; Boswell and Chase-Dunn, *Spiral of Capitalism*, 17–50.

43. Wallerstein, *Modern World-System*, 1:32–35, 51–90, 147–95, 230, 232; Wallerstein, *World-Systems Analysis*, 23–27.

44. Boswell and Chase-Dunn, *Spiral of Capitalism*, 39, table 1.3.

45. Wallerstein has written extensively on world-systems theory; for the discussion here, see *Modern World-System*, vols. 1, 2, and 3.

46. Bradshaw and Wallace, *Global Inequalities*. Although first published in 1989 and updated in a second edition in 1996, Shannon's *Introduction*, 155–86 is a good overview of the development of the theory and offers a summary of the criticisms. Wallerstein answers some of these critiques in *World-Systems Analysis*, 1–22.

47. World-systems theory today is one of the most important conceptual tools in the social sciences. The concept of globalization, for example, is an acknowledged derivation from world-systems theory. For contemporary studies using world-systems theory, see the following studies: Wallerstein, *Modern World-System in the Longue Durée*; Arrighi, *Long Twentieth Century*; Chase-Dunn and Anderson, *Historical Evolution of World-Systems*; and Chase-Dunn and Babones, *Global Social Change*.

48. For some of this debate, see Innes, *Creating the Commonwealth*; Newell, *From Dependency to Independence*; and Henretta, *Origins of American Capitalism*.

49. This statement is not limited to France, England, and the Netherlands. In fact, world-systems theory states that all European imperial endeavors beginning in the sixteenth century were capitalist based, including those of the Italians, Spanish, Portuguese, Germans, and so on.

50. Placing the Atlantic World as a subset of a larger global economy follows Coclanis, "Atlantic World or Atlantic/World?" However, Coclanis prefers a neo-Marxist approach rather than a Wallerstenian world-systems approach. See also Gallay, "Charles Town."

51. Alan Gallay, especially, has begun to develop a framework for thinking about these commercial outposts. He calls them "hot spots," or "locals that had extraordinary impact economically, culturally and diplomatically on large regions, which they also linked to the greater world"; Gallay, "Charles Town."

52. For a discussion of the global experiences of these European immigrants, see Games, "Beyond the Atlantic." Carson in *Making an Atlantic World*, 61–64, makes the point that these early European colonists understood the value of adopting and using indigenous practices in their colonial projects. For a detailed treatment of a Southern American colony as a trade factory, see Kupperman, *Jamestown Project*.

53. Verner W. Crane's 1929 *Southern Frontier* was the first to note the disturbance to Southern Indian life caused by colonization. He also noted the Indian slave trade as being particularly disruptive. In more recent years the contributors to Ethridge and Hudson's *Transformation* understand colonial turmoil to have

been a key cause for the transformation of Southern Native peoples. Some studies tracking the movements and amalgamations of people during the contact era are DePratter, "Chiefdom of Cofitachequi"; the essays in Ethridge and Hudson, *Transformation*; Galloway, *Choctaw Genesis*; Hickerson, "Historical Processes"; Johnson, "Chickasaws"; Jenkins, this volume; Knight, "Formation of the Creeks"; Kowalewski and Hatch, "Sixteenth-Century Expansion"; Ramenofsky, *Vectors of Death*, 42–71; Regnier, "Stylistic Analysis"; Rogers, "Chronology and the Demise of Chiefdoms"; Schroedl, "Cherokee Ethnohistory"; Smith, *Archaeology of Aboriginal Culture Change*; Smith, *Coosa*; Worth, "Lower Creeks"; Worth, *Timucuan Chiefdoms*; and Waselkov and Smith, "Upper Creek Archaeology."

54. The classic anthropological examples of this are Chagnon, *Yanomamo*, and Rappaport, *Pigs for the Ancestors*. Ferguson's *Yanomami Warfare* offers a detailed case study to challenge these static conceptions of warfare by placing Yanomami conflicts in historical context.

55. Wolf, *Europe and the People without History*; Silverblatt, *Modern Inquisitions*, 3–4; and Blackhawk, *Violence Over the Land*, 9, 13, 276–80. Recent scholarship is recasting violence during the colonial era as actions of much more complex motives than European struggles over land or Native resistances. For examples, see Calloway, *One Vast Winter Count*; Richter, *Ordeal of the Longhouse*; Stannard, *American Holocaust*, and Ferguson, *Yanomami Warfare*. For the South, see Ethridge, *Creek Country*, 215–42; Oatis, *Colonial Complex*; and Waselkov, *Conquering Spirit*.

56. In the 1990s historians Richard White and James Merrell offered their now-famous frameworks for historicizing European and Indian interactions and the generative powers of these interactions for building "middle grounds" and "new worlds." Their studies reshaped the terrain of American history by underscoring that American imperialism involved not just Europeans but Indians and Africans as well; White, *Middle Ground*; and Merrell, *Indians' New World*. Although not central to their analyses, neither White nor Merrell shied away from close looks at episodes of violence born out of this colonial context. In fact, the first chapter in White's *Middle Ground*, "Refugees: A World Made of Fragments," shows the beginnings of the *pays d'en haut* to have been the result of extremely violent encounters — fueled by the fur trade and disease — in which the Iroquois pushed the Algonquian-speaking Indians of the Northeast into the Great Lakes Region; White, *Middle Ground*. For a good overview of the contributions of White and Merrell and other recent developments in American Indian history, see Blackhawk, "Look How Far We've Come."

57. Ferguson and Whitehead, Preface to the Second Edition; and Ferguson and Whitehead, "Violent Edge of Empire."

58. Perdue in *Slavery and the Evolution of Cherokee Society* and Littlefield in *Africans and Creeks* were the first scholars to take in-depth looks at Southern Indian slave practices, both indigenous ideas and imported Euro-American ones. Although Perdue offered a chapter on the Indian slave trade, both studies mostly focus on African-American slavery among the Indians. In more recent years scholars have built on Perdue's and Littlefield's work by examining the complex historical relationship between Indians, African Americans, and Indian citizens of mixed descent. These authors, likewise, focus on Natives and African-American slavery and not on the Indian slave trade. For examples, see Brooks, *Confounding the Color Line*; Frank, *Creeks and Southerners*; Holland and Miles, *Crossing Waters*; Krauthamer, "Particular Kind of Freedom"; Miles, *Ties That Bind*; Naylor-Ojurongbe, "More at Home with the Indians"; Saunt, *Black, White, and Indian*; Sturm, *Blood Politics*; Miles and Naylor-Ojurongbe, "African-Americans in Indian Societies"; Perdue, "Race and Culture"; and Saunt et al., "Rethinking Race."

59. *Invisible Citizens*, the forthcoming compilation of essays edited by Catherine M. Cameron, will be the first sustained look at precontact captivity. The anthology covers captive taking on a global scale.

60. Dye, "Warfare in the Protohistoric Southeast," 137–38. For a recent anthology of the scholarship on trophy taking among American Indians, see the essays in Chacon and Dye in *Taking and Displaying of Human Body Parts*.

61. Alt, "Unwilling Immigrants."

62. Fowler, Rose, Leest, and Ahler, *Mound 72 Area*; and Alt, "Unwilling Immigrants." For an interpretation of Cahokia mortuary practices being used to establish Cahokia preeminence, see Pauketat, *Ancient Cahokia*, 84–95. Others interpret Mound 72 to be a tableau of myth; Brown, "Where's the Power in Mound Building?"; and Kehoe, "Osage Texts and Cahokia Data." For the women retainers, see Ambrose, Buikstra, and Krueger, "Status and Gender Differences"; and Rose, "Mortuary Data and Analysis." The Natchez practiced retainer burials into the eighteenth century. For a summary of the archeology of Natchez mortuary practices, see Lorenz, "Natchez of Southwest Mississippi."

63. Dye, "Warfare in the Protohistoric Southeast," 137–38. Dye's assessment for the increase in captivity as being driven by a loss of population due to disease largely follows Richter's assessment for Iroquois slaving throughout the seventeenth century; Richter, *Ordeal of the Longhouse*, 58. Martin in "Southeastern Indians

and the English Trade," 308–10, was one of the first to note that the commercial slave trade also involved a new kind of slaving.

64. Perdue, *Slavery and the Evolution of Cherokee Society*, 3–18. Snyder's "Conquered Enemies" documents these distinctions among the Creeks. Rushforth's "Little Flesh We Offer You" and "Slavery, the Fox Wars, and the Limits of Alliance" emphasize the role of prisoner and captive exchanges in Indian-European diplomacy among the Great Lakes Indians. Barr in "From Captives to Slaves" examines how men used enslaved Native women for social and political capital and the various forms that bondage took for these women. Kehoe's "'Slaves' and Slave-Raiding" argues that Plains Indians used captives as forced laborers in both pre-and postcontact times, and hence the term "slave" should be applied to this particular kind of precontact bondage. All of these studies remind us that Native categories of slave-captive-kin are not transparent and that we must work at clarifying them in order to fully understand how slavery developed among Native peoples both before and during the colonial years.

65. Lauber, *Indian Slavery in Colonial Times*. The exceptions in Southern history are Crane, *Southern Frontier*; Wood, *Black Majority*; and Perdue, *Slavery*, 19–35. Published well ahead of the recent historical scholarship, Joyce Rockwood Hudson in *Apalachee* portrays a historically accurate fictional account of an Apalachee woman sold into slavery and working on a South Carolina plantation. Although a novel, Hudson attempts to portray something of how an Apalachee woman may have felt about being enslaved and the hardships she would have had to endure as a slave and as her world collapsed around her.

66. Gallay, *Indian Slave Trade*, 23–39, 127–54,170–77, 338–41.

67. Brooks, *Captives and Cousins*, 26–40. Blackhawk critiques *Captives and Cousins* on these grounds; Blackhawk, Review.

68. Snyder in "Conquered Enemies" documents the continued killing of war captives, but she emphasizes the ritual aspects of these killings that she understands to have allowed "for the release of dead kinspeople's souls into the afterlife" (267) A recent flurry of articles on Indian slaving likewise downplays the violence; Rushforth, "Little Flesh We Offer You"; Rushforth, "Slavery, the Fox Wars, and the Limits of Alliance"; Barr, "From Captives to Slaves"; and Kehoe, "'Slaves' and Slave-Raiding."

69. Blackhawk, Review, 89.

70. Bowne, *Westo Indians*.

71. Ferguson and Whitehead make this point in "Violent Edge of Empire," 23.

72. We still do not know all of the reasons for Mississippian Period warfare. Dye in "Warfare in the Protohistoric Southeast," 130–31, lists protecting territory, chiefs legitimizing their authority over other elites through success in warfare, resolution of disputes between chiefs, and political and financial expansion as some prime reasons for Mississippian warfare. However, since revenge and retaliation were such deeply held values for many Southern Indians during the Historic Period, these motives for warfare may have had deep roots in the Mississippian. For discussions on revenge and retaliation, see Hudson, *Southeastern Indians*, 128–83, Ethridge, *Creek Country*, 228–32. The most comprehensive treatment of these principles is still John Phillip Reid's *Law of Blood*.

73. Ferguson and Whitehead in "Violent Edge of Empire" argue that once indigenous people became involved in European trade and colonial politics and military agendas, indigenous warfare became directed by elements outside of a purely Native world. Access to European trade goods, control over the supply and distribution of Indian slaves and trade goods, the use of indigenous mercenaries by the colonizers, as well as mutual military, political, and economic manipulation of each other by Europeans and indigenous inhabitants, all began to figure into indigenous motivations for and strategies of war. This issue may come down to whether one understands indigenous warfare to be culturally (or even biologically) determined or to be determined by political and economic history.

Dye, citing Ferguson and Whitehead, was the first to note the change in Southern Indian warfare during the colonial era in "Warfare in the Protohistoric Southeast." Ethridge in "Making of a Militaristic Slaving Society" examines the militarization of the Chickasaw and the repercussions on the internal civic and military orders of Chickasaw society once trade and warfare became connected.

By way of comparison, Law in "Warfare on the West African Slave Coast," 113, notes that scholars of the African slave trade are somewhat divided over whether or not the endemic warfare among the African kingdoms of the Slave and Gold coasts was "cultural" and not substantively transformed by the slave trade. Law understands African warfare in these areas to have become driven by commercial interests, in particular the capture of war captives to sell to European slavers.

74. Ethridge, "Creating the Shatter Zone," 208–9. Ferguson and Whitehead, "Violent Edge," 18–28, also understand militarization to be a result of the interface between expanding states and indigenous peoples.

75. Hudson and Ethridge, "Early Historic Transformation," 41–42; Gallay, *Indian Slave Trade*, 40–52; and Hall, "Zamumo's Gifts," chapter 5.

There is a standing question about the effectiveness of these early trade guns and whether or not they would have given any group a military edge. Opinions are divided; Heather, "Weapons of War"; and Chet, *Conquering the American Wilderness*. For discussions on the effectiveness of these weapons in Indian warfare, see Bowne, *Westo Indians*, 65–71; and Malone, *Skulking Way of War*.

The question of Native dependency on guns raises larger issues regarding the use of and dependency on trade goods in general. Scholars are not in agreement over the transforming power of the colonial trade system. Examining a contemporary people, Brian Ferguson makes a strong case that not only guns but also metal tools became indispensable after they were introduced to the Yanomami and that the Yanomami still go to great lengths to obtain both and are so intent on gaining and controlling access to western trade goods that this intent infiltrates into as well as directs many aspects of Yanomami life; Ferguson, *Yanomami Warfare*, 21–37. The same can be said for the Southern Natives during the Historic Period. White in *Roots of Dependency* argues that Native dependency on European-manufactured goods resulted in changes in three different Native groups once they became involved in the new economy. Hahn makes a similar case for the Creeks in "Miniature Arms Race" and "Mother of Necessity."

76. Gallay, "Beachheads into Empires."

77. This is not to say that European-manufactured goods did not find their way into the South. Waselkov in "Seventeenth-Century Trade" demonstrates that goods flowed into and out of Spanish Florida throughout the seventeenth century and that although the sale of guns was prohibited, some Indians acquired a few, most likely through an illicit trade between the Spanish and the Indians. More recently, Hall in "Zamumo's Gifts" examines the movement of goods from Spanish Florida into the interior and argues that although these goods came mostly as gifts, they profoundly affected the prestige exchange system of nearby chiefdoms.

78. There has been much work done on the Indians of Spanish Florida. For brief overviews, see Milanich, "Timucua Indians"; Saunders, "Guale Indians"; and McEwan, "Apalachee Indians." Some book-length treatments are Hann, *Apalachee*; *Native American World Beyond Apalachee*; McEwan, *Spanish Missions of La Florida*; Milanich, *Laboring in the Field of the Lords*; Thomas, *St. Catherines*; *Native American Landscapes*; Worth, *Struggle for the Georgia Coast*; and Worth, *Timucuan Chiefdoms*.

79. Milanich, "Timucua Indians," 10, 17–22; Worth, *Timucuan Chiefdoms*, 1:35–43, 126–34, 187–97; 2:1–37; McEwan, "Apalachee Indians," 65–67; and Saunders, "Guale Indians," 40–50.

80. Milanich, "Timucua Indians," 14. Worth in "Bridging Prehistory and History" contrasts the persistence of Indian ways throughout the mission period against the sweeping changes that took place in Native societies in the interior South with the introduction of firearms and the slave trade. He concludes that the concept of acculturation is inadequate to explain these differences and posits that rather one should look at the broader emerging global sociopolitical and capitalist economic system and how the different European regimes fit into this system and how their varying colonial strategies in turn affected Native life.

81. Worth, *Timucuan Chiefdoms*, 2:27–37, 38–65; Worth, "Spanish Missions"; and Saunders, "Guale Indians," 47–50. On the health of Spanish mission Indians, see Larsen et al., "Frontiers of Contact"; Larsen, Ruff, and Griffin, "Implications"; Milanich, *Florida Indians*, 99–231; and Stojanowski, *Biocultural Histories*, 126–52. Stojanowski in *Biocultural Histories* offers an interesting comparison between Apalachees and Guales and notes significant health differences between the two, with the Guales fairing the worst.

82. Worth, *Struggle for the Georgia Coast*, 9, 36, 40, 45. Pirate activity has long held a place in the America imagination, and pirate activity in the Atlantic has been long noted by historians. Although their participation in the North American Indian slave trade is well documented in the historic record, scholars have yet to assess not only the impact of pirate slave raiding on Indian people but also the contacts between pirates and Indians in general. For recent scholarship on Atlantic piracy, see Cordingly, *Under the Black Flag*; and Earle, *Pirate Wars*.

83. Worth, *Struggle for the Georgia Coast*, 15–18; and Saunders, "Guale Indians," 50. For the biological evidence and implications of these movements, see Stojanowski, *Biocultural Histories*, 126–52.

84. Abler, "Beavers and Muskets"; Richter, *Ordeal of the Longhouse*; Starna and Watkins, "Northern Iroquoian Slavery"; and Fox, this volume. The Dutch abandoned their North American project in the mid-seventeenth century, but they were clearly involved in the fur and slave trade up until that time.

85. Richter, *Ordeal of the Longhouse*, 1, 28–45.

86. Starna and Watkins, "Northern Iroquoian Slavery," 41–46, 52–53; and Richter, *Ordeal of the Longhouse*, 32–49.

87. Abler, "Beavers and Muskets," 158–160; and Richter, *Ordeal of the Longhouse*, 56–58.

88. Richter, *Ordeal of the Longhouse*, 51–62.

89. White, *Middle Ground*, 11–13; and Richter, *Ordeal of the Longhouse*, 60–66.

90. Richter, *Ordeal of the Longhouse*, 144; and Wolf, *Europe and the People Without History*, 163–94; and White, *Middle Ground*, 1–49.

91. Drooker, "Ohio Valley"; Pollack, *Caborn-Welborn*, 188–90. Archaeologists have also identified another vacant area that they call the Vacant Quarter, which was an area stretching from the Ohio River to the Mississippi River and south to northern Mississippi. They believe that the Vacant Quarter was abandoned sometime around 1450 and only sparsely populated in the seventeenth century; Williams, "Vacant Quarter"; and Cobb and Butler, "Vacant Quarter Revisited."

92. Drooker, "Ohio Valley," 233; and Smith, "Aboriginal Population Movements in the Postcontact Southeast, 5–7."

93. Jeter first suggested this idea in "From Prehistory through Protohistory," 214–15. The question of Quapaw origins has been in debate among archaeologists for over a decade. For a summary of this debate, see Sabo, "Quapaw Indians of Arkansas," 185–87.

94. For a discussion of the Shawnees and colonial slaving, see Drooker, "Ohio Valley," 124–28.

95. Rountree, "Trouble Coming Southward," 72.

96. Rountree in "Trouble Coming Southward," 66–69 also notes that these movements and disruptions in Virginia were generated by Iroquois slaving.

97. Ward and Davis, *Indian Communities*, 427–30; Davis, "Cultural Landscape," 139. See also Davis, Livingood, Ward, and Steponaitis, "Excavating Occaneechi Town."

98. Davis, "Cultural Landscape," 150–51.

99. Richter, *Ordeal of the Longhouse*, 145–48; Davis, "Cultural Landscape," 145–54; Rountree, "Trouble Coming Southward," 72–78; Rountree and Davidson, *Eastern Shore Indians*, 47–123; Turner, "Socio-Political Organization"; and Meyers, "Adapting to the Shatter Zone."

100. For the coalescence of the Creeks, see Knight, "Formation of the Creeks"; Smith, *Coosa*, 50–81, 96–117; Waselkov and Smith, "Upper Creek Archaeology"; Worth, "Lower Creeks"; Hall, "Zamumo's Gifts"; and Jenkins, this volume.

101. Rodning, "Reconstructing the Coalescence."

102. Turner, "Socio-Political Organization"; Rountree, *Powhatan Indians*, 141; Gallivan, "Powhatan's Werowocomoco," 97; and Scarry and Maxham, "Elite Actors," 53–163. The essays in Rountree's *Powhatan Foreign Relations* detail much about Powhatan relations with other Natives; however, the Indian slave trade figures only marginally in the authors' discussions.

103. Hudson, *Knights of Spain*, 203; Goddard et al., "Small Tribes," 176–77; Hahn, "Mother of Necessity," 93–94; Hann, "Florida's Terra Incognita," 75–79; Worth, *Timucuan Chiefdoms of Spanish Florida* 2:18–21, 34–35; and Hann, *Native American World beyond Apalachee*, 52–68.

104. Bowne in *Westo Indians* mostly covers the Westos once they move to the Savannah River. The Westos' activities in Virginia are still cloudy, but it is reasonable to presume that they were developing, if not already utilizing, the predatory strategy that they later used in Georgia. Westo affairs then could also help account for some of the turmoil of the northern Piedmont in the mid-seventeenth century. The Westos may have also been composed of some Neutrals as well as Eries; Meyers, this volume. The Indian slave trade in Virginia is only now being investigated; Everett, "'They Shalbe Slaves for Their Lives'"; and Shefveland, "Hidden in Plain View."

105. Bowne, *Westo Indians*, 72–88; and Gallay, *Indian Slave Trade*, 53–69.

106. Gallay, *Indian Slave Trade*, 51–52; and Hudson et al., "On Cofitachequi."

107. See also Hudson et al., "On Cofitachequi."

108. For the Occaneechis, see Ward and Davis, *Indian Communities*, 430; and Davis, "Cultural Landscape," 144. For the Westos, see Bowne, "Rise and Fall," 71–73; and Bowne, *Westo Indians*, 89–105. For the Chiscas, see Hahn, "Mother of Necessity," 93, and Hahn, *Native American World beyond Apalachee*, 52–68. For the Iroquois, see Richter, *Ordeal of the Longhouse*, 148–90. Neil Whitehead in "Tribes Make States," 138, sees a similar process in South America where colonial tribal mercenaries became the objects of later European military campaigns.

109. The Tuscaroras, surrounded by Indian enemies because of their slaving, were defeated by a Yamasee-English army in 1713; the survivors migrated to Iroquoia, where in 1722 they joined the Great League as the Sixth Nation. Merrell, *Indians' New World*, 40, 54, 118; and Richter, *Ordeal of the Longhouse*, 238.

110. Gallay, *Indian Slave Trade*, 319–22; and Dunaway, *Slavery in the American Mountain South*, 1–10.

111. Riggs, "Reinterpreting the Chestowee Raid."

112. Gallay, *Indian Slave Trade*, 308.

113. I am currently completing a volume on the Chickasaw involvement in the slave trade, and I have published a summary article of that book and other related articles elsewhere; therefore their involvement is not covered in this volume. I refer readers to these other publications for detailed histories of the Chickasaws as slavers and the subsequent transformation of their society; Ethridge, "Making

of a Militaristic Slaving Society"; Ethridge, "From Chicaza to Chickasaw"; and Johnson et al., "Measuring Chickasaw Adaptation."

114. Smith, "Aboriginal Population Movements in the Postcontact Southeast," 17; Ramenofsky in *Vectors of Death*, 42–71, 137–76, argues that this abandonment is largely due to disease epidemics.

115. Perttula, "Social Changes," 255–69; Swanton, *Indian Tribes*, 296–97; Hickerson, "Historical Processes"; Early, "Caddos"; and Lorenz, "Natchez"; and Galloway, *Choctaw Genesis*.

116. Swanton in *Indian Tribes*, 274–306, was the first to try to make sense of the history of Natives of lower Louisiana and Alabama. Others since then have made strides in placing them within their precontact and colonial historical contexts; Goddard et al., "Small Tribes"; Kniffin, Gregory, and Stokes, *Tribes of Louisiana*, 71–105; and especially Usner, *American Indians*; Usner, *Indians, Settlers, and Slaves*; and Waselkov and Gums. *Plantation Archaeology at Rivière aux Chiens*, 6–62.

117. Gallay in *Indian Slave Trade*, 14–15, 128–34, 142–43, understands the Chickasaws' geopolitical position to have been an important factor in their involvement in the slave trade.

118. Whitehead and Ferguson in "Violent Edge of Empire," 12–16, also understand the "tribal zone" to change indigenous geopolitical landscapes in that not only are emerging states and empires part of the new landscape, but their presence leads to the formation of new kinds of indigenous societies. In particular, they understand societies on the edges of empires and states to be uniformly transformed into "tribes," or decentralized polities. Whitehead, however, in "Tribes Make States," 134–35, posits a variety of decentralized social types for South America that emerged during the colonial era. Of particular interest here, Whitehead states that in the case of South America "no modern groups can be seen as exemplifying pre-Columbian patterns of existence, as has sometimes been the rather naive assumption of ethnographers and archaeologists" (135).

119. Hudson, Introduction, xxxviii–xxxxix.

120. Blackhawk in *Violence Over the Land*, 9, uses the term "foundational experience" in reference to how Euro-American expansion impacted Native people, and he is emphatic that "without recognition, first, of the magnitude of Europe's impact upon the Americas, histories of the nation will remain forever incomplete" (293). Charles R. Cobb recently noted that the scholarship to understand the forces of modernism, capitalism, and globalization on Native societies has gone far in deconstructing the Native as "Other," but he insists that this has been done "at the expense of reifying a homogenized [prehistoric] past of traditional, static

societies" (Cobb, "Archaeology and the 'Savage Slot,'" 563) and that anthropologists and historians uncritically use this static concept of prehistory as a baseline for measuring the impact of colonialism and thus conclude that changes in Native life only occurred once Europeans set things in motion. According to Cobb, all of this serves to support the notion of an unchanging, traditional prehistory. As Cobb puts it, we, in fact, have not dismantled the Other, but rather we have simply construed it into a "pre-Columbian Other." Still, one can subscribe to Cobb's insistence on historicizing prehistory while also acknowledging that European contact was a foundational experience as Blackhawk asserts.

121. For works examining the fall of chiefdoms, see Galloway, "Confederation as a Solution"; Jenkins, this volume; Knight, "Formation of the Creeks"; Anderson, *Savannah River Chiefdoms*; Smith, *Coosa*; Pollack, *Caborn-Welborn*; Scarry, *Political Structure and Change*; and Scarry, "Rise, Transformation, and Fall of Apalachee."

122. Gallay, *Indian Slave Trade*, 51–52

123. The settlement Indians and the *petites nations*, more than any other groups in the interior South, may resemble Richard White's famous "middle ground." White, *Middle Ground*, 50–60.

124. Worth, "Spanish Missions," 51–52.

125. Hickerson, "Historical Processes"; and Perttula, "Social Changes."

126. Johnson et al., "Measuring Chickasaw Adaptations"; Johnson et al., "Chickasaws"; and Lorenz, "Natchez of Southwest Mississippi." For a detailed investigation of the Natchez experience among the Chickasaws, see Lieb, "Grand Village is Silent."

127. Merrell, *Indians' New World*, 92–133; and Hudson and Ethridge, "Early Historic Transformations," 40–46. Worth, in "Spanish Missions," 52, calls this "confederation," but the definition is similar enough to "coalescence" to lump it with coalescence for now. As these responses become clearer, finer distinctions no doubt will be made between them. In a broad cross-cultural comparison Kowalewski in "Coalescent Societies" concludes that coalescence is a wide-spread response to social stresses, and therefore coalescent societies are not necessarily a social type but the result of people responding in a particular way as a social system facing instability breaks apart.

128. Worth, "Yamassee"; Merrell, *Indians' New World*, 92–122; Fitts and Heath, this volume; and Beck, this volume.

129. Perttula, "Social Changes," 257–69; and Hickerson, "Historical Processes."

130. Perttula in "Social Changes," 257–60, and Knight in "Formation of the Creeks" were the first to notice the chiefdom political basis for coalescence.

131. Ethridge, "Ethnohistory"; and Ethridge, "Making of a Militaristic Slaving Society."

132. Hudson and Ethridge, "Early Historic Transformation," 42–43. On the continuities in domestic and subsistence economy, see Muller, *Mississippian Political Economy*; Ethridge, *Creek Country*, 140–57; Pavao-Zuckerman, "Vertebrate Subsistence"; and Gremillion, "Adoption of Old World Crops." On political continuities, see Blitz, *Ancient Chiefdoms*, 9–24; King, "Historic Period Transformation"; Pollack, *Caborn-Welborn*, 199–206; and Foster, *Archaeology of the Lower Muskogee Creek*, 12–17, 264–66. For continuities (and discontinuities) across household structure, see Hally, "'As Caves beneath the Ground'"; Lapham, *Hunting for Hides*, 101–4, 138–41; Wesson, *Households and Hegemony*; and the essays in Cobb, *Stone Tool Traditions*.

133. On the transformation from Mississippian to Historic Period leadership, see Ethridge, "Making of a Militaristic Slaving Society"; Galloway, "Confederation as a Solution"; Galloway, "Dual Organization Reconsidered"; Gallivan, "Powhatan's Werowocomoco"; King, "Historic Period Transformation"; Knight, "Institutional Organization"; Lapham, *Hunting for Hides*, 104–37, 141–49; and Wesson, "Prestige Goods." On the continuing changes in leadership patterns during the colonial era, see Hahn, *Invention of the Creek Nation*; O'Brien, *Choctaws in a Revolutionary Age*; Piker, *Okfuskee*; Saunt, *New Order*; and Waselkov, "Historic Creek Indian Responses."

134. The emergence of an assimilationist elite class among the Southern Indians during the Removal era was first noted by Perdue in *Slavery and the Evolution of Cherokee Society*. More recently, Martin in *Sacred Revolt* and Saunt in *New Order* understand this elite class among the Creeks to have been market-oriented *métis*, whose mind set, life ways, and jockeying for political power were gravely disruptive and divisive forces in Creek society by the last few decades of the eighteenth century.

2 | *Events as Seen from the North*

THE IROQUOIS AND COLONIAL SLAVERY

WILLIAM A. FOX

Warfare among and between Iroquoian-speaking groups and their neighbors had been endemic for centuries or even millennia prior to the arrival of Europeans in the Northeast, as amply attested by archaeological evidence.[1] There is nothing, however, to suggest that such aggression constituted more than lineage-based blood feuding or revenge warfare to maintain the honor of the village.[2] This perpetual unrest among Iroquoian groups may have been exacerbated by the transition to an agricultural economy and the resultant increase in population levels.[3] William Engelbrecht has further proposed a connection "between sacrifice and crops" per Bruce Trigger's suggestion that "the sacrifice of prisoners was linked to crop success, game abundance, and the continuation of the natural world."[4] The construction of multiwalled palisades, often with earthworks, during the fifteenth century and increasing amounts of cracked and burnt human bone in village middens during the sixteenth century suggest intensified conflict.[5] There were some long distance movements in the sixteenth century by groups who formed the Neutral and Huron confederacies.[6] Yet no warfare-related village abandonments have been documented archaeologically.

Such endemic warfare was incomprehensible to many European observers, and later ethnohistorians attributed its intensified seventeenth-century expression to a quest for participation in the European fur trade.[7] Recently, this warfare has been seen to reflect beliefs about death and the replacement of individuals in aboriginal societies — the mourning war.[8] A broader Iroquois political agenda for the latter, the amalgamation of all Iroquoian peoples — "one people and only one land" — was reported by

Father Jogues following his Mohawk captivity.[9] The shatter zone concept provides another explanatory model for the disruptive violence of this period. Such zones constituted "large regions of instability from which shock waves radiate out for sometimes hundreds and hundreds of miles."[10] Instigated by commercial trade and its attendant colonial struggles, this model has focused on the Indian slave trade and its destructive consequences to aboriginal societies throughout the South.

All of these perspectives hold some truth. Yet a layered approach to explaining the explosion of Five Nations Iroquois violence during the mid-seventeenth century may provide a more comprehensive understanding of events, particularly as these culturally shattering events to the North ultimately impacted the Indian societies of the South. The acquisition of European goods for incorporation into ritual had been an important consideration for Native groups since initial contact, and the catastrophic epidemics of the 1630s and 1640s intensified the requirement to recruit replacements for the dead, through mourning wars.[11] Likewise, the English and Dutch provision of firearms to the Mohawk provided a decided advantage to their war parties by increasing the effectiveness of these conflicts. Identifying an underlying social condition, which can explain the availability of young male agents to carry out the public desire for revenge or replacement of the dead, could elucidate the events that confused and frustrated the British during their eighteenth-century attempts to control inter-Indian politics and speak to the earlier seventeenth-century Wars of the Iroquois.[12]

During the latter half of the 1630s the elderly and the very young were the first victims of the devastating epidemics that swept through Iroquoia. This death toll would have included elder matrons and sachems, leading to a destabilization of Iroquoian villages and society in general. Fear of witchcraft was rampant as was anger toward real or imagined perpetrators.[13] Mesquida and Wiener have argued convincingly that the ratio of men aged fifteen to twenty-nine versus men older than thirty in a society is an accurate predictor of the outbreak of war or "coalitional aggression," as they term it. They note that "a relatively large number of young men in a society, usually caused by rapid population growth, is therefore suggested as being at the origin of the formation of aggressive young male coalitions. We propose that changes within societies in the relative numbers of young men contribute importantly to the periodicity of violent conflicts."[14]

This demographic profile may have triggered the sporadic precontact violence documented among Ontario Iroquoian groups following the population boom of the fourteenth century. However, it may equally well explain the apparently anomalous level of aggression reported among the Neutral in the early 1640s that involved the capture of hundreds of Fire Nation prisoners in a massive escalation of a long-term conflict, which appears to have evolved into a mourning war. In this case decimation by disease and famine rather than a rapid population increase may have tipped the scale in favor of the angry-young-man demographic. Indeed, the same scenario may help to explain the collective aggression of the Five Nations, which escalated in the 1640s. This aggression would have been exacerbated by an additional tool of war, the firearm, leading shortly thereafter to the dispersal of the Ontario Iroquoian-speaking confederacies.[15]

It is proposed here that a coalitional aggression demographic evolved rapidly among Iroquoian-speaking groups during the late 1630s and 1640s that fueled the warfare. Traditional power structures and control mechanisms in Iroquoian society had been weakened by epidemic losses. Aggressive young men — the warriors (as opposed to sachems) — prevailed, and their aggressions required direction away from the village. Combined with a weapon of spiritual as well technological superiority, the Mohawk and then all Five Nations succeeded to an unprecedented degree in their wars. Iroquois war parties defeated and dispersed the Huron, Petun, and Neutral confederacies in 1649, 1650, and 1651, respectively, and then the Erie Nation during the period between 1654 and 1657. As each nation fell, individuals, lineages and village populations that were not captured and forcibly removed from their homelands made survival decisions. Some joined adjacent groups with whom they had personal or political connections, while some left the region for more distant refuges, and some opted to join the Iroquois.[16]

Father Lalemant's 1660 observation concerning the Five Nations Iroquois is telling in this regard:

If anyone should compute the number of pure-blooded Iroquois, he would have difficulty in finding more than twelve hundred of them in all of the Five Nations, since these are, for the most part, only aggregations of different tribes whom they have conquered — as the Hurons; the Tionnontatehronnons, otherwise called the Tobacco Nation; the Atiwendaronk, called the Neutrals when they were still independent; the Riquehronnons, who are the Cat Nation; the Ontwagannhas, or Fire Nation; the Trakwaehronnons, and others, — who, utter Foreigners although they are, form without doubt the largest and best part of the Iroquois.[17]

It has been suggested that a significant component of the late seventeenth-century Western Seneca of Ohio were in fact made up largely of Neutrals. Add to this the early seventeenth-century osteological evidence for some of the first *métis* among the Neutral and Seneca, and by all accounts the Seneca were a coalescent nation from the mid-seventeenth century onward. There is no doubt that the midcentury conquests of adjacent Iroquoian-speaking confederacies by the Five Nations Iroquois shattered the Native political map in the lower Great Lakes region and sent reverberations into the upper Great Lakes or *pays d'en haut*.[18] It is evident, however, that indigenous social factors played a dominant role in these events.

The Early Seventeenth Century in Iroquoia

There can be little doubt that the aggressive Richahecrians known to midcentury Virginians can be equated with the Westo peoples, a seminal participant in the Native slaving raids of the South from the late 1650s to the early 1680s. William Green in his insightful paper concerning the Eries and Westos argues cogently for the joint identity of the two.[19] But just who were the Eries by 1660? In order to begin answering this question, we must reel back to the first half of the seventeenth century and review the material culture of undoubted Erie village and cemetery sites.[20] To anyone familiar with the contemporary material culture of the adjacent Neutral, Erie artifact assemblages would be lost on a Neutral site of the period because the assemblages are so similar, particularly the mortuary vessels.[21] In a comprehensive review of cartographic, ethnohistoric, and ethnographic information, Pendergast proposes that the Kahkwas, located immediately adjacent to the southeasternmost Neutral group, were "a component of the Erie confederacy." The difficulty in identifying the affiliation of the Kakwas has been a function of both very limited contemporary European documentation concerning the Eries and the cultural similarities between the various groups that constituted the Neutral and Erie confederacies.[22]

As to the Neutral, Lennox and Fitzgerald observed, "the Neutral should be investigated, not as a homogeneous cultural entity, but as a collection of individual, territorial communities or tribes, each with its own distinctive identity." Indeed, the Neutral confederacy appears to have been constituted of eight or nine groups in a series of villages that at times extended from present-day southern Ontario into New York State east of the Niagara River. Cooper has discussed the individuality of these "village clusters" in some detail with regard to the southeastern Neutral of the Niagara Peninsula. Considerable confusion exists about the identity of this frontier Neutral group's neighbors near present-day Buffalo, New York. Earlier researchers identified these peoples as Neutrals or Eries or some other allied group such as the Kakwas. Given conflicting historical documentation and the similarity of the material culture on archaeological sites confidently identified with the Neutral and Erie confederacies, this confusion is hardly surprising. Half a century ago, MacNeish proposed that based on ceramic typology "shortly after the time period of the Southwold Earthworks (ca. 1500 CE), the Eries evidently separated from the Neutral." As the material culture of each of the groups that made up the Neutral confederacy becomes better defined, artifact attribute clines may be defined geographically from north of Lake Ontario to south of Lake Erie, such that the archaeological definition of Neutral versus Erie will become even further clouded. The point is that despite occasional conflict, the Neutrals and Eries were closely related peoples, closer than they were to their Seneca neighbors to the east.[23]

In order to comprehend the Eries of the late 1650s, we must look to the north of Lake Erie in the homeland of the powerful and populous Neutral Confederacy. Early seventeenth-century French observers noted this confederacy's neutrality in relation to the endemic warfare that characterized Five Nations Iroquois and Huron relations as well as their alliance with the Odawa in wars against the Gens de Feu, or Fire Nation. The latter was a collective term for Central Algonquian-speaking groups later known as the Kickapoos, Mascoutins, and Fox, among others, who occupied lands at the western end of Lake Erie and along the Detroit-St. Clair River corridor.[24]

The Recollect priest, Father Daillon, in his 1626 visit to the Neutral noted twenty-eight "boroughs, towns or villages, built like those of the Huron country" as well as "many little hamlets of seven or eight lodges."[25] Father Lalemant noted the Neutral in the Jesuit Relation of 1641–42: "according to the reckoning of the Fathers who have been there, there are at least twelve thousand souls in the whole extent of the country, which relies upon being still able to furnish four thousand warriors, not withstanding the wars, famine, and sickness which for 3 years have been unusually prevalent there."[26]

Population estimates of up to forty thousand are documented. The 1641 "Nouvelle France" map reported "quarante Bourgs" (forty villages) for the Neutral as compared to only seventeen for the Huron. Compare this number to four contemporary villages at most for the Seneca and probably a total of no more than fifteen for the entire Five Nations Iroquois confederacy at this time. The Neutral Confederacy was not only "very populous" by comparison to neighboring Iroquoian groups, but also it was more cosmopolitan or wide ranging in its contacts with foreign peoples, particularly to the south. For instance, Neutral groups had close ties with the proto-Shawnee Fort Ancient peoples in the Ohio Valley, and some may have had direct connections as far away as what is now central Alabama. In addition, the Hurons through the Nipissings and the Petuns through the Odawas maintained long-distance connections with other Algonquian-speaking nations far to the north and west, respectively. The Five Nations Iroquois appear to have had more limited contact with other Native groups beyond their immediate neighbors.[27]

Based on settlement pattern and artifact evidence from southwestern Ontario and northwestern Ohio, it appears that the animosities between at least one of the Neutral confederacy groups, probably the Oheroukouarhronon, or People of the Swamp, and at least one of the constituent groups of the Fire Nation, probably the Totontaratonhronon, was of some antiquity. The exact timing and basis of deteriorating relations between Neutrals and other Algonquian-speaking groups in southwestern Ontario cannot be ascertained at present, although villages of both groups began to build earthwork defenses as early as the fifteenth century. Also, the 1500 CE western Neutral citadel known as the Lawson site contains considerable burnt and fractured human bone in its middens that indicate some sort of animosity with external groups. By the late sixteenth century this particular group moved east to the Beverly Swamp environs, north of present-day Hamilton, where they became known as the People of the Swamp.[28]

For Native groups in the Northeast warfare consisted of raids and skirmishes. Champlain's frustration with Huron fighting tactics in the 1615 campaign against the Five Nations Iroquois (Oneida or Onondaga) underlines the limited extent of such battles. Thus the capture of hundreds of Central Algonquian-speaking prisoners by the Neutrals in the early 1640s stands in stark contrast to typical warfare of the time.[29] It is a possibility that this phenomenon was a form of mourning war borne of epidemic-related population loss in the late 1630s. Yet whatever its cause, it marks the first recorded large-scale forcible incorporation of alien peoples into an Iroquoian-speaking population.

The 1640s were a pivotal period for Native relations in the lower Great Lakes region. Trade competition between European nations resulted in the arming with muskets of Five Nations Iroquois warriors, particularly the Mohawk. While the efficacy of these primitive firearms is debated, there is little doubt that they provided a substantial advantage to the users, especially when turned against the general population of an Ontario Iroquoian village. Moreover, in 1648–49 the Iroquois armament advantage was combined with nontraditional military tactics to rout the Hurons. A chance event in December 1649 — the sort that often determines victory or defeat on the battlefield — resulted in the dispersal westward of the major portion of the Tionnontatehronnons (Petuns) and Kiskakon Odawas in 1650. Although the Neutral had enjoyed a relatively peaceful relationship with the Five Nations Iroquois until the late 1640s, in 1651–52 the epidemic-depleted Neutral confederacy finally succumbed to the Seneca. Many of the Neutral refugees settled with the Seneca, and archaeologists have identified their artifacts on at least three post-1660 Seneca sites. Large segments of several Seneca villages in the Genesee River region consisted of "adopted" Neutral peoples.[30]

During these turbulent times the Jesuits retreated from Huronia in 1650 and did not return to the region until 1656 when they established a mission to the Onondaga. All information about the Neutral Confederacy's abandonment of their territory comes from second-and third-hand reports by Native informants. Consequently, we do not have a clear sense of how the Neutral abandonment of their territory proceeded and even less so as to whether there were different strategies implemented by different groups. We do know that individuals dispersed widely as one Neutral woman was identified among the Huron in Quebec, and in July 1653 eight hundred Neutrals were recorded in the Detroit vicinity to the west. That some of the Neutral People of the Swamp may have been among those who joined the Seneca is suggested by the subsequent location of the Sonontoua (Seneca) village of Outinaouatoua adjacent to the Beverly swamp as documented by Galinee in 1667. Indeed, it is very likely that Ontario Iroquoian populations predominated among the occupants of Five Nations Iroquois villages established along the north shore of Lake Ontario between 1660 and 1680.[31]

Substantial groups of Neutral could also have fled south to the neighboring Erie confederacy as suggested on the Sanson map of 1656, thus bolstering Erie numbers during the four-year conflict with the Five Nations.[32] Father Francois le Mercier in September of 1654 reports that "the Cat Nation [Erie] is very populous, having been reinforced by some Hurons, who scattered in all directions when their country was laid waste, and who now have stirred up this war which is filling the Iroquois with alarm."[33] These refugee Hurons are likely to have arrived via the Neutral territory and with Neutral refugees, most likely accompanied by many more of the latter. Unfortunately we have no recorded first-hand observations of the Eries by Europeans prior to their major defeat by the Iroquois (primarily Onondaga) in 1656 and subsequent dispersal and adoption into the Five Nations. We know, however, that certain groups from the Neutral Confederacy (certainly the Omiagarhronnons) were familiar with nations to the south in the Ohio Valley and beyond and that the western Neutral People of the Swamp were proficient in the capture of large numbers of enemy peoples.[34]

With a possible Neutral-Erie connection in mind, we should consider two pieces of historical evidence. One is Father Ragueneau's statement in 1645 that the Eries moved far inland to escape their enemies, and the second is the location of the Attioundarons, a Native group spanning the Appalachians to the northeast of the colony of Virginia on the "Nouvelle France" map of 1641. As Heidenreich indicates, Attiouendaronk is what the Huron called the Neutral and the meaning of the word is "people of a slightly different language" or, more literally, "their words are some distance away." While the *Enrie Nation Du Chat* (The Erie) are identified to the north of the enigmatic Attioundarons on the 1641 map, it may well be that the appellation represents a Neutral-Erie population who had moved to the south, consistent with Green's hypothesis. This possibility, plus the archaeological data supporting strong Southern connections on the part of several Neutral groups, may explain Father Le Jeune's 1639 observation concerning "the neutral Nation, which is a main gateway for the Southern tribes."[35]

There is no doubt that Ontario Iroquoian-speaking peoples joined the Erie Confederacy during the first years of the 1650s, making the Eries a coalescent nation similar to the Five Nations Iroquois. The coalescence of people brought together a variety of personal and political agendas. Some of these imported agendas derived from recent traumas and appear to have been the underlying motivation in the Erie-Seneca war (1654–57). Based on the reports about a major battle at a fortified Erie village, the defenders were armed with muskets by the early 1650s.[36] The Erie, an aggressive coalescent group, may have migrated to the Virginia frontier in the mid-1650s to join a related population already resident in the region and familiar with the economic needs of the English colonies. This migrant group would have been armed with muskets, accustomed to large scale enemy capture, and bereft of a constraining social structure; it made them prime candidates for a prominent role in commercial slaving. The most suggestive evidence for the Erie origins of the Westos comes from Father Jean de Lamberville's letter from Onnontague (Onondaga), penned on August 25, 1682. He reports that "six hundred men, women, and Children of the nation of the chats [Eries], near Virginia, surrendered voluntarily (to the Iroquois), for fear that they might be compelled to do so by force."[37] According to colonist Thomas Newe, the Carolinians in concert with the Shawnees (Savannah) were still pursuing the Westos in 1682.[38] This return north and surrender near Virginia by a group of Eries following the Westo War of 1680 seems more than coincidental in terms of the Erie identity to the Westo.

Slavery among the Iroquois

Some of the first historical references to captives being used as slaves among the Iroquois come to us from the pen of Father Herosime Lalemant in 1646 and 1647. The former communication is related to a plea for the return of a captive Huron girl convert, and the latter concerned the sufferings of Father Isaac Jogues as a "servant to some hunters."[39] Next, we hear from Father Francesco Bressani, concerning his capture, torture, and servitude in his relation of 1653.[40] In his December 1, 1657, relation from the Onnontague Mission, Father Paul le Jeune defines three classes of captives among the Iroquois. These included those who voluntarily had integrated within Five Nations communities following their capture, those captives who had fallen from esteemed status in their own villages, and those young women and girls who had not yet married into their captive communities.[41] Father Lalemant, describing a captured Iroquois "Captain" in 1663 noted that he "commonly has nine slaves with him, namely, five boys and four girls."[42] Subsequent Jesuit references to slaves of the Iroquois throughout the remainder of the seventeenth century indicate that this displaced and powerless class of individual was ripe for conversion, as echoed in the eighteenth century by Father Nau. He noted in his 1735 relation that "the majority of the adults whom we instruct for baptism in the village are slaves taken in war."[43] Starna and Watkins first proposed the mourning-war complex as the mechanism for the acquisition of war captives to serve as slaves during the early to mid-seventeenth century, suggesting that this indigenous "slave system . . . lost its formal structure in the chaos of the late seventeenth century."[44]

What exactly constituted the slave system of the Iroquois? European writings from the sixteenth to eighteenth centuries are replete with descriptions of war captives and their fate. The latter ranged from almost immediate death by a variety of techniques to a delay in their demise until arrival at their enemy's village where they were tortured to death to the sparing of their lives, usually following torture. Those spared would take on a variety of roles in their new community. Similar to Father Jogues's experience and Soto's use of Native slaves during his sixteenth-century *entrada* through the South, many were used as "burdeners." The particular domestic roles of individuals in villages were determined by the matriarch of their adoptive family house.[45]

While some adopted captives assumed prominent roles in their new societies, it is Starna and Watkin's thesis that all were subject to the "ultimate sanction or coercive factor: death." However, slave status was not inherited, and the children of a slave parent were considered as "free members of the society they were born into." This naturalized status of slave offspring appears to have been acknowledged by many Northeastern Native groups. On the other hand, Ferris suggests that various states of servitude may have been transient over an individual's lifetime and that the "death" of some slaves as reported by Europeans may have been metaphorical, a prerequisite of their assumption of a new identity.[46]

Adopted captives could play a role in the larger arena of European-Native politics as "prisoners," where their return was often a salient issue in inter-Native and European-Native peace negotiations. But because of their status in their new community and possibly because of their attachment to their fictive kin, the return of such prisoners as part of a peace treaty constituted a delicate diplomatic matter for Native negotiators. Finally, the above observations characterizing slavery among the Iroquois clearly indicate that as argued by Perdue for the Cherokee, slavery among the Iroquois was not chattel slavery.[47]

Recent scholarship proposes that the seventeenth-century Wars of the Iroquois against New France and her Native allies were a response to French policies that "threatened their survival" and not a response to a mercantile desire on the part of the Iroquois to compete in the Euro-American economy. Likewise, one can argue a purely Iroquois motive in their late seventeenth-and early eighteenth-century forays into the South as these raids appear to have been based in Iroquois values and perpetuated by the angry-young-man demographic generated by the continuing epidemic cycles.[48] Indeed, Governor Beauharnois alluded to such in a 1741 harangue to the Senecas that encouraged them to attack the Southern Native groups by arguing, "but what would become of your young men, and where could they go to divert themselves?"[49]

As each new group was incorporated into Iroquois society, they brought with them their own agendas for revenge, as when the Susquehannocks in the late 1670s "were returning south with their new Iroquois friends to even the score" against Virginia Piedmont groups.[50] The inability of the Five Nations to "naturalize" the vast numbers of captives returned to Iroquoia during the latter half of the seventeenth century is reflected in the migration of significant numbers of "Iroquois" to Christian settlements along the St. Lawrence River (primarily the Huron), the establishment of the Ohio Seneca to the west (primarily the Neutral), and probably also the establishment of the north Lake Ontario shore Seneca, Cayuga, and Oneida communities (probably the Neutral and Huron).[51] Such peoples were not being sold or traded into the commercial slavery system. Rather, because they were not required to support Native communities in the Five Nations Iroquois homeland, they had the option of migration and eventually began to break away from the Five Nations.

As argued by Brandao, the Iroquois were fully occupied throughout the latter half of the seventeenth century in complex political negotiations and tactical war maneuvers dedicated to protecting their sovereignty in the face of European imperial intrigues and ambitions. They suffered terribly from cyclical epidemics and the casualties of war and required the periodic unleashing of young male war parties to bolster their numbers with enslaved captives. Fluctuating population numbers among the Five Nations throughout the first half of the eighteenth century allowed little or no surplus for contribution to the Euro-American slave economy, despite the regular predations of Iroquois war parties. While doubtless aware of a growing demand for slave labor in the English colonies and even French Canada, there is no documentary evidence supporting Five Nations Iroquois participation in the Euro-American slave trade between

1670 and 1720. Indeed, the only known reference to the trafficking of slaves involves the 1731 sale of a lame black man in Pennsylvania by an Iroquois war party returning home with two more healthy blacks and a mulatto.[52]

Certainly a coalition of Iroquoian-speaking peoples (the Westos) actively participated in the Indian slave trade for a generation until they too became victims of the slaving wars in the South. Some remnants of the Westos apparently retreated north to join the Five Nations Iroquois, possibly the Mohawk. Others joined various groups forming the Creek Nation, perhaps because of relations established some fifty years earlier by Neutrals of the Niagara region. Neutral-Westo warriors may even have been influential in Henry Woodward's successful brokering of an English alliance with the Creeks in 1685.[53]

The Five and then Six Nations Iroquois continued to raid into the South during the early to mid-eighteenth century for two reasons. First, the Great Peace of Montreal in 1701 with the French and their Native allies effectively closed the east, north, and west to their war parties. Second, the French encouraged (and revenge traditions dictated) the Iroquois continue to divert their young men to the south, especially following the adoption of the Susquehannocks in 1677 and the Tuscaroras in 1715. There can be no doubt that early eighteenth-century Iroquois attacks on Southern groups such as the Catawbas, Cherokees, Creeks, Chickasaws, and Choctaws contributed to the shattering of traditional polities and the emergence of new coalitions in the South.[54] However, Iroquois' actions were directed to their own cultural preservation from external threats to and internal stresses in their society. If any of their young men participated in the Euro-American slave trade, it was to a very marginal extent.

Notes

Commentary on earlier drafts of this paper was received from Dr. Neal Ferris, Charles Garrad, and Dr. Conrad Heidenreich. While their thoughts considerably improved the document, none other than the author can be held responsible for the content.

1. Molto, Spence, and Fox in "Van Oordt Site" consider evidence regarding the

fate of what appears to have been an unsuccessful fifteenth-century war party in Neutral Iroquois territory. See also Ritchie, *Prehistoric Fortified Village Site*, concerning evidence for the violent death of six adult males on a New York State Owasco village site. Overall, the archaeological evidence of violence in Ontario and New York state Iroquoian villages and cemeteries suggests conflicts ranging from raids and ambushes to massacres as defined by Keeley, *War before Civilization*, 65–67.

2. Brandao, *Your Fyre Shall Burn No More*, 36–37; and Snow, *Iroquois*, 127.

3. Warrick in "Precontact Iroquoian Population of Southern Ontario," 444, provides convincing evidence for a fourteenth-century "population explosion" among the Ontario Iroquois.

4. Engelbrecht, *Iroquoia*, 37.

5. Lennox and Fitzgerald, "Culture History," 441 and figure 13.27; and Brandao, *Your Fyre Shall Burn No More*, 46.

6. William Fitzgerald has argued that the Neutral movement east was motivated more by hostile relations with Central Algonquian groups to the west than interest in the European goods trickling in from the east. Fitzgerald, "Contact, Neutral Iroquoian Transformation," 38–40 and figure 5.1.

7. Perdue, "Cherokee Relations with the Iroquois"; Hunt, *Wars of the Iroquois*, 4; and Trigger, *Children of Aataentsic*, 617–27.

8. Havard, *Great Peace of Montreal*, 47–49; Richter, "Ordeals of the Longhouse," 16; and Viau, *Enfants du Neant*, 43.

9. Heidenreich, "History of the St. Lawrence-Great Lakes Area," 489.

10. Ethridge, this volume.

11. White, *Middle Ground*, 98–104. Snow provides evidence in *Iroquois*, 94–100 and table 6.1, to indicate that smallpox and measles epidemics had reduced the Mohawk population by more than half by 1634. See also Trigger, *Children of Aataentsic*, 499–501, for similar epidemic-related impacts on the Huron.

12. Trigger, *Children of Aataentsic*, 630–32; Dunn, "Effects of the Mahican-Mohawk Wars," 95; Jennings, *Ambiguous Iroquois*, 81; Snow, *Iroquois*, 113; Perdue, "Cherokee Relations with the Iroquois," 148; and Richter, "Ordeals of the Longhouse," 15.

13. Trigger, *Children of Aataentsic*, 532, 526–38.

14. Mesquida and Wiener, "Human Collective Aggression"; and Mesquida and Wiener, "Male Age Composition," 187 (quote).

15. Thwaites, *Jesuit Relations*, 27:25, 21:195, and 20:49; and Havard, *Great Peace of Montreal*, 33.

16. Havard, *Great Peace of Montreal*, 39; and Trigger, *Children of Aataentsic*, 797. I have argued for the association of muskets with Missipisheu and hunting magic among the Ojibway and Cree of what is now northern Ontario and Manitoba in my "Dragon Sideplates from York Factory." The present-day regions of Green Bay, Detroit, and Quebec City are destinations noted by the Jesuit chroniclers in Thwaites, *Jesuit Relations*, 38:181

17. Thwaites, *Jesuit Relations*, 45:207.

18. Garrad, Abler, and Hancks, "On the Survival of the Neutrals." Jackes has provided clear osteological evidence concerning the mixed-race genesis of a thirty-year-old woman interred ca. 1640 at the Neutral Iroquois Grimsby cemetery in her " Osteology of the Grimsby Site," 29–31. Saunders has documented a young female displaying some negroid traits from the Seneca ca. 1590 Tram village cemetery and an early middle-aged European male and three young adult females of mixed race from the ca. 1620 Dutch Hollow village cemetery in Sempowski and Saunders, *Dutch Hollow and Factory Hollow*, 32–36.

19. Bowne, *Westo Indians*, 34–36. Crane in "Historical Note" was the first to suggest an Erie-Iroquoian identity for the Westos; see Smith, *Archaeology of Aboriginal Culture Change*, 132; and Meyers this volume. Subsequently, this conclusion was cogently argued by Green in " Erie/Westo Connection."

20. Among the seminal archaeological works on the poorly known Eries are the 1907 volume by Parker, *Excavations in an Erie Indian Village*; the 1949 report by Carpenter, Pfirman, and Schoff, "28th Street Site"; and White's synthesis "Erie."

21. Kenyon's *Grimsby Site* is an important pictorial record of Neutral Iroquois material culture. Parker's report *Excavations in an Erie Indian Village* illustrates Erie mortuary vessels in plates 6, 9, 18, and 26–30 and figures 5, 13, 16, 17, and 22, while mortuary vessels are pictured in plates 1 and 4–7 in Carpenter, Pfirman, and Schoff, "28th Street Site." All are very similar to Neutral ware illustrated by Kenyon from the Grimsby site.

22. Pendergast, "Kakouagoga or Kahkwas," 133 (quote), 134.

23. Lennox and Fitzgerald, "Culture History," 456 (quote), figure 13.3; Noble, "Neutral Indians," 156; Cooper, "Neutrals on the Frontier," 370; and MacNeish, *Iroquois Pottery*, 85 (quote), figure 23.

24. Biggar, *Works of Samuel de Champlain*, 99–100; Thwaites, *Jesuit Relations*, 21:193; and Heidenreich, "Analysis of the 17th Century Map," figure 1.

25. Langdon, "Father Joseph de la Roche Daillon Letter," 3.

26. Thwaites, *Jesuit Relations*, 21:191.

27. Lennox and Fitzgerald, "Culture History," 410; Heidenreich, "Analysis of

the 17th Century Map," 69, figure 1, 105; Snow, *Iroquois*, 88, table 5.1, 96, table 6.1; Thwaites, *Jesuit Relations*, 21:189, 16:253; Sempowski, "Early Historic Exchange," 60–61; and Kuhn and Funk, "Mohawk Interaction Patterns," 82. Drooker in *View from Madisonville*, 333, and Fox in "Thaniba Wakondagi," 139, both present archaeological evidence for probable direct contact between proto-Shawnee and Neutral groups during the early seventeenth century. Fox in "North-South Copper Axis," 94, has documented early seventeenth century contact between the Neutral of the Niagara Peninsula in Ontario and a group whose descendants occupied the Creek town of Tukabahchee in central Alabama during the eighteenth century.

28. Fox, "Of Projectile Points and Politics"; Lennox, *Hamilton Site*, 358, and Stothers, "Indian Hills," 52, have presented archaeological evidence regarding the animosity between the western Neutral and the Fire Nation during the sixteenth and early seventeenth centuries. Heidenreich in "Analysis of the 17th Century Map," 100–1, identifies the occupants of the Maumee River Valley as the Totontaratonhronon peoples. See also Stothers, "Protohistoric Time Period," 72. Fitzgerald, "Contact," 39, and Murphy and Ferris, "Late Woodland Western Basin Tradition," 262–63, speak to the Neutral-Fire Nation conflict in southwestern Ontario. Ferris in "In Their Time" and Lennox and Fitzgerald, "Culture History," 441, discuss the enhanced fortification of southwestern Ontario Native communities during the fifteenth century. Wintemberg in *Lawson Prehistoric Village Site*, 58, suggests that some of the fractured and scorched human bone scattered across the site derived from prisoner torture, although this claim has been questioned by Ferris, "In Their Time," 65n3.

29. Biggar, *Works of Samuel de Champlain*, 66–74; and Trigger, *Children of Aataentsic*, 624–25.

30. Brandao, *Your Fyre Shall Burn No More*, 100; Engelbrecht, *Iroquoia*, 159; Keeley, *War Before Civilization*, 51; White, "Neutral and Wenro," 410; Thwaites, *Jesuit Relations*, 54:81; Fox, "Horned Panthers," 287; and Wright, *Neutral Indians*, 57. Thwaites, *Jesuit Relations* 35:107–17, 40:15–19, describe how the warriors of the Petun village of Etharita (Mission of St. Jean) assumed that the Iroquois had been defeated by the Huron in November of 1649 and, tired of awaiting the Iroquois arrival, left for Huronia on December 5. The Iroquois approached the Petun by a circuitous route and arrived at the undefended mission village on December 7, whereupon they sacked the village and took numerous prisoners, killing the elderly and children. Two days later, the Petun war party returned to discover the devastation. This event precipitated the Petun-Huron-Odawa decision to leave for the west the following year.

Fox in "Odawa," 473, has proposed that the original homeland of the Kiskakon Odawa encompassed the historic location of the Iroquoian Petun and Huron nations along the southern shoreline of Georgian Bay.

31. Thwaites, *Jesuit Relations*, 36:117–19; Wright, *Neutral Indians*, 58; Garrad, Abler, and Hancks, "On the Survival of the Neutrals," 16; and Ferris, "In Their Time," 108; and Coyne, *Exploration of the Great Lakes*, 41–49.

32. White, "Neutral and Wenro," 410. Garrad, Abler, and Hancks in "On the Survival of the Neutrals," 13–14, do not agree with White's interpretation of the 1656 Sanson map, suggesting that the name "Attiouandarons" south of Lake Erie refers to the Andastes.

33. Thwaites, *Jesuit Relations*, 41:83.

34. Thwaites, *Jesuit Relations*, 21:195, 27:25–27.

35. Thwaites, *Jesuit Relations*, 33:63; Green, "Erie/Westo Connection," 8, 10; Heidenreich, "Analysis of the 17th Century Map," 86 and figure 1, 100–1; and Steckley, "Early Map 'Novvelle France,'" 21. See also Johnson, "Protohistoric Monongahela," and Meyers, this volume, who identify the "Attioundarons" with the Monongahela peoples. Quote from Thwaites, *Jesuit Relations*, 16:253.

36. Thwaites, *Jesuit Relations*, 42:181.

37. Thwaites, *Jesuit Relations*, 62:71.

38. Bowne, *Westo Indians*, 101.

39. Thwaites, *Jesuit Relations*, 28:297, 34:117, 31:71–81.

40. Thwaites, *Jesuit Relations*, vol. 39.

41. Thwaites, *Jesuit Relations*, 43:293–95; and Starna and Watkins, "Northern Iroquoian Slavery," 50.

42. Thwaites, *Jesuit Relations*, 48:171.

43. Thwaites, *Jesuit Relations*, 68:277.

44. Starna and Watkins, "Northern Iroquoian Slavery," 52.

45. Lafitau, *Customs of the American Indians*, 2:145; Thwaites, *Jesuit Relations*, 39:63, 31:71–73; and Perdue, *Slavery and the Evolution of Cherokee Society*, 3, 15.

46. Starna and Watkins, "Northern Iroquoian Slavery," 41, 52; Neal Ferris, personal communication (2007); Ferris, "In Their Time," 77.

47. Havard, *Great Peace of Montreal*, 55–57, 71, 100; and Perdue, *Slavery and the Evolution of Cherokee Society*, 12–15.

48. Brandao, *Your Fyre Shall Burn No More*, 130 (quote), 151, table B.1.

49. Aquila, "Down the Warrior's Path," 218.

50. Merrell, "Their Very Bones Shall Fight," 117.

51. McConnell, "Peoples 'In Between,'" 95–98; and Conrad, "Iroquois Frontier."

52. In Neilson's "Slavery in Old Canada," 23, he states incorrectly that the Iroquois (Five Nations) were involved in the Carolina slave trade; however, he does note the importance to the French of Pawnee slaves captured by their Native allies in the early eighteenth century. William Starna, personal communication (2006), made the point about the lack of any documentary evidence about Iroquois involvement in the commercial sale of Native people. On the sale of the lame black man, see Aquila, "Down the Warrior's Path," 217.

53. Bowne, *Westo Indians*, 106–7, 110–11; and Green, "Erie/Westo Connection," 9.

54. Havard, *Great Peace of Montreal*; and Beauchamp, *History of the New York Iroquois*, 156.

3 | *From Refugees to Slave Traders*

THE TRANSFORMATION OF
THE WESTO INDIANS

MAUREEN MEYERS

During a period of constant change on the colonial frontier, the actions of one Native group reverberated throughout the South. The Westo Indians arrived at the falls of the James River in 1656; their origins prior to this arrival have long been debated. Their stay in Virginia was significant locally and regionally, and the effects of this brief sojourn had long-ranging consequences for Native Southern peoples as far south as Florida. After defeating the rival Pamunkeys at the James River in 1656, the Westos secured an agreement with Virginia traders to leave the area and procure Native slaves from the interior in exchange for guns. Within a few years they appeared in the Savannah River Valley and quickly and forcefully made their presence known.[1] Through the capture and trade of local groups, the Westos became a feared presence in the valley.

Eventually, however, their control over regional trade threatened many English colonists who later armed the Savannah to annihilate the Westos. The Westos had greatly altered the lives of Natives within the interior South during a twenty-five-year time span, yet they had disappeared by the end of the seventeenth century. Little is known about them historically, and even less is known about them archaeologically. This chapter examines the origins of the Westos and their history while in Virginia, their possible relations to other Native groups in the mid-Atlantic region during the early and mid-seventeenth century, their role in colonial Virginia, and their actions beginning in 1656 that had resounding consequences far beyond Virginia.

The Westos' relations with Virginia colonists affected the fortunes of early settlers, and their enslavement of Southern Indian tribes initiated commercialized slaving there. Ethridge suggests that a shatter zone — a "region of instability from which shock waves radiated out for sometimes hundreds and hundreds of miles" — existed in the South during the seventeenth century.[2] Indeed, the effects of this shatter zone may have encompassed the entire Eastern Woodlands. Out of the shatter zone arose militaristic Indian slaving societies, with resultant intensified internecine warfare, migration, coalescence, and in some cases extinction. The Westos are significant because their history illustrates the effects of this zone on the Eastern seaboard region.

Although we could view this shatter zone as a straightforward social collapse with devastating consequences for Indians, such a notion would obscure the reasons behind Natives' decision to enslave their rivals. The strategies of both Natives and colonists varied across time and space. I suggest there are "contextual moments" within the shatter zone, especially during its development, in which we can identify a more dialectical relationship between Natives and colonists and in which actions of both groups had consequences for each other. To identify these ramifications, we need to reconstruct local, regional, and macroregional sociopolitical climates of both Natives and colonists in order to examine the reverberations of their relationship across both time and space. In so doing, however, we must keep in mind that what we are reconstructing is but one part of the shatter zone in one specific place and time; still, by piecing together the differing parts of the shatter zone across the South, we begin to see its effects at multiple scales and to understand its historical impact.

Westo Origins

Scholars have debated Westo origins since the early twentieth century and recently have reopened the debate. Verner Crane first argued that the Westos were the same group as the Richahecrians (also spelled Rickahockans), who appeared in Virginia in 1656 (see map 1). Arriving from the mountains, they settled on the James River. Crane suggests that the Westos or Richahecrians were displaced Northeastern Indians, either Eries or other Iroquoian-speakers. Evidence to support this connection was made most strongly by Mason in 1963, who noted that during Henry

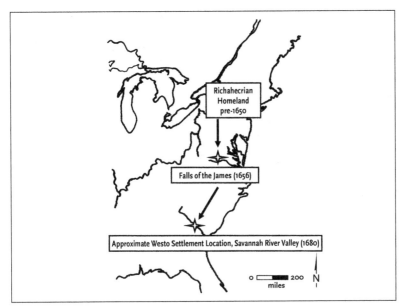

Map 1. Location of Richahecrian pre-1650 northeastern homeland, Richahecrian settlement at falls of James in 1656, and approximate location of 1680 Westo settlement.

Woodward's 1674 visit to a Westo village along the Savannah River, he described the houses as long structures made of bark as opposed to conventional Southern wattle-and-daub structures; such bark structures, or longhouses, were common to Northeastern groups.[3]

Bowne presents strong evidence that the Westos were displaced Eries. The Eries lived west of the Five Nations Iroquois and were a coalescent society; as one of the last groups to "hold out against the aggression of the Five Nations," they incorporated displaced groups such as the Huron, Neutral, and Wenro. Because of the coalescent nature of the Eries, Bowne suggests that a faction of the group, known as the Richahecrians, moved to Virginia in 1656 following their defeat by the Five Nations Iroquois.[4]

Bowne also discusses numerous references to the Westos as cannibals, and rather than dismissing such references, he notes a connection between cannibalism and a Northeastern custom known as the mourning war that included "ritual torture of prisoners. . . intended to help ease the grief of those who had lost relatives to war." During the seventeenth century the mourning war became inextricably tied to European trade that led to much Indian captive raiding and displaced many Northeastern peoples.[5] Bowne suggests that some of these displaced people migrated south. Instead of heading for the Chesapeake Bay region already controlled by the Susquehannocks, they found it more advantageous to continue south to the Virginia Fall Line where Europeans had not yet established trade with Northern Indian groups.

Green offers additional evidence that the Eries and the Richahecrians were the same group: South Carolina trader Henry Woodward's description of a Westo town along the Savannah River in 1680, the multiple accounts of Richahecrians settling in Virginia the same year the Eries were defeated by the Iroquois, and the similarity between Southern names for the Westo and Northern names for the Eries. Green further suggests that the Eries moved as a response to threats from their enemies and later acted as middlemen, trading marine shell from Virginia for beaver pelts from the North.[6]

There is evidence that suggests that groups other than the Eries made up the Richahecrians-Westos. It may be that the Westos were a splinter group from the mixed populations that made up the Neutral Confederacy. The Westos also may have contained some people from the Neutrals, Eries, and Wenros, all of whom were part of the Neutral Confederacy.[7]

Little is known about the Wenros (Wenro is a short form for the Huron "Wenrohronon")except that their main village was near the site of an oil spring at present-day Cuba, New York; they prized oil for medicinal purposes, and this strategic location would have allowed them to control access to this oil spring. The Wenros were the first victims of the Five Nations Iroquois during the Beaver Wars of the mid-seventeenth century. They had protected themselves against Iroquois predations through an alliance with the Eries to the west and the Neutrals to the north. This alliance ended in 1639 for unknown reasons and left the Wenro vulnerable. The Senecas later defeated the Wenros during the early 1640s.[8] Afterwards, most Wenros subsequently moved to Ontario, where they joined the Neutral Confederacy. The Huron Confederacy provided refuge for approximately six hundred Wenros. Another remnant group continued to fight the Iroquois until 1643 when they too fled to the Neutrals. Ultimately most of the Wenros were destroyed when the Iroquois overtook the Huron Confederacy in 1649 and the Neutrals in 1651.[9]

The Neutrals had stronger ties to the Eries. Yet these ties were not always friendly ones as attested by Jesuit records that note Neutral attacks on Erie villages during the mid-seventeenth century in which Neutrals took hundreds of Erie prisoners.[10] In the first quarter of the seventeenth century, the Neutrals expanded their territory west from southern Ontario and encroached onto the lands of various Algonquin-speaking groups, sparking tensions. In 1635 they gave refuge to Aouenrehronon, an Iroquoian-speaking group from the western end of Lake Erie, who had also encroached on Algonquin territory. The Neutrals drove out the Algonquians from Ontario in the 1630s and 1640s. With the Algonquin groups dispersed, tensions between the Iroquois and the Neutrals escalated, especially after the Iroquois obtained guns from the Dutch. These tensions culminated in the western Iroquois attack and defeat of the Neutrals in 1650. Afterwards, many Neutrals were absorbed into the Five Nations, but some small groups fled west across the Great Lakes to the Hurons; another group reached the Susquehannocks in Pennsylvania. Many Neutrals also joined the Eries, who treated them as slaves. The Iroquois defeated the Eries in 1656, and the Neutral ceased to exist.[11]

A third possible origin for the Richahecrians-Westos is that they were formerly with the Five Nations Iroquois. There are four lines of evidence to support this supposition. First, the Five Nations Iroquois were better equipped than Eries with guns. As Daniel Richter states, "plentiful supplies and dextrous [sic] use of firearms gave Iroquois a considerable advantage over their Indian enemies . . . this was especially true in battles with less well armed Hurons and *poorly armed Neutrals, Petuns, and Erie*." [12] Also, it seems likely that only the Iroquois could have produced enough well-armed warriors to defeat the Pamunkeys in 1656. Second, after the Iroquois defeated the Eries, those not incorporated into the Five Nations were few in number. In contrast, based on documentary sources, Alan Gallay has estimated that the Westos comprised a population of a few thousand.[13] Third, in 1661 the Jesuit priest Lalemont recorded the presence of Iroquois warriors in Virginia who had come "to avenge Iroquois warriors who were killed there eight or nine years ago."[14]

The Lalemont record suggests one of two things. If Lalemont's time estimate of eight to nine years is correct, then the killings occurred in 1652 or 1653, before the Richahecrians appeared on the James River in 1656. But there is some historical evidence that the Iroquois had been in the region prior to 1656. If the date was a miscalculation, then the incident Lalemont refers to may be a battle that took place in 1656 between the Pamunkeys (Powhatan Confederacy) and Richahecrians at the Battle of Bloody Run (see below). Although the Richahecrians-Westos were victorious, undoubtedly they must have lost some warriors during the battle. Finally, Bowne notes, "there is some evidence that versions of the term 'Rickahakians' were used and understood by early Virginians as a generic term for aggressive native groups beyond the borders of the colony about whom the colonists had very little information."[15] Therefore it is plausible that any reference to Richahecrians written by Virginians could refer to Five Nations Iroquois because the Virginians used the term as a generic reference to hostile Northern Indian groups.

Northern Trade and Southern Migrations

One of the many questions surrounding the Richahecrian migration is why they chose to move south, particularly because most of the Northern groups displaced by the Iroquois traveled farther north or west. However, southern migrations were not necessarily new patterns, and there is archaeological and ethnohistorical evidence for the presence of Northern groups in Virginia before the mid-seventeenth century.[16] In fact, there is some evidence that Northern groups may have moved into the mid-Atlantic region as early as the late sixteenth century. Green suggests that a group of Richahecrians settled in southern Virginia as early as 1585 and that the group appearing at the falls of the James River in 1656 were related to them.[17] On John Smith's 1608 map the town of Ricahokene is shown as one of four Weapemeoc villages located on the north side of Albemarle Sound. The Smith map also notes the town of Righkahauck on the Chickahominy River which notation Green interprets as representing a movement north by the same group.[18]

Additionally, thirteen years later, in 1621, Smith noted that "a few of the westerly Runnagados had conspired against the laughing king [of the Accomacs], but fearing their treason was discovered, fled to Smith's Isles where they made a massacre of Deere and hogges; and thence to Rickahake betwixt Cissapeak and Nansamund [on the James River] where they are now under the command of Itoyatin."[19]

Itoyatin was the brother and successor of Powhatan, head of the Powhatan Confederacy. Green suggests that the group under Itoyatin participated in the Jamestown Massacre of 1622, after which they fled back to the mountains.[20]

Archaeological evidence for such a group has been found in the upper James River region of Virginia. Turner describes Gaston ware, a ceramic type typical of the upper James, as a sand and crushed quartz-tempered type characterized by simple stamping.[21] Archaeological excavations and analysis suggests that Gaston ware is "a significant ware in a critical area of the Powhatan chiefdom, namely the upper reaches of the James River."[22] Gaston ceramics are associated with the Powhatan, Appomattox, Arrohattoc, and Weanock groups, most of which are listed as groups inherited by Powhatan as part of the Confederacy. They are also associated with such Iroquoian-speaking groups to the south as the Nottoway, Meherrin, and Tuscarora. These ceramic affiliations lend credence to the proposition by Turner that Powhatan, his father, and his brother Opechancanough were Pamunkeys from the south or southwest of Jamestown and that the incorporation of these other groups into the Confederacy resulted from alliance and not warfare.

By the mid-seventeenth century maps from that era show a group called the Attioundaron to have been first located in both Huron and Neutral territory and in the upper Ohio River Valley. Bruce Trigger asserts that this is a name used by Hurons and Neutrals when referring to one another; it means "people who speak a slightly different language." William Johnson suggests that the Ohio River Valley Attioundarons may have been Monongahela dispersed by the Seneca Iroquois in 1635 and that during the early seventeenth century they were known as the Massowomacks. Both Johnson and Pendergast hold that the Massowomacks resided around the Chesapeake Bay and raided and traded beaver pelts and whelk shell. Indeed, they likely acted as middlemen between the Neutral Indians and the more southern Eastern Shore Algonquians.[23]

Fox, on the other hand, suggests in this volume that they may have been a confederation of Eries and Neutrals. Originally from the Ohio Valley, during the late Prehistoric Period they began trading with their northern Iroquoian neighbors, and assumed the middleman position by the early seventeenth century.[24]

According to Johnson, the Seneca Iroquois dispersed the Massowomacks in 1635. The Seneca had previously been excluded from the trade in shell and beaver, but after Henry Fleet began trade with the Natives in 1631 in the Chesapeake Bay region, Johnson notes that, "the Seneca destroyed or dispersed other groups who exercised control of the beaver resources in the upper Ohio Valley and the Upper Great Lakes." After the 1635–36 dispersal of the Massowomack-Monongahela-Attioundaron, many of the dispersed people moved into Susquehannock territory where they became known as the Black Minquas.[25]

There is also archaeological evidence for a Northern-Mid-Atlantic trade connection. Shell, considered of religious importance to many Iroquoian-speaking groups, was one of the most significant Native trade items in the seventeenth-century mid-Atlantic region. Historic Period Neutral, Huron, and Petun sites have large numbers of lightning whelk and snow whelk shells; the latter type originated in the Chesapeake Bay region. Archaeological evidence from Virginia suggests that northern Iroquoian speakers, likely the Attiondaron-Massowomack-Monongahela, were trading shell to the north. The Abbyville site, located at the confluence of the Dan and Staunton Rivers, offers such evidence. A Historic Period Native occupation at Abbyville is indicated by the presence of shell-tempered pottery with pot shapes and decorative motifs different from that made by the surrounding Piedmont peoples (Dan River or Occaneechi).[26]

In addition, copper spirals and a beaver pelt effigy were recovered from graves at the site. Copper and brass spirals and hoops are indicative of a trade "between the Five Nations Iroquois and the Susquehannock and protohistoric Monongahela and Madisonville phase Fort Ancient people between about 1550 and 1640."[27] Work by Martha Sempowski suggests there are two sets of spiral artifacts, that may indicate two trade routes: one between the Seneca and other Five Nations and another pertaining to the Susquehannock trade, "perhaps via the south branch of the Potomac

River." Beaver pelt effigies are also found at Monongahela, Seneca, and Oneida sites, and they may have been used as counters in the beaver pelt trade. Interestingly, such effigies are not found on Susquehannock sites in the upper Potomac or Susquehanna river drainage, suggesting that the Northern traders may have bypassed the Susquehannocks altogether.[28]

Dutch beads found at the Abbyville site date the site to the first half of the seventeenth century. It is possible that two separate historic occupations occurred, the evidence being that beads dating between 1620 and 1650 were found on a section of a site termed the Northern Terrace and earlier beads, dating to the Dutch Period I (1609–24), were more common on another area termed the Center Terrace. The earlier beads include large striped beads, flush eyes, and chevrons likely supplied by the first influx of the Dutch East India Company and private Dutch traders along the Hudson River. In addition, green-cored redwood beads comprise sixty percent of the Abbyville Center Terrace assemblage. These types that date to the early seventeenth century are also "found in greatest number in western New York on Niagara Frontier and Seneca Iroquois sites." William Fitzgerald, however, dates these green-cored redwood beads to post-1624, a time when these beads outnumbered other colors on Neutral and Huron sites in southern Ontario.[29] Thus these bead types are tied to Northern groups through time; they are found on both Niagara Frontier and Seneca Iroquois sites as well as on Neutral and Huron sites in southern Ontario where they are more popular.

The ceramic, metal, and bead artifacts found at Abbyville also indicate a Northern connection to the mid-Atlantic region. Their associated dates indicate that this connection was in place not long after Fleet's Potomac River voyage opened up Native trade in Virginia. The presence of Dutch beads and beaver pelt effigies indicates that the beaver pelt trade was moving south during the early seventeenth century. Based on archaeological and documentary evidence, it appears that Northern, Iroquoian-speaking groups (the Monongahelas-Massawomacks-Attioundaron) were procuring shell and beaver pelts from Virginia and trading them north to the Neutrals and other groups in exchange for European goods.

Johnson also notes that the Seneca Iroquois were excluded temporarily from the shell and possibly beaver pelt trade sometime after 1610, most likely around 1630 when the Massowomacks were making their inroads into Virginia. Sempowski's work shows that Seneca Iroquois sites in western New York contain little marine shell prior to 1560. Between 1560 and 1595 there is a dramatic increase in shell, yet it decreases to precontact levels between 1590 and 1630. As it decreases at Seneca sites, it increases at Huron, Petun, and especially Neutral sites. Lennox and Fitzgerald state that most of this shell is coming from the Chesapeake Bay region. As noted earlier, in 1635 the Seneca defeated the Massowomacks, reopening Seneca access to the shell and beaver pelt trade. Indeed, the amount of shell in Seneca graves increases substantially after 1635. The early seventeenth-century villages shown on Smith's maps may be indicators of shell procurement sites occupied by Northeastern groups. Green suggests that the Westos also began acting as middlemen in marine shell trade soon after their arrival in Virginia in 1656. In any case when the Westos arrived at the James River in 1656, they may have been following an already established and well-known trade route.[30]

The Battle of Bloody Run

The Richahecrians, who later became known as the Westos, estimated to have numbered about six to seven hundred people, settled at the falls of the James River in 1656 (see map 2).[31] The Virginia colonists immediately organized a militia and solicited military aid from the Pamunkeys, the largest group in the Powhatan Confederacy to attack the newcomers. The Pamunkeys likely had their own reasons for attacking the Richahecrians; they may have been trying to solidify their control of the area south of the James River. In addition, if the Westos were allied with the Susquehannocks in some form, this alliance may have been enough to provoke the Pamunkeys who were enemies of the Susquehannocks.

This battle, which occurred at the Richahecrian settlement on the James River, is known as the Battle of Bloody Run. The English and Pamunkey militia, led by Colonel Edward Hill, made their way to the Richahecrian settlement. When the English stopped to rest, the Pamunkeys, led by Totopotomoy, continued on and attacked the town. The Richahecrians drove back the Pamunkeys and in the fray they killed Totopotomoy. The creek near the battle site became known as Bloody Run, and historic maps of

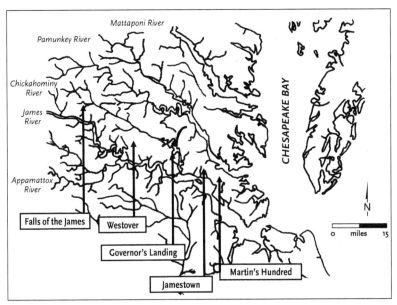

Map 2. Eastern Virginia, showing location of falls of the James, Westover Plantation, and nearby colonial sites, 1656.

Richmond show that the name was used into the early twentieth century.[32] Upon arriving at the scene, the English militia retreated, evidently wanting to evade the same fate as the Pamunkeys. Twenty years later, the English would live to regret this retreat as the queen of the Pamunkeys used the English failure at the Battle of Bloody Run and the lack of compensation for Pamunkey losses by the colonial government to refuse Pamunkey warriors to aid the colonists during Bacon's Rebellion.[33]

That the Pamunkeys were the only Native group to join the Virginia colonists in attacking the Richahecrians is reflective of the changing nature of seventeenth-century Native politics. During the early seventeenth century the Pamunkeys had "politically dominated the Indians of the Virginia coastal plain."[34] This dominance had culminated under the leadership of Powhatan, who forged the Powhatan Confederacy from the Pamunkeys and other groups. The confederacy's power diminished following Powhatan's death, but the Pamunkeys held the balance of power for a few more decades under the leadership of Powhatan's brother Opechancanough. The latter's death in 1644, combined with multiple colonists' reprisals

From Refugees to Slave Traders 91

against the Powhatans after the 1622 Jamestown Massacre, helped to break apart the once-powerful coalition of Indian groups that comprised this paramount chiefdom.

In 1646 Opechancanough's successor Necotowance, known as the King of the Indians, signed a treaty with the Virginia government that ceded much of the Powhatan territory to the English. In 1649 Totopotomoy replaced Necotowance. However, historical documents refer to Totopotomoy simply as the King of the Pamunkeys rather than King of the Indians, indicating the shifting political alliances and dissolution of the confederacy.[35] Totopotomoy, unlike his predecessors, was an English ally, thus explaining the presence of the Pamunkeys at the Battle of Bloody Run. The fall of the Powhatan Confederacy undoubtedly left a political, economic, and military vacuum in the mid-Atlantic region, soon to be filled by militarized slaving societies such as the Richahecrians.

Colonists and Traders along the James River in the 1650s

Following the Richahecrians' victory at Bloody Run, the Virginia government sued for peace with them in 1656. The colony was also eager to open trade with interior Indians, especially those south of Jamestown such as the Occaneechis. Some aspiring traders saw their chance in the Pamunkey and English defeat to seize control of the Virginia Indian trade. They not only had Edward Hill, the failed militia leader, replaced with the trader Abraham Wood but also made sure that the 1656 peace agreement with the Richahecrians designated Wood's residence along the Appomattox River as one of only three places on the western border where Indians would be allowed to trade.[36] Bowne suggests that Wood through his new role as militia leader and with the knowledge that the colony wanted peace with the Richahecrians first initiated a Virginia trade relationship with them.[37]

However, there were other wealthy Indian traders located in the region, and some had plantations closer to the Richahecrian town than Wood. It is also likely that some of these traders had agreements with the Richahecrians. For example, Thomas Stegge II owned a plantation at the falls of the James River in 1656 (see map 3). His plantation was known as both Belvidere and the Falls Plantation. Stegge's plantation was located in

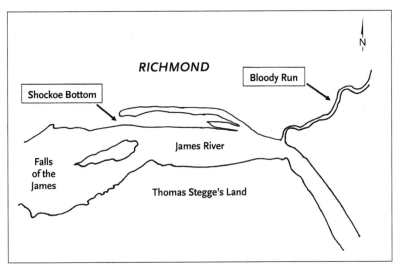

Map 3. James River at Richmond, showing Bloody Run, Thomas Stegge's land, Shockoe Bottom, and location of falls, 1656.

the area immediately below present-day Mayo's Bridge, which is directly across the river from Bloody Run. It had been owned by his father Captain Thomas Stegge I, and his son inherited the property after his father's death at sea defending the English colony against encroaching Dutch traders in 1651. The elder Stegge had been born in England, and at the time of his death he had become a successful merchant, primarily through the Indian trade. Thomas took over his father's business and expanded it throughout Virginia and into North Carolina. The junior Stegge became a successful businessman and Virginia citizen. In 1664 he became a member of the Council and served as auditor for the County until 1670. At the time of his death in 1671 he was well known as having a successful trade "with the Indians in southern Virginia and Western North Carolina."[38]

The junior Stegge had no children and in 1670 he convinced his nephew William Byrd I to come over from England to assist him in his business. Upon his death in 1671 he bequeathed his land and trade business to his nephew, who continued to run it successfully. According to Lutz, Byrd's "trading operations extended far into the wilderness over trails which penetrated 400 miles as far as the haunts of the Catawbas and Cherokees." Additionally, Byrd I added to his property by acquiring tracts on both sides of the James River. By 1673 Byrd's plantation at the falls was "an active trading post" with caravans composed of up to fifteen men and one hundred pack horses carrying goods. Marambaud notes that near the Falls Plantation, a well-known trading path emerged, providing these caravans access to as far as South Carolina. Although no accounts state that Byrd traded Indian slaves, it is known that he owned them; he also imported white indentured servants and African and West Indies slaves. He later became the chief owner of a slave ship that was later captured by French privateers.[39]

The economic successes of Byrd I thrust him into the political sphere. In 1676 he was a captain in the Henrico County militia and later was promoted to colonel. He was also a member of the House of Burgesses. He was appointed to the Virginia Council in 1680 and eventually served as its president.[40]

Yet Byrd's primary occupation was as an Indian trader, and his main competition in the Indian trade was Abraham Wood. Both men sent out parties to explore west and south from the Richmond area; indeed, in 1671 the Batts and Fallam party sponsored by Wood almost crossed paths near West Virginia with another sponsored by Byrd.

Wood and Byrd I were acquaintances as both served on the Virginia Council for fifteen years between 1655 and 1670 along with other colonists involved in the Indian trade such as Stegge, the trading family of Theodorick Bland and his sons, and Edward Hill. These traders formed at least two separate partnerships. In one partnership, despite the fact that Wood had replaced Hill as militia leader, Hill and Wood were closely aligned. The Blands, Stegge, and Byrd I formed a second partnership. At the time of the 1656 Richahecrian intrusion, the junior Stegge would have had an advantage in that his property was located directly across from Bloody Run where the Richahecrians had chosen to establish a village. Wood and Hill, on the other hand, would have been at a disadvantage in forging any kind of relationship with the Richahecrians because of Hill's actions against them at the Battle of Bloody Run.

Other actions by the Virginia Council would have also contributed to Stegge's advantage in securing a trade agreement with the Richahecrians. In 1656 trade restrictions that had been in place and intermittently enforced since the Jamestown massacre of 1622 were lifted, allowing individuals to trade directly with Natives. As already noted, specified trading establishments were designated by trade regulations such as Wood's plantation. In conjunction with this law specific Indians were required to obtain a trading license that would stipulate with whom they were to trade.[41]

Considering that Stegge and Bland were allies, it is possible that if they had established trade relations with the Richahecrians, the name of one of their plantations would be on the license. We also know that one of Bland's plantations was called Westover because in 1688 Byrd I bought it from the Bland brothers. Westover had originally belonged to Theodorick Bland, who had bought it around 1656. When he died in 1671, the plantation was conveyed to his sons, Theodorick and Richard. The brothers later sold it to Byrd I.[42] This reference to Westover could help account for the transition from the name of Richahecrians to Westos. "Westo" may be the shortened version of "Westover" as written on a trade agreement. (The first recorded use of the name does not occur until 1670 when South Carolina natives warn the British about the Westo.)[43]

A trade agreement between the Richahecrians and the Stegge-Byrd-Bland partnership would have been particularly helpful at this point because their other trading partner Abraham Wood was negotiating a trade agreement with the Occaneechi Indians of North Carolina. A separate agreement with another partnership would have afforded the Richahecrians some form of trade protection from the competing Occaneechis. Even so, Occaneechi competition may have been one of the reasons behind the Richahecrians southern slaving campaigns, begun as early as 1659, and their later migration out of Virginia in the mid-1660s.

Most scholars agree that the Richahecrians moved to the Savannah River in order to raid the Spanish mission Indians and low country groups. However, one of the many questions surrounding the Richahecrians was how did they know where to go to obtain Southern slaves, particularly if they were from the North? One answer may be found in the documents of James Needham. Needham was allied with Wood, with Wood sponsoring Needham at least once to find a trading path west to the Cherokees. Needham later formed a friendship with Henry Woodward, another Indian trader located in South Carolina who would enter into an exclusive agreement with the Westos in 1674 after they had moved to the Savannah River. Woodward had traveled to Virginia on occasion; Morrison noted, "there is indication that Dr. Woodward in 1671 traveled up, by the paths as they were, from Carolina to Virginia."[44] Woodward and Needham were acquaintances, so it is possible that the Virginia colonists had close ties with those in South Carolina, and such ties may have been used to the advantage of both Virginia and South Carolina colonists.

The Virginia Colony and the End of the Westo

Sometime in the 1660s the Richahecrians moved south and settled on the Savannah River near present-day Augusta. Here they became known as the Westos. Some evidence of this southern migration is recounted in John Lederer's account of his 1672 journey to North Carolina when he encountered Richahecrians on Occaneechi Island. However, there is evidence that they were raiding groups in present-day Georgia and Florida as early as 1659. And according to John Worth, Indians from Virginia — most likely the Westos, whom the Spanish called Chichimecos — were raiding and displacing many Indian groups north of Florida by 1661. Worth suggests that the Westos initially went to the Tama and Guale provinces along the Georgia and Florida coasts in order to procure slaves. Fleeing the Westo slavers, Southern groups fled to interior Spanish missions. But soon the Chichimecos began attacking the missions themselves, using the Savannah River location as their vantage point. Such raiding by Westos continued through the 1660s. Because of these slave raiders, Worth states that "interior Georgia became a vast buffer between the musket-bearing Chichimecos on the Savannah River and the established mission provinces along the southeastern Georgia coastline." By the time the English landed at Charles Town in 1670, Native groups were seeking safety from alliances with Europeans; indeed, the local Cusabos greeted them with "English are our friends, Westo are not."[45]

By the 1670s circumstances in South Carolina are recognized by historians as providing the fateful blows to the end of the Westos. During this time other Southern groups were acquiring guns and competing with the Westos for slaves to trade to the English. Indeed, the Occaneechis became a real threat, and in 1670 they even killed some Westo guests in their town. After Charles Town was established, the Westos secured a trade agreement with Henry Woodward, thus opening trade relations with the English in South Carolina. Bowne notes that the relationship with Woodward and the South Carolina Lords Proprietors resulted in the Westos obtaining guns and ammunition but without the expense and risks of transporting slaves to Virginia.[46]

The Westos reign came to an end when a group of aspiring Charles Town planters and business men, dubbed the Goose Creek Men, staged a trade coup against the Lords Proprietors and the Westo monopoly. The Goose Creek Men hired Savannah (Shawnee) mercenaries to annihilate the Westos and thus open trade into the interior. By 1682 only about fifty Westo warriors remained, and by 1715 they disappeared from the documentary record.[47]

Although it appears that South Carolina's colonists were responsible for the demise of the Westos, actions by the Virginia colonial government should not be overlooked. From the 1650s through the 1670s, the Virginia Council passed several laws intended to regulate the Indian trade. In addition to those already mentioned, in 1656 all freemen were granted the right to trade with Indians, but they were forbidden to trade guns, powder, and shot. This latter prohibition was revoked in 1658–59. However, colonists began to feel unsafe at the thought of armed Natives, so the Council passed another law requiring participants in the trade to obtain a commission from the governor of the colony.[48]

In 1662 another law passed that prohibited trade with Northern Indians. The passage of all such laws would have been beneficial to the colonists engaged in trade with the Westos because the laws both sanctioned the selling of guns to them and essentially gave the Westos and the Occaneechis (once they migrated south) sole rights to trade with Virginia colonists, hence limiting competition with other groups. However, by 1665 tensions between the Indians and Virginians began to rise, and the sale of arms was once again prohibited, this time with strict fines for offenders. Then in 1676 with an increasing number of Indian raids that would precipitate Bacon's Rebellion, "it was provided that all who supplied the aborigines with arms, powder and shot should not only forfeit their whole estates but suffer death in addition."[49]

Bacon's Rebellion, often cited by American historians as the first American rebellion against representatives of the English Crown, can also be directly linked to the Indian slave trade. Nathaniel Bacon was a planter and new to the Indian trade when he received a commission from Governor Berkeley.[50] He owned property in Henrico County, including some at the falls of the James River. In September 1675 Susquehannocks raided several plantations and farmsteads including that of Bacon and Byrd I, resulting "in the killing of Bacon's overseer and at least one of Byrd's servants."[51] Ultimately the consequence of these attacks was Bacon's Rebellion.

In April 1676 Byrd I, Bacon, and others discussed Governor Berkeley's ineptitude "in the face of a much-feared combination of Indians from New England to the Chesapeake."[52] Their fear may not have been of bodily harm from Indians but rather that these Northern Indian incursions would disrupt their trade. In fact, these Indian traders may have taken advantage of the Susquehannock hostilities to break the Occaneechi monopoly of the Virginia trade, much like the Goose Creek Men would later break the Westo trade. It could also be that these Virginia traders hoped to reestablish their trade alliance with the Westos, now living on the Savannah River, and engaged in widespread slaving in partnership with Woodward and South Carolina.

Although Bacon threatened all Indians, curiously, those whom he attacked were the Occaneechis, enemy and recent murderers of the Westos, and, as the rebellion proceeded, the Pamunkeys, who had fought the Richahecrians as English allies twenty years earlier. His men also attacked other Indian traders, including the failed Bloody Run militia leader Edward Hill, who was despised by the poor farmers who made up the majority of Bacon's forces; they even beat his pregnant wife with a cane. Byrd, who initially assisted Bacon, still managed to remain neutral during the conflict, likely saving his life; he moved to Westover shortly thereafter, away from his James River Falls plantation.[53]

One result of Bacon's Rebellion for groups like the Westos was a clear message that Indians would no longer control the trade. Although the Susquehannocks were largely diminished and driven north as a result of the rebellion, the colonists' willingness to wage war on any Indians would have dampened trade with Virginia. Combine this willingness with the fact that traders in Virginia would have had to forfeit lands if they were found trading guns to Indians, and the Virginians trade with the Westo looked less viable.

If Stegge, Byrd, Hill, and Wood were bound in some partnership to trade with the Westos, the partnership would have unraveled during the 1670s. Stegge died in 1671, Byrd moved to Westover and away from the James River, Hill was disgraced by Bacon's men (who destroyed his accounts), and Wood faded from the scene by the late 1670s.[54] Moreover, once the Occaneechis were dislodged, both Byrd and Wood became more interested in trading with the Cherokees and Catawbas than with the Westos. This way they would not have to compete with Charles Town for Westo trade. Also at this time the trade in African slaves to Virginia increased exponentially and was much more profitable for Byrd I whose Shockoe Bottom warehouse at the falls of the James River became infamous as an African slave-trading venue. Altogether, the circumstances in Virginia aligned against the Westos. While one reason for their turning to South Carolina colonists for a trade relationship may have been the threat of the Occaneechis and the cost of slave transport to Virginia, the political and economic situation in Virginia also contributed to their decision to trade with South Carolina.

The work presented here has attempted to integrate the colonial Virginia political climate with the movements and actions of the Westos. First, Westo origins may be Erie, Wenro, Huron, Neutral, or even Five Nations Iroquois, although there is not sufficient evidence at this time to state definitively who they were. Earlier seventeenth-century incursions into Virginia by the Massowomack and Monongahela would have made Virginia known to Northern groups. Second, influenced by geography, newly enacted laws, and relations with other groups, multiple Virginia colonial traders may have been engaged in an alliance with the Westos. One consequence of a possible trading partnership between the Westos and the Indian traders Stegge, Bland, and Byrd may have been the institution of the name "Westo" (derived from Westover) as moniker for the

Richahecrians. Third, the demise of the Westos—instigated by South Carolina traders—also may have been caused by Virginia colonists and their actions including Bacon's Rebellion.

The Westos exemplify the myriad of relations and factions among not just Natives but also Natives and colonists within the Eastern Woodlands. Virginia was a literal and symbolic meeting place of these relations. The evidence from the Abbyville site shows that Virginia was important to the Northern beaver and shell trades before the mid-seventeenth century; it may be these trade routes that lured the Richahecrians to Virginia in 1656. The Virginia colonists in turn had ties with South Carolinians such as Henry Woodward, and these relations need to be explored further as they may have helped to direct Westo movements southward. This move precipitated Indian slaving in that region. In addition, the fact that the Westos could make their way down the east coast suggests that long-held social institutions such as trade, likely dating to the Archaic Period, connected the South with the Northeast more intimately than we realize.[55]

The shatter zone is a useful framework to better understand the interconnections of Natives and colonists in the seventeenth century. By its very effects, we can trace the relations among different groups. The Westo are emblematic of its far-reaching consequences as seen at the local scale. At the same time we need to reevaluate our perceptions of Native groups as powerless in the face of Europeans. The Westos demonstrated a flexibility and adaptability that is rather astounding. To originate in the upper Northeast; move south almost to Florida; negotiate with the French, Dutch, English, and Spanish; and successfully survive, if only for a time, testifies to a Native agency and self-determination that is oftentimes overlooked in American histories. Until now, perhaps we have been too focused on European effects on Native peoples and have failed to consider that Natives in fact had some hand in shaping their destiny despite Europeans.

Notes

This research was based on a project supported by the Savannah River Archaeological Research Program. I would like to thank Ann Jeter for suggesting a possible link between Westo Indians and Westover Plantation.

1. Bowne, this volume.

2. Ethridge, "Creating the Shatter Zone," 208.

3. Tooker, "Problem of the Rechahecrian Indians"; Swanton, "Westo," 936; Swanton, "Identity of the Westo Indians"; Swanton, *Early History*; Mason, "Reconsideration of Westo-Yuchi Identification"; Juricek, "Westo Indians"; Worth, "Prelude to Abandonment"; Worth, *Struggle for the Georgia Coast*; Green, "Erie/Westo Connection"; Bowne, "Rise and Fall of the Westo"; Crane,; Crane, "Historical Note"; and Crane, "Westo and Chisca."

4. Bowne, *Westo Indians*, 37 (quote); and Fox, this volume.

5. Bowne, *Westo Indians*, 39–53, 59 (quote).

6. Green, "Erie/Westo Connection," 10.

7. Fox, this volume.

8. Brose, "Penumbral Protohistory," 62.

9. Richter, *Ordeal of the Longhouse*, 1, 62.

10. Deale, "History of the Potawatomis."

11. Noble, "Neutral Indians," 11

12. Richter, *Ordeal of the Longhouse*, 64 (quote) (emphasis added), 94.

13. Gallay, *Indian Slave Trade*, 41.

14. Aquila, "Down the Warrior's Path."

15. Bowne, *Westo Indians*, 34

16. Fox, this volume.

17. Green, "Erie/Westo Connection."

18. Green, "Erie/Westo Connection."

19. Tooker, "Problem of the Rechahecrian Indians," 265.

20. Green, "Erie/Westo Connection," 7.

21. Turner, "Protohistoric Native American Interactions"; and Coe, *Formative Cultures*, 105–6.

22. Mouer, "Ocaneechee Connection"; and Turner "Protohistoric Native American Interactions," 9 (quote).

23. Johnson, "Protohistoric Monongahela"; and Pendergast, *Massawomeck*.

24. See the 1656 Sanson map "Nouveau Mexique" and the 1663 Du Val map "La Floride" in Cumming and DeVorsey, *Southeast in Early Maps*, plates 31 and 33. Trigger, *Huron*; Johnson, "Protohistoric Monongahela," 67; and Fox, this volume.

25. Johnson, "Protohistoric Monongahela," 80 (quote).

26. Wells, *Abbyville*; and MacCord, "Summary and Conclusions."

27. Johnson, "Protohistoric Monongahela," 77 (quote); and Bradley and Childs, "Basque Earrings and Panther's Tails."

28. Sempowski, "Early Historic Exchange"; and Johnson, "Protohistoric Monongahela," 76 (quote), 77.

29. Lapham, "Glass Beads from the Abbyville Sites," 197 (quote); and Fitzgerald, "Contact."

30. Johnson, "Protohistoric Monongahela"; Sempowski, "Fluctuations through Time"; Sempowski, "Early Historic Exchange"; Lennox and Fitzgerald, "Culture History"; and Green, "Erie/Westo Connection."

31. Bowne, "Rise and Fall of the Westo"; Alvord and Bidgood, *First Explorations*, 155; Swanton, *Early History*, 94–95; and Crane, "Westo and Chisca."

32. See the map in Ellyson, *Richmond Directory*.

33. Force, *Tracts and Other Papers*, 2:14.

34. McCartney, "Cockacoeske, Queen of Pamunkey," 173.

35. McCartney, "Cockacoeske," 175.

36. Bowne, "Rise and Fall of the Westo Indians," 61. The other places were Fort James along the Chickahominy and Fort Royal, interestingly also known as Fort Rickahock, along the Pamunkey River to the north; Robinson, *Southern Colonial Frontier*. The latter fort's name suggests it may have been designated to deal primarily or exclusively with Northern Indians, although this conclusion is speculative. The documentary record so far reveals little about these forts, their function, and their duration. Lauber in *Indian Slavery in Colonial Times*, 119, notes that Thomas Smallcomb was a lieutenant stationed at Fort Royal on the Pamunkey and owned several Indian slaves when he died in 1646, probably killed in the war with Opecancanough.

37. Bowne, "Rise and Fall of the Westo Indians," 63.

38. Lutz, *Chesterfield*, 51

39. Lutz, *Chesterfield*, 52–53 (quotes); Marambaud, *William Byrd of Westover*, 16; and Wright, "William Byrd I and the Slave Trade." Abraham Wood, likewise, owned Indian slaves.

40. Stanard and Stanard, *Colonial Virginia Register*.

41. Bruce, *Economic History of Virginia*, 385–86; and Hening, *Statutes at Large*, 1:410, 415, 525.

42. Marambaud, *William Byrd of Westover*, 17. Within two years Byrd I had built a mansion there, but he moved after Bacon's Rebellion in 1676, seeking safer areas along the James River. He later returned, and he died there in 1704. His son William Byrd II inherited the properties and continued his father's Indian trade business into the mid-eighteenth century.

43. I have not found this trade agreement; however, it seems a likely proposition. Milling, *Red Carolinians*.

44. Morrison, "Virginia Indian Trade."

45. Crane, "Historical Note"; Mason, "Reconsideration of Westo-Yuchi"; Juricek, "Westo Indians"; Cumming, *Discoveries of John Lederer*; Bowne, *Westo Indians*, 24; Worth, "Prelude to Abandonment," 51 (quote); Worth, *Struggle for the Georgia Coast*; and Cheves, *Shaftesbury Papers*, 167 (quote).

46. Bowne, "Rise and Fall of the Westo Indians," 69.

47. Milling, *Red Carolinians*; Robinson, *Southern Colonial Frontier*; and De-Vorsey, "Colonial Georgia Backcountry."

48. Bruce, *Economic History of Virginia*, 386–87.

49. Bruce, *Economic History*, 388.

50. Billings, *Sir William Berkeley*, 233.

51. Billings, *Sir William Berkeley*, 234; and Brown, *Good Wives*, 159 (quote).

52. Billings, *Sir William Berkeley*, 235.

53. Billings, *Sir William Berkeley*, 237, 246; Brown, *Good Wives*, 165; and Marambaud, *William Byrd*, 15.

54. Stanard and Stanard, *Colonial Virginia Register*.

55. Goad, "Copper and the Southeastern Indians."

4 | "Caryinge awaye their Corne and Children"

THE EFFECTS OF WESTO SLAVE RAIDS ON
THE INDIANS OF THE LOWER SOUTH

ERIC E. BOWNE

One of the most difficult questions in early Southern history is how were the dozens of large chiefdoms encountered by Spanish explorers in the mid-1500s transformed into the coalescent societies of the eighteenth century. Most explanations of this transformation are gradualist: over the course of the century and a half following the first appearance of Spaniards, Southern peoples gradually accommodated to European colonists. Yet there is an alternative explanation. A group of Northern Indians invaded the homeland of the Southern Indians in 1656 and remained there until about 1682, during which time they inflicted great violence upon many of the peoples who lived there. The Westos, a relatively small group, played an inordinately large role in transforming the Southern Indians, and they did so in a surprisingly brief period.

As Alan Gallay has argued, the European trade in Indian slaves was an important economic component of the early colonial South and the building of the English empire. Between approximately 1660 and 1715, as many as fifty thousand Indians were captured by other Indians and sold into slavery in the Virginia and Carolina colonies.[1] Indian slaves made up only a small fraction of Carolina's population because Indian slaves were often resold to sugar plantations on the Caribbean Islands, where they had little opportunity to escape.[2] Unfortunately, few records were kept concerning the shipping of Indian slaves. The semiclandestine nature of the Indian slave trade was in part an attempt by merchants to avoid the taxation and regulation of the English crown.[3] Despite the lack of well-documented quantification, it is apparent from existing records that Indian slavery had drastic effects on Native social and political organization in the lower

South. It is also apparent that during the early decades of this trade, the Westo Indians were the preeminent slave raiders in the region.

The group that would be known in the South as the Westos first entered the historical record in the 1630s as the Eries.[4] Sometime prior to or just after European contact, the Erie confederacy converged around the southern shore of present-day Lake Erie and most likely was composed of not only Eries but Neutrals as well.[5] In the 1640s the Eries pursued a trading partnership with the Susquehannocks of northern Chesapeake Bay. The Eries exchanged beaver pelts with the Susquehannocks for European-manufactured items, including firearms, that the latter obtained from the Virginians.[6] Other Native groups, most notably the powerful Five Nations Iroquois of present-day New York, were also at that time engaging in trade with Europeans at various colonial outposts throughout the Northeast. By 1650 the insatiable European demand for beaver pelts had led quickly to plummeting beaver populations, greatly increasing competition between Native groups participating in the trade.[7] The violent conflicts resulting from this competition collectively became known as the Beaver Wars.

The Eries, despite their access to European guns, fared poorly in the Beaver Wars. After a protracted struggle with the Five Nations Iroquois, the Eries abandoned their homeland and moved south beyond the easy reach of their enemies in 1656. Shortly after arriving on the southwestern frontier of Virginia, the Eries (known to Virginians as the Richahecrians) forged a trading partnership with Abraham Wood.[8] The Virginians desired not only beaver pelts but also Indian slaves to work their tobacco fields.[9] By 1659 the Richahecrians were staging raids against the Native peoples in Spanish Florida. Southern Indians provided good targets for slave raids because they had no access to large numbers of European firearms. After years of raids along the Spanish frontier, in the mid-1660s the Richahecrians moved to the Savannah River along the present boundary of Georgia and South Carolina where they continued to raid the Spanish missions as well as surrounding groups.[10]

The term "Westos" was originally recorded by settlers in the Carolina country in 1670 where local Indians used this word to refer to the slave-raiding Richahecrians. Between 1663 and 1674 the Westos assaulted Indian groups in the area in order to steal corn and capture Native peoples whom they transported to Virginia and sold into slavery. Terrified local Indians were forced to seek the protection of the newly established Carolina colony against further assaults. In 1674, however, the Lords Proprietors of Carolina, in collaboration with the English trader Henry Woodward, established trade with the Westos, stipulating that slaves were to be captured only from interior, nonallied Indians.[11]

Between 1674 and 1680 the Lords Proprietors fought bitterly with Carolina planters over control of the Indian trade. The proprietors' monopoly on trade with the Westos infuriated the planters because the export of deerskins, beaver pelts, and Indian slaves was the most lucrative economic activity occurring in the colony at that time. The Westos' military advantage over other Indian groups had to be challenged, however, before the planters could usurp control of the trade from the Lords Proprietors. In 1680 a group of planters financed a secret war against the Westos, forcing the group to abandon their fortified town on the Savannah River. By 1682 there were reported to be only fifty Westo warriors remaining in the South. Several thousand Southern Indians had been enslaved before the end of the Westo War in 1682. Yet up until that war, the Westos had been the principal Indian slavers in the region.[12] Westo slave raids then dramatically affected Native peoples of the lower South.

Westo aggression also had a significant effect on the social geography of Spanish Florida during the early 1660s.[13] At its height the Spanish mission system in Florida amounted to no more than about forty towns of Christian Indians located throughout three provinces that included approximately twenty-six thousand Indians, three hundred Spanish soldiers, and a small number of priests.[14] These missionaries and their Native flocks were thinly spread from coastal missions as far north as South Carolina and as far west as the Apalachicola River. This dispersion over such a wide area made them particularly vulnerable to the depredations of the Westos. Moreover, because it was illegal to trade arms and ammunition to Native peoples along the Spanish borders, the Indians were at a military disadvantage against the Northern invaders. When the Westos armed with European guns arrived in the lower South, they encountered Native peoples with only bow and arrows and little experience with the loud and destructive weapons of the Europeans. Such weapons in the hands of determined Indian slave raiders had a destabilizing effect on the region's population.[15]

The Westos first raided the Guale missions in 1661, targeting the outermost missions of the Spanish mission system and hence the most vulnerable. Westo raiding was directly responsible for the 1662 abandonment of the mission town of Talaje and probably also for the relocation of the Satuache mission closer to Santa Catalina, the principal town of Guale.[16] The Spanish mission system, however, offered Natives some semblance of a place of retreat and at least the promise of military protection against the Westos. Westo raiding also forced some interior groups into Spanish Florida. Natives directly adjacent to the missions but farther from potential Spanish help also presented an appealing target for Westo slave raids. These slave raids resulted in not only a contraction of the mission frontier but also an emptying of much of the population that lived on the boundary of the missions in present Georgia and Florida. Evidence for the movements of these refugees into Spanish Florida comes from census counts taken throughout the 1660s by friars who made a distinction between mission Indians and so-called pagan Natives from the interior provinces.[17]

The Westos perhaps also supplied the major impetus behind the formation of the Yamasees, a confederacy of diverse Native peoples first recorded in 1662. The population of the Yamasees was composed in large part of refugees from the chiefdoms of Altamaha, Ocute, and Ichisi, all located in present-day central Georgia and all of which broke apart due to Westo raiding. The Yamasees initially coalesced around 1663 along the lower coast of South Carolina between the Westos and the Spanish missions of Guale. They became allies of the Spanish, although resisting Catholic conversion. They would later leave the Spanish and move closer to the Carolinians; they eventually supplanted the Westos as the preeminent slavers of the region.[18]

By 1667 the Westos also were attacking Indian settlements along the coast of present-day South Carolina. When the Carolina colony was founded in 1670, the Westos had so harried local Indians that the latter sought the protection of the English newcomers. In the coming decades

Carolinians would refer to these local groups as settlement Indians. With no other available respite from the slavers, these small Indian societies became intimately associated with the Carolina colony, living among the settlers and performing menial tasks. Many of them learned European trades such as blacksmithing, and Indian-made pottery was widely used in colonial settlements.[19] As Carolina's Lords Proprietors noted in 1682, the settlement Indians were "of great use to ye Inhabitants of our province for the fetching in againe of such Negroe Slaves as shall Runn away from their masters and allsoe for fishing, fouleing, and hunting."[20]

Early reports from the colony often mention the willingness of Natives to trade food to the English in exchange for protection against the slave raids of the Westos.[21] The ravaged coastal groups were "affraid of ye very footstep of a Westoe," who "doe strike a great feare in these Indians havinge gunns and powder and shot and doe come upon these Indians heere in the tyme of their crop and destroye all by killing Caryinge aweaye their Corne and Children and eat[ing] them."[22] That local Natives believed the Carolinians might offer some respite from the devastating slave raids is apparent in the welcome the Englishmen received upon arrival at Port Royal: "Ye distressed Indians ... were glad and crying ... English are good friends Westoes are nought, they hoped by our Arrivall to be protected from ye Westoes, often making signes ... wee should [engage them] with our guns."[23]

As noted above, some relief for coastal Natives came with the 1674 trade agreement between the Westos and the Carolinians that stipulated slaves should be taken only from interior, nonallied groups. The coastal peoples, now clustered around Charles Town and under the cursory protection of the Carolinians, were no longer an easy target for the Westos. Although after 1674 they would continue to take an occasional captive from along the coast, the slave raiders now turned their attention to the Indian provinces of interior South and North Carolina. The Westos may have sought a trade agreement with the Carolinians before they began to enslave in earnest the chiefdom of Cofitachequi, located along the Wateree River in present South Carolina.[24] Before they attacked the largest remaining Indian province in the region, the Westos likely hoped to be on amicable terms with the English, the only group capable of defending Cofitachequi against the slave raiders.

Cofitachequi had been on good terms with the English since the founding of the colony and on ill terms with the Westos for at least as long. In 1670 Henry Woodward, the same trader that brokered the Lords Proprietors' deal with the Westos, made a journey to Cofitachequi, "14 days trauell after ye Indian manner of marchinge," and met with the so-called emperor.[25] When Hernando de Soto's expedition visited Cofitachequi in 1540, it was the seat of a large paramount chiefdom ruled by a woman known as the Lady of Cofitachequi.[26] In the 130-year interim between Soto's and Woodward's visits, Cofitachequi must have undergone some fundamental changes similar to those experienced by other Southern native societies of the time. Yet during his trip to Cofitachequi in 1670, Woodward "contracted a league with ye Emperor & all those Petty Caciques betwixt us & them, soe that some few weeks after my returne, our Provision failed us . . . [and] had not [we] releved ye General wants by what Provisions wee procured of the Natives [of Cofitachequi] it had gone very hard with us."[27]

It appears that the emperor of Cofitachequi exerted a certain influence over several villages at least as late as 1670. The emperor of Cofitachequi and his petty caciques, however, disappeared from the written record during the middle years of the 1670s, and the old province of Cofitachequi soon became known as the country of the Catawbas.[28] It is sometimes assumed that disease crippled the chiefdom of Cofitachequi before the English arrived on the Carolina coast. Yet by studying Woodward's account, one can see that was not the whole story. Likely some time shortly before or after Woodward and the Westos met, the province of Cofitachequi became one of the principal targets of Westo slave raids. Archaeological evidence supports the idea that significant depopulation did not occur in the Carolina piedmont until after 1650.[29] The Westo slave raids were at least partially responsible for the downfall of the Cofitachequi polity. If this was indeed the case, then Westo depredations also provided some impetus for the formation of the Catawba Confederacy.

Bearing the Yamasee and Catawba examples in mind, it also seems possible that Westo aggressions were one of the important factors that led to the political coalescence of the groups that would later be collectively called the Creek Confederacy. These groups, known first to the Spanish as Apalachicolas and later to the English as Lower Creeks, likely included a number of refugees from Westo slave raids along the Spanish frontier during the 1660s. It is difficult, however, to pinpoint precisely when the political entity known in the eighteenth century as the Creek Confederacy formed; not only was it a gradual process not directly reflected in the archaeological record, but it also occurred far from Spanish or English observers. The confederacy was a social entity as well as a political one, and even before the eighteenth century a widespread similarity in material culture was evident in Creek towns despite the generally independent nature of those towns.[30] It is likely that the social foundation for the Creek Nation developed in the period following European contact but prior to the arrival of the Westos in the lower South. Westo slave raids then served as a potent mechanism that accelerated the development of the Creek Nation as a political entity.

This scenario is an alternative to the currently popular theory that the social and political aspects of the confederacy developed together, and both did so gradually.[31] The archaeological evidence indicates that a social base for the confederacy was in place before the eighteenth century, but as noted above, it is silent concerning politics. It has only been assumed that social similarity was indicative of political cohesion, and this is a weak assumption. As chiefdoms went into steep decline after European contact, there was little reason to form or maintain widespread political relationships based on mutual defense. The advent of the slave trade, however, changed things. It is not difficult to imagine that despite the lack of written evidence the volatile nature of the commercial slave trade forced neighboring groups into nonaggression pacts for the purpose of mutual defense.

It is not simply coincidence that we see the formation of the coalescent societies in the South during the height of the slave trade. During the seventeenth century groups that would later become part of the Creek Nation were known by names such as the Ocheses, Hitchitis, Ocmulgees, and Cowetas, as well as dozens of others. The terms "Upper Creeks," "Lower Creeks," and "Creek Confederacy" were not used by the English until the eighteenth century. The same was true of the Catawba Confederacy. Before the eighteenth century Carolinians referred to the peoples who would come to be known as Catawbas by a variety of names, including Esaws, Waterees, Congarees, and Sugarees.[32] Certainly the people still identified themselves by a variety of names during the eighteenth century, but the umbrella terms such as Catawba, Creek, and so on seem to have had real meaning for the constituents of these polities. In other words, although various groups made up the coalescent societies, there was some recognition of the larger polities by the constituents of the polities, outside Indian groups, and Europeans. Although this evidence is not conclusive, it supports the idea that the development of the well-known Indian confederacies of the eighteenth century occurred, at least in part, as a reaction to the Indian slave trade.

By 1700 the South was nearly unrecognizable in comparison to when the Westos first began launching slave raids into Georgia and Florida in 1659. Despite a century of Spanish colonial occupation and Native population losses due to epidemic diseases, something of the Mississippian world was still intact, including the political diversity of the chiefdoms. By the beginning of the eighteenth century, however, much of that diversity had disappeared. When Westo depredations reached their height between 1660 and 1680, several thousand Indians from the region were captured and sold, primarily by the Westos.[33] Refugees of Westo raids and those of their successors were left with only two options. The first was to seek the protection of the Spanish or English settlers. The second was to join with other Native groups in order to form polities large enough to lend a measure of protection against slavers. During the seventeenth century these aggregates of various Native peoples developed essentially new social identities, becoming the Indian peoples of the Old South: Creeks, Catawbas, Chickasaws, Choctaws, and Cherokees.

In the four decades since the Westos had been forced to abandon their homeland near Lake Erie, the South had taken on many of the characteristics common in the Northeast during the Beaver Wars. First, the number of Native polities in the South decreased dramatically, with only larger aggregate polities surviving. Second, virtually every male Indian in the region possessed a firearm by the beginning of the eighteenth century, a fact that John Lawson noted on his journey through the Carolina backcountry in 1701 as did Thomas Nairne on his foray to the Mississippi River in 1708. Finally, the commercial hunting and slaving economy had the ability to affect groups located far from European settlements, even groups who had little if any direct contact with Europeans themselves. For example, LaSalle encountered Natives in possession of European guns during his exploration of the Mississippi River in 1682 — sixteen years before Nairne became the first Carolinian to see the great river.[34]

The notable military advantage of the Westos was an integral part of the engine that propelled these changes, creating a powerful stimulus for other Native groups to attempt to acquire firearms.[35] By the time the Westos were defeated in 1682, the need for European arms and ammunition had become pervasive in the South. When the coalescent polities that developed because of Westo aggression obtained significant numbers of firearms, they began their own slaving campaigns against neighboring groups, thus widening the shatter zone. Like Westo raiding, these raids continued to destroy many small Native societies, forcing the refugees and others into one of a handful of larger polities that were increasing their numbers through coalescence. The dramatic lessening of social diversity by 1700 is a testament to the "success" of the second generation of Southern Indian slavers. Aggregate groups like the Creeks and Catawbas survived the final turbulent quarter of the seventeenth century, but many of their neighbors, including the Guales, the Mocamas, the Timucuas, and the Calusas, did not.[36] Much work remains to be done before we can adequately answer the question: what shaped Native peoples of the eighteenth-century South? The history of the Westos, however, allows a crucial glimpse into this important period in Southern history.

Notes

1. Gallay, *Indian Slave Trade*, 294–99.

2. Gallay, *Indian Slave Trade*, 200, 300–1, 306.

3. Gallay, *Indian Slave Trade*, 301.

4. Thwaites, *Jesuit Relations*, 8:115.

5. Fox, this volume.

6. Weslager, *Dutch Explorers*, 117; Hoffman, *Observations on Certain Ancient Tribes*, 195–245; and Green, "Erie/Westo Connection."

7. Trigger, "Early Iroquoian Contacts"; Starna, "Seventeenth Century Dutch-Indian Trade," 247; and Richter, *Ordeal of the Longhouse*, 57.

8. Thwaites, *Jesuit Relations*, 47:47–59; Alvord and Bidgood, *First Explorations*, 155; and Crane, *Southern Frontier* (1929), 112.

9. Worth, *Struggle for the Georgia Coast*, 17; it is also possible that some of these English slavers were selling Indian slaves abroad.

10. Don Alonso de Aranguiz y Cotes, "Letters to the Crown," November 9, 1659, AGI 839; and Worth, *Struggle for the Georgia Coast*, 18.

11. Cheves, *Shaftesbury Papers*, 166, 168, 194, 200–1, 456–62.

12. Cheves, *Shaftesbury Papers*, 445–46; Salley, *Records in the British Public Records Office*, 1:100, 104–7, 115–16; Salley, *Narratives of Early Carolina*, 182–83; and Gallay, *Indian Slave Trade*, 294–96.

13. Worth, this volume.

14. Bushnell, "Ruling 'the Republic of Indians,'" 138.

15. For a more detailed discussion of the Westos' predatory strategies, see Bowne, *Westo Indians*.

16. Worth, *Struggle for the Georgia Coast*, 19.

17. Worth, *Struggle for the Georgia Coast*, 18–20. For a fuller discussion of the contraction southward of the missions system due to Westo raiding, see Worth, this volume.

18. Worth, *Struggle for the Georgia Coast*, 15–20, 24; and Worth, "Yamasee," 245. For a discussion of the Yamasees, see Worth, this volume; and Jennings, this volume.

19. Cheves, *Shaftesbury Papers*, 166; and Lawson, *New Voyage*, 10, 175, 200.

20. Salley, *Records in the British Public Records Office*, 1:174.

21. Cheves, *Shaftesbury Papers*, 166–68, 194, 200–1.

22. Cheves, *Shaftesbury Papers*, 334, 194.

23. Cheves, *Shaftesbury Papers*, 167–68.

24. For a discussion of the collapse of the chiefdom of Cofitachequi, see Beck, this volume.

25. Cheves, *Shaftesbury Papers*, 186–87 (quote), 201.

26. Hudson, *Knights of Spain*, 172–84.

27. Cheves, *Shaftesbury Papers*, 187.

28. For a discussion of the coalescence of the Catawba Confederacy, see Beck, this volume; and Fitts and Heath, this volume.

29. Davis, "Cultural Landscape," 143.

30. Waselkov, "Macon Trading House"; Knight, "Formation of the Creeks";

Waselkov and Smith, "Upper Creek Archaeology"; Worth, "Lower Creeks"; and Jenkins, this volume.

31. Waselkov, "Macon Trading House," 194.

32. Braund, *Deerskins and Duffels*, 6–7; and Merrell, *Indians' New World*, 92–133.

33. Gallay, *Indian Slave Trade*, 295–96.

34. Lawson, *New Voyage*, 33, 38, 175; Nairne, *Nairne's Muskogean Journals*, 37–38; and Ethridge, "Making of a Militaristic Slaving Society."

35. Bowne, *Westo Indians*, 65–71; and Hahn, "Miniature Arms Race."

36. Worth, *Struggle for the Georgia Coast*, 11.

5 | Catawba Coalescence and the Shattering of the Carolina Piedmont, 1540–1675

ROBIN A. BECK JR.

When English surveyor John Lawson crossed the Carolina Piedmont in 1701, its social landscape had been transformed dramatically from that observed by the Spaniards Hernando de Soto and Juan Pardo a century and a half before. Where the latter explorers saw large regional polities under the nominal sway of chiefs, Lawson recorded scant evidence of such hierarchies, though the reorganization of formerly distinct Piedmont peoples within the lower Catawba Valley was well underway. This reorganization heralded the opening phases of Catawba Indian coalescence, but to grasp the temporal and spatial contexts of this beginning requires closer attention to the Piedmont's social landscape during the two centuries prior to Lawson's journey.[1] Drawing from the records of the Soto and Pardo expeditions and from the writings of Lawson's seventeenth-century predecessors John Lederer and Henry Woodward as well as from archaeological data, I suggest that shifting tides of power and prominence among the sixteenth-century Piedmont chiefdoms forged a subsequent haven in the lower Catawba Valley and that the "shattering" of these chiefdoms after the middle of the seventeenth century made Catawba coalescence possible.

Three chiefdoms — Cofitachequi (also known as Canos), Joara (also known as Xualla), and Guatari — dominated the Carolina Piedmont during the mid-sixteenth century. The first of these, Cofitachequi, occupied the Wateree Valley in central South Carolina and was seemingly the only one of regional prominence during the time of Soto's expedition.[2] Indeed, Cofitachequi's long reach prior to 1540 likely had a dampening effect on the expansion of competition along its peripheries. By 1567 when Juan

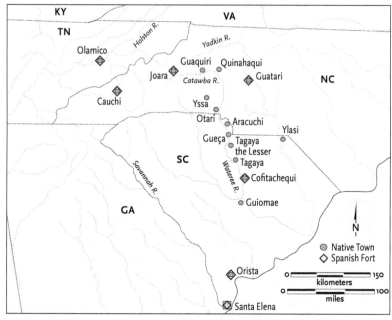

Map 4. Native towns and polities of the Carolina piedmont, ca. 1540–68.

Pardo revisited a short stretch of Soto's path, Cofitachequi's shadow was significantly diminished, and Joara and Guatari were flourishing on the upper Catawba and central Yadkin rivers, respectively (see map 4). But it was in that central, interstitial region between these chiefdoms — near the heart of the triangle they formed in the lower Catawba Valley — that Piedmont peoples forged a coalescent society that became the Catawba Confederacy in the 1700s. The aim of this chapter is to reveal the historical interrelatedness of these episodes and to unravel the patterns of social process within particular details of Piedmont history.

The Paramount's Shadow: Cofitachequi in 1540

On April 30, 1540, Hernando de Soto and a vanguard of soldiers encamped along the Wateree River. For seventeen days since departing the Ocute polity in modern Georgia, Soto and his army had traversed across the uninhabited wilderness, or *despablado*, of the central Savannah River where the expedition nearly met its end. After nearly starving in the wilderness, they finally had arrived at a town called Hymahi, which was near the junction of the Wateree and Congaree rivers in central South Carolina and to which they bestowed the name *Soccoro*, or "Relief."[3] This village was the first place in the Carolina Piedmont to experience the invasion from Europe. After resting for a few days at Hymahi, Soto and his vanguard left and traveled for a day, making the aforementioned camp on the lower Wateree. The next day, May 1, they came to a canoe landing or crossing on the west bank of the river; on the east bank was the town of Cofitachequi.[4] Soto's subsequent reception by its female *cacica* — borne upon a litter by her principal men — was among the most renowned episodes of the expedition and was described by all of its chroniclers. The rest of the army arrived shortly thereafter, and most stayed until May 7. One of the four accounts of the expedition penned by a Portuguese writer known as the Gentleman of Elvas, states that Cofitachequi was "a very pleasing and fertile" land with "excellent fields along the rivers, the forest being clear and having many walnuts and mulberries."[5]

While the name Cofitachequi has generally been applied to the entire polity, both in the expedition's accounts and by most subsequent scholars, the place where the *cacica* welcomed Soto was probably not the principal center of her chiefdom. At Cofitachequi Soto and his personal secretary Rodrigo Rangel entered the mortuary temple where they found many pounds of pearls wrapped among the bodies as well as European goods such as rosary beads and metal axes that had likely been obtained from Ayllon's failed attempt to settle the Carolina coast in 1521.[6] The *cacica* observed the Spaniards' excitement over the pearls and told them "do you think this is a lot? . . . Go to Talimeco, my town, and you will be unable to carry them on your horses." Soto seems to have accepted this invitation, for Rangel subsequently writes that "in the temple or oratory of Talimeco, there were breastplates, as well as corselets and helmets, made from raw and hairless hides of cows, and from the same very good shields. This Talimeco was a town of great importance, with its very authoritative oratory on a high mound; the caney, or house, of the cacique very large and very tall and broad, all covered, high and low, with very excellent and beautiful mats."[7]

The Muskogean translation for Talimeco is literally "chief town." During the time of Pardo's expeditions, the term *mico* appears to have been applied to the leaders of multicommunity polities, so it is significant that Talimeco (or, rather, Cofitachequi) was the only place in the Carolina Piedmont for which the Soto chroniclers recorded this designation.[8]

In the century prior to Soto's *entrada*, Cofitachequi had emerged as the dominant polity in this region, and at Soto's time it was the only one in that region that could accurately be referred to as a chiefdom. Cofitachequi was probably centered at the Mulberry site (38KE12) in the lower Wateree Valley. Although there are other Mississippian mound sites along this section of the Wateree, Mulberry alone can be dated with certainty to the sixteenth and seventeenth centuries. About 1450 CE several other mound centers and their polities flourished in the valleys east, west, and south of the lower Wateree. The Hollywood and Rembert sites were major powers along the central Savannah, as was the Scott's Lake site on the upper Santee; it is possible that the Town Creek mound on a tributary of the Pee Dee River in North Carolina was also in use as were several mounds along the upper Broad River.[9]

Within a few decades, however, all of these centers were abandoned, and vast regions such as the central Savannah and the upper Broad Rivers were almost entirely emptied. Although climatic factors may have played a role in these changes, increasing warfare and competition, such as characterized the Late Mississippian Period across most of the Southern United States, were also undoubtedly significant.[10] In any event Cofitachequi rose to prominence after this time, and it seems quite likely that this rise came at the direct expense of its neighbors in the Carolina Piedmont.

Based on the descriptions of the Soto accounts, as well as on these archaeological data, Cofitachequi has recently been identified as a paramount chiefdom or a paramount complex chiefdom.[11] As usually conceived, the paramount chiefdom has varying degrees of regional authority over neighboring simple and complex chiefdoms and thus is marked by at least two levels of regional administrative hierarchy above the local community. I have argued elsewhere that Mississippian chiefdoms, even the largest like Cahokia and Moundville, had no more than a single level of regional hierarchy and that Mississippian chiefdoms probably did not administer other Mississippian chiefdoms. However, the notion of paramount chiefdoms should not be dismissed. When such polities emerged in the precontact South, they tended to inhibit or actively preclude the con-solidation of nearby rivals and thus undermined and destabilized — rather than controlled and administered — existing polities on their peripheries. The paramount chiefdom of Cofitachequi may only have administered a territory of large towns and hamlets along the lower Wateree and neigh-boring streams, but its prominence from 1450 CE until the arrival of Soto's army appears to have had a profound dampening effect on the expansion of chiefly power in other portions of the Carolina Piedmont. This effect may be the most evident hallmark of paramount chiefdoms.[12]

By 1540 CE Cofitachequi may already have slipped from the peak of its prominence. Soto's Native interpreter Perico, for example, claimed that some headmen of the polity "had rebelled against [the *cacica*] and kept the tribute." Moreover, a "plague" of mysterious nature and origin had struck two years earlier; the Gentleman of Elvas attributed the abandon-ment of several large towns in Cofitachequi's immediate vicinity to it.[13] Researchers have debated how to interpret Elvas's reference to plague: was this an episode of epidemic disease that decimated the populations of these abandoned towns or an agricultural blight that infected maize fields? Or was it just a miscommunication between the Spaniards and their Native interpreters?[14] While the mystery is unlikely to be resolved, there seems to have been problems within the polity, and these would only have been exacerbated by the sudden appearance of Soto and his men. But Cofitachequi, if in the early stages of decline from what had been paramount status, was hardly toothless. Rangel writes that the chief of Altamaha, named Çamumo and a subject of Ocute, "ate and slept and walked continually armed, and that he never took off the weapons, because he was on the frontier of another *cacique* called Cofitachequi, his enemy."[15] The Ocute chiefdom was located in the Oconee Valley of eastern Georgia, nearly one hundred and fifty miles from the Wateree.

When Soto's *entrada* left Cofitachequi, having first consumed all of the food they could find, they journeyed north along the Wateree-Catawba River, keeping the *cacica* as their hostage both to guarantee safe passage and to help obtain maize from her potentially uncooperative subjects. After several days they came to a region called Chalaque, which in the Muskogean language means "people of a different speech."[16] Here the expedition found little maize; the Gentleman of Elvas notes that this was "the poorest land in maize seen in Florida."[17] Nor was there a principal town in this region, so the army made camp in the open each night. Chalaque occupied most of the lower and middle Catawba Valley, north of what is now the South Carolina state line. Regardless of whether this place was part of the polity of Cofitachequi, the *cacica* seems to have had little success obtaining either food or shelter for the expedition through Chalaque.[18] Significantly, this thinly populated place lacking evidence of chiefly hierarchy would become the heart of the Catawba Confederacy during the early 1700s.

After traversing Chalaque in a little under a week, Soto arrived at a village named Xualla. Recent archaeological investigations have identified the Berry site (31BK22) on a tributary of the upper Catawba River near Morganton, North Carolina, as the location of this town. Rangel's account refers to Xualla as "a town on a plain between some rivers; its *cacique* . . . so well provisioned, that he gave to the Christians however much they asked for: *tamemes* [burden bearers], corn, little dogs, *petacas*, and however much he had." He also writes that the army occupied the town for four days. According to the Gentleman of Elvas, however, they stayed only two days because there was little food there. Biedma agrees, noting that the village had "little population." Perhaps Rangel as Soto's personal secretary entered Xualla with an advance party led by Soto. In fact, Rangel states that Baltasar de Gallegos, one of Soto's captains and "most of the people of the army" departed Cofitachequi for Ilapi — a subject village along the Pee Dee River — to seize its maize, rejoining Soto at Xualla two weeks later. Both the Gentleman of Elvas and Biedma were likely in Gallegos's detachment and therefore when they arrived at Xualla, they found that the grain stores had been exhausted by the vanguard. Although a headman, or *cacique*, did reside at Xualla in 1540, there is little documentation from Soto's *entrada* to suggest that he had regional authority such as that accorded the *cacica* of Cofitachequi. That would change by 1567.[19]

Soto left Xualla on May 25 and "crossed that day a very high mountain range, and they spent the night in a small forest." The *entrada* probably took a northwesterly route from Berry toward the headwaters of the Toe and Nolichucky rivers. It was here, along the treacherous, densely wooded slopes of the Appalachian Mountains, that the *cacica* of Cofitachequi — together with her personal attendants and most of the freshwater pearls that Soto had personally taken from her ancestors' mortuary — slipped into the forest and made good her escape. The Gentleman of Elvas reports that she returned to Xualla, where she took for her husband a Spanish slave who had deserted the expedition, and that they had both decided to make their way back to Cofitachequi.[20]

Some scholars have used the time and place of her escape to infer that the mountainous territory north and west of Xualla represented the outermost extent of her chiefdom.[21] However, it seems just as likely, especially given her inability to find food and shelter for Soto through Chalaque, that the Appalachians simply provided the first and best opportunity for her to elude the Spaniards' grasp. But with her escape and the *entrada*'s Appalachian ascent, Soto and his chroniclers took leave of the Carolina Piedmont. More than twenty-five years would pass before another European crossed this region when Juan Pardo explored the Carolinas in 1566–68. In his explorations Pardo negotiated a landscape of one old and two new chiefly powers.

A Crowded Landscape: Canos, Joara, and Guatari in 1567

In 1565–66 after his successful expulsion of the French from La Florida, Pedro Menéndez de Avilés founded a pair of small colonies on the southern Atlantic coast: San Agustín, established September 1565 in northern Florida, and Santa Elena, founded April 1566 on Parris Island, South Carolina. The latter was to be the principal site of Menéndez's colonial ambitions.[22] When Philip II received news of this success, he ordered that immediate reinforcements be sent to Menéndez's colony. In July 1566 Captain Juan Pardo arrived at Santa Elena with a company of two hundred and fifty men and began to fortify the settlement. Because the Santa Elena colony was ill prepared to feed this contingent of soldiers for very long, Menéndez ordered Pardo to prepare half of his army for an expedition into the interior lands that lay behind the Atlantic coast. Pardo's task was to explore this region, to claim its lands for Spain while pacifying local Indians, and to find an overland route from Santa Elena to the silver mines in Zacatecas, Mexico. Pardo left with one hundred and twenty-five men on December 1, 1566.

Of this, the first of Pardo's two expeditions into the interior, we have but a single eyewitness account, a brief and rather inattentive relation written by Pardo himself. This document provides few details about social relations in the Carolina Piedmont during the post-Soto era, other than the names of the places that the expedition visited and how their respective leaders received Pardo and his men. By combining this document with records of the second expedition, however, it is possible to reconstruct a basic itinerary for the first.[23]

After departing Santa Elena, Pardo and his company traveled north for several days across South Carolina's lightly populated inner Coastal Plain. The first town of note was called Guiomae, clearly the same as Soto's Hymahi.[24] Two days later, they arrived at the important town of Canos, where Pardo says that he "found a great number of *caciques* and Indians." Fortunately Juan de la Bandera (Pardo's scribe) made two records of the second expedition and says in the shorter of these that the Indians referred to this place as "Canosi and, for another name, Cofetazque."[25] Thus, the place named Canos in the Pardo accounts is the same as Soto's Cofitachequi. Here, as at most of the important towns that Pardo entered, he told the *cacique* and his subjects to construct a house for the expedition and to fill it with a quantity of maize.

Pardo continued north from Canos through the Catawba Valley, pausing briefly at several small towns before leaving the Catawba for the South Fork of the Catawba where he came to a town called Yssa (or Ysa). Yssa was probably located at or near the Hardins site (31GS29) near modern Lincolnton, North Carolina.[26] Yssa is the same name as Esaw, one of the core groups that later made up the Catawba coalescence, and transposed as Nassaw, it was one of their most important towns in the early eighteenth century.[27] By this date, however, its location had shifted east to the main course of the lower Catawba; significantly, the lower and middle Catawba was thinly inhabited at the time of Pardo's expeditions, much as they had been when Soto's chroniclers referred to this region as Chalaque.

After two or three days travel from Yssa, Pardo arrived in the chiefdom of Joara, situated along the upper Catawba River in the foothills of the Appalachians; this is the same place as Soto's Xualla, though as will be seen, its political stature in the Carolina Piedmont had changed significantly in the years since Soto's brief occupation. During the fifteenth and sixteenth centuries the upper Catawba was among the most densely populated regions of the North Carolina Piedmont.[28] Over fifty archaeological sites with Burke phase ceramic components (1400–1600 CE) have been identified within this area and range in size from five hundred square meters to almost five hectares. As noted, the political center of the Joara chiefdom was at the town of the same name, which is the archaeological site known as the Berry site, near the modern city of Morganton, North Carolina. Berry is the largest known Burke phase site and is one of the only recorded sites in the upper valley with a platform mound.

Pardo's command from Menéndez had been to press over the mountains and forge a route to Mexico. At Joara, however, he could see that there was snow on the peaks that lay ahead, so he decided to halt his westward push and continue exploring the Piedmont regions. Pardo was at Joara for fifteen days, writing that its people "demanded Christians from me to catechize them." Here he constructed a small fort christened Fort San Juan, leaving it with thirty soldiers under the command of his sergeant Hernando Moyano; this outpost was the earliest European settlement within the interior of what is now the United States. Excavations at the Berry site have recently identified the burned remains of Fort San Juan, flanking the northern periphery of the site.[29]

Before leaving the Catawba River altogether, Pardo went northeast through the upper Catawba Valley, spending several days at the towns of Guaquiri and Quinahaqui, located near the westward bend of the river. After traveling east through an unoccupied region between the Catawba and Yadkin basins, the company arrived at Guatari, located in the central Yadkin Valley near present-day Salisbury, North Carolina. Pardo found thirty *caciques* and many Indians waiting to meet the company at Guatari, a clear indication of the town's political prominence in 1567. During the early eighteenth century a much-reduced Guatari, John Lawson's town of Watery, had moved to the lower Wateree River valley, giving this river its name. Pardo stayed at Guatari for a little more than two weeks, departing quickly when he received word from Santa Elena of a possible French military threat. He left four soldiers and the company's cleric, Father Sebastian Montero, to catechize the Indians, and it was here that Montero founded the first mission in the interior of North America. Pardo crossed back to the Catawba-Wateree valley and passed through several villages just south of the North Carolina state line before returning to Canos; the company arrived in Santa Elena on March 7, 1567.[30]

During the six months that Pardo was at Santa Elena, Moyano still at Joara became involved in the violent struggles between Joara and its adversaries across the mountains. According to the account of Francisco Martinez, who recorded the testimony of four solders at Santa Elena in July 1567, Moyano left Fort San Juan on two occasions, taking twenty men — and probably a large group of warriors from Joara — into present-day southeastern Virginia and eastern Tennessee where they attacked two Native villages. Martinez's informants claimed that more than two thousand Indians were killed during the attacks, but this is certainly an exaggeration. Moyano's company traveled on to Chiaha, also called Olamico, a powerful chiefdom in the Tennessee Valley. At Chiaha they constructed a small fort and waited for Pardo's second expedition to commence.[31]

On the second expedition Pardo left Santa Elena at Menéndez's command on September 1, 1567, taking one hundred and twenty soldiers with him. As already noted, an official scribe named Juan de la Bandera who kept two detailed accounts of the journey accompanied this second expedition. The longer of these is particularly useful because of the data it offers on interpolity relations across the Carolina Piedmont.

Pardo returned to Canos or Cofitachequi on September 10. Bandera notes that an impressive group of *orata* were awaiting the army at Canos and that all of them provided help to build a large house for the Spaniards there per Pardo's earlier request or had donated some maize to feed the army. In the longer of his two documents Bandera carefully distinguishes between the terms *mico* and *orata*: while the latter apparently refers to village headmen (he recorded the names of more than one hundred and twenty *orata* during the second expedition), the former may have applied only to those chiefs with regional authority. In fact, Bandera explains that *mico* was the term for a great lord (*un gran señor*) and *orata* a term for lesser lords (*un menor señor*). Only three *micos* are noted in his longer account: Joara Mico, Guatari Mico, and Olamico (Chiaha).[32]

There was no *mico* present at Cofitachequi in 1567, though this was the only place in the Carolina Piedmont to which the Soto chroniclers applied the term in 1540. The former paramount chiefdom, which for a century was able to preclude the expansion of chiefly power on the margins of its territory, clearly had waned since its entanglement with Soto. This diminishment left room for two younger polities — Joara and Guatari — to claim its northern frontier. Still, the town of Canos remained an important place, particularly considering that at least thirteen *orata* met there to receive Pardo; these included the leaders of Ylasi, Vehidi, Yssa, and Cataba. Ylasi is probably the Ylapi of the Soto accounts and is where Baltasar de Gallegos took most of Soto's army to seize some maize belonging to the *cacica* of Cofitachequi. Located on the Pee Dee River just below the present-day South Carolina state line, Ylasi appears not to have been a subject of Canos in 1567, for while the Ylasi *orata* wanted credit for helping to build the house for Pardo there, he was holding his maize contribution within a house he had built for that purpose in his own town. Vehidi may refer to the Indians later known as the Pee Dee, who gave their name to this river before they joined the Catawba during the 1720s. Two of the *orata* at Canos, the aforementioned Yssa and one named Cataba, were leaders of key constituents in the later Catawba coalescence, and this Cataba is actually the first recorded use of the name that would come to represent most Piedmont peoples after 1725.[33]

Pardo's company continued north from Canos and visited several towns — Tagaya, Gueça, Aracuchi, and Otari — along the lower reaches of the Catawba River, just above the Fall Line. Each of these towns was certainly a subject of Cofitachequi in 1540, though it is unclear whether any of them remained so in 1567. People in each town had built their own wooden house for Pardo. Indeed, all of the towns along the Wateree-Catawba built such houses, probably as much an explicit showing of their own relative autonomy as an act of compliance with Pardo's command. Gueça refers to the Waxhaws, another people who interacted with the Catawba during the early eighteenth century. Seven *orata* came to see Pardo at Gueça, including a Suhere Orata, whose name was anglicized to Sugaree in the early 1700s. The Sugaree lived along Sugar Creek, a tributary of the lower Catawba, and later were among the core peoples of the Catawba coalescence. Leaving Otari, Pardo and his company traveled through an uninhabited stretch of the lower and middle Catawba River before stopping at Quinahaqui and Guaquiri. At Quinahaqui Pardo was met again by the headmen of Yssa and Cataba as well as by another *orata* whose name Uchiri (Usheree or Ushery) the Virginia colonists would later apply to all Catawban peoples for a brief time around 1700.[34]

That Soto and Pardo found such sparse populations in the middle Catawba valley is puzzling, given that David Moore's analysis of ceramics recovered from archaeological sites in this region shows that nearly a dozen sites date to the Low (1400–1600 CE) or Iredell (1600–1725 CE) phases. Both phases are distinguished by a Lamar ceramic ware that Moore calls Cowans Ford and that shares many attributes with contemporaneous Burke phase ceramics of the upper Catawba River. Moore suggests that Low phase sites near the bend of the Catawba could be good candidates for Quinahaqui and Guaquili, but these appear to have been the only Low phase sites of the mid-sixteenth century. Without radiocarbon dates and with many of the identified Low phase sites currently beneath Lake Norman, it is impossible to be more specific about the timing of particular sites, much less to suggest their place in the social landscape of the Catawba valley.[35]

On September 24 Pardo arrived at Joara and Fort San Juan, where he learned that his sergeant Moyano was under siege at Olamico (also known as Chiaha). The army went to Moyano's aid with only a few days rest and then continued to explore the Appalachian summit of western North Carolina and eastern Tennessee for most of the next six weeks. After receiving news that several *orata* were planning to ambush the army, Pardo and his officers decided to turn back. They improved the Chiaha garrison and built another at Cauchi, situated along the Pigeon River west of Asheville, North Carolina. They returned to Joara on November 6 and recuperated at Fort San Juan for three weeks.[36]

While the company rested, no fewer than twenty-five *orata* and their *mandadores*, or principal men came to see Pardo at Joara, a clear consequence of the burgeoning status enjoyed by this chiefdom and its leader

Joara Mico. These visiting *orata* arrived at Joara in three groups. In the first were leaders from the villages of Quinahaqui, Guaquiri, Catape (Cataba?), and Yssa Chiquito, the latter a hamlet of Yssa. In the second were eighteen *orata* of villages whose locations are unknown. Some of these had met with Pardo at Cauchi as he was returning across the mountains, and Hudson suggests that they may have traveled to Joara from communities on the upper Broad, Saluda, and Savannah rivers. It is also quite possible that many of these *orata* came from other Burke phase communities along the upper Catawba and nearby Yadkin valleys. Bandera specifically notes that five of the *orata* in this group were *caciques* of Joara Mico, such that their communities probably formed the core of the Joara polity and were almost certainly located nearby. Finally, just before the company left Joara, two leaders called Chara Orata and Adini Orata — though nominally subjects of Guatari — came to switch their allegiance to Joara. In order to prevent hostilities between Guatari and Joara, Pardo convinced the men to continue giving their obedience to Guatari.[37]

Leaving thirty men at Fort San Juan, Pardo and his company departed from Joara on November 24. After a significant detour south to Yssa, where they remained for nearly two weeks, the company entered Guatari on December 15. Like Cofitachequi in 1540, the *mico* at Guatari was a woman; thus of the three *micos* who met with Soto and Pardo as they crossed the Carolinas, two were women. This is rather extraordinary, given the lack of complementary evidence — archaeological or documentary — for women holding the highest seats of political leadership in other Southern chiefdoms. In his account of the first expedition, Pardo reported that thirty *orata* received him at Guatari, the most at any town during the two expeditions. Bandera does not say how many visited during the second expedition, but clearly the number was much less impressive. Upon his arrival Pardo told the *mico* to summon her subjects to help the Spaniards build a fort; from Bandera's list of formal gifts that Pardo made that day, it seems that about seven of the subject *orata* came at the *cacica*'s behest. While at first this number looks quite low, it is close to the number that Bandera describes as *caciques* of Joara Mico. I suggest that the chiefdoms of Guatari and Joara probably administered about a half-dozen core villages each, making them comparable in size to the archaeological site clusters that David Hally has identified as chiefdoms in northwest Georgia and eastern Tennessee.[38]

The Guatari chiefdom may have been associated with the archaeological Caraway phase (1500–1700 CE). Like the Burke and Low phases of the Catawba River, Caraway is a manifestation of South Appalachian Mississippian, and Caraway ceramics are related to the Lamar cultural tradition. Caraway phase wares may have derived from pottery of the Pee Dee culture, a Middle Mississippian ceramic tradition whose people occupied the Pee Dee River and its tributaries from the twelfth through the fifteenth centuries. Most Pee Dee sites seem to have been abandoned by 1500 CE, about a century after the burning of the final structure atop Town Creek's mound. If the abandonment of Town Creek and other sites in its general vicinity were related to the rise of Cofitachequi, then Pee Dee peoples probably moved a short distance to the north, since most sites belonging to the Caraway phase are located on the central Yadkin River and its tributaries. I suggest that Town Creek and the Pee Dee culture may have been ancestral to Guatari and the Caraway phase and that Guatari rose to prominence in the central Yadkin as Cofitachequi's dampening effect began to wane. Moreover, this hypothesis suggests that all three of the Piedmont's sixteenth-century chiefdoms — Cofitachequi, Joara, and Guatari — were specific expressions of the South Appalachian Mississippian tradition, having more in common with one another than with groups farther east along the Carolina Piedmont.[39]

Pardo completed Fort Santiago at Guatari on January 6, 1568. Leaving a corporal named Lucas de Canizares in command of the fort and its sixteen men, he departed on the following day with the rest of his army and marched five days before arriving at Aracuchi along the lower Catawba River. The expedition then turned east and made a detour to the town of Ylasi on the Pee Dee River, reaching it in five days. Heavy rains delayed their departure by four days, but they left for Canos on January 21 and arrived on January 23. Pardo remained at Canos for eighteen days, building another garrison that he christened Fort Santo Tomás where he stationed thirty men.[40] After departing Canos and the Carolina Piedmont, he built a strong house at the Coastal Plain village of Orista and then returned to Santa Elena with fewer than a dozen men on March 2,

1568. In the end all of the forts at Joara, Chiaha, Cauchi, Guatari, Canos, and Orista would fall to native attack within just two or three months of Pardo's return to Santa Elena.[41] While the expeditions were thus an unmitigated failure from the perspective of the Spanish Crown, they provide modern historians and anthropologists with the most observant and detailed records of the Piedmont's sixteenth-century chiefdoms.

Two brief Spanish accounts of the Carolina Piedmont from the early seventeenth-century suggest that Joara and Cofitachequi remained prominent for several decades after the fall of Pardo's garrisons. In 1605 a sea captain named Francesco Fernández de Ecija questioned some Natives along the coast of South Carolina about interior lands. One of them told Ecija that near a high mountain far from the coast was "a very big village which is called Hoada [a lexical variant of Joara], and which has many Indians."[42] Several towns were noted as lying between Hoada and the sea, including Guatari, Guaca (Gueça), and Lasi (Ylasi) of the Pardo expeditions. Then in 1628 a small force of ten Spanish soldiers and sixty Indians led by Pedro de Torres penetrated the Carolina Piedmont as far as "Cofitachiqui," where he was "regaled by the *cacique*, who is very respected by all the remaining *caciques*, and all obey him and recognize vassalage."[43] These observations are the final recorded glimpses of the territory covered by Soto and Pardo until the 1670s by which time most of the social landscape had changed.

The Soto and Pardo accounts illuminate, if all too briefly, the politically fluid and dynamic landscape of the sixteenth-century Carolina Piedmont, particularly in the regions of the Catawba-Wateree and Yadkin-Pee Dee basins. It was a crowded landscape marked by complex webs of allegiance and competition, regional prominence and decline. There is little evidence that epidemic disease had any impact on the area's populations during or prior to this time, apart from the Gentleman of Elvas's sketchy reference to "plague" at Cofitachequi. Even if Elvas's statement does refer to an epidemic, its effects appear to have been quite localized given the crowded landscape that Pardo's expedition encountered, and it had little impact on the character of Piedmont politics given the pattern of chiefdom cycling from 1540 to 1567. Three chiefdoms flourished in this area in the sixteenth century: Cofitachequi, located on the Fall Line of the Wateree

River; Joara in the Appalachian foothills where the Catawba River enters the Piedmont; and Guatari, located along the central Yadkin. Both Joara and Cofitachequi rose to regional prominence near ecotones — resource-rich areas where major physiographic provinces meet — that provided exceptional conditions for the consolidation of chiefly power.[44] Guatari's emergence took place well to the north of the Fall Line, but as discussed above, its location along the central Yadkin valley was strongly conditioned by the particular circumstance of its proximity to Cofitachequi.

It was in the interstitial region between these three well-populated chiefdoms, along the lower and central Catawba River and its tributaries, that those towns and villages first identifiable as constituencies of the Catawba coalescence — towns with names such as Yssa, Cataba, Suhere, and Uchiri — existed during the mid-sixteenth century. Parts of this region may have been subject to Cofitachequi when Soto passed through the Carolina Piedmont, though the place referred to as Chalaque where subsequent coalescence actually unfolded appears to have been a sparsely populated province where the *cacica*'s chiefly stature provided little benefit for the expedition. During Pardo's time Cofitachequi, or Canos, cast a diminished shadow in this interstitial zone, such that the *orata* of its towns and villages seem to have moved quite freely among the chiefly centers of Canos, Joara, and Guatari or else simply avoided them altogether. But why should the lesser players of the sixteenth-century stage have become the leading actors of the early 1700s? And why should the seat of power or influence have shifted to the lower Catawba River? Satisfactory answers to these questions lay shrouded behind a curtain of ethnohistorical silence, but the observations of early English explorers do reveal clues about both the collapse of the Piedmont chiefdoms and about the origins of the shatter zone that made Catawba coalescence possible.

The Shattering of the Carolina Piedmont: 1650–75

On May 20, 1670, the German physician John Lederer commenced the second of his three explorations beyond the falls of the James River in Virginia. This trip would be the only one of the three to venture into the North Carolina Piedmont and, if it is to be believed, to revisit a portion of the route that Soto and Pardo had taken over a century before. Lederer's account of his discoveries has been a source of historical controversy, often discounted thanks to his detailed description of a "brackish" lake on the lower Catawba River where no such body of water could have existed.[45] As Steve Davis observes, however, Lederer introduces the Native towns he claims to have visited in a narrative and geographic order that corresponds with Lawson's account from 1701.[46] It may be that Lederer did not personally visit the lower North Carolina Piedmont but rather received his information from Native informants. Yet given that his is the only account of this region until Lawson, it cannot be ignored. Here I will use Lederer's narrative to gain some perspective on this region's social landscape in the late 1600s, recognizing that it is impossible to verify all of the details of his account.

Lederer entered the Carolina Piedmont shortly after his departure from Akhenatzy Island, better known to history as Occaneechi, located on the Roanoke River near present Clarksville, Virginia, and bestriding the famed Trading Path to the interior. The people of this island, the powerful Occaneechis, dominated Virginia's trade with the interior by at least 1670 and, as Robbie Ethridge has observed, were probably among the earliest "militaristic slaving societies" to form in the colonial South.[47] I will return to the slaving issue and to the Occaneechis' role therein as this is one of the keys to the collapse of the Piedmont chiefdoms and to the creation of a seventeenth-century shatter zone across most of the former territories of the Piedmont chiefdoms. The Occaneechis could be brutal in maintaining control over the interior trade, and Lederer's account offers a well-known case in point. He says that he "slunk away" from the island in the early morning hours, fearful of awakening his sleeping hosts. During the previous night these hosts held a "Ball" for the "Rickohockan Ambassadour," who had arrived with a small retinue, "but in the height of their mirth and dancing, by a smoke contrived for that purpose, the *Room was suddenly darkened, and for what cause I know not, the Rickohockan and his Retinue barbarously murthered."[48]

From Akhenatzy Lederer passed through several Piedmont towns far to the northeast of the territories traversed by Soto and Pardo, including Oenock (or Eno) and Shakori in the upper Neuse basin.[49] Here "their

Government is Democratick; and the Sentences of their old men are received as Laws, or rather Oracles, by them." Forty miles southwest of Shakori, Lederer arrived at Watery — the Guatari of the Pardo expeditions — apparently in the same general vicinity of the central Yadkin or its tributaries. Lederer observed that the mode of government at Guatari differed "from all the other Indians of these parts: for they are Slaves, rather then Subjects to their King."[50] Clearly Guatari still retained some features of a chiefly hierarchy, though there is nothing in Lederer's description to suggest that its "King" enjoyed the regional authority of a sixteenth-century *mico*.

Thirty miles west of Watery, still in the vicinity of the central Yadkin, Lederer came to Sara, stating that it was "not far distant from the Mountains, which here lose their height, and change their course and name: for they run due West, and receive from the Spaniards the name of Suala." Earlier in his account, he claimed that "*Sara* in the Warrennuncock dialect" was translated as "*Sasa* or *Sualy*." On its face Lederer's town of Sara seems to be the same as the sixteenth-century Joara, or Xualla, only moved one hundred miles to the east of the upper Catawba River. Sualy, it should also be noted, is the name that James Mooney's Cherokee informants used in reference to the Sara, or Cheraw, calling them the Ani-Suali and whom Mooney identified with Joara-Xualla. It is possible that the low mountains that Lederer describes here are the Uwharries, which are more a range of eroded hills in the central Piedmont and that this word itself is a linguistic remnant of Joara-Xualla. If such an interpretation is accurate, then both the Guatari and Joara chiefdoms had collapsed by the time of Lederer's journey, and major population movements had splintered the landscape of the Carolina Piedmont prior to 1670. This view of events does correspond with the archaeology of the upper Catawba River, which was probably depopulated by the mid-1600s.[51]

From Sara Lederer traveled south-southwest for two or three days before arriving at Wisacky, Pardo's Gueça, probably located in much the same general area as during the 1560s. It is here that Lederer discusses the lake called Ushery by which his testimony has so often been discounted. It is difficult to accommodate his description of this lake, but it is worth noting his observations about the village of Ushery, which Bandera had recorded as Uchiri in 1567; even if Lederer did not actually visit the lower Catawba but obtained these details secondhand from native informants, they still provide a clear example of the political changes that accompanied this shatter zone's formation. Lederer notes that Wisacky was "subject to a neighbour-King" named Ushery, and that his village was "more populous then any I had seen before in my March."[52] Ushery, a town that was hardly worthy of notice in 1567, may have been the only place on the North Carolina Piedmont with authority over neighboring villages in 1670. Moreover, Lederer's account provides the first documented notice that the lower Catawba Valley had emerged as a seat of political power. Even so, Ushery and its neighbors did not enjoy great security. According to Lederer, "this Prince, though his Dominions are large and populous, is in continual fear of the Oustack-Indians seated on the opposite side of the Lake; a people so addicted to Arms, that even their women come into the field, and shoot Arrows over their husbands shoulders, who shield them with Leathern Targets. . .They are a cruel generation, and prey upon people, whom they either steal, or force away from the Usheryes in Periago's, to sacrifice to their Idols."[53] This brief note about "Oustack-Indians" may be an early reference to the Westos, perhaps the most infamous of the South's slaving societies, who by this time were living southwest of the lower Catawba on the central Savannah River.[54]

Lederer's narrative describes a southern Carolina Piedmont that was dramatically different from the crowded landscape of 1567. The former centers of political power and population — particularly Joara and Guatari, where Pardo was received by at least fifty-five *orata* and two *micos* — were greatly reduced, scattered, or else entirely wiped away. A new political center was forming at Ushery in the neighborhood of the lower Catawba, a place that the Gentleman of Elvas described as the poorest in Florida in 1540 and that was marginal at best during the 1560s. It appears clear by comparing Lederer's account to Bandera's long relation that the native population of the southern Piedmont, as measured in the number and density of towns, was significantly thinned. Archaeological data corroborate this view as the upper Catawba River, one of the most densely settled parts of the Piedmont during the fifteenth and sixteenth centuries and the seat of Joara's chiefdom, was probably abandoned by the mid-1600s. What accounts for the scale of these transformations?

It is certainly possible that the introduction of novel European diseases, especially smallpox, had a significant role in the shattering of the Piedmont's chiefdoms. However, Paul Kelton has persuasively argued that, prior to the late 1600s, the social geography of the South was ill suited to the widespread dissemination of most contagions and that the first wide-spread smallpox epidemic probably did not occur until 1696. Archaeological data from the northern Piedmont region support this interpretation, as there is no evidence for significantly increased mortality rates until after 1675.[55]

If epidemics were not the principal factor in these transformations, then Lederer's account does provide clues about another, and equally devastating, source of catastrophic change. The Oustack and Akhenatzy Indians, or the Westo and Occaneechi, were two of the first Southern slaving groups to ravage the Carolinas; Ethridge has used the phrase militaristic slaving society to describe these Native slavers who emerged as the English, Dutch, and French pursued capitalist economic strategies in their trade for furs and slaves across the Eastern Woodlands. In 1670 when they were noted by Lederer, the Westos lived in a fortified town named Hickauhaugau, situated on the west bank of the Savannah River near modern Augusta, Georgia. Prior to settling the Savannah, they occupied the falls of the James River in Virginia where they were known as the Richahecrians. The Westos seem to have been a group of well-armed Erie and Neutral Indians — known to the Five Nations Iroquois as the Richahecrians — who were displaced from their original home along Lake Erie during the 1650s. Less is currently understood of Occaneechi origins, though a Virginian named Edward Bland reported their presence along the Roanoke River in 1650; they relocated to the Trading Path only after the Westos left Virginia.[56]

Both of these peoples were heavily outfitted with firearms relative to other groups in the interior, and they initially enjoyed a tremendous military advantage over their more isolated neighbors, including the well-populated chiefdoms of the Carolina Piedmont. It seems evident that the towns of these chiefdoms presented easy nearby targets for groups

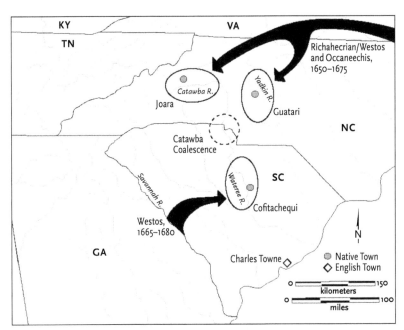

Map 5. The shattering of the Carolina Piedmont chiefdoms, ca. 1650–80.

such as the Westos and Occaneechis, both of who lived just to the north along Virginia's frontier from 1650–75. Thus slave raiders from Virginia and places farther north probably moved into Carolina, where they targeted the polities of Joara and Guatari, especially during the time prior to Lederer's second expedition. This interpretation accounts for the apparent population losses between 1570 and 1670 in terms of slaving rather than epidemic disease and also provides a geographic explanation for the rising significance of the lower Catawba valley and its southern location. If Piedmont chiefdoms farther north like Joara and Guatari took the brunt of early assaults, then the lower Catawba River — with a smaller density of towns and therefore fewer targets — became a relatively sheltered locale, particularly during these initial years of the rapidly expanding shatter zone (see map 5).

A similar fate to that of these northern chiefdoms awaited Cofitachequi. In 1670, about the same time that John Lederer set out to explore the interior of Virginia and North Carolina, Henry Woodward departed the newly founded colony of Charles Towne and went north along the

Santee-Wateree River. Eventually he came to "Chufytachyqi [that] fruit-full Province where ye Emperour resides . . . It lys West & by Northe nearest from us 14 days trauell after ye Indian manner of marchinge. I there contracted a league [with] ye Emp[eror] & all those Petty Cassekas betwixt us & them."[57]

From Woodward's description, and from several documentary references to an Emperor Cotachico, it is obvious that some form of chiefly hierarchy remained at Cofitachequi.[58] However, the scale of this hierarchy is far from clear. Was the position of the "Emperor" a relic or remnant—as Lederer's Watery King appears to have been—or did this position imply the regional authority of a sixteenth-century *mico*? An unknown number of "Petty Cassekas" met Woodward at Cofitachequi, much like the *orata* who met with Pardo there in 1567. Yet there was no *mico* during the time of Pardo's visit or any reason to believe that all of the *orata* who came there were subjects of Canos Orata. Thus there is nothing in Woodward's account to suggest that these headmen from locales between Cofitachequi and Charles Towne were subjects of the former in 1670.

Even so, Cofitachequi may have retained some authority over other villages along the lower Wateree River. The town reportedly had one thousand bowmen at its command, and if this number is even reasonably accurate, then Cofitachequi likely drew military support from neighboring villages. Cofitachequi was known as an enemy of the Westos, who had moved to the Savannah in the late 1660s. Charles Towne settler William Owen asserted the Cofitachequi emperor's "friend[ship] with us is very considerable against ye Westoes if ever they intend to Molest us he hath often defeated them and is ever their Master."[59] Such claims aside, the Westos had begun to assault Native groups living near Charles Towne. Another colonist, Stephen Bull, wrote in 1670 that these local Indians were "expectinge protecon under us [which] wee have promised them [against] another sorte of Indians that live backwards in an intier body & warr [against] all Indians they are called Westoes & doe strike a great feare in these Indians havinge gunns & powder & shott & doe come upon these Indians heere in the tyme of their cropp & destroye all by killinge Caryinge aweye their Corne & Children & eat them & our neibouringe Indians."[60]

In October 1674 Woodward made a journey to the Westo town of Hickauhaugau; after this visit the Westos and the Carolina colony began a trading partnership that lasted for six years. The partnership guaranteed for the Westos exclusive legal right to trade for guns with Carolina.[61] In exchange Carolina was guaranteed a plentiful supply of "deare skins, furrs & younge slaves." This agreement proved disastrous for the Native peoples of Cofitachequi, and it is no coincidence that this polity disappears from the documentary record immediately after Woodward's visit to the Westos. Eric Bowne directly attributes their disappearance to Westo predations.[62] The Westos' interest in Cofitachequi and the lower Wateree would likely have provided a respite to the people of the lower Catawba River, people like the Uchiri, Yssa, Cataba, and Suhere. And while Cofitachequi did persist as a regional polity for a short time longer than either Joara or Guatari, it too was completely shattered by 1675.

Neither the Westos nor the Occaneechis had an opportunity to fully turn their attention to the new society coalescing along the lower Catawba River as both were themselves destroyed by 1680: the Occaneechis during Bacon's Rebellion in 1676 and the Westos in the Westo War of 1680. If the Piedmont chiefdoms shielded this region during the early slaving era when the Occaneechis and Westos dominated the trade, then colonial uprisings in Virginia and Carolina dispatched the slave catchers shortly after the chiefdoms were shattered, inadvertently maintaining the lower Catawba as a shelter in the broader cultural context of the Piedmont shatter zone. This is not to suggest, of course, that the peoples of this evolving Catawba coalescence were simply the passive and quiescent beneficiaries of others' actions. Rather, the specific details of Piedmont history provided opportunities for peoples in the lower Catawba Valley to experiment with novel modes of integration during a time of unprecedented change.

The transformations of this period were not unprecedented because of population movements or chiefdom collapse. During Cofitachequi's ascendance in the late fifteenth century, for example, several potentially competing polities collapsed across the Carolina and Georgia piedmonts, and vast stretches of otherwise attractive riverine territories were largely abandoned. In a very real sense then shatter zone conditions were nothing novel to the Late Mississippian world. What was unprecedented was the fact that no chiefdoms took the place of those that collapsed and the fact that population movements in this new shatter zone often meant the forced removal of Native peoples from their Piedmont homes to plantations in Carolina, Virginia, and the West Indies. A new political economy based on guns and furs — instead of labor and surplus maize — underwrote the process of Catawba coalescence and rendered obsolescent the chiefdom as a political institution. This chapter illustrates the degree to which social process unfolds through the particularities of history, and thus the degree to which Catawba coalescence was inextricably bound to the particular and contingent histories of Cofitachequi, Guatari, and Joara.

Notes

1. Davis, "Cultural Landscape."

2. Although Cofitachequi was actually located just south of the Fall Line and thus within the Coastal Plain, it is impossible to understand the social history of chiefdoms across the Carolina Piedmont — as well as the process of Catawba ethnogenesis — without considering Cofitachequi's regional prominence.

3. Gentleman of Elvas, "True Relation," 81; Rangel, "Account," 275; and Hudson, *Knights*, 171–72.

4. Rangel, "Account," 278.

5. Gentleman of Elvas, "True Relation," 83.

6. Hudson, *Juan Pardo Expeditions* (2005), 69, 73.

7. Rangel, "Account," 279–80.

8. Hudson, *Juan Pardo Expeditions* (2005), 62, 69. Pardo encountered three such chiefs, two of whom governed polities in the North Carolina Piedmont.

9. I define chiefdom as a hierarchically organized polity that integrates multiple communities. See Anderson, *Savannah River Chiefdoms*, 6; Beck, "Consolidation and Hierarchy," 641; DePratter, "Chiefdom of Cofitachequi," 208, 211; and Ward and Davis, *Time Before History*, 132–33

10. Anderson, *Savannah River Chiefdoms*, chapter 7.

11. Hudson, *Knights of Spain*, 174–75.

12. Anderson, *Savannah River Chiefdoms*, 8–9, 70; Beck, "Consolidation and

Hierarchy"; and Beck, "Persuasive Politics." For a discussion of the Moundville chiefdom's dampening effect, see Steponaitis, "Contrasting Patterns."

13. Gentleman of Elvas, "True Relation," 85, 86 (quote).

14. DePratter, "Chiefdom of Cofitachequi," 215–17.

15. Rangel, "Account," 272.

16. Swanton, *Final Report*, 50.

17. Gentleman of Elvas, "True Relation," 86.

18. DePratter, "Chiefdom of Cofitachequi," 218–19.

19. On the archaeology of Joara (Xualla), see Beck, "From Joara to Chiaha"; Beck and Moore, "Burke Phase"; Beck, Moore, and Rodning, "Identifying Fort San Juan"; and Moore, Beck, and Rodning, Afterward. Rangel, "Account," 279 (quote), 281 (quote); Gentleman of Elvas, "True Relation," 86; and Biedma, "Relation," 231 (quote).

20. Rangel, "Account," 281 (quote). Beck, "From Joara to Chiaha"; and Hudson, *Knights of Spain*, 190–93. Gentleman of Elvas, "True Relation," 86–87; and Rangel, "Account," 281, simply notes that the she "turned back."

21. Baker, "Historic Catawba"; and Hudson, *Knights of Spain*.

22. Hoffman, *New Andalucia*; Hudson, *Juan Pardo Expeditions* (2005); Lyon, *Enterprise of Florida*; Lyon, *Santa Elena*; and Paar, "Witness to Empire."

23. DePratter, Hudson, and Smith, "Juan Pardo's Explorations"; and Hudson, *Juan Pardo Expeditions* (2005).

24. Hudson, Smith, and DePratter, "Hernando De Soto Expedition," 72; and Hudson, *Juan Pardo Expeditions* (2005), 34.

25. Pardo, "Pardo Relation," 311 (quote); and Bandera, "Short Bandera Relation," 301 (quote).

26. Keel, "Salvage Archaeology."

27. Merrell, *Indians' New World*, 94. See also the chapter by Fitts and Heath, this volume.

28. Beck and Moore, "Burke Phase"; and Moore, *Catawba Valley Mississippian*.

29. Martinez, "Martinez Relation," 320; Pardo, "Pardo Relation," 312(quote); and Beck, Moore, and Rodning, "Identifying Fort San Juan."

30. Hudson, *Juan Pardo Expeditions* (2005), 26; Pardo, "Pardo Relation," 312; and Bandera, "'Long' Bandera Relation," 259.

31. Beck, "From Joara to Chiaha"; and Martinez, "Martinez Relation."

32. Hudson, *Juan Pardo Expeditions* (2005), 63; and Bandera, "'Long' Bandera Relation," 215, 263.

33. Bandera, "'Long' Bandera Relation," 260–61; Bandera sometimes records Cataba as "Catapa." Hudson, *Juan Pardo Expeditions* (2005), 43, 77.

34. Hudson, *Juan Pardo Expeditions* (2005), 76, 77, 84; and Merrell, *Indians' New World*, 47, 92. While Hudson notes that "Uchiri" may have been a reference to the Yuchi, Usheree is a better match given its clear affiliation with the Catawba coalescence. Merrell also suggests that the Virginians arrived at "Usheree" by adding the suffix *ri* to "Esaw." However, the Bandera account makes it quite clear that Yssa (Esaw) and Uchiri (Usheree) were distinct groups in 1567.

35. Moore, *Catawba Valley Mississippian*, 132–51, 181.

36. Pardo, "Pardo Relation," 313–14; and Bandera, "'Long' Bandera Relation," 277.

37. Bandera, "'Long' Bandera Relation," 278, 279 (quote) (emphasis added); Hudson, *Juan Pardo Expeditions* (2005), 88–89; and Beck and Moore, "Burke Phase," 201.

38. Bandera, "'Long' Bandera Relation," 277, 284; and Hally, "Chiefdom," 246.

39. Coe, *Town Creek*, 163–67; Hally, "Overview of Lamar"; Moore, *Catawba Valley Mississippian*, 133; Ward and Davis, *Time before History*, 132–37; Oliver, "Settlements of the Pee Dee," figure 40; Davis, "Cultural Landscape," figure 2.

40. Bandera, "'Long' Bandera Relation," 292.

41. Beck, Moore, and Rodning, "Identifying Fort San Juan"; and Hudson, *Juan Pardo Expeditions* (2005), 173–77.

42. Hann, "Translation of the Ecija Voyages," 10.

43. Worth, "Late Spanish Military Expeditions," 114.

44. Beck and Moore, "Burke Phase"; and Hally, "Overview of Lamar Culture."

45. Lederer, *Discoveries*, 21; Alvord and Bidgood, *First Explorations*, 63–64; Davis, "Cultural Landscape," 140; and Hudson, *Juan Pardo Expeditions* (2005), 184–85.

46. Davis, "Cultural Landscape," 140.

47. Ethridge, "Creating the Shatter Zone," 210.

48. Lederer, *Discoveries*, 17.

49. Davis, "Cultural Landscape," 140.

50. Lederer, *Discoveries*, 18–19.

51. Lederer, *Discoveries*, 5, 19; Mooney, *Myths of the Cherokee*, 380; Rights, *American Indian*, 119; and Moore, *Catawba Valley Mississippian*, 194. The mountains to which Lederer refers run southwest, not due west. A lengthy treatment of the Sara Indians is beyond the scope of this chapter. In the colonial documents of Virginia

and the Carolinas, they are referred to as the Saraw and later as the Charraw or Cheraw. Hudson's *Juan Pardo Expeditions* (2005), 184–85, links the Sara Indians with the Chara Orata briefly noted in the Pardo accounts, but doing so means dismissing Lederer's apparent equating of Sara and Sualy-Xualla-Joara. Rudes, Blumer, and May in "Catawba and Neighboring Groups" specifically associate Sara with Joara. Byrd in "Journey," 289–90, notes that prior to 1700 the Sara lived on the Dan River south of the Virginia state line but that Iroquois predations drove them south to the Pee Dee River, where they remained until the 1720s. Davis in "Cultural Landscape" has argued that "no archaeological evidence exists for placing the Sara south of the Dan River before the eighteenth century" (140), but he leaves unspecified precisely what form such archaeological evidence might take. Lederer's testimony is relatively clear, and it seems possible that Joara and Sara reference the same people and that Joara had moved east to the vicinity of the Yadkin River prior to 1670. Byrd's account relates that they moved yet again, north to the Dan River, sometime between 1670 and 1700, perhaps to be nearer the Virginia colony

52. Lederer, *Discoveries*, 20.

53. Lederer, *Discoveries*, 20–21.

54. Bowne, *Westo Indians*, 33; Mooney, *Siouan Tribes*, 70; and Swanton, *Early History*, 292.

55. Kelton, "Great Southeastern Smallpox Epidemic"; Ward and Davis, "Impact of Old World Diseases"; and Ward and Davis, *Indian Communities*, 430–32.

56. Ethridge, "Creating the Shatter Zone," 208; Bowne, *Westo Indians*, 23, 37–38; and Meyers, "Site Location Model." See also Bowne, this volume, and Meyers, this volume.

57. Cheves, *Shaftesbury Papers*, 186–87.

58. Cheves, *Shaftesbury Papers*, 201.

59. Cheves, *Shaftesbury Papers*, 223 (quote), 249, 256.

60. Cheves, *Shaftesbury Papers*, 194.

61. Bowne, *Westo Indians*, 85.

62. Bowne, *Westo Indians*, 85–86; and Cheves, *Shaftesbury Papers*, 462 (quote).

6 | *"Indians Refusing to Carry Burdens"*

UNDERSTANDING THE SUCCESS OF CATAWBA
POLITICAL, MILITARY, AND SETTLEMENT
STRATEGIES IN COLONIAL CAROLINA

MARY ELIZABETH FITTS AND CHARLES L. HEATH

The trader Eleazer Wiggan stood before the South Carolina Board of Indian Trade Commissioners on Thursday, October 24, 1717. He had managed to sustain his career in Indian country despite the temporary revocation of his trading license for instigating the Cherokee attack on the Yuchi community of Chestowee in 1713 and despite the hazards of the 1715 Yamasee War. Back in the good graces of the board and serving as trade factor to the Catawba, Wiggan reported that these inhabitants of the Carolina Piedmont were "refusing to carry Burdens any more," referring to the common practice of Indian couriers transporting deerskins and trade goods between Charles Town and their own settlements. Two weeks later, the commissioners had procured packhorses for the Catawba trade.[1] Charles Town officials were clearly interested in appeasing the Catawba, but why was this the case?

The Yamasee War, which ultimately forced both the British and the Southern Indians to recognize that they had underestimated each other, instigated the negotiation of a new political climate in the region. During the previous century demographic and political turmoil had cascaded through the South as Indian communities began to participate in the fur and Indian slave trades.[2] In this colonial shatter zone the British market for Indian slaves encouraged some groups to intensify previously episodic raiding activities, a practice that has been described as militaristic slaving.[3] The Yamasee War forced the British to confront the results of this historical process and to undertake diplomatic maneuvers intended to bring political order to the region.

This task was complicated, however, by demographic changes that had occurred during the late seventeenth century. Forced to find solutions to the danger and chaos of the shatter zone, Southern Indians enacted a variety of strategies to both protect themselves from their enemies and to benefit materially through the acquisition of European commodities. One widespread practice to accomplish these ends was the coalescence of previously distinct groups into confederated polities.[4] Although many American Indian societies in eastern North America such as the Iroquois, Catawba, Cherokee, Creek, and Seminole absorbed refugees into their ranks, the ways in which differences between the host community and newcomers were addressed varied based on the specific political histories and cultural understandings of the groups in question. The coalescence of American Indian groups during the colonial period therefore can be understood as a historical phenomenon that had distinct but interrelated political and social aspects.

In the following discussion we examine the case of Catawba coalescence from an anthropological perspective through the use of both documentary and archaeological evidence. A first step in this process is tracing the history of the name Catawba and its referents, an undertaking that supplies clues to the political and social circumstances of Catawba coalescence. We next use the geopolitical concept of the shatter zone to describe the context within which members of the Catawba community made their political and economic choices during the late seventeenth and early eighteenth centuries. With the establishment of Charles Town in 1670 some of these choices involved participation in violent intra- and inter-Indian or colonial conflicts at the perpetual request of South Carolina officials as well as the Indian slave trade. We employ the term "ethnic soldiering" to describe the role that the Catawba played for the British, and we consider its significance in the process of social coalescence taking place in the lower Catawba River Valley.[5]

In addition, the political and military strategies of Carolina Piedmont peoples were enacted within a historically contingent landscape of towns and trails. To characterize this demographic and geographic space, we present the results of a settlement pattern analysis based on pottery assemblages from ten archaeological sites in the lower Catawba Valley near present Fort Mill, South Carolina. Because fragments of ceramic vessels are durable manifestations of the knowledge that potters acquired as members of specific communities, similarities and differences between pottery assemblages from contemporaneous sites can be used to assess the character of the sociopolitical landscape in the lower Catawba River Valley. We use the results of this settlement analysis, in conjunction with documentary references, to propose that the core population of the coalescent Catawba society in the lower Catawba River Valley was of local origin and would have possessed an advantageous familiarity with the social and physical terrain of the region. Moreover, by preferentially establishing new towns along the main trading path that passed through the region, these Carolina Piedmont Indians also appear to have been enacting a strategy to best access the flow of trade materials and information through their territory. Taken together, due consideration of these political, military, and settlement strategies provide a better understanding of how the Catawba not only managed to survive the trials of the colonial shatter zone but also emerged from this crucible as a regionally important polity throughout the colonial era.

Naming Catawba

Anthropological approaches to ethnicity often emphasize the emic, or the self-naming aspect of identity construction.[6] Nevertheless, the choices of group members are informed by their perceptions of "external" social categories and contexts. Given this situation, it is not surprising that names expressing ethnic identity tend to change through time in a dialectical fashion.[7] The issue of translation adds another wrinkle to the study of this process in colonial contexts, and the case of the name Catawba is no exception. Tracking the changes in this term from early Spanish to later English transpositions and finally to its enduring political usage is important for the study of the ascendancy of the Catawba Nation in the colonial shatter zone. This practice not only provides a *terminus ante quem* for the core ethnic groups of the polity, but it can also be used as evidence for changes in the composition of the Catawba community during the late seventeenth and early eighteenth centuries.

It is not possible to fully understand the history of the name Catawba without also considering the history of the name Esaw. When John Lawson traveled through the upper Wateree River Valley in 1701, he set out to visit the "Esaw Indians, a very large Nation containing many thousand People," and only inadvertently encountered a group he identified as the Kadapau. The earliest European references to names considered renderings of Catawba and Esaw were made during the Juan Pardo expeditions of 1566 and 1567. Expedition records identify Native officials named Yssa Orata and Cataba Orata; the Spanish used the title *orata* to refer to a minor chief.[8] Both names appear to have been translated from Catawban, consisting of a set of dialects distantly related to Siouan languages.[9] The names Cataba and Yssa therefore are names with very similar linguistic backgrounds that were used to refer to the leaders of two distinct groups that Spanish observers perceived to have equivalent political status.

During the following century there appears to have been a shift in the relative political importance of the Yssa and Cataba groups. While the Cataba are not specifically mentioned in colonial documents from the extended period between the visits of Pardo (1566–67) and Lawson (1701), English records dating to the late seventeenth century contain references to the Yssa, transposed as Esaw. At the turn of the eighteenth century it would seem that the names Esaw and Kadapau continued to distinguish two groups, with Esaw also referring to the totality of groups living in the lower Catawba Valley.[10]

Through a dynamic process of self-identification and external reference, the situation reported by Lawson reversed over the next twenty years. The first step in this process may be manifest in the appearance of the name Nassaw, which was recorded on a deerskin map created by a Catawba leader and presented to South Carolina Governor Francis Nicholson in 1721. In 1728 Colonel William Byrd of Virginia noted that the first Catawba town English traders encountered on their way to the Cherokee was called Nauvasa. The derivation of Nassaw appears to be similar to that of Yssa and Esaw: all three are glosses of the Catawban word for "river," *iswa*. Nassaw, however, contains the preposition *nea*, an abbreviation of the term meaning "people" in Catawban. The use of the preposition *nea* seems to constitute an assertion of identity and a recognition of difference as it suggests that some people were considered "people of the river" and by implication others were not. At the time the deerskin map was drawn and presented to Governor Nicholson, the lower Catawba Valley was the center of the Catawba coalescence and the locality where displaced groups from various regions had joined the emerging polity. Transposing *iswa* into *nea-iswa*, or Nassaw as the English later recorded it, provides a possible linguistic clue as to the processes of coalescence and the emergence of a unified polity.[11] But how did a group named Catawba come to be understood as the host community of this polity?

The Kadapau, as Lawson called them, appear to have been the northernmost group he encountered in the Catawba Valley. After leaving the Kadapau village to travel northward along the Virginia-Cherokee trading path with the Virginia trader John Stewart, whom he had met at the village, Lawson does not record the presence of any settlements until his arrival in Sapona Town on the Yadkin River.[12] In fact, it seems that for the Virginians, the well-trod trading path itself came to be named for the Catawba. The nineteenth-century anthropologist James Mooney observed that "the great trading path from Virginia to Georgia was commonly known as the Catawba path," as evidenced by a 1733 map of North Carolina produced by Edward Moseley on which this trail is labeled "Indian Trading Road from the Cataubous and Cherokee Indians to Virginia."[13] When the name Catawba became synonymous with the trail, members of diverse groups integrated into the nascent polity may have been more likely to use this name, if only when communicating with outsiders such as Indians from other polities, English traders, and colonial officials.

It is also possible that another form of pragmatism informed the adoption of Catawba as the name for the coalescent polity forming in the lower Catawba Valley. While Esaw seems to have served a similar purpose at the turn of the eighteenth century, their participation in the seventeenth-century Indian slave trade may have made this name a liability for lower Catawba Valley peoples and English alike during the period of diplomacy that followed the Yamasee War. For example, in 1693 Cherokee leaders went to Charleston and identified the Esaw as enemies who had attacked them and sold captives into slavery; accusations that colonial authorities were complicit in such attacks were registered in the early 1700s. From this perspective the naming of the Catawba Nation appears to have been a process informed partly by the politics of the colonial shatter zone.

Militarism and Coalescence

The demographic and political coalescence that took place in the lower Catawba Valley during the late seventeenth and early eighteenth centuries is not a unique phenomenon, especially for societies experiencing increased levels of warfare and decreased population stability.[14] Both these conditions accompanied the English slave trade, which created shatter zones of political and demographic transformation on multiple continents.[15] The English market for American Indian slaves as a labor force for New World plantations intensified throughout the seventeenth century, in part because enslaved American Indians cost less than African slaves, especially if traders could avoid paying taxes.[16] This demand, coupled with the rapid adoption of firearms by Indian societies, led to a significant escalation of conflict in the Eastern Woodlands. During the mid-to late-seventeenth century Northern Indian raiding parties headed southward, and Southern peoples responded in a variety of ways. Some became militaristic slaving societies themselves, while others took a defensive stance, forming alliances with colonial governments, neighboring villages, and refugees from shattered tribes.

Inhabitants of the lower Catawba Valley were participating in the Indian slave trade by the late seventeenth century. When English slavers based in Charles Town sought to break the Westo monopoly of the interior slave trade in 1680, they enlisted the Esaw to help subdue the well-armed Westos. The Esaw are also recorded as having captured Winyah, Cherokee, and Westo slaves.[17] The fierce reputation Catawba warriors later enjoyed during the eighteenth century may stem in part from these early exploits. The political and militaristic prominence of the Esaw during the late seventeenth century also may explain why John Lawson expected to encounter "the powerful Nation of Esaws" but did not anticipate meeting the Kadapau.[18]

Unlike other militaristic slaving societies of the seventeenth century, however, the Esaw did not become the focus of catastrophic retaliatory violence. Instead, they appear to have joined a coalition of communities depicted on the deerskin map presented to the governor of South Carolina in 1721. This political body, possibly modeled after the Iroquois

Confederacy and formed during or just after the Yamasee War, is mapped with the town Nassaw at its geographic center.[19] Some members of the Yuchi, another Southern militaristic slaving society that adopted a tactic of "strategically repositioning" themselves during the early eighteenth century, may have joined the Catawba Confederacy.[20] The balance of Catawba allies, however, consisted of Carolina Piedmont groups that are not known to have been slaving societies, such as the Wateree, Sucah, and Nustie. James Merrell suggests that members of these groups may have agreed to join the confederacy for protection, not only from other raiding parties and colonial militias but also from the Catawba themselves. Regardless of whether their decision to join the coalescent Catawba polity was based on friendship, coercion, or something in between, Carolina Piedmont peoples ultimately put aside their differences as they came to understand in light of crushing British victories in the Tuscarora War (1711–15) and Yamasee War (1715–18) that the Carolina colony was not as fragile as the piedmont groups seem to have originally believed.[21]

One of the strategies employed by members of the lower Catawba River Valley polity in response to the chaos of the shatter zone was to serve as ethnic soldiers for the fledgling South Carolina colony. From the perspective of South Carolina officials, the Catawba formed a living bulkhead between the coastal British settlements, the seemingly unpredictable Cherokees to the west, and Northern Indian raiders, primarily from the Iroquois Confederacy. As well as a strategic buffer, the Catawba acted as a ready-reserve force and a psychological weapon to suppress potential African slave insurrections in the Carolinas.[22] Ferguson and Whitehead's concept of ethnic soldiers can be used to describe the role that the Catawba played for the British during and after the Tuscarora War. According to Ferguson and Whitehead, in many colonial settings ethnic soldiers, typically culled from an existing indigenous warrior class, are "drawn into the service of state agents by varying combinations of coercive and seductive measures." Such measures included, but are not restricted to, overt force and preferential trade relationships. Expanding empires and states often use ethnic soldiers as auxiliary combat troops, as raiders to procure something the state desires, or as a means of furthering the geopolitical interests of the empire. Moreover, ethnic soldiers frequently perform internal policing functions that control subversive activities or enslaved populations.[23]

The English enlisted the Catawba as ethnic soldiers in the late seventeenth century when Charles Town officials courted Catawba warriors as military allies, first against the Westos and later against the Savannah-Shawnees.[24] After French-allied Iroquois warriors raided South Carolina settlements in 1709 and 1710, British officials hired the Catawba to both take the war north and to defend the periphery of the colony. Catawba contingents also fought with Carolina militiamen, British regulars, and other Indian auxiliaries in the Franco-Spanish attack on Charles Town in 1706 and again in the Tuscarora War of 1711–15.[25] Although we have no direct documentary evidence of Catawba motives for their support of the Carolina colonists during the Tuscarora War, they seem to have participated out of a desire to capture marketable slaves and other spoils of war.[26]

For a brief period in the Yamasee War the Catawba allied with the Yamasee coalition but quickly realigned themselves with the Carolinians after suffering brutal losses of men, women, and children at Goose Creek in 1715.[27] To cement their restored alliance with the British, Catawba warriors later destroyed several warring Waxhaw villages and reportedly subjugated the warring Cheraw.[28] Later in the Seven Years' War (1756–63), Catawba men joined English forces and served on several expeditions in the Ohio Valley, patrolled in the Broad River Valley, and supported major actions against the Savannah-Shawnees and the Cherokees. Catawba warriors continued to serve with North and South Carolina regiments in the American Revolution and then as soldiers for the United States well into the modern era.[29]

Militarism and ethnic soldiering are common strategies of societal self-preservation for peoples subject to frequent attacks by polities exhibiting superior military force. Carolina Piedmont Indians certainly had to fight or be destroyed by their often numerically superior Northern Iroquois, Cherokee, and Chickasaw enemies throughout most of the eighteenth century. The Catawba's apparently well-deserved reputation as formidable warriors likely protected them from many potential attacks from either fearful European colonists or other Indian enemies. This issue was critical during the heyday of the Indian slave trade when other militaristic slaving societies preyed on weaker victims across the South. That the Catawba continued to pursue this militaristic strategy despite its deleterious effects in terms of casualties and stress due to perpetual cycles of violent retribution, especially from the Northern Iroquois, speaks to the degree to which the Catawba considered it a vital element of group survival.[30]

Ethnic soldiering was also a collective activity that served to unite groups with different backgrounds under the protective umbrella of the Catawba identity. Participation in military expeditions would have promoted coalescence and group solidarity among the constituent elements of the multiethnic Catawba Nation in a variety of ways. For example, the planning and execution of such undertakings required continuous communication between towns, and it is easy to imagine that the resulting stories of battles and heroes would be transformed into a trove of collective memory and historical consciousness.[31] On a more banal but no less important level, members of the coalescent Catawba community also were negotiating on a day-to-day basis the value, meaning, and utility of mass-produced European goods that were the material spoils of war and slaving. Colonial officials typically paid chiefs, war leaders, warriors, and families with presents of arms, trade goods, or food supplies for their alliances and martial services as well as for their tracking and recovering escaped African slaves. Charles Town officials also paid for services rendered by European craftsmen, doctors, and apothecaries for gun repairs, saddle repairs, medicines, and medical treatment.[32] Whatever their linguistic, political, or cultural differences, all members of the Catawba Confederacy would have had access to the same kaolin pipes, trade beads, clasp knives, and trade guns.

The British strategy of factionalizing the native peoples of the Carolinas, adopted as early as 1681, was thwarted by the resilience of the Catawba Confederacy. Using inhabitants of the lower Catawba River Valley as ethnic soldiers, particularly during the Tuscarora War, diminished the effectiveness of this factionalizing strategy by providing Carolina Piedmont Indians the opportunity to identify and craft responses to British machinations.[33] Yet while militaristic slave raiding and ethnic soldiering played a role in Catawba coalescence, these actions do not by themselves explain the unique character of this historical process. In order to examine other conditions that contributed to Catawba coalescence, we next utilize archaeological evidence to characterize the landscape within which it took place.

Old Trails, New Towns

Archaeology cannot provide information about short-term ephemeral events such as a dispute between two parties that escalates into large-scale internecine warfare that may play a large role in historical causation. Nevertheless, the consequences of such an event and the context out of which it arose can be visible in the physical materials produced and altered by people who changed their behavior from one set of circumstances to another.[34] For example, while it may be difficult to trace the passage of the Juan Pardo expedition of 1566 using material evidence, archaeological methods can be used to identify Pre- and Postcontact Period differences in the location of lower Catawba River Valley communities. This information can in turn be used to consider social and economic aspects of Catawba coalescence that are not accessible through the documentary record.

The following diachronic investigation of Catawba settlement locations and pottery assemblages considers the physical remains of Catawba communities not as isolated habitation sites but as the remains of groups of people who interacted with each other. Pottery is understood to be a physical product of knowledge and skills obtained by an individual within a historically contingent community of practice. From this perspective most pots when created for daily use within a regime of domestic production are relatively conservative tools in that their manufacture is a "self-evident and undisputed" aspect of the social world. Changes in ceramic distributions therefore can be understood in terms of the movement and transformation of communities of teachers and learners.[35]

The archaeological materials from which the following interpretations are drawn consist of pottery assemblages collected from the surface of ten habitation sites in the lower Catawba Valley (see map 6).[36] Two of these sites can be identified as the remains of Catawba towns mapped in 1756 by John Evans, who was sent to determine how many Catawba warriors would be available to fight in the Seven Years' War.[37] The pri-

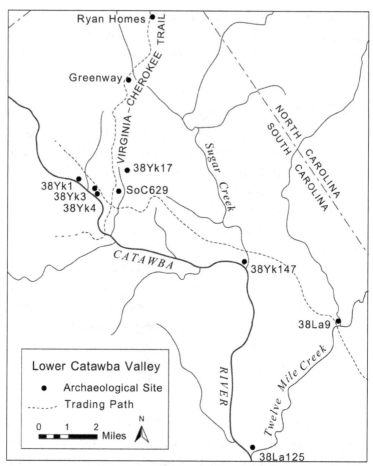

Map 6. Locations of archaeological sites in the lower Catawba Valley from which the analyzed pottery assemblages were collected. The ten assemblages are separable into four groups: those from sites dating primarily to the Late Woodland (38Yk4), Mississippian (38La9 and 38La125), and early Historic periods (SoC629, 38Yk17, Ryan Homes, and Greenway), and those that cannot be ascribed to a single category (38Yk1, 38Yk3, and 38Yk147).

mary settlements of the Catawba Nation at that time were located just south of present Fort Mill, South Carolina (see map 7). Patterns in the variation between pottery assemblages were identified using correspondence analysis, and these patterns were then employed to develop a rough chronological ordering of the archaeological sites.[38] The ten assemblages

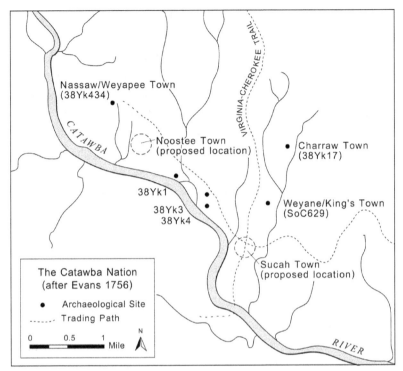

Map 7. A region of the lower Catawba Valley thought to approximate the area mapped by Evans in 1756, showing paths, recorded archaeological sites, and proposed locations of villages.

are separable into four groups: those from sites dating primarily to the Late Woodland Period (38yk4), Mississippian Period (38La9 and 38La125), colonial period (SoC629, 38yk17, Ryan Homes, and Greenway), and those from sites that cannot be ascribed to a single chronological period (38yk1, 38yk3, and 38yk147) (see map 6).

Perhaps the most straightforward and significant characteristic of the pottery assemblages is that they collectively represent settlement in the project area over a span of roughly seven hundred years. This is not to say that community relocation on a small scale did not take place through time, but there is no archaeological evidence for seventeenth-century depopulation of the lower Catawba River Valley.[39] Independent of this issue is a series of posited seventeenth- and eighteenth-century population movements into the area. It has been suggested that people from the

"Indians Refusing to Carry Burdens" 153

upper Catawba River Valley moved southward during the second half of the seventeenth century to command an advantageous position for trade with Virginia and Carolina.[40] After Bacon's Rebellion (1676), which ended Occaneechi control over the northern Carolina Piedmont, refugee Siouan groups moved southward to avoid escalating Iroquois raids. At the end of the seventeenth century some of these refugee groups may have been living among the communities of what was then known as the Esaw Nation. By the 1740s the remnants of the Sissipahaw, Shakori, Sara (Cheraw), Eno, and Keyauwee had joined the Catawba Confederacy.[41] Both archaeological and documentary evidence suggest that the core population of the coalescent Catawba society, however, was of local origin.[42] Unlike some groups that participated in the Indian slave trade such as the Yuchi and Westo, the Esaw and Kadapau did not relocate hundreds of miles from their precontact territories. For some militaristic slaving societies, mobility became a strategy that protected them from reprisals and ensured that their victims were strangers. Yet the fact that the peoples of the central Carolina Piedmont remained largely in their precontact homeland meant that they could use their familiarity with its geographic and sociopolitical terrain to their advantage.[43]

The pottery assemblages assessed for this study also provide tantalizing information as to the character of the sociopolitical landscape in the central Carolina Piedmont prior to the development of the colonial shatter zone. Specifically, the potters who produced these assemblages did not, with any frequency, attach an appliqué ring of clay parallel to but slightly below the rims of their cooking jars. This absence of appliqué rim strips from the 1,100 sherds examined despite the presence of other late Mississippian Period attributes such as complicated stamping and bold incising may relate to the nature of the relationship between the inhabitants of the lower Catawba River Valley and the Cofitachequi polity. The Spanish perceived this political entity, which is often classified as a late Mississippian chiefdom, to be more centralized, ranked, and powerful than those surrounding it.[44] The types of pottery most likely produced by inhabitants of the main town of Cofitachequi are those described by Depratter and Judge as the Wateree River Valley Mulberry series, which date from 1450 to 1550.[45] In the Wateree Valley the production of appliqué strips, as well as the use of complicated stamped paddles to decorate pottery, appear to continue into the seventeenth century. The seeming disconnect between the pottery traditions of the Mississippian people living in the Wateree River valley and those living in the lower Catawba region may suggest that two different communities of potters lived in these areas.[46] Given this pattern, it seems interactions between lower Catawba River Valley groups and the political center of Cofitachequi were limited, perhaps diplomatic in character. The possible linguistic difference between inhabitants of the central Wateree and lower Catawba Valley regions in the sixteenth century, as noted by Beck in this volume, would be consistent with this seeming synchronic discontinuity in kinship networks as inferred from pottery production practices.[47]

The Cofitachequi polity disappeared from the political landscape of the South by the late seventeenth century, but descendants of the Yssa and Cataba groups remained in the lower Catawba Valley. These communities were connected to each other, as they were generations earlier, by a network of trails and rivers. Trails in particular figure prominently in the writings of European prospectors and traders who traveled through the Carolina interior. These thoroughfares were clearly a vital element of infrastructure that linked native communities together on a regional scale. Although John Lawson observed a Saponi "ambassador" among the Waxhaw, encountered an Esaw war captain who was heading off to visit with the Congaree and Savanna, and found it necessary to weigh down one of his Indian guides "with a good heavy Pack. . .by which Means we kept Pace with him," Lawson still found it "very odd, that News should fly so swiftly among these People."[48] Indeed, comments made by the Virginian trader John Stewart suggest that some members of this community were connected to an extensive communication network through which they were informed of events that had taken place 125 to 175 miles away.[49]

The most important trail that passed through the lower Catawba Valley crossed the river at Nation Ford and was considered to be, at least from the Virginians' perspective, the main trading path to the Cherokee. Using historic maps and modern topography, it is possible to trace the route of this Great Trading Path, or Virginia-Cherokee Trail, by proceeding from a small extant portion of a wagon road that was originally a portion of the trail.[50] This is a useful exercise because it allows for a comparison of settlement locations based on their proximity to the trading path and the Catawba River (see map 6). While Mississippian Period settlements (38La9 and 38La125) seem to have existed throughout the study area in the general vicinity of the river, late seventeenth-and early eighteenth-century settlements (SoC629, 38Yk17, Ryan Homes, and Greenway) are clearly oriented along the Virginia-Cherokee trading path.[51] As people increasingly chose to establish new towns along this regionally significant trade and communication corridor, they affirmed their optimism for the incipient networks and for the coalescent, multiethnic communities that were forming along its margins. Moving close to the trail enabled members of the Catawba Confederacy not only to monitor the varied activities of trading parties, explorers, and colonial dignitaries but also afforded them the option of physical control over their movements and hence over a large swath of territory.[52]

James Merrell identifies the Catawbas' willingness to "cross the cultural divide" between themselves and Euro-Americans as the ultimate secret of their survival.[53] During the late seventeenth and early eighteenth centuries ethnic soldiering and the preferential establishment of new towns along a key trading path were two strategies enacted by the members of the coalescent Catawba polity that would seem to support Merrell's assertion. Yet as the piedmont Indians' refusal to carry deerskins and other trade items for Eleazer Wiggan demonstrates, this engagement did not amount to an appeasement of colonial interests. Members of the emergent Catawba Nation would travel this path actively, negotiating their manner of travel along the way.

We have endeavored in the preceding discussion to describe Catawba sociopolitical coalescence as a specific case of a common strategy for survival in the colonial shatter zone of eastern North America. At the same time we have been interested in this process as a unique historical phenomenon brought about by specific strategies and conditions that contributed to the emergence of the Catawba Nation as a regionally powerful militarized polity after the Yamasee War. The transformation of the Esaw Nation, which can be characterized as a late seventeenth-century militaristic slaving society, into the Catawba Nation was made possible by the political decision to form the Catawba Confederacy. At the same time new towns were being established adjacent to the main trading path that passed through Catawba lands, suggesting that members of this polity understood and affirmed the importance of this long-distance transportation route for access to — and possibly a certain measure of control over — the markets created by the extension of nascent global capitalism into the Americas. Serving as ethnic soldiers for the Carolina colony enabled the Catawba to maintain their military prominence and political clout throughout the first half of the eighteenth century and likely promoted social coalescence and group solidarity among the constituent elements of the multiethnic Catawba Nation.

Despite the importance of social coalescence for the success of the Catawba Nation, little is known about how this process actually took place. Future ethnohistorical and archaeological research will allow for a better understanding of how cultural differences were mediated within the Catawba Confederacy. When refugees arrived in the lower Catawba Valley, they may have settled down with individuals most similar to themselves, creating intragroup segregation that in turn may have encouraged cultural persistence. Such behavior would be visible archaeologically as spatial differences in materials associated with food preparation, pottery production, and the organization of social space. Excavations at Catawba towns inhabited during the first half of the eighteenth century should yield information to address this and other topics relevant to the Catawbas' continued survival as a sovereign nation. For in addition to militarism and diplomacy day-to-day activities ranging from trade to the preparation of meals to the negotiation of kin relationships were the contexts in which the Carolina Piedmont peoples engaged challenges brought about by the violence, demographic turmoil, and political economy of a colonial shatter zone.

Notes

This chapter is a synthesis of papers prepared by the authors in the course of their studies at the University of North Carolina–Chapel Hill. We are grateful to Steve Davis and Brett Riggs of the Research Laboratories of Archaeology for pointing us in the direction of important resources, helping with access to collections, and providing many useful comments and suggestions on previous iterations of our work. We would also like to thank the following individuals for their assistance at various points along the way: Thomas Blumer, Margaret Scarry, Carole Crumley, John Scarry, John Marcoux, Theresa McReynolds, Michelle Schohn, Michael Scholl, Mark Plane, and Ben Shields. In addition, the comments of Charles Hudson and two anonymous reviewers were invaluable in identifying loci of ambiguity and overstatement in the presentation of our ideas. In spite of these generous attentions, any errors of fact or judgment found herein are our own.

1. McDowell, *Journals of the Commissioners*, 55, 221 (quote), 223–24. While one can imagine motivations for Wiggan to fabricate the Catawbas' refusal, the official response to his comments, whether or not they reflected Catawba desires, shows that the commissioners found the request both plausible and in need of appeasement.

2. Gallay, *Indian Slave Trade.*

3. Ethridge, "Creating the Shatter Zone." Examples of militaristic slaving societies include the Westos, Chiscas, and Occaneechis. For the Westos, see Bowne, "Bold and Warlike People." For the Chiscas, see Hahn, "Mother of Necessity," 93–94. For the Occaneechis, see Davis, "Cultural Landscape," 142.

4. Kowalewski, "Coalescent Societies."

5. Ferguson and Whitehead, "Violent Edge of Empire."

6. Barth, *Ethnic Groups and Boundaries.*

7. Nagel, "Constructing Ethnicity."

8. Lawson, *New Voyage*, 49; and Hudson, *Juan Pardo Expeditions* (1990), 61–63.

9. Gatschet, "Grammatic Sketch"; and Rudes, Blumer, and May, "Catawba and Neighboring Groups," 301, 315. Cataba is derived from the Catawba name *yi kátapu*, which can be translated as "people in the fork of the river." Similarly Yssa is believed to be a Spanish rendition of *iswa*, the Catawban word for river.

10. Baker, "Historic Catawba," 44–46; Hudson, *Juan Pardo Expeditions* (1990), 75; and Lawson, *New Voyage*, 49.

11. Waselkov, "Indian Maps," 306; Rights, "Trading Path," 56; and Mooney, *Siouan Tribes*, 69. Given the existence of a convincing etymology for the two-syllable word "Nassaw" in Catawban, its similarity to the German "Nassau," used to name a port in the Bahamas, is taken to be an instance of linguistic homology. Also, the diversity of these groups is most conspicuously suggested by James

Adair's observation in *History of the American Indians*, 246, that "above twenty" languages were spoken within the Catawba Nation in 1743.

12. Lawson, *New Voyage*, 49–53.

13. Gallay, *Indian Slave Trade*, 338; and Mooney, *Historical Sketch*, 21–22.

14. Kowalewski, "Coalescent Societies," 117.

15. Cohen, *Geography and Politics*; East, "Concept and Political Status"; Hartshorne, "Politico-Geographic Pattern"; Hartshorne, "United States"; Hensel and Diehl, "Testing Empirical Propositions"; Kelly, "Escalation of Regional Conflict"; Ferguson and Whitehead, "Violent Edge of Empire"; Riggs, "Reinterpreting the Chestowee Raid"; Oatis, *Colonial Complex*, 4–6; and Slotkin, *Fatal Environment*, 1–48. Adopting a theoretical construct developed in another academic discipline or realm of discourse is always a potentially hazardous practice given the potential for importing unwarranted assumptions and implications. In the case of the shatter zone, the utility of the concept seems to outweigh such concerns for at least two primary reasons. First, by emphasizing the role that colonizing states play in destabilizing indigenous political networks, the shatter zone concept calls into question the uncritical use of the direct historical approach for linking archaeological materials and the American Indian societies described in documentary sources. Second, the shatter zone concept is also a welcome means of characterizing the colonial period milieu in contradistinction to the trope of the "frontier." While the Eurocentric nature of the frontier concept has been recognized, its continued use by historians of the colonial period seems to stem in part from the need for a way to characterize the unique contextual qualities of the time. The shatter zone concept fills this interpretive void as a narrative device without reinscribing the myth of the frontier. Although Slotkin insists on the existence of "real" frontiers, he details the creation of a nationalist myth from ideas and stories of the colonial period. Frontiers certainly existed in the minds of Euro-Americans, and the concept is important in that it shaped colonial, and later national, policies.

16. Gallay, *Indian Slave Trade*, 299–306. The methods used to avoid paying taxes on American Indian slaves resulted in a sparse documentary record of these transactions. Some American Indian slaves obtained by South Carolina were shipped to New England, most likely in small coastal vessels. Others may have been sent to the West Indies.

17. Hewatt, *Historical Account*, 127; and Baker, "Historic Catawba," 45.

18. Lawson, *New Voyage*, 49. Lawson sets out to find groups such as the Congaree, Wateree, and Esaw, but does not mention the Kadapau until his party

arrives within their village. His silence would seem to imply his ignorance of their existence up to that moment.

19. Waselkov, "Indian Maps," 320–24; and Fitts, "Mapping Catawba Coalescence," 13–14. We propose that members of the Piedmont groups would have chosen to organize themselves in a way that was both compatible with existing political divisions, and, based upon the knowledge they possessed, seemed to yield the greatest amount of success to its members. Admittedly, this interpretation posits that Catawba leaders approached community governance from a pragmatic subject position.

20. Waselkov, "Indian Maps," 323. This is inferred from the presence of the name "Youchine" on the deerskin map a Catawba headman presented to Governor Nicholson in 1721.

21. Merrell, *Indians' New World*, 71, 105.

22. Hudson, *Catawba Nation*; Bentley, "Slaveholding Catawbas"; and Willis, "Divide and Rule."

23. Ferguson and Whitehead, "Violent Edge of Empire," 22 (quote), 21–22.

24. Brown, *Catawba Indians*, 60–68; Corkran, *Carolina Indian Frontier*; Gallay, *Indian Slave Trade*, 53–54; Milling, *Red Carolinians*, 233; Silver, *New Face on the Countryside*, 89; and Speck, "Catawba Nation."

25. Blumer, *Bibliography of the Catawba*, 2.

26. Oatis, *Colonial Complex*, 88; and Gallay, *Indian Slave Trade*, 267–70. After John Barnwell's 1712 attack on the Tuscarora town Torhunta, most of "Essaw Captain Jack's Company," apparently satisfied with their "very considerable" plunder, packed up and returned home despite Barnwell's attempts to convince them to press on to the next military target. Captain Jack's company consisted of 155 warriors who were identified as Wateree, Sugaree, Catawba, Suteree, Waxhaw, and Congaree.

27. Hewatt, *Historical Account*; Le Jau, *Carolina Chronicles*; and Merrell, *Indians' New World*, 76–77.

28. Merrell, *Indians' New World*, 103–4; and Milling, *Red Carolinians*, 235.

29. Heath, "Catawba Militarism," 87–88, 92. Catawba warriors also fought in the War of 1812, the Mexican War, possibly the Seminole Wars, and the American Civil War. Dozens of men and women, primarily volunteers, later served with U.S. forces in World War I, World War II, and the Vietnam War.

30. Merrell, *Indian's New World*, 118–21.

31. Merrell, *Indian's New World*, 113; and Cattell and Climo, "Meaning in Social Memory."

32. McDowell, *Journals of the Commissioners*.

33. Baker, "Historic Catawba," 169; Merrell, *Indian's New World*, 72; and Gallay, *Indian Slave Trade*, 276–77.

34. Smith, "Patterns in Time," 89–91.

35. Crown, "Learning to Make Pottery"; Kamp, "Prehistoric Children"; Wallert-Pêtre, "Learning How to Make the Right Pots"; and Bourdieu, *Outline of a Theory of Practice*, 164.

36. Six of these sites were surface collected by archaeologists from the Research Laboratories of Archaeology (RLA) at the University of North Carolina–Chapel Hill in the 1940s, 1960s, and 1970s. More recently, surface collections have been made at four sites in the vicinity of Fort Mill as part of the Catawba Project currently undertaken by RLA archaeologists Stephen Davis and Brett Riggs.

37. Merrell, *Indians' New World*, 163.

38. Fitts, "Mapping Catawba Coalescence," 20–41. Correspondence analysis converts abundances — in this case pottery sherd counts — into standardized chi-square residuals that are subjected to multidimensional scaling, effectively collapsing all the variation present into two dimensions. The results allow for the identification of pottery attributes that occur in frequencies greater or less than would be expected if they were present in equal amounts at every site.

39. Fitts, "Mapping Catawba Coalescence," 43–45; and Moore, *Catawba Valley Mississippian*, 47–48. Moore proposes that the upper Catawba Valley was depopulated before the mid-seventeenth century. While the available data are limited, demographic collapse within the lower Catawba Valley does not appear to have taken place.

40. Brown, *Catawba Indians*, 7; Hudson, *Juan Pardo Expeditions* (1990), 25; Moore, *Catawba Valley Mississippian*, 21; and Fitts, "Mapping Catawba Coalescence," 32–37. This movement has been interpreted as the relocation of the Yssa and Cataba towns. Hudson proposes that Yssa was located near present Lincolnton (or Denver), North Carolina, on the South Fork of the Catawba River. To date no archaeological site has been identified as the specific location of this community.

41. Davis, "Cultural Landscape," 142–43, 152.

42. Waselkov, "Indian Maps," 302; and Fitts, "Mapping Catawba Coalescence," 39–40. Adair in *History of the American Indians*, 246, identifies "Kátahba" as "the standard, or court-dialect" of the Catawba Nation, and Nassaw is depicted at the center of the confederacy on the deerskin map. Further, the pottery assemblages examined for this project indicate change in production practices through time,

but wholesale population replacement does not seem to have occurred. The relatively small size and collection method of these assemblages limit their utility for identifying subtle differences that may be attributable to matrilocal kin groups; pottery types attributable to distinct refugee groups were not identified.

43. Gallay, *Indian Slave Trade*, 193. In passing Gallay observes that from an American Indian perspective, outsiders, or "Others," were not afforded the same rights as community members. Anthropologists recognize this type of logic as common among humans in general, and it is also clearly demonstrated in the European treatment of both Native Americans and Africans.

44. Hudson, *Juan Pardo Expeditions* (1990), 65.

45. DePratter and Judge, "Wateree River Phases," 58.

46. As previously observed by Moore, *Catawba Valley Mississippian*, 168.

47. While future archaeological research may help clarify the character of Cofitachequi-Catawba Valley relations during the sixteenth and early seventeenth centuries, the existence of late Mississippian pottery in the lower Catawba Valley supports the interpretation that local groups formed the demographic core of the eighteenth century coalescent Catawba Nation.

48. Lawson, *New Voyage*, 37, 42–49.

49. Hudson, *Catawba Nation*, 30.

50. Rights, "Trading Path," 71–72; and Fitts, "Mapping Catawba Coalescence," 18–20.

51. Fitts, "Mapping Catawba Coalescence," 35–37.

52. Merrell, *Indian's New World*, 160–62; and Oatis, *Colonial Complex*, 135.

53. Merrell, *Indian's New World*, 281.

7 | *"The Greatest Travelers in America"*

SHAWNEE SURVIVAL IN THE SHATTER ZONE

STEPHEN WARREN AND RANDOLPH NOE

Both anthropologists and historians have made much of sacred geography and the power of place in American Indian cultures. Historian Colin Calloway writes that for the Shawnees "tribal homelands were hallowed ground. They drew both physical and spiritual sustenance from it." Historian James Taylor Carson expands his focus, writing that for American Indians from the South "removal triggered a crisis of cosmology because it upset the spiritual systems of ritual and power that [Southern] Native Americans had written into the landscape." To the Southwest anthropologist Keith Basso's powerful assessment of Western Apache "place-making" makes clear the "moral significance of geographic locations."[1] In *Where the Lightning Strikes* anthropologist Peter Nabokov universalizes these ideas. Nabokov contends that American Indian "attitudes and ethics about beings and forces that reside in the natural environment . . . remain a bedrock of American Indian belief systems."[2] Taken together, these general and specific examples about American Indian religiosity converge on a sweeping thesis: that American Indian cultural identity emanates from the land itself.[3]

Such correlations between place and identity inadvertently exclude transient townspeople from the central paradigmatic discussions of American Indian identities.[4] Woodland Indians, most of whom endured a series of voluntary and forced removals from successive homelands, continue to occupy unstable ground among scholars. As exiles permanently torn from their homelands, they occupy an unhappy place in American Indian history. Northern Woodland towns affiliated with Shawnees, Delawares, and Kickapoos are unlike many western American Indian communities.

As such, they challenge widely accepted assumptions, perhaps because colonial-era Woodland Indian towns are so unlike many of the place-bound communities west of the Mississippi whose land base still includes many of their sacred sites.[5] Shawnee history challenges the story of these place-bound communities. Lasting over three hundred years, the long Shawnee diaspora meant that infusing new landscapes with sacred meaning became a perilous luxury. Movement became a colonial survival strategy. In 1779 town chiefs from Chillicothe, Ohio, admitted as much when they told the British that "we have always been the frontier."[6]

For nearly two hundred years Shawnee migrations aroused both the awe and suspicion of their Indian and non-Indian neighbors in the colonial South. In Edmond Atkin's 1755 *Report*, for instance, he described the Shawnees as "Stout, Bold, Cunning and the greatest Travellers in America." Just three years earlier, in 1752, a Cherokee named Tasattee observed that the Shawnees were "a People of no Settlement but rambling from Place to Place with Nothing but Lyes." Those who knew them almost always commented on Shawnee mobility. To Atkin and Tasattee the Shawnees were dislocated peoples, separated from their own sacred geography, and as such, they were often viewed as profane and morally suspect.[7]

During the Historic Period Shawnee identity became synonymous with movement. As a result, identifying a precise precontact Shawnee homeland remains elusive. Tenuous archaeological connections between the Fort Ancient peoples (1000–1650 CE) and the Historic Period Shawnee may offer some insight as to why the Shawnees moved easily to a mobile pattern of life.[8] Fort Ancient's geographic position, situated along one of "the great conduits of human civilization in North America," the Ohio River, could help to explain why the Shawnees quickly developed a reputation as travelers, border-crossers, and intermediaries in the early Historic Period.[9]

In fact, the Ohio Valley was a cross-cultural center for commerce and trade from as early as Fort Ancient times into the Protohistoric-early Colonial period (1550–1675 CE) and beyond. The Hardin Village site is one of the only Fort Ancient sites that dates to the early colonial era that has been systematically investigated. Hardin Village contains material items from Algonquians, Iroquoians, Southern Indians, and Europeans. For example, Hardin Village blends stone burials attributed to the Shawnees and "historic trade items, such as brass or copper beads and bracelets" in an "an Iroquoian style."[10] Archaeological evidence, including trade goods and excavated burials, indicate that the historic Shawnees blended traits of both the Woodland and Mississippian cultural traditions.

Ethnographic evidence from the twentieth century further complicates precise links between the Fort Ancient peoples and the Shawnees. From the 1930s through the 1950s anthropologist Erminie Wheeler-Voegelin worked with Shawnee informants who described Shawnee ceramic traditions that derived from the Woodland, Fort Ancient, and Tennessee-Cumberland Aspect of the Middle Mississippi phase.[11] Such varying understandings of Shawnee material culture clearly reflect the range and diversity of Shawnee movements in the Colonial period. Ceramic traditions illustrate that history and geography shaped Shawnee identities as the Fort Ancient world fell apart in the seventeenth century.[12]

Establishing an early colonial Shawnee homeland is further complicated by the fact that European observers only set foot in the Ohio Valley after the devastation of warfare and disease had obliterated the Fort Ancient peoples, and hence we have scant documentary records of their lives before this time. In 1674 an English indentured servant named Gabriel Arthur became the first European to arrive in the Ohio Valley. Native survivors of the shatter zone were not surprised to see him. Between 1539 and 1543 news of Europeans first emerged when the Hernando de Soto expedition explored much of the South as far north as Tennessee. Since the Soto expedition European trade goods had filtered into the Ohio Valley via two routes. From the East, over the Appalachian Mountains, trade goods arrived through the Susquehannock and Iroquois. From the South, through the Cumberland Gap, Cherokee intermediaries regulated the trade with Europeans.[13]

In spite of more than a century of trade, Arthur believed that the people he encountered lived in a state of nature, free from European trade and material culture. Arthur traveled with a group of Tomahitan Cherokees who served as guides for the Virginia traders. They were sent by Arthur's master Abraham Wood, who may have hoped that the Tomahitans would return with Indian slaves from the Ohio country. Suggestive evidence indicates as much, for the Tomahitans, according to Wood, hoped to "give a clap to some of that great nation, where they fell on with great courage." In the ensuing melee the Tomahitans were "curagiously repullsed by theire enimise." The Shawnees wounded Arthur with flint-knapped arrows, and he became their captive after an arrow to his thigh allowed the Shawnees to overtake him. His captors saved his life only after they "scowered his skin with water and ashes, and when they discovered his skin to be white, they made very much of him."[14]

As a slaver turned prospective trader, Gabriel Arthur was a lucky man. His survival depended on the Shawnees' desire for European arms. Arthur reported that when he "made signes that if they would lett him return, he would bring many things amongst them . . . [they] seemed to rejoyce att it." Arthur's "knife and hatchet" were of particular interest to his captors. For more than a century the Ohio Valley peoples had transformed European kettles into strips of copper and brass. These became pendants, bracelets, and beads. At least initially functional items such as kettles were valued far more for their aesthetic value than their functionality. But with the rise of the slave trade and the Iroquois wars, the Shawnees and their neighbors saw in Gabriel Arthur's arrival what they had longed for: direct contact with European traders who could forestall their enemies.[15]

Fort Ancient peoples smuggled small amounts of arms and metal goods into the Ohio country. Nevertheless, the archaeological evidence and the historical record confirm that as mediators of the trade with Europeans, both the Iroquois and the Cherokees generally succeeded in preventing firearms, hatchets, and knives from flowing into the Ohio Valley towns. Like Gabriel Arthur, Father Jacques Marquette believed that iron and other European war implements were entirely absent from the Fort Ancient world. In 1673 Marquette meditated on the inherent weakness of the Shawnees on a trip down the Mississippi. Marquette believed that the Iroquois continually attacked their Ohio towns "because they have no fire-arms."[16]

By the 1670s the Shawnees came to depend on direct access to European traders as well as multiple alliances with other Indian communities. Across the Woodland Indian world, from Illinois to Maryland, various people banded together into mobile heterogeneous communities with a shared interest in survival. They searched for safe harbors free from disease, the slave trade, and intertribal warfare yet close enough to colonizers interested in trade. European witnesses marveled at the geographic range of these mobile communities. Shawnee townspeople in particular epitomized these trends. In 1709 the Carolina trader John Lawson remarked that the Shawnees "to this day are a shifting, wandering people, for I know some Indian nations that have changed their Indian settlements many hundred miles, sometimes no less than a thousand. As is proved by the Savanna [Shawnee] Indians."[17]

Between 1661 and 1673 Iroquois war parties, which thrust into the Ohio Valley and dispersed the Native people living there, were one of the principal causes of these migrations. The Iroquois had two essential missions in the Ohio country. First, their hunters had to expand westward in search of fur-bearing animals that had been overhunted within the Iroquois homeland, which ranged from the Mohawk River in the east to the Genesee River to the west. Second, virgin soil epidemics such as smallpox devastated the Iroquois, forcing them to search for captives who might replace their fallen kin. The mourning wars and the intertribal competition brought on by the fur trade led to the disappearance of some Ohio peoples, including the Eries and the Wenros (see Fox and Meyers, this volume). In contrast, the Shawnees fled the Ohio country and did not return until warfare between Indian groups had largely subsided in the 1740s.[18]

Hundreds, if not thousands, of migrations across the woodlands reveal an essential point about Shawnee identities that can and should extend to other Eastern Indian populations. The Shawnees and their neighbors had a limited attachment to place. During the colonial era they had become transient peoples. Diplomatic considerations outweighed any long-standing attachments to homeland. The vicissitudes of trade and alliance determined migration patterns. Yet movement did not always equal cultural loss. Divorced from both a land-based polity and a sacred landscape, the Shawnees managed to avoid coalescence into either Southern Indian or Iroquoian coalescent communities. They maintained their separateness because of language, ritual, cosmogonic myth, and the kin groups that are unique to the Shawnee people. Indian societies such as the Shawnees that were both ripped and pulled from their geographic moorings maintained their distinctiveness through beliefs and practices that were not linked to place and that could be sustained in a wide variety of geographic contexts.

Shawnee history thus offers an extreme example of processes occurring among a host of Algonquian, Iroquoian, and Muskogean peoples, including the Delawares, Mahicans, Tuscaroras, Alabamas, and Coushattas. But unlike their neighbors, the Shawnees traveled among a wider range of language families and cultures. And through it all Shawnees maintained a sense of their own unique identity.

The Shawnees avoided coalescence and cultural extinction in part through their towns. During the Colonial period as historian Richard White points out in *Middle Ground*, "the units called tribes, nations, and confederacies were only loose leagues of villages." Information on the towns of the Creek Confederacy offers a good analog to Shawnee political organization in the early Colonial period. Like the Shawnees, the Muskogees' *talwas*, or square ground towns, were the "most important symbolic space" for a Creek person.[19] *Talwas*, which would be analogous to *hotewes* in Shawnee, made it possible for small numbers of Shawnee people to disperse and still survive independently. For a Creek one's loyalties were first and foremost to their towns, and a person claimed their identities from their towns.[20] A person was, for instance, a Tukabatchee, a Coweta, a Cusseta, or an Okchai.[21] Anthropologist Peter Nabokov writes that "throughout [Creek] history their spatial relationships have emphasized a civic identity. Since the precontact era of their mound-building ancestors, their sense of sacred space is aligned to each town's 'heart' — its annually renewed sacred fire."[22]

Even today, ethnographic research shows that *talwas*, reinvented as ceremonial grounds in eastern Oklahoma, defend local identities against larger tribal identities that have been imposed on Native people since the Indian Reorganization Act. Today's ceremonial grounds act like the seventeenth-century towns of old. Anthropologist Jason Baird Jackson has found that within the Creek Nation "members of the Arbeka Ceremonial Ground are identified closely with the Creek 'tribal town' of Arbika, live in the region near their 'square ground,' and trace their history back to a settlement of the same name in Alabama."[23] As Jackson's research attests, towns moved over a vast geographic area. With each relocation, the town square allowed for the cultural survival of historic Woodland peoples.

Shawnee Places and their Meanings in Colonial History

Set adrift by epidemic disease in the 1640s, followed soon after by Iroquois war parties in the 1660s and 1670s, Shawnees on the Ohio River began to disperse throughout the Midwest and the South. No other Algonquian tribe rivals the geographic, cultural, and linguistic range of Shawnee settlements. Simultaneous Shawnee migrations in the late seventeenth and early eighteenth centuries illustrate the weakness of place as a marker of identity. Local decision making, centered in tribal towns, was normative. Towns and the kin groups associated with them were transient polities that resisted amalgamation within larger coalescent communities.

Early European maps of Shawnee towns dating from 1683 to 1721 reveal four major clusters of Shawnee settlements. Between 1675 and 1685 a group of Shawnee towns were located among the groups that were beginning to form the Upper Creeks on the lower Coosa and Tallapoosa rivers in modern Alabama. Another cluster of Shawnee towns existed between 1683 and 1721 along the Cumberland River in and around Nashville, Tennessee. A third cluster of towns was located along the Savannah River near modern Augusta, Georgia, between 1687 and 1707. Finally, in 1681 a group of Shawnees, approximately two hundred in number, settled in Fort St. Louis near modern Utica, Illinois.[24]

By the 1660s Shawnee towns were symbolic and portable rather than place bound and unmovable, markers of identity.[25] One reason that such a transition was possible may have been because Shawnee townspeople shared a common membership in one of the five society clans, or divisions. The Shawnees have five major divisions that are patrilineal descent groups. They are the Kispokotha, Thawekila, Chalagawtha, Pekowitha, and Mekoche. Each one of the divisions also maintains six exogamous patrilineal clans, which operate as fictive kin groups.[26]

The divisions fulfilled different functions.[27] For example, chiefs came from either the Thawekila or Chalagawtha divisions, while the Kispokothas regulated war. According to contemporary tribal elder George Blanchard, "at one time we lived in different clans so if you needed something you traveled to visit them. If you needed medicine you visited the Mekoches, if you needed war you visited the Kispokothas."[28] The Shawnee towns that dotted the colonial South then were also kin groups based on these divisions.

Many historic Shawnee towns derive from these divisional kin groups. In fact, divisional identities seem to have organized the Shawnee diaspora. For example, the Shawnees at Fort St. Louis, who became known as the Starved Rock Shawnee, were members of the Mekoche, Chalagawtha, and Pekowitha divisions.[29] Following their exile in Starved Rock, these divisions relocated to Pennsylvania between 1690 and 1710. In contrast, the Kispokotha and Thawekila divisions organized the Shawnee diaspora in the South. Small numbers of Pekowitha Shawnees joined the Thawekilas who settled along the Savannah River, but by 1707 they became the first to abandon South Carolina. Curiously, there is no evidence to suggest that either the Mekoche or Chalagawtha Shawnees migrated to either Alabama or South Carolina following the Iroquois wars.[30] It is clear that these kin groups fragmented and coalesced with each other throughout the Colonial period. Like all human families, the Shawnee divisions were porous and unstable markers of identity. Even so, the long Shawnee diaspora tended to follow these broad divisional patterns.

Nevertheless, scholars usually follow the tribal model of Shawnee identity first established by anthropologist Erminie Wheeler-Voegelin. From the 1930s through the 1970s Wheeler-Voegelin argued that the separate though intersecting functions of the five divisions proved the existence of a Shawnee "tribe" at the time of contact.[31] Yet the separate functions of the Shawnee divisions might also confirm a broader notion of Shawnee coalescence. Coalescent communities, like tribes, create hierarchies of power by assigning differential values to kin groups. Moreover, there is very little evidence that Shawnee towns operated as a unified polity during the Historic Period. Shawnee culture must then be separated from Shawnee politics.[32] Their world was simultaneously parochial and cosmopolitan, driven by kin groups that shared a language and a host of cultural practices. In the historical reconstruction of Shawnee towns that follows, Shawnees managed to avoid coalescence. Their stories provide powerful testimonies to the resilience of the Shawnee people and dedication to their culture.

For example, the Starved Rock Shawnees numbered only two hundred people, and yet they avoided merging with the eighteen to twenty thousand Indian people who gathered together at Starved Rock. Minet, an engineer who accompanied La Salle into the Great Lakes region, believed that the Starved Rock Shawnees came from the "Spaniards of St. Augustine [who] had chased [the Shawnees] from their land." Simultaneously, "the Iroquois had succeeded in ruining" them. Algonquians and Siouans from more than thirteen different communities gathered together in a defensive alliance there. The French under La Salle played a vital diplomatic role in bringing these disparate groups together. After emptying the Ohio Valley of their enemies, Iroquois warriors crossed the Wabash River and entered the Illinois country. Then in March 1684 the Iroquois attacked the confederacy at Starved Rock. The Algonquian alliance held their ground, and the Iroquois failed to disperse them.[33]

Eight years after the Iroquois attack, the Starved Rock Shawnees grew tired of the French alliance. As "Southerners" in the Great Lakes Algonquian world, the Shawnees were unlike the primary architects of the middle ground as they absorbed elements of both the Southern and Iroquoian groups. In contrast, the Ottawa, Potawatomi, and Miami peoples occupied a geographic and cultural position at the center of the Algonquian world. Additionally, some Shawnees rejected French and Algonquian overtures because of the endemic violence in the Great Lakes region. In 1682 one group of Shawnees chastised La Salle for his attempts to consolidate Algonquian peoples at Starved Rock. According to these Shawnees, "they would be devoid of sense to leave it [their homes] and expose themselves to be tomahawked by the Illinois or burnt by the Iroquois."[34]

In 1692 the Starved Rock Shawnees migrated to the Maryland-Pennsylvania border. Their journey began when Delaware and Mahican runners enticed the Starved Rock Shawnees to move back east. Several years later, approximately one hundred of the former Starved Rock Shawnees, accompanied by Mahican and Minsi [Delaware] allies, traveled to New York in order to enter into an alliance as subsidiary towns of the Iroquois.

Shawnee leaders stated that "we come to renew the Covenant chain of peace with you; and desire we may be as one heart, one blood, and one soul with the English, the Mohawks, and the Mahikanders, and all the Indians of this Government." However, the reports of this episode are conflicting. Maryland officials believed that some members of the Starved Rock Shawnee had hoped "to join the Sinniquos [Senecas] in their war." But, a French trader then living in Pennsylvania reported that "ye five nations [the Iroquois] . . . had a design of carrying off the Shawanah Indians . . . [as] colonies of a nation that were their enemies." Neither the French nor the English completely understood the complicated relationship between the Iroquois and their Algonquian neighbors in Pennsylvania. First, the Shawnees regarded the Delawares as "grandfathers" in an inter-Indian kinship system. Kin ties and a long history of residence near one another made living alongside the Delaware preferable to life among enemy Algonquian Indians, including the Illinois. Second, the Iroquois covenant chain granted smaller tribes such as the Shawnees, Delawares, Nanticokes, and Conoys considerable autonomy, far more than would have been possible under the French-Algonquian alliance at Starved Rock. Historian Daniel Richter argues that smaller Algonquian groups in Pennsylvania "serve[d] both as allies in campaigns against Southern Indians and as bulwarks against counterraids."[35]

Delaware and Mahican intermediaries made the Shawnee migration from Starved Rock possible. In 1791 the noted Mahican diplomat Hendrick Apaumat remembered that "our ancestors near 200 years ago rescued them [the Shawnee] from the mouth of the many nations as well as the Five Nations who were ready to swallow my younger brother, Shawany, for which kind deliverance they ever have felt themselves under the greatest obligation to obey our voice." In the early 1770s John Heckewelder, the Moravian missionary to the Delaware, wrote that the Shawnees "sent messengers to their elder brother, the Mohican, requesting them to intercede for them with their grandfather, the Lenni Lenape [Delaware] that he might take them under his protection." Heckewelder contended that the Shawnees were "a restless people, delighting in wars. They could not have survived without Delaware and Mahican assistance."[36]

The year 1675 marked the arrival of a group of Shawnees at Tukabatchee, the Upper Creek town on the lower Tallapoosa River.[37] The Shawnees arrived after the Iroquois defeat of the Susquehannocks and their Algonquian allies. Townspeople affiliated with the Kispokotha division organized the migration to Tukabatchee.[38] Louis LeClerc de Milfort, a Frenchman living within the Creek Nation at the end of the eighteenth century, believed that "an Indian tribe which had just been destroyed by the Iroquois and Hurons [which] came to implore the protection of the Muskogees, which from now on I shall call the Creeks. The Creeks took them in and assigned them land in the center of the nation. They built a town called Tukabahchee."[39]

Apparently sometime after the group of Kispokotha Shawnees settled in Tukabatchee, another group of Shawnee migrated to the town. In the nineteenth century the Creek *métis* George Stiggins described the "Ispocoga" (Kispokotha) and Shawnee as two different "nations" brought together at Tukabatchee through an elaborate ritual exchange.[40]

Stiggins posited that the Shawnee constituted a large nation that coalesced with the five divisions of the modern Shawnee. In his opinion "Shawnee" became the umbrella term by which the five divisions came to identify themselves in the nineteenth century. According to Stiggins, coalescence between the Shawnees and Kispokothas took place during the Busk, or Green Corn Ceremony, typically held in August. Residents of Tukabatchee proudly displayed the sacred brass plates described in their origin stories. The sharing of these ritual objects during the most sacred time of the year made it possible for the Kispokothas, then living on the Tallapoosa, to join with the Shawnees. To conclude their compact, "they deposited with the keepers of the national square of one of their groups their calumet Tobacco Pipes Belts and war club called by them *Attussa*," along with the twelve sacred brass plates of the Ispocoga Nation.[41] According to Stiggins, ultimately the union between the Ispocogas and Shawnees did not last. Stiggins related that "through some unknown reason or occurrence which the Ispocagas attributes to the instable and fickle disposition of the Shawanose . . . [they] formed a resolution to recede from the union . . . and when they moved they carried off six of the sacred brass plates . . . which the Shawanose have retained possession of ever since, for they were seen by some Creeks first in the care of the old prophet at tippaconoe [Tenskwatawa] . . . and not long since they were still in his possession over the Mississippi."[42]

At the time that the Kispokotha Shawnees settled in Tukabatchee, Thawekila Shawnees settled towns along the Savannah River and revealed yet another divisional and cultural context for Shawnee settlement.[43] The Savannah River Shawnees lived among Uchean, Iroquoian, Muskogean, Siouan, and Algonquian speakers. Once the Shawnees moved to the area, the Shawnee language became the trade language of the region. According to the Episcopal minister Francis Le Jau, "that language [the Savannah tongue] is understood all over these Northern Parts of America, even in Canada."[44]

The Thawekilas along with a small number of Pekowithas had begun migrating to the Savannah River in the 1670s and 1680s. According to Le Jau, the Shawnees "settled near this province Even before the nations of the Westos were destroyed and to this day they keep about the places where the Westos lived." Upon their arrival South Carolina traders enlisted them to drive out the Westos (see Bowne, this volume). Following Westo displacement, the Shawnees as well as other Southern Indians groups emerged as slave traders for the labor-hungry British.[45]

The Thawekila Shawnees moved their town and their identity with each eighteenth-century cataclysm. In 1715, after the Yamasee War, Thawekila townspeople fled westward, away from the Savannah, Oconee, and Ocmulgee rivers. Between 1715 and 1731 the Thawekila Shawnees, settled with the Lower Creeks on the lower Chattahoochee River.[46] Between 1730 and 1733 the Thawekila Shawnees migrated again. One branch returned to Pennsylvania and established a village named Sewickley on the Youghiogheny River. The other branch moved within the Upper Creek Confederacy to Sawanogi at the confluence of the Coosa and Tallapoosa Rivers.[47] As late as the close of the eighteenth century, Southern Superintendent of Indian Affairs Benjamin Hawkins noted that Shawnees at Sawanogi within the Upper Creek Confederacy still retained "the manners of their countrymen to the N.W."[48]

Like the Thawekilas, the Pekowitha Shawnees who had moved with them to the Savannah River were also caught in the shatter zone. As early as 1707 they chose to move north to the Maryland-Pennsylvania border.

Led by a Shawnee "king" named Opessa, the Pekowitha Shawnees began to lose ground to their Catawba enemies in colonial Carolina during the first decade of the eighteenth century. At a 1707 conference with Pennsylvania governor John Evans, Opessa confessed that "he was happy to live in a country at peace." Catawba slaving had taken a toll on his people. He reported that "upon our return from hunting, we found our town surprised, and our women and children taken prisoner by our enemies." The Pekowitha Shawnees moved closer to diverse coalescent populations of Algonquian-speakers, which included Conoy and Nanticoke speakers from the Tidewater region and Delaware and Mahican speakers from the coasts of Delaware, New Jersey, and southern New England. Now situated along the border between the colonies of Maryland and Pennsylvania, these refugees lived near each other and paid tribute to the Iroquois.[49]

The move toward former enemies — the Iroquois — offered the Pekowitha Shawnees respite and protection from Catawba slavers and a chance for peace. On June 8, 1710, Opessa joined five Seneca leaders at Conestoga, Pennsylvania, to sue for peace with the colonists of Pennsylvania. Opessa and the Senecas offered the Pennsylvanians eight wampum belts to ensure that "room to sport and play without danger of slavery might be allowed them." Opessa acknowledged that until now his people had been "hitherto strangers to this place they now came as people blind." He hoped that from then on the Pennsylvanians "will take them by the hand and lead them, and then they will lift up their heads in the woods without danger or any fear."[50]

Opessa's town, also known as Old Town, was situated at the headwaters of the Potomac River in the northwest corner of Maryland. Life on the border between European empires and powerful Indian groups shaped the Pekowitha Shawnees' identity. Linguistic skill, geographic range, and military prowess made it possible for Shawnees to disappear and reemerge in a host of guises. Opessa's life as a Shawnee "king" and an inveterate enemy of the Catawba became even more complicated when in 1711 he voluntarily abandoned both his chieftainship and his town and sought a home among Sassoonan's band of Delawares. Some rumored that Opessa's love for a Delaware woman inspired his decision. Others said that he became Delaware out of a very real fear that both the English and the

Iroquois were about to kill him for his role in the deaths of several white indentured servants.[51]

The Pekowitha experience parallels that of the Starved Rock Shawnees. Intermarriage between the Shawnees and the Delawares was and is extensive, making differences between the two groups sometimes difficult to discern. Opessa took advantage of these alliances and became Delaware, only to appear later in 1725 as the new chief of the Shawnees at the headwaters of the Potomac. Such cross-cultural flexibility, driven by disease and the incessant warfare associated with the early colonial slave trade, seems unthinkable today. Modern American Indian communities are national in orientation and their members, most of whom are multiethnic, have been made to declare exclusive membership. Consequently, we tend to graft contemporary national and tribal identities onto past American lives. Opessa's story, like that of all Shawnees, is more complex; the malleable nature of his identity is perplexing to us today.

Between 1680 and 1720 the four clusters of Shawnee towns shared one thing in common. Each one lived within the orbit of a much larger geopolitical power. The Algonquian alliance at Starved Rock, the Creek Confederacy of present-day Alabama and Georgia, and the Iroquois confederacy that guided both the residence patterns and the alliances of Indian communities in New York, Maryland, and Pennsylvania structured the migration patterns of smaller groups such as the Shawnees.

Place and Identity in Shawnee Cosmology

For many Shawnees involved in the early colonial migrations, sacred geography was not a fundamental component of their identities. Cultural survival depended on geographic mobility. As Absentee Shawnee ceremonial singer Sherman Tiger reminded me in June of 2006, "Grandma's everywhere." Ceremonial Chief Andy Warrior elaborated on Tiger's point, commenting that "the things we do between the day we're born and the day God calls us home — all that in between, it's the Shawnee way . . . All that in between is how I view what it means to be Shawnee."[52] For both Andy Warrior and Sherman Tiger, lived experience and ritual action rather than sacred places reconstitute being Shawnee.

The geographer Yi-Fu Tuan reminds us that "religion could either bind a people to a place or free them from it." Shawnee cosmogonic narratives and the rituals that inform their particular identity freed members from an attachment to place.[53] And geotemporal contexts, while thickly described, fail to guide us toward a better understanding of motivation in history. What motivated the Shawnees to travel so far beyond their own central place, the lands along the Ohio and Scioto Rivers, and into the South? Shawnee cosmogonic myths offer some clues. Sacred Shawnee stories emphasize transience, mobility, and alliance. For example, an 1824 account provided by Tenskwatawa, the Shawnee Prophet and the brother of the famed warrior Tecumseh, includes these words about travel and destiny:

They [the Shawnees] were then lowered in a basket with the old man carrying a pack on his back which contained all the things the Great Spirit had entrusted to him for the benefit of the Indians. They arrived on the shore of a great lake and the old man told them that that his heart was "in a northern direction . . . a great distance" which was their destination. After prayer and fasting for 12 days, the water dried up and they began a journey to the island. Calakaatha led them to the opposite shore . . . After a 12 day march, they reached their destination.[54]

Tenskwatawa's emphasis on migration then turns to conflict with other Southern Indians, such as the Creeks and Catawbas.[55] In his account the Shawnees destroyed the Creeks when they first met because the latter doubted the power of Shawnee medicine. The Shawnees then brought the Creeks back to life and "compromised with them, calling them thereafter their brothers."[56] Migration and warfare, hallmarks of the colonial South, had become sacred elements of Shawnee identity.

A contemporary cosmogonic story collected from Absentee Shawnee elder George Blanchard supports Tenskwatawa's emphasis on both transience and alliance. According to Mr. Blanchard,

while we were out hunting it'd get real cold and they'd start telling stories. They said that at one time there was a good kill . . . a lot of deer . . . they were sitting there feasting and they had their fill. Across the water there was another group that sounded Shawnee so the men with the good kill went over there and shared their meat with them. We became stronger that way . . . we would pick up another band of Shawnees . . . and we got too big for our britches. The society clans were separate back in the old days. But now we're all one big group.[57]

In 1934 anthropologist Truman Michelson collected a number of stories from Shawnee informants about the Shawnee divisions. Their words echo Mr. Blanchard's in that both stories question the cohesiveness of the Shawnees as a political unit. They reveal a weakened sense of unity among the five Shawnee divisions. The stories begin with the separate creation of the divisions in a variety of locations. In one story Joe Billy, an Absentee Shawnee informant of Truman Michelson, Erminie Wheeler-Voegelin, and Carl Voegelin, claimed that the Chalagawtha division was created on a different, though unnamed, continent. Billy then explained how the autonomous Shawnee divisions came together as the Shawnee people. According to Billy, the divisions "were worshipping at the same time but in separate camps. As they were worshipping they understood the words used in the prayers and the same terms and usages prevailed." Both camps became angry, believing that the neighboring group mocked their prayers to Kokumthena, "Our Grandmother," the Shawnee female deity. Before fighting began, someone interceded between the two divisions and convinced them that they "were worshipping the same person in the same language and manner . . . and it proved that their usages and rites were the same absolutely." From that point forward they identified each other as Shawnees.[58]

Taken together, these narratives convey a "historical philosophy" regarding Shawnee identity.[59] While the particular details of their stories sometimes diverge, the Shawnees could inhabit shattered worlds sometimes within larger Indian communities, sometimes independently, because their cosmogonic stories made warfare, alliances, and travel inherent characteristics of "being Shawnee." A consistent emphasis on transience and alliance reflect the colonial era realities of the Eastern Woodlands. As such, they signal a profound schism between pre-Columbian Fort Ancient peoples and the historic Shawnees.

Exploring the links between the pre-Columbian and colonial peoples of the Eastern Woodlands remains a daunting task. Unfortunately, many of the connections have been lost to us. But at the very least this research ought to suggest that there are multiple horizons of migration that can be traced back to deep time.[60] For the Shawnees migration reveals less about the power of place than the ongoing recreation of a distinctive cultural identity associated with Shawnee ceremonial life. As North Ground ceremonial chief Andy Warrior once stated, "what we do here [on the ceremonial ground] makes us Shawnee."[61] To his mind the performance of ritual rather than the places where rituals are conducted has perpetuated Shawnee identity into the twenty-first century.

Shawnee towns, mobile, migratory, and hence separated by geographic, colonial, and geopolitical contexts, functioned as autonomous political units and maintained a sense of their own distinctiveness as Shawnee peoples. During the early colonial years Potawatomi, Delaware, Miami, Kickapoo, Mahican, and other groups were composite communities. They were diverse multiethnic groups shattered and then reconstituted by the simultaneous assault of European disease, the Indian slave trade, and Iroquois warfare. Nevertheless, Shawnees accustomed to smallness, to clan identities, and to diplomacy for survival alternately joined and resisted amalgamation into larger Indian polities. The history of these people and their towns reminds us that any discussion of "tribal" identities must first be historically situated in order for it to have any analytical value.

Notes

1. Calloway, *Shawnees*, 8; Carson, "Ethnogeography," 769; and Basso, *Wisdom Sits in Places*, 61. Unlike Basso, Carson acknowledges the Indian Removal Act as the initial act in cultural genocide directed at place. Quite rightly American Indian histories diverge along the Mississippi as the Indian Removal Act separated groups east of the Mississippi from the land.

2. Nabokov, *Where the Lightning Strikes*, xiii.

3. For general examples of the intersection of place, religion, and identity, see Martin, *Land Looks After Us*. See also Feld and Basso, *Senses of Place*.

4. Richard White prefers villages; White, *Middle Ground*, 17. But the model of Creek towns makes more sense for the Shawnees because they functioned as political units in which diplomatic, religious, and political leadership are inter-

twined. For an ethnohistorical description of Creek towns, see Ethridge, *Creek Country*, 94–97.

5. Many anthropologists and historians continue to argue that American Indian identities derive from the land itself. I cannot speak for the communities west of the Mississippi, but my guess is that scholars have failed to grasp the profoundly different notions of place and identity east and west of the Mississippi. Taos Pueblo, for example, is the oldest continuously inhabited village in North America. To cite another example, the recent conflict between the Navajo Nation and the Arizona Snowbowl Ski Resort in Arizona confirms that sacred geography is of fundamental importance to many American Indians, particularly those in the western United States. Native intellectual Vine Deloria argues that space is "determinative of the way that we experience things" and further that "American Indians hold their lands — places — as having the highest possible meaning, and all their statements are made with this reference point in mind"; Deloria, *God is Red*, xvi, 61. Woodland Indian history tells a different story, one in which ritual performance, intertribal alliances, and linguistic diversity enabled small mobile communities to resist amalgamation into larger Southern and Iroquoian syntheses.

6. Calloway, "We Have Always Been the Frontier," 39. Anthropologist Erminie Wheeler Voegelin in *Mortuary Customs* suggests that "the frequent shifts in location of the Shawnee have not only acted directly against diffusion, but have brought the Shawnee into contact with such a variety of cultures that they have become aloof of all of them and highly conscious of the desirability of preserving their own" (379).

7. Atkin, *Appalachian Indian Frontier*, 65; and McDowell, *Colonial Records*, 363. My interpretation of migration and the absence of sacred geography among the seventeenth-and eighteenth-century Shawnees is inspired by Basso, *Wisdom*.

8. Henderson, Jobe, and Turnbow, *Indian Occupation*, 172. Henderson argues that "the occupants of the late Fort Ancient Madisonville phase sites can probably be at least partially identified with the Shawnee." More recently, archaeologist Penelope Drooker, like Henderson, has contended that there is a high probability of a Fort Ancient-Shawnee linkage; Drooker, *View from Madisonville*. In 1948 anthropologist Erminie Wheeler-Voegelin conducted exhaustive research on the possible links between the Shawnees and the Fort Ancient people. Wheeler-Voegelin stopped short of making the connection explicit, writing that "since there are no known descriptions of ceramic remains from definitely identified historic Shawnee sites," such a connection remains elusive; Wheeler-Voegelin and Neumann, "Shawnee Pots," 10. However, both the Miami and Illinois are the

closest linguistic relatives to the Shawnees. Historic ceramic evidence definitively links both the Miami and Illinois to the Fort Ancient. Therefore linguistic evidence offers the strongest possible connection between the Fort Ancient and the Shawnees. See Shackelford, "On a Crossroads."

9. Hinderaker, *Elusive Empires*, 3–19.

10. Henderson, Jobe, and Turnbow, *Indian Occupation*, 11.

11. Wheeler-Voegelin and Neumann, "Shawnee Pots," 10.

12. This reshaping is in contrast to the protohistoric descendants of the Mississippian chiefdoms who continually reaffirmed their connections to their pre-Columbian forbearers. Patricia Galloway, James Carson, and Greg O'Brien, among others, spell out some of these enduring characteristics. Carson discovered that the Choctaws maintain a "moral economy" that includes a chiefly political organization, a gendered division of labor, matrilineal kinship, and a Mississippian cosmology. Greg O'Brien used the Choctaw understanding of power and authority to link them to their Mississippian ancestors; Carson, *Searching for the Bright Path*, 1–5; Galloway, *Choctaw Genesis*; O'Brien, *Choctaws in a Revolutionary Age*.

13. For Gabriel Arthur's journey into the Ohio Valley, see Williams, *Early Travels*, 35–36. See also Henderson, "Early European Contact," 231.

14. Williams, *Early Travels*, 36. For more on Virginians in the Indian slave trade, see Gallay, *Indian Slave Trade*, 53, 303–8.

15. Olafson, "Gabriel Arthur." Olafson speculates that the Shawnees were the historic descendants of the Fort Ancient people.

16. Thwaites, *Jesuit Relations*, 59:144–45; and Marquette, "Relation of the Voyages." For more on iron and European daggers at For Ancient sites, see Drooker, *View from Madisonville,* 170.

17. Lawson, *New Voyage*, 130–31.

18. Alfred W. Crosby made the initial argument regarding 1492 and the subsequent collapse of American Indian populations caused by virgin soil epidemics; Crosby, *Columbian Exchange*. The first historian to chronicle the so-called Iroquois wars, dating from 1640 to 1701, was Hunt in *Wars of the Iroquois*. For primary sources on the Iroquois wars in the Ohio Valley, see Thwaites, *Jesuit Relations*, 47:145. For more nuanced analyses of the relationship between the Iroquois and their neighbors, see Tanner, *Atlas of Great Lakes*, 29. See also White, *Middle Ground*; and Richter, *Ordeal of the Longhouse*.

19. White, *Middle Ground*, 17. See also Martin, *Sacred Revolt*, 31.

20. Ethridge, *Creek Country*, 94–97.

21. Piker, "Crossing Frontiers," paragraph 3. For a more extensive treatment, see Piker, *Okfuskee*.

22. Nabokov, *Forest of Time*, 133.

23. Jackson, "Opposite of Powwow," 187, 239.

24. For the six Shawnee villages on the Cumberland River near modern Nashville, see Louis de la Porte de Louvigny, "Carte de Fleuue Missisipi," and Guillaume Delisle, "Carte de la Louisiane"; both maps are reproduced in Tucker, *Atlas and Supplement*, plates XIII and XIV, respectively. Delisle refers to the Cumberland as "Riviere des ancious Chaouanons." The Delisle map records one Shawnee village at Tukabatchee within the Upper Creek Confederacy. Delisle also records one Shawnee village on the upper Savannah River. Like the Cumberland, he defines the Savannah River as the "r. de Chaouanons." Both Minet and Jean-Baptiste Louis Franquelin used La Salle's 1684 map as the basis for their map of the Eastern Woodlands. In both maps Shawnees are located at Starved Rock in 1684, the year of the Iroquois assault on that multiethnic defensive village; Minet, "Carte de la Louisiane"; and Franquelin, "Carte de L'Amerique Septentrionnalle," Tucker, *Atlas and Supplement*, plates VII and XIA.

25. Callender, "Shawnee," 580; and Clark, "Shawnee Indian Migration."

26. They are the Turkey, Turtle, Rounded feet, Horse, Raccoon, and Rabbit name group. For more information, see Voegelin and Wheeler-Voegelin, "Shawnee Name Groups," 617.

27. Contemporary Shawnee spellings of the divisions are *kesepokofi, pekowefi, mekoga, galikifi,* and *hifiwakela.*

28. Author's interview with George Blanchard, October 27, 2005.

29. Hanna, *Wilderness Trail*, 1:145. Hanna notes that the Pekowitha, Kispokotha, Chalagawtha, and Mekoche all had towns in colonial Pennsylvania. Towns were frequently named after one of the five divisions. According to my own compilation of these towns, Pekowitha and Mekoche villages predominated. The basis for my own reconstruction of Shawnee villages in Pennsylvania derives from a host of sources, including Clark, "Shawnee Indian Migration."

30. A longer discussion of each one of these divisional migrations appears in this chapter.

31. As early as 1935 both Erminie Wheeler-Voegelin and Carl Voegelin argued that the Shawnees were "an Algonkin-speaking tribe composed of five major divisions"; Voegelin and Wheeler-Voegelin, "Shawnee Name Groups," 617. For more on the Shawnees return to Ohio between 1745 and 1774, during which period cooperation between the various Shawnee towns constituted a tribal polity, see

Wheeler-Voegelin, *Ethnohistory of Indian Use and Occupancy*, 2:464–68. Between the 1950s and the 1970s Wheeler-Voegelin worked exhaustively on behalf of the Indian Claims Commission for which tribal polities were the basic organizing principle. Wheeler-Voegelin organized documents relating to each of the Great Lakes "tribes" into hundreds of ringbinders that were arranged chronologically. Thus the intellectual basis for the commission and the documentary record used to support it confirmed the existence of tribal polities. Historians tend to follow Wheeler-Voegelin's understanding of the Shawnees as a unified tribe. For examples, see Edmunds, *Shawnee Prophet*, 7–8; and Calloway, *Shawnees*, 8. John Sugden adopts a more nuanced view of Shawnee identity, writing that "the Shawnee 'tribe' was really a loose confederation of villages linked by a common language and culture, ties of kinship, and a rudimentary notion of unity"; Sugden, *Blue Jacket*, 7–8. For my own discussion of the relationship between the five divisions and the tribe as a whole, see Warren, *Shawnees and Their Neighbors*, 13–17.

32. Between 1745 and 1774 most, though not all, Shawnees lived in Ohio in towns along the Scioto and Ohio rivers. Following their early colonial pattern, their towns were typically named after the division with the largest number of residents in the community. Some Shawnees remained in Alabama at Tukabatchee and Sawanogi within the Upper Creek Confederacy. By 1774 and the Battle of Point Pleasant, many Ohio Shawnees voluntarily removed west of the Mississippi River. Thus the evidence for Shawnee political unity rests on their brief, though not complete, thirty-year period of geographic proximity in modern Ohio. However, the Shawnees return to Ohio must be placed in the much larger context of the long Shawnee diaspora that extended well into the nineteenth century. For one example of that discussion, see Warren, *Shawnees and Their Neighbors*, 69–70.

33. For the Minet account of the Shawnee migration to Starved Rock, see Minet, "Voyage Made from Canada." For the impact of the Iroquois wars on the Shawnees, see Wheeler-Voegelin and Tanner, *Indians of Ohio and Indiana*, 1:34; and Hunt, *Wars of the Iroquois*, 139. For the members of the alliance and the number at Starved Rock, see White, *Middle Ground*, 24.

34. White, *Middle Ground*, 49.

35. Browne, *Archives of Maryland*, 8:518. See also Richter, *Ordeal of the Longhouse*, 362n46, 343–44n42; and Hanna, *Wilderness Trail*, 1:142. For the intertribal kinship system, see Speck, "Delaware Indians as Women." For the relationship between the Iroquois and the Algonquians in Pennsylvania, see Richter, *Ordeal of the Longhouse*, 239.

36. Apaumat, "Narrative of an Embassy," 77; and Heckewelder, *History, Manners, and Customs*, 86.

37. Archaeologist Vernon J. Knight believes that Shawnee migrants settled Tukabatchee between 1675 and 1677; Knight, *Tukabatchee*, 24.

38. Anthropologist John R. Swanton made the initial scholarly claim that Tukabatchee was settled by Kispokotha Shawnees. Like Swanton, Charles Hanna and Noel Schutz have made similar claims based on the synonymy between "Ispokogi" and "Kispokotha." For these arguments, see Swanton, *Early History*, 296; Hanna, *Wilderness Trail*, 1:93; and Schutz, "Shawnee Myth," 423–26. Albert Gatschet in *Migration Legend*, 1:147, contends that in Muskogee Tukatachi means "town of survivors," or alternately "town . . . of foreign origin." Both Tecumseh and Tenskwatawa were members of the Kispokotha division. Historian John Sugden argues that kin ties between Tecumseh and the townspeople of Tukabatchee inspired his visit there in 1811; Sugden, *Tecumseh*, 14, 240–41. Shawnee cosmology, as revealed by the Kispokotha Shawnee Tenskwatawa, also confirms a link between the Creeks and the Kispokotha Shawnees at Tukabatchee. Several sets of Tukabatchee plates have been excavated. Those closely associated with Tukabatchee were excavated by relic hunters "near the falls of the Tallapoosa" sometime before 1930. For more on these plates, see Brannon, "Sacred Creek Relics," 3. Archaeologist William A. Fox argues that the brass plates were almost certainly made from French copper basins owned by Neutrals in lower Ontario. In Fox's view "there was communication ca. AD 1600–1650 between what is now the Niagara region of Ontario and central Alabama, either direct or indirect, and perhaps through Shawnee 'middlemen'"; Fox, "North-South Copper Axis," 90–91, 94. The authors wish to thank archaeologist Vernon J. Knight for these citations and insights into the Tukabatchee plates. The Shawnee Prophet mentions these brass plates in his description of the origins of Shawnee-Creek relations in the South; Kinietz and Wheeler-Voegelin, *Shawnese Traditions*, xv–xvi.

39. Clark, "Shawnee Indian Migration," 33. Milfort in *Memoir*, 184, claimed that the Creek town of Tukabatchee, then situated on the Tallapoosa River in present-day Elmore County, Alabama, was founded between 1675 and 1685. Historian Angie Debo maintains that "a tradition of Creek-Shawnee friendship [goes] . . . back to the dim days of their legendary history"; Debo, *Road to Disappearance*, 56.

40. For more on Stiggins, see Woodward, *Reminiscences*, 7.

41. To this day members of the Kispokotha division exhibit items that represent the symbolic alliance between the Shawnees and Creeks during the fast that precedes the Busk, the current War Dance. Today, Shawnees refer to this ceremo-

nial event as *Helenewekawe* (Men's Dance). The use of horses and guns seems to have led to the name War Dance. According to Absentee Shawnee elder George Blanchard, the War Dance is actually intended to promote peace.

42. Stiggins, "Historical Narration," 30. Knight in *Tukabatchee*, 24, dates the Shawnee departure to the eighteenth century because a recognizably Shawnee identification does not appear in the documents at that time. Even today, Shawnees, Creeks, and Yuchis continue to honor their historic ties to one another. Shawnees continue to visit the Peach, Fish Pond, and Arbeka Creek ceremonial grounds. Indeed, the Fish Pond ceremonial chief is half Shawnee; interview with George Blanchard (Absentee Shawnee), Little Axe, Oklahoma, August 5, 2005. Andy Warrior, the North Ground Chief of the Absentee Shawnee Group, stated that he is more Creek and Yuchi than Shawnee. Chief Warrior's uncle is Simon Harry, the ceremonial chief of the Yuchis at the Duck Creek ground. Each of these ceremonial ground chiefs shares Stomp Dance ceremonialism, similar planting and harvest ceremonies, and a vibrant alliance that has endured for centuries. For example, Absentee Shawnee ceremonial singer Scott Miller joked that "we know that alligators didn't swim up and down the Ohio River . . . we must have picked up the dance from the Yuchis." In 1789 botanist and explorer William Bartram also noticed similar cultural anomalies at work within the Creek synthesis. Bartram in "Observations," 13, noted that there were "almost as many languages or dialects as there are towns."

43. In 1731 the traders James Le Tort and James Davenport described the Shawnees then living in the Alleghany Mountains of Pennsylvania as "Asswikales [Thawekilas] 50 families; lately from S. Carolina to Ptowmack, and from thence thither, making 100 men." In that same year the governor of Pennsylvania addressed "Chiefs of ye Shawanese and Assekelaes." His differentiation between the two chiefs suggests a corollary to the Tukabatchee case described by Stiggins. Both sources define them as independent polities whose coalescence as a single "Shawnee" polity remained incomplete during the Colonial period; for Davenport and Le Tort, see Hanna, *Wilderness Trail,* 1:296, 298. For the Pennsylvania Governor, see Hazard, *Pennsylvania Archives,* 1:299–302.

44. Le Jau, *Carolina Chronicles*, 49.

45. A French census of 1760 and 1761 describes these Savannah River Shawnees as "Savanalis [Little Shawnee] opposite to Mucklassee on sharicula savanalis"; Swanton, *Early History*, 319; and Jemison, *Historic Tales of Tallagega*, 21. Swanton has argued that "sharicula" was a mistranslation of Thawakila. For the Shawnee role in the slave trade, see Gallay, *Indian Slave Trade*, 55–57. Le Jau is quoted in

Gallay, *Indian Slave Trade*, 372n55; for the primary source, see Le Jau, *Carolina Chronicles*, 68.

46. Edmond Atkin writes that "on the breaking out of the Indian War in 1715, they [the Shawnee] fled westerly with the Lower Creeks," and since the Lower Creeks moved to the lower Chattahoochee at this time, it is reasonable to assume that the Shawnees did likewise; Atkins, *Indians of the Southern Colonial Frontier*, 65; Swanton also tracks the Shawnee movements from the Savannah to the Chattahoochee before their move to the Tallapoosa; Swanton, *Early History*, 318–19. Charles Hanna first identified the Lower Creek town of Sawokli on the Lower Chattahoochee River as Shawnee. Citing Gatschet, Hanna acknowledges, though, that *sawokli* translates as *sawi*, "raccoon," and as *ukli*, "town " (Raccoon Town); Hanna, *Wilderness Trail*, 1:11. Such linguistic evidence thus supports the archaeological evidence that Sawokli was a Hitchiti rather than a Shawnee town; Worth, "Lower Creeks"; and Foster, *Archaeology of the Lower Muskogee*, 67–68. The Shawnee town on the lower Chattahoochee then has not yet been identified.

47. Swanton, *Indians of the Southern United States*, 184; Alford, "Shawnee Indians," 22. Patricia Galloway first recognized this as the date for the Shawnee migration from the Chattahoochee to the Tallapoosa river: a letter of Artaguette, the commandant of Mobile, to Maurepas, the minister of the Navy, October 17, 1729, states that "several councils have been held among the nations of these quarters in order to establish there eleven villages, that is seven of Shawnee, whom the Koasati are to place where they judge proper." Galloway writes that "this gives a date for the settlement among the Upper Creeks of the Shawnees who had lived on the Chattahoochee"; Rowland, Sanders, and Galloway, *Mississippi Provincial Archives*, 4:28, 30n16.

48. Hawkins, *Sketch*, 33.

49. For more on the Delaware and their linguistic relatives, see Goddard, "Delaware," 213–15; Grumet, *Northeastern Indian Lives*; and Hanna, *Wilderness Trail*, 1:150

50. Hazard, *Register of Pennsylvania*, 1:190.

51. Hanna, *Wilderness Trail*, 150.

52. Author's interview with Sherman Tiger, Shawnee, Oklahoma, June 2006. Warrior, "Interview with Andy Warrior."

53. Tuan, *Space and Place*, 152.

54. Kinietz and Wheeler-Voegelin, *Shawnese Traditions*, 3–4.

55. Kinietz and Wheeler-Voegelin, *Shawnese Traditions*, 6. Swanton in *Social Organization*, 627, corroborates the Shawnee Prophet's belief that the alliance

was built upon the Creeks' need for the Shawnees' supernatural and medicinal powers.

56. The Prophet's account also suggests that the five divisions of the Shawnees were autonomous political units who shared a common culture. According to the Prophet, "finding that other nations had sprung up, the Shawanese, Pickaways, and Kishpookoo divisions or tribes of the Shawnee Nation began to war upon the Catawba Indians. In their first expedition, they took two female Catawba prisoners who found their way into the possession of one of the Mekoce family"; Kinietz and Wheeler-Voegelin, *Shawnese Traditions*, 7.

57. Author's interview with George Blanchard, October 27, 2005. Mr. Blanchard argued that the survival of the Shawnee divisions depended on movement. Now place bound in Oklahoma, "a lot of people nowadays don't know" their division.

58. Manuscript 2719, received from Joseph Nocktonick, Shawnee, Oklahoma, 1934, Truman Michelson Collection, Ethnology, Linguistics, Text, Etc., National Anthropological Archives, s1.

59. Nabokov, *Forest of Time*, vi–ix.

60. Recognition of these migrations also places the Indian Removal Era in a larger and longer context of geographic mobility.

61. Author's interview with Andy Warrior, Little Axe, Oklahoma, June 2005.

8 | Tracing the Origins of the Early Creeks, 1050–1700 CE

NED J. JENKINS

In the last few years several authors have written on the origins of the Creeks. Most have discussed Creek ancestry primarily in terms of seventeenth- and eighteenth-century origins, reviewing the literature for evidence of refugee movements into the Creek homeland.[1] Charles Fairbanks and Vernon Knight are prominent exceptions in that they look at the archaeological evidence in order to understand Creek origins — methodology that I also use in this study to trace the people who became known as the Creeks.[2] By better understanding regional archaeology and artifact attribute distribution through space and time, we can better ascertain what groups actually comprised the core of the early Creeks.

I propose the groups who formed the core of the population that would become the Upper Creeks (ca. 1350–1675 CE) were comprised of three primary groups: (1) a Savannah Variant group of Georgia origin that evolved into the local Shine II Lamar phase; (2) a Moundville Variant group who started its exodus to the upper Alabama River Valley around 1450 CE, completing their final removal to the upper Alabama River around 1650 CE; and (3) the central Alabama Terminal Woodland population that probably became a part of early proto-Creek society once it fused with the intrusive Savannah Variant population ca. 1350–75 CE. At approximately 1450 CE the Shine II Lamar and Moundville groups began a fusion process that was complete by 1600 with the development of the Atasi phase.

I further suggest that some portion of the late Moundville III group that settled the upper Alabama River continued eastward to the middle Chattahoochee River Valley (where they are known archaeologically as the Abercrombie phase people). Here around 1500 CE they settled among a local Stewart phase Lamar group, founding the historically known *tal-was* of Cusseta and Coweta. The fusion of local Lamar (Stewart phase) and intrusive Late Moundville III (Abercrombie phase) resulted in the Blackmon phase (ca. 1600 CE). This similar parentage explains why the Blackmon phase and the Atasi phase have very similar ceramic content. The Blackmon phase can be considered the beginning of the historic Lower Creeks, and the Atasi phase can be considered the beginning of the historic Upper Creeks. This scenario also begins to explain the close relationship between the two historic divisions as both the Blackmon phase and the Atasi phase were derived from the same Moundville and Lamar Variant stock.

The final stage of Creek coalescence occurred during the seventeenth and early eighteenth centuries when refugees from around the South sought asylum with the Creeks. The Blackmon and Atasi phase people lived in the rich Fall Line environment along the Chattahoochee and Tallapoosa rivers, which meant that they had plenty of resources for additional people. Moreover, the *insitu* Creek core population could offer more organized protection to Koasati, Shawnee, Natchez, Alabama, Yuchi, and many other historic groups fleeing Native slave raiders.[3]

A Note on Taxonomic Terminology

In the following discussion I refer to prehistoric groups as they are known archaeologically through their taxonomic names of "variant" and "phase" such as the Moundville Variant and Abercrombie phase. "Phase" is a conceptual term that links periods of time to the common use of a certain technology, decoration style, or other aspect of artifact manufacture across a region. Phases may be fifty to two hundred and fifty years long, although they are usually thought of as representing segments of a cultural continuum.[4]

The more inclusive taxonomic term encompassing phases is "culture," or "variant." Whereas some archaeologists prefer the term "culture" for this taxonomic category, I prefer the term "variant."[5] Most recently, Krause characterized variant "as a mid-range taxon with less content, greater time span, and greater spread than a phase, but having less time span than a tradition and less spatial spread than a horizon. Thus defined, the variant fits securely within the logic of the Willey and Phillips system."[6] "Variant" then is used herein as a taxonomic term, characterized by multiple phases related by very similar content, temporal proximity, and usually (but not always) spatially contiguous. In this sense the Savannah Variant, for instance, refers to a series of phases usually occurring tangentially in space and time and defined by the diagnostic Savannah ceramic series. Used in this way Savannah Variant is a *taxonomic term* that does not necessarily dictate cultural relatedness. The same is true for the Etowah Variant, the Moundville Variant, the Lamar Variant, and other variants used in this discussion.

When working with taxonomic constructs, we should address the position of whether they (or ceramic style) may correlate with actual ethnic groups. My basic position is that shared ceramic styles of material culture were often products of long-term interaction within or between groups. Thus groups that exhibited shared ceramic style belonged to a social group with a common history and sustained interaction. It is logical that the degree of social interaction is reflected by the degree of ceramic stylistic similarity between sites. A high degree of stylistic similarity between sites is believed to reveal a shared or collective identity. In this sense style may have served as communication or even an aspect of ideology and group identity. Ceramic attributes, types, and varieties are the taxonomic building blocks of components and subsequent phases and document ceramic similarities. Phases serve to document the similarity among components and communities, while the variant may emphasize the degree of ceramic similarity between phases, together providing the mechanism for discussion of traditions-histories and processes of social interaction and integration.

It should be recognized, however, that the cycling process, budding or fissioning, and subsequent fusion often would have resulted in the creation of a hybrid or coalescent ethnic group. For example, when the Moundville chiefdom cycled or fissioned ca. 1450 CE, as we will see, a large segment of this ethnic group moved to the upper Alabama River Valley where they remained a distinct group until after the Soto *entrada*. Shortly thereafter, the Moundville group fused with the local Lamar Shine

II group, resulting in the creation of a coalescent ethnic group. Thus the Moundville ethnic group had been a distinct entity from 1050 CE until ca. 1575 CE when they fused with Lamar to form the Early Creeks — a hybrid ceramic complex and ethnic group. Cycling then was central to both ethnic and ceramic change. A similar process is seen among the late seventeenth-century Creeks as many divergent groups moved to the Coosa, Tallapoosa, and Chattahoochee river valleys. By approximately 1700 CE all of these groups had lost their original ceramic complexes and were manufacturing the Lawson Fields or Tallapoosa phase complex.

Cycling, Budding, and Fissioning

To understand the Creek coalescence, one must take a deep view of history and look into Creek prehistory where the roots of the coalescence can be found in the Early Mississippian Period. One of the salient characteristics of the Mississippian Period was the movement of people. David Anderson discusses late Mississippian population movement in terms of the "cycling," or the rise and fall, of chiefdoms. He describes chiefly polities as characterized by a fair degree of instability with movement acting as a safety valve for social tension among competing elites. Anderson details chiefdom cycling as, "the recurrent process of the emergence, expansion, and fragmentation of complex chiefdoms amid a regional backdrop of simple chiefdoms." Within this definition fissioning is part and parcel of the cycling process. When a chiefdom fissioned, elite males and their dependents (forming a basic fissioning unit) would move a moderate distance from the parent community. In this chapter I propose a distinction between fissioning and something I define as "budding." Both entail an out-movement of people from a village or population center. Fissioning occurred late in a chiefdom's life and is a product of instability as the chiefdom reorganized or fragmented as a result of competition among elites for power and prestige. The nature of the office of the chief itself appears to have been a primary cause of much of the organizational instability observed in chiefly societies.[7]

Budding, I propose, is a process that occurred early in the life of a chiefdom. It is a process whereby lineage segments of a chiefdom moved, forming a new but related chiefdom. Using ethnographic evidence, Jenkins and Krause discuss a probable mechanism of fissioning units that may be applicable to budding. Jenkins and Krause put forward that a unilateral descent group's dispute over succession would occur most frequently between half brothers, that is, a high-ranking man's descendents by separate wives.[8] Each of the male descendents of the chiefs' sisters having a claim to power might identify himself as a potential leader and could call on relatives for support. Because only one competitor could win, however, the loser may have chosen to establish an independent settlement beyond the parent community's reach. The competitor would found a colony or independent chiefdom that retained social, ceremonial, and economic ties while establishing an independent or partially independent local authority structure. By successfully manipulating affinal alliances and kin ties through war, trade, or other economic enterprises, a shrewd political leader might gain wealth and support to further his ambitions and consolidate his new power. A successful Mississippian leader then might bud from the parent group with kin support into a hinterland territory beyond the parent group's reach, but not so spatially removed as to sever social and community ties.[9] Service, who first defined chiefdoms, notes such a process when he states that, "chiefdoms tend to expand by a sort of budding off of families that have low potentiality in the inheritance scheme."[10]

Budding and fissioning then were similar processes and therefore functioned in a similar manner as safety valves for chiefly competition among the elite. However, I understand budding to have been a process of the Early and Middle Mississippian chiefdoms and that it was a mechanism for population movements, sometimes over long distances. Understanding how and why budding occurred and worked is central to understanding early Mississippian movements and the seemingly simultaneous appearance of early Mississippian communities across the southern United States.

Budding also may have been linked to the procurement of nonlocal goods as prestige items and redistributive products. It is clear from Paul Welch's analysis of the Moundville economy, for example, that the procurement of nonlocal resources was important in the Moundville economy and was tied not only to the flow of trade goods but also to the redistribution of chiefly prestige items.[11] Hence competitive descendents would have actively sought external resources or goods, offering procurement services and prestige goods to the parent polity. This process is in line with Service's early formulation of the chiefdom concept in which he understood chiefdoms to develop at the nexus of regional exchange and an increase in local specialization and that small neighboring societies, or parts of them, voluntarily join an adjacent chiefdom because of the benefits of participation in the exchange network. In addition, Service states, "The fact that there is frequently a continuous belt of chiefdoms suggests the possibility that the cycle of expansion by incorporation and subsequent disintegration is a common cause of the origin and spread of many chiefdoms."[12]

Fissioning is a similar process to budding, except that fissioning usually involved the fragmentation of the chiefdom. A good example of fissioning discussed in this chapter occurred within the Moundville chiefdom in west Alabama during the late Moundville III phase (around 1450 CE). At this time the Moundville chiefdom partially dissolved, with occupation at the Moundville site practically ceasing and several mound centers being established elsewhere in the Warrior River Valley while a large segment of the Moundville population moved to the upper Alabama River Valley. Another significant example of fissioning also discussed later occurred at the Etowah chiefdom of northeast Georgia around 1350–75 CE. At this time a large population segment moved a great distance to the headwaters of the Choctawhatchee River near Troy, Alabama.

Anderson and Blitz and Lorenz have offered a climatic explanation for the growth and subsequent fissioning of chiefdoms.[13] Anderson, with tree-ring specialists David Stahle and Malcolm Cleveland, examined bald cypress growth patterns in the Savannah River Valley of South Carolina and Georgia dating within the range 1000–1600 CE. Patterns revealed favorable rainfall amounts from 1152 to 1200 CE with few shortfalls. This time frame of favorable rainfall correlates well with the period of extensive Early Mississippian budding discussed above. In addition, a longer continual span of favorable rainfall also occurred between 1251 and 1358 CE at a time when multiple mound centers proliferated across the southern United States. Sites such as Moundville and Etowah were at their maximum size and complexity during this time frame. The time of the appearance and spread of Early Mississippian chiefdoms corresponds to the climatic epoch known as the Medieval Warming Period (1000–1300 CE), which was an episode of wetter, warmer weather in the northern hemisphere.[14]

Following the years of favorable rainfall came dry years. A highly stressful span from 1359 to 1377 CE was followed by another devastating drought between 1407 and 1476 CE. The latter drought corresponds to the ca. 1450 date proposed for the fissioning (collapse) of Moundville, while the earlier date corresponds to the ca. 1350–75 date for the fissioning of the Etowah chiefdom.

If Anderson's patterns of climate conditions apply to areas slightly west of the Savannah River drainage, then they provide an explanation for the simultaneous fall of many Southern chiefdoms. These alternating periods of favorable growing seasons and drought stresses would no doubt have affected corn surpluses, stability among elites, interregional alliances, and the scale of warfare for the control of surplus.

Blitz and Lorenz offer an interesting model of how the Medieval Warming Period could have affected Mississippian polity growth for the years 1000–1300 CE. The model links this period's subsistence surpluses, which were created by favorable rains, to the booming pattern of Southern Ceremonial Complex (SECC) prestige-goods exchange. According to Blitz and Lorenz,

> in periods of high rainfall, larger crop yield could sustain greater numbers in residence at a center. Surpluses could be mobilized by leaders for feasting and hosting visiting elites from neighboring polities. Alliances between polities within a river valley could have been cemented by prestige-good exchange and elite marriage, creating kinship ties between polities and allies for support in times of need. At the interregional scale a prestige-goods network, such as the SECC inter-regional styles, would best maintain polity alliances. Thus, when rainfall was adequate, polities grew in size and political integration expanded in scale . . . The opposite climatic scenario, extended drought periods leading to continual harvest shortfalls, could destabilize polities dependent on surpluses to subsidize political and social integration.[15]

An important impact of reduced maize production would have been a polity's inability to support its population. Failure to amass surplus grain during successive drought years would have resulted in the belief that their leader was incompetent. If alliance networks were no longer maintained, SECC prestige items would no longer be distributed as tokens of alliance, and marriageable spouses would no longer be exchanged between centers, thus removing the "social glue" that obligates affinal kin in different polities to support one another. Indeed, around 1450 CE the flow of prestige goods slowed in the Black Warrior River Valley, followed by the fissioning of the Moundville system. As alliance systems collapsed, we might expect evidence of regional warfare to supplement crop shortfalls with tribute demands. Such demands seem to have been the case in the mid-sixteenth century as Luna and Soto observed eastern Tennessee River Valley polities paying tribute to the core province of Coosa.[16]

Woodland Predecessors, 100 BCE–1100 CE

The Woodland Stage in central Alabama is characterized by a thousand years of two different groups living contiguous to one another. We can trace one group who made check-stamped pottery through the Cobbs Swamp, Henderson, and Autauga phases. This group we refer to as the Pintlalla Cultural Tradition (see table 2). At the beginning of the Middle Woodland Period (100 BCE–500 CE), check-stamped pottery had a continuous spatial distribution down the Coosa, Tallapoosa, and Alabama rivers. Around 200 CE Pintlalla tradition people were pushed down the Alabama River to the vicinity of Pintlalla Creek by a group making plain pottery that were moving down the Coosa. This group who made plain pottery for eleven hundred years is referred to as the Elmore Cultural Tradition, and the Calloway, Dead River, Hope Hull, and Unions Springs phases document the local evolution of this group once they were in central Alabama (see map 8). The Pintlalla and Elmore people lived adjacent to one another for a thousand years in apparent harmony, responding to the same technological innovations and outside influences. Then sometime between 1000–1050 CE the people of the Autauga phase (Pintlalla) moved up the Alabama River into the lower Tallapoosa River Valley and nearby drainages, partially fusing with the Union Springs phase (Elmore)

Table 2. Late prehistoric and protohistoric culture sequences

	Upper Alabama	Lower Tallapoosa	Middle Coosa	Middle Chattahoochee	Warrior Valley	Upper Choctawhatchee	Middle Tombigbee
1700 CE	Tallapoosa	Tallapoosa	Childersburg	Lawson Field	Abandoned	?	Abandoned
	Alabama River	Atasi	Woods Island	Blackmon			Summerville IV
1600 CE			Kymulga	Abercrombie	Moundville IV		
	Big Eddy	Big Eddy		Stewart	Late Moundville III	?	Summerville II & III
1500 CE				Bull Creek			
1400 CE	Unoccupied	Shine II Early Lamar	?	Singer	Early Moundville III		
		Shine I		Rood III	Moundville II	Walnut Creek (Savannah)	
1300 CE							
	Brannon	Late Autauga Union Springs Brannon		Rood II	Moundville I	Union Springs	Summerville I
1200 CE			Ellis	Rood I			
1100 CE	Late Autauga Middle Autauga				West Jefferson		Cofferdam
							Gainesville
1000 CE				Averett			Catfish Bend
	Early Autauga	Hope Hull			Carthage	?	
900 CE				?			

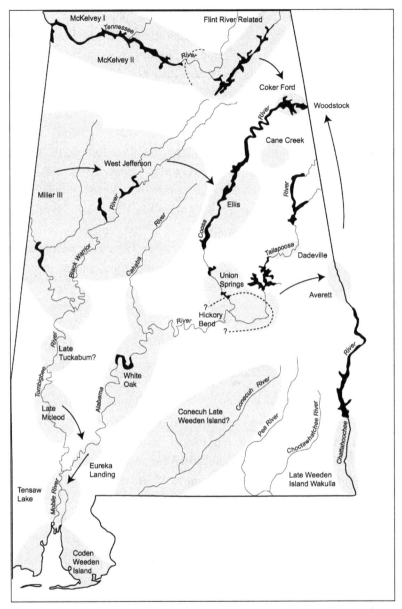

Map 8. Selected Terminal Woodland manifestations, ca. 1050–1300 CE.

group.[17] The Union Springs phase and Autauga phase Late Woodland groups were numerous in central Alabama, and because of this diversely rich environment, these Late Woodland groups may not have suffered significant population pressure; in fact, their populations seem to have expanded during the Medieval Warming Period. Both continued well into the Mississippian Period.

On the middle Chattahoochee River the Terminal Woodland is represented by the Averett phase (see map 8). No local Chattahoochee Valley origin can be found for the Averett ceramic complex, so it most likely represents a displaced Hope Hull phase group from the lower Tallapoosa (see map 8). Averett ceramics are very much like Hope Hull ceramics in terms of paste, vessel shape, a dominance of plain pottery, and a minority red-filmed surface treatment.[18] A portion of the Hope Hull phase group moved to the Middle Chattahoochee as a result of the Autauga intrusion into the lower Tallapoosa River area.

The Mississippian Transition, 1100–1300 CE

In central Alabama the beginning of the Mississippian Stage witnessed the intrusion of a small Moundville-related Brannon phase group into the upper Alabama River Valley area at approximately 1100 CE. This ceramic complex is very similar to the Rood I complex that appears contemporaneously in the lower Chattahoochee River Valley (see map 9).[19] The Brannon phase intrusion seems almost transitory in nature because it is so slightly represented archaeologically. Radiocarbon and thermoluminescent dates extend the Terminal Woodland in central Alabama to at least 1300 CE.[20] These dates along with feature associations indicate that the Early Mississippian Brannon phase people lived side by side with Woodland Autauga and Union Springs phase people. In central Alabama, then, Mississippian groups (characterized by many new traits including shell-tempered pottery) lived contemporaneously with Terminal Woodland groups.

In addition, the Early Mississippian Shine I phase people, a relatively small group characterized by pyramidal mounds, agriculture, and predominantly coarse, plain shell-tempered pottery, also may have lived alongside larger Terminal Woodland, Autauga and Union Springs phase populations in the lower Tallapoosa Valley. I do not believe the Shine I

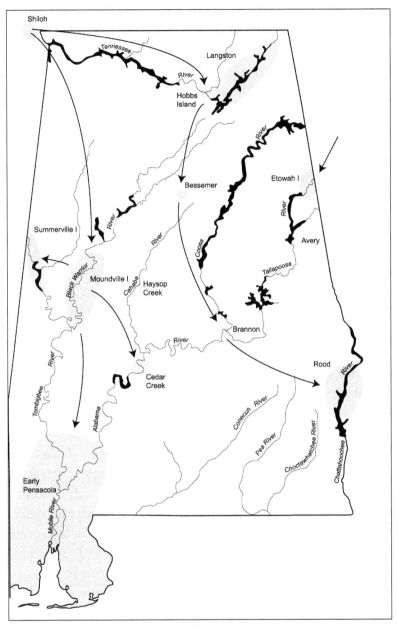

Map 9. Selected Early Mississippian manifestations, ca. 1050–1250 CE.

phase or Brannon phase groups to have been sufficiently numerous to acculturate the more populous late Woodland groups. Their ceramic traditions seemingly fade into obscurity. However, it now seems likely that these groups fused during the Middle Mississippian Period (ca. 1350–75) with an intrusive Savannah Variant group from the east (Walnut Creek complex).

The Introduction of the Lamar Variant in Central Alabama

The two Mississippian populations that later would form the larger, more visible components of the historic Creek population were the Lamar Variant people (best known from Georgia) and the Moundville Variant people from the Black Warrior River Valley in western Alabama. Both fused in central Alabama to form the core of the Upper Creek population. The Lamar Variant is comprised of a group of contemporaneous phases with similar content extending across much of Georgia, central Alabama, and north central Florida. Lamar Complicated Stamped is the most prevalent decorated ceramic type. The genesis of the Lamar Variant can be traced to the Early Mississippian Etowah Variant of north Georgia where the Etowah chiefdom first appeared at approximately 1050 CE.[21] Etowah Variant ceramics (Early Etowah and Late Etowah phases) are characterized by sand-tempered rectilinear complicated stamping, and they are placed into the more encompassing South Appalachian Tradition.[22] By 1200 CE the Etowah ceramic complex had been replaced by the predominantly curvilinear complicated-stamped pottery known as the Savannah Variant. And by 1400 CE the Savannah Variant had evolved into the Lamar Variant. Throughout this sequence the Mississippian Period, South Appalachian Tradition expanded from north central Georgia and southward into the Coastal Plain.[23]

I use the term "Savannah" or "Savannah Variant" here in a manner consistent with Hally's use of "Savannah Culture" that includes those regions of Georgia comprising the Wilbanks, Scull Shoals, Beaverdam, and Hollywood phases.[24] In addition, I use the term "Savannah" to refer to those Savannah-related complexes within the Chattahoochee and Savannah river drainages as well as those recently recognized in central

Alabama.[25] However, I do not use the term "Savannah Culture" since all of the phases of Savannah may not represent a single cultural system.

The Georgia Valley and Ridge and Piedmont physiographic provinces were the developmental heartland of Lamar (or Lamar Variant). Throughout north Georgia Lamar evolves out of local Savannah-related complexes. However, Lamar Variant phases also appeared in Alabama by the Late Mississippian Period. Throughout the middle Coosa, lower Tallapoosa, and lower Chattahoochee rivers in Alabama, the Late Mississippian Lamar Variant phases (Shine II, Stewart, and Bull Creek phases) appear, but only recently have their immediate South Appalachian Tradition predecessors been recognized. Until recently, Lamar on the middle Chattahoochee appeared to have been a site-unit intrusion into an area in which the Terminal Woodland Averett phase constituted the primary preceding population.[26] Farther down the Chattahoochee, Lamar follows a late Rood complex, or Knight's middle period, at the Singer Moye site. More recently, Blitz and Lorenz indicate Lamar first appearing in this area of the lower Chattahoochee during the Singer phase, 1400–50 CE (see maps 9 and 10).[27] The Late Rood (Singer-Moye) phase most likely developed into early Lamar as a result of interaction with late Savannah groups moving into the area. As noted earlier, intrusions of small Savannah groups occurred during or following the collapse of the Etowah chiefdom (ca. 1350–75 CE), with subsequent absorption of those groups by resident late Rood groups.

Recent reexaminations of the ceramics from the Walnut Creek site also reveal some Lamar predecessors in central Alabama. The Walnut Creek site, first reported by Brooms and Chase — and located just east of Troy, Alabama, at the headwater of the Choctawhatchee River, revealed a large, twelve-acre site with clear affiliation to the north Georgia Savannah Variant.[28] Another large site with a similar complex is located less than one mile away.[29] The Walnut Creek ceramic complex is most like that of the Savannah Variant, Wilbanks phase of the Etowah River Valley.[30] More specifically, the Walnut Creek ceramic complex appears most like what one might expect in a terminal Wilbanks phase component.[31] This Wilbanks-like Walnut Creek complex has no predecessors in the Troy, Alabama, area and thus is a likely product of a site-unit intrusion from

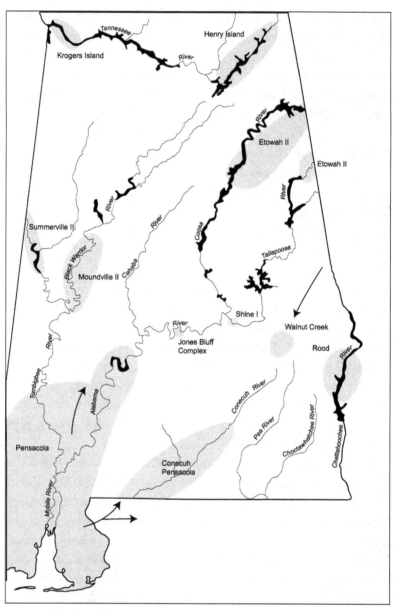

Map 10. Selected Middle Mississippian manifestations, ca. 1250–1400 CE.

the Etowah River Valley of north Georgia similar to that on the lower Chattahoochee at Singer-Moye. The nearest complex of comparable age in the Troy area is the Terminal Woodland Union Springs phase, a morphologically very different complex of local origin.

The extreme isolation of these Wilbanks-like sites in Alabama gives the impression of fissioning groups. The locality does not even have good bottomland suitable for horticulture. If the collapse of the Etowah chiefdom was a product of internal rivalry or factionalism brought about by succession to chieftainship, it is probable that the losing faction was forced to flee.[32] It is also likely that the winner of the dispute remained in the Etowah Valley while a group on the Coosawattee River eventually merged with a Dallas population around 1350–1400 CE, together forming the chiefdom of Coosa.

Although the Walnut Creek phase group may have been the losers in the Etowah Valley confrontation, they were able to reconsolidate their power as they merged with the Terminal Woodland Autauga and Middle Mississippian Shine I groups in the lower Tallapoosa to become the Lamar Variant, Shine II phase around 1400 CE. Although a transitional complex between Walnut Creek and Shine II has not yet been clearly isolated, the Walnut Creek complex is very similar to the Shine II ceramic complex except for the coarser gray paste and appliqué rims of the Shine II ceramic complex. A fusing of the local Autauga complex with the Walnut Creek complex would have produced a ceramic complex very similar to Shine II.

In fact, David Chase notes the association of a minority of Walnut Creek phase ceramics with the Shine II component at the Jere Shine site.[33] Recent examinations of Chase's original Jere Shine collection reveal important hints to the origin of Shine II. Although the collection needs a detailed reanalysis, cursory examination reveals the appliqué rim strips typical of Shine II phase to be virtually absent at the Jere Shine site. Instead, many of the rims are punctated or pinched, identically to those of the Walnut Creek phase near Troy forty miles to the south. In addition, a few sherds of Walnut Creek Complicated Stamped are also present.[34]

Considering this ceramic evidence, it looks as though within fifty years or less of their arrival in southeast Alabama, the Savannah Variant, Walnut

Creek group had moved forty miles north into the lower Tallapoosa Valley, incorporating the small Shine I phase chiefdom as well as the Terminal Woodland Autauga (Hickory Bend subphase) population. Future archaeology should better define the timing and evolution of early Shine II (1350 and 1400 CE). The Lamar Variant, Shine II phase of the lower Tallapoosa River Valley is fully Mississippian and is characterized by developed corn agriculture and a chiefdom political organization.[35] Truncated pyramidal mounds, no doubt, served as the residences of the elite, around which compact villages were located. Like Shine I, villages around these mounds have dense compact middens near the river.[36] Indeed, one can see that the central Alabama region does not appear to have become fully or at least extensively Mississippianized until approximately 1400 CE with the development of the Lamar-related Shine II phase. It is at this time that Late Mississippian Period sites were concentrated in central Alabama River valleys. However, this period seems to have been more of a "poor man's" Mississippian, with fewer prestige goods than found at Moundville or Etowah.

Another later intrusion of Lamar Variant people into Alabama occurred after European contact when people from the fallen paramount chiefdom of Coosa migrated south. The province of Coosa, centered in northwest Georgia in the Coosa River Valley, had emerged by ca. 1400 CE. At its height one hundred and forty years later (around 1540), Coosa was a paramount chiefdom composed of a series of linked Lamar Variant and Dallas Variant polities stretching for approximately four hundred kilometers along the Coosa and Tennessee River valleys from northeastern Alabama through northwestern Georgia and into the Tennessee River Valley. (The Dallas Variant extends through the southern Ridge and Valley province of eastern Tennessee into portions of north Georgia and Alabama). These polities were probably largely independent chiefdoms that were unified (perhaps only briefly) by Coosa, the chiefdom represented by the largest and geographically most central site cluster in the parmountcy and situated in the upper Coosa River Valley at the Little Egypt site.[37]

The Coosa polity arose in the Coosawattee River Valley. The earliest phase of the Lamar Variant from the Coosawattee River Valley is the Little Egypt phase. It is interesting that the assemblage is dominated by shell-tempered Dallas Variant ceramics (seventy-one percent) and not

Lamar.[38] This dominance no doubt reflects the initial formation of the Coosa chiefdom that would have been contemporaneous with the early Shine II phase of the lower Tallapoosa River Valley. Judging from the dominance of shell tempering during the Little Egypt phase, it is entirely possible that the early Dallas population was dominant over the early Lamar people in the area. If this were true, then it might follow that the Dallas polity, centered in the adjacent Tennessee River Valley, founded Coosa in the Coosawattee River Valley during the Little Egypt phase. As stated by Smith, "it is worth noting that Little Egypt [the site] was the forth mound center since 1000 CE in the Coosawattee Valley, suggesting that political power had been unstable there."[39]

In other words, the Coosawattee Valley situation was marked by serially occupied mound centers presumably ruled by different linages. All of the mound centers in the valley demonstrate spatially varying percentages of Lamar and Dallas ceramics that may indicate a struggle between Dallas and Lamar people for control of the region during this brief period.[40] In the following Lamar Variant, Barnett phase (1475–1575 CE), when Lamar ceramics dominated the assemblage, the local Lamar population no doubt commanded control of the chiefdom. In addition to the paramount center at the Little Egypt site, six other villages and at least three smaller settlements are known for the Coosawattee River Valley and may have made up the central chiefdom in the Coosa Paramountcy. This cluster of towns and settlements was the largest population concentration in the Ridge and Valley province in the sixteenth century, and this growth may explain the rise of Little Egypt as the dominant power in the region. Given this population base, conquest of neighboring chiefdoms might have been relatively easy, and as more groups were incorporated, the military advantage grew.[41] When Coosa fell after the Soto *entrada*, some of these Lamar Variant and Dallas Variant people moved into central Alabama.

Lamar Variant in Central Alabama:
The Shine II phase, 1400–1575 CE

David Chase first defined the Shine II phase as a result of salvage investigations at the Jere Shine site, located on the lower Tallapoosa River just north of Montgomery.[42] During the Shine II phase there was a substantial

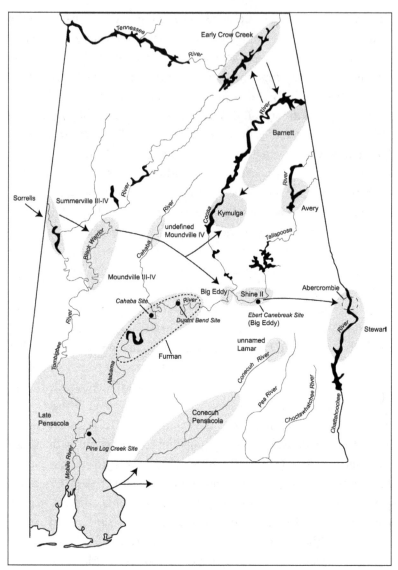

Map 11. Selected Late Mississippian and Early Protohistoric manifestations, ca. 1400–1600 CE.

increase in the number of mounds with compact villages along the lower Tallapoosa River. These sites include the Jere Shine site (1Mt6), Kulumi (1Mt3), Tukabatchee (1Ee32), and possibly Muklasa (1Mt10). Another large Shine II component is found at the Hickory Bend site (1Mt56); however, the mound identification is uncertain. A small Shine II mound was once present at the Jenkins site (1Mt48), but it has washed away. The Tukabatchee site, the easternmost Shine II site, has a large compact midden with one mound located within a tight horseshoe bend of the Tallapoosa, while the westernmost site, the Jere Shine, has five mounds and associated middens. Hence the primary territory of the Shine II phase extends from the Jere Shine site near the junction of the Coosa and Tallapoosa Rivers to Tukabatchee in the big bend of the Tallapoosa, being approximately forty miles upriver from the Jere Shine site (see map 11).

Recall that Shine II is a blend of the intrusive (proto-Lamar) Savannah Variant Walnut Creek with the local Autauga and Shine I phases. Chase's original description of the Shine II complex, however, emphasized the Lamar aspect of the ceramic assemblage.[43] As stated earlier, contrasting Shine II Lamar from the Jere Shine site with other Shine II sites indicates the Kulumi Lamar complex is most like Middle Lamar, 1450–1550 CE, while Jere Shine site is most like Early Lamar, 1400–50.[44] Chase obtained one radiocarbon determination from the Jere Shine site. An uncalibrated date of 1380–+50 (DIC-2709) was recovered from Burial 25. Burial 25 also contained a Spaghetti Style gorget that can aid in dating the site.[45] Muller refers to the Spaghetti Style as the Williams Island Style and dates it to the late thirteenth or early fourteenth century, while Calvin Jones contends the three Spaghetti Style gorgets found at Lake Jackson, Florida, date to the period 1240–1476 CE.[46]

In the mid-1960s Chase conducted excavations at the Kulumi site, located three to four miles upstream from the Jere Shine site. Chase's excavations indicated a generally stratified site. In 1982 Craig Sheldon and I returned to the area of Chase's excavations in hopes of better defining the cultural stratigraphy. Although unpublished, this work accomplished these goals. A small late Middle Woodland Calloway phase component was concentrated at the one-meter depth, followed by major Late Woodland, late Autauga, and Mississippian Shine I components. A major Shine

II component was concentrated in the upper zone along with a sparse veneer of Historic Creek.

In the process of working up a detailed history of the central Alabama cultural sequence, Sheldon and I revisited the tables and materials from our 1982 excavation.[47] The tables indicated that the upper twenty-cm zone contained the expected Shine II Lamar complex. However, an unexpected shell-tempered complex was in complimentary association. A close examination of the decorated shell-tempered pottery in the collections indicated this additional shell-tempered complex to be most like a very Late Moundville III complex.[48] The Moundville III complex at Kulumi most likely was derived from the nearby upper Alabama River Valley complex defined as the Big Eddy phase, a phase in the Moundville Variant.

Moundville Variant

The Moundville Variant is characterized by a distinctive combination of ceramic types, with coarse and fine shell-tempered wares possessing distinctive vessel forms that change throughout the six-hundred-year span of the Moundville Variant. Our most detailed Moundville Variant sequence is from the Moundville site, although this sequence seems to be mirrored in other areas, especially in the central Tombigbee.[49] Spatially the Moundville Variant extends from the Shiloh phase of the western Tennessee Valley east to the Hobbs Island phase, and then southward to the Black Warrior River Valley Moundville and Bessemer phases, and west to the Summerville I phase of west Alabama-east Mississippi (see map 9). Poorly defined early Moundville Variant (Moundville I–related) phases also can be found in the Cedar Creek phase of the lower Alabama River, the central Cahaba Haysop Creek phase, and the central Alabama Brannon phase (see map 9).[50] Throughout its existence the Moundville Variant was an exciting cultural phenomenon. Understanding and modeling how and why this occurrence grew and moved will no doubt be a subject of future study.

The Moundville Variant appeared earliest in the Shiloh phase of the western Tennessee River Valley and budded around 1050 CE to form the Moundville I phase of the Black Warrior River Valley. The Moundville I phase population was adjacent to a moderately sized Terminal Woodland,

West Jefferson phase population. The West Jefferson phase population is viewed by this author as a Terminal Woodland population in the process of Mississippianization, possessing cottage industries of shell working (microliths), chunky-stone manufacture, and the procurement of greenstone serving as mechanisms of acculturation (for the extent of the West Jefferson phase, see map 8).[51] The acculturation of such a group would have been important toward producing surplus corn and thus fueling the prestige economy.

There is no evidence that the Moundville I phase evolved out of the *insitu* West Jefferson phase, and there is clear evidence that the Moundville I phase has considerable temporal overlap with the West Jefferson phase, indicating that they were contemporaries. When West Jefferson ceramics occur at Moundville, for instance, they are in association with Moundville I ceramics. Although the early Moundville Variant (Moundville I–related phases) is geographically widespread, it is the most highly developed at the Moundville site, which is near present-day Tuscaloosa, Alabama. By the Moundville II phase the Moundville Variant becomes more restricted to the Black Warrior River Valley and adjacent central Tombigbee Valley (see map 10).[52]

During the Moundville I phase the Moundville chiefdom budded down the Black Warrior and Tombigbee rivers to the Mobile Bay-Delta to form the Pensacola Variant (see map 9). During Moundville I, a competitor of chiefly descent from Moundville moved his lineage and followers to Mound Island in the Mobile Delta around 1100 CE (Andrews Place phase). By the Bottle Creek I phase the Pensacola complex had become better established with its own local distinctive identity. The Bottle Creek polity offered marine shell, salt, and exotic lithics to the parent Moundville polity. The importation of marine shell peaked at Moundville shortly after the establishment of the Bottle Creek polity (the Moundville I–II transition between 1150 CE and 1350 CE) and just before the Moundville chiefdom fissioned.[53] Although maintaining strong Moundville influences, the local character of Bottle Creek I and II emerged after sustained interaction with Lower Mississippi Valley Plaquemine cultures of the Lower Yazoo Basin and Natchez Bluff regions.[54] By the Middle Mississippian the Pensacola Variant, which refers to Bottle Creek I, II, and related phases, eventually extended as far north as the middle Alabama River Valley, east to the Choctawhatchee Bay and the Conecuh drainage, and west to the Mississippi Sound (see map 10).[55]

A closely related Moundville I group also budded from Shiloh to the lower Chattahoochee River. In this case the Moundville I group first budded from Shiloh to the Tennessee Valley (Hobbs Island phase) and then moved through the Bessemer phase area of the upper Black Warrior River drainage and into central Alabama in the form of the Brannon phase on the upper Alabama. From there, it continued to the lower Chattahoochee River to form the Rood Variant around 1100 CE (see map 9). Rood I ceramics are virtually identical to Shiloh, Bessemer, Brannon, and Moundville I ceramics.[56] At this time Rood I phase mound centers were built at the Cool Branch, Mandeville, and Rood's Landing sites on the middle Chattahoochee.

A recent study may suggest that there was also a relationship between the Moundville Variant people in the Chattahoochee Valley and those in west Florida (known archaeologically as the Tallahassee Hills Fort Walton phase). In this study Scarry and Payne indicate that the initial occupation of the Lake Jackson site, located near Tallahassee, Florida, was in the late twelfth or early thirteenth century, which is late compared to Moundville or to the Early Mississippian centers of the Chattahoochee Valley. They state that "this dating leaves open the possibility that the Lake Jackson chiefdom was a secondary construction influenced directly or indirectly by earlier chiefdoms to the north and west. It also means that it is possible that the Lake Jackson chiefdom was a result of population movement (of several possible scales) from existing chiefdoms."[57]

Scarry also provided a disc of ceramic images to this author from Lake Jackson that are helpful in evaluating the similarities between the Tallahassee Hills Fort Walton assemblage and that from the contemporaneous Chattahoochee Valley Cemochechobee site (Rood II). The images on the disc are quite similar to those from the Cemochechobee site, Rood II phase (as defined by Blitz and Lorenz).[58] Blitz and Lorenz date Rood II from 1200 to 1300 CE, which corresponds to the initial occupation of the Lake Jackson site (see table 2). Based on this data, I propose that the founding of the Lake Jackson site and chiefdom was a product of chiefdom budding from the Rood II phase of the lower Chattahoochee River Valley during the late twelfth or early thirteenth centuries. It is also important that the only gorget style (three specimens) found at the Lake Jackson site is the Spaghetti type, likely indicating an affiliation between the areas from which they are most numerous — the Big Eddy phase and the Dallas areas. Hence there is likely a linguistic affiliation between the Big Eddy phase (Alabama speakers), Dallas Variant (Koasati speakers), Rood II, and Lake Jackson (Apalachee speakers) phases.[59]

West of Moundville, in the central Tombigbee Valley of present-day western Alabama and eastern Mississippi, the Summerville I–IV and Tibbee Creek-Sorrells phase sequences are representative of the Moundville Variant (see maps 9, 10, and 11). The Black Warrior Valley population must have maintained a close relationship with the central Tombigbee populations, as this is the only area where another Moundville I–IV–like sequence can be recognized. The Lubbub center, located on the Tombigbee in west central Alabama, was probably a product of budding, from Moundville to the Lubbub locality during Moundville I (around 1150 CE). After this initial budding, secondary single mound centers and farmsteads grew and were virtually continuous between the Lubbub Creek site and the Lyons Bluff site, another major center upriver from Lubbub Creek near the Tombigbee in present-day eastern Mississippi.[60]

The Moundville Variant is most strongly manifested in the Black Warrior Valley in the Moundville I–IV phases of the Middle Mississippian chiefdom today known as Moundville.[61] In the Black Warrior River Valley we see the development of a paramount chiefdom through four stages; Initial Centralization, (1050–1250 CE), Regional Consolidation (1200–1300 CE), The Paramountcy Entrenched (1300–1450 CE), and Collapse and Reorganization (1450–1650 CE; see table 2 for the corresponding ceramic sequences).[62] The Moundville site was first occupied during the Initial Centralization Stage (1050–1200 CE, Moundville I). Welch observed that "right from the beginning of the Moundville I phase, settlement on the high, flood free terrace at Moundville was different in kind from settlements elsewhere in the valley."[63] It is by far the largest site in the valley at this early date. Although the Asphalt Mound is the only mound verified by excavation for this stage, several other mounds at Moundville may have been utilized because late Moundville I components are known from their upper levels. A fairly large population lived along the river bluff and along Carthage Branch. No pre-Moundville, West Jefferson phase component has been found at Moundville as all West Jefferson materials from primary contexts have been found in direct association with Moundville I phase materials.[64]

During Regional Consolidation (1200–1300 CE, late Moundville I and Moundville II), the basic plan of the center was established, including the layout of the central plaza and the positioning of the mounds. At this time Moundville became the political center of the valley. The sheet midden accumulated during this time indicates that the Moundville site carried its densest population between 1200 and 1300 CE. This is also the time when the palisade was first built and maintained (being rebuilt six times) until 1300. At this time Moundville assumed the character of a large palisaded town, drawing residents from a broad area. The acquisition of nonlocal goods and raw materials also intensified and peaked during this interval. Outside the Moundville central site three other mound sites in the Black Warrior Valley that date to the late Moundville I phase were abandoned at this time.[65] These people undoubtedly moved to Moundville. However, population increase at Moundville was associated not only with the abandonment of local mound centers but likely with the fall of the Shiloh chiefdom and partial abandonment of the western Tennessee River Valley along with the final absorption of the local West Jefferson population. The initial building of the palisade at this time may indicate that the position of the elite was less secure or that the sociopolitical environment was becoming less secure.

During the Paramountcy Entrenched (1300–1450 CE, Moundville II and early Moundville III), most of Moundville's resident population vacated the center, and the palisade ceased to be maintained. As residential spaces were vacated across the site, a series of cemeteries were established and the number of burials at the site peaked during this interval. In essence, Moundville became a necropolis, a center of mortuary ritual for the region as a whole. The mounds on the southern portion of the site ceased to function as burial grounds, and the focus of mortuary ritual, including that of the elite, shifted to offmound cemeteries. Conversely, those earliest occupied mounds in the northern portion of the site, those nearest the river, show vigorous use. And although long-distance exchange declined somewhat, the prestige-goods economy continued to function. Much of the iconographically rich SECC material from elite contexts at Moundville seems to date from this time.

During the Parmountcy Entrenched era the once-thriving center of Moundville was radically transformed to a largely vacant and unpalisaded ceremonial center. People had moved up and down the Black Warrior so that by the end of the Moundville II phase there were seven probable late Moundville II mound centers in use. At this time the "tributary economy was in full swing, as numerous second-order administrative centers mobilized the labor and agricultural surplus of a farmstead-based population numbering perhaps 10,000 people." Both north and south of Moundville, second-order mound sites peaked at eight, reflecting the increasing rural population and the virtual emptying of the primary center.[66]

No doubt, by the removal of the palisade the elite believed the sociopolitical climate to be secure. However, I would like to point out that the dispersal of the population and the virtually unpopulated primary center would have left the entire Moundville system exposed to attack. Chiefs, cult paraphernalia, exotics, cornfields, and most of the population were largely unprotected. Interestingly, early in this stage the chiefdom of Coosa, located one hundred miles to the east, rose to prominence. And most important to this study, it was at the end of this stage (ca. 1450 CE) that a portion of the Moundville population removed to the virtually unpopulated upper Alabama River Valley, adjacent to the Shine II Lamar territory.

During Collapse and Reorganization (1450–1650 CE, late Moundville III and Moundville IV), Moundville continued to be utilized for mortuary ritual but on a much smaller scale, and several additional mounds at the primary center were abandoned. Mortuary mounds no longer received tombs of the elite, and fewer burials were being placed in the offmound cemeteries. Nucleated villages began to appear adjacent to the second-order mounds up-and downriver from Moundville. However, most, if not all, of the secondary mounds ceased to be used by the mid-1500s. As we will see, by this time much of the population began moving to the upper Alabama River Valley, and it is probable that all of the mounds at Moundville were abandoned by the end of the sixteenth century.

The dependence on maize also dropped significantly during this time, with people depending more on wild foods. Subsequently the population suffered from a high pathogen load exacerbated by malnutrition.[67] Because the chiefdom was especially vulnerable during this time, the apparent decline of corn in the Moundville IV diet could have been a product of external attack with consequent robbing and plundering of cornfields. More likely it was the result of the dry periods during the Little Ice Age. A decline in cultivated species has also been found in Summerville IV and Sorrells contexts on the central Tombigbee.[68] And in the Savannah River area, Anderson documented dry periods during portions of the fourteenth, fifteenth, and sixteenth centuries that produced shortfalls in corn production and thus acted as a likely contributor to chiefly cycling.[69] This dry period of the Little Ice Age may have occurred across much of the middle South contributing to the instability of many chiefdoms.

As Moundville was going through its decline and reorganization, the Soto *entrada* passed through the Black Warrior Valley encountering the province of Apafalaya and, unknowingly, the once mighty chiefdom of Moundville in collapse. Much of the grandeur that had once been Moundville's now was found by Soto in the province of Tascalusa in central Alabama.

Big Eddy Phase, 1450–1575 CE

The Big Eddy phase refers to a group of sites with mounds located on the upper Alabama River from about three miles southwest of Montgomery and northeast to the junction of the Coosa and Tallapoosa Rivers (see map 11).[70] Following the river, this area is approximately twenty-five miles in length. Big Eddy phase sites include Big Eddy, Charlotte Thompson, mounds in Thirty Acre Field, Jackson Lake, and Fort Toulouse mound and village site.[71] In addition, there were two mounds (now destroyed) that once existed on the bluff of the present site of Montgomery (most likely Big Eddy phase sites).[72] The known Big Eddy mound total is approximately eight.[73]

An isolated late Big Eddy village also is at the Ebert-Canebrake site, located at the junction of Calebee Creek and the Tallapoosa River. Although a Big Eddy site, Ebert-Canebrake is about thirty-five miles east of the center of the Big Eddy phase territory and on the eastern end of Shine II phase territory (see map 11). Additionally, the ceramics from this site include a Lamar minority that consists primarily of Lamar Plain (Lamar Complicated Stamped is virtually absent), indicating some interaction with Lamar Variant Shine II people nearby. Radiocarbon dates range from 1300 to 1600 CE.[74]

The towns and mound centers constituting the Big Eddy phase were almost certainly the chiefdom or province of Tascalusa visited by the Soto *entrada* in 1540. Tascalusa's central town of Atahachi is probably the Charlotte Thompson site, situated approximately three miles below Montgomery in a big bend of the Alabama River. Spanish artifacts from both the Soto and Luna expeditions are present from top to bottom in the mound at the Charlotte Thompson site.[75]

I have argued elsewhere that the Big Eddy complex is part of the Moundville Variant.[76] The population forming the Big Eddy phase was an apparent product of a site-unit intrusion from the Black Warrior River Valley because the ceramics of this phase are like those of the late Moundville III phase.[77] Although we now have a much better understanding of the relationship between the Big Eddy phase and Moundville III phase, problem-oriented excavations need to be undertaken at Big Eddy phase components to further explicate this relationship.

It is interesting that by far the most numerous shell gorget type found within the Big Eddy phase area is the Spaghetti Style. The other area producing the greatest number of this gorget style is the Dallas Variant, Koasati area of the lower eastern Tennessee Valley. From the spatial distribution of this gorget style, Lankford concludes "there must have been ongoing communication between the two polities of these areas and that it most certainly implies alliances, intermarriages, and probably even a common Language."[78] If Moundville Variant peoples did indeed speak a dialect of Alabama, the Dallas, Koasati, and Big Eddy phase people were probably linguistically related, and we know that the later Alabama and Coushatta spoke related languages.[79] Tristán de Luna artifacts found in the Charlotte Thompson mound indicate that Big Eddy phase mound building continued until the late sixteenth century.[80] In the Black Warrior Valley Late Moundville III mound sites of comparable age with similar ceramics are found at the White site, the Stephen's Bluff mound, and Snow's Bend mound.[81]

Finally, along the middle Alabama River, the Furman phase was a product of a movement of Pensacola Variant peoples up the Alabama River and interacting with Big Eddy phase people (see map 11). At the Durant Bend site, for example, the ceramic complex shows a blending of the Big Eddy and Pensacola complexes.[82] Durant's Bend was the Furman phase community nearest to Big Eddy phase communities. The Furman phase most likely represents the province of Mabila where Soto encountered a massive Indian resistance.

The Abercrombie Phase, 1500–1600 CE

The Abercrombie phase area is located sixty miles east of the Tallapoosa River on the middle Chattahoochee River near the Fall Line (see map 11). The appearance of this complex on the middle Chattahoochee is another part of the equation in our understanding of the early Creeks. The Abercrombie phase is contemporaneous with the Stewart phase, and both date from 1500 to 1600 CE. The Abercrombie phase is the last ceramic phase characterized by mound building along the central Chattahoochee. Abercrombie phase components are found at the Abercrombie and Kyle sites on the Chattahoochee.[83]

The first discussion of Abercrombie as a phase was by Frank Schnell. Schnell does not discuss many specifics of phase content, but instead he contrasts the Abercrombie ceramic complex with contemporaneous complexes along the middle and lower Chattahoochee. He notes that although the Abercrombie phase bridges the protohistoric gap, there are no trade goods in the majority of components with it. Knight and Mistovitch expand on Schnell's initial description of Abercrombie and give a brief discussion of the phase in terms of space, time, and content. They emphasize the presence of a very few early Spanish beads with a beginning date of 1550 CE for the Abercrombie phase. Marvin Smith believes that the general lack of trade goods is more likely attributable to the relative lack of excavation. However, taking Schnell's observation that the majority of Abercrombie contexts have not yielded trade goods, it is probable that at least part of the Abercrombie phase is prehistoric. There remains an extensive amount of excavated material from the Abercrombie site in the Columbus Museum awaiting analysis. The study of this material should produce a better understanding of the temporal parameters and cultural relationships of the Abercrombie phase.[84]

The Abercrombie phase is an intriguing phenomenon for two primary reasons. First, morphologically the shell-tempered ceramic complex represents a distinct break with the preceding South Appalachian Tradition, Lamar-related Bull Creek and Stewart complexes of the area.[85] Second, Abercrombie settlement and demography show an apparent severe reduction in site frequency and distribution from the previous Lamar-related phases. Known Abercrombie components are restricted to Russell County, Alabama, and Muscogee County, Georgia, with the two major sites being the Abercrombie and Kyle sites, although similar materials have also been reported at site 1He34 and by 9cla83.[86]

Because the Abercrombie phase dates to the contact era, this seeming severe population loss has been attributed to the spread of European-introduced epidemic disease into the southern United States.[87] However, I view this so-called reduction as a direct result of the movement of a Moundville Variant group from the west into the area, those who settled two major *talwas*, known historically as Cusseta and Coweta. The Abercrombie phase did not evolve out of the local Lamar Variant, Stewart phase. Rather, Abercrombie has its origin in the central Alabama Big Eddy phase, and specific morphological parallels in the ceramics can be found between the Big Eddy and Abercrombie phases. Because the Big Eddy phase was the product of the decline of Moundville, the ultimate origin of the Abercrombie phase was the Late Moundville III phase of the Black Warrior Valley. The Abercrombie phase then is the easternmost extension of the Moundville Variant.

The Abercrombie phase can be considered the archaeological documentation of the Cusseta migration legend as told by Tchikilli in the early eighteenth century. This legend states that the Cusseta migrated from the west to the Chattahoochee River. The Cusseta's western origins could well have been the Moundville chiefdom. The Cusseta migration legend, as given in a speech by Chigelly in 1735 and recorded by Thomas Causton, explains the origins of the Cusseta people from a mystical point in the west.[88] After resolving a brief dispute, the Apalachicola and Cusseta peoples decided to "be all one." Chigelly asserted that the Cusseta and Coweta were the people thus recognized to be the head towns of the Upper and Lower Creeks. In addition, the Cusseta credited themselves with the establishment of the Coweta and taught them to build mounds and even gave them their name. In time the Coweta earned the distinction as one of the four foundation towns of the Creek Confederacy along with Cusseta, Abhika, and Tuckabatchee. It thus seems fitting that the word Coweta is derived from the Muskogee verb *vytv*, "to go," for this migratory group of people.[89] John Worth argues that available historical evidence indicates the Coweta and Cusseta were Muskogee-speaking migrants into the central Chattahoochee River Valley where they met the indigenous Stewart phase Lamar people who probably spoke Hitchiti. In addition, Worth argues that the Abercrombie site (1Ru11) is the Coweta Tallahassee town while Kyle's Landing Mound (9Me2) is the Cusseta town.[90] The archaeology clearly shows that the Stewart phase was an *in situ* development and the product of continuity with the preceding Bull Creek phase.[91]

Because Abercrombie phase people occupied the same sites or area as Stewart phase people at the Chattahoochee River Fall Line, the Abercrombie and Stewart complexes were most likely contemporaneous or at least partially contemporaneous (beginning ca. 1500 CE and lasting until 1600 CE).[92] In fact, both Stewart phase and Abercrombie phase complexes co-occur at the Abercrombie site (1Ru61).[93] A plural society then existed on the middle Chattahoochee much like that of the contemporaneous Big Eddy and Shine II phases of central Alabama. By approximately 1600 CE the Stewart and Abercrombie ceramic complexes had morphologically fused, thereby evolving into the Blackmon phase ceramic complex.

Kymulga Phase, 1500–1650 CE

The other major cluster of towns that became part of the historic Creek Confederacy was on the Coosa River in Alabama. These towns had their roots in the Kymulga phase of the central Coosa River Valley (see map 11). The Kymulga phase was first defined by Rick Walling, with additional interpretation by Knight. Knight estimated the Kymulga phase to date from 1500 to 1650 CE. The Kymulga phase ceramic assemblage is quite interesting in that three parent complexes are evident within the Kymulga assemblage that have distinctly different origins: Big Eddy-Late Moundville III, Lamar, and local Terminal Woodland Ellis phase (who made grog-tempered pottery).[94]

It is clear that the Kymulga phase complex is a product of a plural society. Because the assemblage is comprised of predominantly shell-tempered Late Moundville III ceramics, it is considered part of the Moundville Variant and more closely related to Moundville than Lamar. Knight suggests that the Kymulga phase people are related to the historically known Abhika group of Creek towns that resided in this area.[95] By the seventeenth century, however, the Abhikas were probably comprised of the people of both the Kymulga and Coosa chiefdom who had moved downstream.

The Hernando de Soto *entrada* through Central Alabama, 1540 CE

At the time of the Soto *entrada* into central Alabama in 1540, plural societies existed in the areas that would later form the Creek Confederacy. These communities formed when the people of the once-great Moundville chiefdom moved east and fused with local groups to form new polities. On the middle Chattahoochee the Moundville Variant, Abercrombie phase people and the Lamar Variant, Stewart phase people coexisted. On the Coosa were the blended Kymulga phase people. On the lower Tallapoosa and upper Alabama the Lamar Variant, Shine II; Moundville Variant, Big Eddy; and Pensacola Variant, Furman phase people lived in separate but spatially close polities. Additionally, on the Black Warrior descendents of the Moundville chiefdom continued to live in their homeland but in greatly reduced circumstances (see map 11).

Taking this archaeological evidence then, one can see that during the late summer of 1540 Hernando de Soto encountered a central Alabama cultural landscape comprised of three provinces, or chiefdoms. Reaching the area after an arduous sixteen-month journey through the length of Georgia and parts of Florida, South Carolina, Tennessee, and finally Alabama, Soto entered the rich environment of central Alabama near the

peak of fall harvest. Soto likely anticipated a chance for rest and plentiful food after his trip through the Appalachians as he entered the mild
mid-September climate of central Alabama. He confiscated food stores,
demanded burden bearers, and took the chiefs hostage in the manner to
which he was accustomed. Surely he had no inkling of what was about
to transpire during the following three weeks as Tascalusa, "a powerful
lord and very feared in the land," guided him down the Alabama River
to the province of Mabila.[96] The chronicles indicate that Tascalusa had
some degree of authority over all three provinces. He was clearly the
most prominent regional political figure and was likely the chief of a
paramount chiefdom that included all three provinces, Talisi, Tascalusa,
and Mabila.

The province of Talisi probably was situated within the lower Tallapoosa
River Valley where the river flows along the Fall Line.[97] This part of the
Tallapoosa is environmentally diverse with the Piedmont uplands situated
to the north and the wide Tallapoosa floodplain to the immediate south
in the Coastal Plain. Spatially and temporally the province of Talisi most
likely correlates with the Shine II phase. To reach this area Soto traveled
four days across a frontier from the province or village of Tuasi.[98] The
drainage divide trail that he followed may be the same as that followed by
Andrew Jackson in 1814 to reach the same section of the Tallapoosa from
Fort Strother, located on the middle Coosa River.[99] The principal town of
the province of Talisi was also called Talisi. This may be site 1Ee32, located
within the big bend of the lower Tallapoosa River three miles south of the
modern town of Tallassee, Alabama. A large Shine II phase midden and
mound is situated here within the neck of the river and surrounded by a
large stretch of bottomland along the lower Tallapoosa River.[100]

Soto stayed at Talisi town for ten days. Here, according to Garcilaso, he
learned that the primary town of Tascalusa was located twelve or thirteen
leagues distant. From Talisi Soto was guided down the Tallapoosa River
Valley by Tascalusa's emissaries, passing through Casiste and then Caxa
(Caxa is most likely either the Shine II sites of Jere Shine, 1Mt6, or Kulumi,
1Mt3). The appearance of the name Casiste on the Tallapoosa in the Soto
record is important as the next appearance of this name in the historic

documents is the Spanish version, Kashita, which refers to a town on the middle Chattahoochee.[101]

The Ebert-Canebrake site may be Casiste. As mentioned earlier, the ceramics on this site, although situated in the Shine II phase area, are late Big Eddy phase, Moundville Variant that are normally found thirty miles to the west on the upper Alabama River. Current excavations also indicate the site to be a very compact village of daubed houses situated inside a possible palisade.[102] I believe the site to have been an administrative outpost founded for the purpose of collecting tribute from the Talisi province during the lifetime of chief Tascalusa. The outpost could also have served as a jumping-off point for the Moundville Variant people who migrated to the Chattahoochee River and established Coweta (the Abercrombie site) and Kashita (the Kyle site) as discussed above (see map 11).

Upon reaching the nearby Alabama River, Soto spent the night on the eastern shore opposite the village of Humati (most likely the Jackson Lake site) within the upper Alabama River Valley and in the province of Tascalusa. Spatially and temporally the Big Eddy phase coincides with the province of Tascalusa and most likely represents this polity (see map 11). From the camp at Humati Soto continued down the Alabama River to a new town called Uxapita. This town may be the now destroyed mound pair that once sat on the bluff at Montgomery near where I-65 now crosses the Alabama River. The next and last site visited within the province of Tascalusa was the capital Atahachi, which the chroniclers called "a new town."[103] Atahachi may likely be the now-destroyed Charlotte Thompson site that was excavated by C. B. Moore at the beginning of the twentieth century.

Here Soto met Tascalusa. Rangel describes Tascalusa's regal bearing: "on Sunday, the tenth of October, the Governor entered the town of Tascaluca, which was called Atahachi, a new town; and the cacique was on a mound to one side of the plaza, about his head a certain headdress like an almaizar, worn like a moor, which gave him appearance of authority, and a pelote or blanket of feathers down to his feet, very authoritative, seated upon some high cushions, and many principals of his Indians with him."[104] Garcilaso described Tascalusa as, "the tallest Indian and of the finest figure that these Castilians saw in all their travels through La

Florida."[105] Tascalusa was a noble and impressive cacique, representing the grandeur that had once been Moundville's, from which his predecessors originated.

After a two-day stay at Atahachi, Rangel indicates that the army proceeded for two days across open country, encountering no people and spending the night in the open.[106] According to the scenario presented here, this would put Soto's army moving into the province of Mabila as represented by the Furman phase area (see map 11). The two-day march through an empty region may represent a buffer zone between the provinces of Tascalusa and Mabila. However, the archaeology indicates otherwise as there is a major Furman phase community at Durant Bend and a smaller community at site 1Au7, both within this suspected buffer zone.[107] After the march the Soto party arrived at Piache, "a high town, upon the bluff of a rocky river," where the army spent two days building canoes to cross the river while withstanding an attack by the chief of Piache.[108] Piache was surely a town in the Mabila province. The location of Piache is not clear, but a likely location is the white chalk bluffs at Selma, Alabama. The area has undergone extensive building and disturbance, and although no sixteenth-century sites have been found on the Selma bluffs, the 1733 Baron de Crenay French map locates a village named Panchy in this general locality.[109]

The information pertaining to the distance traveled between Piache and the town of Mabila is not clear. Rangel states that "on Saturday, the sixteenth of October, they departed from there [Piache] and went into a forest," but he does not elaborate on distance traveled. He indicates they spent the next night at an unnamed palisaded village. The only Furman phase village in the vicinity of Selma that might be a candidate for the unnamed palisaded village is the historic site of Cahaba, twelve to fifteen miles downriver from Selma. After departing the unnamed village, the army arrived at another palisaded village after only a two-hour march.[110] This village was Mabila. Current survey efforts, however, have not located another Furman phase village within a two to three hour march from Cahaba that could be Mabila. Chief Tascalusa guided the Spaniards to Mabila where Soto's army encountered a very large Native force hiding within the houses of the palisaded town. The ensuing battle killed at least several thousand Indians. Garcilaso de la Vega indicates approximately eleven thousand Natives were killed, but he was prone to exaggeration. Rangel indicates three thousand Indians were killed.[111]

The chiefdom of Tascalusa, represented by the Big Eddy phase as argued here, seems to have been one of the most highly organized provinces, or chiefdoms, encountered by the Soto *entrada*. Even though Soto only spent two days at Tascalusa's principal town of Atahachi, there is a good amount of description for it. In organizational terms Atahachi was a nucleated town with an obvious hierarchical social organization. It is significant that Tascalusa's emissaries met Soto at the neighboring province of Talisi (the Shine II phase), indicating that Tascalusa could freely send such messengers into Talisi and probably held some sort of influence or control over the province. His emissaries accompanying the Soto army through Talisi and then with Tascalusa through Tascalusa and into Mabila may imply that Tascalusa controlled not only his province but also the provinces of Talisi and Mabila. If such is the case, then this may account for the large minority of Big Eddy phase pottery on the Jere Shine and Kulumi sites (both Shine II) sites as well as the late Big Eddy single component Ebert-Canebrake site well in Shine II territory. After the battle of Mabila the process of mound building continued until at least some time shortly after 1560, as evidenced by the Spanish items of Luna and Soto origin found in the Charlotte Thompson mound (the probable site of Atahachi).[112]

After the battle of Mabila, Soto continued northwest and next encountered the province of Apafalaya on the Black Warrior River. Apafalaya was clearly a mere echo of its former glory. Although it was "well provisioned," there are no descriptions of grandeur, no mounds being used, and no chiefs with entourages. There is only one chief, Apafalaya, even mentioned at this town. Talicpacana and Moçulixa, two other towns in this area also mentioned in the Soto narratives were surely the later villages reported in central Alabama by Marcos Delgado in 1686 as Pagna (Pacana) and Qulasa (Muklasa).[113]

But what effect did the Soto expedition through central Alabama have on Native inhabitants? Perhaps the most immediate consequence was the losses in the battle of Mabila. According to the Spanish accounts, this battle killed up to three thousand Natives. If the words of Garcilaso are credible, it may have been that Tascalusa assembled warriors from several provinces for this battle, meaning that the populations of those provinces over which Tascalusa had influence were all affected. Such population losses would have had long-term effects on food production, among other things. Also, it seems probable that the introduction of European pathogens by Soto's army would have led to a large loss of life. Such disruptions may have resulted in the hierarchical collapse of communities and polities along with a loss of knowledge as elders died before passing along their knowledge of medicine history, custom, and social organization.[114]

Alabama River Phase, 1575–1700 CE

After Soto's *entrada* the people of central Alabama began to reorganize their lives. The material culture of the upper Alabama River Valley for this time period is known as the Alabama River phase. Spatially this phase extends from the junction of the Coosa and Tallapoosa rivers and down the Alabama River within Monroe County (see map 12). The Alabama River phase is the result of both a direct local development out of the Big Eddy phase and the final abandonment of the Black Warrior Valley. Consequently, Alabama River phase and Moundville IV phase ceramics are virtually indistinguishable.[115]

Mortuary structures and mound building, indicative of a ranked society or chiefdom, were no longer present during the Alabama River phase. These were replaced with compact villages without mounds. In addition, there was a change from elaborate burial accoutrements to burials with little or no grave goods, and by the early seventeenth century a distinctive form of burial interment had appeared — burial (frequently multiple) in large urns.[116] Mound building and other public works were discontinued; thus we may presume that the organizing social and political force behind them, at least in part, had also collapsed.[117]

People also experienced a period of poor health. An exhaustive study of 182 individuals from the Warrior, Tombigbee, and Alabama rivers indicate a dramatic increase in porotic hyperostosis and other infections during the period of the Summerville IV, Moundville IV, and Alabama

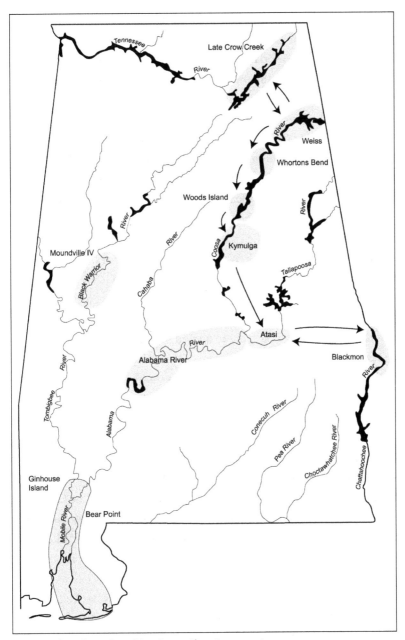

Map 12. Selected Late Protohistoric manifestations, ca. 1600–1700 CE.

River phases.[118] As noted by Hill, "this pattern indicates that nutritional stress was essentially a way of life, at least by the later part of the proto-historic period."[119] Her data indicate increasing hyperostosis from late Mississippian through the protohistoric. And as indicated by Brannon, seventy-five percent of urn burials contained remains of children and infants. This increase in porotic hyperostosis and infection correlates with the pattern of the increased use of noncultivated wild species that has also been noted within the middle Tombigbee River Valley.[120]

The Alabama River phase developed out of the in situ Big Eddy phase, but it was also a product of the movement of people out of the Black War-rior Valley. When Soto reached the Black Warrior, people were manufac-turing very Late Moundville III or early IV ceramics.[121] Soto encountered several villages in the Black Warrior valley with names very similar to those that would later appear in central Alabama. Within the province of Apafalaya on the Black Warrior, Soto passed through the towns of Taliepacana and Moçulixa, and once in the province of Chicaza in present-day Mississippi, he met a cacique named Miculasa and passed through another province subject to Chicaza — Alimamu — that was most likely in the vicinity of Line or Tibbee Creek near Starkville, Mississippi.[122]

The next documentary evidence for these towns comes one hundred and forty years later, in 1686, when the Marcos Delgado expedition reached the junction of the Coosa and Tallapoosa Rivers. Delgado noted the towns of Pagna (Pacana), Qulasa (Muklasa), and Aymamu (Alabama) were "all of one nation." According to Delgado, these people had migrated to central Alabama "from the interior" region, fleeing from the Chata and many wars.[123] The ceramics indicate that all of these named groups on the upper Alabama came from the Warrior and Tombigbee River Valleys. We know that the Black Warrior Moundville IV complex was manufactured after 1575, and more recently Knight and Steponaitis proposed a terminal date of 1650 (see map 12).[124] In the central Tombigbee River Valley of the Gainesville Reservoir area, the Summerville IV phase ceramics also were being manufactured during this time.[125] Just northwest of the Gainesville Reservoir along Tibbee Creek, a tributary of the Tombigbee, is the Sor-rells phase that has a very similar complex to Summerville IV.[126] On the upper Alabama River of central Alabama, the comparable complex is the Alabama River phase.[127]

All of these are late Moundville Variant phases. Hence during the seventeenth century late Moundville Variant phases extended in an arc, basically following the Black Prairie from east central Mississippi to central Alabama. The upper Alabama at the juncture of the Coosa and Tallapoosa rivers became the core of the Alabama coalescence, although the Alabama River phase extended from the junction of the Coosa and Tallapoosa Rivers and down the Alabama River within Monroe County (see map 12).

By the early eighteenth century the Alabama River phase people living near or at the junction of the Coosa and Tallapoosa rivers became collectively known as the Alabamas, and they spoke a Muskogean language now known as the Alabama language.[128] Because the people who made up the early eighteenth-century Alabama originated from Moundville Variant peoples — Sorrells, Summerville IV, Moundville IV, and Alabama River — it stands to reason that the Moundville chiefdom spoke a language that is most closely related to the historic Alabama.

Ocmulgee Fields Variant: Atasi phase, 1575–1700 CE

By approximately 1575 CE on the lower Tallapoosa, the Shine II phase was replaced by the Atasi phase. Although the Atasi phase ceramics have been described as "perfectly intermediate in style between Shine II Lamar and local Historic Creek," we now understand the content and the processes that formed the previous Shine II phase.[129] Recall that Shine II was a plural society composed of both Lamar Variant people and a minority of Moundville Variant people. Moundville Variant people migrated to the upper Alabama River Valley when Moundville fell to form the Big Eddy phase. By the late Big Eddy phase (1500–75) a minority of late Big Eddy phase people may have been living among Shine II people along the lower Tallapoosa River. Thus the Atasi phase ceramic complex developed as a product of this Shine II plural society and consequently demonstrated attributes in common with Big Eddy-Late Moundville III phase ceramic complexes.[130] There is likewise a Lamar Variant aspect of the Atasi phase parentage evident in the ceramics, specifically the predominance of sand-over-shell tempering with shell tempering being most prevalent early in the phase.[131] This blend of Moundville and Lamar variant ceramic traditions probably reflects a linguistic and cultural blending of these groups.

I think it no coincidence that the Atasi phase developed within that part of the lower Tallapoosa River Valley between Calebee Creek and the big bend of the Tallapoosa River. It is here that the Ebert-Canebrake site is found, a single component Moundville Variant, late Big Eddy phase site in the midst of contemporaneous Lamar Variant, Shine II phase sites.[132] In other words, the plural Atasi society formed on the foundation of the plural Shine II society on the lower Tallapoosa. The Atasi phase people would form part of the core of the historic Upper Creeks.

Blackmon Phase, 1600–1700 CE

The core of the historic Lower Creek on the Chattahoochee River comes to us archaeologically as the Blackmon phase. Before the initial recognition of the Blackmon phase, there were no criteria for distinguishing Blackmon phase assemblages from the earlier Abercrombie and Stewart phases that were contemporaneous. Blackmon phase ceramics are a blend of the coarse sand-tempered late Stewart complex, Lamar Variant, and the primarily shell-tempered Abercrombie complex, Moundville Variant.[133]

During the late Blackmon phase, sometime between 1685 and 1695, a majority of middle Chattahoochee River Valley people moved to the Macon, Georgia, area as a result of conflicts with the Spanish. It was during this time that the English and Spanish were actively competing for political influence and trading partners among the Creeks. This European rivalry resulted in an English trading house being built at Macon in 1685 and Spanish Fort Apalachicola being built on the Chattahoochee just south of Coweta in 1690. From Fort Apalachicola the Spanish burned several nearby Creek villages. Consequently the late protohistoric components in the Macon area are a product of a transported late Blackmon phase complex from the Chattahoochee River Valley. From their Ocmulgee location these groups conducted slave raids against the Florida mission Indians, and these raids led to the destruction of the Spanish missions and the dispersal of the north Florida Indians. These groups returned to the Chattahoochee in 1716 after the Yamassee War.[134]

The Blackmon phase ceramic complex is morphologically similar to the Atasi phase ceramics of the Tallapoosa River Valley. This similarity makes sense given that both have parent complexes of similar origins (the Moundville and Lamar variants). The Stewart phase ceramic complex has a similar developmental history as the Tallapoosa River Valley Shine II complex, while the origin of the Abercrombie phase is to be found in the central Alabama Big Eddy phase. Hence the Blackmon and Atasi ceramic complexes are morphologically comparable due to similar origins. In addition, during the Blackmon phase several groups of Koasati from east Tennessee (making shell-tempered late Dallas ceramics) moved into the Chattahoochee Valley. The most obvious result of this final mixing is the addition to the assemblage of Dallas ceramics, specifically McKee Island Cord Marked and Crow Creek Noded.

Chickasaw Connections

In the last few years evidence has accumulated indicating a connection between the Sorrells and Summerville IV complexes of the central Tombigbee River Valley and a portion of the historic Chickasaw ceramic assemblage. As previously discussed, the Sorrells and Summerville IV ceramic complexes have their origin in the Moundville Variant. They are the central Tombigbee River Valley counterpart to Moundville IV of the Black Warrior River Valley and the Alabama River phase complex in central Alabama. Aided by the earlier work of James Atkinson, Jay Johnson has built a convincing case in which the primary Chickasaw population at some time moved northward out of the Tombigbee River bottoms into the Black Prairie Hills of north central Mississippi. These people were making a ceramic complex most like the Sorrells-Summerville IV complexes except that during this time the tempering agent changed from live shell to fossil shell that is plentiful in the Black Prairie. Johnson completes the movement out of Tombigbee Valley early; he states that "by 1450 the major river terraces and the bottom of the Tombigbee had been abandoned and the population had relocated to the uplands of the Black Prairie." He points out that no diagnostic Chickasaw types and the potential proto-Chickasaw type, Alabama River Appliqué, are found on Mississippian Period sites excavated in preparation for the Tennessee-Tombigbee Waterway. Furthermore, the Yarborough site (22C1814), located in the bottoms of one of the major tributaries of the Tombigbee River as it crosses the Black Prairie in Clay County, is the only non-upland site in northeast Mississippi to have yielded any prehistoric or protohistoric Chickasaw pottery types.[135] However, it should be noted that Alabama River Appliqué is diagnostic of the Summerville IV phase of the middle Tombigbee Valley, the late Moundville III and IV phases of the Warrior, and Summerville IV sites along the Tombigbee.[136] Because the Summerville IV phase ends at approximately 1650, the end of this phase should date the final abandonment of the Tombigbee Valley.[137]

Although it is clear that the Tombigbee Valley was not abandoned by 1450, some populations may have moved out at that time. Abandonment did not occur until around 1650 or maybe 1680 if we take Marcos Delgado's encountering the Aymamu (Alabama) and Qulasa (Muklasa) on the upper Alabama to reflect the last movement of people out of the middle Tombigbee River Valley area and the Pagna (Pacana) from the Black Warrior River Valley. It is important that a segment of the Summerville IV-Sorrel's phase people and the late Moundville III and IV people of the Black Warrior and elsewhere manufactured virtually the same ceramic complex. It appears that when the central Tombigbee River Valley was abandoned, the Alabama group, or at least part of it, moved to the upper Alabama River Valley, while the remainder of the group moved with the people of Chicaza north into the rolling hills of the Black Prairie to become the historic Chickasaws.[138]

There was also another group on the upper Tombigbee that Atkinson identifies as part of the early historic Chakchiuma (ca. 1700), whose town was found on the northern edge of Starkville, Mississippi. Based on their ceramics, these people were a late Moundville Variant-derived group. The ceramics are similar to very late Summerville IV, Sorrells, or Moundville IV phase assemblages. Although it is difficult to determine that these ceramics were indeed a Chakchiuma product, Atkinson correctly points out the similarities between these ceramics and those of the Alabama River phase and historic Creek. During the Soto *entrada* the chief of the Sacchuma, who may have been part of the Paramountcy of Chicaza, was named Miculasa.[139]

As we have seen, Miculasa (Moçulixa) was the name of a town on the Black Warrior encountered by Soto and the name of a late seventeenth-or early eighteenth-century Creek town (Muklasa) on the lower Tallapoosa. This duplication of names in the Tombigbee, Black Warrior, and lower Tallapoosa rivers should reinforce the notion that the people from these three areas were closely connected, with the eighteenth-century towns on the lower Tallapoosa-upper Alabama rivers originating from the sixteenth-century towns on the Black Warrior-middle Tombigbee river areas.

During the Early Mississippian Period between 1050–1100 CE, the Moundville Variant appeared over a broad area of the middle South. The earliest fluorescence of the Moundville Variant was in the Shiloh phase of the western Tennessee River Valley. In an area between forty-four km up river and twenty-four km down river from the Shiloh site are at least five and possibly nine other Shiloh phase mound sites that taken together contain as many as forty-five mounds. Current radiocarbon evidence indicates that the Shiloh phase chiefdom fissioned between 1300 and 1400 CE.[140] However, initial fissioning may not have meant total abandonment. As we have seen, after the initial fissioning at Moundville ca. 1450, it was another two hundred years until the Black Warrior River Valley was completely abandoned.

In this chapter I have posited that before its final fissioning the Shiloh phase went through a process I have dubbed budding, which resulted in the spread of the Moundville Variant southward into many of the river drainages of present-day Alabama. These early Moundville Variant phases, related by a very similar content, are generally contemporaneous with the Black Warrior River Valley Moundville I phase (see table 2). The Medieval Warm Period may have been one important variable contributing to the spread of early Moundville Variant polities to the areas of the Hobbs Island, Bessemer, Tibbee Creek, Summerville I, Moundville I, Haysop Creek, Brannon, and Cedar Creek phases. In all of these areas communities manufacturing early Moundville ceramics represented not only stark technological change but also organizational transformations or discontinuities when contrasted with the local ceramically diverse Terminal Woodland groups. I suggest here that these morphologically similar, yet geographically distinct, early Moundville Variant phases are very alike because they have a common origin and are products of budding from the western Tennessee Valley Shiloh phase. The budding of segmented lineages from the Shiloh area created a belt of Moundville I related chiefdoms, and as these chiefdoms budded further into the hinterlands, they evolved into distinct yet ethnically related groups.

For instance, by 1100 CE an early Moundville Variant group had budded to the lower Chattahoochee River Valley (via the Bessemer and Brannon phases) where it quickly evolved into the Rood Variant.[141] A similar process produced the Pensacola Variant. By 1200–50 CE the Black Warrior River Valley paramount chiefdom of Moundville had become the dominant as well as most populous and complex manifestation of the early Moundville Variant. Soon after its rise to prominence the Moundville chiefdom budded down the Tombigbee River to the Gulf Coast to form the Pensacola Variant, which evolved into a distinctive complex as a result of interaction with lower Mississippi River Valley Plaquemine populations.

In the Black Warrior River Valley, between 1200 and 1450 CE, the Moundville chiefdom consolidated, reaching its height of complexity and power. At 1200 CE for the first time it was enclosed by a palisade, while other Moundville Variant phases across the region disappeared, with the exception of those within the central Tombigbee River Valley. And although Moundville imported metamorphic lithics in large quantities from the Coosa Valley, Moundville Variant population centers were confined to the Black Warrior and central Tombigbee River valleys.[142]

By 1450 CE Moundville began a period of collapse and fissioning, which was within one hundred years of the disappearance of the palisade, with a substantial depopulation of the Moundville central town.[143] Significantly, the fissioning of Moundville resulted in the fragmentation and removal of a relatively large segment of the Black Warrior River Valley population to the upper Alabama River Valley. I refer to this Late Moundville III group on the upper Alabama as the Big Eddy phase. Big Eddy phase communities of the upper Alabama River Valley were established less than ten miles from the Shine II phase communities of the lower Tallapoosa River Valley.

The close geographical proximity of these two distinct groups (and their distinct ceramic complexes) resulted in the eventual mixing of Shine II and late Big Eddy populations, and in the case of the Ebert-Canebrake Big Eddy people settled a town within the Shine II territory. I propose here that the Big Eddy phase represents the chiefdom of Tascalusa and that the Shine II phase represents the chiefdom of Talisi, both of which Soto encountered in 1540. In addition, sometime before 1540 CE the Pensacola Variant penetrated up the Alabama River Valley almost to Montgomery, Alabama, in the form of the Furman phase. The Furman phase was the most northern manifestation of the Pensacola Variant, probably constituting the province of Mabila. This was the situation in central Alabama on the lower Tallapoosa and upper Alabama rivers at the time of contact. The three provinces of Talisi, Tascalusa, and Mabila — all geographically close and all related through their historic Moundville connections — may have been united under the paramount chiefdom ruled by the chief Tascalusa. Savannah Variant groups from the east also migrated into present-day Alabama during the Mississippian Period.

At approximately the same time as the development of the Moundville chiefdom ca. 1050 CE, the Etowah chiefdom appeared in the upper reaches of the Coosa River drainage. With the decline of Etowah around 1350–75 CE its subsequent fissioning would result in the formation of the sixteenth-century paramount chiefdom of Coosa, centered in the nearby Coosawattee River Valley. At the same time a Savannah Variant, Wilbanks phase group migrated southward to an area near Troy, Alabama. Within less than fifty years they appear to have fused (at least ceramically) with the Terminal Woodland Autauga complex and evolved into the Shine II (Lamar) complex of the lower Tallapoosa River Valley around 1400 CE. Thus both the Little Egypt phase-Coosa province and the Shine II phase-Talisi province formed as a product of the Etowah River Valley cycling process.

Sometime near contact, Big Eddy phase communities from the upper Alabama moved into the middle Chattahoochee River Valley. These towns are known archaeologically as the Abercrombie phase and historically the *talwas* of Cusseta and Coweta. This west-to-east migration also reflects the Cusseta migration legend and their western origins.

Between 1450 and 1575 CE the Big Eddy population (most likely the province of Tascalusa) was a close neighbor to the Shine II population (most likely the province of Talisi) and the Furman phase population (most likely the province of Mabila). During the first half of the sixteenth century and an extended period of favorable rainfall, the chiefdoms of Coosa, Talisi, Tascalusa, and Mabila would have grown into the polities recorded by Hernando de Soto in 1540.[144] On the Chattahoochee the Stewart phase and Abercrombie phase people would have established chiefdoms as well, although Soto did not pass through their territory. After the Soto *entrada* mound building; the exchange of prestige goods, already reduced; and most of the trappings of chiefdom organization had disappeared across central Alabama.

What was the effect then of the Soto *entrada* on the Native polities? It is not clear if the polities of Mabila, Tascalusa, and Talisi were recognizable polities when Tristán de Luna's men ventured through the area twenty years later in 1560.[145] Given the structure of Mississippian chiefdoms, polity organization would have been severely damaged by the debacle with Soto. Soto journeyed through the area at harvest time, and feeding a six-hundred-plus army would have adversely affected the supply of corn for that winter and probably any surpluses that would have been stored for the next year. In addition, the numerous people killed in the battle of Mabila may have been warriors from all of these provinces. And lastly, European pathogens could have dealt another blow to population numbers and polity organization. All of these combined factors likely resulted in the hierarchical collapse of communities and polities as well as a loss of organization that would include storage and dispersion of food reserves. It is important to recognize that not long after the Soto and Luna expeditions, both the Atasi and Blackmon phases developed (ca. 1575–1700 CE, see table 2), and the archaeology of these phases indicate that the chiefdoms Soto did not encounter on the Chattahoochee were probably devastated to the point of collapse.

It is probable that Spanish contact resulted in chiefdom collapse and fusion or partial fusion of the Big Eddy and Shine II populations, thus resulting in the development of the Atasi population. In terms of ceramic taxonomy the development of the Blackmon phase on the Chattahoochee and the Atasi phase of the lower Tallapoosa (ca. 1575–1600) signal the development of the early Okmulgee Fields Variant and the people we refer to as the Creeks.[146] Along the upper Alabama River, the Alabama River phase begins around 1575 CE. By 1650 only a few villages remained in the Black Warrior River Valley, and by 1680 the Alabama removed from the central Tombigbee following earlier Late Moundville III kinsmen to central Alabama. As previously stated, ceramically the Alabama belong solidly within the Moundville Variant. They removed to central Alabama with the Muklasa and Pacana, and all became known as the Alabamas, speakers of the Alabama language.[147]

The southward movement of the Koasati to join the Alabama during the seventeenth-century may also have its roots in the prehistoric movements of Moundville Variant peoples. The Koasati people most likely have their origins in the east Tennessee Dallas Variant. A plausible connection between them and the Moundville Variant people on the upper Alabama is that when the Shiloh chiefdom fell ca. 1300 CE, a Moundville Variant population moved up the Tennessee Valley to fuse with a late Hiwassee Island group.[148] This migration could also help explain the close parallels in grammar and vocabulary between the Koasati language and the Alabama language as both possibly could have their origins in the Moundville Variant.[149]

Between the time of the Soto and Luna expeditions, the province of Coosa began a period of collapse. Late Dallas towns from the eastern Tennessee River Valley and upper Coosa River Valley towns began moving south, settling first on the upper and middle Coosa and then along the lower Tallapoosa or middle Chattahoochee. In the lower Tallapoosa River Valley the *talwas* of Hoithlewaulee, Tuskegee, Okfuskee, and Kulumi represented them.[150]

With the arrival of the Coosas, Coushattas (Koasatis), and later some Natchez, Shawnees, Yuchis, and others in the seventeenth and eighteenth centuries, the central Coosa, the lower Tallapoosa, upper Alabama, and the Chattahoochee formed a culturally diverse region, the homeland of a truly coalescent society. Yet the core of the Creek population was the people of Lamar, Moundville, and probably local Late Woodland descent. The rich Fall Line environment of the central Alabama region permitted room for many refugee groups caught in the shatter zone of disease, slaving, and warfare.[151]

Thus the Creeks were formed. When Carolina traders entered south central Georgia to find late Blackmon phase people, the traders never really understood who these people were. In 1670 traders from Charleston stopped at Ochese Creek and bartered manufactured goods for deerskins. They referred at first to the Indians as Ochese Creek and then eventually simply as Creeks.[152] As stated in the editors' introduction to Hahn's *Invention of the Creek Nation*, "when English colonists first coined the term 'Creek Confederacy,' they were trying to make political sense of a group of Indians that was very important to them but one they did not understand very well."[153]

Only now are we poised to begin to understand the deep historical roots of the Creek coalescence. The Creek Confederacy, famous during the Historic Period as a pluralistic society that welcomed refugees, formed from a pluralistic core group of Lamar and Moundville segmented lineages. Migrations, fusions, and coalescences then were nothing new to the core people of the Creek Confederacy. These processes had been a part of their history for at least five hundred or more years at the time of contact. That they would put these old ways of dealing with neighbors and stresses to a new use makes sense, and indeed the innovative use of old ways is what we see in the shatter zone as the Creek Confederacy became the preeminent coalescent society.

Notes

1. Smith, "Aboriginal Population Movements in the Early Historic Period Southeast"; Smith "Aboriginal Population Movements in the Postcontact Southeast"; Waselkov and Smith, "Upper Creek Archaeology"; Worth, "Lower Creeks"; and Hahn, *Invention of the Creek Nation*.

2. Fairbanks, "Creek and Pre-Creek"; Fairbanks, "Abercrombie Mound"; Fairbanks, "Some Problems"; Knight, "Ocmulgee Fields"; and Knight, "Formation of the Creeks."

3. Because of the addition of these smaller nonlocal groups into the Creek home-land, the multiethnic historic Creeks have been referred to as a coalescent society of late seventeenth-and early eighteenth-century origin; Hudson, Introduction, xxxvi. For discussions on the various groups who joined the Creek Confederacy during the Historic Period, see Worth, "Lower Creeks"; Waselkov and Smith, "Upper Creek Archaeology"; and Smith, "Aboriginal Population Movements in the Postcontact Southeast."

4. Definition from Glossarist, "Archaeology Explorer," *http://www.glossarist.com/ glossaries/humanities-social-sciences/archaeology.asp*, accessed July 29, 2007.

5. Lehmer, *Introduction to Middle Missouri Archaeology*; Jenkins, "Archaeo-logical Investigations in the Gainesville Lake Area"; and Jenkins and Krause, *Tombigbee Watershed*.

6. Krause, "History of Great Plains Prehistory," 63.

7. Anderson, *Savannah River Chiefdoms*, 1–52, 9 (quote).

8. Jenkins and Krause, *Tombigbee Watershed*, 127–28. See also Service, *Origins of the State*, 78.

9. Anderson, *Savannah River Chiefdoms*, 87–93; and Blitz and Lorenz, *Chatta-hoochee Chiefdoms*, 140. In this discussion of budding I assume that the societies in question had a kin-based segmentary organization in which lineages were grouped into larger corporate units based on the concept of common descent.

10. Service, *Primitive Social Organization*, 157.

11. Welch, *Moundville's Economy*; and Welch, "Control over Goods."

12. Service, *Primitive Social Organization*, 136, 142, 143 (quote). In the case of Moundville the data from Bottle Creek suggest that the Moundville people were most active in extralocal exchange fairly early in the polity's lifespan; Welch, "Control over Goods," 86.

13. Anderson, *Savannah River Chiefdom*; and Blitz and Lorenz, *Chattahoochee Chiefdoms*, 131–33.

14. Lamb, "Climate History."

15. Blitz and Lorenz, *Chattahoochee Chiefdoms*, 132.

16. The documents relating to Soto and Luna are in Clayton, Knight, and Moore, *De Soto Chronicles*, and Priestly, *Luna Papers*. For a discussion of the location of Coosa, see Hudson et al., "Coosa."

17. Terminal Autauga ceramics are over ninety percent plain with minorities of pinched and a brushed type referred to as Anderson Incised. The paste is coarse sand-tempered gray ware, which was smoothed while leather hard. This smoothing resulted in the slightly protruding dark coarse sand paste referred to

as a salt and pepper effect. This paste is very similar to both Lamar and Ocmulgee Fields. See Chase, "New Pottery Types From Central Alabama"; Chase, "New Pottery Types from Alabama"; Chase, "Brief Synopsis"; Chase, "Prehistoric Pottery of Central Alabama"; Dickens, "Archaeology of the Jones Bluff Reservoir"; Jeter, "Late Woodland Chronology"; and Jenkins and Sheldon, "Native American Culture Change."

18. Chase, *Averett Culture*; Chase, "Reappraisal of the Averett Culture"; Schnell and Wright, *Mississippi Period Archaeology of the Georgia Coastal Plain*; and Blitz and Lorenz, *Chattahoochee Chiefdoms*, 137. Averett components also can be accompanied by a minority of Etowah Valley ceramics.

19. Blitz and Lorenz, *Chattahoochee Chiefdoms*, 68.

20. Sheldon, Mann, and Cottier, "Late Woodland-Mississippian Culture Contact in Central Alabama."

21. Hally and Rudolph, *Mississippi Period Archaeology of the Georgia Piedmont*; and Hally and Langford, *Mississippi Period Archaeology of the Georgia Valley and Ridge Province*.

22. Caldwell, "Trend and Tradition."

23. Hally, "Overview"; Hally and Langford, *Mississippi Period Archaeology of the Georgia Valley and Ridge Province*; Hally and Rudolph, *Mississippi Period Archaeology of the Georgia Piedmont*; and Schnell and Wright, *Mississippi Period Archaeology of the Georgia Coastal Plain*.

24. Hally and Rudolph, *Mississippi Period Archaeology of the Georgia Piedmont*, 51, 55.

25. Mann, "Reappraisal"; and Jenkins, "Early Origins."

26. Schnell and Wright, *Mississippi Period Archaeology of the Georgia Coastal Plain*, 28.

27. Caldwell, "Investigations at Rood's Landing"; and Ferguson, "South Appalachian Mississippian." For the middle period at the Singer Moye site, see Knight, "Ceramic Stratigraphy"; or more recently Blitz and Lorenz, *Chattahoochee Chiefdoms*, 70.

28. Brooms, "Archaeological Inventory"; Chase, "Prehistoric Pottery of Central Alabama"; Mann, "Reappraisal"; and Jenkins, "Early Origins."

29. Jason Mann of Troy State University is currently restudying this material. Further research should examine how this complex relates to the lower Tallapoosa Valley Shine II Lamar forty miles to the north.

30. The only decorative treatments (fifteen to eighteen percent) are concentric circle and bull's-eye complicated stamped. Etowah complicated stamped is absent.

Rims are predominately unmodified, although a minority may be fingernail or reed punctuated. No rim straps or appliqué rims are present. Tempering is fine brown sand, although a gray coarser Lamar like paste occurs as a minority. A minority complex found in direct association is a sand-tempered late Rood III or early Singer phase complex of the lower Chattahoochee River Valley. This complex is characterized by plain standard jars with small strap handles and Columbia Incised. No Cool Branch Incised is present. For these ceramic types, see Hally and Rudolph, *Mississippi Period Archaeology of the Georgia Piedmont*, 56–61; Sears, *Wilbanks Site*; and Wauchope, *Archaeological Survey*.

31. Blitz and Lorenz, *Chattahoochee Chiefdoms*, 69–70.

32. Anderson, *Savannah River Chiefdoms*, 84–87.

33. Chase, "Prehistoric Pottery," 88. Terminal Autauga ceramics that were found also at the Jere Shine site were predominantly plain. Anderson Incised (which is actually combed or brushed) and Autauga Pinched together comprise less than eight percent of the assemblage. The Autauga paste is gray with particles of dark sand and difficult to sort from Lamar ware.

34. Three sherds of Walnut Creek Complicated Stamped are also present in the Autauga zone at the nearby Kulumi (1Mt3) site; however more of the Shine II rims at this site are appliqué rims and are thus later.

35. One partially excavated house at 1Mt3 is round and semi-subterranean; notes on file at Auburn University, Montgomery, Alabama.

36. In contrast, Terminal Woodland Autauga sites extend up tributary streams and lacked mounds.

37. Smith, "Rise and Fall of Coosa."

38. Hally and Langford, *Mississippi Period Archaeology of the Georgia Valley and Ridge Province*, 68–71.

39. Smith, "Rise and Fall of Coosa," 147.

40. Langford and Smith, "Two Late Lamar Sites," table 5.

41. Smith, "Rise and Fall of Coosa," 147–48.

42. Chase, "New Pottery Types from Central Alabama"; Chase "Pottery Typology Committee"; and Chase "Brief Synopsis."

43. Chase notes that Shine II Lamar ceramics include Lamar Plain, Lamar Complicated Stamped, Lamar Roughened, and a minority of Fort Walton Incised (zone punctuated) and Walnut Creek, sand-tempered bull's-eye complicated stamped wares. He also notes a "Dallas-like pottery which is shell tempered and often burnished"; Chase, "Prehistoric Pottery," 87–88. More recent analysis of the Lamar material from the Kulumi site (1Mt3) by Jenkins and Sheldon in "Native American

Culture Change" indicates that Lamar Complicated Stamped may comprise 16 to 18 percent of the coarse sand-tempered Shine II complex. The minority bold incised and zone punctuated although sparse may comprise up to 4 percent of the complex in one unit. Leon Check Stamped comprised a maximum of 1.3 percent.

44. Hally, "Overview," 147. The Jere Shine Lamar is characterized by a form of early Lamar rim mode. Rim forms at Kulumi more frequently have either a narrow appliqué strip or a broad appliqué strip as wide as 14 mm. Rim sherds at the nearby Jere Shine site do not display appliqué rims, a finding that means that they are earlier than those from Kulumi. The Jere Shine site Lamar rims are identical to those found on Walnut Creek phase rims with no appliqué rim strip.

45. For the date, see Chase, "Prehistoric Pottery," 88. On the Spaghetti Style gorget, see Wesson, Wall, and Chase, "Spaghetti Style Gorget," 135.

46. Muller, "Southern Cult," 20; and Jones, "Southern Cult Manifestations."

47. Jenkins and Sheldon, "Native American Culture Change."

48. This complex includes Mississippian Plain *var. Warrior* and Bell Plain *var. Hale* with minorities of Carthage Incised *vars. Carthage, Fosters,* and *Poole.* Another distinctive minority is Alabama River Appliqué. The primary Bell Plain vessel shapes are the diagnostic Late Moundville III short-necked and flaring rimed bowls. Beaded rims on burnished black hemispherical bowls are present as well as human head medallions (rim riders). No engraved types are present. The percentage of shell tempered pottery varies from thirty to forty percent among units. See Jenkins and Sheldon, "Native American Culture Change"; and Steponaitis, *Ceramics,* figures 51a, 51e, 51n, and 51p. The Kulumi complex is slightly later than the Big Eddy phase components illustrated by Clarence Bloomfield Moore since Bell Plain effigies and Carthage Incised *var. Akron* are absent from the Kulumi site; Moore, "Certain Aboriginal Remains." An identical late Big Eddy phase component is also present at the Jere Shine site, 1Mt6. It should be emphasized that decorative modes remained within their distinctive temper groups, that is, complicated stamping was always on coarse sand-tempered paste and Carthage Incised usually occurred only on a shell-tempered paste.

49. Knight and Steponaitis, "New History," 7–9. The ceramic content of early Moundville Variant phases is characterized by the diagnostic Moundville Incised *var. Moundville. Var. Carrollton* is a minority early but increases in frequency through time, becoming the primary decorated type by 1200 CE. A coarse shell-tempered ware dominated by globular jars of Mississippian Plain comprises approximately ninety percent of the assemblage early in the sequence but decreases very gradually through time as Bell Plain increases. Moundville Incised (the arch

motif) is the most numerous decorated type of the early Moundville Variant. A fine shell-tempered, black-burnished ware comprises the types Bell Plain, Carthage Incised, and Moundville Engraved. These occur as minorities early in the sequence but increase through time to twenty-seven percent (at Moundville) by Moundville III times. Moundville Engraved and Carthage Incised, usually bowls or bottle forms, are most numerous about midway through the sequence. Moundville Engraved is most numerous toward the end of the first half of the sequence. Carthage Incised is rare in the early portion of the Moundville Variant but becomes the major decorated type during the late Moundville Variant. The beaded rim first occurs at the midpoint of the sequence and is most prevalent toward the later part of the sequence. Importantly, the short-neck bowl is diagnostic of the late Moundville III time frame. Alabama River (Campbell) Appliqué and Barton Incised vars. *Demopolis* and *Cochran* are diagnostic of the late Moundville Variant. The deep flaring rim bowl is also an important form at the end of the sequence. A diagnostic house type of the early Moundville Variant is the depressed floor, or basin house; however, the basin house quickly disappeared as the wall trench house became more prevalent. The PA and ECB Tracts at Moundville are good excavated examples of early Moundville Variant components, while the Bessemer site is only slightly later. See also Scarry, *Excavations on the Northwest Riverbank*; Welch, "Occupational History"; and Jenkins, "Terminal Woodland/ Mississippian Transition."

50. Jenkins and Krause, *Tombigbee Watershed*; and Jenkins, "Terminal Woodland/Mississippian Transition."

51. Jenkins, "Terminal Woodland/Mississippian Transition."

52. Knight and Steponaitis, "New History"; Jenkins, "Terminal Woodland/ Mississippian Transition"; and Jenkins, "Early Origins."

53. Welch, *Moundville's Economy*, figure 6.4.

54. Fuller, "Out of the Moundville Shadow," 62. Plaquemine interaction was very important in the evolution of Pensacola ceramics. One can only wonder what other aspects of Pensacola culture, such as language, were affected.

55. For the Pensacola Variant, see Stowe, "Pensacola Variant"; and Fuller, "Bear Point Phase." For the Conecuh drainage, see Jenkins and Mann, "Archaeological Study." For discussions about the Pensacola Variant west to the Mississippi Sound, see Blitz and Mann, *Fisherfolk, Farmers, and Frenchmen*.

56. Jenkins, "Prehistoric Chronology"; Jenkins, "Terminal Woodland/Mississippian Transition"; and Blitz and Lorenz, "Early Mississippian Frontier." Early Rood I ceramics are morphologically very similar to Moundville I ceramics, with

shell-tempered Moundville Incised as the dominant decorated type. Moundville Incised and the sand-tempered equivalent Cool Branch Incised are characterized by the distinctive arch incised on the shoulder of the standard form; Blitz and Lorenz, *Chattahoochee Chiefdoms*, 68, 137.

57. Scarry and Payne, "Chronology of Mound Construction."

58. Blitz and Lorenz, *Chattahoochee Chiefdoms*, 68. For another discussion of the relationship of early Rood and early Fort Walton, see Schnell, Knight, and Schnell, *Cemochechobee*, 243–46.

59. Scarry and Payne, "Chronology of Mound Construction"; and Lankford, *Looking for Lost Lore*. This may help explain Martin's observation in "Languages," 71, that the Apalachees are closest linguistically to the Alabama Koasati.

60. Blitz, *Ancient Chiefdoms*, 39–68.

61. Steponaitis, *Ceramics*; and Little and Curren, "Moundville IV Phase."

62. Knight and Steponaitis, "New History."

63. Welch, "Outlying Sites," 162.

64. Scarry, *Excavations on the Northwest Riverbank*; Scarry, "Domestic Life," 73; and Knight and Steponaitis, "New History," 12–14.

65. Knight and Steponaitis, "New History," 14–17.

66. Welch, "Outlying Sites," figure 7.7, 163; and Knight and Steponaitis, "New History," 20 (quote).

67. Schoeninger and Schurr, "Human Subsistence," 125, 132; and Knight and Steponaitis, "New History," 22. In addition, Hill notes a dramatic increase in porotic hyperostosis for the Black Warrior and Tombigbee valleys; Hill, "Proto-historic Aborigines."

68. For Summerville IV, see Caddell, "Plant Resources," 273. For Sorrells, see Caddell, "Plant Remains from the Yarborough Site."

69. Anderson, Stahle, and Cleveland, "Paleo Climate."

70. The early Big Eddy phase ceramic complex is shell tempered and included Mississippian Plain *var. Warrior*, Bell Plain *var. Hale*, and Carthage Incised *Vars Akron, Carthage, Poole*, and *Fosters* and are executed on the diagnostic Late Moundville III short-necked bowl as illustrated in Steponaitis, *Ceramics*, figures 51m, 51o, and 51q. Alabama River Appliqué occurs as a minority, and Moundville Engraved appears to be absent. Moore illustrates Late Moundville III ceramics diagnostic of this phase. One miniature vessel of Carthage Incised *var. Fosters* was recovered from the Charlotte Thompson site. The bottle form of Carthage Incised *var. Carthage* was recovered at Thirty Field Mound. Several bird effigies characteristic of Carthage Incised *var. Akron* were found by Moore at Charlotte

Thompson and Thirty Acre Field; Moore, "Certain Aboriginal Remains," figures 41, 42, 59, and 68. These bird effigies are outward facing as described by Steponaitis for the Moundville III phase; Steponaitis, *Ceramics*, 125.

71. Almost no sites in the Big Eddy area have been recently excavated by trained archaeologists; the latest excavations were those conducted by David Chase at the Jackson Lake site during the late 1960s. The Jackson Lake field notes and artifacts are curated by Auburn University in Montgomery, Alabama. The ceramics are those of the early Big Eddy phase complex (see note 70 above for a description of Big Eddy ceramics), associated with a minority of coarse sand-tempered Lamar Variant ceramics, specifically Lamar Plain and Lamar Complicated Stamped.

72. Blue, *Brief History*, 4.

73. The adjacent Shine II mound total is also eight, and it may be of interest that the number of secondary mound centers in the Warrior Valley during the Moundville III phase peaked at eight as well; Welch, "Outlying Sites."

74. Marisa Fontana, personal communication, September 2003. Also, Craig Sheldon and John Cottier of Auburn University as well as Cameron Wesson of the University of Illinois–Chicago have conducted excavations at this site.

75. Sheldon, *Southern and Central Alabama Expeditions*, 23–25; Moore, "Certain Aboriginal Remains," 329; and Little and Curren, "Moundville IV Phase," 70.

76. Jenkins, "Archaeological Investigations in the Gainesville Lake Area," figures 19, 20, and 21; and Jenkins and Krause, *Tombigbee Watershed*, figure 24.

77. Steponaitis, *Ceramics*, 114–25.

78. Lankford, *Looking for Lost Lore*.

79. Martin, "Languages," 71.

80. Little and Curren, "Moundville IV Phase," 69–70; and Moore, "Certain Aboriginal Remains," 330–32.

81. Welch, "Outlying Sites," 158–59; Hayward, Curren, Jenkins, and Little, "Archaeological Investigations at Stephens Bluff"; and DeJarnette and Peebles, "Development of Alabama Archaeology."

82. Amanda Regnier, personal communication, August 2004.

83. Blitz and Lorenz, *Chattahoochee Chiefdoms*. Of the excavations conducted by Peter Brannon, David Chase, Joseph Mahan, Ed Kurjack, and Frank Schnell, only Kurjack and Brannon have been reported; DeJarnette, *Archaeological Salvage*; and Brannon, "Aboriginal Remains."

84. Schnell, "Late Prehistoric Ceramic Chronologies," 21–22; and Knight and Mistovitch, *Walter F. George Lake*, 225.

85. Abercrombie phase is characterized by a burnished reduced-fired fine

shell-tempered ware most like Carthage Incised *vars. Carthage, Poole,* and *Fosters* executed on the Moundville III short-neck bowl and flaring rim bowl; Steponaitis, *Ceramics,* figures 51m, 51o, 51q, and 53h. The type Alabama River Appliqué (or Campbell Appliqué *var. Alabama River*) is a distinctive minority, which no doubt has its origins in the Middle Mississippi Valley; Jenkins, *Gainesville Lake Area Ceramic Description*; and Sheldon and Jenkins, "Protohistoric Development." An important type, seeming to appear late in the phase, is Rood Incised, which morphologically duplicates Carthage Incised in all aspects except temper. This type is clearly a sand-tempered copy of Carthage Incised; Knight and Mistovitch, *Walter F. George Lake,* 225.

86. For site 1He34, see Hurt, "Archaeological Survey of the Chattahoochee Valley," 60. For Site 9cla83, see Belovich, Brose, and Weisman, "Archaeological Survey at George W. Andrews Lake," 228.

87. Smith, *Archaeology of Aboriginal Culture Change*; Smith "Aboriginal Depopulation in the Postcontact Southeast"; and Worth, "Lower Creeks," 269.

88. Gatschet, *Creek Migration Legend.* Gatschet interprets the legend to mean that the Cusseta migrated from the Red River area in east Texas.

89. Hahn, *Invention of the Creek Nation*, 10–29.

90. Worth, "Lower Creeks," 272–73. See also Hawkins, *Letters of Benjamin Hawkins*, 54, 63.

91. An important regional constant in this section of the Chattahoochee Valley is that the percentage of complicated stamping decreases through time. In the Stewart Complex the amount of Lamar Complicated Stamped is lower, approximately twenty to forty percent with a higher percentage of incising; Schnell and Wright, *Mississippi Period Archaeology of the Georgia Coastal Plain*, 21. I suspect that the higher percentage of incising is due to these people copying the intrusive Carthage Incised motifs on a sand-tempered paste. It may be important to remember that both times a shell-tempered complex (early Roods I and Abercrombie) was introduced to the Chattahoochee; the acculturation process subsumed the shell-tempered complex to a sand-tempered complex.

92. The radiocarbon dates from the Abercrombie site (1Ru61) date both the Abercrombie and Stewart complexes 1390–1660 and 1420–1620 CE at the two-sigma range; Blitz and Lorenz, *Chattahoochee Chiefdoms*, table 4.1.

93. Blitz and Lorenz, *Chattahoochee Chiefdoms*, 72.

94. Walling, *Lamar in the Middle Coosa Drainage.* For an additional interpretation, see Knight, "Ocmulgee Fields." The complex is unusual in that the incised complicated stamped and burnished plain decorative treatment crosscut the shell,

grit, and grog temper groups. The presence of the short-neck bowl is important because it is also a diagnostic vessel shape of the Late Moundville III phase; Steponaitis, *Ceramics*, 117. Like most western Alabama shell-tempered Mississippian complexes, ninety percent of this complex is plain, with seven percent incised or punctuated. Only two percent of the complex is complicated stamped. Shell is the dominant temper group (fifty-five percent), followed by grit (twenty-nine percent) and grog (ten percent); Walling, *Lamar in the Middle Coosa Drainage*, tables 8 and 10. Incised motifs on short-necked bowls and flaring rim bowls are most like those that occur in late Moundville III; Walling, *Lamar in the Middle Coosa Drainage*, figure 3. Alabama River Appliqué is a minority in this assemblage; Walling, *Lamar in the Middle Coosa Drainage*, figure 6, lower right.

95. Knight, "Ocmulgee Fields," 186.

96. Rangel, "Account," 288.

97. This location of Talisi differs from that of Hudson in *Knights of Spain*, 228, who places it in the vicinity of Childersburg, Alabama.

98. Rangel, "Account," 288.

99. Owsley, *Struggle for the Gulf Borderlands*, 82–83.

100. Knight, *Tukabatchee*, figure 3.1.

101. Garcilaso, "La Florida," 327. Worth in "Lower Creeks," 272, notes the relationship between the Soto period Casiste and the later Kashita, but following Hudson, he places Casiste on the middle Coosa River; Hudson, *Knights of Spain*, 229.

102. John Cottier, personal communication, August 2007.

103. Biedma, "Relation," 228; and Rangel, "Account," 290. On the mound pair at Montgomery, see Blue, *Brief History*, 4.

104. Rangel, "Account," 290–91.

105. Garcilaso, "La Florida," 328.

106. Rangel, "Account," 291.

107. Nance, *Archaeological Sequence*; and Dickens, "Archaeology of the Jones Bluff Reservoir."

108. Rangel, "Account," 291. For the location of Piache, see Hudson, *Knights of Spain*, 234.

109. Swanton, *Early History*, plate 5.

110. Rangel, "Account," 292.

111. Garcilaso, "La Florida," 351; and Rangel, "Account," 294. On Garcilaso, see Galloway, "Incestuous Soto Narratives," 34.

112. Little and Curren, "Moundville IV Phase"; and Sheldon, *Southern and Central Alabama Expeditions*.

113. Galloway, *Choctaw Genesis*, 120–22; and Boyd, "Expedition of Marcos Delgado," 26.

114. Rangel, "Account," 294; Garcilaso, "La Florida," 352–53; and Saunt, "History until 1776," 128. On introduced diseases, see Smith, *Archaeology of Aboriginal Culture*; Larsen, Schoeninger, Hutchinson, Russell, and Ruff, "Beyond Demographic Collapse." See also Kelton, this volume, for a counterargument.

115. The ceramic attributes of these phases have most recently been best summarized by Little and Curren, "Moundville IV Phase." Like the earlier Big Eddy complex, the Alabama River complex is comprised of roughly seventy percent Mississippian Plain. Large rectangular and triangular strap handles, four to a jar, are characteristic of this time frame. The percentage of Bell Plain seems to be slightly higher than previously. Both Alabama River Appliqué and Barton Incised *var. Demopolis* are slightly more numerous that previously, but together they never comprise over two percent of the assemblage. Engraving is absent in Moundville IV and the Alabama River phase. Carthage Incised *vars. Carthage, Fosters,* and *Poole* occur largely on deep flaring rim bowls with motifs occurring on interior rim surfaces. An examination of the curated collections in the Alabama Archives and History in Montgomery indicate that the subglobular bottle with simple base form also occurs. An evolved form of the short-necked bowl occurs that is weakly carinated with a neck that slants outward instead of straight down. The line width of Carthage Incised of this time frame is generally narrower and less well executed than previously. A very small amount (less than a quarter percent) of red-and red-and-white filmed pottery continues from Late Moundville III; Steponaitis, *Ceramics*, 129. This ware is no doubt derived from Nodena and also ancestral to Kasita Red Filmed.

116. Sheldon, "Mississippian-Historic Transition," 78–80; Curren, *Protohistoric Period in Central Alabama*; and Little and Curren, "Moundville," 68. At one time the distinctive burials from this time frame were referred to as the Burial Urn Culture; Brannon, "Urn-Burial"; and Brannon "Aboriginal Remains." In this burial form both infants and multiple defleshed adults were interred in large vessels. The vessels containing the deceased were usually Mississippian Plain *var. Warrior* or less frequently Alabama River (Campbell) Appliqué and Barton Incised *var. Demopolis*. Urn burial is clearly a horizon style most commonly associated with Late Mississippian-Protohistoric Period and the late Moundville Variant in particular. The urn covers are well made, reduced-fired flaring bowls of Carthage Incised *var. Fosters*.

117. Peebles, "Rise and Fall of Mississippian in Western Alabama."

118. Hill, "Protohistoric Aborigines," figure 2.3.

119. Hill, "Protohistoric Aborigines," 29.

120. Brannon, "Urn-Burial," 230; Caddell, "Plant Resources," 273; and Caddell "Plant Remains from the Yarborough Site."

121. Little and Curren, "Moundville IV Phase."

122. Garcilaso, "La Florida," 379–81; Hudson, Smith, and DePratter, "Hernando de Soto Expedition."

123. Boyd, "Expedition of Marcos Delgado," 26.

124. Little and Curren, "Moundville IV Phase," 68–70; and Knight and Steponaitis, *Archaeology of the Moudville Chiefdom*, figure I.2.

125. Mann, "Classification of Ceramics from the Lubbub Creek"; Jenkins and Meyer, "Ceramics of the Tombigbee-Black Warrior River Valleys"; and Blitz, *Ancient Chiefdoms*.

126. Hudson, Smith, and DePratter, "Hernando de Soto Expedition." For the Sorrells ceramic complex, see Marshall, "Lyon's Bluff Site (22OK1) Radiocarbon Dated"; Solis and Walling, *Archaeological Investigations at Yarborough*; and Blitz, *Ancient Chiefdoms*.

127. Sheldon, "Mississippian-Historic Transition"; and Sheldon and Jenkins, "Protohistoric Development."

128. For a discussion of the Alabama coalescence, see Shuck-Hall, this volume. On the Baron De Crenay Map of 1733, the area is referred to as Pays Des Alibamons; Swanton, *Early History*, plate 5.

129. Knight, "Ocmulgee Fields," 184.

130. The incised surface treatments of the Atasi ceramic complex are predominantly western Mississippian (Moundville Variant) in origin. Complicated stamping is gone, and like western Mississippian complexes, the ceramics are predominantly plain, with incised motifs very much like those of the late Moundville III-Big Eddy phase. Like the Moundville fine ware, a significant number of Atasi phase vessels were reduction fired and burnished; Knight and Smith, "Big Tallassee," 65.

131. The weak carinated bowl (no sharp break at the shoulder) was introduced into the Tallapoosa River Valley at this time. Although the carinated bowl appears to have been present in earlier north Georgia Savannah and Lamar complexes, it did not occur in the Tallapoosa Valley until the Atasi phase; Sears, *Wilbanks Site*; and Wauchope, *Archaeological Survey*, figures 32 and 38. The Atasi phase casuela does not have the pronounced shoulder angle characteristic of the later Tallapoosa phase.

132. Another Atasi phase site, the Big Tallassee, is located six or seven miles upriver from the Ebert-Canebrake site and across from Tuckabatchee; Big Tal-

lassee and Atasi sites are type sites for the Atasi phase; Knight and Smith, "Big Tallassee."

133. Schnell, "Late Prehistoric Ceramic Chronologies," 67–69; Knight and Mistovitch, *Walter F. George Lake*, 225–26; and Knight, "Ocmulgee Fields," 189. Mistovitch and Knight developed a very workable type-variety nomenclature for Protohistoric and Historic Creek ceramics; Mistovitch and Knight, "Excavations at Four Sites." Based on their analysis of the Blackmon site, approximately fifty-five percent of the Blackmon assemblage is shell-tempered plain. Shell-tempered cob marked and brushed together comprises no more than three percent of the complex, while Fortune Noded and McKee Island Cord Marked together comprised less than one half percent. A rare shell-tempered incised mode occurs that is very similar to the sand-tempered Ocmulgee Fields Incised except that the line width is broader. Approximately forty-four percent of the complex is sand tempered, with thirty-two percent plain and ten percent untempered Toulouse Plain. Lamar Incised *var. Ocmulgee Fields* accounts for less than one half percent. Complicated and check stamping are rare; Mistovitch and Knight, *Excavations at Four Sites*, table 10. Like the Atasi phase complex, at least ninety percent of the Blackmon complex is plain and has the general character of a Mississippian complex from the west except for a very small amount of brushed, cob marked, check stamped, and complicated stamped.

134. Waselkov, "Macon Trading House"; Mistovitch and Knight, *Excavations at Four Sites*, 39; Schnell, "Beginnings of the Creeks"; Worth, this volume; and Kelton, this volume.

135. Johnson, "Chickasaws," 85–90, 89 (quote); and Atkinson, "Historic Chickasaw." For the Yarborough site, see Solis and Walling, *Archaeological Investigations*.

136. Mann, "Classification of Ceramics from Lubbub"; and Blitz, *Ancient Chiefdoms*.

137. Johnson, "Chickasaws," figure 4.1.

138. Boyd, "Expedition of Marcos Delgado," 26.

139. Atkinson, "Historic Contact Indian Settlement." Chakchiuma ceramics are characterized by deep flaring rim bowls with very fine line Carthage Incised motifs; in addition, Alabama River Appliqué occurs as a minority.

140. Welch, *Archaeology at Shiloh Indian Mounds*, table 8.1, 277.

141. Blitz and Lorenz, "Early Mississippian Frontier"; Blitz and Lorenz, *Chattahoochee Chiefdoms*; and Jenkins, "Terminal Woodland/Mississippian Transition."

142. Gall and Steponaitis, "Composition and Provenance."

143. Knight and Steponaitis, *Archaeology of the Moundville Chiefdom*, 21.

144. Anderson, "Chiefly Cycling," 179.

145. On the Luna expedition, see Priestly, *Tristán De Luna*; and Priestly, *Luna Papers*.

146. The early Ocmulgee Fields Variant has a generally western Mississippian appearance as over ninety percent of the assemblage is plain. Burnished incising (often fired in a reducing environment) is the most important decorative treatment; Rood Incised is a sand-tempered copy of late Big Eddy Carthage Incised motifs. Complicated stamping is gone, replaced by cob marking and brushing. The late Ocmulgee Fields assemblage is characterized by increases in frequency brushing during the subsequent Tallapoosa phase of the Lower Tallapoosa River Valley and the Lawson Field phase of the Chattahoochee River Valley. Together the Atasi, Blackmon, Tallapoosa, and Lawson Field ceramic complexes comprise the Ocmulgee Fields Variant.

147. Boyd, "Expedition of Marcos Delgado," 26.

148. Evidence for the possible interaction between early Moundville or Shiloh groups, and Hiwassee Island groups is that Hiwassee Island vessel shapes, decorative modes, and handle styles are very similar to early Moundville styles. Additionally, Moundville Incised *var. Moundville* is a part of the Dallas ceramic complex as illustrated in Lewis and Kneberg, *Hiwassee Island*, plate 57, lower right; further, the Dallas Decorated type shares attributes of motif and vessel form with Carthage Incised and Bell Plain; Lewis and Kneberg, *Hiwassee Island*, plates 52a, 52b, and 54.

149. Martin, "Languages," 71–72.

150. Smith, "Rise and Fall of Coosa," 145. An eighteenth-century Creek occupation occurs in the upper level of the old Kulumi site, 1Mt3, which is located on the south bank of the Tallapoosa and which also contains a large earlier Shine II phase component. A single component, later Kulumi occupation, is located on the north bank.

151. See Milner, this volume, for the Natchez dispersal; see Warren, this volume, for the Shawnee movement to Creek country. On the Indian slave trade, see Ethridge, "Shatter Zone"; Bowne, *Westo Indians*; and Gallay, *Indian Slave Trade*.

152. Crane, "Origin of the Name of the Creek Indians"; and Wright, *Creeks and Seminoles*, 2.

153. Green and Perdue, Series Editors' Introduction, xi.

9 | Alabama and Coushatta Diaspora and Coalescence in the Mississippian Shatter Zone

SHERI M. SHUCK-HALL

History is replete with diasporas. Often defined as a voluntary or involuntary migration out of an ancestral homeland, a diaspora identifies a people who migrate through shifting and ephemeral political borders in search of a new space and yet retain some kind of connection (emotional and otherwise) to their past homelands.[1] The political and social landscape from which diasporic groups eventually flee can be described as a shatter zone.[2] As previous chapters in this volume have examined, the geographic boundaries of a shatter zone are often chaotic, violent, and claimed by many. However, people living in a shatter zone are not doomed to an existence of disempowerment and social degradation; they also rebuild their homes, renew cultural practices, and most importantly, recreate their lives.

The shatter zone model described in this volume and its association with diasporic movements provides a useful framework for examining the link between the ancient Mississippians and the historic Native peoples of the colonial South. From 1500 to 1700 the European invasion radically altered the world of Native Southern peoples. The Mississippian chiefdoms collapsed, and their political orders changed. They suffered from debilitating disease and physical displacement, both of which contributed to the breakdown and transformation of Southern peoples. The Mississippian social order (ca. 900–1700 CE) with its centralized hierarchical chiefdoms diminished; highly organized power relations that were necessary for building ancient political edifices evaporated. Well-established trading networks among ceremonial centers declined, and a new type of European commerce that was focused on the acquisition of European goods, especially guns, in exchange for American Indian slaves arose. The last stage of this centuries-long instability initially resulted in fragmentation as the weakened Mississippian chiefdoms, unable to withstand the strain, collapsed. Mapping a course of survival, peoples from fallen chiefdoms began a history of long and short migrations within the shatter zone and eventually merged into the well-known coalescent societies of the eighteenth century, including the Creeks, Choctaws, Chickasaws, and Catawbas.

The Alabamas and Coushattas, two Southern peoples often neglected in previous scholarship, provide an example of diaspora and coalescence in the shatter zone.[3] They were among many Mississippian groups that experienced traumatic social and political change in the sixteenth and seventeenth centuries. Indeed, the shatter zone in which they lived revolutionized their world. As disease and slave raids devastated their respective communities, they embarked upon a diasporic migration and created a new Native community that remains cohesive to this day. This chapter will trace how the Southern shatter zone motivated American Indian diasporas and the eventual creation of new social entities by examining the case of the Alabamas and Coushattas, two separate and distinct peoples who coalesced but nevertheless retained vestiges of their Mississippian past.

Mississippian Origins

Like the ancestors of many Southern peoples, the forbearers of the Alabamas and Coushattas can be located in the precontact era that archaeologists call the Mississippian Period, the era of the ancient chiefdoms of the South. Both the Alabamas and Coushattas shared similar political and socioeconomic characteristics typical of Mississippian chiefdoms, yet they lived hundreds of miles apart and developed quite separately. As Ned Jenkins discusses in this volume, the historic Alabamas most likely evolved out of the Moundville paramount chiefdom that dominated western Alabama and eastern Mississippi for almost five hundred years prior to European contact (1000–1450 CE). The Moundville Variant had developed out of the Shiloh chiefdom in the western Tennessee Valley; Shiloh then budded and part of its inhabitants migrated to the Tombigbee and the Warrior river valleys between 1050 and 1100 CE.[4] By 1300 CE those on the Black Warrior had become Moundville, a large complex chiefdom that extended fifty kilometers along the river. It looks as though sometime during its early formation, some people from Moundville moved to the Tombigbee River and formed a series of simple chiefdoms, influenced by, but not under, the authority of Moundville.[5] The center of Moundville was located near present-day Tuscaloosa, Alabama, and it encompassed over three hundred acres of fertile floodplain; it included twenty-six earthen mounds, a central plaza, a palisade, and scattered settlements throughout the valley. Moundville's rulers and nobles strictly controlled the nonelite society, who was responsible for providing food and tribute.[6]

Toward the end of Moundville's preeminence, between 1300 and 1450 CE, the chiefdom's center began to show signs of stress. Long-distance exchange started to decline, and soil depletion and exhausted resources further strained the chiefdom. These factors may have led to an out-migration of Moundville's inhabitants; they were leaving the center for the hinterlands. By 1450 settlement patterns began reverting to nuclear villages away from the mound center indicating that they were becoming increasingly independent of Moundville.[7] As discussed in other chapters of this volume, such periods of instability were common historical trajectories for Mississippian chiefdoms, but the reorganization that followed Moundville's collapse is only now coming to light.

As reconstructed by Jenkins, Moundville had collapsed one hundred years before the Soto *entrada*. Many of the people had dispersed down the Tombigbee and east to the Tallapoosa, Alabama, and Chattahoochee river valleys where they formed other chiefdoms such as the famous Tascalusa chiefdom, which was on the upper Alabama River. However, some Moundville descendents stayed on the Black Warrior River and formed the simple chiefdoms of Taliepacana, Moçulixa, Apafalaya, and perhaps others (see map 13).[8]

Unlike their Moundville ancestors, these people relied more heavily on wild foods rather than on the large-scale production of maize. By the sixteenth century these simple chiefdoms suffered from a general decline in health resulting from malnutrition.[9] Meanwhile, those groups on the Tombigbee had moved slightly west by the time of Soto and were organized into several simple chiefdoms, including the Alibamu and Miculasa,

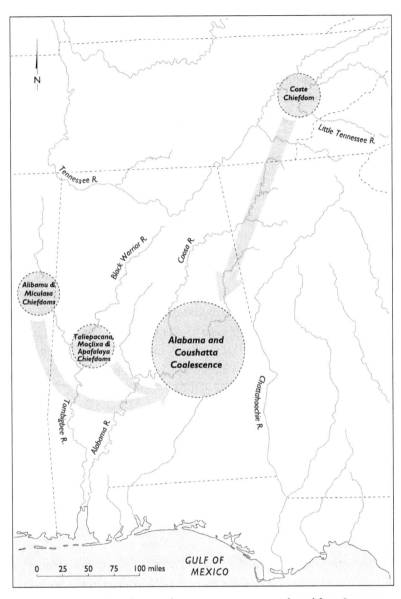

Map 13. Alabama and Coushatta coalescence, ca. 1500–1700. Adapted from *Journey to the West*, Shuck-Hall, p. 26, by permission of the University of Oklahoma Press.

whom Soto encountered. These two chiefdoms were apparently under the authority of Chicaza when Soto saw them. The Chicaza would later form the core of the historic Chickasaws, but the Taliepacana, Moçulixa, Apafalaya, Alibamu, and Miculasa simple chiefdoms would later form the historic Alabamas.

The historic Coushattas most likely were once part of the more distant Coste chiefdom, whose main town was on Bussell Island in the Little Tennessee River.[10] Coste was a simple chiefdom closely affiliated with the larger and more powerful Coosa paramount chiefdom. Coste dwellings circled an open-air ceremonial court, public buildings, and other community structures atop earthen mounds, which were comparable to those found at Moundville. Recent archaeological studies suggest that Coste may have originated from the Moundville Variant at Shiloh in western Tennessee. Instead of budding and migrating to the Black Warrior and Tombigbee river valleys as had the Alabamas' ancestors, Coushatta ancestors budded to the north and created the Coste chiefdom in the eastern Tennessee Valley sometime between 1050 and 1100 CE. In addition to the similarities between Coste (Dallas phase) and Moundville (Moundville II–III) ceramics, Jenkins sees another piece of enticing evidence suggestive of an ancient connection between Moundville and Coste (and hence the historic Coushattas and the Alabamas) to be the Spaghetti Style shell gorget found in both Dallas phase sites and Moundville phase II–III sites.[11]

These simple chiefdoms that would eventually form the historic Alabamas and Coushattas encountered Spanish conquistador Hernando de Soto in the 1540s. Inhabitants of the Coste chiefdom first met the Spaniards on July 1, 1540. The chief of Coste "came forth to receive them in peace" and invited the Spaniards to take shelter in one of the villages.[12] The invitation quickly turned sour when Soto's men, without permission of the chief, took corn from some barbacoas. Unnoticed by the Spaniards, the chief left to gather and arm his men at the main town on Bussell Island at the mouth of the Little Tennessee River. Once Soto arrived, he deflected the chief's anger, eventually capturing him and at least ten of his principal men. The Spaniards stayed for several days and left when the chief met Soto's demands for a guide and porters.[13]

After the battle of Mabila, Soto later traveled through territory along the Black Warrior River. On November 18, 1540, the Spaniards approached Taliepacana. The main town had twenty households and a white-capped mound; its inhabitants had fled, so Soto and his men stayed there for a few days. Soto described neighboring Moçulixa as nine miles north, with the main village located along a high bluff facing the Black Warrior. The people of Moçulixa had evacuated with their food supply, but later they harassed and unsuccessfully invaded the Spaniards' camp. Days later, Chief Apafalaya, who controlled one of the largest mound centers of the same name in the valley outside of Moundville (at Snow's Bend site), met Soto. Based on archaeological evidence, Apafalaya had nuclear settlements with fortifications. Chief Apafalaya had considerable control over the surrounding area, especially as supplies were abundant. Soto took the chief as a prisoner, demanding that he act as an interpreter and guide as the Spaniards left for the Tombigbee Valley.[14]

The chiefs of the Alibamu and Miculasa chiefdoms controlled settlements along the Tombigbee River and met Soto as he entered the chiefdom of Chicaza in the winter of 1541. After considerable delay the chief of Chicaza agreed to meet the Spaniard on January 3. The chief appeared before Soto on a litter held up by his subjects. With him were the chiefs of Alibamu and Miculasa, apparently holding tributary status in Chicaza. Archaeologists have not found the locations of Miculasa or Alibamu, but Charles Hudson suggests that Alibamu (Alibamo) may have been northwest of the main town of Chicaza, near Line Creek, and included numerous small towns each with at least fifteen households. After Soto battled with the Chicazas (which likely included warriors from both Miculasa and Alibamu), the inhabitants of Alibamu led the Spaniards into a trap in April 1541. Armed Alibamu warriors, stationed at their square fortification on Line Creek, outnumbered Soto's men; despite Soto's poor military strategy, his army managed to escape and continued northwest.[15]

Alabama and Coushatta ancestors who appear in these historical records left by Soto's men revealed that their respective settlements along the Black Warrior, Tombigbee, and Little Tennessee rivers all had characteristics of simple chiefdoms. Soto met with their chiefs directly, not groups of noble representatives. There is also no description of these communities treating the chiefs as divine and peerless such as those found in the paramount chiefdom of Coosa. Indeed, it is likely that the chiefdoms of Coste and the chiefdoms of Alibamu and Miculasa were under the subjection of their neighboring paramount chiefdoms, Coosa and Chicaza, respectively.[16] Descriptions also demonstrate that their settlement patterns were those of less populated households, often surrounding a mound and sometimes fortified; absent were the grand plazas and centers for trade. This was the political and cultural landscape of the Alabama and Coushatta ancestors on the eve of their diaspora and coalescence.

Eve of Diaspora

After Soto's attempted conquest of the South, Alabama and Coushatta ancestors may have suffered from the devastating effects of introduced European diseases. Although there is neither documentary nor archaeo-logical evidence for disease epidemics in the interior South before 1696, the oral tradition of the Alabamas and Coushattas recounts how disease spread through their communities long before European settlement in the South. According to their memory, disease befell their people, "causing much trouble and grief everywhere." Their ancestors met in a council to discuss how to eliminate disease from the earth and then collected all of the sickness and placed it in a clay pot. A snipe agreed to take the pot to the sky where it would remain never to return to earth. To the people's disappointment the snipe dropped the clay pot, and when it shattered on the ground, "sickness scattered to all parts of the world again."[17] This memory may echo the early tragedy and suffering from epidemic diseases brought by Soto and other Spaniards. Even before the bulk of European settlers made contact with the Alabamas and Coushattas, pestilence had damaged their weakened chiefdoms.[18]

A few decades after Soto's *entrada* Southern peoples witnessed a second phase of European contact. The Spanish Crown had staked its claim in the Americas, and in 1565 ordered Pedro Menéndez de Avilés to explore and to settle the Floridas. By September 1565 Spain funded the construction of its first fortified settlement at St. Augustine and one year later established Santa Elena (present-day Parris Island); these coastal outposts facilitated Spanish forays into the interior. The Juan Pardo expedition, launched from Santa Elena in 1566, traversed present-day Georgia, North Carolina, South Carolina, and eastern Tennessee. Along his journey Pardo explored the region that eventually would mark the arrival of Spanish colonists and soldiers. Franciscans soon followed and constructed missions in northern Florida and members of coastal chiefdoms settled within these missions.[19]

The Spanish colonization of the South by Spanish Florida paled in comparison to the more successful English colonies, especially as England stepped up its efforts in penetrating the region. After many failed attempts and financial disasters in the Americas, England finally founded the Southern colonies of Jamestown, Virginia, in 1607 and Charles Town, Carolina, in 1670. Settlers in Charles Town recognized that their colony was a buffer to Spanish Florida, and they courted Native allies in order to buttress their military presence against the Spanish. More importantly, the English Crown expected the colony to extract and export local raw materials and resources. These resources included Indian slaves, and Charles Town soon became a commercial center for the Indian slave trade.[20]

Indian slaves were one of the most sought-after commodities throughout the seventeenth century. Alan Gallay has analyzed how various Native communities quickly adapted to this new market. The English, like most Europeans at the time, viewed slavery as a moral, socially acceptable, and legal institution. Natives too understood forms of bondage to be an accepted social institution. Yet with the arrival of a European market for slaves, Indian groups began to consider slaves a commodity that could be exchanged for trade goods, a mind-set that bore full fruit much later when profits from the deer trade declined in the eighteenth century.[21] Prisoners of war were no longer subject to conventional rules of warfare and captivity; instead, Natives brought captives to Charles Town and sold the prisoners to the English in exchange for trade goods such as textiles, metals, weapons, and alcohol. The English then sent the slaves to planters in the North American colonies and the English West Indies.[22]

Many Natives profited from slaving, but many also feared that they too would be vulnerable to slave raids. And as the slave trade widened into the interior South, the Alabamas' ancestors were among many who suffered from its expansion. Those simple chiefdoms on the Black Warrior and Tombigbee Rivers, including the Alibamu, Miculasa, Taliepacana, Apafalaya, and Moçulixa, began to break apart sometime in the seventeenth century, most likely caused by the disruptions from Soto's *entrada*, disease, and slaving. In this area the premier slavers in the middle to late seventeenth century were the Chickasaws, who by this time had moved away from the Tombigbee River and were living at present-day Tupelo, Mississippi. They had earlier established a lucrative relationship with traders from Charles Town, and English agents armed Chickasaw warriors with muskets and led some slaving expeditions against enemy towns. Chickasaw men actively raided Native communities in and around the Mississippi River Valley, as far south as the Gulf of Mexico and perhaps as far east as the Black Warrior River.[23] In 1699 Pierre Le Moyne d'Iberville, French explorer and founder of Louisiana, noted that the Chickasaws "were going among all the other nations to make war on them and to carry off as many slaves as they could, whom they buy and use in extensive trading, to the distress of all these Indian nations."[24] The Chickasaws' years of successful slaving had convinced the French that this group was the dominant Native force in the South.

Indian slavery also had an impact on the people of the Coushatta chiefdom of Coste on the Little Tennessee River. After the paramount chiefdom of Coosa fell in the sixteenth century, the Coste chiefdom also shifted to a smaller community organization. Later documentation describes Coste as a small town, devoid of the large-scale organization that characterized their previous chiefdom. This reduction likely left them more vulnerable to slave raids.[25] The group that threatened Coste was undoubtedly the Westos, who had moved to the Savannah River sometime in the 1660s.[26] As recounted elsewhere in this volume, the Westos had established a profitable slaving partnership with Virginian and Carolina traders. Westo warriors relentlessly raided Native communities throughout the lower South, and they quickly became the enemy of the Florida mission Indians, the coastal Indians, and interior groups such as the Cussetas, Cowetas, Cherokees, and Savannah (who later helped annihilate the Westos in 1682).[27]

The Westos' aggressive participation in the capture and sale of Indians slaves led many groups, including the Coushattas, to fear their very name.[28]

And after the Westos were eliminated from the interior slave trade, the Coushattas then had to fight off raids by Cherokee slavers, who occupied territory in the Appalachian Mountains in Tennessee and western South Carolina and apparently became involved in the slave trade soon after the Westo monopoly shattered. The Coushattas dwindling population at Coste was especially vulnerable to enemy raids. Throughout the late 1680s the Cherokees repeatedly captured the greatly outnumbered Coushattas and sold them to Carolina traders.[29]

Slavers mainly targeted and captured women and children; the men who survived were often tortured and killed. The frequency of slave raids, coupled with losses from disease, was the breaking point for these chiefdoms. In all cases people quit their ancestral lands for safer ground where they could regroup and revitalize their severely damaged populations. They all chose a path of diaspora not only to escape the effects of the shatter zone that engulfed them, but also to shape a new landscape on their own terms.

According to archaeologist Ned Jenkins, sometime in the seventeenth century the Alibamu and Miculasa people on the Tombigbee, as well as the people of Taliepacana, Moçulixa, and perhaps Apafalaya on the Black Warrior, migrated to the northern Alabama River near its confluence with the Coosa and Tallapoosa rivers (near present-day Montgomery, Alabama).[30] This group became known collectively as the Alabamas. The Coushattas, who may have followed the southward path of the scattered Coosas, also quit their homeland in Tennessee and migrated to the same location as the Alabamas sometime in the seventeenth century. By the start of the eighteenth century Europeans and Creeks alike considered the Coushattas as part of the "Alabama Nation."[31] Although they blended their lives with the Alabamas, the Coushattas retained a separate identity.

Both the Alabamas and Coushattas were drawn to the upper Alabama River valley (see map 13). The new location along protective bluffs near the confluence of the Alabama, Coosa, and Tallapoosa rivers provided a better position for the Alabamas and Coushattas to make alliances with their western neighbors who were coalescing into the Upper Creeks. Recognized by outsiders as the Alabama Nation, the Alabamas and Coushattas now comprised a larger polity, and they were less vulnerable to raids. By the start of the eighteenth century they also were better located for trading with the English and later the French.

Coalescence

Why did the Alabamas and Coushattas coalesce after their respective diasporas? The answer can be found in their oral traditions and their Mississippian roots. Although the exact dates of the Alabama and Coushatta diaspora and coalescence are unknown, their shared memory recounts their migrations. Passed down through generations, their oral history describes how a group of their ancestors who lived in an underground cave wanted to see the surface of the earth. After camping three times during their long journey, they discovered the tree of life at the cave's entrance. The Alabamas emerged out of one side of the tree's roots, and the Coushattas surfaced on the other side. Once they saw the light of day, their ancestors discovered the Alabama River that lay before them. The Alabamas and Coushattas established their villages in two bodies. Though they had different origins, they had "always remained near each other."[32] Although separate people, the origin story places them as close entities; they both emerged from the Cosmic Tree, symbolic of their creation and the center of their world. This memory marked the beginning of their new existence together, an existence that they created out of a shatter zone.

The linguistic evidence supports this origin story as the Alabamas and Coushattas shared similar linguistic traits undoubtedly owing to their Mississippian origins. Alabama and Coushatta (Koasati) languages are part of the Eastern Muskogean language family, whose speakers include the Apalachees, Mikasukis, Hitchitis, Creeks, and Seminoles; the western branch includes the Choctaw and Chickasaw languages.[33] Although Alabama and Koasati are different, many linguists describe them as a pair of dialects, or a subdivision of a single language.[34] These shared linguistic links are more than likely based on their common ancestry in the Moundville Variant that allowed the Alabamas and Coushattas to communicate and to connect socially and politically, leading to the creation of lasting bonds. More importantly these linguistic similarities would have been a "pull factor" for the Coushattas as they left the Little Tennessee River.[35]

As observed by Marcos Delgado in 1686, Alabama and Coushatta refugees had established their towns and villages along the Coosa-Tallapoosa-Alabama confluence. Delgado referred to the Coushatta as "Qusate" and the Alabama as "Pagna." The Coushatta towns had around five hundred warriors, but Delgado's estimates failed to include the number of women and children, who were a substantial part of the population. The main Coushatta town was Coosada. Part of the Coosada also founded the town of Tubani, nine miles northwest of the main forks of the Alabama River; Delgado noted that this latter town had two hundred warriors. Taskigi (Tuskegee) was also a Coushatta town, which was located near the French Fort Toulouse at the forks of the Alabama River. Soto found the town of Tasqui near the Hiwassee River in Tennessee during his *entrada*; Charles Hudson believes it is probable that this town is the same as Taskigi, where the Koasati language was spoken.[36]

The Alabamas supported more towns compared to the Coushattas, and in the late seventeenth century had over five hundred warriors. Delgado identified the Alabama town of Pagna (Pakana) at the forks of the Alabama River. This town in the heart of the Alabama Nation proved to be a major diplomatic player in the eighteenth century. He also named the town of Culasa (possibly the same as the later-known Miculasa), located south along the Coosa River. By 1702 this village had one hundred and fifty warriors and had relocated closer to the confluence of the Alabama River (possibly on the Tallapoosa). Towassa (listed as Tuave by Delgado) was located near the juncture of the Alabama River system and joined the Alabamas near Fort Toulouse and had approximately one hundred warriors in the late seventeenth century. Delgado also listed Aymamu (Alibamu) as another town, but records about this town as well as archaeological findings are absent. An explanation may be found in Charles Levasseur's account of his travels to Alabama in 1700. Levasseur identified the town of Little Okchai as another Alabama town, possibly part of the original Alibamu town that was located at Okchai on the east side of the Coosa River shortly after 1686. Little Okchai became a significant town in the Alabama Nation by the mid-eighteenth century. Levasseur also identified Tomopa as an Alabama town that was located near the juncture of the Alabama River system. Kinship ties with residents of these Alabama and Coushatta towns were common, with many sharing both Alabama and Coushatta family members.[37]

As they created a community, Alabama and Coushatta men and women further secured their connections through intermarriage, thus creating extensive kinship ties. It is not clear when Alabamas and Coushattas first began to intermarry, but it is likely that it occurred after their movement to central Alabama and increased over decades of living in close proximity to one another. Clans common to both the Alabamas and Coushattas included the Beaver, Wildcat, Lion or Panther, Bear, Alligator (now extinct), Turkey, and Daddy Longlegs. The Alabamas' clans also included the Wolf (now extinct), Bird, Skunk, Salt, and Wind (also now extinct, with Chief John Abbey, who died in 1910, being the last Wind clan member). The merging of Alabama and Coushatta *ayiksa* (matriclans traced through the mother's family) was one mechanism of coalescence. It was a way to weave disparate people into one. One point is clear: like many Southern peoples, the Alabamas and Coushattas drew strength, stability, and cohesion from their complex kinship systems and marriage rules that specified marriage outside of one's clan. Their systems of kinship likely survived centuries of separation during the Mississippian Period and later served as a mechanism to counteract the disruptive effect of their diasporas and resettlement. Today, many Alabamas and Coushattas in Texas and Coushattas in Louisiana continue to share common surnames and clans despite living on different reservations.[38]

The overall picture that emerges from the earliest historical documents and maps is of small Alabama and Coushatta communities that merged and relocated frequently. Delgado recognized the coalescence and union of the Alabamas and Coushattas as early as 1686, but his references to them clearly indicate two entities. About twenty years later the English and the French referred to the two groups collectively as the Alabama Nation; the Coushattas were often absent in written records. What can explain their absence from many of the early accounts? One can speculate that in the beginning years of coalescence, the Alabamas, who supported more towns and warriors, admitted the Coushatta refugees into their polity but that they placed them in a subordinate political position. The Alabamas might have continued to employ ancient Mississippian political institutions. Early eighteenth-century Alabama chieftains, such as Deerfoot and Opoyheatly, were important leaders with whom Europeans primarily negotiated for trade and diplomacy within the Alabama Nation. Such negotiations included the invitation to the French to build Fort Toulouse in the heart of the Alabama Nation in 1717. Even at this late date the Coushattas seem to have had a reduced political role.[39] Despite the unequal balance of power between the Alabamas and Coushattas, town leaders acted cooperatively and generally benefited from sharing common interests. This characteristic would have resembled, though on a much smaller scale, the macro social organization of the Mississippian chiefdoms.[40]

Following migrations, the Alabamas and Coushattas recreated a lasting and interlocking community. This union resulted in a new polity, social order, and even worldview.[41] Moreover, their alliance created a united front, and it provided them with increased power, the ability to confront their enemies, and a claim to political sovereignty. This strategy was necessary in order to survive in the shattered South.

From Slaves to Slavers

The Alabamas and Coushattas, who both had migrated from a landscape of chaos, rampant with disease and slave raids, shared a common goal: to create new trade networks and alliances that would promote order and stability, power and sovereignty. Like many diasporic groups that find refuge in new spaces, the Alabamas and Coushattas faced possible hostility or attack from their new neighbors. Yet many peoples who bordered the Alabama Nation, including the Tallapoosas, Abhikas, Cowetas, and Cussetas (collectively known as the Creeks), were in a similar situation. They too had fewer numbers and sought alliances to protect their autonomy, especially as the English expanded their interests into the Southern interior. This situation may have been the genesis of the close relationship that developed between the Alabamas and Coushattas and the Creek Confederacy.

One example of the early formation of this alliance was the joint English

and Indian slave raids during Queen Anne's War (1702–13). The Alabamas and Coushattas were among many migrant newcomers who saw
opportunity in the slaving expeditions against Spanish Florida.[42] Alabama
and Coushatta participation in the slave trade had social, political, and
economic dimensions. Because slaving was a part of warfare, warriors
could build experience in battle and exercise their military prowess as well
as establish good relations with other allied Creek warriors. Moreover,
given the snowball effect of slaving, it was important for warrior-slavers
to establish preeminence in the Southern interior, especially because there
was additional incentive to exchange captives for trade goods.

Though little evidence remains, one can speculate that those who were
not sold into slavery may have been incorporated into the Alabama and
Coushatta community in order to strengthen the captors' numbers, much
as the Iroquois did through the mourning wars. As Paul Kelton suggests,
by the late seventeenth century Native communities had been devastated
by the Great Southeastern Smallpox Epidemic (1696–1700) and then by
the disease episodes that followed the slaving paths.[43] The Alabamas and
Coushattas were on the Upper Path of the pathogens, so they undoubtedly were among those affected, though, as discussed earlier, they had
probably suffered from some European diseases before this period. The
Alabama and Coushatta slave raids then would have been motivated by
several incentives: to rebuild trade networks previously damaged after
the collapse of the Mississippian world, to solidify their relationship with
their Creek neighbors, to establish hegemony over surrounding territory
in central Alabama, to replace gradually their population loss from the
smallpox epidemic by prisoner-adoption, and to purchase European goods
on which they were quickly becoming dependant.

Based on documentary evidence, the primary targets of the early eighteenth-century slave raids were the missionized Apalachees of Spanish
Florida.[44] Just as slavers had once raided Alabama and Coushatta settlements in the late seventeenth century, Alabama and Coushatta warriors
attacked Apalachee communities between May and September of 1702.
According to Don Hyacinthe Roque Perez, a Spanish officer stationed on
the Gulf coast deep in Apalachee territory, a combined Native force of
three thousand warriors quickly overwhelmed a small Spanish garrison

and the Apalachee warriors. Armed with English muskets, the slavers included the united Alabama-Coushattas, Cherokees, Tallapoosas, Abhikas, and Cowetas.[45] According to reports, the allied warriors eventually forced more than two thousand Apalachees to surrender and took the survivors to Carolina's coast, presumably to sell them to English slave traders. A year later, on September 15, 1703, Carolina governor James Moore called for the organization of "our Fri[e]ndly Indians to our interest, and ye gaining others thereunto, as well as Encouraging our fri[e]nds, & destroying our enemies."[46] For at least five more years the Alabamas and Coushattas continued to join these allied raids against Florida's coast, including an attack on the Spanish fort at Pensacola.[47] In Don Hyacinthe's words, "all these nations gathered together had caused tremendous havoc in the province."[48] They demonstrated to potential rivals and especially to potential slavers that these allied groups formed a powerful force and that they feared no one.

These ventures with the English also were lucrative for the Native allies, and the Alabamas and Coushattas created beneficial trade relations with Charles Town traders. The seeds of the play-off system that would later characterize Indian-European trade relations throughout the South in the eighteenth century were sown at this time. Even during the war the English worried that the Spanish agents in St. Augustine would "incite our Indians to trade with them" and that "our Indians are in Love with their liberality and Conversation."[49] European fears such as this one, coupled with the increasing leverage of Native communities, especially the Creek Confederacy, would only grow in the following decades.

The Alabama-Coushatta alliance with their neighbors during the war was a potential risk to Alabama and Coushatta independence. Still, the Alabamas and Coushattas maintained their autonomy and identity. They did not succumb to the power or dictates of their Creek allies despite their alliance with Creek towns throughout the eighteenth century; the Alabamas and Coushattas always remained outsiders. Before their coalescence in the 1680s the Alabamas and Coushattas were separately weak and vulnerable to attacks and slave raids in the shatter zone; they were among the hunted and enslaved. During the last decades of the seventeenth century and the first decade of the eighteenth century, however, the united Alabamas and Coushattas turned the tables and ironically reaped rewards from the very same Indian slave trade. Indeed, it was the Alabamas and Coushattas' previous existence in a shatter zone, coupled with their shared Mississippian past, that acted as a catalyst to alliance building and future unions that proved essential and beneficial with the growth of imperial European rivalries in the eighteenth century.

In the Mississippian period the precursors of the Alabamas and Coushattas lived apart. After ancient ceremonial centers, centralized tribute, and trade networks disintegrated, a shatter zone developed that created a new reality for the Alabama and Coushatta people. This new reality had political, socioeconomic, and cultural ramifications. By the end of the seventeenth century displacement and depopulation precipitated the collapse of the old order. Internal and external pressures led to smaller-scale communal organization based on clans and villages. This process of fragmentation left many groups like the Alabamas and Coushattas weak and exposed.

Socioeconomic dislocation accompanied political decentralization. The well-organized and hierarchical societies capable of massive communal projects collapsed, and mound building and many other macrosocial activities ceased. The relatively stable semiurban society of the chiefdoms became the overwhelmingly rural and transient village-based life that we know about in the Historic Period. Yet these new settlements could not survive alone in the shatter zone. Hence in the case of the Alabamas and Coushattas we see the building of alliances that were grounded in precontact Mississippian connections and subsequent coalescences into larger polities.

The analysis resulting from the present case study of the Alabamas and Coushattas can be applied to many other groups that also endured shatter zone conditions and subsequently decided to abandon their ancestral homelands and create new kinds of societies. As this chapter and others in this volume show, such diasporic movements are inextricably linked with the shatter zone. The Alabamas and Coushattas migrated east and south, respectively, escaping chaos and instability by uniting along the Alabama River in central Alabama. The Alabama-Coushatta alliance created needed strength and order in a rapidly changing world.

By 1700 their newfound security resulting from this union transformed the Alabamas and Coushattas from victims to perpetrators in the slave trade as they too reaped the rewards of new European markets. By conducting slave raids with their allies in Spanish Florida, the Alabamas and Coushattas ultimately aided in the widening of the shatter zone. But these slaving ventures also gave the Alabamas and Coushattas incentives to build pan-Indian alliances, one of which would later transform into the Creek Nation. The Alabamas and Coushattas, along with other remnant peoples who became their neighbors, redefined their new space by recreating social and political networks. And in an era where slaving turned friends into foes, cooperation became a key element to survival. Diasporic peoples depended on such relationships if they were to rebuild communities and prosper.

Looking at their oral traditions, the Alabamas and Coushattas' memory of their origins can be seen to echo their experiences in the shatter zone. Traditional telling describes how their ancestors emerged from a cave at nightfall, and upon surfacing they heard the screech of an owl. Many were frightened of the strange noise and returned to the security of the cave, never to return; this part of the story explained why the Alabamas and Coushattas' numbers were so few.[50]

Rooted in this oral history is the endurance of two peoples who fled from dislocation, disease, and the onslaught of neighboring rivals engaged in the Indian slave trade. Survivors coalesced to form a new community in the South. Some Alabamas and Coushattas undoubtedly remained behind, lost to history. Yet many sought the strength of unity as they crossed paths in their migrations, and these successful groups formed the basis on which Alabama and Coushatta identity now rests. Their diaspora and coalescence in the seventeenth century marked the beginning of their history as an allied people, a relationship that eventually developed into a common identity as they joined in future migrations west.

Notes

1. Lavie and Swedenburg, *Displacement*, 15.
2. Ethridge, "Creating the Shatter Zone."
3. The Alabamas and Coushattas are often lost in "Creek" history. Though they

were allies of many Creek towns, the Alabamas and Coushattas had a separate identity and historical experience. For more details, see Shuck-Hall, *Journey to the West*.

4. Sheldon, "Mississippian-Historic Transition," 9; Jenkins, this volume.

5. Jenkins, this volume.

6. The Moundville Archaeological Park and the Jones Archaeological Museum are located fourteen miles south of Tuscaloosa, Alabama. Knight and Steponaitis, "New History."

7. Knight and Steponaitis, "New History"; Anderson, *Savannah River Chiefdoms*, 148–50; Peebles, "Rise and Fall"; and Peebles, "Moundville."

8. According to Jenkins, the chiefdom of Tascalusa most likely correlates with the ceramic Big Eddy phase on the upper Alabama River; these simple chiefdoms were controlled by a single-level elite subgroup and established smaller, nonpalisaded towns and villages; Jenkins, this volume. Moundville, on the other hand, was a "complex chiefdom," with an apical chief and other villages and perhaps simple chiefdoms under the apical chief's authority. See Ethridge, this volume, for a brief discussion of simple and complex chiefdoms.

9. The Alibamu and Miculasa simple chiefdoms on the Tombigbee River acted independently of the Moundville chiefdom during its paramountcy and likely were unaffected by Moundville's collapse; Jenkins, this volume; Sheldon, "Mississippian-Historic Tradition," 120; Galloway, *Choctaw Genesis*, 63–64; Cottier, "Alabama River Phase," 120; Steponaitis, *Ceramics*, 169; Anderson, "Fluctuations," 250; and Anderson, *Savannah River Chiefdoms*, 7, 13, 149.

10. The variant spellings of Coushattas are "Coste" or "Acoste" in the Spanish documents, "Conchatys" by the English, and sometimes "Conchaques" by the French. Swanton first identified Coste as Koasati (Coushatta); Swanton, *Early History*, 201. DePratter, Hudson, and Smith identified the site on Bussell Island as Coste; DePratter, Hudson, and Smith, "Hernando de Soto Expedition," 114. See also Biedma, "Relation," 232.

11. Ned Jenkins argues that the Coste origins can be found in the Moundville Variant. Such an origin would help explain Alabama-Coushatta similarities in their ceramics and languages prior to their coalescence; Jenkins, this volume; Smith, *Archaeology of Aboriginal Culture Change*, 139; Lewis, Sullivan, and Lewis, *Prehistory of the Chickamauga Basin*, 1:13, 6–7, 245; and Smith, *Coosa*, 80.

12. Rangel, "Account," 282.

13. Gentleman of Elvas, "True Relation," 88–91; Rangel, "Account of the Northern Conquest," 282–83; and Hudson, *Knights of Spain*, 205–7.

14. Hudson, *Knights of Spain*, 256–59.

15. There is still much speculation on the ancient Tombigbee chiefdoms; Blitz, *Ancient Chiefdoms*; and Hudson, *Knights of Spain*, 262–65, 271–74. For a discussion of the Chicaza paramount chiefdom, see Ethridge, "From Chicaza to Chickasaw."

16. For a discussion of simple versus complex chiefdoms, see Anderson, *Savannah River Chiefdoms*, 1–11.

17. Martin, *Myths and Folktales*, 8–9.

18. Paul Kelton offers a counterargument by suggesting that European epidemic diseases made no significant impact on Native communities until after 1696; Kelton, this volume.

19. Hudson, *Juan Pardo Expeditions* (1990), 3–18; and Reinhartz and Saxon, *Mapping of the Entradas*, 75.

20. Hinderaker and Mancall, *At the Edge of Empire*, 73–75; and Gallay, *Indian Slave Trade*, 29, 46.

21. For a discussion on the shift of the Native mind-set regarding capital, see Snyder, "Captives of the Dark and Bloody Ground"; and Gallay, *Indian Slave Trade*, 29, 46. See also Galloway, this volume, for a discussion of how Native peoples blended the European trade system with their indigenous economic system.

22. Gallay, *Indian Slave Trade*. See also Kelton, this volume.

23. Ethridge, "Making of a Militaristic Slaving Society."

24. Iberville, *Gulf Journals*, 119.

25. Lewis, Sullivan, and Lewis, *Prehistory of the Chickamauga Basin*, 1:6–13, 245.

26. The Occaneechis may also have been raiding this far west during the seventeenth century.

27. September 30, 1683, British Public Records Office, South Carolina Colonial Entry, bk. 1:257–58, scdah; Hinderaker and Mancall, *At the Edge of Empire*, 73–75; and Gallay, *Indian Slave Trade*, 55–57. For Westo raiding in the lower Appalachians, see Bowne, *Westo Indians*, and Beck, this volume.

28. Entry for June 1 and 4, 1680, Salley, *Journal of the Grand Council*, 84–85.

29. June 3, 1684, British Public Records Office, South Carolina Colonial Entry, bk. 1:289–90, scdah; and Salley, *Journal of the Commons House for 1703*, 75–76. With Coste and the other chiefdoms on the Little Tennessee gone, the Cherokees soon settled this area; Hudson, *Juan Pardo Expeditions* (1990), 105.

30. Scholars do not yet have an exact date as to when the people from the Tombigbee and Black Warrior moved near the Alabama River except that it took place between Soto's *entrada* and 1700. For more details, see Jenkins, this volume.

31. Marcos Delgado in 1686 noted these same villages on the upper Alabama; he also noted that the Coushattas had established villages among the Alabamas by this time as well; Boyd, "Expedition of Marcos Delgado"; Guillaume Delisle, "Carte de la Louisiane et du Cours du Mississippi," Richard Yarborough Collection, CAH; January 13, 1693, Salley, *Journals of the Commons House for 1693*; and Knight and Adams, "Voyage."

32. Martin, *Myths and Folktales*, 3 (quote); and Swanton, *Early History*, 192.

33. Ned Jenkins has argued that the Alabama language is most closely associated with that spoken in the ancient Moundville Culture. He also suggests that the Alabamas had lived near the Creeks for two hundred years when their language was first recorded and classified as part of the Eastern branch but was likely a Western Muskogean language prior to their diaspora. See Jenkins, this volume.

34. Lupardus, "Language of the Alabama Indians," 1, 4; and Sylestine, Hardy, and Montler, *Dictionary*, xi–xii.

35. Considering their ancient connections, it is possible that the Coushatta and people who made up the Alabamas had kept some sort of connection over the centuries. This bond may have directed the Coushatta migration south to the Alabama River. In the middle of the shatter zone, surrounded by slavers on all sides and unable to trust anyone, the Coushattas chose to reunite with long-lost kinsmen from the Early Mississippian Period, that is, with people whom they could trust and from whom they could expect the warm and obliging welcome due a kinsperson. Their ancient ties then may have reformulated with the rise and fall of Mississippian chiefdoms.

36. For more details on Taskigi, see Hudson, *Juan Pardo Expeditions* (1990), 109. Treaty of Friendship and Commerce with the Alabama Indians, March 27, 1760, British Public Records Office, Class 5, f. 221–27, LC; Boyd, "Expedition of Marcos Delgado," 14; Delisle, "Carte du Mexique et de la Floride," 1703, Map Collection, HNOC; Nicholas de Fer, "Le Cours de Missisip[p]i, ou de St. Louis," 1718, Map Collection, HNOC; Pedro Oliver to Baron de Carondelet, December 1, 1793, Kinnaird, *Spain in the Mississippi Valley*, 4:231; Knight and Adams, "A Voyage"; Galloway, *Choctaw Genesis*, 177–79; Smith, *Coosa*, 80; Romans, *Concise Natural History*, 332; and Wright, *Historic Indian Towns*, 186, 60, 162, 150–51, 50–52, 17.

37. Hudson, *Juan Pardo Expeditions* (1990); Treaty of Friendship and Commerce with the Alabama Indians, March 27, 1760, British Public Records Office, Class 5, f. 221–27, LC; Boyd, "Expedition of Marcos Delgado" ; Delisle, "Carte du Mexique et de la Floride," 1703, Map Collection, HNOC; Nicholas de Fer, "Le Cours de Missisip[p]i, ou de St. Louis," 1718, Map Collection, HNOC; Oliver to de Caronde-

let, December 1, 1793, Kinnaird, *Spain in the Mississippi Valley*, 4:231; Knight and Adams, "A Voyage"; Galloway, *Choctaw Genesis*; Smith, *Coosa*; Romans, *Concise Natural History*; and Wright, *Historic Indian Towns*. There is much speculation and thus some disagreement among scholars on the names, identities, and locations of Alabama towns.

38. Ernest Sickey's Testimony to the U.S. Claims Court, November 29, 1983, no. 123, 50, Richard Yarborough Collection, CAH; Kniffen, Gregory, and Stokes, *Historic Indian Tribes*, 223–26; Kimball, *Koasati Dictionary*, 10, 27, 50, 274–75; Martin, *Myths and Folktales*, 3; and Sylestine, Hardy, and Montler, *Dictionary*, 75, 472. For a discussion on marriage as a mechanism of coalescence, see Milne, this volume.

39. Pénicaut, *Fleur de Lys* (1988), 63–64, 164–65; and Lamothe Cadillac to Pontchartrain, Fort Louis, October 26, 1713, Rowland and Sanders, *Mississippi Provincial Archives*, 2:162–65.

40. Blitz and Lorenz, *Chattahoochee Chiefdoms*, 12–22; and King, *Etowah*, 1–10.

41. For more details on the permanent ties created between the Alabama and Coushatta peoples, see Shuck-Hall, *Journey to the West*.

42. For a discussion of the consequences of these slaving expeditions on Spanish Florida, see Worth, this volume.

43. Kelton, "Great Southeastern Smallpox Epidemic"; and Kelton, this volume. For the mourning wars, see Richter, *Ordeal of the Longhouse*. See also Fox, this volume.

44. La Harpe, *Historical Journal*, 62–63. For a brief but detailed study on the Apalachee chiefdom, see Scarry, "Apalachee Chiefdom."

45. Steven Hahn has argued that these alliances (excepting the Cherokees) created a unified front in the view of the English, who saw these peoples as part of the "Creek Nation." For a detailed study of the development of the Creek Nation, see Hahn, *Invention of the Creek Nation*.

46. Salley, *Journals of the House of Commons for 1703*, 121 (quote); and La Harpe, *Historical Journal*, 62–63, 66–67, 76, 79.

47. La Harpe, *Historical Journal*, 62–63, 66–67, 76, 79; Salley, *Journals of the House of Commons for 1703*, 79; September 2, 1703, Journal of the Commons House of Assembly, Green Copy no. 2, f. 293, 295, SCDAH.

48. La Harpe, *Historical Journal*, 62–63, 66–67, 76, 79.

49. Salley, *Journals of the House of Commons for 1701*, 4–5.

50. Martin, *Myths and Folktales*, 3.

10 | *Violence in a Shattered World*

All other trades are contained in that of war.
CORMAC MCCARTHY, *Blood Meridian*

Violence was instrumental in creating the shatter zone of the American South. The shatter zone itself was a site of near-constant violence and featured long-distance raids for the express purpose of capturing slaves for sale at market. Yet violence also gave the people of the South a way to put their shattered world back together. Muskogee origin stories, for instance, tell of extraordinary, epic violence that helped to determine who was or was not Creek. From the Mississippians to the coalescent societies of the eighteenth century, indigenous communities developed their own ideas about the appropriate use of intercultural violence. These "cultures of violence" offer a fresh perspective on the European conquest of the South and its lasting impact on Native life. This chapter presents several snapshots of intercultural violence and contextualizes these cases in order to illustrate the multifaceted role of violence as it shattered the Native South and then worked to reorder it. The violence that tore through this region had parallels in other areas, but the wrecked legacy of the Mississippian world provides a unique case study of living and surviving in a shatter zone.

Violence in the Mississippian World

Chiefdoms that dominated life in the ancient South developed a culture of violence that reflected their values; they went to war for chiefly reasons. Warfare was not endemic to Mississippian society, but chiefdoms existed in constant tension with one another. Warfare was an integral part of Mississippian worldviews, and sacred art objects often depicted stylized weapons of war, including axes, swords, maces, and arrowheads. These objects exemplify the connection between warfare and social stratification as they are often associated with the burials of elites and chiefs. Mississippians apparently connected their chiefs to the supernatural forces that brought success in warfare.[1]

Mississippian warfare and religious beliefs intersected in crucial ways, though the details of the relationship remain blurred. Some of the major symbols of Mississippian religion, such as the falcon-impersonator and the forked-eye, both of which appear as motifs on sacred objects found throughout the South, have been associated with warfare before and during the era of European colonization.[2] Though an integral part of the Mississippian religious world, warfare was not necessarily endemic. There were different ways that a chiefdom could establish dominance over its neighbors. In the South chiefs seemed to prefer a pattern of prolonged skirmish warfare that gradually weakened their adversaries' resolve and forced them to capitulate. Warfare between chiefdoms was the outward manifestation of a broader culture of violence that permeated many aspects of Mississippian life.[3]

Chiefs had wide-ranging powers, and coercion was an unpleasant fact in the Mississippian world. Burials of large numbers of commoners, perhaps slaves, with elites at places like Cahokia attest to the coercive nature of Mississippian society. Moreover, because chiefdoms were inherited only through a handful of lineages, the death of a chief could set factions within a chiefdom against one another as they vied for supremacy, effectively weakening a chiefdom from within.[4]

In the Mississippian South chiefdoms instigated wars for a variety of reasons. Understanding how these conflicts were conceived and conducted provides the basis for understanding the Mississippian response to the Spanish intrusions of the sixteenth century. Though prolonged skirmishing and small-scale raids characterized the late prehistoric South, large campaigns akin to those employed in Europe were not altogether absent.[5] Mississippian society was a hierarchical society, marked by stark social inequalities. Chiefs were believed to be the earthly relatives of the sun or at least its representatives. They commanded unwavering respect; they were often elevated during ceremonies and diplomatic meetings, and their living quarters were located on mounds. Ordinary Mississippians were fiercely loyal to both their chiefs and chiefdoms. Mississippian societies also maintained a hierarchical military structure: war councils and priests of the cult of war supported the chain of command. Individual warriors reported to captains, members of the lower elite whose actions were determined by chiefs, council members, and priests.[6]

One theory about Mississippian warfare holds that Mississippians fought primarily for access to scarce resources, most likely arable land. Another posits a psychological interpretation of warfare. Mississippian societies were ranked, and success or failure in combat was a major factor in determining a lineage's fortunes. David Anderson, working on the Savannah River chiefdoms, has moved beyond previous interpretations of interchiefdom violence. He views warfare and its constant threat as part of an ongoing competition among factions of rival elites. Elite rivalry over territory, tribute, and trade fed a larger "cycling" process, through which some chiefdoms held sway for decades, eventually only to be usurped by others.[7]

There are a number of ethnohistorical clues as to Mississippian motivations for pursuing war. Early European accounts, whose authors perhaps were sizing up Natives as possible military adversaries, point to warfare as a method of exacting tribute from a neighboring chiefdom. This was evident at the chiefdom of Chicaza in which the chief, whose name was Chicaza, complained to Spanish conquistador Hernando de Soto in 1541 that "one of his vassals had risen against him, withholding his tribute, and asked that he protect him against him, saying that he was about to go to seek him in his land and punish him as he deserved."[8] In an example drawn from reminiscences of the 1559–61 Luna expeditions, the chiefdom of Napochies ceased paying tribute to the nearby paramount chiefdom of Coosa. According to Agustín Dávila Padilla's account,

> in ancient times the Napochies were tributaries of the Coza people, because this place (Coza) was always recognized as the head of the kingdom and its lord was considered to stand above the one of the Napochies. Then the people from Coza began to decrease while the Napochies were increasing until they refused to be their vassals, finding themselves strong enough to maintain their liberty which they abused. Then those of Coza took to arms to reduce the

rebels to their former servitude, but the most victories were on the side of the Napochies. Those from Coza remained greatly affronted as well from seeing their ancient tribute broken off, as because they found themselves without strength to restore it.[9]

When the Spanish under Pardo returned to the area later in the 1560s, Coosa had regained some of its status, but not its full former glory.[10] Power plays might begin with something as simple as the withholding of tribute and could lead to outright warfare between two chiefdoms.

Mississippians engaged in conflict for a number of material and cultural reasons. The Mississippians' culture of violence reflected their hierarchical worldview, and chiefdoms went to war to enforce tributary relationships, to demonstrate military prowess and dominance, and to capture elite trade goods that included art objects made of copper and other precious materials. Elite rivals could rise up against other elites and chiefs under whose authority they lay, individual chiefs could take autonomous towns or those belonging to their neighbors, or more rarely, chiefdoms could come into direct confrontation with each other.

Because of violence's connection to chiefly and priestly power, Mississippians imbued it with spiritual significance. Mississippian art seems to confirm the centrality of violence. Recent pioneering work by David Dye has combined insights gleaned from careful art historical analysis with the documentary and pictorial record left by sixteenth-century Europeans. The result has been an admittedly conjectural but rich portrayal of a Mississippian culture of violence.[11] The Mississippian world was dominated by the ideologies of chiefly and priestly power. One way to increase power and prestige was through warfare, and Mississippian art reflects a fascination with combat and its associated rituals. Art objects created for elites depict more than earthly combat. Warrior heroes, whether mythical or real, often appear in aggressive poses, brandishing ceremonial weapons in a cosmic effort to maintain order (see figure 1).[12]

Earthly warfare as a reflection of cosmic combat between order and chaos was carefully initiated. Warriors underwent dramatic rituals to purify themselves before fighting: these often included prolonged fasts followed by ceremonial feasts, abstinence from sex, sleep deprivation,

Figure 1. Mississippian shell gorget featuring a mythical warrior. Courtesy: National Museum of the American Indian, Smithsonian Institution, photo no. T150853. Photo by David Heald.

and physical separation from the community. In addition, warriors took special potions and used sacred objects to prepare for combat. Warriors performed similar rituals upon their return from battle.[13] The rituals of combat and their associated paraphernalia yield a depiction of Mississippian violence that provides earthly concerns such as access to labor and surplus resources with a spiritual backdrop. The exact nature of the connection between mythic violence and actual violence remains somewhat obscure, but it is clear that warriors in this world tried to emulate the actions of warriors on a cosmic level. And, in fact, warfare in the Mississippian world appears not to have required competition over resources or land; competition between rival chiefs and priests was integral to the way that Mississippians perceived their world and lay at the heart of Mississippian cultural violence.

An example from a Virginian postcontact paramount chiefdom — the renowned Powhatans under the leadership of Powhatan — can illuminate some key aspects of the Mississippian culture of violence.[14] Though Powhatan's land was at the very edge of the Mississippian world, the Powhatans' preparations for combat seem to reflect a Mississippian worldview. John Smith, who was held captive by Powhatan shortly after the establishment of Jamestown, described Powhatan preparations for war: "when they intend any warres, the Werowances [sub chiefs] usually have the advice of their Priests and Conjurers, and their allies, and ancient friends, but chiefely [sic] the Priests determine their resolution."[15] Priests and conjurers, who had access to sacred knowledge, were essential to Mississippian warfare. In Smith's account the holy men's opinions carried as much weight as consultations with military allies.

Mississippian societies could launch small-scale raids, but they could also field large well-organized armies. Chiefs exerted control over both skirmishing parties and large forces. In their confrontations with each other and later with the Spanish, both of these patterns of fighting appeared. Accounts of the Soto expedition describe coordinated attacks from different directions by multiple squadrons, which used drums as signals and moved in formation. Different groups, spread across a wide geographical range, employed similar tactics and even allied together across political lines to resist incursions such as the one led by Hernando de Soto.[16]

Shattering the World

Mississippian violence, as widespread and sophisticated as it was, did not prepare the chiefdoms for the type of threat posed by Spanish intruders. The Spanish Christians' ideas about violence were honed by centuries of conflict over Iberia. In their conquest of the Canaries, the Caribbean, and large swaths of the mainland Americas, the Spanish refined a worldview that allowed for savage violence against people who were considered "heathens." Soto's army disembarked at present-day Tampa Bay, Florida, in 1539 with both the technology — armor and horses — necessary to militarily engage the Mississippians in order to "conquer" them. Additionally, the Spaniards had the religious and cultural justifications for doing so.[17]

Disease soon followed these European encounters and certainly played a role in the creation of the shatter zone of the South.[18] However, it is impossible to overlook the fact that violence was also instrumental in shattering the Mississippian world. Whereas disease mostly affected the elderly and young, violence most affected males of military age and adult women, who were often the ones taken as captives and potentially sold into slavery. Yet one key factor sets disease apart from violence. The Spanish had much less control over the spread of disease than they had over the violence they brought with them. The story of violence shattering the South is a story of human cruelty, not biological bad luck.

Violence marked the earliest Spanish forays into mainland North America. Witness Juan Ponce de León's demise at a poisoned arrow's tip. Yet it was not until the arrival of Hernando de Soto's army that violence began to shatter the South. The kind of all-consuming violence that Soto imported was unknown to the chiefdoms that inhabited the region. Chiefdoms had gone to war against one another before but never with the amount of death imported by the Spanish.[19] The culture of violence that the Spanish brought with them to the South rested upon certain assumptions. Non-Christians could be subjected to biblically justifiable "wars by fire and blood" (*a fuego y a sangre*) that reinforced a militant form of Christianity born in late medieval Iberia. On a sacred level the men who performed such heroic conquests could expect to be rewarded with membership in the illustrious military brotherhood of the Order of Santiago. On a practical level they could also claim title to the land and labor of those vanquished.[20]

One of the most dramatic episodes of the clash between the Spanish and Mississippian cultures of violence occurred in October 1540 at the battle of Mabila. Lured to Mabila where a surprise attack awaited the Spanish army, Soto engaged the army of Tascalusa, the leader of a paramount chiefdom of the same name that was located in present-day central Alabama. It would be difficult to decide on a victor in this battle as both Tascalusa's army and Soto's army suffered tremendous losses. Soto's secretary Rodrigo Rangel, who had more than twenty arrows pulled out of his armor at the end of the day, described the fighting: "There was so much virtue and shame this day in all those who found themselves in this first attack and the beginning of this bad day. They fought valiantly, and each Christian did his duty as a most valiant soldier . . . In effect, the Indians ended up with the town and all the property of the Christians and with the horses that they left tied within, which they then killed."[21]

A false Spanish retreat drew the warriors of Mabila temporarily from their palisade, and Soto launched a furious counterattack: "the adelantado [Soto] encircled them on many sides until all the army arrived, and they entered it through three sides setting fire, first cutting through the palisade with axes; and the fire traveled so that the nine arrobas [about two hundred and twenty-five pounds] of pearls that they brought were burned, and all the clothes and ornaments and chalices and moulds for wafers, and the wine for saying mass, and they were left like Arabs, empty-handed with great hardship."[22]

The Spanish eventually routed the people of Mabila and their allies, but the casualties were high on both sides. The Spanish lost their pearls, much of their clothing and baggage, and twenty-two men, including seven notable soldiers, among them a relative of Soto. In addition, around one hundred and fifty men were wounded, and the expedition halted as they recuperated. As bad as the day was for the Spanish, it was much worse for the Mississippians. Most of Mabila's defenders, perhaps as many as three thousand men and women, died in the battle, refusing to surrender. Soto abandoned his plans to establish a colony in the area and continued his march to the northwest.[23]

The battle at Mabila undoubtedly contributed to Soto's dawning realization that large-scale colonization in the region would be difficult if not impossible. Overall the expedition gained very little for Spain except that Spain now recognized that another European power founding a colony in what they dubbed La Florida could pose a serious threat to the riches of New Spain. About twenty years later, in 1565, Spain established a toehold at St. Augustine and attempted to colonize through the mission-system strategy.

For Mississippians the losses at Mabila and other battles combined with the general disruptions caused by the Spanish presence and the toll taken by disease heralded the beginning of the end of their way of life. When English and French men and women began to arrive in the South in the second half of the seventeenth century, the chiefdoms were already stressed, and some had already collapsed. People abandoned the temple mound centers and Mississippian social structures in general. The story might end there but for the fact that scholars have begun to link the Mississippian world to the colonial world in some enlightening ways. Mississippian chiefdoms may have started to decline, but the cult of the warrior continued into the colonial era, with Southern warriors continuing to imbue violence with sacred significance and to prepare for battle in ritualized ways. As in Mississippian times warriors in the colonial era still acquired masculine prestige through their exploits in warfare except that now the spoils of war included wealth in arms, trade goods, and strikingly, Indian slaves for sale on the European market.

Violence and Slaving in the Shatter Zone

The Indian slave trade was never an exclusively European institution. In the late seventeenth and early eighteenth centuries, Native peoples joined colonizers in subjugating and enslaving other Natives.[24] Several groups, including Westos, Savannahs (Shawnees), and Yamasees, became slave raiders. This sort of violence was neither wholly Native nor wholly English but came into being because of the specific conditions in the shatter zone. These conditions included a market that valued Indian slaves, the pitting of Native groups against each other by Europeans, the arrival of slaving peoples such as the Westos, and the arms race that developed among the region's indigenous communities. Further study might also point to Mississippian-era animosities that continued into the colonial era. The shatter zone of the South was not a "middle ground" in the way that Richard White has applied the term to the Great Lakes and Midwest. Nor was it stable: groups that allied with the English, for example, could easily end up being victimized by other English allies. Few Native communities were untouched by the violence metastasizing through the South.

The slave trade of the South was an adaptation of older forms of violence to the conditions of colonial Carolina and by extension the Atlantic World market. The story of what slave raiding meant to Westos, Savannah, and Yamasees is not an easy one to uncover and must necessarily involve some speculation. That the story is tentative or speculative does not detract from the fact that it is essential to understanding how colonization worked in the South.[25]

Native societies throughout the Eastern Woodlands were in motion and in cultural flux during the seventeenth century. Native ideas about violence were shifting rapidly as small-scale raids and captive-driven mourning wars spun into predatory trading and slave-raiding expeditions covering long distances. Westos, Savannahs, and Yamasees all had experience with captive taking before contact. The Westos came from a cultural milieu and region that rewarded the theft of trade goods and celebrated skilled captive takers. The Savannah are not usually associated with long-range slave raiding before their time in the South, though there is some evidence they came to the South to avoid Iroquois depredations. The Yamasees were among the earliest victims of Virginia and Carolina's Indian slave trade until they became slave raiders themselves in the late seventeenth century.[26]

The origins and colonial history of the Westos are covered elsewhere in this volume.[27] For my discussion a summary here will suffice. The Westos were a splinter group of Eries who moved by 1656 to the falls of the James River in Virginia where they became known as the Richahecrians and, after an initial confrontation, engaged in a profitable trade with the English.[28]When the Eries arrived in Virginia, they were armed and well aware of the skills necessary to thrive in the world between the Native interior and the colonial market. They soon dominated Virginia's Southern trade. Their Virginia experience prepared the Westos to become the premier Indian slavers of the South.[29] Within a couple of years of their arrival in Virginia, the Eries, now Richahecrians, were undertaking long-distance journeys for slaves and furs that brought them to the outskirts of Florida's missions. The Spanish called the raiders Chichimecos, a blanket term that the Spaniards applied to any number of Native groups that lived outside of the Spanish sphere of influence.

As elite white Virginians struggled to develop a plantation economy, they were plagued by a perennial labor shortage. To satisfy the demand for labor, wealthy planters increasingly turned toward chattel slavery. The limited and sporadic availability of African slaves in seventeenth-century North America made Indian slavery attractive. Later, when Charles Town was established, Carolina's planners envisioned it as a plantation colony from the outset, and its chronic labor shortage was much more severe than that of Virginia.[30] When the English planters spread out from Charles Town in the 1670s, they came into contact and conflict with the Westos, who were already engaged in the Indian slave trade and were eager to gain greater access to European goods. Authorities in Carolina recognized the importance of maintaining cordial relations with the Westos, while the Westos recognized the threat and opportunity of the new English arrivals. As recounted by Eric Bowne in this volume, the voyage to the Westos by Henry Woodward in 1674 inaugurated a short-lived but profitable trade between the Westos and Carolina that had serious consequences for Native people in the region.[31]

The Westos' skill at raiding coastal and interior communities was enhanced by the fact that they were the only firearm-equipped indigenous group in the area. Their reputation as cannibals also helped. They may or may not have actually been cannibals, but the Westos were already terrifying enough by 1670 for coastal peoples to welcome Carolina's first English settlement.[32] In the years after 1670 the Westos sold their captives exclusively to the English at Charles Town, orienting the Southern Indian slave trade to Carolina. The type of violence unleashed by the Westos could only have existed within the specific historical circumstances that obtained in the shattered world of the early South: Europeans prized Indian slaves, and Native people sought firearms to help capture slaves, while nobody much cared about the long-term consequences. The Westos' exploitation of the conditions of the shatter zone, and their complicity in its creation, may have served as an example to other groups in the region such as the Savannahs.

The story of the Savannahs before they migrated to the fringe of Carolina is not well known.[33] The specific Shawnee community that became the Savannahs probably had roots in the Ohio and Cumberland valleys in the seventeenth century. Iroquois pressure on the Shawnees began around this time, and violence intensified throughout the 1660s and 1670s. Shawnees responded to Iroquois raids by abandoning the Ohio and Cumberland country. Hundreds of Shawnees relocated to Fort St. Louis in central Illinois while others moved into the South.[34] At least one community of Shawnees settled on the Savannah River. It is almost inconceivable that the Shawnees had no experience as captive takers before their involvement in the slave trade as most indigenous peoples in eastern North America engaged in the practice on some level.[35] Like the Westos before them, it is also highly unlikely that the Savannahs moved accidentally into the English sphere of influence. The Savannahs' migration to Carolina's backcountry indicates a desire for trade.[36]

Dr. Henry Woodward witnessed an early Savannah appearance on the fringe of Carolina. Woodward recorded a critical early meeting between Savannahs and Westos near the close of his "Woodward's Faithfull Relation." Eric Bowne suggests that this was an advance party of Shawnees looking for potential settlement sites near sources of English trade.[37] Woodward's description of the meeting is as spare as his treatment of the Westos in general, but it does provide some clues about Shawnee motives and the extent of Shawnee migrations. The Shawnees, or Savannahs, were returning from trading with the Spanish at Florida, though the travelers were apparently disappointed with Spanish unwillingness to provide them with guns. They passed along a rumor of an impending attack on the Westos, perhaps in an effort to curry favor with the powerful group.[38]

In 1680 the Westo War erupted. The causes of the war are tied up in the politics of English Carolina: essentially Woodward and the proprietors intended to regulate trade with Indians while a planter faction known as the Goose Creek Men desired to expand the trade as far inland as possible.[39] To achieve this goal, the Goose Creek Men armed the Savannahs. The Savannahs proceeded to defeat and to enslave much of the Westo population. Gov. John Archdale would later write that "the Hand of God was eminently seen in thining the *Indians*, to make room for the *English*. As for Example in *Carolina*, in which were seated Two Potent Nations, called the *Westoes*, and *Sarannah*, which contained many Thousands, who broke out into an unusual Civil War, and thereby reduced themselves into a small Number, and the *Westoes*, the more Cruel of the two, were at the last forced quite out of that Province, and the *Sarannahs* continued good Friends and useful Neighbors to the *English*."[40]

In the aftermath of the war the Savannahs became an important Carolina ally and one of its most prominent slave raiders. Young colonist Thomas Newe described the Savannahs in 1682 as "the most potent Kingdome of the Indians armed by us."[41] This distinction would eventually shift to a third group: the Yamasee.

The Yamasees did not replace the English position of the Savannahs swiftly. In the 1680s both groups occupied prime locations in operating between the Indian world of the interior and the English world of Charles Town. From 1680 to 1710 the story of the Savannahs is nebulous to a frustrating degree. It is clear that the Savannahs and Carolina saw some advantage in maintaining a relationship, and it is equally clear that Savannahs were beginning to detest living in the South. John Lawson in an account of his 1701 trip described the Savannahs as a "famous, warlike, friendly Nation of Indians."[42] A few years later, however, this relationship had begun to fray as reflected in the proceedings of the Commons House of Assembly when they refer to the Savannahs during 1707 and 1708 as the "Revolted Savanas" and the "deserted Savanas."[43] These references point to the desertion of the Savannahs from Carolina. The Savannahs' relationship with Carolina was obviously deteriorating. It may have been that the Savannahs were fleeing Catawba slavers at this time, and hence they recognized that an alliance with Carolina did not guarantee safety from other English-sponsored slavers. The dangers of getting drawn too close to Carolina's Indian trade were becoming clear to the Savannah. Some of these Savannahs subsequently moved to Maryland and Pennsylvania. Such movements by the Shawnees were not unusual as Shawnee communities were oftentimes far apart during the colonial era and individuals and families regularly moved between far-flung settlements.[44]

The Yamasees are among the least understood communities of the early modern South, though the situation is beginning to change owing to recent archaeological discoveries and the work of John Worth, William Green, Chester DePratter, and Bobby Southerlin. The Yamasees were a loose coalition of refugees from the Mississippian chiefdoms of Ocute, Altamaha, Ichisi, and perhaps others. Though they lived close to, and occasionally within, the confines of the Spanish mission system, they appear not to have accepted Catholicism to any significant extent. In fact, their insistence on indigenous religion was one of the factors that marked them as Yamasee to the Spanish authorities.[45] The Yamasees' first exposure to the Indian slave trade was probably as the victims of raids by Westos and Savannahs. As a response to these raids, pirate attacks, and a disagreement with the Spanish governor in 1683, the Yamasees left Spanish Florida and relocated closer to Carolina, near the Scottish colony of Stuart's Town on the coast.[46]

Within a couple of years of their relocation the Yamasees became one of Carolina's principal Indian allies. This role brought certain benefits, including access to English trade and some immunity from enslavement. In return, like Carolina's other Indian allies, they were expected to provide Indian slaves. From the 1680s until 1715 Yamasees did just that. What little is known about Yamasee life ways and economy suggests that the Yamasees represented an early incarnation of the fluid social organization and coalescent identity that would characterize most Native societies in the South in the era of colonization.[47] Yamasees sought and received English and Spanish trade goods and paid for them with Indian slaves taken from Spanish missions.

The Yamasees' career as slave raiders began with a 1685 raid on the Timucuan mission of Santa Catarina de Afuyca and continued through the devastating Florida raids of the first decade of the eighteenth century and the Tuscarora War of 1711-13. English slaver Thomas Nairne recorded one raid on Spanish Florida before his relationship with the Yamasees soured, and he was put to death by the excruciating *petit feu* method. In 1706 Nairne accompanied Yamasee warriors on a slave raid into Florida. The route of the raid and description of it were recorded in 1720 on the Herman Moll "New Map of the North Parts of America." The legend reads, "Explanation of an Expedition in Florida Neck by Thirty-three Iamesee Indians Accompany'd by Capt. T. Nairn." The raid was difficult, involving six days of rowing and swimming over the St. John's River, but it was a success. Nairne and the Yamasees took thirty-five slaves and killed thirty-three Florida Indians. Clearly Nairne understood firearms to have made the difference as he recounted that on the raid, "a very Numerous body of Indians came against them, they being but 33 men. Yet put them presently to flight; they having no Armes but Harpoos, made of Iron and Fish bones; they were all Painted."[48]

Certain narrative strands run through the Westo, Savannah, and Yamasee stories. All moved intentionally into the vicinity of Carolina's planters and traders. The Westos, Savannahs, and Yamasees were pushed out of prior locales by armed aggressors, and each community in turn became an armed aggressor. Their late seventeenth-and early eighteenth-century histories are ones of multiple movements and alliances. In these and other ways all adapted to life in the shatter zone at the same time as their violence helped to shatter it further.

One change to Native life that requires further exploration is the changing meaning of captivity. At various points and for many groups, captivity stopped serving a social purpose and began to serve an economic one. One might question whether social and economic motivations can be so easily separated. Economics alone cannot explain why adoption of captives slowed and why the sale of captives to slave traders picked up. Certainly Native Southerners had an indigenous form of slavery and captivity, and as argued earlier in this chapter, violence was part and parcel of life for Natives before contact. Yet the practice of traveling long distances to secure slaves for eventual sale was absent before extensive contact with Europeans and the opening of a commercial market for Indian slaves. The shatter zone left many indigenous communities with hard choices. They had to choose between being enslaved by people working for Carolina planters and traders or trading for arms and enslaving their neighbors.

Slave raids were at once Indian and European undertakings. Native communities had no trouble figuring out which people to target as each group already had allies and enemies. By the time Carolina was founded, the English were savvy enough to recognize the benefits of exploiting existing Indian rivalries. Europeans thus exploited intra-Indian animosities in the service of colonial interests, and slave raids became a common feature of colonial life and military strategy in the South.

One long-term effect of such European strategies and Native choices was the incessant intra-Indian conflicts that cleared the way for the gradual domination of the region by the English. In the shatter zone, then, Native groups used violence as a strategy of group survival, only to be circumscribed by the colonial institutions that this violence subsidized. Even so, Indians of the South also used this violence as a tool of regeneration.

Violence and Regeneration in the Indigenous South

The trade in Indian slaves had a profound impact on the indigenous South and reshaped the region in ways that are only now becoming clear. Somewhat paradoxically, violence can be a generative as well as a destructive force. Richard Slotkin used the phrase "regeneration through violence" to point out that America's national myth rested on violent acts and stories. Slotkin's regeneration was a Euro-American cultural phenomenon. Yet regeneration through violence in the colonial era was not a whites-only phenomenon.[49] Violence was indeed a central feature of Native nation building and national identity in the colonial era.

For example, Southern Native origin stories that detail emergence of social orders speak of violence on a grand scale. Creek origin stories are perhaps the best documented. Regarding the origins of the eighteenth-century Creek Confederacy, the work of John Worth, Ned Jenkins, and others have brought Creek origins into sharper focus.[50] It is no longer in dispute that the confederacy was made up of people descended from Mississippian chiefdoms. The exact lines of connection, however, are still being sorted out. Examining the role of violence in Native life is useful for exploring the connection between the South's ancient chiefdoms and modern Native American nations. As we have seen, violence functioned as a social glue in the Mississippian world. Most chiefdoms held similar ideas about violence, and though bands of warriors and armies representing the various chiefdoms fought against one another regularly, all participants abided by certain cultural rules. The arrival of Europeans disrupted these rules, and violence as an instrument in the slave trade disrupted many other aspects of Native life as well. Instead of annihilation and extinction, though, new kinds of societies emerged. These new societies were built by the descendants of the Mississippian era. When the Mississippian world began to collapse, Native peoples of the South began to rebuild their lives, and Indian nations began to coalesce in the crucible of this violence. This violent birthing is reflected in their origin stories.

Creek origin stories are rife with legendary violence, indicating that violence was a feature of Creek national formation. One of the earliest recorded origin stories was recited by Chigelly, the headman of Coweta, to English authorities at Savannah in 1735.[51] The Chigelly legend is full of supernatural and human violence. In the story the Cussetas' (Kasihtas') western migration is forced because "the earth became angry and ate up their children." Red, the Creek color of war, appears repeatedly: the Cussetas come upon a "red, bloody river"; they witness a mountain emitting "red smoke"; and they cover red poles with the scalps of slain enemies, noting that Cusseta (who had gathered the most) was the oldest.[52]

The Chigelly legend also speaks of physical violence. The nations determine the oldest group by going to war. In an effort to kill a wild beast tormenting the Coosas, the Cussetas use a motherless child as bait. The legend also boasts of some conquests against people with flattened heads in which the Cussetas killed all but two villagers and a white dog (this may have some otherworldly significance as white was associated with peace in Muskogee cosmology). Eventually they are persuaded by another group, the Apalachicolas, to lay down their arms. The story concludes with Creeks and Georgians reaching a tenuous peace, but with the admission that "the Cussetaws first saw the red smoke, and the red fire, and make bloody towns, they cannot yet leave their red hearts, which are, however, white on one side and red on the other." After the speech concluded, the Creek delegation gave it to the interpreter for Georgia, painted in red and black on a buffalo skin.[53]

The naturalist William Bartram recorded another version of Creek origins in 1773 when he was at the mounds of Ocmulgee. According to Bartram, "this place [Ocmulgee] is remarkable for being the first town or settlement, when they sat down or established themselves after their emigration from the west, beyond the Mississippi, their original native country." Bartram retold the legend of the journey before the Creeks "sat down": "on this long journey they suffered great and innumerable difficulties, encountering and vanquishing numerous and valiant tribes of Indians, who opposed and retarded their march." Following a valiant last stand, the Creeks "recovered their spirits" and achieved victory in a "memorable and decisive battle." They "subdued their surrounding enemies, strengthening themselves by taking into confederacy the vanquished tribes." This example demonstrates that Creek violence against outside enemies helped to create a Creek national identity.[54]

The English, who established Charles Town in 1670, soon entered the Creek narrative. The Creeks understood that the English were "a powerful, warlike people" and immediately dispatched diplomats to the colonial capital to "offer their friendship and alliance." Bartram also wrote of a treaty, established between the Creeks and South Carolina that ostensibly was never violated. The Creeks did not simply promise peace; they offered valuable services to the English in the early years of the eighteenth century; "they never ceased war against the numerous and potent bands of Indians, who then cramped and surrounded the English plantations," according to the story told by Bartram. During the harrowing years of the Yamasee War (1713–15), many Creek towns remained staunchly allied to the English, fighting off numerous enemies and pursuing the defeated hostile tribes "to the very gates of St. Augustine." In the 1770s the Creeks claimed that their violent acts had paved the way for English Carolina's very existence. In this reckoning Creek violence not only helped define Creek identity but also advanced English colonial goals.[55]

The "Bartram legend" asserted a claim to the Macon Plateau vicinity and explained the role of violence in forging Creek identity. Bartram's consultants were correct in their contention that the Creeks and English had signed a treaty. The treaty, dated at Coweta on August 15, 1705, used strictly formulaic language to bind the Creeks, represented by twelve leaders, whom the English called "Kings, Princes, Generals, etc.," in "Hearty

Alliance with, and Subjection to the Crown of England."[56] The Yamasee War as remembered in 1773 is not a correct rendering, and the Creeks played a significant role in the conflict.

Another Creek origin story was recorded by Benjamin Hawkins in 1798. This version is shorter than the others, but it still focuses on the role of violence in the origins of the Creeks. After the main Muskogee towns chose which clans would lead them, "some other Indians came from the west, met them, and had a great wrestle with the three towns; they made ball sticks and played with them, with bows and arrows, and the war club. They fell out, fought, and killed each other."[57] After these hostilities subsided, as in the Chigelly legend, the Creek towns agreed to go to war against a common enemy for four years, counting the scalps accumulated as a method for determining which would be the principal town. The next trial for the Kasihta people involved the flat-headed people, though in this particular legend, mounds factor in as well. The flat-headed people were "in possession of the mounds in the Cussetuh fields."[58] The Cussetas attacked and took the mounds and from that location moved out along the rivers of Georgia.

Creeks and other Native Southerners had found an indigenous answer to the problem of English colonization. Violence was deeply ingrained as an element of precontact Mississippian life and continued through the colonial era, although its practice exceeded masculine prestige and status. Creek nation building, the making of English Carolina, and the creation of the United States all rested on violent ideas. Perhaps one of the reasons the Creeks, Cherokees, and the United States battled on the field and in the courtroom in the nineteenth century is that each nation believed it had earned its place in the South through violence and thereby could lay legitimate claim to its national territory.

No one should be surprised to learn that violence accompanied European colonization in the South. Violence radiated from European colonies throughout the Atlantic World. What set the North American South apart from the rest of the mainland was the legacy of the Mississippians. When chiefdoms disintegrated as the result of disease and new forms of violence inherent in a commercial trade in slaves, they left behind a shattered world. This shatter zone helped to breed an insidious form of violence that eventually permeated the region and Indian life. But this violence was as regenerative as it was destructive, and early modern Creeks and other Native peoples used violence, both physical and legendary, to stake claims to their territories and to make nations suited to their time and place in the American South.

Notes

1. Anderson, *Savannah River Chiefdoms*; and Dye, "Warfare in the Protohistoric Southeast."

2. Emerson, *Cahokia and the Archaeology of Power*, 217; and Howard, *Southeastern Ceremonial Complex*, 43–44. The falcon in particular may have "served as the model for the Cherokee Tlanuwa, which killed men with their sharpened beaks." The falcon was revered by Southern Indians above other birds; it struck quickly, attacking other birds in flight, no matter their size. See Hudson, *Knights of Spain*, 24.

3. Dye, "Warfare in the Protohistoric Southeast," 126–29.

4. Hall, "Cahokia Site," 97–98; and Hudson, *Knights of Spain*, 28.

5. Dye, "Warfare in the Protohistoric Southeast," 129.

6. Hudson, *Knights*, 24; Dye, "Warfare in the Protohistoric Southeast," 133–34.

7. Larson, "Functional Considerations"; Gibson, "Aboriginal Warfare," 130 (quote); and Anderson, *Savannah River Chiefdoms*, 134–35.

8. Garcilaso, "La Florida," 106. Incidentally, this may have been a trick intended to force Soto to divide his army. Still, it demonstrates that tribute collection was a legitimate reason to go to war.

9. Dávilla Padilla, "Historia," 232 (quote).

10. Anderson, *Savannah River Chiefdoms*, 101–10.

11. Dye, "Art, Ritual, and Chiefly Warfare."

12. Gorgets, effigy pipes, ceremonial maces and raptor talons, copper repoussé plates, engraved whelk shells, and monolithic axes are among the items assembled at Chicago's Art Institute's Hero, Hawk, and Open Hand exhibit in 2004–5. The motif of combat runs through much Mississippian art, across various regions, and throughout a period of several hundred years. See, for instance, the gorget featured in Dye, "Art, Ritual, and Chiefly Warfare," 190. It depicts a mythic warrior holding a severed head and brandishing a mace.

13. Dye, "Art, Ritual, and Chiefly Warfare," 191–92, 198.

14. Although the Powhatan chiefdom existed during the early colonial years, some of the patterns of violence can be useful for understanding precontact chiefdom violence.

15. Smith, *Captain John Smith*, 145.

16. DePratter, "Late Prehistoric and Early Historic Chiefdoms," 49–53.

17. Elliott, *Empires of the Atlantic World*, 17–20; Elliott, *Imperial Spain*, 32; Lomax, *Reconquest of Spain*, 99–100; Hudson, *Knights of Spain*, 7; and Bennassar, *Spanish Character*, 23–24.

18. Kelton, this volume.

19. Hudson, *Knights of Spain*, 243–48.

20. Hanke, *Spanish Struggle*; and Poole, "War by Fire and Blood."

21. Rangel, "Account," 293. Rangel's account is generally considered one of the most accurate of all the Soto narratives; Galloway, *Hernando de Soto Expedition*.

22. Rangel, "Account," 293–94. The pearls had been carried from Cofitachequi in South Carolina. Soto intended to use them to prove the value of further colonizing efforts in the South. For students of colonial history this action may recall the events of the Pequot War of 1637 when English forces surrounded a fort on the Mystic River and burned it, killing the Pequot noncombatants who fled.

23. Hudson, *Knights of Spain*, 244–47.

24. The fact that this enslavement happened further demonstrates the inadequacy of shorthand terms like European, English, African, and Native American to describe the peoples involved in the immensely complex situation of the colonial South. The peoples who inhabited the South in the late seventeenth and early eighteenth centuries understood race in a way specific to their historical circumstances (as do we all).

25. Gallay's recent *Indian Slave Trade* marked a watershed moment in the general awareness of the scope and significance of the Indian slave trade. Like all "big books," *Indian Slave Trade*'s lasting contribution will be measured by the quantity and quality of the studies that come in its wake. Gallay has shown that Native Americans became slavers; I am concerned with why they did so.

26. For the movements of populations in the South, see Smith, "Aboriginal Population Movements in the Early Historic Period"; and Smith, *Archaeology of Aboriginal Culture Change*. On cultural changes, see Ethridge and Hudson, *Transformation*; and Hudson and Tesser, *Forgotten Centuries*.

27. Bowne, this volume; Fox, this volume; and Meyers, this volume.

28. For the origins of the Westos, see Bowne, *Westo Indians*, 37–53; Juricek,

"Westo Indians"; Smith, *Archaeology of Aboriginal Culture Change*, 131–32; and Gallay, *Indian Slave Trade*, 41–42.

29. Richter, *Ordeal of the Longhouse*, 32–38, 62; Richter, "War and Culture"; Smith, *Archaeology of Aboriginal Culture Change*, 132; and Bowne, *Westo Indians*, 39–41, 49–52. Most of these accounts can be traced to Jesuit accounts of life in New France; Gallay, *Indian Slave Trade*, 41–43; Bowne, *Westo Indians*, 72–75; and Worth, *Struggle for the Georgia Coast*, 17.

30. It bears mentioning that the phrase labor shortage is relative in this usage. Carolina's planters needed labor to turn the sort of profit they believed befitted the climate of their new colony.

31. Bowne, this volume; and Bowne, *Westo Indians*, 80–88.

32. Bowne, *Westo Indians*, 79; Crane, *Southern Frontier* (1981), 6.

33. For a discussion of the Shawnees, see Warren, this volume.

34. As important as the Shawnees were to nineteenth-century American history, it is surprising so little has been written about them in earlier time periods; Howard, *Shawnee*, 1–23; Clark, *Shawnee*, 5–27; and Wheeler-Voegelin and Tanner, *Indians*, 1:30–37.

35. Namias, "Captives"; and Perdue, "Slavery."

36. In the parlance of immigration studies Carolina's potential for trade was a pull factor that attracted Native Americans from surrounding regions.

37. Bowne, *Westo Indians*, 85. Given the Shawnees' history of organized, methodical migrations, this explanation makes sense.

38. Woodward, "Woodward's Faithfull Relation," 133–34.

39. Gallay, *Indian Slave Trade*, 60–61.

40. Archdale, "New Description," 88–89.

41. Newe, "Letters of Thomas Newe," 182.

42. Lawson, *New Voyage*, 48. For a useful discussion of colonial authors' propensity to employ "warlike" to describe people, see Gallay, *Indian Slave Trade*, 173–75.

43. Entries for June 5 to July 19, 1707, Salley, *Journal of the Commons House for 1707*; references to the revolt and desertion of the Savannah occurs on pages 26–28. Gallay relied on these journals in *Indian Slave Trade*, 210–12.

44. For a discussion of mobility as an adaptive strategy employed by the Shawnees in the shatter zone, see Warren, this volume.

45. Worth, "Yamasee"; Green, DePratter, and Southerlin, "Yamasee in South Carolina"; and Worth, *Struggle for the Georgia Coast*, 18–20. See also Worth, this volume.

46. Worth, "Yamasee," 248–49.

47. Worth, "Yamasee," 250.

48. For a description of Nairne's death, which may have been brought about by the insertion of many small splinters of wood just under his skin and lighting them, see Oatis, *Colonial Complex*, 1. Oatis's work provides a description of Yamasee origins but does its most effective work in describing the results of the breakdown of the Yamasee-South Carolina alliance. The Yamasee War has been the subject of some important recent scholarship; Schrager, "Yamasee Indians"; Ramsey, "Heathenish Combination"; Rayson, "Great Matter to Tell"; Durschlag, "First Creek Resistance"; and Ramsey, "Something Cloudy in Their Looks." The map in question appeared in Moll's *World Described*.

49. Slotkin, *Regeneration through Violence*. Recent generations of historians and anthropologists have been more willing to recognize that violence can produce new social orders at the same time as it destroys old ones. A prime example of this approach is Poole, *Unruly Order*. Ferguson and Whitehead's *War in the Tribal Zone* brings together many of the most recent theoretical interpretations of violence. Ned Blackhawk offers a searing reassessment of the role of violence in the West in his *Violence over the Land*.

50. Jenkins, this volume; and Worth, "Lower Creeks."

51. For a discussion of the Chigelly origin story, see Hahn, "Cussita Migration Legend."

52. Gatschet, *Migration Legend*, 244–46.

53. Gatschet, *Migration Legend*, 248, 250–51, 235–36. The buffalo skin made its way to the Georgia colonial office in London where it disappeared from the historical record.

54. Bartram, *Travels*, 35. For the importance of Ocmulgee to the formation of Muskogee identity, see Hall, "Making an Indian People," 19–21.

55. Bartram, *Travels*, 35 (quote).

56. "South Carolina Treaty with the Creeks at Coweta," Vaughan, *Early American Indian Documents*, 90–91.

57. Hawkins, "Sketch," 82.

58. Hawkins, "Sketch," 83.

11 | *Razing Florida*

THE INDIAN SLAVE TRADE AND
THE DEVASTATION OF SPANISH
FLORIDA, 1659–1715

JOHN E. WORTH

Beginning in 1659 and intensifying through the first decades of the eighteenth century, Native peoples and Spaniards living in the broad region of the greater Spanish Florida experienced a reign of terror originating in the English colonies to the north that was pivotal in what would become the almost complete geographical and social reorganization of the entire region. The direct and indirect impact of European contact spread across much of this region because of early Spanish exploration, colonization, and missionization. However, the juggernaut sparked by English colonists in Virginia and the Carolinas ultimately provoked transformations that were far more rapid and substantial than might ever have been the case in the context of an expanding Spanish colonial system alone. In retrospect the English traders and Natives far to the north bear greater responsibility for the wholesale transformation of the lower Southern landscape by the early eighteenth century than did the Spaniards in St. Augustine, whose antiquity and proximity were initially unrivaled by English advances that postdated the Spanish presence by several generations.

The source of this reign of terror was the Indian slave trade, which began its direct push southward in western Virginia in the 1650s and reached its zenith in South Carolina after the 1670s.[1] Intersocietal warfare and the enslavement of captives on at least a small scale were endemic in the late prehistoric South long before European contact. The English introduced two new forces that would ultimately shatter the fragile and already-damaged social fabric of the seventeenth-century South: a vast and expanding commercial market for slaves and ample supplies of the perfect tool to ensnare both slaves and slavers, the flintlock musket. During the space of just over half a century, the English funneled firearms and munitions into the hands of a few pivotal allied Native groups. These groups in turn terrorized the many people without firearms across greater Spanish Florida. They ultimately reached as far as the very walls of Spanish St. Augustine and even deep into the southern portion of the Florida peninsula. Using their newfound military might, Indian slave raiders killed as many as were necessary and captured as many as were possible. The captives were destined for transport and sale to English traders along the Virginia and Carolina frontier, who in turn shipped Florida Indian slaves to the Caribbean and other destinations.

In broad view the slave trade reaped both economic and political benefits for the English colonies, for in sponsoring Indian raids against Spanish mission Indians, the power and extent of Spanish Florida was diminished and eventually devastated. The intricately organized and delicately balanced colonial system encompassing dozens of previously disparate Indian chiefdoms under the overarching paramountcy of Spanish St. Augustine was swept almost completely away by the effects of increasingly aggressive slave raids, compounded by ongoing population declines due principally to epidemic depopulation.[2] From a far-flung mission system encompassing more than twenty-five thousand Indians in the mid-seventeenth century, Spanish Florida by 1706 was reduced to a handful of refugee missions with just over four hundred Indians huddled around the terrorized residents of St. Augustine. Subsequent raids pushed unconverted (and hence unprotected) south Florida Indians to the Keys, and many ultimately fled to Cuba in 1711 and were followed irregularly by others as late as 1760.

St. Augustine survived another half century, but it did so primarily as an isolated coastal colonial outpost surrounded by a devastated mission zone well over one hundred miles in radius on all sides. The remainder of Spanish Florida was quickly exploited as hunting grounds and eventually even resettled by the very Indians who had terrorized the region for decades and later by the English themselves to the north in what eventually became Georgia. By the 1715 Yamasee War greater Spanish Florida had become a hostile wasteland traversed by armed slave raiders in search of anyone they could find to counter increasing debts to English traders.

The Indian slave trade was self-limiting and dwindled in importance after the near total devastation of all unarmed groups across the South. When all potential victims were either dead, gone, or themselves armed, English firearms were increasingly turned toward the burgeoning deer population. Prowess in hunting slaves was equally advantageous in the deerskin trade. Whether the victims were Indians or deer, commercial hunting had become entrenched as the lifestyle of survival for the groups that remained after the chaotic decades of the slave trade. Not only had the entire social geography of Spanish Florida been violently reformulated through the devastation and extinction of many groups, but also the survivors — the slave-raiders themselves — had largely been transformed from sedentary agriculturalists who hunted on the side to highly mobile commercial hunters who farmed on the side. The slave trade did not result solely in a reduction of population and a physical reshuffling of the social landscape; it also wrought more fundamental changes in the very fabric of social organization among the remaining groups.

Origins of the Slave Trade in Greater Spanish Florida

The beginning of the Southern Indian slave trade can be dated to the late 1650s, when a mobile and armed band of Erie Indians originally from the town known by the French as Rigue arrived in western Virginia near the falls of the James River. This group, known as Riquerrons, had been routed by the Onondaga in January 1656 and fled their palisaded town when they ran out of ammunition for their guns. Following initial skirmishes that same year, expansionist Virginia traders quickly established trade relations with the Riquerrons (or Richahecrians), who subsequently pushed far to the south in search of Indian slaves along the frontiers of Spanish Florida.[3]

These Eries were not the first immigrants from the far northern hinterland beyond Spanish Florida, but they were evidently the first to possess firearms. Further, they seem to have been the first to be linked directly to the commercial slave trade. During the early 1620s an unrelated group called the Chisca migrated from their original homeland in southwestern

Virginia far to the south and into Spanish Florida.[4] Probably representing the first domino effect of the Iroquois Wars in the South to enter Spanish Florida, the refugee Chiscas seem to have maintained a sort of "parasitic" existence in and along the margins of the Spanish mission system, initially settling along the St. Johns River Valley in central Florida before being expelled for insurrection and general troublemaking in 1650. They ultimately settled in the northwest Florida panhandle, where they remained a thorn in the side of Spanish Florida for decades to come. Documentary accounts explicitly indicate they captured their first firearm shortly before 1676 from the Richahecrians themselves and thus were almost certainly not involved as raiders in the English slave trade prior to that point. The Chiscas were more victims than participants in the earliest English-sponsored slaving along the deepest Florida frontier.

The arrival of the Richahecrians was a very different affair altogether. In 1659 fugitives from the interior began to arrive in Spanish Florida with horrific stories of Northern raiders with painted faces and English firearms, characteristics that earned them the designation Chichimecos by Spanish Floridians, referring to the group that ravaged northern New Spain during the previous century.[5] In 1661 these immigrant Erie slavers made their first direct assault against the Guale mission province in coastal Georgia, and additional raids in 1662 along the northern Guale frontier may have coincided with the establishment of a primary base of operations along the Savannah River. In direct consequence, by no later than the following year, a new confederacy called the Yamasees seems to have emerged among refugees from destroyed chiefdoms in central Georgia and perhaps elsewhere.[6] By the late 1660s the Yamasees and other groups along the lower South Carolina coast had fled south into the Mocama mission province, receiving Spanish protection in exchange for participation in the annual *repartimiento* labor draft. When Charles Town was established in 1670, the northern Florida missions were already in a state of contraction, aggregation, and outright retreat in the face of Richahecrian slave raids.

Yet another name was bestowed on the Eries at Augusta by the early Carolina settlers, and this name — Westo — has survived the test of time to become the preferred denomination for the immigrant Eries from Rigue.

In 1674 Carolina pioneer Henry Woodward established formal contact with these Virginia-based slavers who had previously dominated Carolina's western and southern frontier. Three years later, Woodward's trade was formalized, though strictly controlled by the proprietary Carolina government. With this new Carolina connection the Westos continued to ravage the Spanish mission frontier, additionally pushing many unwitting groups along the Carolina frontier into English alliances.[7] By spring 1680 all mainland missions along Florida's northern frontier had been relocated east or south to the barrier islands in defense against the Westo slavers. Nevertheless, not long after an aggressive and successful Westo-led slave raid on the Guale capital, an independent group of Carolina traders called the Goose Creek Men along with Henry Woodward and the proprietary government launched their own campaign to eliminate the Westos' stranglehold on the slave trade and used a group of immigrant Shawnees called the Savannah to wage war against the Westos. By May 1681 fugitive Westos were reported to Spanish authorities to be flooding into Coweta along the western frontier, and English reports two years later suggested that not fifty Westos remained alive, scattered and virtually powerless.[8] Within a few short years Westo power had been destroyed, ending their two-decade monopoly on the Southern Indian slave trade. The damage was done, however, and the remnants of Spanish Guale and Mocama were easily swept away by successive pirate raids in 1683 and 1684. The Yamasees fled the failed Spanish protection, aggregating with other groups in the deep interior. Within the space of twenty-three years the entire coastline of present-day Georgia was wholly depopulated, in large part due to the effectiveness of the Westos in the early Indian slave trade.[9]

Yamasee and Creek Slaving

After a brief interval dominated by the Savannah replacements for the Westos, two pivotal events in 1685 combined to usher in the next phase of the Indian slave trade. First, after the 1684 establishment of a short-lived Scottish colony along the southern Carolina frontier at Stuart's Town, the bulk of the Yamasees who had fled to the interior in 1683 returned to the South Carolina coast, allying themselves with the Scots to initiate a bold new slave raid into the heart of the Florida mission territory.[10] The 1685 Yamasee raid on the Timucuan mission of Santa Catalina de Afuyca was a benchmark, marking the entry of the once-allied Yamasees into the slave raids against Spanish Florida. Later that same year, Henry Woodward embarked on a mission to establish formal trade relations with confederated towns of the powerful Apalachicola province in western Georgia, later to be known as the Uchises by the Spanish and the Lower Creeks by the English.[11] By August, Woodward had used Yamasee allies to make successful contact with the Apalachicola, and within short order at least two stockades were constructed in the northern reaches of the province to house the English and their trade goods.[12]

Spanish retaliation to both these Carolina advances resulted only in minor retreats of various Indians into areas of effective English control and evidently only hardened the resolve of the Creek and Yamasee slavers. Two successive expeditions by Spanish provincial lieutenant Antonio Matheos to Apalachicola in the fall and winter of 1685 only resulted in the burning of four unrepentant towns, and the 1689 construction of a Spanish fort near an Apalachicola town eventually provoked just two years later a wholesale migration of all the Creek towns eastward to the Ocmulgee River where English trade continued unabated.[13] To the east, following two successive Spanish retaliatory raids in the fall and winter of 1686 in which Stuart's Town was destroyed, the Yamasees moved north and inland from the barrier islands of Georgia and South Carolina, ultimately settling just inland from Port Royal.

From these new bases the Yamasees and Lower Creeks waged an effective campaign of terror against Spanish Florida. Over the next few years more aggressive raids pushed deeper and deeper into Spanish territory, eventually bringing the Spanish mission system to its knees. Though small-scale raiding appears to have been increasingly common during this period, it was the full-scale assaults against major population centers that sparked prominent mention in the ethnohistorical record. In 1691 a combined force of Yamasee and Creek warriors attacked mission San Juan de Guacara along the modern Suwannee River, killing or capturing many of the town's Timucuan residents and burning the town itself. San Juan was never reestablished, and two of its nearest neighboring missions soon relocated westward toward the garrisoned Apalachee province, leaving a vast gap in the western chain of Spanish missions.[14]

The pace of raiding against Spanish Florida increased significantly beginning in 1702 as slaving for the first time became a component of outright warfare waged by Carolina against Florida at the outbreak of Queen Anne's War. In May a one-hundred-man force of Creek warriors descended upon the Timucua mission Santa Fé, nearly destroying the mission and returning with many prisoners and scalps.[15] A Spanish lieutenant was subsequently killed on his horse as he chased the raiders with a small Timucuan force. In the early fall a larger force of four hundred Creeks, Chiscas, Westos, and others under the leadership of three English officers set out from Hitchiti town in middle Georgia to invade the Apalachee missions, and on the same day some eight hundred Apalachees, Chacatos, and Timucuans set out northward under Spanish leadership to exact revenge on the Creeks. The two forces met along the lower Flint River, and during what was subsequently known as the Battle of the Blankets (the Creeks laid a trap by arranging blankets to feign sleep as a lure for the Spanish-allied forces), the Spanish forces were completely routed, with the loss of perhaps three hundred who were killed or captured and some two hundred who deserted and fled on foot.[16]

Later that same fall South Carolina Governor James Moore launched a massive invasion of eastern Spanish Florida, using some five hundred Yamasee and Creek warriors who accompanied the English land-based force in a two-pronged assault that reached to the very walls of the Castillo de San Marcos itself. The entire remnants of the Guale and Mocama mission provinces were overrun, pushing Florida's northeastern boundary even farther to the south. This siege was followed just over a year later by yet another ambitious series of raids, this time against Florida's westernmost missions in Apalachee. In 1704, accompanied by more than one thousand Creek warriors and a force of fifty Englishmen, Moore and his Indian allies completely decimated the province, killing hundreds, enslaving more than a thousand, and forcing over two thousand into exile. Some fourteen villages were reduced to ashes, and the entire province was abandoned. Shortly after the Spanish evacuation, the remaining western-most Timucuan missions were similarly destroyed, and despite regrouping and additional defenses the eastern Timucuan missions, after repeated attacks, finally withdrew between August 1705 and May 1706.[17]

By summer 1706 what had been a total mission population of sixty-five hundred Indians a quarter century earlier had been reduced to just over four hundred refugees huddled in and around St. Augustine, leaving the western border effectively unoccupied and undefended.[18] While many of the more than six thousand lost during this time were undoubtedly victims of disease or had voluntarily entered exile outside the formal bounds of Spanish Florida, a substantial portion of this number were victims of the slave raids carried out in large part by Yamasees and Creeks operating out of Georgia and South Carolina. And this number does not include the many thousands captured or killed in the unconverted regions in the southern Florida peninsula during the subsequent few years.

The western mission chain of Spanish Florida had stood as a bul-wark against the worst hostilities of the slave raiding through the last decade of the seventeenth century, but even when gaps in the Camino Real (the road that connected the line of missions across present-day north Florida) were opened up as missions were relocated for protection, the presence of the Apalachee and Timucua missions still provided a magnet to confine slave raids to northern Florida. There is no evidence of any substantial penetration of the southern Florida peninsula until the 1704 decimation of Apalachee. From that point on, south Florida increasingly became a target for slaving. The long-lived policy of isola-tionism and resistance under which the Calusa and other unconverted south Florida chiefdoms had lived for so many decades as neighbors of Spanish Florida ultimately proved to be their downfall in the context of English-sponsored slaving from the far North. What had successfully kept the forces of Spanish colonialism at bay for nearly two centuries also ensured that these groups possessed neither the firearms to defend themselves nor the political relationships to garner Spanish support and protection. Backed by Spanish troops, Florida's mission Indians with-stood the onslaught of English-sponsored slave raiding for nearly half a century between 1659 and 1706, but the unallied Indians of south Florida were almost wholly decimated during the seven years between 1704 and 1711. What had withstood nearly two centuries of European presence was annihilated in less than a decade.

Enslaving South Florida and the Yamasee War

With the 1704–06 collapse of the western mission chain, peninsular Spanish Florida lay completely open and utterly vulnerable for continued raids by armed bands of Yamasees and Creeks, who rapidly plunged deep into the heart of south Florida. Spanish documents are largely silent as to the details of this newest wave of attacks, though subsequent accounts indicate that as early as 1704, the chief of Cayo Hueso, or Key West, was granted permission to immigrate with his people as refugees from such raids to Cuba. The Florida governor later lamented in 1715 that he had been unable to prevent the coastline of Carlos and the rest of south Florida from being overrun three years earlier and had only been able to save those in the immediate environs of St. Augustine.[19]

Details of one memorable slave raid that probably took place during these first few years after the collapse of the missions were recorded by Carolina Indian trader Thomas Nairne and subsequently published posthumously. Accompanying a band of thirty-three Yamasee raiders on an expedition upriver and south along the then-unguarded St. Johns River, the party disembarked and traveled overland through the central Florida Lake District and deep into south Florida, ultimately capturing some thirty-five slaves before being counterattacked by thirty-three Indian warriors armed only with spears, all of whom were killed.

In a letter accompanying a newly drawn map of the Southern borderlands as early as 1708, Nairne reported that the Florida peninsula had been largely depopulated of its Native inhabitants, noting that the Yamasees at that time were "now obliged to goe down as farr on the point of Florida as the firm land will permit." He noted that "they have drove the Floridians to the Islands of the Cape, have brought in and sold many hundreds of them, and dayly now continue that trade so that in some few years thay'le reduce these barbarians to a farr less number."[20] Nairne's comment that the south Florida Indians had been driven beyond the reach of dry land, past the Everglades, and into the Florida Keys is confirmed by details of the 1720 Moll map on which his earlier Yamasee raid was also reported. The map shows "many villages" located in the southeastern tip of the Florida peninsula, confirming subsequent evidence regarding the retreat of these surviving refugees.[21]

During the rampages of 1704–11 the surviving south Florida Indians seem to have fled largely in two directions: south to Miami and the Keys and north to St. Augustine. Both areas ultimately became safe havens for refugees. As late as 1707 only five mission towns were listed at St. Augustine, and all were comprised of refugee Guales, Timucuans, and Apalachees from the northern mission territories. But in a 1711 census a total of eight towns were recorded, including one town consisting of more than a hundred Ais and other coastal south Florida Indians.[22] Many more refugees from the rest of south Florida congregated in the southeastern corner of the peninsula and the Keys where they were protected from the land-based raiders. By 1711 this refugee band included the chief of the Calusa and most or all other neighboring chiefs and many of their surviving vassals, many of whom ultimately requested permission to immigrate to Cuba.

This migration was not without precedent, for Cuban and Spanish records reveal the sporadic presence of south Florida Indians in and around Havana from as early as 1688, with their numbers increasing through the 1690s.[23] By the time of the devastating raids that pushed the Calusa and other south Florida Indians to the Keys, Havana seems to have been familiar territory. In the spring of 1711 a Franciscan friar visiting Key West baptized the dying Calusa chief, who requested transport for his vassals to Cuba. Soon thereafter, a Spanish vessel returned and picked up some two hundred and seventy Indians, including fifty vassals of the Calusa chief, as well as two hundred and twenty other Indians including the chiefs of Jove, Miami, Tancha, Muspa, and Rioseco (or Jeaga). The Calusa chief, who was actively engaged in distant warfare with the Yamasees upon the boat's arrival, sent his brother-in-law the Great Captain and evidently came to Havana later to be baptized as Phelipe V. Nevertheless, after being settled together at the bluff called La Cabaña overlooking the bay, within a few months he along with three other chiefs and up to two hundred Indians perished from rampant epidemics of typhus and smallpox. The survivors were divided up among private citizens around Havana, while others were evidently sent inland, with only sixteen or eighteen ultimately returning to their homeland in Florida.[24]

The depopulation of most of south Florida by Yamasee and Creek raiders between 1704 and 1711 and the resultant flight of survivors either north to St. Augustine or south to the Keys resulted in a substantial falloff in the number of available slaves in the Carolina market, a condition that reached crisis proportions in 1712 and 1713.[25] Based on the firsthand testimony of the Indians themselves, it was precisely the depopulation and final evacuation of south Florida that precipitated this abrupt drop in supply. And it was the subsequent threats of Carolina traders against heavily indebted Yamasees that ultimately sparked the 1715 Yamasee War, which radically changed the political and economic landscape of the South. As related by Lower Creek war chief Yfallaquisca, otherwise known as Perro Bravo (Brave Dog), in his May 1715 meeting with the governor of Florida,

> the causes that moved them to this were many, but . . . two years ago, when the English saw that now the Indians did not bring them any more Indian prisoners of those that they captured in these parts [Florida], razing the land, whom they went to search for by order of the English along the southern coast, in the provinces of Jororo and Mayaca, of these [Spanish] dominions, in order with these prisoners to continue paying the English for the guns, powder, balls, cutlasses, pistols, cassocks, hats, and other valuables which were given to them in credit, and bottles of firewater, the English told them that if they failed to pay them in slaves, they would take payment by making slaves of the debtors themselves, and their children and wives, and carry them off for sale to other places . . . they resolved to send secret messages to all the provinces about the damages that the English wished to do them, taking away their children and wives as slaves because now they could not find Indian slaves to take along the southern coasts, and that they should be prepared to make war on the English everywhere in case they should place this in execution.[26]

In a very real way, just as the thousands of residents of the Florida missions effectively served as a fundamental component of the glutted market for Indian slaves around the turn of the eighteenth century, the final devastation of south Florida's remaining indigenous populations by about 1712 marked the abrupt end of this short-lived boom-and-bust slave market. This was particularly the case for the Yamasee slavers of coastal South Carolina, who by that time were effectively boxed-in by other slaving societies with continuing access to remaining native populations in the midcontinental region. While greater Spanish Florida had fueled rapid and substantial success for Yamasee slavers between 1685 and 1712, the abrupt void left by its wholesale depopulation left the Yamasees in a state of overwhelming debt.

The overt pressure exerted by English traders over the next few years, combined with several provocative steps taken by English authorities during this period (including a census of allied native populations), resulted in a widespread rebellion that shattered the status quo as of 1715. Not only did this result in the flight of most of the Yamasees to find refuge in St. Augustine among their former victims and the gradual repopulation of the devastated western mission provinces by Creeks and remaining Yamasees alike, but it also shifted the overall dynamic of the Indian slave trade, which never recovered its former strength.[27] Carolina's burgeoning slave economy was irrevocably altered. Before 1715 the Carolina colony exported more slaves than it imported — mostly Indians — while in the aftermath of the Yamasee War, the maximum number of African slaves imported annually jumped more than one thousand percent within just over a decade, rising from one hundred and seventy or less between 1706 and 1716 to as many as seventeen hundred to twenty-four hundred during the late 1720s and 1730s.[28] Also transformed was the role of the commercial slave hunters, whose firearms were increasingly turned to the artificially expanded deer population resulting from the almost total removal of normal human predation in many depopulated regions. The exploitation and eventual exhaustion of the vast pool of Indian slaves captured from Spanish Florida between 1659 and 1715 thus played a pivotal role in setting the stage for an entirely new American South, one that would never again be the same either for European colonists or remaining Southern Indians.

The difference between the pre-Indian and the post-Indian slave trade in the South cannot be measured merely in terms of the number of people or groups victimized, destroyed, or relocated as a result of half a century of slave raiding by the Westos, Yamasees, Creeks, and others. Slavers experienced tremendous and ultimately irrevocable cultural changes. To be sure, the introduction and spread of a vast commercial trade in manufactured goods provided by the English had its effect on the slave raiders as primary consumers of these materials. Historical and archaeological evidence make it abundantly clear that all such groups assimilated a wide range of European goods into their daily lives, from tools and weapons to cloth and jewelry. Yet trade goods were neither the primary cause nor the primary result of change during the slave-trade years.

As I have argued elsewhere, it was a far more fundamental shift in production on a local scale that resulted in such extensive cultural transformations among the slave raiders who ultimately survived this turbulent era.[29] Specifically, the introduction of the two elements mentioned above — firearms and a commercial demand for slaves — fostered the emergence of a small number of warlike groups that specialized in commercial slave raiding and hunting. It was the strategic funneling of flintlock muskets to selected groups that paved the way for the emergence of a new social order. Firearms provided unparalleled military might in the seventeenth-and early eighteenth-century South, especially when concentrated in the hands of a few strategically positioned groups who were in a position to provide ready access to abundant sources of Indian slaves, particularly along the Spanish mission frontier.

Nevertheless, the adoption of English guns by these groups resulted in an immediate and near total dependency on English traders for ready supplies of gunpowder and shot. Thus these groups were linked to the expanding network of English commerce. Because Indian slaves were the preferred and most valuable commodities that could be provided by these guns, slave raiding quickly became the primary productive activity of these interior groups, rapidly supplanting agricultural production as a means of providing for security and political and economic well being.

Aggregate chiefdoms that had probably been just on the verge of re-establishing a more traditional chiefly agricultural economy after more than a century of disruptions in the deep frontier were suddenly transformed into commercial hunters working as primary producers on the far colonial periphery of northern Europe. Farmers who supplemented their staple crops with secondary hunting found themselves drawn into a new economic system in which warfare and hunting were primary and in which farming was only secondary.

This is not to say that the reduction in agricultural production had anything to do with the prolonged absence of males on slaving expeditions, especially since women likely played a substantial role in farming activities at many stages in the agricultural cycle. Instead, in a world in which commercial slaving and hunting took increasing priority over agricultural surpluses in defining indigenous political power and socioeconomic status, the totality of farming activities shifted from a central role to a more peripheral one. Surplus production was now directed toward communal slave raids and individual hunting, and surplus agricultural productivity probably dropped off to a minimum. Chiefs whose hereditary power was based principally on the management of human labor on lands owned by the chiefly lineage were devalued as primary productivity took place farther and farther from chiefly territories and under far less centralized control. The agricultural chiefdoms were now supplanted by new social formations such as the coalescent societies described in this volume. Chiefs who had always been at the center of a very small world were now thrust onto the periphery of a colonial world centered in Europe.

All these changes amounted to a fundamental transformation in the cultural landscape of the South, paralleling comparable changes in Europe and elsewhere, all ultimately leading to the development of the world we see today. It is no coincidence that virtually all of the major second-generation slave-raiding groups are still in existence, and all of their initial victims are essentially extinct. The Creeks, combined with absorbed remnants of the Westos and the Yamasees, were and are the survivors of this turbulent era in which virtually all their neighbors — the Guales, the Mocamas, the Timucuans, the Apalachees, the Calusas, and many others — are but distant memories now relegated to the domain of historians and archaeologists.

In the final analysis the Southern Indian slave trade seems aptly characterized as a powerful shock wave radiating out from the English colonies along the middle Atlantic coastline, one which was a catalyst for rapid and far-reaching changes throughout greater Spanish Florida. In this sense Spanish Florida formed an important component of what has been characterized as a colonial shatter zone resulting from the introduction of and competition for commercial trade along a colonial frontier.[30] This shock wave emanating from Virginia and South Carolina almost literally swept away most of mid-seventeenth-century Spanish Florida, including all of its surrounding mission provinces and many adjacent groups and virtually all groups to the south. No surviving groups remained unchanged, including victims and aggressors. And while many colonial transformations occurred both before and after the passage of this particular shock wave, I doubt that many can compare to the speed and power of the Indian slave trade in terms of its effect on the residents — Indian, European, and African alike — of greater Spanish Florida.

Notes

1. For example, see Gallay, *Indian Slave Trade*.

2. For a synthetic overview of the Spanish colonial system in Florida, see Worth, *Timucuan Chiefdoms*.

3. Hahn, "Invention of the Creek Nation," 63–66; Hahn, *Invention of the Creek Nation, 1670–1763* , 17; Bowne, "Rise and Fall"; and Bowne, *Westo Indians*, 37–53. See also Fox, this volume; and Meyers, this volume.

4. Worth, *Timucuan Chiefdoms*, 2:18–21, 34–35, 208n48; Worth, "Spanish Missions," 47, 281–82n27; Hann, "Florida's Terra Incognita"; Hann, "Visitations and Revolts," 31–75; and Galloway, Jeter, Waselkov, Worth, and Goddard, "Small Tribes," 176–77.

5. Worth, *Struggle for the Georgia Coast*, 15–20.

6. Worth, "Yamasee Origins"; Worth, "Yamasee"; and Worth "Struggle for the Georgia Coast."

7. Worth, *Struggle for the Georgia Coast*, 26–27; and Bowne, "Rise and Fall," 69–70.

8. Crane, *Southern Frontier* (2004) 19–21; Worth, *Struggle for the Georgia Coast*, 30–34; Hahn, "Invention of the Creek Nation," 102–4; Hahn, *Invention of the Creek Nation*, 34–35; and Bowne, "Rise and Fall," 70–73.

9. Worth, *Struggle for the Georgia Coast*, 47–50. See also Bowne, this volume; Meyers, this volume; Fox, this volume; and Jennings, this volume.

10. Worth, *Struggle for the Georgia Coast*, 42–47; Worth, *Timucuan Chiefdoms*, 2:40–41; and Hann, *History of the Timucua*, 272–74.

11. Crane, *Southern Frontier* (2004) 33–36; Hahn, "Invention of the Creek Nation," 116–19; and Hahn, *Invention of the Creek Nation*, 6, 49–52.

12. Hahn, "Invention of the Creek Nation," 129–35; and Hahn, *Invention of the Creek Nation*, 40–47.

13. Crane, *Southern Frontier* (2004) 35–36; Hahn, "Invention of the Creek Nation," 119–56; Hahn, *Invention of the Creek Nation*, 49–52; and Worth, "Lower Creeks," 278–86.

14. Worth, *Timucuan Chiefdoms*, 2:42–43, 141–42; and Hann, *History of the Timucua*, 265–66.

15. Hann, *History of the Timucua*, 293–94; Worth, *Timucuan Chiefdoms*, 2:144; and Hahn, *Invention of the Creek Nation*, 60–61.

16. Francisco Romo de Uriza to Governor of Florida, Letter Regarding the Expedition against the Creeks, October 22, 1702, AGI, 858; Manuel Solana to Governor of Florida, Letter Regarding the Expedition against the Creeks, October 22, 1702, AGI, 858; Swanton, *Early History*, 120–21; Crane, *Southern Frontier* (2004) 74; Hahn, "Invention of the Creek Nation," 198–203; and Hahn, *Invention of the Creek Nation*, 62–63.

17. Worth, *Timucuan Chiefdoms*, 2:145–46; Hann, *Apalachee*, 60–62, 264–317, 385–397; and Arnade, *Siege of St. Augustine*.

18. Worth, *Timucuan Chiefdoms*, 2:147–49.

19. Francisco de Corcoles y Martínez to Spanish Crown, Letter Regarding the Arrival of the Yamasees, July 5, 1715, AGI, 843; and Hann, *Missions to the Calusa*, 402–3.

20. Thomas Nairne to Lords Proprietors, Letter Regarding the Indians of Carolina, July 10, 1708, Sainsbury, *Records in the British Public Records Office*, 7:193–202.

21. Herman Moll, "A New Map of the North Parts of America Claimed by France," 1720, HL.

22. Worth, *Timucuan Chiefdoms*, 2:147–49.

23. For example, see Worth, "History."

24. Juan Francisco de Guëmes y Horcasitas to Spanish Crown, Letter Regarding the Keys Indian Mission, July 26, 1743, AGI, 860; Joseph María Monaco and Joseph Xavier Alaña, Report to the Governor of Havana Regarding the Proposed Mission to the Keys Indians (unpublished translation by R. W. Childers in possession of the author), 1742, AGN, Jesuitas III-17; Gerónimo Valdés, Autos Regarding

the Transport of Indians from Carlos, Coleto, and the Keys to Havana, March 5–April 18, 1711, AGI, 860.

25. Hahn, *Invention of the Creek Nation*, 74–80.

26. Francisco de Corcoles y Martinez, Francisco Menéndez Márquez, and Salvador García de Villegas, Autos Regarding the Arrival of the Yamasees, May 28–29, 1715, AGI, 843.

27. Hann, "St. Augustine's Fallout"; Hann, *History of the Timucua*, 306–11; Worth, *Timucuan Chiefdoms*, 2:149–50; and Worth, "Yamasee," 252.

28. Gallay, *Indian Slave Trade*, 299, 346.

29. Worth, "Spanish Missions"; and Worth, "Bridging Prehistory and History."

30. Wolf, *Europe and the People Without History*; and Ethridge, "Creating the Shatter Zone."

12 | *Shattered and Infected*

EPIDEMICS AND THE ORIGINS OF
THE YAMASEE WAR, 1696–1715

PAUL KELTON

South Carolina's Native slave trade certainly shattered indigenous societies, but it was not the only aspect of colonialism doing the shattering. While South Carolina's Native slave trade was at its height, epidemics of the Atlantic World's most lethal germs ravaged the South and its inhabitants. During the nineteen years before the Yamasee War erupted in 1715, epidemic after epidemic struck the South and devastated both raiding groups allied with the English and their victims. South Carolina's trading partners along the Upper Path — an exchange route that stretched across the deep South from the Savannah to the Tombigbee — especially suffered.[1] Upper Path groups including the Yamasees, Lower Creeks, Upper Creeks, and Chickasaws each lost over fifty percent of their populations between 1696 and 1715.

While scholars of the Native slave trade have not entirely ignored disease, the connection between the noxious commerce in human captives and epidemics needs further explanation.[2] By focusing on South Carolina's relations with its Upper Path allies, this chapter will show how disease-induced depopulation and enslavement were connected in two highly significant ways. First, English-inspired commerce in indigenous captives with its high volume of human traffic served as a primary mechanism for the spread of infectious germs throughout the South. Second, the epidemics that spread along the routes of slave trading and raiding caused the commerce in human captives to collapse and thus sowed the seeds of the Yamasee War.

Few topics in the history of the colonial South have engendered as much debate as the issue of virgin soil epidemics and the timing of their occurrence. Some scholars maintain that European explorers and would-be colonizers brought a variety of deadly new diseases with them as early as the sixteenth century and that these diseases caused a massive population collapse among indigenous peoples long before the English ever arrived on the scene.[3] I have argued elsewhere that virgin soil epidemics were much more limited in scope until English commerce integrated the entire region into the Atlantic World in the late seventeenth century.[4]

Whatever the outcome of this debate, no one should doubt that the nineteen-year period leading up to the Yamasee War was a particularly deadly time for Southern Natives. Documentary evidence makes it clear that several waves of diseases swept through the region with deadly consequences for its indigenous inhabitants and that English commerce in indigenous captives enhanced Native vulnerability to imported germs. An examination of the disease history of Upper Path slave raiders from 1696 to 1715 indeed reveals a startling story of biological catastrophe.

The Great Southeastern Smallpox Epidemic, the first historically documented virgin soil epidemic to have a regionwide impact, was clearly linked to the Native slave trade (see map 14). This tragic event began in Virginia in 1696, then spread south into the Carolina piedmont, and finally reached Charles Town by February 1697. Over the course of the next year the virus entered into South Carolina's trade network and exploded into an even more massive epidemic.[5] One Carolinian commented on what must have been a truly horrific site: "smallpox . . . has been mortal to all sorts of the inhabitants & especially the Indians who tis said to have swept away a whole neighboring nation, all to 5 or 6 which ran away and left their dead unburied, lying upon the ground for the vultures to devouer."[6]

For some Carolinians worried about possible Native hostilities due to the escalating slave trade, the epidemic was a blessing. Because so many indigenous peoples died, colonial officials expected that trade would diminish and that Carolina settlers would have "no Reason to Expect any Mischeif from ye Indian Trade, the Small-pox hath killed so many of them that we have little Reason to believe they will be Capable of doing any Harm to us for severall Years to Come."[7] The epidemic did in fact have a vast geographic spread involving numerous Native communities. Governor Joseph Blake informed the colony's proprietors that smallpox had "swept off great Numbers of [indigenous peoples] 4 or

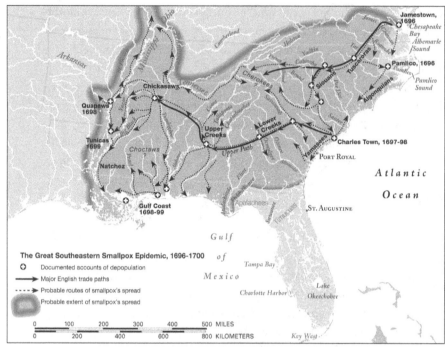

Map 14. The Great Southeastern Smallpox Epidemic, 1696–1700. Adapted from *Epidemics and Enslavement*, Kelton, 142, by permission of the University of Nebraska Press.

500 Miles Inland as well upon ye Sea Cost as in our Neighbourhood."[8] The governor's remarks revealed that he and his fellow colonists had just witnessed one of the worst demographic catastrophes to have ever happened in the South.

Blake's comments underestimated the geographic extent of the Great Southeastern Smallpox Epidemic. After arriving in South Carolina sometime before February 1697, the virus made an overland trip from South Carolina to the Mississippi Valley and Gulf Coast where the French found Natives reeling from the disease from 1698 through 1700.[9] Smallpox undoubtedly arrived there by way of South Carolina's Upper Path trading allies. Thomas Nairne's 1708 journal provides unambiguous evidence that the nasty virus had spread along the slave trade's most important avenue. Nairne, an official from South Carolina, traveled the Upper Path and provided the most detailed observations of the Southern interior since Hernando de Soto's expedition in the sixteenth century. The traveling Carolinian reported that the inhabitants along the Upper Path could remember a time when their communities grew too large and had to send out colonies, whose inhabitants deferentially referred to their parent community as "grandfather." In recent times, however, the reverse had been the case. Upper Path communities ravaged by smallpox were forced to unite their communities "for want of inhabitants."[10] There was no smallpox epidemic between 1700 and the time of Nairne's visit, thus indicating that the Great Southeastern Smallpox Epidemic was a seminal event in the coalescence of peoples into the emerging Yamasees, Lower Creeks, Upper Creeks, and Chickasaws.

The Great Southeastern Smallpox Epidemic was just the beginning of a devastating period in which Upper Path communities experienced wave after wave of imported diseases. European records made note of several "pestilences," "plagues," "distempers," "grievous sicknesses," and other vaguely identified outbreaks that were followed by a return of smallpox in 1711 (see table 3). Upper Path communities were highly vulnerable to several of these epidemics, which served as potent aftershocks for peoples who had suffered steep losses during the 1690s. Just as with the Great Southeastern Smallpox Epidemic, subsequent outbreaks spread west by way of trade caravans that regularly departed from Charles Town. In addition, germs reached the Upper Path by way of captives taken from Gulf Coast and Mississippi Valley peoples whose bodies carried diseases that the French and Spanish introduced (see map 15).

On the Carolina coast, at the eastern terminus of the Upper Path, the Yamasees had especially suffered from the outbreaks following the Great Southeastern Smallpox Epidemic. Slave raids and intercourse with the English kept the Yamasees vulnerable to infection.[11] The Scottish trader John Stewart, for example, reported in a 1711 letter that he was among the Yamasees at an earlier time when they returned home from their enemy's country and suffered from a "raging pestilence."[12] While the exact year of the epidemic and the particular disease involved cannot be discerned from Stewart's cryptic letter, the "raging pestilence" could have been a result of the 1699, 1703, or 1704 epidemic that hit the Gulf Coast. Even more certain, some Yamasees became infected with a deadly disease during their participation in the Tuscarora War (1711–13), a war that occurred during a time in which the whole colony of South Carolina was reeling

Table 3. Aftershock epidemics of the South

DATE	LOCATION	DESCRIPTION	CAUSE
1699 January–March	Gulf Coast	"plague"	typhus or influenza (conjectural)
1699 August–November	Charles Town	"Infectious, Pestilentiall & Mortal Distemper"	yellow fever
1703 [unknown]	Florida	170 Apalachees perished at Mission San Luis	unknown
1704 July–September	Mobile	"plague"	typhus, influenza, or measles
1706 summer–fall	Charles Town	"pestilential fever"	yellow fever
1706 [unknown]	Louisiana	"general sickness"	yellow fever (conjectural)
1708 summer	Pensacola	"plague"	unknown
1709 February	South Carolina	"strange distempers" involving paralysis of arms and legs	unknown
1711 winter	South Carolina	"many spectacles of sickness and mortality"	unknown
1711 May–1712 March	South Carolina	several direct references to smallpox	smallpox
1711 fall–1712 winter	South Carolina	"Pestilential ffeavers" "Pleurisy" and "Malignant Feavers" "spotted fever"	yellow fever, influenza (conjectural), measles, or typhus (conjectural)

Source: The following sources were consulted to reconstruct the epidemics listed above: 1699 GULF COAST: Iberville, *Gulf Journals*, 20–21. Because the outbreak occurred in winter, the disease was more likely to be a cold-weather one such as typhus or influenza than yellow fever. The disease was possibly responsible for the grave illness that Spanish soldiers at Pensacola suffered after receiving a visit from the French. See Iberville, *Gulf Journals*, 94.

1699 CHARLES TOWN: Governor Joseph Blake et al. to Lords Proprietors, January 17, 1700, Salley, *Commissions and Instructions*, 129. The disease involved was certainly yellow fever because it had caused fatality rates more severe than one would expect from malaria and because it occurred in the summer time and did not spread outside of Charles Town. John Duffy agrees; Duffy, *Epidemics in Colonial America*, 143.

1703 FLORIDA: Hann, *Apalachee*, 167. The epidemic likely spread to other Apalachee missions as well.

1704 MOBILE: Bienville to Pontchartrain, September 6, 1704; and Bienville, "Memoir [1726]"; both are in Rowland and Sanders, *Mississippi Provincial Archives*, 3:24, 536; and La Harpe, *Historical Journal*, 47. Yellow fever does not appear to be the responsible disease because whatever the illness was it spread widely and struck inland peoples; measles seems the most likely culprit, but typhus or influenza cannot be ruled out.

1706 CHARLES TOWN: This is one of the best-documented single epidemics in the early eighteenth century, and all sources indicate that yellow fever was involved, although the simultaneous occurrence of another disease cannot be ruled out. For its occurrence in South Carolina, see "Account of the Invasion made by the French and Spaniards upon Carolina," Sainsbury, *Records in the British Public Records Office*, 5:172; Mr. Auchinleck to Secretary, October 29, 1706, SPG, ser. A, vol. 3; Entry for November 20, 1706, Salley, *Journal of the Commons House for 1706*, 5; Francis Le Jau to Secretary, December 2, 1706, Le Jau, *Carolina Chronicle*, 17–18; Lords Proprietors to Governor Nathaniel Johnston, March 8, 1707, Salley, *Commissions and Instructions*, 189; Thomas Hasell to Secretary, September 6, 1707, SPG, ser. A, vol. 3; and Hasell to Secretary, November 30, 1707, SPG, ser. A, vol. 3.

1706 LOUISIANA: French sailors including Louisiana's founder Iberville contracted yellow fever and died in the Caribbean during the summer of 1706; later it was reported that the French in Louisiana suffered from a "general sickness" during 1706; La Harpe, *Historical Journal*, 54; and King Louis XIV to De Muy, June 30, 1707, Rowland and Sanders, *Mississippi Provincial Archives*, 3:56.

1708 PENSACOLA: Bienville to Pontchartrain, October 12, 1708, Rowland and Sanders, *Mississippi Provincial Archives*, 2:41, 55. Spanish soldiers died of this "plague."

1709 SOUTH CAROLINA: Le Jau to Secretary, February 18, 1709; Le Jau, *Carolina Chronicle*, 49, 53.

1711 SOUTH CAROLINA: Gideon Johnston to Secretary, January 27, 1711, Klingburg, *Carolina Chronicle*, 67, 91; and Le Jau to Secretary, February 9, 1711, Le Jau, *Carolina Chronicle*, 85.

1711–12 SOUTH CAROLINA (smallpox): May 15, 1711, and October 26, 1711, Transcripts, *Journal of the Commons House of Assembly*, SCDAH; Gideon Johnston to Secretary, November 16, 1711, in Klingburg, *Carolina Chronicle*, 99; Hasell to Secretary, March 12, 1712, SPG, ser. A, vol. 7; Commissary Johnston's Notitia Parochialis, 1711–12, SPG, ser. A, vol. 7; and "An Act for the More Effectual Preventing the Spreading of Contagious Distempers," Cooper, *Statutes at Large*, 2:382.

1711–12 SOUTH CAROLINA: Mr. Dennis to the Secretary, October 7, 1711, SPG, ser. A, vol. 6; and Gideon Johnston to Secretary, November 16, 1711, Klingburg, *Carolina Chronicle*, 99. One of the many illnesses to strike South Carolina during this period was a disease that appeared in August and let up when the cold weather set in; this disease course makes a diagnosis of yellow fever likely. Early modern Europeans often identified influenza as pleurisy because it often led to pneumonia. For reference to pleurisy, see

Gideon Johnston to Secretary, November 16, 1711, in Klingburg, *Carolina Chronicle*, 99; Le Jau to Secretary, January 4 and February 20, 1712, Le Jau, *Carolina Chronicle*, 104, 108; Mr. Dennis to Secretary, February 26, 1712, SPG, ser. A, vol. 7; and Hasell to Secretary, March 12, 1712, SPG, ser. A, vol. 7. Malignant fever may also be a reference to influenza or possibly typhus. For reference to malignant fever, see Hasell to Secretary, March 12, 1712, SPG, ser. A, vol. 7; and "An Act for the More Effectual Preventing the Spreading of Contagious Distempers," Cooper, *Statutes at Large*, 2:382. Both typhus and measles involve small macular eruptions. For reference to spotted fever, see "An Act for the More Effectual Preventing the Spreading of Contagious Distempers," Cooper, *Statutes at Large*, 2:382.

from disease.[13] The Anglican minister Gideon Johnston remarked in fall 1711, "N[e]ver was there a more sickly or fatall season than this for the small Pox, Pestilential ffeavers, Pleurisies and fflex's have destroyed great numbers here of all Sorts, both Whites, Blacks, and Indians."[14] The "Indians" to whom Johnston referred certainly included the Yamasees.

In 1713 another Anglican minister, Francis Le Jau, claimed that all of South Carolina's "allies and neighbors" had decreased and especially pointed to the Yamasees as a declining people. The Yamasees, Le Jau claimed, were "formerly very numerous but by degrees they are come to very little they could muster 800 fighting men and now they are hardly 400."[15] A census that South Carolinian officials compiled in 1715 reaffirmed Le Jau's estimate. The English counted 413 men among a total of 1,215 Yamasees.[16] Considering the Yamasees adopted substantial numbers of captives and even incorporated two communities of Guales who fled from Florida in 1702, their losses were likely in excess of the fifty percent that Le Jau indicated.[17]

Following the course of the Upper Path across the upper Savannah River Valley (around present-day Augusta, Georgia), germs and slave raids produced a fluid situation in what was already a highly dynamic area of Native settlement. In 1704 the Apalachees from northern Florida moved into the upper Savannah Valley. At the beginning of the eighteenth century approximately eight thousand Apalachees lived in northern Florida, but within a period of four years, blistering slave raids drove the Apalachees who had not been taken captive from their homeland.[18] A particularly severe raid occurred in 1703 when Lower Creeks burned three Apalachee towns and returned with over five hundred captives. In 1704 slave-seeking

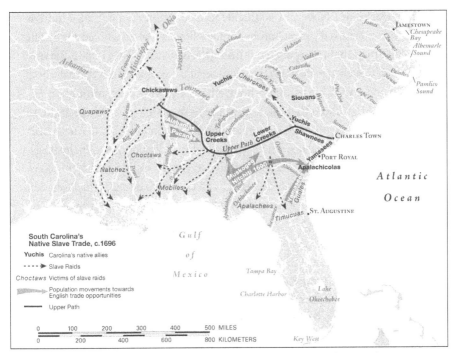

Map 15. South Carolina's Native slave trade, ca. 1696. Adapted from *Epidemics and Enslavement*, Kelton, 201, by permission of the University of Nebraska Press.

Carolinians and their Native allies returned and destroyed five missions. Several months later, an independent Creek raid of six hundred warriors served the finishing blow, attacking the remaining Apalachee towns and forcing the survivors to flee.

As a result of these and other raids the entire population of Apalachees was gone from their homeland.[19] Hundreds certainly ended up dead because of the violence, and at least a thousand were sold to the English as slaves, while others were adopted into Upper Path communities by their Native captors.[20] Some managed to avoid captivity and fled to St. Augustine. Approximately eight hundred individuals made their way to the French at Mobile.[21] Another thirteen hundred agreed to surrender to the English and their Native allies and relocated near the Fall Line of the Savannah not far from where the Upper Path crosses the river.[22] There the Apalachees soon fulfilled a vital role in South Carolina's Upper Path trade network. "These people are seated very advantageous for carrying our trade," Governor Nathaniel Johnson remarked in 1708. "Indians seated upwards of seven hundred miles off are supplied with goods by our white men that transport them from [the Savannah River] upon Indians' backs."[23] Such service would also have kept the Savannah River Apalachees in contact with kinspeople who lived among adoptive communities.

The Apalachees that made it to the Savannah arrived there amid an intense experience with slave raids and germs. In Florida the Apalachees faced constant threats of enemy raids, suffered disruptions to their subsistence routines, and remained confined to germ-ridden Spanish missions. Epidemics, too, took their toll. In 1703 an unknown disease struck Mission San Luis, which served as the central base for the Apalachee province. The outbreak appears to be one of the Atlantic World's deadliest germs because it took the lives of 170 individuals in San Luis alone. It probably spread to outlying villages as well. For those survivors who took up residence on the Savannah, hunger, demoralization, and diseases continued to have a devastating impact. From a population of some 1,300 individuals who relocated on the Upper Path in 1704, the Apalachees had fallen to 638 by 1715.[24] Disease-induced mortality was not solely to blame for such losses. Slaving also contributed. Some, especially women and children, fell into the hands of English slave dealers, while others fled to Creek communities where many of their relatives lived. But one or more of the numerous epidemics that struck the region from 1704 to 1712 certainly accounted for a significant portion of the Apalachees' losses.

The Apalachees' neighbors to the west also faced an onslaught by disease that reverberated along the Upper Path. The Lower Creeks, Upper Creeks, and Chickasaws all experienced destructive epidemics during the years leading up to the Yamasee War. In his 1708 journey, for example, Thomas Nairne not only found evidence that smallpox had preceded him but commented that "other European distempers" had also swept through the towns sometime prior to his arrival.[25] Unfortunately, neither Nairne's journal nor any other European sources reveals what those "other European distempers" were, when exactly they struck, and from where they came. As part of Carolina's vast trade network Creeks and Chickasaws were vulnerable to diseases introduced from the east, but because of their raiding on the Gulf Coast, they were also vulnerable to epidemics from disease that struck the Gulf Coast in 1699, 1703, 1704,

1706, and 1708. The 1703 epidemic in particular had a high likelihood of infecting Upper Path communities because that was the year of one of the massive raids against the Apalachees. If any of the captives were infected, their germs would have disseminated widely among Carolina's Native allies. Similarly, the 1704 epidemic around Mobile had a great potential to spread into the Upper Path because Carolina's indigenous allies were engaged against Mobile Bay area communities.[26]

Some evidence suggests that between 1696 and 1715 the Lower Creeks declined by more than sixty-eight percent because of the Great Southeastern Smallpox Epidemic and subsequent outbreaks. In 1690 John Stewart asserted that the various Muskogee and Hitchiti towns that had coalesced along the Ocmulgee, Oconee, and Ogeechee rivers and their tributaries numbered some 2,500 men. After Stewart made his observations, the numbers of Lower Creeks plummeted, and they became increasingly concentrated in fewer towns, just as Thomas Nairne indicated for Upper Path peoples in general. By 1715 the Lower Creeks had become concentrated on the Ocmulgee River with the exception of some Apalachicolas who alternated locations between the lower Savannah and lower Ogeechee rivers. Together, residents of the Ocmulgee and the Apalachicolas could field only 795 warriors, a sixty-eight percent decrease from the number of warriors that their ancestors could field just twenty-five years before.[27] If the entire Lower Creek population declined by the same percentage as did their warriors alone, then they declined from 8,188 people in 1690 to 2,620 people that South Carolina recorded in its 1715 census. Because Lower Creeks were actively taking in various groups as well as adopting captives, the rate of depopulation was probably even greater than sixty-eight percent. A rate of decline of around seventy-five percent seems a more reasonable estimate, making the core Lower Creek population around 10,500 before the Great Southeastern Smallpox Epidemic in 1696.

The Upper Creeks and Chickasaws were farther removed from South Carolina, so one would expect that they would have declined by a somewhat lesser percentage than the Lower Creeks. Nevertheless, some evidence on the Chickasaws suggests that communities on the western half of the Upper Path declined by a similar percentage as did the Lower Creeks. In 1692 the French reported that the Chickasaws could field as many as two thousand, whereas in 1715 the English counted only seven hundred warriors, a sixty-five percent decline in population from just twenty-three years earlier. Most of those losses probably occurred during the Great Southeastern Smallpox Epidemic, but aftershocks reduced the Chickasaws' number of villages from nine in 1701 to just six in 1715.[28] The warfare involved in Chickasaw slaving certainly played a role in the high death toll for Chickasaws, but they would not have declined by as much as they did without suffering repeated epidemics. If the rate of depopulation of the Chickasaws was indeed sixty-five percent, then the nineteen hundred Chickasaws that the English counted in their 1715 census represented the survivors from a population that numbered around fifty-five hundred in the early 1690s. The Chickasaws also appeared to have been incorporating some of the groups from the Yazoo Basin and adopted at least a portion of their captives, so their rate of depopulation likely exceeded sixty-five percent.[29]

The Upper Creeks also faced substantial losses from the usual high death toll associated with slave raiding, from military losses from French-allied Choctaws, and from their long-standing rivals the Cherokees, making their combined rate of depopulation from slaving, warfare, and germs similar to that of the Chickasaws. The 4,886 Upper Creeks that the English counted in 1715 conceivably represented the survivors of a population that declined by as much as sixty-five percent or of a population that once numbered 13,960 before becoming incorporated into South Carolina's trading network.[30]

If people on the central and western portion of the Upper Path declined by as much as the conjectured seventy-five percent that the Lower Creeks appeared to have declined, then one arrives at pre-1696 populations of 7,600 for the Chickasaws and 19,544 for the Upper Creeks.[31] Regardless of the specific rate of decline for the Upper and Lower Creeks and Chickasaws, these numbers indicate that their populations suffered severely from the biological consequences of being incorporated into the larger Atlantic World and its flow of traders, slaves, and germs.

It was no coincidence that Upper Path communities as well as other Native groups revolted against South Carolina after these periods of epidemics, slaving, and depopulation. As I have shown elsewhere and as John Worth argues in this volume, the potential supply of captives on the eve of the Yamasee War was far from what it had been just nineteen years earlier, and epidemics left Native slave raiders with few viable options to relieve themselves of the debts that they had accumulated.[32] As traders resorted to abusive behaviors such as beatings, rapes, and kidnappings to intimidate their debtors, tensions mounted that ultimately erupted into warfare.

Yet epidemics also played a less obvious but no less important role in precipitating the Yamasee War. Upper Path communities suffered major depopulation in the years leading up to their revolt against South Carolina, thereby adding more demand for the short supply of captives. Upper Path peoples depended heavily on adopting prisoners to replace lost kinsmen, a fact borne out by the marked heterogeneity of their communities.[33] English claims to these captives, especially those that had already been adopted, thus represented a real threat to the survival of Upper Path communities. English traders may have thought they were simply taking slaves that were rightfully owed to them, but in Native eyes they were kidnapping people who had been transformed or who could be transformed from captives into kinspeople. The offense then was quite deep.[34]

English slave traders had interfered with aboriginal practices of capture and adoption as soon as they showed up with their exotic goods. They encouraged a higher level of warfare, the capture of more women and children, and the disempowerment of women in determining the fate of those captives.[35] While the Native South remained well populated with numerous communities, there were plenty of captives to go around. That changed after the Great Southern Smallpox Epidemic. Even when thousands of captives from Florida were being brought north during the early 1700s, South Carolinians and their allies had disputes about the status these conquered people would have.

The Yamasees, for example, took several slaves during the 1702 English invasion of St. Augustine. They complained that South Carolina governor James Moore, Sr., did not give them liberty to dispose of their captives as they saw fit but instead insisted that the captives be sold to agents whom the South Carolina government had authorized, presumably Moore's selected men.[36] The sources do not clearly explain what the Yamasees wanted to do with these captives, but given their heavy losses from the Great Southeastern Smallpox Epidemic, earlier slaving of them by the Westos, and subsequent disease episodes, they had a tremendous incentive to adopt as many captives as they could. During the 1702 invasion the Yamasees convinced two Christianized communities to flee Florida and to incorporate with them, hinting that their participation in the English-sponsored raids had the dual motives of acquiring captives for trade and adoption. English demands certainly undermined the Yamasees' prerogative in determining the fate of their own captives. Yamasee men expressed their peoples' complaints to South Carolinian officials, but they were likely relaying the concerns of their female kin, who had seen so many of their loved ones laid in their graves by the mysterious and invisible actions of microbes. The resentment of women undoubtedly escalated as so many captives became English slaves rather than Yamasee kinsmen.

As the eighteenth century progressed, English sources revealed some startling episodes of traders taking people against the will of the communities to which they belonged. In December 1706, for example, charges against the trader John Musgrove came up for consideration in the Commons House of Assembly. He allegedly enslaved twenty-two people belonging to the Apalachees and another nine from the Lower Creeks. In addition, Musgrove threatened the lives of a headman and another man belonging to the Tuckesaws, a Lower Creek town, unless they gave him four captives. Musgrove claimed that he was due these slaves because the Tuckesaws had taken away his Native wife as well as the wife of another English trader, but the Tuckesaws claimed that the women in question left on their own accord — a female prerogative in the matrilineal societies of the South. The Tuckesaws agreed to Musgrove's lower demand of three Indian slaves as compensation, but another trader had absconded with two of those captives, leaving Musgrove greatly disgruntled. The Assembly declined to arrest Musgrove and to bring him to trial but did require him to remain in Charles Town. Within six months, though, he was again conducting his business among Natives.[37] Musgrove's actions demonstrated what were likely common occurrences. Englishmen laid claim to peoples that their Native clients did not want to see enslaved.

Such abuses continued unabated in the years leading up to the Yamasee War. In September 1710 the Commissioners of the Indian Trade, a body created by the South Carolina Commons House of Assembly to regulate trade with Natives, began to hold regular meetings in which they heard several cases involving the illegal enslavement of Natives and trader interferences with indigenous practices of capture and adoption. From September 21, 1710 to August 1, 1711 the commissioners heard cases involving thirteen Natives that Englishmen allegedly had taken without the consent of the indigenous communities that claimed them.[38] Information regarding these cases is scant, but the few details suggest that some, if not all, of the abducted Natives had been adopted into indigenous communities. One case, for example, involved John Cochran's theft of "a free Indian Brother" who resided in a Yamasee town.[39] Other cases involved Cornelius Macarty taking "the Wife and Child" of a Native man while he was off to war and George Wright stealing a "free Woman that had a Husband in Tomatly Town." In one instance the board freed an Apalachee man name Massony, whom John Musgrove was holding as a slave. The board ordered that Musgrove had to prove that the headman of Tomolla (either a Yamasee or Apalachee town) had declared Massony a slave in order to reclaim him. This judgment tacitly acknowledged the prerogative of Native communities to determine the fate of their own captives, although it mistakenly placed such power in the hands of a male rather than a female leader. It is not known whether Musgrove actually complied with the board's order.[40]

To deal with the incessant complaints about traders, the commissioners established new rules in August 1711. Such policy changes acknowledged that South Carolinians had been heavily involved in kidnapping adopted kinspeople and regular citizens of Native towns and keeping other captives from being adopted. Traders could only acquire slaves from their Native client's town and only after their client had been home for three days with his captives. The commissioners reiterated proprietary limitations on buying only slaves taken in war and most importantly excluded "*those taken in War and made free by their respective Masters*"; such individuals "*shall be deemed free Men and Denizens*" of their new community.[41] In other words, traders had to respect the wishes of the Native community regarding the fate of its captives. They were to wait until a community had a chance to decide what to do with incoming captives, and they were not to touch those captives who had been adopted.

When Carolina's allies returned from the Tuscarora War, however, traders ignored the new regulations as they failed to wait for their clients to return to their home villages. In April 1712, for example, charges were brought against Samuel Hilden for buying multiple slaves before they had been brought to their captor's towns. An Apalachicola man named Wenoya verified the charges. Wenoya, one of the Lower Creeks who participated in South Carolina's 1712 campaign against the Tuscaroras, informed the commissioners that Hilden had stopped him and forced him to surrender one slave for goods valued at one hundred and sixty deerskins. Later, Hilden appeared before the commissioners and confessed to buying six slaves from Apalachicolas but pleaded ignorance that his actions were against trade regulations.[42]

Hilden was not the only one involved in such practices. Three other traders were charged with forcing captives from their Native captors the first day they brought them into the Yamasee town of Pocataligo. Carolinians continued to interfere with the captives of warriors returning home from South Carolina's 1713 campaign against the Tuscaroras. In May 1714 the so-called Coosata King, who participated in the expedition, complained that Theophilus Hastings had persuaded him to send seven of his prisoners from North Carolina with Colonel Alexander Macky to be left at the plantation of John Stanyarn, another leading South Carolinian involved in the slave trade. Coosata King informed the board that he could "hear Nothing of them." Hastings admitted that he had sold the slaves, and the board ordered him to compensate Coosata King with two hundred deerskins for each adult slave and sixty skins for each of the two children. Another trader, John Jones, also interfered with Creek men as they brought prisoners back from the Tuscarora War. Jones defied the commissioners instructions by stopping two Lower Creeks at the Apalachee town on the Savannah River and buying Tuscarora slaves from them before they returned home. John Jones was specifically mentioned by name in early 1715 when the commissioners learned of Creek discontent with several traders and of their plot to kill Jones and his ilk.[43]

The most egregious misconduct of traders continued to be the kidnapping of captives who had undergone the transformation into kinspeople. From August 1711 until April 1715 traders either took or threatened to take fourteen Natives that belonged to indigenous communities.[44] In some of these cases Carolinian traders simply took people away from their clients as payment for debts.

One of the most complicated cases involved the trader John Wright, whose actions particularly alienated the Lower Creeks. One of Wright's misdeeds involved a "free" woman named Ahele, identified as a "Creek Indian" and "kinswom[an] of the Soogela King." Wright allegedly took this woman away and either detained or sold her. When he sent goods to the Cussita Captain "for satisfaction," the Native leader refused them.[45] There is no way to tell whether the Cussita Captain and Soogela King were members of the same clan, but the former man's refusal of gifts from Wright had much significance. Southern Natives considered their relatives who had been captured to be dead and such deaths demanded retaliation.[46] The offending party could give gifts to assuage the family's grief, but when the Cussita Captain refused Wright's gesture, it was a message that Ahele's abduction would be considered an act that would call for revenge. Wright obviously did not understand this custom as he continued to take part in the abduction of kinspeople from their communities. He ultimately paid for his actions with his life; Wright was among the first South Carolinians that the Yamasees executed in their revolt.[47]

That revolt began on April 15, 1715. On that day Yamasees and some Lower Creeks killed Wright and other visiting Carolinians who were sent to investigate rumors that Natives were planning to rebel. Within a matter of days Natives killed the Carolinian traders working among the Apalachees and Lower Creeks. They then raided the settlers around Port Royal, killing or capturing over one hundred English and Africans and causing the survivors to flee to Charles Town for safety. The uprising radiated west along the Upper Path, where traders working among the Upper Creeks and Chickasaws wound up dead as well. By early May Cherokees and the Piedmont groups became involved in the conflict. They killed Carolinian traders and even sent their warriors into outlying English settlements, coming very close to the prosperous Goose Creek plantations. With South Carolina's former allies taking up arms against it, the colony's future was in jeopardy.[48]

In their own words, the Yamasees — who began the conflict and fought for the longest period — revolted against South Carolina because of a profound fear of enslavement.[49] The English indeed gave the Yamasees and others along the Upper Path ample reasons to believe their fears would become reality. English records provide numerous examples of

Englishmen taking kinspeople away from their communities. Kidnapping was not an action of a kinsman but rather of an enemy. It was an action that demanded retaliation. That Carolinians had committed such crimes against communities that had lost fifty percent or more of their population over the previous nineteen years was all the more threatening. Even if disease had not depleted South Carolina's allies so substantially, indigenous peoples would have seen kidnapping as an act of war. Epidemics, however, had made kidnapping the only alternative for market-oriented traders, who absconded with kinspeople as payment for the debts that their Native clients owed. South Carolina's Native trading partners could not find enough captives to supply the traders, and the few enemies that they did capture were more valuable to them as adopted kinspeople than as exchange items. Englishmen displayed such cruelty in taking these valuable members away from their own disease-depleted allies that it is no wonder that the Yamasees and other Natives eventually launched a large-scale pan-Native revolt to destroy the colony that had done so much damage to them.

South Carolina, of course, avoided destruction. After suffering severe losses in the early stages of the war, the English managed to do what so many other European colonies accomplished in their conquest of the Americas. They exploited the intense rivalries that existed among Native groups. By early 1716 the English had managed to win the Cherokees over to their side, and together they obliterated the Yamasees and forced the Lower Creeks to retreat to the Chattahoochee River. Through 1716 and 1717 Cherokee attacks wore down the resistance of Upper Path communities, who in 1718 welcomed a return to peaceful relations with their former English allies. Some Yamasees who had managed to escape to Florida continued to conduct raids against the English into the 1720s, but by then the war named after them had essentially come to an end. South Carolina never rebuilt its slave trade network. A multitude of English traders involved in that noxious commerce were wiped out in one quick stroke, and those that returned to Native villages after the conflict focused their attention on acquiring deerskins, a resource that was in much greater supply than captives. The Yamasee War may have left a bad taste in the mouths of South Carolinians for enslaving indigenous peoples, but the epidemics that followed the course of English commerce made the Native slave trade unsustainable over the long term and laid the foundation for the explosive war that ultimately ended it.[50]

Notes

1. For simplicity, the name "Upper Path" is being used to denote what were in actuality several interlocking paths that integrated the Yamasees, Savannah River groups (Apalachees, Shawnees, and Yuchis), Lower Creeks, Upper Creeks, and Chickasaws into South Carolina's trade network. These branches had various names. Since the Upper Path was the most voluminous slave-trading route and since its name appears more frequently in the sources, I have chosen it as a convenient label. For more on the location of trading paths in the early colonial South, see Cumming and DeVorsey, *Southeast in Early Maps*.

2. Alan Gallay and Steven Oatis have expanded our insights into the Native slave trade; Gallay, *Indian Slave Trade*; and Oatis, *Colonial Complex*. This chapter explores that trade's epidemiological importance.

3. Anthropologist Henry Dobyns has made the boldest estimates of population decline during the Protohistoric Period (1492–1670 CE); Dobyns, *Their Number Become Thinned*. Ramenofsky offers support to Dobyns's views in *Vectors of Death*. Others have greeted Dobyns's and Ramenofsky's conclusions with a great deal of skepticism; Henige, *Numbers from Nowhere*.

4. Kelton, *Epidemics and Enslavement*.

5. Kelton, "Great Southeastern Smallpox Epidemic."

6. McCrady, *History of South Carolina*, 1:308.

7. Joseph Blake and Council to Lords Proprietors, April 23, 1698, Salley, *Commissions and Instructions*, 105.

8. Blake and Council to Lords Proprietors, April 23, 1698, Salley, *Commissions and Instructions*, 105.

9. Kelton, "Great Southeastern Smallpox Epidemic," 34–35.

10. Thomas Nairne to Ralph Izard, April 15, 1708, Nairne, *Nairne's Muskhogean Journals*, 63.

11. For a discussion of Yamasee involvement in the slave trade, see Jenkins, this volume; and Worth, this volume.

12. John Stewart to Queen Anne, October 1711, Archives Nationales de France, Archives des Colonies, ser. C13C, 2:72, LC; I wish to thank Alan Gallay for a photocopy of this letter.

13. For a more detailed account of the epidemics associated with the Tuscarora War, see Kelton, *Epidemics and Enslavement*, 163–82.

14. Gideon Johnston to Secretary, November 16, 1711, Klingburg, *Carolina Chronicle*, 99.

15. Le Jau to Secretary, August 10, 1713, Le Jau, *Carolina Chronicles*, 184.

16. "An Exact Account of the Number and Strength of All the Indian Nations That Were Subject to the Government of South Carolina . . . in the Beginning of the Year 1715" (hereafter cited as "Carolina Census of 1715"), included in letter from Governor Robert Johnson to Lords Commissioners of Trade and Plantations, January 12, 1720, Sainsbury, *Records in the British Public Records Office*, 7:233–50. The letter and census is also reprinted in Merrens, *Colonial South Carolina Scene*, 56–66.

17. For a discussion of the effects of slaving on the Indians of Spanish Florida, see Worth, this volume; Oatis, *Colonial Complex*, 47; and Crane, *Southern Frontier*, (1929) 76.

18. Barnwell Map, 1722, Colonial Office 700, NAUK; Hann, *Apalachee*, 167.

19. For secondary accounts of these actions, see Worth, this volume; Hahn, *Invention of the Creek Nation*, 58–65; Gallay, *Indian Slave Trade*, 144–49; and Oatis, *Colonial Complex*, 49–51.

20. Alan Gallay suggests that Carolinians ended up with between two and four thousand Apalachee slaves, but he does not take into consideration the number that must have been adopted into the communities of Carolina's Native allies. He also bases his number on the dwindling number of free Apalachees on the Savannah but does not consider the possibility that they suffered from disease or that they relocated to live in the interior; John Hann puts the number enslaved at little more than one thousand; Gallay, *Indian Slave Trade*, 146–49; Hann, *Apalachee*, 168–69.

21. Hann, *Apalachee*, 167.

22. James Moore, Sr., the English commander of the attack on the Apalachees, counted thirteen hundred, while Thomas Nairne who also participated in the attack counted sixteen hundred; Moore, "Account of What the Army Did"; and Thomas Nairne to Doctor Marsden, August 20, 1704, SPG, ser. A, vol. 2.

23. Nathaniel Johnson et al. to Lords Proprietors, September 17, 1708, Sainsbury, *Records in the British Public Records Office*, 5:208.

24. Hann, *Apalachee*, 167; and "Carolina Census of 1715."

25. Nairne to Ralph Izard, April 15, 1708, Nairne, *Nairne's Muskhogean Journals*, 63.

26. Bienville to Pontchartrain, September 6, 1704, Rowland and Sanders, *Mississippi Provincial Archives*, 3:20–22.

27. John Stewart to William Dunlop, April 27, 1690, Stewart "Letters," 30; and "Carolina Census of 1715."

28. Nine villages in 1701; La Harpe, *Historical Journal*, 26–27; six villages in 1715; "Carolina Census of 1715"; and Tonty, "Memoir," 60.

29. For the Chickasaw involvement in slaving, see Ethridge, "Making of a Militaristic Slaving Society."

30. "Carolina Census of 1715."

31. I agree with Peter Wood that the late seventeenth and early eighteenth centuries represent a time of significant depopulation for peoples of the Upper Path; Wood, "Changing Population." My estimate of 5,500 to 7,600 Chickasaws fits with Wood's estimate of 5,400 and 10,800 Chickasaws, but I believe Wood undercounts the number of Creeks. Wood estimates a total of 15,000 Natives in the homeland of the Lower and Upper Creeks in 1685, while I put the total number of Lower and Upper Creeks prior to 1696 between 30,044 and 22,148 based on a rate of depopulation between seventy-five percent and sixty-eight percent. I derive my rate of depopulation from John Stewart's estimate of Lower Creeks in 1690, a source that Wood did not consider (see note 27 above).

32. That South Carolina's Native allies were having a more difficult time acquiring captives due to disease-induced depopulation, see Kelton, *Epidemics and Enslavement*, 179–201.

33. Boyd, "Diego Peña's Expedition," 26.

34. Scholars have long identified debt, trader's abuses, and native fears of enslavement as causes for the Yamasee War; more recently scholars have debated the underlying origins of the conflict. Richard L. Hann puts the conflict in the larger context of the Columbian Exchange. He emphasizes that a declining population of potential slaves helped bury the Yamasees under a mountain of debt, but he does not include the impact of epidemics on South Carolina's own allies. He also argues more unconvincingly that Yamasee debt stemmed from declining deer populations without much evidence for a deer shortage; Hann, "'Trade Do's Not Flourish.'" William L. Ramsey persuasively characterizes the conflict as deriving from a fundamental misunderstanding between Carolinian traders and their Native clients about proper economic behavior. Driven by market imperatives to pay off their debts, traders violated Native expectations of reciprocal exchange. Ramsey, moreover, sees South Carolina officials failing miserably to ameliorate the market-generated tensions that their colonial regime produced. Ramsey's analysis, though, dismisses an epidemiological context that documentary sources clearly reveal and in which the growing indebtedness occurred; Ramsey, "'Something Cloudy in Their Looks.'" For interpretations that take a multicausal approach but that unfortunately also omit the conflict's epidemiological context, see Oatis, *Colonial Complex*, 113–39; Gallay, *Indian Slave Trade*, 329–35; and Hahn, *Inven-*

tion of the Creek Nation, 74–80. It must be mentioned that I agree with Hahn's assessment that taking adopted captives by traders was instrumental in driving South Carolina's allies to revolt.

35. Perdue, *Cherokee Women*, 63, 68–70.

36. Entry for April 28, 1703, Salley, *Journal of the Commons House for 1703*, 75.

37. Entry for December 11, 1706, Salley, *Journal of the Commons House of Assembly for 1706*, 21–22; and Gallay, *Indian Slave Trade*, 213–214.

38. McDowell, *Journals of the Commissioners*, 3–5, 11–12.

39. McDowell, *Journals of the Commissioners*, 11.

40. McDowell, *Journals of the Commissioners*, 4–5, 11, 12 (quote).

41. McDowell, *Journals of the Commissioners*, 15–16 (emphasis added).

42. McDowell, *Journals of the Commissioners*, 23–24.

43. McDowell, *Journals of the Commissioners*, 25, 53 (quote), 57, 65.

44. McDowell, *Journals of the Commissioners*, 26–27, 28, 33, 38, 42, 47, 49, 50, 58, 60.

45. McDowell, *Journals of the Commissioners*, 28, 42, 47–48 (quote), 58. The Soogela King most likely was the headman of the Lower Creek town of Savacola that sometimes appears in English documents as "Sowagles" or variants thereof; see Map of South, Colonial Office 700, NAUK; and Glover, "Captain Glover's Account."

46. Nairne to Izard, April 15, 1708, Nairne, *Nairne's Muskhogean Journal*, 62.

47. McDowell, *Journals of the Commissioners*, 60.

48. The events of the Yamasee War are covered in Oatis, *Colonial Complex*, 112–39; Gallay, *Indian Slave Trade*, 327–38; and Hahn, *Invention of the Creek Nation*, 81–120.

49. Yamasee explanations for going to war against South Carolina can be found in the following primary sources: Letter of Captain Jonathan St. Lo and Enclosure, July 12, 1715, Colonial Office 700, NAUK, 1:2451; Córcoles y Martínez to King Philip V, July 5, 1715, Audiencia of Santo Domingo, PKY, 834, f. 4. (I wish to thank Steven Hahn for providing a photocopy of this letter and Ryan Gaston for helping with the translation); Swanton, *Early History*, 100; and Colonel Caleb Heathcote to Lord Townsend, July 16, 1715, O'Callaghan, *Documents Relative*, 5:433.

50. Most historians agree that the Yamasee War marked the end of South Carolina's Native slave trade; Gallay, *Indian Slave Trade*, 338 and 346; and Ramsey, "'All and Singular the Slaves.'"

13 | *Choctaws at the Border of the Shatter Zone*

SPHERES OF EXCHANGE AND
SPHERES OF SOCIAL VALUE

PATRICIA GALLOWAY

In 1995 I published *Choctaw Genesis*, which had started out as an introduction to the book on eighteenth-century Choctaw history that I had originally set out to write. The central argument of *Choctaw Genesis* was that the genesis of the eighteenth-century Choctaw ethnos took place precisely in those forgotten centuries when happenings in the South were relatively invisible to European observation but were being affected by the results and implications of early European contacts during the late sixteenth and seventeenth centuries.[1] Driven by population effects from European disease, European violence, and internecine warfare in aid of slaving and attracted by relatively unused farmlands and the rich hunting available in what had been an interior buffer zone, several population groups left their former homes to join a "native" core population already living on the headwaters of the Pearl River (present-day Mississippi). So-called Alabama River-phase people came from central Alabama and Summerville-phase people came from western Alabama across the Tombigbee River (resulting from the proximal effects of Spanish and English pressures). They were joined perhaps somewhat later by Plaquemine peoples from south central Mississippi (perhaps resulting from Spanish pressures further west) and even later, at the turn of the eighteenth century, by Mobile–Tensaw delta, Doctor Lake–phase people coming from southwestern Alabama directly in flight from European-armed groups to their east.[2] Clearly this scenario suggests many of the features of Ethridge's proposed shatter zone effects, but it lacks detail. I will try to place the Choctaw ethnogenesis process more precisely with respect to this concept and especially to its implications for traditional and emergent economic activity.

The microregion of the Choctaw homeland is now east central Mississippi. During the eighteenth century the Choctaws clearly dominated at least the whole southeastern quarter of the present state, if not quite its whole southern half. During the late eighteenth century, after the expulsion of the Natchez and their congeners, the Choctaws also controlled the lower Yazoo basin and the Natchez region. I have argued, and so far sparse archaeological findings have tentatively confirmed, that the east central Mississippi area was mostly unpopulated during late prehistory when the whole of the region was a relatively rusticated zone between the sophisticated and hierarchically organized chiefdoms of the Mississippi River and those of the Mobile–Alabama–Black Warrior axis. A few modest simple chiefdoms marked by single-mound centers were to be found at advantageous environmental locations (broader floodplains and swaths of good soil) down the center of Mississippi. Among these modest mounds was Nanih Waiya, the traditional Mother Mound of the Choctaws. The slight archaeological evidence suggests that these groups may have participated in a marginal way in the prestige-goods exchanges taking place over the region, but their economies seem to have been localized, and the region was underpopulated in comparison to the regions to east and west.[3] This underpopulation meant that the region's soil, though not as good as found in other regions, was not as exhausted as those that had supported large populations. Further, its game populations were comparatively quite robust during the period in question. The scene was set.

Enter Europeans bearing disease and destruction. Spaniards traipsed by and through in the sixteenth century; Spaniards, Englishmen, and Frenchmen settled in the seventeenth and eighteenth. When the European focus sharpened at the turn of the eighteenth century, the region was bordered to the east and northeast by English colonies, to the southeast by Spanish colonies, and to the southwest and west and northwest by French colonies, all of them bickering with one another and clashing more or less violently with their Indian neighbors.

The Indian neighbors of the Choctaws by the eighteenth century were Alabamas and small tribes (including the Naniabas, Mobilians, and Tomes) to the east, Chickasaws to the north, Tunicans to the northwest, Natchez to the west, and more small tribes (including the Pascagoulas, Biloxis, Acolapissas, and Bayougoulas) to the southwest and south.[4] Buffered by these neighbors, the Choctaws were also located in a significantly remote area, at least as far as European transport was concerned; it was not convenient to large waterways or the coast; they were not even convenient to major east-west inland trading paths. This remoteness protected them from the deleterious effects of direct European contact and would continue to protect them considerably, making them into a clear *beneficiary* of their location on the fringes of the Southern shatter zone.

We need a clearer picture, however, of how the emergent Choctaws were affected by various aspects of the shatter zone, especially those connected with trade in guns and other European-manufactured items, Indian slaves, and deerskins. To begin with, these effects impinged dialectically on the process of ethnogenesis. For Hernando de Soto the region of the Choctaw homeland on the upper Pearl was far too much of a backwoods to compete with the promise of Mabila or Quizquiz, which is why the people of Nanipacana may have fled there for refuge when loony Luna appeared on the scene. Yet some or all of these people may have returned for a time to the Mobile-Tensaw Valley. Joel Martin has argued just how important this period of inattention was for interior Southern Native groups as it gave them a chance to recover, regroup, and forge new political and economic arrangements as well as to assimilate some of the new European trade goods into their own cultural contexts before the active penetration of the region by English traders.[5]

The earliest appearance of the Choctaws by name in European documents did not come until almost a hundred years later with the interior machinations of Spaniards from the Apalachee presidio and Englishmen from South Carolina in the middle and late seventeenth century. Did the Choctaws participate as suppliers to the demand for dried meat from Apalachee in the seventeenth century, conveying their products to the presidio through the agency of Native traders along well-worn trading paths already used for at least hundreds of years? If so, they were not credited with it, yet they had appeared in the reports of their eastern neighbors as an enormous threat. In the late seventeenth century Englishmen like

Henry Woodward and John Stewart reported the Choctaws' importance and their potential for trade as well as their dangerousness. The Choctaws did not, however, appear explicitly in French documentation of their exploration of the Mississippi Valley west of Choctaw country until the end of that century. This delayed contact makes sense in terms of the shatter zone scenario: the primary effects of early and sporadic trade, slaving, and internecine Indian warfare were taking place to the east. At the same time Spanish settlement and creation of another shatter zone in the Southwest ("storms brewed in other men's worlds") that was buffered by large plains and desert regions did not impinge directly enough on the Mississippi Valley to create the same effects pushing from the west. In that direction the Choctaws were still effectively cloaked from view by the Mississippi River groups.[6]

In 1702 the French plunged into both *terrae incognitae* and *medias res* at the same time when Henri de Tonti (or Tonty) was sent by Pierre Le Moyne d'Iberville from Mobile Bay into the interior to bring back Choctaw and Chickasaw representatives for discussions and treaty making. After arriving for the first time on the Gulf coast in 1699, Iberville and those he left behind between trips had begun to hear from their coastal Indian hosts about the powerful Choctaws in the interior and to meet a few of their representatives.[7] La Salle had already learned of the Chickasaws seventeen years before.[8] Iberville also knew that by the end of the century, the Chickasaws (abetted by a particularly dangerous Englishman) had been staging slave raids for the English of Carolina throughout the region and even across the Mississippi. Iberville had asked Tonti to make his skills at Indian diplomacy available to the new colony, but Tonti had been unable to accost the Englishman on a previous trip escorting missionaries down the Mississippi in 1700. This time, traveling up into Choctaw and Chickasaw country from the coast, Tonti had the whole trading-slaving-warfare scenario revealed to him progressively — almost a textbook example of where a shatter zone edge fell across a degree of ethnic continuity.[9]

Before reaching Choctaw country proper, Tonti and his guides, a "Chaqta chief" and two Indians from each of the small Tome and Mobile groups of the Mobile Valley, passed through a country with many small crossings of creeks before they reached a hillier country. It was February, hunting season; it was not surprising that they met with Choctaws camped at outlying and apparently permanently established hunting lodges who presented them with a deer for food. We do not know whether these Choctaws' hunting was of normal intensity for subsistence or significantly intensified for extractive purposes, only that they had meat to spare. As Tonti and his party traveled among the villages, they found the Choctaws "very satisfied that you [Iberville] want to have peace made for them with the Chicacha." Tonti remarked that one of the villages to the east-northeast on the border of Choctaw country could not at that time plant because the Chickasaws, Conchaques (Abhikas), and Alabamas (all by now well documented as in the orbit of trade with the English of South Carolina) "do not give them any rest." Tonti gave to the village chief "nearest the Chicacha" a gun and received "food supplies & skins" or "the things that we need" from him. In his travels Tonti, an experienced trader and Indian diplomat formerly based in the Illinois country, spoke in terms of *paying* his escort, promising them guns and ammunition and an additional bonus of "6 knives, 2 hatchets, & 2 fathoms of large *rassades* [beads]" to serve as messengers, but we do not know how his escort viewed these promises.[10]

On the way to seek a meeting with the Chickasaws, still with a Choctaw chief in escort, Tonti was told that there were two slaving parties led by an Englishman out against the Choctaws. A short time later, received with ceremony by the chief of the first Chickasaw village, he met another Englishman, whom Tonti observed as dressed in mixed European and Indian dress "like a savage." The man attempted to converse with Tonti in Shawnee and claimed that the slaving and internecine warfare was a result of Chickasaw initiative. Tonti, however, thought otherwise, particularly when he acted with a Chickasaw chief to free a young enslaved Choctaw. He observed that the Englishman's cabin in the village was full of slaves and that the man was able to claim a portion of the French gifts presented to the Chickasaws. The man also told Tonti that should the Chickasaws go over to the French, he would have the Conchaques destroy them.[11]

On the way back to the Choctaws and thence to Mobile, Tonti and his party, increased by five Chickasaw men of rank, three Chickasaw women, and two (Chickasaw?) hired (*louez*) carriers, nearly encountered a larger Chickasaw-Chakchiuma raiding party that had already killed and captured several Choctaws. This raiding party made the Chickasaw diplomats hesitant to accompany Tonti through Choctaw country until he promised them a safe escort home. Tonti advised Iberville by letter that he felt certain a French trade house on the Tombigbee would attract Chickasaws, Conchaques, and Alabamas, while Choctaws might come to Mobile to trade.[12]

Two things are remarkable in this sudden view into the interior: the established nature of the English presence, contrasted with its apparent fluidity. That the Englishman had a claim to a portion of the French diplomatic presents to the Chickasaws suggests that he enjoyed some kind of special standing among them; we cannot assume without further evidence that he was appropriating payment for a debt. Tonti at least believed that there was a real chance for the French to wedge into the situation and upset the Chickasaw-English alliance, and the Englishman did not contradict him but rather reinforced that belief. From documentary evidence we know that at this juncture the English believed that the whole region was at risk of loss.[13] At the same time, the Choctaws were defending themselves and already accumulating deerskins to trade (possibly with the English as reported by Sauvole in 1699). Apparently this defense and hunting depended on the use of indigenous weapons, for they had no guns.[14]

How bad had slaving become by this time? In a speech to the Choctaw and Chickasaw negotiators when they arrived at the French settlement, Iberville pointed out to the Chickasaws that it had not profited them much because although they had killed eighteen hundred Choctaws, they had only enslaved five hundred while they had themselves suffered the loss of eight hundred men.[15] The Choctaws had fortified "border" towns, while the Chakchiumas seem to have vacillated between the Choctaws and Chickasaws: Tonti saw abandoned Chakchiuma old fields on the Choctaw side of the borderlands, while the living Chakchiuma town that formed a base for a party of slavers was on the Chickasaw side: fluidity again.

Perhaps most striking is the cultural fluidity (one might almost say hybridity) of the mysterious Englishman "a jean." His appearance was deplored by Tonti: "holding a gun in his hand and a saber at his side. He had on a rather dirty blue shirt, no pants, stockings, or shoes, a scarlet wool blanket and some discs at his neck like a savage" — hardly the model of a capitalist merchant in the English colonies.[16] Yet that very appearance, added to the man's mastery of multiple Indian languages — at a minimum Shawnee and Chickasaw — suggests that to operate effectively in Indian country a European trader might choose to assimilate to Indian culture, that the interface between cultures was articulated to fit Native expectations. Further, the red wool blanket (presumably one of the coveted English "strouds") and the discs (gorgets?) were certainly marks of prestige in Indian dress of the era, whether traded or of indigenous make.[17] Tonti says nothing of the Englishman's trading for anything but slaves, and in fact both Tonti and Iberville said pointedly to the Chickasaws and Choctaws that, in contrast to the English, the French desired to enslave nothing but deer.[18]

The syncretic manner and conduct of the Englishman was only one sign of a persistence and dominance of Indian practices and customs even in the wake of severe disruption. Tonti still expected to establish relations with the interior tribes by gift, and whatever he may have thought of his other transactions in "hiring" bearers and messengers, there is no evidence to prove that they understood the gifts given as placing a specific value on their labor. Each of the chiefs he met emphasized that they could not speak for anyone but their own villages, attesting to segmentary autonomy, which continued to allow preconfederation group identifications to persist through the nineteenth century and later as the tripartite Choctaw divisional structure. As noted above, the Choctaws were not held back from effective hunting by lack of guns; their settled hunting camps attested to a persistent and effective Native subsistence practice. Their gifts of meat to the French party on several occasions suggest that if there was increased hunting for the deerskin trade, it had also begun to provide an abundance of meat. Finally, the presence of women in the diplomatic party that returned with Tonti suggests that women continued to play an active political role in the region.

Thus the French had arrived in the nick of time to provide a counterweight to the English that would free the Choctaws from slaving pressure by providing them with guns to add to their armament. The Choctaws, however, had already been undertaking self-defense with indigenous arms and were already in the process of preparing to take in additional refugees from similar raiding to the east in the form of groups from the very Mobile and Tome whose representatives accompanied Tonti as guides.[19] Although they had lost members to slaving, the Choctaws were replacing them through acceptance of refugees at a greater rate than that of their population losses and without the expense and danger of long-distance mourning wars like those the Iroquois had fought.[20]

The key to the Choctaw ability to resist Chickasaw pressure even without the help of the French lies in the very process of confederation or coalescence that characterized Choctaw ethnogenesis, suggesting that the process was at least partly a positive shatter-zone effect. The terminological variability is worth discussing briefly. I have previously discussed the Choctaw ethnos by the end of the process as a confederation, chiefly because the constituent ethnicities were preserved largely in the form of autonomous villages and village groups. Accordingly, I think this terminology is worth preserving. For "Choctaw" to be an ethnicity, however, the confederated people had to recognize themselves in some sense as belonging to something larger than a single village or a group of them. Perhaps Charles Taylor's notion of a social imaginary, borrowed and generalized from Benedict Anderson's imagined community without the sense of nationalism, fits the situation here: "that common understanding that makes possible common practices and a widely shared sense of legitimacy."[21] The Choctaws' view of themselves as a unity was emergent at this time, marked by vigorous external boundary maintenance and eventually characterized by a unified pottery style, an "official" language, and a single burial mode. Yet how did the emergence of a new social imaginary in this sense relate to the pressures of the shatter zone?

It was especially important that the constituent groups that joined to become Choctaw shared significant cultural commonalities. Their "little tradition" of subsistence and dwelling practices was substantially uniform as was their segmentary political organization with its gendered distribution of political responsibilities (and this set of political practices may have been reinforced to a pernicious degree by confederation as would be seen in the Choctaw civil war at midcentury). In this context of persistent tradition it is significant that through the development of confederation and in spite of the presence of Europeans on the borders of the region, there was still an exclusive adherence to a nonmarket, non-monetized economy.

This economic pattern brings up one of the most significant issues about shatter zone effects, that is, the argument that by 1700 the Native economies of the South, whatever they may have been like, were as shattered as the Native polities and thus vulnerable to the inroads of replacement by a capitalist market economy. Did this happen to the Choctaws? Certainly Carson and O'Brien have had their reservations about this replacement, suggesting instead that Choctaw market participation even in the nineteenth century was significantly embedded in traditional social practices, while White's "middle ground" in the Midwest included fur trade exchanges that were themselves embedded in indigenous practices and imaginaries.[22] I wish to argue here that in spite of the fact that regional upheaval had played a major role in the emergence of the Choctaw Confederacy on the border of that shatter zone, during the eighteenth century, capitalism did not play a significant part in the Choctaw understanding of the proper functioning of their economy.

In 1702 when guns were especially important to both Chickasaws and Choctaws, most were given to chiefs as gifts, at least by the French.[23] When they were traded, however, they were not being traded to anyone in exchange for money but for *stuff*: in the Chickasaw case for people (Indian slaves) and in the Choctaw case for deerskins. In fact, throughout the eighteenth century all the Indian trade lists drawn up by Englishmen and Frenchmen alike were always framed in terms of objects for objects: so many deerskins for such and such a European article. Further, persistent European efforts to establish a kind of standard deerskin "currency" constantly failed as Choctaws and other Southern Native groups objected to Europeans' failure to take context into account in assessing value.[24] Is it then accurate to argue that deerskins (or deerskins and duffels) became *currency* to all intents and purposes, thus ushering in currency as universal solvent along with commodity fetishism? Should we say that with respect to what each saw as "foreign" stuff, both parties to the trade commoditized the other side's production?

It is difficult to tackle the literature on Southern Indian-European exchanges in any critical analytic way because in much of the existing historical discourse (and in most European sources), it has been so frequently cast in lay (and ethnocentric) terms of "trade" and (lately) of "consumerism" and "Atlantic economy" that *presuppose* a neoclassical market-based economic model without addressing the issues of economic theory directly, while nevertheless backhandedly recognizing a mixed character for the trade by speaking of it as a "diplomatic tool," a phrase that cuts in many different directions. An example is the article "Indians and the Economy of Eighteenth-Century Carolina" that historian Peter Mancall wrote in partnership with two economists, Joshua Rosenbloom and Thomas Weiss, as a small part of a joint ongoing effort to define the colonial economy of Carolina.[25] The article's underlying theory is an economic utilitarianism that assumes that individuals invariably minimize their efforts to maximize their gains. The editor of the book containing this article even describes the authors' approach in terms of their appreciation of Indians' perspicacity in that they "grant Indians agency and proceed under the assumption that Native Americans were economic actors operating to optimize their material well-being subject to their social and environmental constraints."[26] Other historians, like White in *Middle Ground*, have made arguments about Indian values suggesting that the notion of Indians having had an "income" of eight pounds sterling "per head" during the eighteenth century (based on the skins they sold, the services they performed, and the money spent on them by the colonial government), if interesting in terms of the economy of European colonies, is simply nonsense in terms of the Indians' view of the matter and especially not much use for understanding why Native people did what they did. Neoclassical economic assumptions, even about Europeans in the colonies and the early Republic, are now much more nuanced by a more serious awareness of the family and community considerations that affected the enterprise of merchants and manufacturers as well as farmers by precluding a consistent maximization of profits.[27]

The vast (and getting vaster) anthropological literature on non-monetized economies and theories of value, as well as the burgeoning literatures of subaltern studies and decolonization, have offered plenty of examples of the questioning of a simplistic neoclassical economic view in other parts of the world. Such questioning arises from anthropological literature based upon analyses of very visible and well-documented nineteenth-and twentieth-century indigenous experiences vis-à-vis a completed capitalist world-subsuming economy. How much less effective at coercing indigenous people the barely nascent capitalism (not even yet named or theorized) of the early eighteenth century might be is not considered here in detail.[28] Instead, I would like to unpack these issues and open the conversation for some serious discussion of how economic theory really does fit into the shatter zone discourse by juxtaposing this initial episode of struggle and trading along the edge of the shatter zone involving Choctaws, Chickasaws, Frenchmen, and Englishmen with the work of economist C. A. Gregory. Gregory argues for a more complex substantivist view of what happens when capitalism is layered onto a noncapitalist economy in his 1982 study of Papua, New Guinea.[29]

Gregory drew upon the political economy theories of Ricardo, Marx, and Sraffa for the framework of his argument. He did so well before the recent development of a critical economics of intangibles and, under Bourdieusian influence, an expanded interest in notions of social capital and the "embeddedness" of markets in traditional social arrangements. Gregory also made significant use of anthropological and economic-anthropological analyses of non-European "gift economies" by Mauss, Lévi-Strauss, Polanyi, and Sahlins to argue that far from being displaced by a capitalist economy, the existing gift economy of Papua, New Guinea, "effloresced" by embedding new trading practices into existing social patterns. By analyzing the gift economy in a holistic way that demonstrates how production, consumption, distribution, and circulation are intimate parts of clan-based societies having multiple spheres of exchange, Gregory pointed to a more nuanced explanation of the reception, alteration, and management of market capitalism among non-Western peoples.

As originally developed by Paul Bohannan in analyses of the Tiv and Mae-Enga, the notion of spheres of exchange captures the idea that in economies where there is no universal measure of value conversion in the

Table 4. Spheres of exchange among the Tiv

EXCHANGE SPHERE	ITEMS EXCHANGED	CONDITION OF REMOVAL OF ITEM FROM SPHERE
supreme	rights in human beings other than slaves, especially dependent women and children	death
prestige	slaves, cattle, a specific kind of white cloth, brass rods	death, consumption, conversion exchange outside sphere
subsistence	food including chickens and goats, household utensils bound up with food preparation, tools again involved with subsistence, and raw materials used for producing any other items in the category	consumed, used up, sacrificed

Source: Bohannan, "Some Principles of Exchange and Investment"

form of a currency, objects of exchange may be ranked rather than valued and may only be exchanged in certain appropriate ways that, presaging Bourdieu's "structuring structures," in turn define and are defined by relationships between people. For the famous Tiv case, see table 4.

In general, things are exchanged only within the same sphere, a procedure Bohannan called conveyance that is morally neutral. The items in the supreme sphere cannot be exchanged for anything else and cannot be completely alienated; women married off occasion an obligation to receive women married in, and married women retain rights in their social grouping of origin. The same restriction to sphere is true of the other items with the notable exception of brass rods, which can cross categories in either direction by being used in exchange for subsistence items (though this is considered wasteful) or in very extreme cases for women (though with loss of prestige for all concerned). This is called conversion exchange and is strongly freighted with moral issues.

Gregory points out that these spheres of exchange are themselves ranked in a continuum: the supreme category generally relates to inter-clan exchanges relating to human reproduction and exogamy, which in fact frame the kinship system itself, and to the inalienable land that is held in partitive common as the base of subsistence.[30] The lowest level of exchange tends to be intraclan only and to reflect items and materials that were available to everyone and yet vital to subsistence. The middle category of prestige items is most associated with items and materials brought from afar or requiring special restricted production methods at home under the control of the wealthy or powerful. Prestige items would be personified rather than commoditized, and their exchange restricted to this specific category.

It is not difficult to draw parallels to these three spheres in the South. The supreme sphere would similarly govern marriages, hence kinship, land tenure, and social reproduction, and in this sphere Europeans would participate in only a limited way. For prestige items prior to Europeans, bow wood, minerals, exotic pelts, and perhaps shell ornaments might be brought from afar, while imported copper might be wrought locally along with nonfunctional pottery vessels. In the European era prestige items might include guns, metals, and fine cloth that could be made into garments locally, as well as silver gorgets, faience containers, and brass containers that might be modified to local taste. Although Europeans participated in this middle sphere more than in the supreme one, they were probably not the primary players whatever they may have thought. There is no evidence that Southern Native people chose to *trade* in prestige items with Europeans, though ample evidence (compare La Salle's near burial in a pile of furs by the Quapaws in 1682) that they did choose to exchange them by *gift* for the sake of the relationship they established. Further, the Choctaws were not alone among Southern Indians, whatever their mortuary ritual, in burying a broad range of prestige items with their owners, much to the chagrin of Europeans who thus saw their gift "investment" (which was really an investment in a relationship) die with individual allies.

The lowest or subsistence sphere, on the other hand, was where Europeans participated most fully via exchange of objects. As they themselves observed, the deerskins they primarily wanted were a byproduct of meat provisioning, and that activity was so basic and so open to everyone that food hospitality was an invariably observed feature of Southern Indian behavior toward strangers.

Exchange activities related to all these spheres have been considered before in some way in historical and archaeological literature, the supreme one under kinship, the middle under prestige goods, and the lowest in discussions of subsistence. Yet as soon as we consider that such a structure is a political economy, with the spheres ranked in this way and exchange activities articulated to match, it becomes significant to talk not only of what might be exchanged but also with whom specifically and when, and what might be the meaning of such exchanges.[31]

Other economic anthropologists have thus suggested further nuance to Bohannan's model, adding dimensions to the spheres in the form of *modalities of exchange* (sharing, buying, delayed-return, exact equivalent) and the role of *relationships in exchange* (in which the kinship or other relationship between the parties and the history of relations between them can dictate the character of the exchange).[32] David Graeber has looked carefully at the notion of value, how it is constructed, both emergent from and creating human relationships; the role of human action in creating value; and how value might accrue historically to objects, particularly heirlooms that inhabit the prestige sphere and come to be personified through not only the labor required to create them but also through the history of their ownership (like that of Kula shells, for example).[33] Annette Weiner's research has further elaborated the concept of "inalienable possessions" underlying objects that become so bound up with lineal or group identity that efforts must be made to keep them in spite of economic and political vicissitudes.[34]

Studies of the fur and skin trades and the "penetration of the market economy" into the Native economies of Southern North America have not attempted extended studies of the Native economies as non-Western phenomena. Instead, like Braund or Mancall, Rosenbloom, and Weiss, they have framed these phenomena implicitly or explicitly in terms of the neoclassical economics model, or like Usner and White, they have used an informal substantivist framework not explicitly articulated to accommodate the notion of spheres of exchange. Graeber, drawing from both Gregory's and Weiner's work, however, argues that when integration into another economy takes place such that the society of interest remains peripheral and autonomous with respect to the external market, the society may experience, as Gregory showed for Papua, New Guinea, a creative cultural flowering as "new means are mainly being put to very old ends; more specifically, a vast flow of new resources is put to the task of pursuing traditional forms of value."[35]

I would like to explore this context of traditional regimes of value in the light of the recent economic anthropological scholarship by attempting a sketch of the Choctaw exchange spheres ca. 1700–65. The data are very sparse and mostly reveal only a non-Choctaw point of view, but suggestions can at least be made to support the viability of such an undertaking.

First, a word about sources and the possibilities they offer for observation, which seriously constrains what can be reconstructed. I am going to draw on four well-attested observations. The first we have already seen, that of Henri de Tonti in 1702. This document is about understanding the interior situation and the trading and defense arrangements of the Choctaws and Chickasaws vis-à-vis the already-present English. It witnesses slaving, defense, and some trade, and it establishes the French as a source of guns for the Choctaws. The second source is the so-called French "Anonymous Relation" that describes Choctaw culture and that was made famous by John Swanton. I date this document to the 1730s before the first Chickasaw war of 1736. This record is all about looking for what Choctaws might want in trade. As a result it observes material culture at the basic household level and how household goods change hands in some detail; the observations unusually include something of the preferences of women. The third document is the report of an embassy to the Choctaws in 1746 by Jadart de Beauchamp. This document is about the Choctaws' fulfilling their side of the *lex talionis* bargain struck with the French in 1738 by providing justice for the murder of three Frenchmen. This rendering of justice is supported by a history of nearly fifty years of French presents, of chiefs with medals and commissions, and of French learning about the Choctaw practice of punishment. Beauchamp harks back to the French saving the Choctaws from enslavement in 1702 and to the French having given justice to the Choctaws in the Barthelemy murder case in 1738. The fourth document is the record of the 1765 Mobile Congress, at which the Choctaws negotiated the terms of their new relationship with the victorious English after the end of

Table 5. Sources for observations

DOCUMENT	OBSERVER	SITUATION	SPHERES REPRESENTED
Tonti 1702	Henri de Tonti, experienced diplomatist	French intervention into a dynamic slaving and trading situation	supreme (rights in human beings: slaving), prestige? (guns), subsistence (deer)
Anonymous 1730s	Unknown French trader	Choctaws host trader who observes opportunities for trade	subsistence
Beauchamp 1746	Jadart de Beauchamp, major of Mobile	French intervention into a civil war	supreme (*lex talionis*), prestige (medals, guns?)
Mobile Congress 1765	English and French officials including governor, military officers, interpreters, and Indian agents	English host Choctaws but on Choctaw land	supreme (land), prestige (chiefs' gifts, medals), subsistence

the French and Indian War. This document is a record of an attempt to set up the English idea of a disciplined colony in which the Indians are supposed to grant land in exchange for trade. Grudgingly the Choctaws are given some limited presents and granted a gunsmith and a commissary but only on condition that the gunsmith's services be provided after approval by both chiefs and commissary.[36]

In all four sources the observers were European, but their perspectives were by no means the same (see table 5). The roles of those who participated in the reported exchanges overlapped somewhat in that most of the Europeans occupied official government positions and most of the named Choctaws were of some rank, while the items of exchange and the spheres of exchange observed varied. In many cases, where it was perfectly clear what the Frenchman made of the exchange, as with Tonti's so-called hiring of bearers or messengers, it is problematic to specify how the Choctaw recipient perceived the situation. Nevertheless, if it was the case that exposure to European trading practices was truly as seductive as some have argued, we would expect to see perceptible change in Choctaw exchange practices over these sixty-some years. Carson and O'Brien have already argued that such changes were only superficial until well into the nineteenth century at the earliest, but they have not explored exchange practices as a system in detail.

To use these documents, I coded the exchange events reported in them, under the categorical headings of things exchanged, the parties to the exchange and their relationship, the occasion of the exchange, the apparent modality of the exchange, and the social value of the exchange. Listed below are the general subcategories that emerged for these elements:

1) relationship (all of these relationships also existed in the intergroup situation, and hence I have assumed that they at least partly represent Native practice)

   a) kinship

   b) marriage

   c) fictive kinship

   d) undefined (refers to the situation in which the relationship itself is in question; there does not appear to be any exchange situation at all in which at least a potential relationship between the parties is not involved)[37]

2) occasion (there are no negative kinds of occasions here because the documents do not address themselves to a situation of active enmity, but clearly one would also need to account for the absence of any occurrence of hostility, as for example that it precluded exchange)

   a) alliance (active construction of alliance)

   b) hospitality (where relations are established)

   c) other

3) modality

   a) sharing (no return on the immediate occasion)

   b) delayed-return (no return on the immediate occasion)

   c) exact exchange (something of equivalent value immediately exchanged on each side; note that buying in which money is involved is not at issue in these documents)

   d) other (includes repudiation)

4) social value

   a) supreme (social reproduction)

b) prestige (agency or power)

c) subsistence (physical reproduction)

In describing events in terms of things exchanged and parties to the exchange, narrative description was used because many of the events were complex, and consequently it was unclear how, or if, I should decompose them, as an example from the 1702 Tonti document shows:

The English agent "a jean" has multiple Choctaw captives

Tonti promises or gives a ransom for one of them to the Chickasaw chief

The Chickasaw chief frees the captive (how is not specified)

The Chickasaw chief turns the captive over to Tonti

The Choctaw captive is freed by Tonti

Tonti gives presents to the Chickasaw chiefs

The Chickasaw chiefs turn over some of the French presents to the English agent

The document frames this sequence as three separate events, and clearly there were many different ways to segment the events presented in all four of the texts. A major concern, however, was simply to segment them sufficiently to see how the four facets above — relationship, occasion, modality, and social value — mapped onto the exchange events. The scale of the documents' contribution to the discussion that follows can perhaps be discerned by noting that my segmentation yielded sixteen events from the 1702 document, forty-two from 1735, twenty-four from 1746, and twenty-four from 1765. I coded not only the exchange of material objects but also the exchange of intangibles such as information, obligation, and honor when it was clear from the explicit speech of participants that exchange was understood as taking place.

Looking at the data in this way of course quickly exposes, as it should, the major import of each document: all of them record Europeans and Choctaws working on some part of new relationships in terms appropriate to each group's values and negotiating a colonial regime that included what Europeans saw as trade along with other relationships viewed from various standpoints. Fortunately all three spheres are approximately represented in these four documents, but all three do not appear in every document. The major drawback of using European documents here is that their authors are pursuing colonial ends, and with the exception of the author of "Anonymous Relation" they do not see, report, or recognize the granular exchanges that characterize and constitute all social relations that define kinship, roles, gender, lineages, households, and villages. Even when seen through the eyes of Europeans, however, the described exchanges make it clear that maintaining appropriate relationships was far more important to the Choctaws than the trade that made some of the relationships visible.[38]

After having tallied the exchange events, I made a list of objects exchanged, after which I attempted to construct categories based on the objects' correlations with the features of the exchange. The resulting categories were as follows:

PEOPLE: This category is about life (fertility and increasing numbers of people) and death or signs of death. I include the act of committing people to do something since such commitment risks them and obligates the group to which they belong.

LAND: Europeans could not give this. Neither did the Choctaws appear prepared to alienate land but rather to share or lend it to Europeans to use.

GUNS AND MUNITIONS: Guns and powder and ball were mentioned repeatedly. They were significant to two contexts, for defense of ethnos and land and as a means of production (in both respects they mapped onto the previously used bows and arrows, which were explicitly cited as having been replaced by guns for both). Interestingly, French lists of imports destined for the Indians indicated that almost a third of the guns the Choctaws received from the French were received as gifts, not in trade, though it would be impossible now to define how the two transmission modalities might parse onto the two spheres.[39]

PERSONAL ADORNMENT: Limited evidence indicates that Native items were still in use for this purpose, especially for ceremonial contexts. Europeans, however, were most focused on this category when it came to trade and gifts.

PRESENTS: When documents mention French and English "presents," that term included items of personal adornment, domestic goods, and means of production or defense. Though some were slightly more special, the presents were almost the same as the items procured for the trade, but they seem to have excluded items intended specifically for women except perhaps cloth yard goods. In this category I also place events such as the negotiation of access to presents that depended in turn to some degree on the rank of the Choctaw participant as perceived or negotiated by Europeans. French documents (though not these) hint that French leaders always received in return for their presents symmetrical presents that were also similar to but perhaps a notch more special than the things the Choctaws traded, such as fine deerskins, furs, and perhaps special foodstuffs.

TRADE: Trade goods brought to Louisiana for the Choctaws were almost the same as the goods given as presents except that they included such items intended specifically for women as ready-made shirts, thread, needles, and awls. In return Choctaws traded deerskins, occasionally furs, and some foodstuffs.

RANK BADGES: Native forms, symbols, and objects, including tattoos and feather ceremonial regalia, still seem to have been in use. Europeans tried to parallel them by offering medals and gorgets (parallel to shell gorgets) and commissions (parallel to oral recitations of standing). The Choctaws retained their own ceremonialism surrounding the allocation of these items, notably renaming ceremonies that changed the relationship between giver and recipient as well as the recipient's status. Medals received a full Native treatment that involved ceremonial practices for display, return, and repudiation.

DOMESTIC MANUFACTURES: The author of the "Anonymous Relation" lists most domestic manufactures when indicating materials and objects as well as the gender division of labor in their production. Many of these things were certainly laden with meaning, but because they were mostly the domain of women and were all shared within the scope of kinship, moiety, or village, they did not seem to impinge much on European trade and thus these meanings were not detailed even in the "Anonymous Relation."

FOOD: Food was reported in many contexts and was constantly being proffered as a duty of hospitality. Interestingly, it seems that a visitor was frequently presented with food shortly after passing over a border onto Choctaw land. Another observation supported by the documents is that men presented the Europeans with raw food (game), while women presented cooked or processed food.[40]

The next step in the analysis is to use these categories to construct spheres of exchange. Again, by referring to the contexts in which the exchanges took place, it is possible to group the categories as follows:

PEOPLE, LAND, AND GUNS AND MUNITIONS (FOR DEFENSE): Both people and land called forth huge effort and commitment. French guns were originally provided for the defense of both people and land against the guns provided to others by the English; this fact is cited repeatedly in these documents as a main basis for the relationship with the French, perhaps reflected by guns being frequently conveyed to the Choctaws from the French as gifts. What the Choctaws clearly described as the usufruct grant of land to the English, even though to the Choctaws' way of thinking it alienated no land, required naming ceremonies and formal statements of standing to accomplish. With respect to people the issue of subsistence labor does not seem to fit here.

RANK BADGES, PERSONAL ADORNMENT, AND ACCESS TO EXTERNAL TRADE AND PRESENTS: Rank badge distribution was clearly connected with power in that in the European-Choctaw case it was always orchestrated by the powerful on both sides in such a way as to maintain their positions and construct a social imaginary to suit their concerns if possible. Items of personal adornment were set aside for people of rank in the form of a sort of outfit referred to by the French as a chief's present. Access to trade on *both* sides emerged from formal negotiations connected with establishing rank and standing, and those negotiations could include the material evidence of gifts.

FOOD, DOMESTIC MANUFACTURES, AND GUNS AND MUNITIONS (FOR HUNTING): All of these items were central to the practical reproduction of material culture. Where European items were not involved, all these things, including deer, were freely shared within the appropriate kinship or community group and via customary hospitality practices. Here guns acted as a domestic means of production, with the product of hunting also being distributed in accord with kinship relations. Surpluses generated here could enter the trade via these relationship pathways, and gifts could be brought into the domestic sphere through similar means.

Choctaws at the Border of the Shatter Zone 353

The above information is summarized in table 6.

What is clearest about such an analysis is that although European goods were integrated into Choctaw culture, the process through which this integration happened was not such as to sweep all previous economic practices aside. The system of economic practices suggested by the four documents I analyzed was still intact well past the middle of the eighteenth century; indeed, something similar at least in part had probably accommodated distant trade for centuries before the coming of Europeans. More importantly, as part of a cultural imaginary that had survived the upheavals of population disaster and population displacements, this indigenous economic system was capable of incorporating and accommodating the interventions of the European trade by slotting Europeans and their offerings into a system that had evolved to support a lifestyle that Europeans of the colonial period had little desire to alter. It was a system that classified people and objects both functionally and relationally but was underdetermined enough to accommodate ongoing negotiated change.

Europeans' decisions interacted with the system and became part of its evolution. For example, because no presents were set aside for women by the French, women were forced to trade to get the things they wanted, and when a new colonial regime was negotiated with the English, women speaking through men took the opportunity to ask specifically for presents designed for them. Further, when the Choctaws were attacked by neighbors bearing firearms, they sought the same weapons in order to defend themselves; the guns they acquired from the French for self-defense, funneled through a Janus-faced system of ranks viewed differently from both sides, soon were fired in the harvest of deer for food provisioning and the deerskin trade. It is significant that the deerskin trade was in fact "down market" in terms of the Choctaws' exchange spheres: far from being inalienable or bound up with the identities of elites or the cosmological security of the Choctaw ethnos, deerskins were almost a byproduct of woodland management for food harvest. What was inalienable — or *immeuble* (immovable) in Marcel Mauss's terms — was land, and in 1765, even after having gone through a complex and vexing ceremony, the English only got the use of it from the Choctaws, not ownership.[41]

Table 6. Suggested Choctaw spheres of exchange, ca. 1700

EXCHANGE SPHERE	ITEMS EXCHANGED	APPROPRIATE RELATIONSHIP OF EXCHANGE PARTNERS	APPROPRIATE MODALITY	SOCIAL VALUE
Supreme (land and people)	1) mates, offspring; 2) land; 3) weapons for defense	1) opposite moiety; 2) same lineage or fictive kin; 3) fictive kin	Delayed-return	social-genealogical reproduction
Prestige (rank badges, adornment, access to trade and presents)	rank badges, personal adornment, metal containers, horses	allied foreigners (established relationship, fictive kin)	Delayed-return, exact exchange	agency/power, identity
Subsistence (production, domestic)	1 & 2) deer, corn, ceramics, mulberry bark for fiber; 3) woven cloth, sewing implements, weapons for hunting	1) relative; 2) nonrelated Choctaw; 3) non-Choctaw	1) sharing (implicit delayed-return); 2) delayed-return; 3) exact equivalent	physical reproduction

Finally, we need to discuss the 1702 Chickasaw-Chakchiuma-English slave raids against the Choctaws once more as an attack on the second element of the supreme sphere of exchange, people. First, we should recall that in 1702 the Choctaws were still in the process of active confederation and population expansion. It was a time when exchange of spouses and reproduction of children was especially important, perhaps of central importance, for the nascent nation. In that context the taking of slaves for export to European colonies was an attack on the heart of the confederation formation process because this trade preyed especially on women and children due to the Europeans' difficulty in keeping male Indian slaves in bondage. Thus the trade limited the number of wombs for reproduction. People enslaved and sold away fell out of the supreme sphere as though they had died. Just to take Tonti's slaving numbers:

Choctaws at the Border of the Shatter Zone 355

eighteen hundred killed and five hundred enslaved equals twenty-three hundred lost, perhaps three-fourths men and one-fourth women and children. If there were fifty villages as some tallies suggest, then forty-six people would have been lost in each village. For a population of fifteen thousand it would be out of a village population of three hundred, or 15.3 percent; for a population of twenty thousand, it would be 11.5 percent of four hundred people. In other words, these numbers were significant and as a loss to social reproduction with no comparable return possible would have been seriously felt.

Such effects, however, would not have been so uniform. When we also consider that, as Tonti observed, it was the northeastern and eastern villages that were most exposed to such attack, it is clear that there would have been more need of additional population in those regions in order to amplify the Concha and Chickasawhay populations. This population adjustment is exactly what seems to have happened through the Choctaws' absorption of additional refugees in the early eighteenth century. It is therefore not hard to understand why the Eastern Choctaw division subsequently clung so steadfastly to French alliance, while the southern Choctaws were more flexible. In addition, it is worth repeating Iberville's famous statement that he wished to enslave only deer, not people. To the Choctaws that would have translated to a desire to offer items in exchange for plentiful resources from the subsistence sphere as opposed to the English-backed raid on the supreme sphere.

Perhaps even more significant, one of Iberville's first acts in earnest of the Choctaw alliance was to bestow young French boys on the Choctaw chiefs; it was a practical act whose eventual efficaciousness had been well proven in Canada. These boys were to be fostered and adopted in order to become interpreters, with several of them eventually marrying into the group and becoming Choctaw "countrymen." I would suggest that this was a *literally* effective act because at a time of threat to the Choctaw population, the French symbolically and actually *gave* people — a gift at the supreme level — rather than taking them away.

It does seem to me that slaving such as the Chickasaws carried out must have tampered seriously with an economic system such as I am suggesting here. Without having analyzed the Chickasaw case in full, I think it is possible to suggest that from the Chickasaw side the commodification of Choctaw people through entering into active slaving as a serious pursuit might well have skewed a previous indigenous concept of the treatment of captives and the Choctaw concept of the loss of them. Such a loss I have suggested pertained to the supreme sphere. In the Choctaw scheme elaborated here (though this Choctaw case is not represented in the documents used for deriving the structure), one might argue on the basis of the literature on North American captive enslavement practices that either captives would normally be secured from enemies and kept in order to further genealogical reproduction or killed in order to assert social reproduction, both acts in aid of the maintenance of land and people but remaining in the supreme sphere. If people were taken captive and exchanged for subsistence goods in some kind of exact exchange, as I propose was the case with the Chickasaw slave raiding, this would clearly mean that the Chickasaws were modifying such a system.

It would be interesting therefore to look in detail at any evidence for how this process was negotiated between Chickasaws and Englishmen at its beginning because existing categories would have to have been used. For example, when the Choctaws held French-enslaved Africans who had been recaptured from the Natchez before returning these slaves to the French in 1730, there seemed to be a great deal of confusion over how the return should be done. In general, it seems to have been accomplished with prestige gifts, including horses and ceremonial suits of clothes, rather than as a subsistence trade. Accordingly, the Choctaws could see the exchange as a reassertion of right relationship in the prestige sphere followed by the return of people between fictive kin at the supreme level. Such a view required the Choctaws to treat the Africans as something like French children and the French to act rather like the Tiv using brass rods to "trade up" for people. Even the French seem to have seen it as something like fee for service rather than actual purchase of the enslaved Africans.[42]

The middle exchange sphere was perhaps more fluid and is clearly in need of much more close analysis in the context of "shatter zones," "tribal zones," and "frontier exchange economies." It reflects in part the category of Indian presents so assiduously given and maintained by the policy-ridden French and so much avoided by the entrepreneurial English, who insisted that Indians trade for such goods, as Jacobs has pointed out.[43] In Gregory's argument this category represents the exchange of symbolic goods that establishes the reproduction of other relationships, including the right of access to the supreme category as well as to the lower one. This category of exchanges, as we know from the vast documentation of the eighteenth century including our 1765 document here, set up and maintained fictive kinship relationships that facilitated such access on both sides. It was the French gifts that began with Tonti and Iberville, more frequent even when cut off for some years than were gifts from the English, that served to establish the French as intracommunity neighbors with whom mutual needs for easily available subsistence items could be met by simple exact equivalent exchange.

This subsistence sphere of exchange that includes food, clothing, and shelter and the utensils and tools for obtaining and preparing them, centered on relatives, and generosity was valued as niggardliness was despised. In the light of the spheres of exchange framework, we can thus explain why the trade in deerskins was not precisely seen as such by Choctaw people and why fictive kinship had to be established for it to be possible at all. The relationship between subsistence and kinship also underlines the importance of the French lists including so many guns as gifts. And to return to the issue of slaving, one might even suggest that a wrong relationship between supreme and subsistence spheres is what Iberville meant when he spoke of the French wish to enslave animals (subsistence sphere) rather than people (supreme sphere treated as subsistence sphere: "eating" people).

I would assert then, against the argument that Native cultural logic will necessarily be profoundly remade under survival pressures in the violence of the tribal (shatter) zone, that the strength of what used to be called the playoff system, whereby Southern tribes used different European groups against one another to retain their own agency, lay at least in the Choctaw case in their unique historical situation. For the Choctaw a sequence of events at the turn of the eighteenth century made them able to acquire guns soon enough to counter internecine warfare more effectively and to become a refuge for additional groups of people who joined their ethnogenesis process. Further, the French ally that they acquired was willing to establish relationships according to Choctaw cultural logic rather than one that insisted on radical alteration of traditional exchange spheres. The Choctaws were thus able to exploit the requirements of the deerskin trade in their own way by giving skins for cloth as items shared among (fictive) kin and fattening on meat from the hunt as well as sharing it generously with those same fictive kin, thereby prospering to such a degree that their population was in resurgence by the end of the colonial period.

Between 1702 and 1763 a sequence of events and contacts made Choctaw relationships with Europeans more complex but possibly no more complex than their relations had been with Native neighbors at the outset. Because the Choctaws were on the border of the shatter zone, perhaps even in a liminal space between shatter zones, not only did the European market economy (such as it was) fail to fully assimilate them during the early or even the late colonial period, but they were even able to adapt external exchange relations to their own cultural practice. I hope to explore the details of what trade meant in this context in greater detail in the future.

Notes

1. The expression "forgotten centuries" was devised by Charles Hudson for the collection *Forgotten Centuries* he edited with Carmen Chaves Tesser.

2. Galloway, *Choctaw Genesis*, figure 9.1, 354.

3. This assertion is based on archaeological evidence that has dated a series of single-mound sites down the center of Mississippi to the Mississippian Period and thus implies that they were so-called simple chiefdoms. For the terminology, see Steponaitis, "Location Theory." See also Lorenz, "Small-Scale Mississippian Community Organization." In the case of those sites such as Lyon's Bluff and Lubbub Creek that have been excavated or at least carefully surveyed, modest trade materials from east or west suggest that these sites did represent a sort of "rusticated" role within what might be construed as a region too distant to fall under the hegemonic influence of a major chiefdom. Additional information may be found in a useful summary of these issues in a report on the rescue observation of such a site: Baca, "Destruction of the Blaine Mound."

4. For information on all these smaller groups, see Fogelson, *Handbook*, vol. 14, *Southeast*.

5. Martin, "Southeastern Indians and the English Trade."" Martin, however, also assumes that this was only a reprieve delaying the steamroller effects of hegemonic capitalism until the American period.

6. For an overview of the shattered Southwest, see John, *Storms Brewed in Other Men's Worlds.*

7. For Iberville's observations as recorded in his ships' logs, see Iberville, *Gulf Journals.*

8. Stubbs, "Chickasaw Contact."

9. For a more detailed discussion of Tonti's trip and a translations of Tonti's reports from the field, see Galloway, "Henri de Tonti."

10. Tonti, "Extract," 167–68.

11. Tonti, "Extract," 168–69.

12. Tonti, "Extract," 170, 172.

13. Various schemes by Carolina representatives, perhaps the most effective by Thomas Nairne some six years later, aimed at eradicating the French presence to obviate this danger. See Nairne, *Nairne's Muskhogean Journals.*

14. For Sauvole's report, see Sauvole, *Journal of Sauvole.* Bows and arrows had worked just fine for almost a millennium in spite of growing populations, and even after acquiring guns, Indians continued to hunt for the trade using these weapons, especially when ammunition for guns was in short supply; White, *Middle Ground,* 135. Archaeological findings on historic sites in the Midwest continue to reveal projectile-point manufacture even after the advent of guns in the region, and the Mississippi Department of Archives and History has in its archaeological collections a projectile point of the eighteenth century fashioned from a shard of European bottle glass.

15. Iberville, *Gulf Journals,* 172.

16. Tonti, "Extract," 168.

17. Galloway, "Medal Chief's *Grosse Lettre.*"

18. This is not to say that the colonizing French never enslaved Indians: they did so on at least two occasions when they carried out punitive wars against Indian groups. In the first instance the victims were the Chitimachas, many of whom were enslaved and became domestic servants in New Orleans, Mobile, and perhaps most famously in Natchez (Antoine Simon Le Page Du Pratz's young Chitimacha slave woman; Galloway, "Natchez Matrilineal Kinship"); and Brightman, "Chitimacha." In the second instance some two hundred and thirty Natchez captured west of the Mississippi by the French and their allies were sent to Santo Domingo as slaves; Galloway and Jackson, "Natchez and Neighboring Groups," esp. 607–9.

Ironically, before the Natchez revolt in 1728 Governor Perier had complained in a letter about Indians who were trafficking in Indian slaves used in the colony; he felt that it stirred up Indian nations and was not useful since Indian slaves weren't good for much and were likely to lead African slaves astray. It was far better he believed to impress Indians with the French virtue of forbidding their enslavement; Rowland and Sanders, *Mississippi Provincial Archives*, 2:573–74. I do not address this issue here because the Choctaws did very little if any documented capturing of slaves for sale, partly because Indian slaving was primarily an artifact of the early colonial period when the Choctaws were not yet in alliance with Europeans who were seeking to buy Indian slaves and partly because they were inconveniently located for the capture or delivery of slaves for sale. On a few occasions the Choctaws doubtless adopted captives, but there is little documentation of such a practice during the colonial period, and any archaeological evidence, given the multiethnic nature of the Choctaw ethnos anyway, would be very hard to disentangle. Later on in this chapter I will address how slave catching fits into the economic structure I am proposing.

19. For an argument about the effectiveness of silent and flashless bows and arrows for night fighting see Gallay, *Indian Slave Trade*, 179–95.

20. Richter, *Ordeal of the Longhouse*, 32–36.

21. Taylor, *Modern Social Imaginaries*, 23–30, 23 (quote); and Anderson, *Imagined Communities*.

22. Carson, *Searching for the Bright Path*; O'Brien, *Choctaws in a Revolutionary Age*; and White, *Middle Ground*, 94–141.

23. At the beginning of the French alliance with the Choctaws in 1702, all guns were given as gifts, but the French strategy with respect to guns was always to make a great many gifts of them (and associated equipment like flints, powder, and bullets) and then to provide free repair of both gift and traded guns by French gunsmiths located at the forts or French settlements (or later in a few villages). With this policy, the likelihood that French traders would then get most of the deerskins the Indians had to trade was high, and accordingly this strategy was continued by the French throughout their tenure in Louisiana. The ratio of guns given to guns traded seems to have remained constant or even increased during the life of the Louisiana colony. For a French list of merchandise to be sent to Louisiana in 1713, see Rowland and Sanders, *Mississippi Provincial Archives*, 2:143–60. This list specified twenty-five guns to be given as gifts to Indians and one hundred to be given to colonial employees as part of their salaries; the French employees could then trade these guns to the Indians for food. In 1722 in spite of an altercation

with the Natchez, Bienville sent to their war chief Tattooed Serpent their regular present, which included eight guns, powder, and ammunition, said to betoken French trust; Rowland and Sanders, *Mississippi Provincial Archives*, 3:327. In 1759 a colonywide list specifies three hundred and fifty guns for general Indian presents and one hundred and fifty for "extraordinary presents." The same list states that the Choctaw trade is allotted two hundred guns, that with other Indians is allotted four hundred, and a projected Cherokee trade four hundred more; Rowland, Sanders, and Galloway, *Mississippi Provincial Archives*, 5:227–41.

24. Braund, *Deerskins and Duffels*, 88–90. Braund, however, assumes that Native "trade" practices were of the "truck and barter" variety that English sources also assume and frequently places the term "presents," used by the Creeks for what they received for their deerskins, in quotes without asking why they used the term.

25. Mancall, Rosenbloom, and Weiss, "Indians and the Economy." This work is connected to the authors' long-sustained work on the colonial economy as participants in the National Bureau of Economic Research's Development of the American Economy Project aimed at uncovering the "sources of economic productivity" in the American economy.

26. Coclanis, *Atlantic Economy*, xvii. In this discourse agency requires autonomy of the methodological individualist kind. Granovetter in "Economic Action" has pointed out that this kind of analysis in modern studies of industrial organization omits the data on personal relations that would enrich economists' view of economic action. This data is omitted because of a view of individuals as rational actors and also because the data are hard to get. The situation is, of course, far worse in the historical case.

27. Mancall, Rosenbloom, and Weiss, "Indians and the Economy," 313. For example, Lamoreaux in "Rethinking the Transition to Capitalism" makes use of a model developed by Peter Temin to argue that customary behaviors always dominate command and instrumental behaviors except in conditions of accelerated societal change. In this way she justifies what she characterizes as a "new consensus" among economists that market capitalism did not begin to dominate among Euro-Americans until after the Revolution. This argument is still a dance of automata, but it does begin to take actual conditions into account, and it certainly shifts the temporal context past the period of interest here.

28. A sampling of the major sources, which begin with the "substantivist" side of the argument against the "naturalness" of markets and capitalism, starts with Mauss, "Essai sur le don," includes the various views of Polanyi, *Great Transformation*; Lévi-Strauss, *Elementary Structures of Kinship*; and Sahlins, *Stone Age*

Economics, with more recent work being Appadurai, *Social Life of Things*; Parry and Bloch, *Money and the Morality of Exchange* ; Akin and Robbins, *Money and Modernity*; and especially Graeber, *Toward an Anthropological Theory of Value* that offers a useful overview of the whole question of cultural value and "economic" behavior including a discussion of Iroquois wampum. Finally, Bell in "White Ethnogenesis and Gradual Capitalism" has written about the "gradual capitalism" that characterized white ethnogenesis in the Chesapeake region in the eighteenth century, a time during which white racial solidarity was more important than thoroughgoing economic individualism.

29. Gregory, *Gifts and Commodities*.

30. Jonathan Parry and Maurice Bloch expand this notion to include the idea that this sphere, because it is responsible for the long-term cycles of social reproduction and maintenance of the social and cosmic order, is also characterized by moral superiority; Parry and Bloch, Introduction.

31. Although most authors have suggested that in principle there could be more than three spheres of exchange in any given system and although empirical research suggests that spheres might be subdivided or split, I will stick here with the three that Bohannan suggested and only indicate where it seems clear that the Choctaw case might require more elaboration.

32. Robbins and Akin, "Introduction to Melanesian Currencies," 9–10. A particularly significant contribution to the study of the importance of relationships is Weiner's *Inalienable Possessions*, which places special emphasis on the economic ramifications of male-female sibling relationships, especially in matrilineal societies (like those of Southern North America) that she studied in the Trobriands, but she also discusses the issue in patrilineal ones elsewhere.

33. Graeber, *Toward an Anthropological Theory of Value*.

34. Weiner, *Inalienable Possessions*. Weiner is most concerned with portable objects, although the most inalienable of group possessions is usually land.

35. Graeber, *Toward an Anthropological Theory of Value*, 148.

36. Documents translated in Galloway, "Henri de Tonti"; "Anonymous Relation"; Galloway, "Choctaw Factionalism and Civil War"; and Galloway, "'So Many Little Republics.'"

37. Granovetter, "Economic Action."

38. O'Brien in *Choctaws in a Revolutionary Age* has already pointed out this issue of appropriate relationships, which would be of especial importance to the Choctaws after the serious impacts of European conquest and disease made it necessary for them to reconstruct their ceremonial relations with land and animals

and to negotiate workable relations with Europeans. From the European point of view it is not so clear whether even the notion of a "right relationship" was at issue. Although both French and English colonials wished to maintain a friendly, cooperative, and profitable relationship with the Indians, one might suggest that for the French the strongest interest was diplomatic security, while for the English the strongest desire was trade profits. I suspect that for European leaders, if not all individual Europeans, Indians' ontological standing made a "right relationship" with them immaterial. Since to Europeans Indians were inferior in spiritual and often in mental understanding, domination could ultimately be the only right relationship. The *appearance* of the right relationship the Indians expected, as it furthered European ends, would suffice if required.

39. See citation of trade lists above, note 23.

40. I do not think this observation is particularly Lévi-Straussian because the observers only report meeting male hunters in the field who presented recently killed game and women in households and villages who presented food usually prepared for the household.

41. Whether they then stole it is, of course, another matter.

42. Letter from Régis du Roullet to Perier, March 16, 1731, Rowland, Sanders, and Galloway, *Mississippi Provincial Archives*, 4:64–71.

43. Jacobs, *Wilderness Politics*.

14 | *Shatter Zone Shock Waves along the Lower Mississippi*

MARVIN D. JETER

The phrase "shatter zone" has been used, albeit rarely, in the field of prehistoric archaeology at least since the 1960s but in contexts related to apparent cultural contacts, boundaries, and conflicts long before historic contact rather than to postcontact slaving.[1] After reviewing the history of earlier usage of this phrase in other fields, it seems to me that we are dealing with a more fluid and changing situation than those described in the traditional literature. Our shatter zone, rather than being relatively stable, stationary, and long-lived, moved inland from the Eastern seaboard ahead of European and later Euro-American expansion.[2]

For most of the period under primary consideration here, the sixteenth and seventeenth to early eighteenth centuries, I contend that the shatter zone had not yet reached the Lower Mississippi Valley (LMV).[3] Instead, it appears that only the Eastern seaboard was accessible for the establishment of European colonial footholds.[4] The Native groups (so-called chiefdoms and tribes) were fragmented in various ways, especially along kinship, ethnic, and linguistic lines, and therefore ripe for exploitation by European "divide and conquer" policies wherever the Europeans could get to them.

Did Eastern Native ethnic conflict include slavery? If so, how far back into prehistory did it extend? We archaeologists certainly do not routinely dig up obvious cases of indigenous slavery; the direct evidence has to come from ethnohistoric accounts of protohistoric and early historic situations. What we offer instead are some more general contexts, interpretations of interrelated masses of evidence about Eastern and Southern cultural traditions and how they eventually were impacted by, and interacted with, the European intrusion. In this way we can take a big-picture, running start on the historic situation. Were there any preexisting practices or long-standing traditions among Eastern and LMV Indians that might have preadapted them for slaving and played into the hands of Europeans bent upon exploitation of resources and peoples?

Of course, the most obvious example is warfare — or at least raiding — by Native peoples. Based mainly on ethnohistoric accounts, Alfred Kroeber famously characterized Eastern tribal warfare as "insane, unending . . . [yet] integrated into the whole fabric of Eastern culture," but warfare can be inferred well back into prehistory.[5] For instance, in one modern archaeological classic, the chapter dealing with the early Late Woodland, or Baytown period, (ca. 400 to 700 CE) in and near northeast Arkansas was entitled "Woodland Conflict."[6]

Elsewhere in the East, Midwest, and South, many archaeologists have documented apparent Late Woodland population increases and climatic fluctuations. These factors probably led to stresses and strains on the old Native Eastern (pre-maize) agricultural system and on hunting territories. They influenced the adoption or intensification of agriculture and the use of the bow and arrow for more efficient hunting and probably for warlike purposes.[7] Arrow points of types common in various parts of Arkansas (ca. 600–1000 CE) and made of Arkansas materials have been found with headless burials in Mississippi, from the northern Yazoo Basin to southeast Mississippi.[8] At the early Caddoan Crenshaw site (ca. 1000–1100 CE) in southwest Arkansas, archaeologists found clusters of human skulls, totaling at least 200, as well as clusters of detached human mandibles, totaling at least 216, though it is uncertain as to whether these represent trophies or some unusual local mortuary program.[9] At a northwest Mississippi site archaeologists found a prehistoric skeleton (probably Late Woodland to Early Mississippian, ca. 1000 CE) with partly healed cut marks on the lower rear of one tibia; the Achilles tendon had been cut with a stone knife, and the unfortunate person had lived for some time after that.[10]

A thorough study of 264 burials from a late prehistoric Oneota culture site in west central Illinois near the Mississippian culture frontier and dating ca. 1300 CE found that evidence for violent death was quite common (forty-three examples), including fourteen individuals with evidence of scalping and eleven who had been decapitated. After an extensive review of the regional and areal literature, the investigators concluded that "there can be little doubt that intergroup aggression was an important fact of life in many parts of prehistoric eastern North America, especially during the millennium preceding European contact . . . consistent with the widespread occurrence of palisaded villages and . . . Mississippian artwork featuring war-related themes."[11]

Mississippian cultures are indeed well known for evidence of warfare, including defensively fortified settlements, especially in probable frontier or peripheral regions, as well as for violent themes in iconography.[12] A recent review of the "Southeastern Ceremonial Complex" (SECC) noted that its imagery emphasizes "prowess in fighting," the "importance of weaponry," and "political domination."[13] Another kind of middle to late Mississippian imagery, a sort of dark side of the SECC, is probably relevant here: the "kneeling prisoner" or "bound captive" stone pipes of the LMV.[14]

A recent article suggested that an extensive "Vacant Quarter" around the Ohio-Mississippi juncture began around 1450 and was preceded by palisaded settlements and other indications of conflicts or avoidances of dangerous situations.[15] The authors proposed that for Mississippian groups similar abandonments were "a widespread phenomenon . . . not a unique event."[16]

Meanwhile, in and near northeast Arkansas major nucleated and fortified (with palisades or moats, or both) Mississippian settlements had developed, probably representing complex chiefdoms. South of the Arkansas River in the LMV archaeological evidence for palisaded or even nucleated villages is lacking so far, and dispersed patterns of smaller settlements seem to have been the norm. In late prehistoric times, however, there was a progression down the LMV of what archaeologists have been willing to call Mississippian culture.[17] The appearance of steady southward advance into lands formerly attributed to other archaeological cultures is so obvious that Philip Phillips felt obliged to caution "against the too easy assumption that Mississippian culture — or the bearers thereof . . . marched down the River in so regular a procession that individual phases can be dated by reference to degrees of latitude."[18] Nevertheless, this apparent southward progress can be roughly mapped and estimated to have occurred at an overall average rate of about sixty-five kilometers per century, comparable to the rate of about one hundred per century for the northwestward spread of Neolithic culture through Europe.[19] In the southern portions of the LMV after about 1200 CE, Mississippian archaeological culture advanced as the apparent northern boundary of Plaquemine culture retreated.[20]

It is uncertain whether this spread represents a kind of "demic diffusion" via population replacement as has been suggested in Europe or simple technological diffusion of shell-tempering for pottery and other Mississippian artifactual traits and lifeways. I have tended to favor the latter alternative, or at most some combination of the two.[21] However, the kinds of bioanthropological analyses, including DNA studies, of skeletal materials that might begin to sort out these possibilities may be precluded by present-day political situations.

This apparent Mississippian culture expansion seems to have lagged behind the southward spread of the chiefdom form of social organization.[22] Neither the chiefly nor Mississippian expansions seem to have been initially fueled by significant maize agriculture but by Native Eastern starchy — and oily — seed plant agriculture, with maize only along for the ride, as it were. Maize does not appear to have become truly dominant until the 1100s CE, or perhaps after 1200 CE in the southern LMV Plaquemine regions. In very late prehistoric times a number of northern LMV peoples adopted stemless arrow points like the "willow-leaf" Nodena type and a later variant of the triangular Madison type. One major use of these points may have been in warfare and raiding.[23]

The Mississippian and southerly Plaquemine traditions continued into protohistoric times. LMV archaeologists often subdivide the Protohistoric period (ca. 1500–1700 CE) into our beloved Early, Middle, and Late subperiods, with the divisions made at 1541 for the arrival of the Hernando de Soto *entrada* and at 1673 for the appearance of the French. The long Middle Protohistoric, a time of great changes among LMV Native American groups, is sometimes called the "Protohistoric Dark Ages" because there were no European observers in or near the LMV for one hundred and thirty years; written documentation is nonexistent.

The Soto chronicles mention a number of instances of conflict between Southern Indian polities. Most relevant here is the situation in which Pacaha, probably represented archaeologically by the Nodena phase of northeast Arkansas, was lording it over adjacent groups, including nearby Casqui, probably the Parkin phase.[24] Casqui, reinforced by the Spaniards, attacked a Pacaha settlement and vandalized the temple.

According to the account by Garcilaso de la Vega, the Casqui invaders freed some of their people who had been captured by Pacaha and crippled by cutting the "nerves," or tendons, of one foot or leg. Garcilaso, however, was not near the Soto *entrada* in time or place. He was born in 1539 in Peru and left in 1560 for Spain, where he lived the rest of his life. He wrote about the *entrada* in the early 1600s, allegedly deriving his story from eyewitness accounts. Garcilaso has a bad reputation as a historian, however, and he likely used literary devices for effect. His account of the alleged crippling of slaves at Pacaha is suspiciously similar to his earlier one about Indians in South Carolina and might be only a set piece. His claim is made even more dubious by the fact that none of the other, better-regarded Soto chroniclers had mentioned crippling of slaves at Pacaha.[25]

Who were the Indians that the *entrada* encountered at Pacaha and elsewhere in the LMV and what kinds of remains did they leave? With these questions we become involved with the difficult effort to mesh archaeological and ethnohistorical data.[26] This task is further complicated by the fact that in the LMV we are really dealing with two rather different ethnohistories. The first was left by the Spaniards of the 1540s and provides specific names for Native settlements, "provinces," and groups; however, those names generally did not survive the Dark Ages in recognizable form. The second was bequeathed by the French starting in 1673; many of the names they recorded have persisted.

The LMV archaeological literature since the 1930s is littered with the mutilated remains of attempts to make linkages of archaeological sites, artifacts, etc., with ethnohistorically named groups.[27] Nevertheless, I have recently suggested yet another reconstruction, proposing that the late prehistoric to protohistoric Tunican homelands extended from the Mississippi Valley in northeastern Arkansas, along the southeastern Ozark border and adjacent lowlands to the Arkansas Valley in west central Arkansas at the time of the Soto *entrada*.[28]

This reinterpretation was based on the simple but previously untried device of not only assuming (with most of my colleagues) that Charles Hudson's revised route for the *entrada* is more or less correct but also that John Swanton's earlier assignments of Indian linguistic families to the names of Indian "provinces," settlements, and people recorded by the Spaniards are also basically correct.[29] A simple mapping exercise then produced coherent geographic clusters of language-family territories, not only for Tunicans and for Caddoans in and near southwesternmost Arkansas but also for another group that previously had not been considered.[30]

I call these people "Northern Natchezans" to distinguish them from their contemporary relatives to the south, who were in the late prehistoric to protohistoric Plaquemine archaeological cultural tradition and became the Natchez proper and other southern LMV groups of the ethnohistoric documents. I suggest that these Northern Natchezans were the principal late prehistoric to middle protohistoric occupants of southeast and east central Arkansas (extending well up the Arkansas Valley) and of the adjacent Mississippi "Delta" lands, from the vicinity of modern Clarksdale (or even farther north) to modern Greenville and southward to merge with other Natchezans.[31]

Although my sympathies are mainly with scientific archaeologists who tend to view oral traditions very skeptically or reject them outright, recent appeals to integrate Native (or other) oral traditions into archaeological and ethnohistorical reconstructions have something to offer.[32] For example, a Tunican homeland along the Ozark front fits nicely with one Tunican tradition of coming originally from a mountainous homeland.[33] Moreover, the new scenario for Northern Natchezans also fits well with a Natchezan tradition of once having occupied a much more extensive territory to the north and east-west in the Mississippi Valley.[34] Yet there are plenty of opportunities for biased picking and choosing among the various oral traditions.[35]

My "Tunicans and Northern Natchezans scenario" is not based on connecting archeological phases to ethnohistoric Indian or linguistic groups, although it has implications for such connections. Instead, its real basis is an attempt to connect the two ethnohistories by getting around their generally dissimilar specific names for Native American groups by going up to the level of language families for the Soto names. In the Southwest, Curtis Schaafsma has emphasized the importance of resolving such problems via historical documents if possible rather than by positing ethnic archaeological assemblages.[36] In my case, questions derived from late protohistoric and historic French and Anglo-American documents about groups such as Tunicans, Natchezans, and Quapaws are addressed through the earlier Spanish documents and knowledge about the linguistic relationships of Indian words in them. The results are applied to the archaeological remains that are now better dated in the relevant locations.

The archaeological Nodena phase of northeast Arkansas is believed to represent the people of the dominant Pacaha province of the Soto chronicles, and the neighboring Parkin phase is generally regarded as the remains of the competing Casqui province.[37] When the Casquis and Spanish attacked the main town of Pacaha, they "found the heads and skulls of their own people impaled on lances by the door of the temple . . . removed them and substituted the heads of Pacahas they had just killed."[38] Despite a number of artifactual similarities between these two phases, Nodena points and various ceramic types, it is possible that the Pacaha peoples were Tunicans and those of Casqui were Northern Natchezans. An earlier archaeological study suggested a "tribal difference" between these phases on the basis of a difference in predominant ceramic pastes.[39] Whether different groups (linguistic and otherwise) were involved here, and whether the Garcilaso account is valid or not, the other accounts certainly attest to enmity between Pacaha and Casqui, thus supporting at least the possibility of enslavement of captives.

After the *entrada* but not necessarily because of it, both of these phases and others like them, such as Kent, Greenbrier, Old Town, Walls, Parchman, and Oliver, obviously representing major population concentrations as suggested by the Soto chronicles, declined during the Dark Ages. The causes have been the subject of much debate. The nucleated populations, living in unsanitary conditions with no knowledge of germs and viruses and no resistance to European diseases, were prime candidates for epidemics. Large numbers of pigs accompanying the Spaniards could have been the disease vectors. However, some have downplayed the role of direct Spanish contact, favoring later indirect transmission of diseases. Others have suggested that severe droughts were a more likely factor. Droughts and unchronicled disease episodes, if not epidemics or pandemics, quite possibly combined in apocalyptic fashion.[40]

In 1673, at the close of the Dark Ages, Marquette and Jolliet found a very different situation. Northeast Arkansas was apparently abandoned except for the Mitchigamea, Illinoian immigrants who may have been there only seasonally or as refugees (see below). The archaeological record, or paucity of it, agrees. Next, the French explorers encountered the Quapaws in a few settlements near the Arkansas-Mississippi river juncture. Their maps also show apparent Tunicans (Tanikoua, Akoroa, and possibly Papikaha) up the Arkansas Valley, apparently based on hearsay rather than actual visits, but no indication of Natchezans in what is now Arkansas.[41]

One map attributed to Jolliet does indicate "Tahensa sauvages" well to the south, apparently in northeastern Louisiana, but again this notation must have been based on hearsay.[42] The location is more or less where the probably Natchezan Taensa were contacted by La Salle nine years later. I suggest that the Taensa were recent arrivals there from Arkansas or northwestern Mississippi.[43] The Northern Natchezans in and near southeast Arkansas had probably entered late prehistoric times with a Plaquemine artifactual assemblage, which gradually changed to a Mississippian assemblage before the first European contacts.[44]

During the one hundred and thirty years of the Dark Ages, remnant groups of Tunicans and Northern Natchezans, or perhaps novel recombinations of them, moved southward, retaining their relative positions (Tunicans generally farther north). They could have reconsolidated their situations and revitalized their cultural heritage at times. Perhaps this process resulted in the archaeological manifestations that we now know as the Menard Complex (former Quapaw phase) along the Lower Arkansas; as clusters of coeval sites near Pine Bluff, Little Rock, and well above Little

Rock in the Carden Bottoms locality; and as sites with similar artifact assemblages near the Mississippi River in northwest Mississippi.[45]

A breakthrough in understanding these sites came with the analyses of materials from the Goldsmith Oliver 2 site at the Little Rock Airport. On the basis of that research I suggested that the Quapaws had not penetrated southward until the early to middle 1600s, significantly later than most researchers had believed. However, even that estimate was probably too early (see the discussion of Siouan migrations below). This late Quapaw arrival would explain the 1673 situation that Marquette and Jolliet reported. In 1682 and later La Salle and his successors did not note Tunicans again in the Lower Arkansas Valley but did find some in the present Vicksburg and Natchez localities. Remnant Tunican groups also appear to have been in or near southeast Arkansas until the 1690s, although they are not reported as residents there after 1700.[46]

In the "Tunicans and Northern Natchezans scenario" the Quapaws along with other Dhegiha Siouans were still in their aboriginal homeland well up the Ohio Valley when the Spaniards were in the LMV in the 1540s. In a related "Very Late Dhegiha Migration scenario," I have suggested that their long-distance migrations occurred much later.[47] These moves would have involved, after descending the Ohio (as in their oral traditions) the Osages and Kansas up the Mississippi-Missouri-Osage river system to southwestern Missouri, the Omahas (or "Upstream People") and Poncas up the Mississippi-Missouri system to the central Plains, and the Quapaws (or "Downstream People") down the Mississippi to the vicinity of the Arkansas-Mississippi juncture where they were described by the French as living in bark-covered longhouses, a house type foreign to the general Southeastern and LMV tradition but well known in the Northeast (and upper Midwest).

This reconstruction involves two major changes from most previous efforts. I suggest that the Dhegiha Siouans' migration had taken place relatively very late, around 1660, and that their homeland up to that time had been significantly farther up the Ohio Valley than most others had suggested. My leading candidate as an ancestral protohistoric archaeological entity was and still is the "eastern Fort Ancient" complex of the eastern Kentucky-West Virginia-Ohio borderlands. Conveniently enough, eastern Fort Ancient occupations seem to end around 1650, and it is the first well-documented complex going up the Ohio Valley that has produced definite and abundant evidence of longhouses.[48]

After years or decades in theoretical exile, migrations have been making a comeback in the archaeological literature. A recent study of prehistoric migrations in the Southwest, with a focus on eastern Arizona, reviewed the worldwide ethnohistoric and anthropological literature relating to migrations as reflected in material culture. Very interestingly, it was found that ceramic decorative styles, often emphasized in archaeological allegations of migrations, were actually relatively poor indicators. Instead, household-and community-related settlement pattern and architectural data were significantly more reliable. Independently a northern New Mexico study also suggested that information about structures was more reliable than ceramics.[49]

In trying to deal with the vexing Quapaw question, I also deemphasized ceramics.[50] Instead, I focused on the ethnohistoric accounts of Arkansas Quapaw longhouses and searched for longhouses in the archaeological record going up the Ohio Valley. I had been strongly influenced by the story of the Erie-Westos winding up a long way from Lake Erie, in bark-covered longhouses in the present Augusta, Georgia vicinity.[51]

Attempting to explain why the Dhegihans left their homeland, I was once again influenced by discussions of the Erie-Westos. The Five Nations Iroquois started attacking their neighbors after getting improved flintlocks from the Dutch and others in the 1640s; the Eries left by the mid-1650s.[52] Could there have been a domino effect down the Ohio drainage? Around 1660 the next, or among the next, to go would have been the Dhegiha Siouans if they were eastern Fort Ancient or some other upper Ohio Valley people. Next may have been the Shawnees, who are reported to have been under attack by the Iroquois later in the 1660s.[53]

The shatter zone then moved south with the Erie-Westos and westward (including northwest and southwest) with the Iroquois, as noted in other chapters of this volume. When Marquette and Jolliet reached northeast Arkansas in 1673, they recognized that like all other Illinoian groups, "the Mitchigamea feared attack from the League of the Iroquois."[54] French explorers of the later 1600s in the LMV were "shadowed by Iroquois war-riors" who were feared by local Indians.[55]

Northerly sources report a similar process. The Hurons and the Pota-watomi were under Iroquois attack by the 1640s, forcing them to flee westward and creating another vacant quarter that extended into parts of Michigan until the French pacified the region in the 1680s and 1690s. The Iroquois eventually even made slave raids among the Chipewyans of west central Canada, over fifteen hundred miles northwest of Iroquoia.[56]

Fear of slaving significantly amplifies the "push" factors that I sug-gested earlier as driving the Dhegiha Siouans out of the Ohio Valley.[57] The complementary "pull" factors may have included the largely depopulated lands along the Mississippi River in northeastern Arkansas and down to the region around the mouth of the Arkansas. When the Quapaws arrived in the LMV, probably with a few European arms of their own, they made some waves themselves. Their oral tradition states that they defeated some Tunicans in the vicinity of the mouth of the St. Francis River, and in the early French documents they are described as being on generally bad terms with Tunicans and some other long-resident groups.[58]

At this point I should mention some arguments against the idea of a very late Dhegiha Siouan migration from well up the Ohio valley. With regard to the source region, some Midwestern archaeologists have argued, on the basis of ethnohistorically recorded legends and beliefs, that in late prehistoric times these Siouans were instead in the American Bottom region of the Mississippi Valley and indeed that they had been responsible for the great Mississippian political and ceremonial center of Cahokia.[59] One has even suggested that their legendary "Ohio" meant "Great River" and therefore really referred to the Mississippi.[60]

Yet was Cahokia really Siouan? Classic Mississippian Cahokia flourished from about 1050 to the 1200s CE but declined abruptly by 1300. It had interacted with and influenced non-Mississippian Oneota culture people to the north.[61] Later, relatively minor and sporadic Oneota occupations appeared in the American Bottom from the 1300s to the 1500s, possibly representing brief small-scale intrusions from the north.[62] Siouan legends about Cahokia, including claims of ancestral connections to the great mound center, may date to those times. Oneota is generally, or arguably, regarded as correlated with late prehistoric to protohistoric Chiwere Siouans, mainly in Minnesota, Iowa, Wisconsin, and the northern parts of Illinois and Missouri, who migrated westward toward the Plains in late protohistoric times — again, quite possibly under pressure from Iroquois or other slavers.[63]

Other data support my position. A linguistic study has suggested that Siouan lexicons did not correlate well with the vocabulary expected for Mississippian chiefdoms.[64] And, where are the Mississippi Valley long-houses? They are apparently known only from Oneota sites as far south as around the Iowa-Missouri state line latitude, well above the American Bottom.[65] Finally, what makes a river "great"? If it is length, then the Missouri-Mississippi drainage is indeed the greatest. But, the volume of water is even more immediately obvious and impressive, and the truly great Ohio contributes much more water than the Mississippi and all its tributaries above the Ohio juncture.[66] My ethnohistorian informants profess no knowledge of any early maps that label the relevant segment of the Mississippi as the Ohio.[67]

On the Arkansas end, some colleagues have suggested that differences in late prehistoric to protohistoric rock art motifs north and south of the Arkansas River in central Arkansas match ethnohistorically recorded Dhegiha Siouan ideas about the cosmos.[68] This match could imply significant time depth for a Quapaw presence in the Arkansas Valley as well as that these northern and southern motifs were created during the same period by different divisions of the Quapaws.

In addition to the difficulties of dating rock art, such ideas about Sky People versus Earth People are by no means unique to Siouans but characterize the general Southern Indian cosmos that contrasted an Upper World with This World.[69] Alternatively, whether or not these motifs were made during the same period, the northern ones might represent the art styles of one non-Siouan group (Tunicans?), whereas the southern ones might have been in the style of another non-Siouan group (Northern Natchezans?). There is simply no ethnohistoric evidence for Siouans occupying the central Arkansas territory in question during protohistoric or even early historic times, whereas some does exist for non-Siouans.[70]

Contemporary Contrasts: the Spanish and French

Before moving to the terminal Protohistoric and early Historic periods in the LMV and the South, brief looks at different kinds of seventeenth-century slaving of Indians may be of interest. The activities of the Spanish in the Southwest and the French in the North add some comparative, and especially contrasting, perspectives. The literature of Spanish conquest indicates that in Florida the Spaniards tended to obey royal edicts against enslaving the Indians, probably because representatives of the king could closely watch Florida colonists. In northern Mexico, New Mexico, and southwest Texas, on the distant frontiers of empire and far from royal supervision, it was a different story. There was no fur trade, but household and craft laborers were needed, and there were fortunes to be made in hacienda ranching and especially in mining. The histories of seventeenth-century Chihuahua and New Mexico are blighted by long chronicles of enslavement of Indians. There were incredible silver mines in Chihuahua and salt mines in dry lake beds in central New Mexico near the Salinas Pueblos such as Gran Quivira; salt was sent down the Rio Grande and used in refining silver. As Florence and Robert Lister put it in their history of Chihuahua, "the entire Spanish colonial system was founded upon Indian labor, sometimes free but more often forced."[71]

Unlike the Dutch and English in the East, the Spanish in the Southwest did much of the slaving with their own military forces relatively near their colonial centers or outposts. As in the South, the Spanish in the Southwest generally did not arm allied Indian groups and send them into the hinterlands. They did deal extensively, however, with groups of roving Apaches and slavers from other such groups as well as more settled Puebloan Indians and Quivirans (probably Wichitas) from the Plains. Slaves were often converted to Catholicism and sometimes treated as household or even family members.[72]

Although there were repeated Indian rebellions, climaxing in the great Pueblo Revolt of 1680 that was put down or revenged brutally by Spanish troops, Southwestern Puebloan Indians were less free to move. There was nothing on the scale of the Eastern shatter zones abandoned by far-fleeing victimized Indian groups, although shorter moves by individuals or small groups did occur and larger groups moved at least temporarily after revolts. As the seventeenth century wore on, more and more emphasis was placed on slaving raids against the hostile Apaches of the adjacent Plains.[73] But there were no discernible seventeenth-century effects of Spanish slaving farther east toward the LMV on groups such as the Caddoans of east Texas.[74]

The French from their established bases in Canada and New France outposts in the Great Lakes country had set up an incipient midcontinental shatter zone by the 1660s. This zone involved mainly the newly armed Illinois as slavers and the Ottawa as middlemen, with most of the raids impacting Plains Indians who lacked guns rather than other Mississippi Valley peoples who were potentially key allies.[75]

Intensifying Contacts in the LMV and the South

The first French LMV contact in 1673 was brief and only got as far south as the mouth of the Arkansas. The belated follow-up by La Salle was also fleeting, though continuing all the way to the mouth of the Mississippi. Both expeditions encountered evidence of continuing inter-Indian rivalries and violence. When the La Salle party made the first European contact with the Taensas in northeast Louisiana in 1682, they found palisades around buildings such as a temple and the houses of a chief and elders, "where on the tip of each there is a skull of one of their enemies whom they have killed." In such an environment enslavement is quite likely, and indeed during this encounter La Salle's assistant Tonti (or Tonty) bought two Koroa (probably Tunican) slaves who had been captured by the Taensas.[76]

It was not until the middle and later 1680s, the 1690s, and especially after 1700 that the French really started moving into the LMV. These French, who were in a precarious geopolitical situation with their own meager population spreading northward from new bases along the Gulf Coast, avoided deep involvement in the Indian slave trade, being more interested in trading directly with Native groups, arming them to some extent, and using them as allies and buffers against the English and Spanish.[77] In 1708 there were only one hundred and twenty-two French soldiers and sailors plus seventy-seven settlers and eighty Indian slaves in the whole Louisiana colony. Even as late as 1726 the census figures for the French enclaves of Louisiana showed only one Indian slave at the Arkansas (Quapaw) settlement, none along the Black and Yazoo rivers, nine at the Natchez, none at the Tunica, one at the Bayougoula, three at the Houma, four at nearby Cannes Bruslées, eleven at the [T]Chapitoulas, and forty-four at and near New Orleans. Most of the slaves were from groups that had warred against the French, but African slaves were already outnumbering Indian slaves by wide margins. With the African influx the French had added incentives to turn away from Native slaves, whose numbers declined after the 1720s. Although there were still over one hundred Indian slaves in the LMV in 1763, most of them were in the unique vicinity of New Orleans.[78]

With the founding of the Carolina colony and Charles Town in 1670, the British set about arming strategically placed Indian groups who roved southward and westward raiding and seeking Indian slaves and thereby at least indirectly disrupting Spanish and French colonial operations. Such English-sponsored slaving by Indians from the East and to a lesser extent Spanish-inspired slaving from Florida started to impact Indian groups allied with the French in Louisiana after about 1680.[79]

Meanwhile, by the late 1690s, if not earlier, British explorer-traders had made their way west to the LMV and failed to enlist the Quapaws as slavers of other trans-Mississippian Indians but succeeded in setting up the Chickasaws as slavers.[80] With this terminal seventeenth-century development, the shatter zone made a quantum leap westward, and the Quapaws once again found themselves, along with their new neighbors, under the guns of raiding and slaving Indians from the East.

Indian slaves eventually were replaced by imported African slaves, and Indian slavers were replaced by a massive American military buildup as the frontier moved farther west in the nineteenth century, resulting in the killing of Indians or the moving of them to make room for Euro-American exploitation of resources by farming, ranching, and mining.

A Concluding Analogy

Using terms borrowed from archaeological studies of lithic (stone tool) technology, the "shattering" first took place near the beachhead "striking platform" points of impact in the coastal and Eastern seaboard zones. The interior zones of the western South and the LMV, however, were affected only by radiating shock wave "ripples."[81] For the migrations of the Dhegiha Siouans down the Ohio and along the Mississippi and its western tributaries, perhaps a better lithic-tech analogy would be linear "radial fractures" away from the primary impact-shatter zone. In the later seventeenth century and especially in the eighteenth, shatter zones of various kinds moved west into the interior (compare the lithic "core reduction" process that involves new striking platforms) ahead of the frontiers of colonization, when peoples such as the Chickasaw became slavers and raiders.

As I concluded in the initial 2002 symposium-paper version of this chapter during the run-up to war in Iraq, "there is something depressingly familiar about all this. In the twentieth century exploitation of resources and Native peoples expanded on a massive worldwide scale, and some resultant 'shatter zone' processes are still very much in evidence here in the twenty-first."

Notes

1. Struever, "Hopewell Interaction Sphere," 92. The theme was revived by Koeppel, "Middle Woodland in a 'Shatter Zone.'"

2. For the history of the use of "shatter zone" and similar phrases in geopolitics and some theoretical considerations, see Hensel and Diehl, "Testing Empirical Propositions." They trace these ideas back to Mahan, *Problem of Asia*. Around World War II such terms were developed by the American geographer Richard Hartshorne and his associates; Hartshorne, "Politico-Geographic Pattern"; and Hartshorne, "United States and the 'Shatter Zone' of Europe." See also Whittlesey, Colby, and Hartshorne, *German Strategy*. Shortly after the war Russell and Kniffen brought the term "shatter belt" into cultural geography in their textbook *Culture Worlds*. Both Russell and Kniffen worked with and influenced Mississippi Valley archeologists and anthropologists. A cursory Internet search reveals that the "shatter zone" phrase is currently used in these and a wide variety of other fields, from geology to the physics of impacts. The latter has furnished concepts that archaeologists use in analyses of stone tool technology, a subject from which I draw an analogy at the end of this chapter.

3. See also Galloway, this volume, who places the Choctaws (just east of the LMV) essentially outside of the shatter zone until the late seventeenth century when the zone's western border reached them.

4. This Eastern seaboard shatter zone could also be regarded as a special case of the "periphery" as defined by Wallerstein, *Modern World System*, vol. 1. For much of the seventeenth century, however, the western South and LMV are more like his "external" zone, which is beyond the active periphery.

5. Kroeber, *Cultural and Natural Areas*, 148.

6. Morse and Morse, *Archaeology of the Central Mississippi Valley*, 181–99. For a discussion of the continuation of violence from the Mississippian period into the contact era, see Jennings, this volume.

7. Nassaney and Pyle, "Adoption of the Bow and Arrow." See also Nassaney, "Bow and Arrow"; and Jeter, Discussant Comments.

8. Brookes, Discussant Comments, 7; and Connaway, Discussant Comments, 25.

9. Schambach, "Mounds, Embankments, and Ceremonialism," 39–40, figures 5.5, 5.6, and 5.7.

10. Connaway, personal communication, 2002; see an account of the Soto *entrada* of 1541 in a nearby region, discussed in the section on protohistoric slavery in this chapter.

11. Milner, Anderson, and Smith, "Warfare," 593–95.

12. Anderson, "Examining Chiefdoms," 228. See also Milner, "Warfare in Prehistoric"; and Milner, *Moundbuilders*.

13. Brown, "Forty Years," 31.

14. Dye, "Art, Ritual, and Chiefly Warfare," figures 8 and 9.

15. Cobb and Butler, "Vacant Quarter Revisited." Lekson in "War in the Southwest" cited a number of comparative Mississippian examples.

16. Cobb and Butler, "Vacant Quarter Revisited," 625.

17. Morse and Morse, *Archaeology of the Central Mississippi Valley*, 201–303, figures 10.1, 11.1, and 12.1. See also Jeter, Rose, Williams, and Harmon, *Archeology and Bioarcheology*, figures 15–22.

18. Phillips, *Archaeological Survey in the Lower Yazoo Basin*, 840.

19. Jeter, Rose, Williams, and Harmon, *Archeology and Bioarcheology*, figures 16–22; Jeter, Discussant Comments, 183–84. Compare with Cavalli-Sforza, "Spread of Agriculture."

20. Jeter, "Outer Limits," 191–92. See also Jeter, Rose, Williams, and Harmon, *Archeology and Bioarcheology*, figures 18–22; and Brain, *Winterville*, 113–30, figures 80–84.

21. Cavalli-Sforza, "Spread of Agriculture"; Jeter, "Tunicans West of the Mississippi" 49; Jeter, "From Prehistory through Protohistory," 187; and Jeter, "Outer Limits," 191.

22. Anderson, "Examining Chiefdoms," 225–27, figure 15.5; this contour map shows chiefdoms originating from the American Bottom (around Cahokia) to northeast Arkansas in the 900s CE, spreading down the Mississippi Valley to the Natchez vicinity by 1000 CE, then eastward across much of the South, and westward into the Caddoan country.

23. Lopinot, "Lifeways"; Morse and Morse, *Archaeology of the Central Mississippi Valley*, 271–303, figure 12.2a-b; and Boszhardt, "Contracting Stemmed," 62.

24. Morse and Morse, *Archaeology of the Central Mississippi Valley*, 284–315.

25. Garcilaso, "La Florida," 312, 400. In a note to Garcilaso's account of the cut tendon (312n18), the editors point out that in 1690 another observer alleged the same practice in the Carolina vicinity. On the reliability of the Garcilaso account, see Dowling, "La Florida del Inca"; and Henige, "So Unbelievable It Has to Be True."

26. Jeter, "From Prehistory through Protohistory," 177–80.

27. See Jeter, "From Prehistory through Protohistory," 196–206, for a review of competing attempts to connect ethnohistorically attested groups with archaeological sites and phases.

28. Jeter, "From Prehistory through Protohistory," 206–9, figure 2.

29. Hudson, "De Soto in Arkansas; Hudson, "Reconstructing the De Soto Route"; and Swanton, *Final Report*, 53–54, 59–61. I am also making the assumption that these were the peoples' names for themselves and their settlements or territories rather than names supplied by guides speaking other languages.

30. Jeter, "From Prehistory through Protohistory," figure 2.

31. Jeter, "From Prehistory through Protohistory," 206–13, figure 2.

32. Mason, "Archaeology and Native North American Oral Traditions"; Schaafsma, *Apaches de Navajo*, 21–26; Echo-Hawk, "Ancient History"; and Warbuton and Begay, "Exploration."

33. Jeter, "From Prehistory through Protohistory," 207–9, 211. The mountainous homeland had been suggested as the Ouachita Mountains or even as a reference to mounds; Brain, *Tunica Archaeology*, 22, 288.

34. Swanton, *Indian Tribes*, 170–71. But, compare to another Natchezan oral tradition (summarized by Swanton, *Indian Tribes*, 182–84) that claimed a very unlikely migration from Mexico.

35. Schaafsma, *Apaches de Navajo*, 23.

36. Schaafsma, *Apaches de Navajo*, 306.

37. Morse, "Nodena Phase"; and Morse, "Parkin Site."

38. Hudson, *Knights of Spain*, 294. See also Morse and Morse, *Archaeology of the Central Mississippi Valley*, 309–11n108, but the source is once again Garcilaso.

39. Morse, *Parkin*, 67.

40. Brain in *Tunica Archaeology*, 293, notes that the Soto expedition lacked children, "those great incubators of pathogens." On the drought, see Burnett and Murray, "Death, Drought, and De Soto," and for technical details, see Stahle et al., "Epic 16th Century Drought." On pigs as vectors, see Ramenofsky and Galloway, "Disease and the Soto Entrada." There is, of course, no historical documentation for epidemics in the Eastern U.S. interior during the Dark Ages, and some have suggested that epidemics did not occur until the 1690s; see Kelton, "Great Southeastern Smallpox Epidemic," 2. However, there is indirect archaeological evidence suggesting that epidemics did occur during the early seventeenth century or even the sixteenth century; see Betts, "Pots and Pox."

41. Phillips, Ford, and Griffin, *Archaeological Survey*, figure 71.

42. DeVorsey, "Impact of the LaSalle Expedition," figure 2.

43. Jeter, "From Prehistory through Protohisory," 210-A11, notes that Phillips in *Archeological Survey in the Lower Yazoo Basin*, 954, 971, was surprised at the Mississippian character of artifacts found at probable Taensa sites in northeastern Louisiana since he had expected artifacts in the southerly Plaquemine-Natchezan tradition.

44. Jeter, "Outer Limits," 191–94.

45. Hoffman, "Kinkead-Mainard Site"; Hoffman, "Protohistoric Period," 27–30; and Jeter, "From Prehistory through Protohistory," 210–11.

46. Jeter, Cande, and Mintz, "Goldsmith Oliver 2"; and Jeter, "Tunicans West."

47. Jeter, "From Prehistory through Protohistory," 213–19.

48. Holmes, "Hardin Village," 96. See also Hanson, *Hardin Village Site*; and Hanson, Buffalo Site.

49. Clark, "Tracking Prehistoric Migrations"; and Schaafsma, *Apaches de Navajo*, 306.

50. Jeter, "From Prehistory through Protohistory," 213–21. Indeed, I deemphasized Arkansas archaeology in general because I did not believe anyone had yet definitively identified the Arkansas Quapaw archaeological record. Since then, a site has been found which appears to represent the Quapaw village of Osotouy

during the early to middle 1700s, if not earlier, and its ceramics so far differ significantly from those of the former Quapaw phase; House, "Wallace Bottom."

51. Smith, *Archaeology of Aboriginal Culture Change*, 22, 41, 132–34.

52. Bowne, *Westo Indians*, 37–44. See also Fox, this volume; Meyers, this volume; and Bowne, this volume.

53. Griffin, *Fort Ancient Aspect*, 28–30. The Shawnees may themselves have been the Fort Ancient people as Griffin thought, or at least the western Fort Ancient people if that archaeological complex was multicultural as suggested by Essenpreis in "Fort Ancient Settlement."

54. Hall, *Archaeology of the Soul*, 7.

55. Ethridge, "Creating the Shatter Zone," 214.

56. Branstner, "Tionontate Huron Occupation," 179; and Ethridge, "Creating the Shatter Zone," 210.

57. Jeter, "From Prehistory through Protohistory," 217. Being ignorant of the literature of Iroquoian slaving at the time of writing, I merely mentioned Five Nations Iroquois warfare and raiding and the threats of same. For the importance of the additional fear factor of slaving, see Galloway, *Choctaw Genesis*, 256; compare with Smith, "Aboriginal Population Movements in the Postcontact Southeast," 3–9.

58. Jeter, "Tunicans West," 65.

59. Hall, "Cahokia Site." See also Kehoe, *Land of Prehistory*. Such attempts to connect Cahokia with historic Siouans leap over a time span of more than five hundred years, a number of cultural discontinuities, and a great deal of space (to the Osage in southwest Missouri and the Plains or in another direction to the Winnebago in the upper Midwest). Also such attempts may be biased toward well-documented Siouan oral traditions, whereas several other Mississippi Valley or eastern U.S. linguistic groups may well have had similar myths; Muller, "Prolegomena," 15, 23–24, 37.

60. Alice Kehoe, personal communication, 2005, and discussion comments at the annual meeting of the American Society for Ethnohistory, Mapping the Shatter Zone symposium, Santa Fe, 2005.

61. Emerson, "Introduction to Cahokia 2002"; Pauketat, "Fourth-Generation Synthesis"; and Hall, "Cahokia Identity."

62. Fortier, Emerson, and McElrath, "Calibrating," 197. According to these authors, the evidence for Oneota occupations in the American Bottom is "ephemeral at best" and probably represents only "temporary intruders" based well to the north or "isolated Oneota homesteads" in a region that was "generally depopulated" by Mississippians after the collapse of Cahokia around 1300 CE. No prehistoric

or protohistoric longhouse remains have been found in the American Bottom; Thomas E. Emerson, personal communication, 2007.

63. Attempts to connect Oneota archaeology with Chiwere-speaking groups go back at least to Griffin, "Archaeological Remains," but as in the case of Fort Ancient culture (see note 53 above), more recent scholarship has tended to suggest multiethnic connections for Oneota culture in general, although some regional variants of Oneota are more or less securely correlated with individual Chiwere groups such as Oto, Ioway, or Missouria. Some scholars also believe that at least some of the Dhegiha Siouan groups were derived from Oneota culture, but I suggest that any Dhegiha-Oneota connections may have been very late additions after the Dhegihas moved from the Ohio Valley, especially among groups such as the Omaha-Ponca who moved near to Chiwere Siouans with an Oneota material culture tradition; see the various chapters in Green, *Oneota Archaeology*. Hollinger in "Residence Patterns" states that "with increasing pressure from the Eastern tribes the Oneota began moving west" (165) and cites probable early spreads of European-derived disease epidemics, followed by increasing changes due to the fur trade as having "shattered" traditional Oneota subsistence-settlement systems (compare with Ethridge's shatter zone model). But as with my earlier discussion of the demise of Fort Ancient culture (see note 57 above), he did not mention slaving as a factor. I now strongly suspect that it was. See also Esarey, "17th Century Midwestern Slave Trade."

64. Mochon, "Language History."

65. Dale Henning, personal communication, 2007. See also Hollinger, "Residence Patterns," 144–50, for a summary of data on Oneota longhouses, with emphasis on finds in Wisconsin.

66. Jeter, Rose, Williams, and Harmon, *Archeology and Bioarcheology*, 4. See also Hayes, "Natural and Unnatural Disasters," especially his schematic diagram of flood potentials of the Mississippi and its major tributaries (498).

67. Helen Tanner and George Sabo III, personal communications, 2006.

68. Sabo and Walker, "Mississippian Developments." These authors concede as conceivable a hypothesis "that a proto-Siouan iconography emanating from the Cahokia area came to be adopted in other areas" so that their Arkansas Valley "Dhegihan cosmogram" might have been produced by Tunicans or Natchezans or some other group or groups. But, as noted above, I strongly doubt that Dhegiha or other Siouans were the originators of Cahokian iconography; instead, I suggest that they may have been the non-Mississippian, Fort Ancient receivers of such influences from Mississippian Cahokia; the Arkansas Tunicans and Northern

Natchezans probably were receiving such influences directly from classic Cahokia without an assist from Siouan middlemen. For a general summary of rock art in Arkansas, see Sabo and Sabo, *Rock Art in Arkansas.*

69. Hudson, *Southeastern Indians*, 122–83. As Hudson notes, there was also a dangerous Lower World, but perhaps its monsters were not regarded as fit subjects for rock art in Arkansas, although there are some likely examples elsewhere such as the Piasa monster seen in the 1670s by Marquette and Jolliet on cliffs north of present Alton, Illinois.

70. The idea of a late prehistoric to protohistoric Quapaw presence in central Arkansas is merely a survival from the defunct archaeological notion of a widespread Quapaw phase. There is no evidence for Siouans anywhere in Arkansas in the narratives of the Soto *entrada* of the 1540s, even though the Spaniards traversed northeast Arkansas and virtually the entire Arkansas Valley within present Arkansas. The French in the 1670s and following decades reported the Quapaw only near the Arkansas-Mississippi juncture; Jeter, "Tunicans"; and Jeter, "From Prehistory through Protohistory," 206–9, figure 2. Even as late as 1722 the Quapaw on the lower Arkansas did not want La Harpe to go up the valley and deal with Indians they did not trust, as noted in Wedel, "Bénard, Sieur de La Harpe."

71. Lister and Lister, *Chihuahua*, 28–33, 34 (quote). See also Bushnell, *Situado and Sabana*, 33–66; Vivian, *Gran Quivira*, 13–30; Bailey, *Indian Slave Trade in the Southwest*; and Brooks, *Captives and Cousins.*

72. Brooks, *Captives and Cousins*, 30–33, 39, 49–50, 123–25.

73. Lister and Lister, *Chihuahua*, 28–34; Vivian, *Gran Quivira*, 25–26. For examples of short moves after revolts, see Schaafsma, *Apaches de Navajo.*

74. Timothy Perttula, personal communication, 2002.

75. Esarey, "17th Century Midwestern Slave Trade."

76. Minet, "Voyage Made from Canada," 61 (quote); La Salle, "Nicolas de La Salle Journal," 107.

77. For a discussion of the French and Choctaw relationship on the edge of the shatter zone, see Galloway, this volume. For the negotiations involving the French (and other Europeans) and the Quapaws, the Osages, and other Arkansas Valley peoples, see DuVal, *Native Ground.*

78. Usner, *Indians, Settlers, and Slaves*, 25, 56–59, 132, table 2. However, by the mid-eighteenth century Frenchmen living on the western frontier of their LMV domain among Caddoans in the Red River Valley around Natchitoches had apparently set up a short-lived small-scale "shatter zone" of their own by trading guns to Indians who brought them Plains Indian women (and children) as slaves — "an

infamous traffic of the flesh" according to a Spanish friar's 1774 report; quoted in Barr, "From Captives to Slaves," 19.

79. Bense, *Archaeology of the Southeastern United States*, 288–312; Kniffen, Gregory, and Stokes, *Historic Indian Tribes*, 51–57, 62–66, 222, 232–33. See also Meyers, this volume; Bowne, this volume; Worth, this volume; and Shuck-Hall, this volume

80. Although the University of Mississippi Department of Anthropology's "Chickasaw Project" is not represented by a chapter in the present volume, relevant publications are beginning to come from it; see Ethridge, "Making of a Militaristic Slaving Society," and Johnson et al., "Measuring Chickasaw Adaptation." See also Galloway, *Choctaw Genesis*, 181–82.

81. Another term borrowed from lithic technological description. Coincidentally and from another perspective, a "ripple effect" on the LMV was described by Gallay, *Indian Slave Trade*, 7.

15 | *Picking Up the Pieces*

NATCHEZ COALESCENCE IN
THE SHATTER ZONE

GEORGE EDWARD MILNE

The South at the dawn of the eighteenth century was a dangerous and complex place for both Natives and newcomers. Slave raids emanating from Carolina and conducted by British merchants and their Indian proxies as well as the lingering effects of epidemics destabilized the region, turning it into a shattered zone. Not all the indigenous peoples who lived there fell into a pattern of contact, disease, war, decline, or dispersal. Some Native communities adapted to and even found ways to benefit from the chaos. The early eighteenth-century Natchez drew upon an established repertoire of diplomatic and social practices in which their women acted as envoys, advocates, and mates for outside groups who came seeking trade or protection. Under this rubric negotiation and compromise were vital for successful relations between cultural groups as well as among individuals.

Compromise and accommodation, evident in every successful marriage, are evident in the pairings that took place in the South among French-speaking newcomers and Native residents. The first recorded Euro-Natchez couple exemplified this trend as they challenged one another's religious beliefs several times throughout their relationship. Jean-François Buisson de St. Cosme, a Québécois in his early thirties, asked his mate the Tattooed Arm if she really believed that she and her kin had descended from the Sun. She admitted to the Canadian that her ancestors had invented the story so that the Great Sun, her people's leader, could exert total authority over the Natchez Nation. Their own name for themselves was the Théoloëls, which translates to the People of the Sun.[1] Nonetheless, the Tattooed Arm had an interest in promulgating the myth; she was the sister of the headman and shared in her brother's prestige. More importantly, according to tradition her male child would rule over the Natchez after her sibling died. Sometime between 1700 and 1706, she gave birth to St. Cosme's son. The boy grew up to become the last Great Sun.[2]

The Tattooed Arm's choice for the father of her child was rooted in her people's long-standing social and political practices. These practices made it only natural that the sister of the Great Sun sought out St. Cosme as a mate because in the past such unions had been the first step in absorbing newcomers into the Natchez world. To these Natives the small bands of French officers, Canadian traders, missionaries, and the Native Americans who traveled with them probably looked and often acted like the indigenous refugees who had come in the recent past seeking the protection of the Great Sun. Perhaps St. Cosme shared some resemblance to these wayfarers after he relocated from the post of Henri de Tonti (or Tonty) on the Arkansas River to the Grand Village of the Natchez.[3] As part of her mission of inculcating such newcomers with a knowledge of the Théoloël order of things, the Tattooed Arm sought to convert St. Cosme to her belief system. Her task was not without setbacks. Their relationship had begun slowly; the Tattooed Arm had pursued the Québécois for some time before St. Cosme responded.[4]

Even after he warmed to her, the Tattooed Arm found St. Cosme a difficult student. She finally managed to extract a grudging compliance from the Canadian to accept her faith. Nonetheless, he needed frequent promptings to keep his promise. Eventually she desisted when she realized that his allegiance to Catholicism was too great for her to overcome. His commitment was indeed powerful; St. Cosme had taken the vows of a Catholic priest a decade earlier at the Seminary of the Fathers of the Foreign Missions in Québec. In 1706 a band of Chitimacha warriors murdered him and several of his French companions as they camped along the Mississippi River. St. Cosme died before he could respond to the reports of his conversion to faith in Thé or of his paternity of the Great Sun; hence, the cleric's side of this story will never be known.[5]

Enough evidence remains concerning the People of the Sun, however, to shed light on the Tattooed Arm's side of the story. Her conversations with the priest and her subsequent union with him exemplified the roles played by high status Natchez women. One of their foremost responsibilities involved incorporating outsiders into their polity through marital unions. Natchez women also participated in the formulation of policy toward outsiders who were in the process of amalgamating with the People of the Sun. This task informed another: that of representing their chiefdom as diplomats to other groups living in the Lower Mississippi Valley. While disruptive forces were tearing at the South during the late seventeenth and early eighteenth centuries, several of these Natchez women were hard at work picking up pieces in the shatter zone.

The Tattooed Arm's career exemplified this work. Her involvement with St. Cosme conformed to a tradition of intermarriage with those who settled among the Théoloëls. Her efforts to convert the priest conformed to her vocation of acculturating newcomers. The Tattooed Arm's ministrations and those of her colleagues took on increasing urgency during the 1720s. Strained relations between the Europeans and Natchez replaced the relative harmony that existed during the early years of contact. She and other elite Natchez women frequently helped to resolve the conflicts that arose between Louisianan and Théoloël villagers.

In the decades following the death of St. Cosme, the Tattooed Arm continued to fulfill her responsibilities as an educator, advocate, and diplomat. The structure of the Natchez's paramount chiefdom informed these offices and lent power and purpose to her work. The Natchez were one of the last functioning chiefdoms in the South at this time. As Ethridge discusses in the introduction to this volume, the inherent structural instability of the Mississippian chiefdoms meant that chiefly institutions must have been in place for absorbing people from fallen chiefdoms and for the dismantling of sociopolitical relations of those chiefdoms that were falling.[6] The Tattooed Arm and women like her were crucial operators within those institutions.

The flexibility of their political and social systems permitted the Natchez to capitalize on the disorder that wracked the South. During the late protohistoric era the Natchez put their old ways to new uses and adapted them to the shifting conditions of the shatter zone. The refugees that the slaving and warfare produced sought shelter among the People of the

Sun, and were admitted into the chiefdom through various processes, one of which was marriage.

Other Native peoples in the South employed similar strategies of banding together in confederations. The Natchez, however, did so during a time when numerous European observers were beginning to travel through Théoloël country. These observers noted the efforts of the Grand Village's chiefs to exert authority over the polity's outlying towns. At least some of these Natchez attempted to maintain political hegemony in a manner unlike the looser and more consensual relationships other Native groups were forging during the same period. These elites employed several long-established means of upholding their leadership position over their compatriots.

One the most impressive of these means was the Théoloëls' religious pageantry, which quickly attracted the attention of European visitors. These rites offered solace to those fleeing the smoldering warfare and Indian slave raids sponsored by the colonial powers along the coasts. European observers were quick to note the similarity between the Théoloëls' theology and their own. Antoine Le Page du Pratz, who penned a three-volume memoir on Louisiana, wrote that they believed in an omnipotent creator.[7] In the afterlife the good were rewarded and the evil punished in places that resembled the Catholics' heaven and hell.[8] French colonizers also pointed out that the Natchez followed a moral code of divine origin that was not unlike those found in the Old Testament. It prohibited theft, murder, and adultery, and it encouraged the Natchez to share their possessions freely among themselves. To plantation manager Le Page du Pratz, these Native beliefs resembled those of Christianity. Other newcomers from the Old World likened the Natchez's religion to the European and western Asian faiths with which the early Church Fathers had successfully competed during the last days of the Roman Empire.

The extent to which Europeans imposed their own preconceptions upon these Native beliefs as they wrote about them will probably never be known; the Natchez left no records of their own. Undoubtedly some of the outsiders saw and heard what they had hoped to see and hear, particularly when it came to stories that served to reinforce their own origin myths. It is safe to say, however, that such perceived similarities encouraged Catholic missionaries. French priests therefore hoped that that they might make easy converts among the Théoloëls.[9]

As the Tattooed Arm admitted to St. Cosme, the claim of direct descent from the solar deity formed the basis of the Great Sun's religious and political status.[10] The legend arose when sometime in the distant past a being named Thé and his wife the White Woman appeared among the Natchez. They shone so brightly that the Natchez thought the two could have come only from the Sun itself. Impressed with the authoritative manner that the shining man spoke, the elders of the Natchez asked him to become their sovereign. At first Thé refused, but he relented on the condition that they follow him to a better land. He then gave them instructions on forming a government. Thé told them not to kill except in self-defense, to avoid drunkenness, lies, and adultery and to respect the property of others. He ordered them to share their food and goods with one another without envy. The Natchez had to promise to build a temple and maintain a sacred fire within it. Thé ignited the first sacred flame by means of his supernatural powers.[11]

Finally, the Théoloëls also had to agree to marry outside their status groups and not allow the sons of the leader to become "princes." Rather, these boys would lose a rank to become mere nobles, but the girls would remain in the royal family. From that time until 1731, the first son born to the Great Sun's sister became the leader of the nation.

Thus the influence of the subsequent White Women proceeded from the injunction of the first Great Sun. The latter's command that the Natchez leaders marry those born into lower ranks prevented the formation of a permanent, hereditary, and exclusive elite lineage. The decree instituted the blending of various social groups that made up the Théoloël polity. To the Europeans the Natchez chiefdom appeared to have an hereditary elite. The Natchez system, however, was matrilineal and exogamous, which defies a like analysis with the European model. In fact, scholars are still not in accord as to how the system worked.

One of the first twentieth-century researchers who documented the system was anthropologist John R. Swanton. Swanton described it as a four-tiered structure that began with commoners (the elites referred to them as *puants*, or "stinkards"), honored men, nobles, and Suns. Although the perspectives of contemporary Europeans, particularly with regard to their observations of Natchez marriage and descent, clouded parts of the picture; most eighteenth-century sources agree that commoners could marry any member of the chiefdom.[12] In contrast, the elites had to choose a mate from the commoner ranks.[13] Consequently, the Great Sun was always the offspring of a stinkard father and a Sun mother.

Complicating the matter further, the Natchez social hierarchy possessed a regressive element; half of the children from these marriages lost status according to a pattern. The male child of a male Sun lost one rank and became a noble, although his daughter remained a Sun. Thus a noble could have been the child either of a Sun father and a stinkard mother or of a stinkard father and a noble mother. Honored people could come from an honored father and a stinkard mother or from a noble mother and a stinkard father.

Swanton's interpretation of Théoloël descent sparked the so-called Natchez Paradox, which spawned a series of anthropological debates that continued for sixty years. Some scholars reasoned that if Swanton's explanation was correct, the Théoloëls would have run out of commoner mates in a few generations.[14]

A number of solutions to the paradox have been put forth over the years. Among these is George I. Quimby's suggestion that the Natchez system perpetuated itself through a long-standing tradition of absorbing foreign elements through intermarriage.[15] This practice would have increased the number of potential wives and husbands for the elite lineage. Derogation of the offspring would also help return some people to the lower marriageable ranks. Vernon Knight argues that the People of the Sun adapted an exogamous clan system in use throughout the region in order to suit their needs. The reduction in male rank over the course of several generations acted as a corrective, guaranteeing that the nobility would remain small in numbers.[16]

Nonetheless, intermarriage spread members of recently adopted groups throughout the entire polity. Thus the Tattooed Arm's selection of Father St. Cosme conforms to Quimby's interpretation. As an outsider with status among his own people, St. Cosme was well situated (at least from a Natchez perspective) to aid in the process of amalgamating the newest set of Lower Mississippi Valley immigrants, the French, into Natchez society.

The Natchez may have been in the process of consolidating their chiefdom when d'Iberville, Penicault, and other European observers encountered them during the first decades of the eighteenth century. The disruptions that plagued the South during the late protohistoric era would have provided a steady stream of refugees to swell the polity's numbers. Such recent recruits may not have had time to sufficiently blend into the general population or to absorb the Natchez political and social ideologies. The reaction of the marginalized leaders from the outer settlements to the policies of the Grand Village demonstrates that respect for the Great Sun was by no means universal. Furthermore, archaeological evidence suggests that several of the towns were new additions to the Natchez polity.[17]

Europeans wrote about the Grand Village as if it were a kind of Théoloël capital city, unaware that it had acquired that role only a few decades before the founding of Louisiana. A much larger settlement to the north that archaeologists call the Emerald site previously held a more important position in the region's paramount chiefdom. During the Emerald site's predominance the Grand Village operated as a tributary of the larger town. In turn it administered its own satellite communities scattered across the lands near St. Catherine's Creek. Excavations undertaken during the 1940s revealed that the Natchez abandoned the Emerald site by the turn of the eighteenth century. The reason for this desertion remains unclear. Perhaps, like their Tunican neighbors to the north, the People of the Sun were escaping from Chickasaw raiders. Some written sources corroborate the anthropological data regarding the previous center of the Théoloël polity; several European authors related Natchez stories about a great temple that once stood at the northern edge of the Natives' homeland.[18]

These movements took place for the most part beyond the gaze of men from the Old World. Up until the late 1600s the Natchez had weathered the protohistoric era relatively removed from the damaging effects of the Indian slave trade. This changed when English-sponsored slave raiders appeared in the Lower Mississippi Valley at the end of the seventeenth century.[19] The Théoloëls' social and political structures not only survived these incursions, but they also profited from the disruption left in the raids' wake as vulnerable Native clans weakened by pandemics and incessant warfare and slaving sought asylum among the People of the Sun.[20] Refugees from fallen chiefdoms like the Koroas, the Tunican-speaking Grigras, and Tioux moved into the Natchez's domain and took up subordinate roles, augmenting that polity's numbers. Consequently, the Théoloëls were well prepared to receive further infusions of immigrants when a new group of wayfarers paddled upriver from the Gulf of Mexico.

In late March 1682 several canoes hove onto the shore of the Mississippi River. They carried an eclectic mix of twenty-three Europeans and over three dozen Natives. The Native contingent included ten women and three children.[21] The Europeans hailed from France, Sicily, and Flanders. Except for two Chickasaw interpreters, most of the Natives came from the Great Lakes and the St. Lawrence River Valley. Among this group were the first people from the Old World to record their visits to the Théoloëls since Hernando de Soto's conquistadors sailed by on their retreat to the Gulf of Mexico.

La Salle's sojourn at a village that he recorded as Natché marked the beginning of a dialogue between people from the Old World and the People of the Sun. Although the meeting was brief and the Franco-Native expedition was small, certain aspects of the dialogue's syntax were already evident. The first was the fact that most of the visitors were Indians but even the Canadians spoke Native languages, dressed in a mixture of buckskins and trade cloth, and held Indian slaves taken from among the Natchez's neighbors. Most importantly, these newcomers entered Natchez country on Natchez terms. They paid their respects to the Great Sun and negotiated with one of his brothers who acted as an intermediary with La Salle. The Great Sun summoned the headmen from other towns to attend a feast to welcome the newcomers. Thus La Salle's encounter with the People of the Sun gave rise to the illusion that the two shared parallel social and political practices, making it easier for the Indians to imagine the French as potential inductees to the Théoloël order.[22]

The first years of the eighteenth century brought a slow but steady trickle of Europeans and Canadians into Natchez country. The Natchez towns were natural waypoints on the Mississippi route from Canada to the French settlements on the Gulf Coast. Their location helped to integrate the Théoloëls into the Mississippi Valley's economy as producers of foodstuffs and peltries and as consumers of European goods. The requests and deportment of the newcomers demonstrated their need for assistance from this secure and prosperous Native group. This dependence conformed to the Théoloëls' practice of absorbing weaker peoples into their polity.

Later, Father St. Cosme's relationship with the Tattooed Arm would reinforce the illusion that his people had embraced the Natchez order of things and acknowledged the Suns' political and social superiority. According to Natchez marriage rules, the sister of the Great Sun could only marry a stinkard, and the priest's union with her implied that he had accepted a lower status for himself and all of the French. If St. Cosme knew about such derogation, he never mentioned it in the few letters he wrote to his superiors in Québec, but then again he failed to mention his relationship with a Théoloël headwoman. On the contrary, he complained that the Natchez "are polygamous, thievish, and very depraved — the girls and women being even more so than the men and boys, among whom a great reformation must be effected before anything can be expected from them."[23] Obviously St. Cosme's attempts to win over the People of the Sun to his faith had met with resistance from more than just the Tattooed Arm.

The female Sun, however, did not fail to attract the attention of other Europeans. Later, in November 1700, the Jesuit Father Gravier traveled to the Grand Village and met with the Tattooed Arm. In his words "this woman Chief is very intelligent, and enjoys greater influence than one thinks." In contrast, the priest showed little respect for the abilities of headmen of the Théoloëls when he wrote that "her brother is not a great genius."[24]

The sporadic visits of French traders during the early eighteenth century strengthened the emerging Théoloël notions about the French as stinkards. In 1714 the La Loire brothers opened a trading post that offered a steady source of prestige goods that came under the Suns' protection.[25] The ruling family's control of food surpluses gave them leverage with the

French during Louisiana's early years. The Suns exchanged corn and game for European goods that the Native leaders used in conspicuous displays or dispensed as gifts to loyal followers.

At the same time there were economic forces at work against both the Suns and the La Loires. Archaeological data suggests that some of the Natchez purchased European manufactures from English merchants residing among the Chickasaws. This alternate source of goods counteracted the centripetal influence of the French-Sun exchange system. A series of excavations undertaken during the 1920s and 1930s identified Fatherland site as the Grand Village of the 1700s. Robert Neitzel conducted further digs during the early 1960s and again in the early 1970s and cataloged the European trade goods found in the Fatherland mounds.

The graves at these sites contained items such as iron axe heads and calumet pipes that conferred political authority. They also held flintlock pistols, cooking utensils, clothing, clasp knives, iron ornaments, farming tools, and jewelry and other trinkets. Later digs uncovered significant caches of European glass beads in the Rice site, the "subordinate" Natchez village of the Jenzenaques.[26] The Rice site also yielded gunflints, musket parts, and silver and brass bells as well as iron axe heads and calumet pipes. More importantly, the quantity of European goods was significantly greater in the gravesites closer to the Chickasaws and therefore to British commerce. These goods also were more widely distributed among the population in the outer districts than in the Grand Village.

The fact that these villages acquired European manufactures in significant quantities suggests that the Grand Village was not their only distribution point. From this data anthropologist Karl Lorenz extrapolated that peripheral settlements enjoyed some degree of autonomy because they too possessed objects that symbolized power, particularly those associated with war and peace such as axe heads and calumets.[27]

The mutually beneficial relationship between the La Loires and the Natchez came to an end in the spring of 1716. Antoine La Mothe, sieur de Cadillac, the governor of Louisiana, upset the diplomatic equilibrium. During the autumn of the previous year he ascended the Mississippi River to investigate rumors of silver mines in Illinois country. In his haste Cadillac failed to come ashore and smoke the calumet with the Suns of the Great Village. On his return trip he repeated the snub by traveling past the Natchez lands without stopping. According to several French officials, this action was tantamount to a declaration of war against the People of the Sun.[28]

Taking advantage of the deterioration in relations with the French, leaders from outlying Natchez towns murdered five Canadian *coureurs de bois* (runners in the woods) who were visiting the trading post during their journey from Québec to Mobile. These marchland towns had received earlier envoys from the Chickasaws, one of which included an agent from Charles Town named Price Hughes. Hughes traveled in Théoloël country in 1714 and 1715. While among the Natchez he promised that if they ejected the French, merchants from Carolina would supply them with all of their wants.[29]

To avenge the murders, Cadillac ordered the King's Lieutenant, Jean-Baptiste le Moyne, sieur de Bienville, Louisiana's second-in-command, to lead an expedition against the Théoloëls. Relying on subterfuge, Bienville lured a group of important Natchez diplomats, including the Great Sun and his brother the Tattooed Serpent, into a trap. After holding the Suns in a makeshift stockade for a few weeks, the lieutenant released his hostages when other Natchez revealed the identity of four of the killers whom Bienville already had in custody. They also promised to bring the head of the leader of the anti-French faction who remained at large.

Despite the apparent break in harmony in this First Natchez War, the conflict did little to disrupt the relationship between the Théoloëls and Louisiana. Only a few Europeans or People of the Sun lost their lives in the war. Those who died came from the fringes of either society; they were either obscure *coureurs de bois* or members of the outlying towns not fully integrated into Natchez society or necessarily loyal to the Grand Village's elite. In some respects the First Natchez War actually strengthened diplomatic ties between the two groups. The Tattooed Serpent, the brother of the Great Sun, and Bienville became well acquainted during the former's imprisonment. The two even shared quarters during the negotiations that ended the hostilities.[30]

Their interactions bore some resemblance to La Salle's encounter three decades earlier when the Sun's brother hosted the French and brokered an agreement between the two peoples. To compensate for the killings, during the summer of 1716 the Natchez helped construct a fort for French troops on the bluffs above the Mississippi. This small outpost, named Fort Rosalie, was to protect communication between Illinois and Louisiana. It quickly became a magnet for hundreds of French colonists and their African slaves.

Between 1718 and 1721 the French government under the auspices of John Law's Company of the Indies transported thousands of Europeans to the Gulf Coast.[31] This influx of immigrants would set off a new round of instability, shattering the peace of the Lower Mississippi Valley. Poor planning and draconian recruitment schemes led to massive casualties among the newcomers as ships from Lorient and La Rochelle dumped their human cargo onto the sands of Dauphin Island, the colony's *entrepôt*. Nonetheless, several established colonists hoped to capitalize on the influx of labor. One of these, Marc-Antoine Hubert, Louisiana's comptroller, had acquired a tract northeast of Fort Rosalie about two miles from the Grand Village where he constructed a mill on the banks of the Petite Riviere du Natchez (nowadays known as Saint Catherine Creek). His enterprise soon employed nearly one hundred workers and slaves to tend his crops.[32]

Other entrepreneurs soon joined the quest for wealth by investing in Louisiana. A Parisian banker named Jean Deucher and his partner Swiss-born Jean-Daniel Kolly saw the fertile soil around Fort Rosalie as a potential source of riches. The two bankers sent Jean-Baptiste Fauçon, sieur Dumanoir, to oversee the development of the enterprise. Through the winter of 1719–20 Dumanoir scoured France's Atlantic ports for recruits. Upon reaching Natchez country a year later with his charges, Dumanoir purchased Hubert's farm as a site for the new concession to save workers the trouble of clearing land for crops.[33]

Within a few months of their appearance in Natchez territory, Dumanoir's colonists began to write about trouble with their neighbors. Another group of settlers had recently moved into the area. These latest arrivals, however, were from the Apple People, a contingent of Théoloëls who were part of the Natchez polity. After the decades of violence generated by the slave trade, the land east of the Grand Village must have looked like a safe haven to the Apple People who had previously dwelled astride the route from Chickasaw country to the great river. These eastern fields stood in the shadow of the Natchez's most powerful town, one that could act as glacis against danger. Sometime between 1716 and early 1723, the Apple Villagers built a new town a few miles west of St. Catherine's Creek, not far from the French post.[34] This district became the focal point of the colonists and of the Natives' first struggle for control over the region.

The first sign of trouble came during the night of February 9, 1722. According to one account a number of "savages of the environs of the concession gathered and came armed with the design to defeat the French of this concession."[35] Throughout the spring and summer the Apple People engaged in low-intensity hostilities marked by sniping incidents, petty thievery, and attacks on livestock.[36] These hostilities, however, affected only two villages: the Concession of St. Catherine and the Apple town. More important for the French settlers, the Suns of the Grand Village recognized that activities of the Apple leaders ran counter to Natchez interests. The narrow scope of the conflict allowed the Théoloël elites to employ long-standing diplomatic practices to rein in the anti-French factions on their marchlands, demonstrating the old systems' resilience in dealing with fractious outliers.

On October 29, 1722, a delegation from several Natchez towns brought word to the St. Catherine's Concession that the Sun of the Apple Village wished to make peace. The diplomats who carried the news included the Sun of the Flour Village, a "female chief," and the wife of the Tattooed Serpent. The Tattooed Serpent had just sung the calumet with Lieutenant Bernaval, the commander of Fort Rosalie. Within a few days the Tattooed Serpent and his entourage came to St. Catherine's to end the hostilities between the Apple Villagers and the plantation's inhabitants. The Sun of the Grigras also accompanied the group and offered his people's assurances to the officials at the concession. These talks and rituals concluded the so-called war on the evening of November 4, 1722.[37] Thus the Natchez elites took charge of the situation and reigned in the Apple Village, thereby restoring the political order.

A French observer, one of the managers of St. Catherine's Concession named Longrais, wrote that a number of women played a role in the autumn negotiations, but he failed to provide details about them and the services they rendered.[38] Were they active negotiators during these visits? Did they formulate policy, were they substitutes for their husbands, or were they more like couriers than diplomats? The author used the term *la femme chef* to describe one of the women. Again, his vagueness leaves unanswered questions: was she the wife of the Great Sun or was she the Tattooed Arm? Longrais, however, named at least one of the women as the wife of the Great Sun's brother the Tattooed Serpent.

The identity of the female chief notwithstanding, the presence of these women in formal delegations mirrored one of the roles played by the Tattooed Arm two decades earlier. The women worked to smooth relations with the newest immigrants to Natchez country, the "villagers" of Saint Catherine's Concession, according to established protocol and to keep the outlying Natchez towns in check. According to Father Charlevoix, a Jesuit who visited the region a year before the hostilities, "ordinarily, an embassy is composed of thirty men and six women."[39]

This latest conflict provided a venue for the traditional style of diplomacy. Unlike the First Natchez War of 1716, the second of 1722 took place in the environs of the Théoloël polity. The struggle was between two sets of villagers new to the scene of the fighting. Despite the fact that one of the villages — St. Catherine's Concession — was inhabited by French and African men and women, it may have been perceived as a candidate for absorption into the Natchez order of things. This intravillage struggle was the type of disturbance that flared up in polyglot societies like the Natchez before the arrival of the Europeans. The Natchez would soon discover that this new town would not play by the rules of the old order; St. Catherine's Concession would not become a Théoloël village.

A few years later, high-status Théoloël women once again played a role in Natchez-French affairs. This time they did so during the elaborate funeral of the Tattooed Serpent in June 1725.[40] The foremost of these actors, the favorite spouse of the Tattooed Serpent, took this opportunity to act once again as a peacemaker. In her first performance the Tattooed Serpent's mate spoke to several of the French elites during a memorial dance that took place a few days before the funeral. She told them not to regret her impending death because she would soon join her husband in the Land of the Spirits. She said to the "chefs et nobles François" that her husband's passing "is as very regrettable for the French as it is for our Nation because he carried both in his heart, his ears were always full of the words of the French chiefs. He walked the same road as the French; and he loved them more than himself."[41]

Two days later, the favorite wife of the Tattooed Serpent addressed the crowd attending the funeral. She exhorted the young people of her nation to "walk in peace with the French like their father and her" and to "never tell lies about them." She turned to the "French chiefs" and told them "be friends always with the Natchez." She reminded them of the affection that she and her husband had shown them, and admonished them to trade fairly with the Théoloëls. After her speech her relatives placed a deerskin over her head and strangled her.[42]

The elaborate rites that took her life required the sacrifices of other Théoloëls besides the spouses and servants of the Tattooed Serpent. Parents from the lower ranks suffocated their infants and tossed the bodies under the feet of the pallbearers as an offering to the departed. After the procession reached the top of the temple mound, the Natchez buried the Tattooed Serpent near one of the walls inside the shrine. The status of the members of his retinue determined the locations of their tombs in the area immediately outside the holy place.

Although the name of the Tattooed Serpent's wife is lost to us, her speeches to the French just before her own death provide some evidence of her career. From the evening of the Tattooed Serpent's death until the close of the ceremonies, this high-status woman was the only Théoloël who spoke directly to the French leaders in attendance at official functions. Although several private dialogues took place between the colonial elites and the Great Sun and other Théoloël notables, only the wife of the Tattooed Serpent aimed her words at the European listeners during the public events. Until her dying day she stayed true to the responsibilities of her office, advocating for peace between the People of the Sun and the French.

According to Le Page du Pratz, some of the Natchez hierarchs were tiring of the bloody nature of their funerals. They had worked out a plan that involved him and some of the highest-ranking Théoloëls. The envoy that the Natchez elite sent, however, was a woman. One morning, sometime after the interment of the Tattooed Serpent, the Grande Soliele, or Female Great Sun, came to call on Le Page du Pratz. The Dutchman had not yet risen from his bed, and although he was not in the habit of receiving visitors in this way, he told his slave to admit her. To his surprise she entered the room with her fifteen-year-old daughter. The two arranged themselves around Le Page du Pratz's bed; the mother sat in a chair and the girl sat on the floor.[43]

The Grande Soliele began by complimenting Le Page du Pratz on his command of the Natchez language and his understanding of their way of life. The Female Great Sun then said that she "was too old to bear children . . . There were no more than two young Suns left to speak (to succeed them) for her brothers because the third had only one leg . . . because of this, the warriors will not obey him nor will the entire Natchez nation."[44] After some further pleasantries she came to the point: she wanted Le Page du Pratz to marry her daughter. She and her brothers, the Suns, came to this decision after assessing the "Beautiful Head's" cultural acumen, intelligence, and leadership.[45] They reasoned that the Grande Soliele's daughter, once married to the Dutchman, would come under the protection of the French.

Upon hearing this proposal, Le Page du Pratz exclaimed, "Do you take me for a 'stinkard?' because the daughters of the female Suns marry only the men of the People, and I pretended not to have the sense of what she had said to me. She responded, no, to the contrary, it was because they wanted to extinguish this practice that I had been brought to their attention, that it was, in effect, to establish among them our [French] practice which was much better."[46]

The European had cause for concern because the spouse of any Sun, male or female, followed their mate to the Land of the Spirits. If he married the girl and she expired before him, Le Page du Pratz stood a very good chance of being strangled at her funeral. The Suns and the Grande Soliele were banking on the idea that the Europeans would not permit the other Natchez leaders to sacrifice the plantation manager as if he were a Théoloël commoner.

Despite her listener's reluctance to accept her offer, the Female Great Sun's discussion with Le Page du Pratz conformed to her role as a spokesperson for the chiefdom. While the proposal corresponded with the established pattern of marriage, it also revealed a significant departure from past practices. After a month of deliberation, in which at least one woman took part, the Suns had turned to a European to amend their custom of spousal sacrifice. The noble woman also divulged that the younger Suns "did not have enough sense to listen to reason on this important affair" and wanted the custom to continue. Nor could they count on "any of the other female Suns to stand against this [practice] to which they consent voluntarily."[47]

The exact part that Le Page du Pratz was to play within the Natchez polity if he married the girl is uncertain. The only clue to his prospective status comes from the Female Great Sun's response to Le Page du Pratz's question about being mistaken for a "stinkard." She stated clearly that she recognized him as a prestigious individual but gave no hint whether he would make policy. She quickly moved on to the motives of the Sun of the Grand Village who wanted to "extinguish" the nation's bloody funeral custom and desired French aid. The Grande Soleile's offer implied that the Suns recognized Louisiana's power, and were indeed willing to take advantage of the fact the Europeans could directly intervene in the Théoloël order of things. In this instance the Suns tried to maneuver an influential Louisianan into a position that would benefit the policies of the Grand Village's leadership.[48]

The Grande Soliele notwithstanding, the Natchez began to lose their veteran negotiators during the 1720s. The death of the Tattooed Serpent in 1725 and the passing of his brother the Great Sun in 1728 deprived them of two adept politicians. The Sun of the Flour Village was the only practiced male diplomat remaining. The Great Sun's nephew, the offspring of the Tattooed Arm and the missionary St. Cosme, became the paramount chief. The new leader, as the Tattooed Arm warned, was young and lacked experience.[49]

This lack of experienced leadership left the Théoloëls at a disadvantage when the next Frenchman who played a part in the Théoloël order of things did so with no intention of furthering the fortunes of anybody but himself. Captain De Chépart, the commandant of Fort Rosalie, sought to acquire real estate east of the post to build a plantation. By 1729 the best land already belonged to other Europeans who had influence at the capital. In the spring of that year the captain moved instead against the Apple Village. As a prelude to an even larger seizure De Chépart evicted an Apple villager from the latter's homestead and replaced him with several African slaves and a Frenchwoman to oversee them.[50]

Captain De Chépart then summoned the Sun of the Apple Village "without any of the compliments." During the meeting De Chépart made the outrageous demand that the Sun of the Apple Village move his entire town so that the captain could continue with his acquisitions.[51] The headman responded, "believing that he would be heard if he spoke reasonably . . . that his ancestors had lived there for as many years as there were hairs in his topknot, and that it was best that they remain there still."[52] When Papin, the French officer's interpreter, rendered the Sun's words into French, De Chépart exploded into a rage and told the headman "within a few days, he would regret not leaving his village." After witnessing the captain's final outburst, the Sun of the Apple Village returned home with his composure intact.[53]

Once back in his town the Indian leader called the elders of the nation and the Great Sun to a meeting to devise a response to De Chépart's demands. They discussed several options, all of which they rejected. Finally, one of the oldest members arose to give his views: "The merchandise of the French gives our youth pleasure, but in effect, it serves to debauch our young women and corrupt the blood of the Nation and make our women arrogant and idle. They do the same to the young men, and the married men work themselves to death to feed their family and satisfy their children."[54] He demanded that the Natchez eject the French from their homeland. The elder's plan met with unanimous approval from the other men in the council. It appears that the young Great Sun agreed with the plan.

From that time on, factionalism disappeared among the Théoloël men, and they conducted themselves with a singular purpose. The People of the Sun no longer acted like an aggregation of villages under the contested leadership of a ruling clan. The anti-French policy of the Apple Village, long at odds with that of the Grand Village's, now became the central guiding principle for the entire nation. Through their opposition to the

French, generated over years of declining expectations that the Europeans would act according to Théoloël standards of civilized behavior and crystallized by De Chépart's arrogant demands, the Natchez united. Although their polity still consisted of numerous towns of disparate groups who had taken refuge with the Théoloëls during the Indian slave-trade era, the Théoloël men determined that the newcomers from overseas would no longer be a part of the Natchez world.

Despite the accord reached by the men of the council, a small but significant sector of the Natchez elite refused to countenance the destruction of the Europeans among them. A handful of Théoloël women, including the mother of the Great Sun, the same Tattooed Arm who bore St. Cosme's child, attempted to thwart the council's plan. The nation's female leaders had been barred from the debates, perhaps because of their relationships with Frenchmen. The women's unions with Europeans rather than reinforcing the power of the Mississippian chiefdom ultimately disrupted it. The Tattooed Arm also may have acted as representative of the French, similar to the Chickasaw *fanimingos*, men who spoke on behalf of outside tribes at the Chickasaw council fires. These were chosen by outsiders in an elaborate ceremony, after which they sought to maintain peace between the Chickasaws and their adoptive nation. One eighteenth-century informant, Thomas Nairne, described their office. If these men failed to keep the peace, they were to "send the people private intelligence to provide for their safety."[55] The relationships of certain Natchez women with French men may have placed them, the Tattooed Arm foremost among these women, in an analogous role as *fanimingos* acting on behalf of the French.[56]

According to Le Page du Pratz, although the plan stayed secret for a while, the uneasiness that pervaded the Natchez villages gave the Great Sun's mother reason to suspect something was afoot. Sometime after the council meeting she asked her son to accompany her to the Flour Village to visit a sick relative.[57] When they reached a secluded spot along the path, the Tattooed Arm stopped and began to interrogate the Great Sun. She reminded him of her years of maternal care and that even though he was the son of a Frenchman, she held her own blood "more dear than that of foreigners."[58] Upon hearing her, the Great Sun revealed the details of the plan to destroy the French. Expressing a fear for his life, his mother tried to dissuade him from participating.

The Tattooed Arm tried several times to warn the colonists of the impending attack. She sent word of the elders' plans through the "young women who were in love with Frenchmen" but to no avail. In another instance the Tattooed Arm stopped a soldier and told him of the plot. He went to De Chépart with the story. The commandant clapped the man in irons for cowardice. She later informed Sub-Lieutenant Massé, who once again relayed the message to the commandant, only to have De Chépart dismiss it as fantasy.[59] In all, De Chépart imprisoned seven Frenchmen, the interpreter Papin among them, who had attempted to alert him to the conspiracy.[60]

In the early morning of November 28, 1729, several hundred Natchez warriors entered Fort Rosalie, ostensibly to pay off old debts and to borrow firearms for a great hunt. They positioned themselves throughout the post and among the surrounding homes. Upon a prearranged signal from the Great Sun, each warrior fell on the nearest Frenchman. In less than an hour all but a handful of the European males at the settlement were dead. The Natchez cornered Captain de Chépart in his vegetable garden. The high-status men thought it beneath them to soil their hands by killing such a lowly character. They called for a lesser individual to dispatch the officer, and a low caste "stinkard" headman soon arrived to club the Frenchman to death.[61]

During the fighting the Théoloëls also captured around one hundred and fifty European women and children.[62] They placed many of them under the supervision of the Great Sun and his wife, the White Woman.[63] Some of the Frenchwomen hauled water and prepared meals in Natchez homes. Others worked as seamstresses, repairing clothing stripped from the dead.[64] Although the Natchez expected labor from their captives, they also appreciated the efforts of those who cooperated with them. Le Page du Pratz's housekeeper was among these prisoners. The Natchez employed her in washing and mending shirts, a chore that she performed so well that they named her Mistress of the Laundry for the female Great Sun.[65]

The transfer of the French captives to the custody of the Great Sun and his wife demonstrated both continuity and change within Natchez political and social practices. On one hand, it was natural that "the White Woman . . . who was regarded as the Empress of the Nation" shared in the governance of her people's prisoners.[66] Her standing as a member of the leading family gave her enormous authority over the average Théoloël. It made sense that she also commanded the labor of French captives. This arrangement contrasted with the practices of warriors from other nations in the Lower Mississippi Valley who usually retained individual possession of the slaves they captured. Thus her control of the European detainees reaffirmed the rule of the Great Sun's entourage.

The fact that the People of the Sun chose to put captured European women and children into slavery also reveals a shift in their earlier practice of usually absorbing foreign elements into their polity. Because they intended to eject the French from the Lower Mississippi Valley, marriages with or adoptions of these women would have been out of the question. In fact, Charlevoix wrote that the Natchez "wanted to remove from the Women and other Slaves all hope of ever recovering their liberty."[67] It is doubtful that they meant to incorporate these women into their polity as full members. Regardless of their captors' motives, the enslavement of the French women and children marked the end of the old system of incorporating non-Natchez groups into the Théoloëls' ranks.

The People of the Sun's ascendancy was short-lived. By late January 1730 the tide had turned in favor of the colonists. First, the Choctaws, allies of Louisiana, launched a surprise attack on the Natchez, recapturing dozens of African slaves and rescuing nearly fifty French captives. Many of the Africans chose to cast their lot with the Natchez. At least two African men helped to defend the Théoloël forts against the Choctaw-French army. The Natchez retreated to their fortresses at the south of the Grand Village. A French army equipped with artillery arrived a few weeks later and settled in for a siege.[68]

Despite their rejection of the French as candidates for adoption and marriage, the Natchez acted in other ways suggesting that they still saw some social parallels between themselves and the Europeans. For instance, the People of the Sun recognized that some of the French women might be able to perform in roles similar to their own female leaders. Madame Desnoyers, the widow of the director of the White Earth Concession, held a position similar to the Tattooed Arm; she had been married to the "Sun" of a French village. In fact, her rank may have saved her when she conspired with her African slaves to avenge the death of her husband. The Natchez did not execute her when one of her accomplices revealed the plot.[69]

During a lull in the fighting the Great Sun ordered Madame Desnoyers to draft a letter containing the conditions by which the Europeans could obtain the release of the French women and children. In exchange for the prisoners he demanded "two hundred muskets, two hundred barrels of powder, two thousand gun flints, two hundred knives, two hundred hatchets, two hundred pickaxes, twenty quarts of brandy, twenty casks of wine, twenty barrels of vermillion, two hundred shirts, twenty pieces of limbourg [trade cloth], twenty pieces of coats with lace on the seams, twenty hats bordered with plumes, and a hundred coats of a plainer kind."[70] The Sun also insisted that the French turn over the chief of the Tunicans and Sieur de Broutin, the previous commandant of Fort Rosalie. He sent a captured soldier to carry the letter to the French commander who refused to treat with the Natives.[71]

European women's forced assistance to the Natchez did not end when Madame Desnoyers finished writing her note. According to Lieutenant Dumont de Montigny, a group of Théoloël headmen held a meeting during which they asked a Natchez-speaking Frenchwoman her opinion concerning the war. They told her that the Théoloëls would make peace if the French recognized the death of De Chépart as revenge for the execution of Old Hair of the Apple Village — the headman of one French settlement for the headman of a Natchez settlement. The unnamed Frenchwoman thought the idea might work, but the records make no further mention of the plan.[72]

The Great Sun's use of Madame Desnoyers as a scribe and his council's consultation with her anonymous countrywoman reveal the Théoloëls' conception of roles of women in war and peace. When the Great Sun employed Madame Desnoyers to write to Louboëy, he employed her in a diplomatic capacity similar to that of his mother. The Great Sun's conference with the anonymous Frenchwoman also mirrored roles taken by Natchez women who had been born into lesser castes or into foreign nations: she became a temporary advisor who shared the perspectives of the outsiders with whom the Natchez would have to negotiate.[73]

As the French siege works crept closer, the Natchez leaders needed to find a way to open negotiations with the French without exposing themselves to enemy fire. The Suns called upon Madame Desnoyers once again.[74] They wanted her to act as their *fanimingo*, representing the Natchez's interests to the decision makers among the French. Madame Desnoyers crossed the battlefield with an offer: the Natchez would release all of the French captives and remove their villages to any place the commandant would designate. Louboëy countered that the Théoloëls must release all of the African slaves and their children as well as all of the European captives. The Great Sun agreed to free his prisoners if the commandant withdrew his artillery to the riverbank and promised that neither the French nor the Choctaws would enter the forts until the next day.[75] The besiegers complied and pulled back their guns to the bluffs along the Mississippi.

The Théoloëls released their French captives. During the night of February 27, 1730, all of the Natchez and at least two dozen Africans slipped out of their forts, crossed the Mississippi, and disappeared into the swamps. At sunrise the French discovered that their enemy had absconded. The colonists decamped and gathered around the ruins of Fort Rosalie to organize a pursuit but the speed with which the Théoloëls traveled foiled their plans.[76]

A year later, an even larger French force finally tracked down the Natchez in another fort that the latter had built on the banks of the Black River. This time, Governor Périer agreed only to spare the lives of those who surrendered. The French began a bombardment of the Indians' stronghold. After several days the Great Sun and other important leaders emerged and turned themselves over to Périer. The Natchez attempted to buy time by turning over twenty Africans. The colonial governor told them that if they refused to capitulate, he would "pound their fort to ashes."[77]

Périer's threat to destroy the fort prompted the Great Sun to order his people's surrender. The French commander agreed not to enter the fort until all of the Natchez had evacuated it. On the morning of January 25 the White Woman in her last authoritative act led the Théoloël women and children into captivity. Some of the warriors surrendered later that day to the Europeans. As many as four hundred and fifty women and children became prisoners; forty-six warriors surrendered.[78]

The French soldiers loaded most of the prisoners onto the demi-galley and the frigate that had accompanied the expedition up the Black River. Périer divided the rest between smaller *bateaux* for the trip to New Orleans. The next day the French set about demolishing the fort. On January 28 Périer and his convoy of prison vessels set sail and arrived at the capital on February 5. Because the ships in the port were too few to hold all of the prisoners, some of the Natchez women and children were locked in the main government building. It was at this time that Le Page du Pratz recognized the Tattooed Arm among those in the improvised jail, imprisoned "despite all she had done to warn the French."[79] It was during her captivity in New Orleans that she told her story to the Dutchman, who included her words in his three-volume history of the colony.

After securing his Théoloël captives, Périer kept his promise; none of the prisoners were executed. He had nearly all of them loaded onto a *Compagnie* ship bound for Saint Domingue. A few stayed behind, enslaved on European plantations along the lower reaches of the Mississippi. The bulk of the Natchez people, the Great Sun and the White Woman included, spent the rest of their days as slaves in the sugar fields near Cap Francis.[80]

Those Théoloëls who escaped captivity sought refuge among the other coalescent societies of the South such as the Cherokees, Creeks, and Chickasaws. The Natchez, the last paramount chiefdom in the South, had once offered hope and protection to those in the shatter zone and allowed them to settle into small client villages as the diplomatic landscape around changed into one that favored nonhierarchical political and social organizations such as those that came to characterize the Creeks and Choctaws.

The position of the Natchez on the edge of the shatter zone and their chiefdom's order sustained them through the era of Indian slaving and widespread disease and into the early eighteenth century. The efforts of the Tattooed Serpent's wife and the Tattooed Arm and her partisans helped to prolong the Natchez tenure in the region. The world around them had indeed changed by the late 1720s, yet the Théoloëls had managed to stave off collapse for three decades after the French settled the region. This accomplishment was no mean feat. They achieved this by utilizing long-standing practices of intermarriage and the diplomatic acumen of Natchez women. It was only after Paris dispatched massive reinforcements, equipped with heavy artillery, that the People of the Sun succumbed. They demonstrated, at least for a time, that some of the Natives found traditional ways with the skill and leadership of their women to deal with the disruptive forces of the shattered zone.

Notes

1. Swanton, *Indians of the Southeastern United States*, 45–48; and Galloway and Jackson, "Natchez and Neighboring Groups," 614.

2. "Grand Soleil, files d'un françois en 1728," BNF, Manuscrits, nouvelles acquisitions, française, tome 2550, fol. 115.

3. Another Francophone, Father Montigny, had ministered briefly to the Théoloëls during the late 1690s; Letter of Father St. Cosme of Québec to the Bishop of Québec, Missionary, January 2, 1699, AM, séries 2, sous séries JJ, tome 56; and Penicault, "Relation, ou annale veritable de ce qui s'est passé dans le pais de la Louisiane," CJC, manuscrit, no. 828, 102 and 120.

4. "Grand Soliel, files d'un françois," BNF, Manuscrits, nouvelles acquisitions, française, tome 2550, fol. 115–16.

5. The first report of St. Cosme's murder placed the blame on the Natchez. Bienville to Minister of Marine, February 20, 1707, AC, ser. C13A, vol. 2, fol. 11. The culprits were later determined to be Chitimachas; La Harpe, *Historical Journal*, 51; and Penicault, "Relation, ou annale veritable de ce qui s'est passé dans le pais de la Louisiane," CJC, manuscrit, no. 828, 102.

6. For a detailed explanation of the Mississippian cycle of consolidation and dissolution, see Galloway, *Choctaw Genesis*, 27–74. For other views of Mississippian coalescence and dispersion, see Blitz, "Mississippian Chiefdoms"; Cobb, "Mississippian Chiefdoms"; Scarry, "Late Prehistoric Southeast"; and Widmer, "Structure of Southeastern Chiefdoms."

7. Le Page du Pratz, *Histoire de la Louisiane*, 2:126–27.

8. "Les sauvages Natchez," BNF, Manuscrits, nouvelles acquisitions, française, tome 2554, fol. 64. See also Father Le Pétit, missionary, to Father d'Avaugour, procurator of the missions in North America, July 12, 1730, Thwaites, *Jesuit Relations*, 68:129–30; and Swanton, *Indian Tribes*, 181.

9. Father Le Pétit to Father d'Avaugour July 12, 1730, Thwaites, *Jesuit Relations*, 68:126; "Nouvelle relation de la Louisiane, 1717" Waggoner, *Le Plus Beau Païs*, 41; and Lafitau, *Moeurs des sauvages*, 120, 153–55. See also MacCormack, "Limits of Understanding." For hopes that the Natchez would quickly convert to Catholicism, see Du Ru, *Journal*, 29.

10. The Tattooed Arm, the mother of the last Great Sun, explained to the missionary Father St. Cosme that the Suns' claim of descent from a solar deity enhanced their authority over the commoners; "Grand Soliel," BNF, Manuscrits, nouvelles acquisitions, française, tome 2550, fols. 115–16.

11. Le Page du Pratz, *Histoire*, 2:326–34. See also "Les Sauvages Natchez," BNF, Manuscrits, nouvelles acquisitions, française, tome 2549, fol. 64; and Pénicaut, *Fleur de Lys* (1953) 90–92.

12. Swanton, *Indian Tribes*, 107. Galloway reduces these rankings to three, Suns, nobles, and stinkards. She argues that low-status individuals who achieved merit in battle or through social service became honored men and that this was not a hereditary class; Galloway, "Natchez Matrilineal Kinship."

13. Dumont de Montigny, *Mémoires historiques*, 1:178–80; Le Page du Pratz, *Histoire*, 2:393–96; Mathurin le Petit, Lettre au d'Avaugour, July 12, 1730, Thwaites, *Jesuit Relations*, 68:135; and Pénicaut, *Fleur de Lys* (1953) 90.

14. Hart, "Reconsideration."

15. Jeffrey Brain agrees with Quimby's assimilation model but disputes his hypothesis that the Natchez had employed it for very long by the time the French arrived; Brain, "Natchez 'Paradox'"; Quimby, "Natchez Social Structure"; Tooker, "Natchez Social Organization"; and White, Murdock, and Scaglion, "Natchez Class." Woods adopted Brain's hypothesis; Woods, *French-Indian Relations*, 26. See also Lorenz, "Natchez," 152–58.

16. Knight, "Social Organization."

17. Tonty, "Relation"; and La Salle, "Récit," 557.

18. For the importance of the Emerald site, see Brain, "Late Prehistoric Settlement Patterning"; and Cottier, "Stratigraphic and Area Test." Swanton surmised that the northern temple might have been the Taensa's structure that Father Davion burned down in 1704; Swanton, *Indian Tribes*, 165. Father Poisson mentioned a connection between the Natchez temple and the Tunicas, who lived north of the Yazoo River at the turn of the eighteenth century; Poisson, aux Akensas, October 3, 1727, Thwaites, *Jesuit Relations*, 67:311.

19. For discussions on the Lower Mississippi Valley Indians and the Choctaws, see Jeter, this volume; and Galloway, this volume.

20. For the effects of European pathogens in North America, see Crosby, *Ecological Imperialism*, 212–17; Crosby, "Virgin Soil Epidemics"; and Diamond, *Guns, Germs, and Steel*, 77–70, 210–13. For an overview of Natchez population trends, see Wood, "Changing Population," 73–79. Kelton questions the role of disease in the decline of Indian populations in the Gulf Coast region; Kelton, "Avoiding the Smallpox Spirits"; Kelton, "Great Southeastern Smallpox Epidemic"; and Kelton, this volume.

21. Tonty, "Relation," 594–95.

22. La Salle, "Récit," 565–66; and Minet, "Voyage Made from Canada," 59.

23. Jacques Graviers, Relation ou Journal du voyage en 1700 depuis le pays des Illinois jusqu'a l'embouchure du fleuve Mississipi, February 16, 1701, Thwaites, *Jesuit Relations*, 65:133.

24. Graviers, Relation ou Journal du voyage en 1700 depuis le pays des Illinois jusqu'a l'embouchure du fleuve Mississipi, February 16, 1701, Thwaites, *Jesuit Relations*, 65:142–43.

25. Penicault placed the post at or near the Grand Village; Penicault, "Relation, ou annale veritable de ce qui s'est passé dans le pais de la Louisiane," CJC, manuscrit, no. 828, 248.

26. The event horizon for the internment of these items ended in 1730 when the French seized the area. For a full listing of grave goods, see Neitzel, *Archeology of the Fatherland Site,* 40–45, 50–51. For further analyses of Natchez archaeology, see Brown, "Historic Indians"; and Brown, "Archaeology Confronts History." See also Albrecht, "Indian-French Relations"; and Muller, *Mississippian Political Economy*, 63–69.

27. Lorenz, "Natchez." Lorenz's work responds to Brown's suggestion that adopted villages like the Grigras should yield different artifacts than "native" Natchez towns; Brown, "Archaeological Study."

28. Duclos to Pontchartrain, June 7, 1716, Rowland and Sanders, *Mississippi Provincial Archives*, 3:208–9. Cadillac left for Illinois without leaving instructions for Bienville, the King's lieutenant and second-in-command, and without revealing his destination; Bienville to Pontchartrain, June 15, 1715, Rowland and Sanders, *Mississippi Provincial Archives*, 3:181.

29. For Hughes's plans for colonizing the Mississippi, see Crane, *Southern Frontier* (1929), 100–8. For Hughes's subsequent capture by the elder La Loire, see Bienville to Pontchartrain, June 15, 1715, Rowland and Sanders, *Mississippi Provincial Archives*, 3:181–82.

30. Memoire en la forme de ce qui est passé dans la premiere expedition que

Mr. Bienville fit aux Natchez en 1716, AC, séries C13A, vol. 4; and Punition des sauvages Natchez en 1716 et etablissent d'un fort françois chez eux, BNF, Manuscrits, nouvelles acquisitions, française, tome 2549, fol. 45.

31. For an overview of Law's impact on the development of Louisiana, see Langlois, *Villes*, 112–22. See also Allain, *Not Worth a Straw*, 67–68; and Woods, *French-Indian Relations*, 62. For France's emigration policies during this era, see Brasseaux, "Image of Louisiana"; and Conrad, "Emigration Forcée."

32. Extrait de l'acte de Société entre la cie des Indes et les associés en la Concession de Ste. Catherine, September 4, 1719, AC, séries G1, vol. 465; Deucher to the Directors, February 6, 1720, AC, séries G1, vol. 465; and Pénicaut, *Fleur de Lys* (1953), 237–39. See also Le Page du Pratz, *Histoire*, 173.

33. Procuration de Kolly et Deucher au Sieur Faucon Dumanoir, December 29, 1719, AC, séries G1, vol. 465.

34. Longrais's Journal, June 15, 1723, AC, séries C13A, vol. 7, fol. 302.

35. Recit du premier attentat des Natchez contre la Concession de St. Catherine, March 9, 1722, AC, séries G1, vol. 465. See also La Harpe, *Historical Journal*, 157.

36. For a narrative of the Second Natchez War, see Woods, *French-Indian Relations*, 73–75.

37. Relation des hostilités commises par les Natchez, November 4, 1722, AC, séries G1, vol. 465; Requête préséntée par Faucon Dumanoir, May 20, 1723, AC, séries G1, vol. 465; Journal de Diron D'Artaguette, October 26, 1722, AC, séries C13C, vol. 2, fol. 189; and Le Page du Pratz, *Histoire*, 1:184–85. See also La Harpe, *Historical Journal*, 157.

38. Relation des hostilités commises par les Natchez, November 4, 1722, AC, séries G1, vol. 465.

39. Charlevoix, *Histoire et description*, 3:417.

40. Le Page du Pratz, *Histoire*, 3:17. Swanton translated and edited their observations as well as those of European informants who had witnessed previous Natchez burial rites; Swanton, *Indian Tribes*, 139–57.

41. Le Page du Pratz, *Histoire*, 3:37–39.

42. Le Page du Pratz, *Histoire*, 51–52. Dumont de Montigny's account of the funeral closely resembles Le Page du Pratz's narrative; Dumont de Montigny, *Mémoires Historiques*, 1:208–39. Nearly all of the longer speeches addressed to the Europeans witnessing the funeral were delivered by Théoloël women, including The Glorious Woman. "The French had named her la Glorieuse because of her majestic bearing, her proud demeanor, and because she associated only with distinguished Frenchmen"; Le Page du Pratz, *Histoire*, 3:36.

43. Le Page du Pratz, *Histoire*, 2:398.

44. Le Page du Pratz, *Histoire*, 2:398. One of the healthy Suns was most likely the child fathered by St. Cosme.

45. Le Page du Pratz explained the reason why the Indians called him this: "they named me this because I was the Chief or Commandant of the Habitants of the Post of the Natchez and because of my hair"; Le Page du Pratz, *Histoire*, 2:400.

46. Le Page du Pratz, *Histoire*, 2:402–3.

47. Le Page du Pratz, *Histoire*, 2:402.

48. Le Page du Pratz did not marry the young female Sun.

49. Le Page du Pratz, *Histoire*, 3:247.

50. Montigny, *Mémoires historiques*, 2:129.

51. Le Page du Pratz, *Histoire*, 3:232.

52. Le Page du Pratz, *Histoire*, 3:233.

53. Le Page du Pratz, *Histoire*, 3:233–34.

54. Le Page du Pratz, *Histoire*, 3:238–39.

55. Nairne, *Nairne's Muskhogean Journals*, 40.

56. For further discussion of this role of *fanimingos* in Indian diplomacy, see Galloway, "'Chief Who Is Your Father,'" 259–64.

57. Galloway, "'Chief Who Is Your Father,'" 246.

58. Le Page du Pratz did not identify the father of the Great Sun except to say that he had been dead for some time. Galloway, "'Chief Who Is Your Father,'" 247.

59. Montigny, *Mémoires historiques*, 2:139; and Le Page du Pratz, *Histoire*, 3:151–54.

60. Périer to Maurepas, March 18, 1730, Rowland and Sanders, *Mississippi Provincial Archives*, 1:62; Broutin to the Company, August 7, 1730, Rowland and Sanders, *Mississippi Provincial Archives*, 1:127–28; Montigny, *Mémoires historiques*, 2:137, 139–40; and Le Page du Pratz, *Histoire*, 3:254.

61. Périer to Maurepas, March 18, 1730, AC, séries C13A, vol. 12, fol. 23–45; Lusser to Maurepas, Journal of a journey that I made to the Choctaws, January 12, 1730 to March 23, 1730, Rowland and Sanders, *Mississippi Provincial Archives*, 1:97–99; Charlevoix, *Histoire et Description*, 2:467–69; Montigny, *Mémoires historiques*, 2:138–46, 319; and Le Page du Pratz, *Histoire*, 3:258.

62. Charlevoix, *Histoire et description*, 2:467.

63. Montigny, *Mémoires historiques*, 2:154; and Le Page du Pratz, *Histoire*, 3:261.

64. Le Page du Pratz, *Histoire*, 3:260–61; and Le Petit to D'Avaugour, July 12, 1730, Thwaites, *Jesuit Relations*, 68:169.

65. Le Page du Pratz, *Histoire*, 3:261.

66. Montigny, *Mémoires historiques*, 2:154.

67. Charlevoix, *Histoire et description*, 2:468–69.

68. Périer to Maurepas, March 18, 1730, Rowland and Sanders, *Mississippi Provincial Archives*, 1:68; Diron to Minister of Marine, February 9, 1730, AC, séries C13A, vol. 12, fol. 368; Diron to Maurepas, March 20, 1730, Rowland and Sanders, *Mississippi Provincial Archives*, 1:78; and Relation of the Last of Attack of the French on the Natchez, January 1731, ASH, séries 67, no. 16.

69. Le Petit to D'Avaugour, July 12, 1730, Thwaites, *Jesuit Relations*, 68:171.

70. Le Petit to D'Avaugour, July 12, 1730, Thwaites, *Jesuit Relations*, 68:191.

71. Diron to Minister of Marine, March 20, 1730, Rowland and Sanders, *Mississippi Provincial Archives*, 1:78; Le Petit to D'Avaugour, July 12, 1730, Thwaites, *Jesuit Relations*, 68:191; and Montigny, *Mémoires historiques*, 2:175–80.

72. Montigny, *Mémoires historiques*, 2:180–82.

73. Le Page du Pratz's Chitimacha slave woman acted in a similar manner by providing the Dutchman with access to the Natchez and Chitimacha hierarchy; Galloway and Jackson, "Natchez and Neighboring Groups," 603.

74. Montigny, *Mémoires historiques*, 2:188.

75. Diron to Minister of Marine, March 20, 1730, Rowland and Sanders, *Mississippi Provincial Archives*, 1:80; and Le Page du Pratz, *Histoire*, 2:291–93.

76. Périer to Minister of Marine, March 18, 1730; Broutin to the Company, August 7, 1730, Rowland and Sanders, *Mississippi Provincial Archives*, 1:70, 135–36; Charlevoix, *Histoire et description*, 2:482; Montigny, *Mémoires historiques*, 2:190; and Le Page du Pratz, *Histoire*, 2:292.

77. Relation of the Last of Attack of the French on the Natchez, January 1731, ASH, séries 67, no. 16.

78. Périer to the Minister of Marine, March 25, 1731, AC, séries C13A, vol. 13, fol. 40; Relation of the Last of Attack of the French on the Natchez, January 1731, ASH, séries 67, no. 16; Charlevoix, *Histoire et description*, 2:493–94; and Périer to the Minister of Marine, March 25, 1731, AC, séries C13A, vol. 13, fol. 38.

79. Périer to the Minister of Marine, March 25, 1731, AC, séries C13A, vol. 13, fol. 41; and Charlevoix, *Histoire*, 2:494–95; Le Page du Pratz, *Histoire*, 3:327 (quote).

80. M. Lancelot to Minister of Marine, March 1731, BNF, Manuscrits, nouvelles acquisitions, française, tome 2610, fols, 63–64v; "Attaque du fort des Natchez par les François en janvier 1731," BNF, Manuscrits, nouvelles acquisitions, française, tome 2551, fol. 113; Charlevoix, *Histoire et description*, 2:496–97; and Montigny, *Mémoires historiques*, 2:208.

Afterword

SOME THOUGHTS ON FURTHER WORK

ROBBIE ETHRIDGE

In this volume we have begun "mapping" the Mississippian shatter zone by delineating its geographic extent, its temporal existence, and its conceptual underpinnings. This volume is more the first word than the last word on the subject. The goal has been to attend to the difficult task of understanding the collapse of the Mississippian world, the changes that took place afterwards, and the forces that caused this transformation. Much remains to be done.

First of all, we must get a better grasp of the inner workings of the Mississippian world. Building on the understanding of the Mississippian era that has been established over the past several decades we must now reconstruct the Mississippian world as an interconnected historical system that informed and sometimes directed the daily concerns of both the *micos* and their rank and file. We must also reconstruct the ups and downs of life, and the historical contingencies of that time and place. It seems to me that we just now are poised to begin discussing the *history* of the Mississippian Period, and this discussion is a necessary step in understanding how and why this world was transformed.

For example, the rich archaeological scholarship on the Mississippian South gives archaeologists and ethnohistorians the tools necessary to begin identifying the changing geopolitical realities over the entire duration of the Mississippian Period from Cahokia to Coosa. Such is necessary in order to understand how these chiefdoms interacted before the shatter zone developed and after they found themselves in it. Ned Jenkins in this volume gives us a model for understanding these processes, and one hopes that others will find his model useful for not only understanding the rises and dissolutions of chiefdoms but also their internal operations.

As we have seen, the relationships among chiefdoms were obviously an important factor in the shatter zone and in the subsequent restructuring of Native life. The breakdown of Native polities prompted short and long migrations of their people. Scholars have already made great strides in understanding the migrations and motivations for these movements, but there is more to do. For example, the deep history of chiefdom relationships appears to have been pivotal as people made decisions as to where they would move. Reconstructing the relationships among Mississippian polities then will be important in our understanding of the postcontact migrations and vice versa. Likewise, the physical presence of militarized slavers surely was an important factor in where people moved as was proximity to Europeans and the trade infrastructure. Local disease outbreaks also must have figured into such decisions. All of these push and pull factors and others identified elsewhere need intensive investigations.

The authors in this volume have identified many of the Indian groups that were caught up in the Mississippian shatter zone and were transformed within it. However, not all such groups have been included in this volume. We still do not know or understand the fate of many of the chiefdoms that existed at the time of the Soto *entrada* such as the host of impressive polities in the lower Mississippi Valley. Although the Mississippian roots of the Creek, Alabama-Coushatta, Catawba, and Choctaw coalescences are becoming clearer, the coalescences of other well-known eighteenth-century Indian polities such as the Cherokees, Chickasaws, Caddos, Yamasees, Tuscaroras, Yuchis, Occaneechis, Powhatans, and others await further clarification.

The question of introduced diseases has been an object of ongoing inquiry for almost two decades, and we must fold this research into other investigations such as the migration studies noted above. Paul Kelton shows us in this volume and in his monograph *Epidemics and Enslavement* that in order to understand the effects of disease we must build multicausal interactive models wherein disease is conjoined with trade, Indian slavery, warfare, and other factors. Disease in and of itself can no longer be used to explain the decline of the Mississippian but must be placed in context with many other factors that impacted Native life after contact.

The role of the Iroquois begs for more scrutiny. Obviously the scholarship on the Iroquois is vast, and their role in Indian slaving has been well established for over a decade. However, the full extent of the impact of Iroquois slaving has yet to be examined, especially the shock waves they sent into and through the South. The repercussions sometimes came in the form of migrants such as the Quapaws, Shawnees, and Westos.

Bowne in his monograph and in this volume has identified the Westos as a militarized slaving society, and they in particular figure prominently in the Mississippian shatter zone. The documentary and archaeological evidence for the Westos is sparse, yet scholars are now able to put them into an historical context that for the first time helps make sense of who they were, why they were in the South, and the consequences of their actions for Native people. We now must examine what, if any, role other migrants played in the fall of the Mississippian chiefdoms and the reconfigurations that followed. We also need to build on current research to develop similar treatments for Southern Indians who became militarized slavers such as the Susquehannocks, Occaneechis, Tuscaroras, and Yamasees.

That the militarized slaving societies controlled access to the early trade system is obvious. However, how they did so is not so clear. As several authors have demonstrated in this volume, violence was certainly one mechanism, and the role of violence and warfare in the shatter zone awaits full-length treatments. Scholars can now reexamine early colonial conflicts within the context of the Indian slave trade, militarized slaving societies, and Europeans hoping to open the trade to a wider field of participants. For example, understanding the militarized slavers as holding monopolies over the trade and blocking other Indian participation casts a new light on the Indian wars of the seventeenth and early eighteenth centuries such as the Tuscarora War and others. This insight can help explain subsequent Indian animosities, and it also helps to explain why in wars such as Bacon's Rebellion the real target of European hostilities were those Indians that blocked European access to the interior populations.

In examining the role of violence and warfare, we cannot turn away from close examinations of the brutal side of Indian life and Euro-American imperialism, nor should we be satisfied with explanations of indigenous violence in terms of simple cultural determinism. A more productive way to think about this violence would be as a mechanism for achieving imperial dominance, a mechanism for capitalist incorporation, and an active, deliberate strategy employed by indigenous peoples to not only control their own lives but to compete with others for access to the new opportunities afforded by Europeans. We also have to be frank about the fact that the contestants in this imperial struggle who were organized into nation states held the advantage — Europeans prevailed decisively in this struggle. The real question is why the Indians did not, and the answer does not lie in archaic notions about racial or military superiority but in sorting out the advantages and disadvantages nation states held in a global economy compared to those held by political organizations such as Mississippian chiefdoms, coalescent societies, and other nonstate social formations.

Since the world-systems model informs much about the Mississippian shatter zone, we must begin to examine the particulars of the precontact Mississippian economy and how and what changed when it came up against capitalist hegemony. We must begin to examine what effect market enterprises had on Mississippian systems of labor, resource procurement and use, subsistence-level economic activities, the prestige-goods economy, and so on. In this volume Galloway gives us an innovative model for understanding how Choctaws viewed the new economic opportunities presented to them at this time. We need similar treatments for others on the edge of the shatter zone. Galloway's model may also be useful for understanding how the new capitalist economic system articulated with and changed the indigenous system of Indian groups who were central to the European trade like the Westos, the Occaneechis, and later the Creeks and Chickasaws.

Such research could also help clarify the relationship between seventeenth-century European traders and their Indian clients. For this task, we also need better representations of the early Southern colonists. Historians are beginning to recognize these men and women as experienced venture capitalists. The colonists came to the South to take advantage of the birth of a capitalist system, to make money, and to do business. We must flesh out the sketches we presently have of traders such as Henry Woodward, Abraham Wood, James Needham, Thomas Nairne, and the Goose Creek Men, not to speak of later players such as George Galphin, James Adair, and Lachlan McGillivray. Likewise, we can now recast our narratives about colonial stalwarts such as William Byrd and Thomas Stegge by determining if and how they were involved in the Indian trade in slaves and skins.

The role that Africans played in these early years of the slave trade and the articulation between the African and Indian slave trade has not been broached in this volume. Given the well-developed historiography on the African slave trade, an inquiry into this is especially promising as one may discover unsuspected parallels and differences between the two systems. On a more general level we need to place the Indian slave trade of the American South into the Atlantic World and global economy at large. The shatter zone concept maintains that the commercial trade in Indian slaves was part and parcel of the emerging global economy, yet the precise ties between them have yet to be explored. Likewise, this volume admittedly does not closely examine the various European colonies, yet they were the beachheads of empire and hence deserve a firmer place in the shatter zone framework.

John Worth paints us a grim picture of the fate of the Florida Indians. We now need a full treatment of the fall of the Spanish mission system. Given the vigorous scholarship on Spanish Florida and the relative abundance of documentary evidence, such study will be especially fruitful for not only understanding the forces at play in the shatter zone but how they played out in different colonial settings. This research will also require that scholars examine the Apalachee and Timucuan chiefdoms as possibly being something different from typical Mississippian chiefdoms. As we have seen, they were not chiefdoms functioning in a Mississippian world, but rather they were chiefdoms in a rapidly changing world and ones responding to numerous colonial pressures. As George Milne makes clear in his essay on the Natchez, the Natchez continued to operate as something of a chiefdom into the eighteenth century precisely because they could put old chiefdom institutions such as marriage to a new service of colonial coalescence. But the question still remains as to just how much the eighteenth-century Natchez chiefdom resembled a sixteenth-century Mississippian chiefdom.

We must also endeavor to understand the geopolitics and the ecology of the new South that had emerged by 1730. This new South not only included Indians, Africans, and Europeans but also colonial settlements, coalescent societies, *petites nations*, settlement Indians, and Indian and European nations as well as all of the ties that bound these entities together. This new South also had new ecological parameters, something that has not been touched on in this volume. Certainly the decline of the Mississippian world and the introduction of exotic animals, plants, and microbes had resounding ecological consequences.

Finally, we will need to develop a new vocabulary for talking about and studying the first two hundred years after initial contact. Over the past fifteen or so years scholars have moved away from shopworn concepts such as assimilation and acculturation in favor of new concepts such as middle ground, new world, creolization, and hybridity to account for the blended world of Europeans, Africans, and Indians that came about after contact. But in the American South this blended world did not truly take shape until the eighteenth century. Therefore we must begin to build new conceptual tools for understanding the processes at play in the first and second century after initial contact before these blended worlds came into being. In this volume we have offered the framework of the Mississippian shatter zone, but we must think of others as well.

We also must devise as precise a terminology for characterizing Indian societies as we have for characterizing European societies. The social typologies of band, tribe, chiefdom, and state are a gross classification and often do a disservice. We need more precise and subtle terminologies that will enable us to further historicize the Native Southern past. We also must develop a fuller vocabulary for describing and understanding the new kinds of Indian political and social systems that emerged in the eighteenth century. We have used some newer terms such as "coalescent society," but even these terms need further refinement.

As we undertake the task of building a new vocabulary and conceptual tool kit, it is important to develop terms and concepts that will foster collaboration between archaeology, history, and anthropology. Historians, for instance, must be as comfortable with "Mississippian chiefdom" as they are with "kingdom" or "city-state" or "nation." Conversely, archaeologists and anthropologists must be comfortable with and conversant in historical scholarship. All of this requires not only compatible vocabularies but also compatible or at the least mutually comprehensible methodologies as well as cross-disciplinary respect.

As all of the chapters in this volume attest, the first two hundred years of European contact were indeed a foundational experience for the Indians of the American South. But they were also foundational years in the formation of the new South that had emerged by 1730 and that included not only Indians but Europeans and Africans as well. In other words, understanding the transformation of the Southern Indians during these two hundred years is necessary for understanding why the history of the American South unfolded as it did.

Bibliography

ARCHIVAL SOURCES

Archives de la Marine. Archives Nationales de France, Paris.

Archives des Colonies. Archives Nationales de France, Paris.

Archives du Service Hydrographique. Archives Nationales de France, Paris.

Archivo General de la Nación México, Mexico City.

Audiencia of Santo Domingo. Archivo General de las Indias, Seville.

Audiencia of Santo Domingo, Archivo General de las Indias. Stetson
Manuscript Collection, P. K. Yonge Library of Florida History, University
of Florida, Gainesville.

British Public Records Office, London.

Colonial Office 700, North American Colonies 7, Carolina 3. Admiralty Office,
National Archives of the United Kingdom (formerly known as the British
Public Record Office), Kew.

Hargrett Library. University of Georgia, Athens.

Map Collection. Williams Research Center. Historic New Orleans Collection,
New Orleans.

National Anthropological Archives. Smithsonian Institution, Washington DC.

Bibliothèque nationale de France. Manuscrits, nouvelles acquisitions
française, Paris.

Collège des Jésuites de Clermont, Paris

Records of the Society for the Propagation of the Gospel in Foreign Parts.
Society for the Propagation of the Gospel, London.

Richard Yarborough Collection. Center for American History, Texas State
Historical Association, University of Texas at Austin.

South Carolina Department of Archives and History, Columbia.

Transcripts of the Colonial Office, class 5, Archives des Colonies, British
Public Records Office. Manuscript Reading Room, Library of Congress,
Washington DC.

PUBLISHED WORKS

Abler, Thomas S. "Beavers and Muskets: Iroquois Military Fortunes in the
Face of European Colonization." In *War in the Tribal Zone: Expanding*

States and Indigenous Warfare, edited by R. Brian Ferguson and Neil L. Whitehead, 158–68. 1992. 2nd ed. Santa Fe: School of American Research Press, 1999.

Adair, James. *The History of the American Indians*. 1775. Edited by Kathryn E. Holland Braund. Tuscaloosa: University of Alabama Press, 2005.

Akin, David, and Joel Robbins, eds. *Money and Modernity: State and Local Currencies in Melanesia*. Pittsburgh: University of Pittsburgh Press, 1999.

Albrecht, Andrew C. "Indian-French Relations at Natchez." *American Anthropologist*, n.s. 48, no. 3 (1946): 321–54.

Alchon, Suzanne Austin. *A Pest in the Land: New World Epidemics in a Global Perspective*. Albuquerque: University of New Mexico Press, 2003.

Alford, Thomas Wildcat. "The Shawnee Indians." In *Old Chillicothe: Shawnee and Pioneer History: Conflicts and Romances in the Northwest Territory*, edited by William A. Galloway, 18–42. Xenia OH: Buckeye Press, 1934.

Allain, Mathé. *Not Worth a Straw: French Colonial Policy and the Early Years of Louisiana*. Lafayette: Center for Louisiana Studies, 1988.

Alt, Susan M. "Unwilling Immigrants: Culture, Change, and the 'Other' in Mississippian Societies." In *Invisible Citizens: Captives and Their Consequences*, edited by Catherine M. Cameron. Salt Lake City: University of Utah Press, 2008.

Alvord, Clarence W., and Lee Bidgood, eds. *The First Explorations of the Trans-Alleghany Region by Virginians, 1650–1674*. Cleveland: Arthur H. Clark, 1912.

Ambrose, Stanley H., Jane Buikstra, and Harold Krueger. "Status and Gender Differences in Diet at Mound 72, Cahokia, Revealed by Isotopic Analysis of Bone." *Journal of Anthropological Archaeology* 22, no. 3 (2003): 217–27.

Anderson, Benedict. *Imagined Communities*. London: Verso, 1983.

Anderson, David G. "Chiefly Cycling and Large-Scale Abandonments as Viewed from the Savannah River Basin." In *Political Structure and Change in the Prehistoric Southeastern United States*, edited by John F. Scarry, 150–91. Gainesville: University Press of Florida, 1996.

———. "Examining Chiefdoms in the Southeast: An Application of Multiscalar Analysis." In *Great Towns and Regional Polities*, edited by Jill E. Neitzel, 215–42. Albuquerque: University of New Mexico Press, 1999.

———. "Fluctuations between Simple and Complex Chiefdoms: Cycling in the Late Prehistoric Southeast." In *Political Structure and Change in the Prehis-*

toric Southeastern United States, edited by John F. Scarry, 150–91. Gainesville: University Press of Florida, 1996.

———. Savannah River Chiefdoms: Political Change in the Late Prehistoric Southeast. Tuscaloosa: University of Alabama Press, 1994.

Anderson, David L., David W. Stahle, and Malcolm K. Cleveland. "Paleo Climate and the Potential Food Reserves of Mississippian Societies in the Southeastern United States." American Antiquity 60, no. 2 (1996): 258–86.

"Anonymous Relation." In Source Material for the Social and Ceremonial Life of the Choctaw Indians, by John R. Swanton, 243–58. Bureau of American Ethnology, bulletin 103, Washington DC: Government Printing Office, 1931.

Apaumat, Hendrick. "A Narrative of an Embassy to the Western Indians, from the Original Manuscript of Hendrick Apaumat." Memoirs of the Historical Society of Pennsylvania 2 (1827), 60–131.

Appadurai, Arjun, ed. The Social Life of Things: Commodities in Cultural Perspective. Cambridge, UK: Cambridge University Press, 1986.

Aquila, Richard. "Down the Warrior's Path: The Causes of the Southern Wars of the Iroquois." American Indian Quarterly 4, no. 3 (1978): 211–21.

Archdale, John. "A New Description of That Fertile and Pleasant Province of Carolina, 1707." In Historical Collections of South Carolina, edited by B. R. Carroll, 85–120. Vol. 2. New York: Harper, 1836.

Arnade, Charles W. The Siege of St. Augustine in 1702. Gainesville: University of Florida Press, 1959.

Arrighi, Giovanni. The Long Twentieth Century: Money, Power, and the Origins of Our Times. New York: Verso, 1994.

Atkin, Edmond. The Appalachian Indian Frontier: The Edmond Atkin Report and Plan of 1755. Edited by Wilbur R. Jacobs. 1954. Lincoln: University of Nebraska Press, 1967.

———. Indians of the Southern Colonial Frontier: The Edmond Atkin Report and Plan of 1755. Edited by Wilbur R. Jacobs. Columbia: University of South Carolina, 1954.

Atkinson, Jim. "Historic Chickasaw Cultural Material: A More Comprehensive Identification." Mississippi Archaeology 22 (1987): 32–62.

———. "A Historic Contact Indian Settlement in Oktibbeha County, Mississippi." Journal of Alabama Archaeology 25 (1979): 61–82.

Baca, Keith. "Destruction of the Blaine Mound, a Mississippian Period Site in the Central Pearl River Valley, Mississippi." Mississippi Archaeology 36 (2001): 1–16.

Bailey, L. R. *Indian Slave Trade in the Southwest*. Los Angeles: Westernlore, 1964.

Baker, Brenda J., and Lisa Kealhofer. "Assessing the Impact of European Contact on Aboriginal Populations." In *Bioarchaeology of Native American Adaptation in the Spanish Borderlands*, edited by Brenda J. Baker and Lisa Kealhofer, 1–14. Gainesville: University Press of Florida, 1996.

——, eds. *Bioarchaeology of Native American Adaptation in the Spanish Borderlands*. Gainesville: University Press of Florida, 1996.

Baker, Steven G. "The Historic Catawba Peoples: Exploratory Perspectives in Ethnohistory and Archaeology." Report prepared for Duke Power Company and other sponsors of Institutional Grant J-100, University of South Carolina–Columbia, 1975.

Bandera, Juan de la. "The 'Long' Bandera Relation." In *The Juan Pardo Expeditions: Explorations of the Carolinas and Tennessee, 1566–1568*, edited by Charles Hudson, translated by Paul Hoffman, 205–96. Washington DC: Smithsonian Institution Press, 1990.

——. "The Short Bandera Relation." In *The Juan Pardo Expeditions: Explorations of the Carolinas and Tennessee, 1566–1568*, edited by Charles Hudson, translated by Paul Hoffman, 297–304. Washington DC: Smithsonian Institution Press, 1990.

Barr, Juliana. "From Captives to Slaves: Commodifying Indian Women in the Borderlands." *Journal of American History* 92, no. 1 (2005): 19–46.

Barth, Fredrick, ed. *Ethnic Groups and Boundaries: The Social Organization of Culture Difference*. Oslo: Scandinavian University Books, 1969.

Bartram, William. "Observations on the Creek and Cherokee Indians." In *A Creek Source Book*. Edited by William C. Sturtevant. New York, Garland, 1987.

——. *The Travels of William Bartram*. Naturalist's Edition. Edited by Francis Harper. New Haven CT: Yale University Press, 1958.

Basso, Keith H. *Wisdom Sits in Places: Landscape and Language among the Western Apache*. Albuquerque: University of New Mexico Press, 1996.

Beauchamp, William M. *A History of the New York Iroquois Now Commonly Called the Six Nations*. Port Washington NY: Ira J. Friedman, 1968.

Beck, Robin A., Jr. "Consolidation and Hierarchy: Chiefdom Variability in the Mississippian Southeast." *American Antiquity* 68, no. 4 (2003): 641–61.

——. "From Joara to Chiaha: Spanish Exploration of the Appalachian Summit Area, 1540–1568." *Southeastern Archaeology* 16, no. 2 (1997): 162–69.

——. "Persuasive Politics and Domination at Cahokia and Moundville." In

Leadership and Polity in Mississippian Society, edited by Brian M. Butler and Paul D. Welch, 19–42. Center for Archaeological Investigations, Occasional Paper, no. 33. Carbondale: Southern Illinois University, 2006.

Beck, Robin A., Jr., and David G. Moore. "The Burke Phase: A Mississippian Frontier in the North Carolina Foothills." *Southeastern Archaeology* 21, no. 2 (2002): 192–205.

Beck, Robin A., Jr., David G. Moore, and Christopher B. Rodning. "Identifying Fort San Juan: A 16th-Century Spanish Occupation at the Berry Site, North Carolina." *Southeastern Archaeology* 25, no. 1 (2006): 65–77.

Bell, Alison. "White Ethnogenesis and Gradual Capitalism: Perspectives from Colonial Archaeological Sites in the Chesapeake." *American Anthropologist*, n.s. 107, no. 3 (2005): 446–60.

Belovich, Stephanie J., David S. Brose, and Russell M. Weisman. *Archaeological Survey at George W. Andrews Lake and Chattahoochee River*. With N. White. Archaeological Research Reports of the Cleveland Museum of Natural History, no. 37, Cleveland, 1982.

Bennassar, Bartolomé. *The Spanish Character: Attitudes and Mentalities from the Sixteenth to the Nineteenth Century*. 1975. Translated by Benjamin Keen. Berkeley: University of California Press, 1979.

Bense, Judith A. *Archaeology of the Southeastern United States: Paleoindian to World War I*. San Diego: Academic Press, 1994.

Bentley, M. M. "The Slaveholding Catawbas." *South Carolina Historical Magazine* 92 (1991): 85–98.

Betts, Colin M. "Pots and Pox: the Identification of Protohistoric Epidemics in the Upper Mississippi Valley." *American Antiquity* 71 (2006): 233–59.

Biedma, Luys Hernández de. "Relation of the Island of Florida." In *The De Soto Chronicles: The Expedition of Hernando de Soto to North America in 1539–1543*, edited by Lawrence A. Clayton, Vernon. J. Knight, Jr., and Edward C. Moore, translated by John E. Worth, 221–46. Vol. 1. Tuscaloosa: University of Alabama Press, 1993.

Biggar, H. P., ed. *The Works of Samuel de Champlain in Six Volumes*. Vol. 3, *1615–1618*. Translated and edited by H. H. Langton and W. F. Ganong. French texts collated by J. Home Cameron. Toronto: The Champlain Society, 1929.

Billings, Warren M. *Sir William Berkeley and the Forging of Colonial Virginia*. Baton Rouge: Louisiana State University Press, 2004.

Blackhawk, Ned. "Look How Far We've Come: How American Indian History

Changed the Study of American History in the 1990s," OAH *Magazine of History*, November 2005, 8–12.

———. Review of *Captives and Cousins: Slavery, Kinship, and Community in the Southwest Borderlands*. *American Indian Culture and Research Journal* 28 (2004): 85–90.

———. *Violence over the Land: Indians and Empires in the Early American West*. Cambridge MA: Harvard University Press, 2006.

Blitz, John. *Ancient Chiefdoms of the Tombigbee*. Tuscaloosa: University of Alabama Press, 1993.

———. "Mississippian Chiefdoms and the Fusion-Fission Process." *American Antiquity* 64, no. 4 (1999): 577–92.

Blitz, John H., and Karl G. Lorenz. *The Chattahoochee Chiefdoms*. Tuscaloosa: The University of Alabama Press, 2006.

———. "The Early Mississippian Frontier in the Lower Chattahoochee-Apalachicola River Valley." *Southeastern Archaeology* 21, no. 2 (2002): 117–35.

Blitz, John H., and C. Baxter Mann. *Fisherfolk, Farmers, and Frenchmen: Archaeological Explorations on the Mississippi Gulf Coast*. Mississippi Department of Archives and History, Archaeological Report Series, no. 30, Jackson, 2000.

Blue, Mathew P. *A Brief History of Montgomery*. Montgomery AL: Privately Printed, 1878.

Blumer, Thomas J. *Bibliography of the Catawba*. Metuchen PA: Scarecrow, 1987.

Bohannan, Paul. "Some Principles of Exchange and Investment among the Tiv." *American Anthropologist*, n.s. 57, no. 1 (1955): 60–70.

Boswell, Terry, and Christopher Chase-Dunn. *A Spiral of Capitalism and Socialism: Toward Global Democracy*. Boulder CO: Lynne Rienner, 2000.

Boszhardt, Robert F. "Contracting Stemmed: What's the Point?" *Midcontinental Journal of Archaeology* 27 (2002): 35–67.

Bourdieu, Pierre. *Outline of a Theory of Practice*. Translated by R. Nice. Cambridge, UK: Cambridge University Press, 1977.

Bowne, Eric. "'A Bold and Warlike People': The Basis of Westo Power." In *Light on the Path: The Anthropology and History of the Southeastern Indians*, edited by Thomas J. Pluckhahn and Robbie Ethridge, 123–32. Tuscaloosa: University of Alabama Press, 2006.

———. "The Rise and Fall of the Westo Indians: An Evaluation of the Documentary Evidence." *Early Georgia* 28, no. 1 (2000): 56–78.

————. *The Westo Indians: Slave Traders of the Early Colonial South*. Tuscaloosa: University of Alabama Press, 2005.

Boyd, Mark F., ed. and trans. "Diego Peña's Expedition to Apalachee and Apalachicola in 1716." *Florida Historical Quarterly* 28 (1949): 3–48.

————, ed. and trans. "Expedition of Marcos Delgado From Apalachee to the Upper Creek Country in 1686." *Florida Historical Quarterly* 16 (1936): 1–32.

Boyd, Mark F., Hale G. Smith, and John W. Griffin. *Here They Once Stood: The Tragic End of the Apalachee Missions*. Gainesville: University Press of Florida, 1951.

Bradley, James W., and S. Terry Childs. "Basque Earrings and Panther's Tails: The Form of Cross-Cultural Contact in Sixteenth-Century Iroquoia." In *Metals in Society: Theory beyond Analysis*, edited by Robert M. Ehrenreich, 7–17. M A S C A Research Papers in Science and Archaeology 8, no. 2. Philadelphia: University Museum of Archaeology and Anthropology, University of Pennsylvania, 1991.

Bradshaw, York W., and Michael Wallace. *Global Inequalities*. Thousand Oaks C A: Pine Forge, 1996.

Brain, Jeffrey P. "Late Prehistoric Settlement Patterning in the Yazoo Basin and Natchez Bluffs Regions of the Lower Mississippi Valley." In *Mississippian Settlement Patterns*, edited by Bruce D. Smith, 331–68. New York: Academic Press, 1978.

————. "The Natchez 'Paradox.'" *Ethnology* 10, no. 2 (1971): 215–22.

————. *Tunica Archaeology*. Papers of the Peabody Museum of Archaeology and Ethnology, vol. 78. Cambridge M A: Harvard University, 1988.

————. *Winterville: Late Prehistoric Culture Contact in the Lower Mississippi Valley*. Archaeological Reports, no. 23. Jackson: Mississippi Department of Archives and History, 1989.

Brandao, J. A. *Your Fyre Shall Burn No More: Iroquois Policy toward New France and Its Native Allies to 1701*. Lincoln: University of Nebraska Press, 2000.

Brannon, Peter A. "Aboriginal Remains in the Middle Chattahoochee Valley of Alabama and Georgia." *American Anthropologist*, o.s. 9, no. 2 (1909): 186–98.

————. "Sacred Creek Relics Found in Alabama." *Arrow Points* 19, no. 1–2 (1930): 3.

————. "Urn-Burial in Central Alabama." *American Antiquity* 3, no. 3 (1938): 228–35.

Branstner, Susan. "Tionontate Huron Occupation at the Marquette Mission." In *Calumet and Fleur-de-Lys: Archaeology of Indian and French Contact in the*

Midcontinent, edited by John A. Walthall and Thomas E. Emerson, 177–202. Washington DC: Smithsonian Institution Press, 1992.

Brasseaux, Carl A. "The Image of Louisiana and the Failure of Voluntary French Emigration, 1683–1731." In *The French Experience in Louisiana*, edited by Glenn R. Conrad, 153–62. Lafayette: Center for Louisiana Studies, 1995.

Braund, Kathryn E. Holland. *Deerskins and Duffels: Creek Indian Trade with Anglo-America, 1685–1815*. Lincoln: University of Nebraska Press, 1993.

Brightman, Robert A. "Chitimacha." In *Handbook of North American Indians*, Vol. 14, *Southeast*, edited by Raymond D. Fogelson, 542–52. Washington DC: Smithsonian Institution Press, 2004.

Brookes, Samuel O. Discussant Comments. In *The Woodland-Mississippian Transition in the Mid-South: Proceedings of the Twenty-Second Mid-South Archaeological Conference*, edited by Charles H. McNutt, Stephen Williams, and Marvin D. Jeter, 7–8. University of Memphis Anthropological Research Center, Occasional Papers, no. 25. Memphis TN: University of Memphis, 2003.

Brooks, James F. *Captives and Cousins: Slavery, Kinship, and Community in the Southwestern Borderlands*. Chapel Hill: University of North Carolina Press, 2002.

———, ed. *Confounding the Color Line: The Indian-Black Experience in North America*. Lincoln: University of Nebraska Press, 2002.

Brooms, Bascom M. "An Archaeological Inventory of 1pk2 within the Walnut Creek Reservoir." Report submitted to the United States Soil Conservation Service, Auburn AL, 1977. Montgomery: Alabama Historical Commission.

Brose, David. "Penumbral Protohistory on Lake Erie's South Shore." In *Societies in Eclipse: Archaeology of the Eastern Woodlands Indians, AD 1400–1700*, edited by David S. Brose, C. Wesley Cowan, and Robert C. Mainfort Jr., 49–66. Washington DC: Smithsonian Institution Press, 2001.

Brose, David S., C. Wesley Cowan, and Robert C. Mainfort, Jr. *Societies in Eclipse: Archaeology of the Eastern Woodlands Indians, AD 1400–1700*. Washington DC: Smithsonian Institution Press, 2001.

Brown, Douglas S. *The Catawba Indians: People of the River*. Columbia: University of South Carolina Press, 1966.

Brown, Ian W. "An Archaeological Study of Culture Contact and Change in the Natchez Bluffs Region." In *La Salle and His Legacy: Frenchmen and Indians in the Lower Mississippi Valley*, edited by Patricia K. Galloway, 49–59. Jackson: University of Mississippi Press, 1982.

———. "Historic Indians of the Lower Mississippi Valley: An Archaeologist's View." In *Towns and Temples Along the Mississippi*, edited by David H. Dye and Cheryl Ann Cox, 176–93. Tuscaloosa: University of Alabama Press.

Brown, Ian W., and Penelope B. Drooker, eds. *Bottle Creek: A Pensacola Culture Site in South Alabama*. Tuscaloosa: University of Alabama Press, 2003.

Brown, James A. "Archaeology Confronts History at the Natchez Temple." *Southeastern Archaeology* 9, no. 1 (1990): 1–10.

———. "Forty Years of the Southeastern Ceremonial Complex." In *Histories of Southeastern Archaeology*, edited by Shannon Tushingham, Jane Hill, and Charles H. McNutt, 26–34. Tuscaloosa: University of Alabama Press, 2002.

———. "Where's the Power in Mound Building? An Eastern Woodland Perspective." In *Leadership and Polity in Mississippian Society*, ed. Brian M. Butler and Paul D. Welch, 197–213. Center for Archaeological Investigations, Occasional Paper, no. 33. Carbondale: University of Southern Illinois University Press, 2006.

Brown, Kathleen M. *Good Wives, Nasty Wenches, and Anxious Patriarchs: Gender, Race, and Power in Colonial Virginia*. Chapel Hill: University of North Carolina Press, 1996.

Browne, William Hand, et al. *Archives of Maryland*. 72 vols. Baltimore: Maryland Historical Society, 1883–1972.

Bruce, Philip Alexander. *Economic History of Virginia in the Seventeenth Century*. New York: Macmillan, 1907.

Burnett, Barbara A., and Katherine A. Murray. "Death, Drought, and De Soto: The Bioarchaeology of Depopulation." In *The Expedition of Hernando De Soto West of the Mississippi, 1541–1543*, edited by Gloria A. Young and Michael P. Hoffman, 227–36. Fayetteville: University of Arkansas Press, 1993.

Bushnell, Amy Turner. "Ruling 'The Republic of Indians' in Seventeenth-Century Florida." In *Powhatan's Mantle: Indians in the Colonial South*, edited by Peter H. Wood, Gregory A. Waselkov, and Thomas M. Hatley, 134–50. Lincoln: University of Nebraska Press, 1989.

———. *Situado and Sabana: Spain's Support System for the Presidio and Mission Provinces of Florida*. Anthropological Papers of the American Museum of Natural History, no. 74, 1994.

Butler, Brian M., and Paul D. Welch, eds. *Leadership and Polity in Mississippian Society*. Center for Archaeological Investigations, Occasional Paper, no. 33. Carbondale IL: Southern Illinois University, 2006.

Byrd, William. "A Journey to the Land of Eden in the Year 1733." In *A Journey*

to the Land of Eden and Other Papers by William Byrd, edited by Mark Van
Doren, 265–313. New York: Vanguard, 1928.

Caddell, Gloria M. "Plant Remains from the Yarborough Site." In *Archaeological
Investigations at the Yarborough Site (22cl814) Clay County, Mississippi*, edited
by Carlos Solis and Richard Walling, 139–143. University of Alabama, Office
of Archaeological Research, Report of Investigations, no. 30, Tuscaloosa,
1982.

———. "Plant Resources, Archaeological Plant Remains, and Prehistoric Plant Use
Patterns in the Central Tombigbee River Valley." In *Archaeological Investigations in the Gainesville Lake Area of the Tennessee-Tombigbee Waterway*. Vol.
4, *Biocultural Studies in the Gainesville Lake Area*, by Gloria M. Caddell, Anne
Woodrick, and Mary C. Hill, 44–51. University of Alabama, Office of Archaeological Research, Report of Investigations, no. 14, Tuscaloosa, 1981.

Caldwell, Joseph R. "Investigations at Rood's Landing, Stewart County, Georgia."
Early Georgia 2, no. 1 (1955): 22–49.

———. *Trend and Tradition in the Prehistory of the Eastern United States*. American
Anthropological Association, memoir 88, 1958.

Callender, Charles. "Shawnee." In *Handbook of North American Indians*. Vol. 15,
Northeast, edited by Bruce G. Trigger, 622–35. Washington DC: Smithsonian
Institution Press, 1978.

Calloway, Colin B. *One Vast Winter Count: The Native American West before Lewis
and Clark*. Lincoln: University of Nebraska Press, 2003.

———. *The Shawnees and the War for America*. New York: Viking, 2007.

———. "'We Have Always Been the Frontier': The American Revolution in Shawnee
Country." *American Indian Quarterly* 16, no. 1 (1992): 39–53.

Cameron, Catherin M. *Invisible Citizens: Captives and Their Consequences*. Salt
Lake City: University of Utah Press, 2008.

Carpenter, Edmund S., K. R. Pfirman, and Harry L. Schoff. "The 28th Street Site."
Pennsylvania Archaeologist 19, no. 1–2 (1949): 3–16.

Carson, James Taylor. "Ethnogeography and the Native American Past." *Ethnohistory* 49, no. 4 (2002): 769–88.

———. *Making an Atlantic World: Circles, Paths, and Stories from the American
South*. Knoxville: University of Tennessee Press, 2007.

———. *Searching for the Bright Path: The Mississippi Choctaws from Prehistory to
Removal*. Lincoln: University of Nebraska Press, 1999.

Cattell, Maria G., and Jacob J. Climo. "Meaning in Social Memory and History:

Anthropological Perspectives." In *Social Memory and History*, edited by Jacob
J. Climo and Maria G. Cattell, 1–36. Walnut Creek CA: AltaMira, 2002.

Cavalli-Sforza, Luigi L. "The Spread of Agriculture and Nomadic Pastoralism:
Insights from Genetics, Linguistics, and Archaeology." In *The Origin and
Spread of Agriculture and Pastoralism in Eurasia*, edited by David R. Harris,
51–69. Washington DC: Smithsonian Institution Press, 1996.

Chacon, Richard J., and David H. Dye, eds. *The Taking and Displaying of Human
Body Parts as Trophies by Amerindians*. Interdisciplinary Contributions to
Archaeology Series. New York: Springer, 2007.

Chagnon, Napoleon A. *The Yanomamo*. Belmont CA: Wadsworth, 1996.

Charlevoix, Pierre-Francois-Xavier. *Histoire et description generale de la nouvelle
France avec le Journal historique d'un voyage fait par ordre du roi dans l'Amerique Septentrionnale*. Vol. 3. Paris: Chez Nyon Fils, 1744.

Chase, David W. *The Averett Culture*. The Coweta Memorial Association Papers,
no. 1, Columbus GA, 1959.

———. "A Brief Synopsis of Central Alabama Prehistory." Paper presented at the
winter meeting of the Alabama Archaeological Society, Auburn AL, 1979.

———. "New Pottery Types from Alabama." *Southeastern Archaeological Conference*, bulletin 10 (1969): 17–25.

———. "New Pottery Types From Central Alabama." *Southeastern Archaeological
Conference*, bulletin 5 (1967): 41–9.

———. "Pottery Typology Committee for Central Alabama." *Southeastern Archaeological Conference*, bulletin 8 (1968): 11–22.

———. "Prehistoric Pottery of Central Alabama." *Journal of Alabama Archaeology*
44, no. 1–2 (1998): 52–98.

———. "A Reappraisal of the Averett Culture." *Journal of Alabama Archaeology*
9 (1963): 49–61.

Chase-Dunn, Christopher, and E. N. Anderson, eds. *The Historical Evolution of
World-Systems*. London: Palgrave, 2005.

Chase-Dunn, Christopher, and Salvatore Babones, eds. *Global Social Change:
Comparative and World Historical Perspectives*. Baltimore: Johns Hopkins
University Press, 2006.

Chet, Guy. *Conquering the American Wilderness: The Triumph of European Warfare in the Colonial Northeast*. Amherst: University of Massachusetts Press,
2003.

Cheves, Langdon, ed. *The Shaftesbury Papers and Other Records Relating to Carolina and the First Settlement on the Ashley River Prior to the Year 1676*. Col-

lections of the South Carolina Historical Society, no. 5. Charleston: South Carolina Historical Society, 1897.

Clark, Jeffery J. "Tracking Prehistoric Migrations: Pueblo Settlers among the Tonto Basin Hohokam." *Anthropological Papers of the University of Arizona* 65 (2001): 14–22.

Clark, Jerry E. *The Shawnee.* Lexington: University Press of Kentucky, 1993.

———. "Shawnee Indian Migration: A System Analysis." PhD diss., University of Kentucky, 1974.

Clay, R. Berle. "Interpreting the Mississippian Hinterlands." *Southeastern Archaeology* 25, no. 1 (2006): 48–64.

Clayton, Lawrence A., Vernon James Knight, Jr., and Edward C. Moore, eds. *The De Soto Chronicles: The Expedition of Hernando de Soto to North America in 1539–1543.* 2 vols. Tuscaloosa: University of Alabama Press, 1993.

Cobb, Charles R. "Archaeology and the 'Savage Slot': Displacement and Emplacement in the Premodern World." *American Anthropologist,* n.s. 107, no. 4 (2005): 563–74.

———. *From Quarry to Cornfield: The Political Economy of Mississippian Hoe Production.* Tuscaloosa: University of Alabama Press, 2000.

———. "Mississippian Chiefdoms: How Complex?" *Annual Review of Anthropology* 82 (2003): 63–84.

———, ed. *Stone Tool Traditions in the Contact Era.* Tuscaloosa: University of Alabama, 2003.

Cobb, Charles R., and Brian M. Butler. "The Vacant Quarter Revisited: Late Mississippian Abandonment of the Lower Ohio Valley." *American Antiquity* 67 (2002): 625–41.

Coclanis, Peter, ed. *The Atlantic Economy during the Seventeenth and Eighteenth Centuries: Organization, Operation, Practice, and Personnel.* Columbia: University of South Carolina Press, 2005.

———. "Atlantic World or Atlantic/World?" *William and Mary Quarterly* 63, no. 4 (2006): 725–42.

Coe, Joffre Lanning. *The Formative Cultures of the Carolina Piedmont.* Transactions of the American Philosophical Society, n.s. vol. 54, pt. 5, Philadelphia, 1964.

———. *Town Creek Indian Mound: A Native American Legacy.* Chapel Hill: University of North Carolina Press, 1995.

Cohen, Saul Bernard. *Geography and Politics in a World Divided.* London: Oxford University Press, 1973.

Connaway, John M. Discussant Comments. In *The Woodland-Mississippian Transition in the Mid-South: Proceedings of the Twenty-Second Mid-South Archaeological Conference*, edited by Charles H. McNutt, Stephen Williams, and Marvin D. Jeter, 24–27. University of Memphis Anthropological Research Center, Occasional Papers, no. 25. Memphis TN: University of Memphis, 2003.

Conrad, Glenn R. "Emigration Forcée: A French Attempt to Populate Louisiana, 1716–1720." In *The French Experience in Louisiana*, edited by Glenn R. Conrad, 125–35. Lafayette: Center for Louisiana Studies, 1995.

Conrad, Victor. "An Iroquois Frontier: The North Shore of Lake Ontario during the Late Seventeenth Century." *Journal of Historical Geography* 7, no. 2 (1981): 129–44.

Cooper, Martin S. "Neutrals on the Frontier: Settlement-Subsistence Patterns of the Southeastern Neutral Iroquoians." PhD diss., University of Toronto, 2005.

Cooper, Thomas, ed. *Statutes at Large of South Carolina*. 10 vols. Columbia SC: A. S. Johnston, 1836–41.

Cordingly, David. *Under the Black Flag: The Romance and the Reality of Life among the Pirates*. New York: Random House, 2006.

Corkran, David H. *The Carolina Indian Frontier*. Tricentennial booklet 6. Columbia: South Carolina Tricentennial Commission and University of South Carolina Press, 1970.

Cottier, John. "The Alabama River Phase: A Brief Description of a Late Phase in the Prehistory of South Central Alabama." In "Archaeological Salvage Investigations in the Miller's Ferry Lock and Dam Reservoir, 1968," by John Cottier, appendix. Unpublished report submitted to the National Park Service by the University of Alabama, Office of Archaeological Research, Tuscaloosa, 1970.

———. "Stratigraphic and Area Test at the Emerald and Anna Mound Sites." *American Antiquity* 17 (1951): 18–31.

Coyne, James H., ed. *Exploration of the Great Lakes 1669–1670 by Dollier de Casson and De Brehant de Galinee: Galinee's Narrative and Map with an English Version, Including All the Map Legends*. Pt. I. Ontario Historical Society Papers and Records, no. 4, Willowdale, 1903.

Crane, Verner W. "An Historical Note on the Westo Indians." *American Anthropologist*, n.s. 20 (1918): 331–37.

———. "The Origin of the Name of the Creek Indians." *Mississippi Valley Historical Review* 5, no. 3 (1918): 339–42.

———. *The Southern Frontier, 1670–1732*. Durham NC: Duke University Press, 1929.

———. *The Southern Frontier, 1670–1732*. 1929. Ann Arbor: University of Michigan Press, 1956.

———. *The Southern Frontier, 1670–1732*. 1929. New York: Norton, 1981.

———. *The Southern Frontier: 1670–1732*. 1929. Tuscaloosa: University of Alabama Press, 2004.

———. "Westo and Chisca." *American Anthropologist*, n.s. 21 (1919): 463–65.

Crosby, Alfred W., Jr. *The Columbian Exchange: Biological and Cultural Consequence of 1492*. Westport CT: Greenwood, 1972.

———. *Ecological Imperialism: The Biological Expansion of Europe, 900–1900*. New York: Cambridge University Press, 1993.

———. "Virgin Soil Epidemics as a Factor in Aboriginal Depopulation." *William and Mary Quarterly* 33, no. 2 (1976): 289–99.

Crown, Patricia L. "Learning to Make Pottery in the Prehispanic American Southwest." *Journal of Anthropological Research* 57 (2001): 451–69.

Cumming, William P., ed. *The Discoveries of John Lederer*. Charlottesville: University of Virginia Press, 1958.

Cumming, William P., and Louis DeVorsey, Jr., eds. *The Southeast in Early Maps*. 3rd ed. Chapel Hill: University of North Carolina Press, 1998.

Curren, Caleb. *The Protohistoric Period in Central Alabama*. Camden: Alabama Tombigbee Regional Commission, 1984.

Daniels, John D.. "The Indian Population of North America in 1492." *William and Mary Quarterly* 49, no. 2 (1992): 298–320.

Dávilla Padilla, Augustín. "Historia de la Fundacion y Discurso de la Provincia de Santiago de Mexico de la Orden de Predicadores par los Vidas de sus Varones Insignes y Casos Notables de Nueve España." Translated by Fanny Bandelier. In *Early History of the Creek Indians and Their Neighbors*, edited by John R. Swanton, 231–39. 1922. Bureau of American Ethnology, bulletin 73. Gainesville: University Press of Florida, 1998.

Davis, R. P. Stephen, Jr. "The Cultural Landscape of the North Carolina Piedmont at Contact." In *The Transformation of the Southeastern Indians, 1540–1760*, edited by Robbie Ethridge and Charles Hudson, 135–54. Jackson: University Press of Mississippi, 2002.

Davis, R. P. Stephen, Jr., Patrick Livingood, H. Trawick Ward, and Vincas Steponaitis, eds. "Excavating Occaneechi Town: Archaeology of an Eighteenth-Century Village in North Carolina." Research Laboratories of Archaeology

Site Report, Web edition, University of North Carolina, 2003. http://www
.ibiblio.org/dig/html/index.html, accessed June 24, 2007.

Deale, Valerie B. "The History of the Potawatomis before 1722." *Ethnohistory* 5,
no. 4 (1958): 305–60.

Debo, Angie. *The Road to Disappearance: A History of the Creek Indians.* Norman:
University of Oklahoma Press, 1979.

DeJarnette, David, ed. *Archaeological Salvage in the Walter F. George Basin of
the Chattahoochee River in Alabama.* Tuscaloosa: University of Alabama
Press, 1975.

DeJarnette, David L., and Christopher H. Peebles. "The Development of Alabama Archaeology: The Snows Bend Site." *Journal of Alabama Archaeology*
16 (1970): 77–119.

Deloria, Vine. *God is Red: A Native View of Religion.* 1973. Golden CO: Fulcrum,
2003.

DePratter, Chester. "The Chiefdom of Cofitachequi." In *The Forgotten Centuries:
Indians and Europeans in the American South, 1521–1704*, edited by Charles
Hudson and Carmen Chaves Tesser, 197–226. Athens: University of Georgia
Press, 1994.

———. "Late Prehistoric and Early Historic Chiefdoms in the Southeastern United
States." PhD diss., University of Georgia, 1983.

DePratter, Chester B., Charles M. Hudson, and Marvin Smith. "The Hernando de
Soto Expedition: From Chiaha to Mabila." In *Alabama and the Borderlands:
From Prehistory to Statehood*, edited by R. Reid Badger and Lawrence A.
Clayton, 108–27. Tuscaloosa: University of Alabama Press, 1985.

———. "Juan Pardo's Explorations in the Interior Southeast, 1566–1568." *Florida
Historical Quarterly* 62 (1983): 125–58.

DePratter, Chester B., and Christopher Judge. "Wateree River Phases." In *Lamar
Archaeology: Mississippian Chiefdoms in the Deep South*, edited by M. Williams
and G. Shapiro, 56–58. Tuscaloosa: University of Alabama Press, 1990.

DeVorsey, Louis, Jr. "The Colonial Georgia Backcountry." In *Colonial Augusta
"Key of the Indian Countrey,"* edited by Edward J. Cashin, 3–26. Macon GA:
Mercer University Press, 1988.

———. "The Impact of the LaSalle Expedition of 1682 on European Cartography."
In *La Salle and His Legacy: Frenchmen and Indians in the Lower Mississippi
Valley*, edited by Patricia K. Galloway, 60–78. Jackson: University Press of
Mississippi, 1982.

Diamond, Jared M. *Guns, Germs, and Steel: The Fates of Human Societies.* New York: Norton, 1999.

Dickens, Roy S. "Archaeology of the Jones Bluff Reservoir of Central Alabama." *Journal of Alabama Archaeology* 17 (1971): 1–107.

Dobyns, Henry F. "Disease Transfer at Contact." *Annual Review of Anthropology,* 23 (1993): 273–91.

——. *Their Number Become Thinned: Native American Population Dynamics in Eastern North America.* Knoxville: University of Tennessee Press, 1983.

Dowling, Lee. "La Florida del Inca: Garcilaso's Literary Sources." In *The Hernando De Soto Expedition: History, Historiography, and "Discovery" in the Southeast,* edited by Patricia Galloway, 98–154. Lincoln: University of Nebraska Press, 1997.

Drooker, Penelope B. "The Ohio Valley, 1550–1750: Patterns of Sociopolitical Coalescence and Dispersal." In *The Transformation of the Southeastern Indians, 1540–1760,* edited by Robbie Ethridge and Charles Hudson, 118–24. Jackson: University Press of Mississippi, 2002.

——. *The View from Madisonville: Protohistoric Western Fort Ancient Interaction Patterns.* Memoirs of the Museum of Anthropology, no. 31, University of Michigan, Ann Arbor, 1997.

Duffy, John. *Epidemics in Colonial America.* Baton Rouge: Louisiana State University Press, 1953.

Dumont de Montigny, Jean François Benjamin. *Mémoires historiques sur la Louisiane contenant ce qui est arrivé de plus mémorable depuis l'année 1687.* 3 vols. Paris: Bauche, 1753.

Dunaway, Wilma A. *Slavery in the American Mountain South.* New York: Cambridge University Press, 2003.

Dunn, S. "Effects of the Mahican-Mohawk Wars on the Transfer of Mahican Land." In *Proceedings of the 1992 People to People Conference Selected Papers,* no. 23, edited by C. F. Hayes III, C. Bodner, and L. Saunders, 85–103. Rochester NY: Rochester Museum and Science Center Research Records, 1994.

Durschlag, Richard. "The First Creek Resistance: Transformations in Creek Indian Existence and the Yamasee War, 1670–1730." PhD diss., Duke University, 1995.

Du Ru, Paul. *Journal of Paul Du Ru (February 1 to May 8, 1700): Missionary Priest to Louisiana.* 1934. Translated by Ruth Lapham Butler. Oakesdale WA: Ye Galleon, 1997.

DuVal, Kathleen. *The Native Ground: Indians and Colonists in the Heart of the Continent*. Philadelphia: University of Pennsylvania Press, 2006.

Dye, David H. "Art, Ritual, and Chiefly Warfare in the Mississippian World." In *Hero, Hawk, and Open Hand: American Indian Art of the Ancient Midwest and South*, edited by Richard F. Townsend, 191–206. New Haven CT: Yale University Press, 2004.

———. "Warfare in the Protohistoric Southeast." In *Between Contact and Colonies: Archaeological Perspectives on the Protohistoric Southeast*, edited by Cameron Wesson and Mark Rees, 126–41. Tuscaloosa: University of Alabama Press, 2002.

Dye, David H., and Cheryl Ann Cox, eds. *Towns and Temples along the Mississippi*. Tuscaloosa: University of Alabama Press, 1990.

Earle, Peter. *The Pirate Wars*. New York: Holtzbrinck, 2006.

Early, Ann M. *Caddoan Saltmakers in the Ouchita Valley: The Hardeman Site*. Arkansas Archaeological Survey Research Series, no. 43, Fayetteville, 1983.

———. "The Caddos of the Trans-Mississippi South." In *Indians of the Greater Southeast: Historical Archaeology and Ethnohistory*, edited by Bonnie G. McEwan, 123–33. Gainesville: University Press of Florida, 2000.

East, G. "The Concept and Political Status of the Shatter Zone." In *Geographical Essays on Eastern Europe*, edited by N. J. G. Pounds, 1–27. Bloomington: Indiana University Press, 1961.

Echo-Hawk, Roger C. "Ancient History in the New World: Integrating Oral Traditions and the Archaeological Record in Deep Time." *American Antiquity* 65 (2000): 267–90.

Edmunds, R. David. *The Shawnee Prophet*. Lincoln: University of Nebraska Press, 1983.

Elliott, J. H. *Empires of the Atlantic World: Britain and Spain in America, 1492–1830*. New Haven CT: Yale University Press, 2006.

———. *Imperial Spain, 1492–1716*. 1963. New York: Penguin, 1990.

Ellyson, Moses. *The Richmond Directory and Business Advertiser for 1856*. Richmond VA: H. K. Ellyson, 1856.

Emerson, Thomas E. *Cahokia and the Archaeology of Power*. Tuscaloosa: University of Alabama Press, 1997.

———. "Contributions of Transportation Archaeology to American Bottom Prehistory." *Southeastern Archaeology* 25, no. 2 (2006): 155–328.

———. "An Introduction to Cahokia 2002: Diversity, Complexity, and History." *Midcontinental Journal of Archaeology* 27 (2002): 135–39.

Engelbrecht, William. *Iroquoia: The Development of A Native World*. Syracuse NY: Syracuse University Press, 2003.

Esarey, Duane. "The 17th Century Midwestern Slave Trade in Colonial Context." Paper presented at the annual meeting of the Midwest Archaeological Conference, South Bend IN, 2007.

Essenpreis, Patricia D. "Fort Ancient Settlement: Differential Response at a Mississippian-Late Woodland Interface." In *Mississippian Settlement Patterns*, edited by Bruce D. Smith, 141–167. New York: Academic Press, 1978.

Ethridge, Robbie. "Creating the Shatter Zone: The Indian Slave Traders and the Collapse of the Southeastern Chiefdoms." In *Light on the Path: The Anthropology and History of the Southeastern Indians*, edited by Thomas J. Pluckhahn and Robbie Ethridge, 207–18. Tuscaloosa: University of Alabama Press, 2006.

———. *Creek Country: The Creek Indians and their World*. Chapel Hill: University of North Carolina Press, 2003.

———. "Ethnohistory." In "The Chickasaws: Economics, Politics, and Social Organization in the Early 18th Century," by Jay K. Johnson, John W. O'Hear, Robbie Ethridge, Brad Lieb, Susan L. Scott, H. Edwin Jackson, Keith Jacobi, and Donna Courtney Rausch, 8.10–8.13. Final report, National Endowment for the Humanities Grant, no. RZ-20620-00, coauthored with Center for Archaeological Research, University of Mississippi, Oxford, 2004.

———. "From Chicaza to Chickasaw: The European Invasion and the Transformation of a Southern Indian Society." Chapel Hill: University of North Carolina Press, manuscript in preparation.

———. "The Making of a Militaristic Slaving Society: The Chickasaws and the Colonial Indian Slave Trade." In *Indian Slavery in Colonial America*, edited by Alan Gallay. Lincoln: University of Nebraska Press, 2010.

———. "Raiding the Remains: the Indian Slave Trade and the Collapse of the Mississippian Chiefdoms." Paper presented at the annual meeting of the Southeastern Archaeological Conference, Chattanooga, 2001.

———. "Shatter Zone: Early Colonial Slave Raiding and its Consequences for the Natives of the Eastern Woodlands." Paper presented at the annual meeting of the Society for Ethnohistory, Riverside CA, 2004.

Ethridge, Robbie, and Charles Hudson, eds. *The Transformation of the Southeastern Indians, 1540–1760*. Jackson: University Press of Mississippi, 2002.

Everett, Christopher S. "'They Shalbe Slaves for Their Lives': Indian Slavery in Colonial Virigina." In *Indian Slavery in Colonial America*, edited by Alan Gallay. Lincoln: University of Nebraska Press, 2010.

Ewen, Charles. "Continuity and Change: De Soto and the Apalachee." *Historical Archaeology* 30, no. 2 (1996): 41–53.

Fairbanks, Charles H. "The Abercrombie Mound, Russell County, Alabama." *Early Georgia* 2, no. 1 (1955): 13–19.

———. "Creek and Pre-Creek." In *Archaeology of the Eastern United States*, edited by James B. Griffin, 285–300. Chicago: University of Chicago Press, 1952.

———. "Some Problems of the Origin of Creek Pottery." *Florida Anthropologist* 11, no. 2 (1958): 53–64.

Feld, Steven, and Keith H. Basso, eds. *Senses of Place*. Santa Fe: School of American Research Press, 1996.

Ferguson, Leland G. "South Appalachian Mississippian." PhD diss., University of North Carolina, 1971.

Ferguson, R. Brian. *Yanomami Warfare: A Political History*. Santa Fe: School of American Research Press, 1995.

Ferguson, R. Brian, and Neil L. Whitehead. Preface to the Second Edition. In *War in the Tribal Zone: Expanding States and Indigenous Warfare*, edited by R. Brian Ferguson and Neil L. Whitehead, xi–xxviii. 2nd ed. Santa Fe: School of American Research Press, 1999.

———. "The Violent Edge of Empire." In *War in the Tribal Zone: Expanding States and Indigenous Warfare*, edited by R. Brian Ferguson and Neil L. Whitehead, 1–30. 1992. 2nd ed. Santa Fe: School of American Research, 1999.

———. *War in the Tribal Zone: Expanding States and Indigenous Warfare*. Santa Fe: School of American Research, 1992.

Ferris, Neal. "In Their Time: Archaeological Histories of Native-Lived Contacts and Colonialisms, Southwestern Ontario AD 1400–1900." PhD diss., McMaster University, 2006.

Fitts, Mary Elizabeth. "Mapping Catawba Coalescence." *North Carolina Archaeology* 55 (2006): 1–59.

Fitzgerald, William. R. "Contact, Neutral Iroquoian Transformation, and the Little Ice Age." In *Societies in Eclipse: Archaeology of the Eastern Woodlands Indians, AD 1400–1700*, edited by David S. Brose, C. Wesley Cowan, and Robert C. Mainfort, Jr., 37–47. Washington DC: Smithsonian Institution Press, 2001.

Fogelson, Raymond D., ed. *Handbook of North American Indians*. Vol. 14, *Southeast*. Washington DC: Smithsonian Institution Press, 2004.

Force, Peter. *Tracts and Other Papers Relating Principally to the Origin, Settlement, and Progress of the Colonies in North America*. 4 vols. Gloucester MA: Peter Smith, 1963.

Fortier, Andrew C., Thomas E. Emerson, and Dale L. McElrath. "Calibrating and Reassessing American Bottom Culture History." *Southeastern Archaeology* 25 (2006): 170–211.

Foster, H. Thomas, III. *Archaeology of the Lower Muskogee Creek Indians, 1715–1836.* Tuscaloosa: University of Alabama Press.

Foster, William C., ed. *The La Salle Expedition on the Mississippi River: A Lost Manuscript of Nicolas de La Salle, 1682.* Austin: Texas State Historical Association, 2003.

Fowler, Melvin C., Jerome Rose, Barbara Vander Leest, and Steven A. Ahler. *The Mound 72 Area: Dedicated and Sacred Space in Early Cahokia.* Illinois State Museum, Reports of Investigations, no. 54, Springfield, 1999.

Fox, William A. "Dragon Sideplates from York Factory: A New Twist on an Old Tail." *Manitoba Archaeological Journal* 2, no. 2 (1992): 21–35.

———. "Horned Panthers and Erie Associates." In *A Passion for the Past: Papers in Honour of James F. Pendergast*, edited by J. V. Wright and J. L. Pilon, 283–304. Archaeological Survey of Canada Mercury Series, paper 164. Gatineau: Canadian Museum of Civilization, 2004.

———. "The North-South Copper Axis." *Southeastern Archaeology* 23, no. 1 (2004): 85-97.

———. "The Odawa." In *The Archaeology of Southern Ontario to AD 1650*, edited by E. C. Ellis and N. Ferris, 457–73. Occasional Publication of the OAS London Chapter, no. 5, 1990.

———. "Of Projectile Points and Politics." *Arch Notes, Newsletter of the Ontario Archaeological Society* 80, no. 2 (1980): 5–13.

———. "Thaniba Wakondagi among the Ontario Iroquois." *Canadian Journal of Archaeology* 26, no. 2 (2002): 130–51.

Frank, Andrew K. *Creeks and Southerners: Biculturalism on the Early American Frontier.* Lincoln: University of Nebraska Press, 2005.

Fried, Morton Herbert. *The Evolution of Political Society: An Essay in Political Anthropology.* New York: McGraw-Hill, 1967.

Fuller, Richard. "The Bear Point Phase of the Pensacola Variant: The Protohistoric Period in Southwest Alabama." *The Florida Anthropologist* 38, no. 2 (1985).

———. "Out of the Moundville Shadow: The Origin and Evolution of Pensacola Culture." In *Bottle Creek: A Pensacola Culture Site in South Alabama*, edited by Ian W. Brown and Penelope B. Drooker, 27–62. Tuscaloosa: University of Alabama Press, 2003.

Gall, Daniel G., and Vincas Steponaitis. "Composition and Provenance of Greenstone Artifacts from Moundville." *Southeastern Archaeology* 20, no. 2 (2001): 99–117.

Gallay, Alan. "Beachheads into Empires, Villages into Confederacies: Atlantic World Trade and the Transformation of the American South." Paper presented at Transformations: The Atlantic World in the Late Seventeenth Century, Harvard University, Cambridge MA, 2006.

———. "Charles Town, South Carolina: Hot Spot in the Atlantic World." Paper presented at the Center for Historic Research, The Ohio State University, Columbus, 2008.

———. *The Indian Slave Trade: The Rise of the English Empire in the American South, 1670–1717.* New Haven CT: Yale University Press, 2002.

Gallivan, Martin D. "Powhatan's Werowocomoco: Constructing Place, Polity, and Personhood in the Chesapeake, CE 1200 to CE 1609." *American Anthropologist*, n.s. 109, no. 1 (2007): 85–101.

Galloway, Patricia. "'The Chief Who Is Your Father': Choctaw and French Views of Diplomatic Relation." In *Powhatan's Mantle: Indians in the Colonial Southeast*, edited by Peter H. Wood, Gregory A Waselkov, and M. Thomas Hatley, 254–78. Lincoln: University of Nebraska Press, 1989.

———. "Choctaw Factionalism and Civil War, 1746–1750." *Journal of Mississippi History* 44, no. 4 (1982): 289–327.

———. *Choctaw Genesis, 1500–1700.* Lincoln: University of Nebraska Press, 1995.

———. "Confederation as a Solution to Chiefdom Dissolution: Historical Evidence in the Choctaw Case." In *The Forgotten Centuries: Indians and Europeans in the American South, 1521–1704*, edited by Charles Hudson and Carmen Chaves Tesser, 393–420. Athens: University of Georgia Press, 1994.

———. "Dual Organization Reconsidered: Eighteenth-Century Choctaw Chiefs and the Exploration of Social Design Space." In *Practicing Ethnohistory: Mining Archives, Hearing Testimony, Constructing Narrative*, by Patricia Galloway, 357–73. Lincoln: University of Nebraska Press, 2007.

———. "Henri de Tonti du Village des Chacta, 1702: The Beginning of the French Alliance." In *La Salle and His Legacy: Frenchmen and Indians in the Lower Mississippi Valley*, edited by Patricia K. Galloway, 146–75. Jackson: University Press of Mississippi, 1982.

———, ed. *The Hernando de Soto Expedition: History, Historiography, and "Discovery" in the Southeast.* Lincoln: University of Nebraska Press, 1997.

———. "The Incestuous Soto Narratives." In *The Hernando de Soto Expedition:*

History, Historiography, and "Discovery" in the Southeast, edited by Patricia Galloway, 11–44. Lincoln: University of Nebraska Press, 1997.

———. "The Medal Chief's *Grosse Lettre*: A Chapter in French Indian Policy." In *Practicing Ethnohistory: Mining Archives, Hearing Testimony, Constructing Narrative*, by Patricia Galloway, 292–310. Lincoln: University of Nebraska Press, 2006.

———. "Natchez Matrilineal Kinship: Du Pratz and the Woman's Touch." In *Practicing Ethnohistory: Mining Archives, Hearing Testimony, Constructing Narrative*, by Patricia Galloway, 97–108. Lincoln: University of Nebraska Press, 2006.

———. "'So Many Little Republics': British Negotiations with the Choctaw Confederacy, 1765." *Ethnohistory* 41, no. 4 (1994): 513–38.

———, ed. *The Southeastern Ceremonial Complex: Artifacts and Analysis, The Cottonlandia Conference Exhibition Catalog*. Lincoln: University of Nebraska Press, 1989.

Galloway, Patricia, and Jason Baird Jackson. "Natchez and Neighboring Groups." In *Handbook of North American Indians*. Vol. 14, *Southeast*, edited by Raymond D. Fogelson, 598–615. Washington DC: Smithsonian Institution Press, 2004.

Galloway, Patricia, Marvin D. Jeter, Gregory A. Waselkov, John E. Worth, and Ives Goddard. "Small Tribes of the Western Southeast." In *Handbook of North American Indians*. Vol. 14, *Southeast*, edited by Raymond D. Fogelson, 174–90. Washington DC: Smithsonian Institution Press, 2004.

Games, Alison. "Beyond the Atlantic: English Globetrotters and Transoceanic Connections." *William and Mary Quarterly* 63, no. 4 (2006): 675–92.

Garcilaso de la Vega, the Inca. "La Florida." In *The De Soto Chronicles: The Expedition of Hernando de Soto to North America in 1539–1543*, edited by Lawrence A. Clayton, Vernon James Knight, Jr., and Edward C. Moore, translated by Charmion Shelby, 25–560. Vol. 2. Tuscaloosa: University of Alabama Press, 1993.

Garrad, C., T. Abler, and L. Hancks. "On the Survival of the Neutrals." *Arch Notes, Newsletter of the Ontario Archaeological Society* 8, no. 2 (2003): 9–21.

Gatschet, Albert S. *A Creek Migration Legend*. 1884. Vol. 1. Library of Aboriginal American Literature, no. 4. Edited by D. G. Brinton. New York: Krause Reprint, 1969.

———. "Grammatic Sketch of the Catawba Language." *American Anthropologist*, n.s. 2 (1900): 527–29.

———. *A Migration Legend of the Creek Indians with a Linguistic, Historic, and Ethnographic Introduction.* 4 Vols. Philadelphia: Brinton, 1884–88.

Gentleman of Elvas. "True Relation of the Vicissitudes That Attended the Governor Don Hernando de Soto and Some Nobles of Portugal in the Discovery of the Provence of Florida." In *The De Soto Chronicles: The Expedition of Hernando de Soto to North America in 1539–1543*, edited by Lawrence A. Clayton, Vernon. J. Knight, Jr., and Edward C. Moore, translated by James Robertson, 25–219. Vol 1. Tuscaloosa: University of Alabama Press, 1993.

Gibson, Jon L. "Aboriginal Warfare in the Protohistoric Southeast: An Alternative Perspective." *American Antiquity* 39, no. 1 (1974): 130–33.

Glover, Captain. "Captain Glover's Account of Indian Tribes." *South Carolina Historical and Genealogical Magazine* 32 (1931): 241–42.

Goad, Sharon I. "Copper and the Southeastern Indians." *Early Georgia* 4 (1976): 49–67.

Goddard, Ives. "Delaware." In *Handbook of North American Indians.* Vol. 15, *Northeast*, edited by Bruce Trigger, 213–39. Washington DC: Smithsonian Institution Press, 1978.

Goddard, Ives, Patricia Galloway, Marvin D. Jeter, Gregory A. Waselkov, and John E. Worth. "Small Tribes of the Western Southeast." In *Handbook of North American Indians.* Vol. 14, *Southeast*, edited by Raymond D. Fogelson, 174–90. Washington DC: Smithsonian Institution Press, 2004.

Graeber, David. *Toward an Anthropological Theory of Value: The False Coin of Our Own Dreams.* New York: Palgrave, 2001.

Granovetter, Mark. "Economic Action and Social Structure: The Problem of Embeddedness." *American Journal of Sociology* 91, no. 3 (1985): 481–510.

Green, Michael D., and Theda Perdue. Series Editors' Introduction. In *The Invention of the Creek Nation, 1670–1763*, by Steven C. Hahn, xi–xii. Lincoln: University of Nebraska Press, 2004.

Green, William, ed. *Oneota Archaeology: Past, Present, and Future.* Office of the State Archaeologist report, no. 20, University of Iowa, Iowa City, 1995.

Green, William G. "The Erie/Westo Connection: Possible Evidence of Long Distance Migration in the Eastern Woodlands during the 16th and 17th Centuries." Paper presented at the annual meeting of the Southeastern Archaeological Conference, Greenville SC, 1998.

Green, William G., Chester B. DePratter, and Bobby Southerlin. "The Yamasee in South Carolina." In *Another's Country: Archaeological and Historical Perspectives on Cultural Interactions in the Southern Colonies*, edited by

J. W. Joseph and Martha Zierden, 13–29. Tuscaloosa: University of Alabama Press, 2002.

Gregory, C. A. *Gifts and Commodities.* London: Academic Press, 1982.

Gremillion, Kristen J. "Adoption of Old World Crops and Processes of Cultural Change in the Historic Southeast." *Southeastern Archaeology* 12 (1993): 15–20.

Griffin, James B. "The Archaeological Remains of the Chiwere Sioux." *American Antiquity* 2 (1937): 180–81.

———. *The Fort Ancient Aspect.* University of Michigan Museum of Anthropology Papers, no. 28, Ann Arbor, 1966 [1941].

Grumet, Robert S., ed. *Northeastern Indian Lives, 1632–1816.* Amherst: University of Massachusetts Press, 1996.

Hahn, Steven C. "The Cussita Migration Legend: History, Ideology, and the Politics of Mythmaking." In *Light on the Path: The Anthropology and History of the Southeastern Indians,* edited by Thomas J. Pluckhahn and Robbie Ethridge, 57–93. Tuscaloosa: University of Alabama Press, 2006.

———. "The Invention of the Creek Nation." PhD diss. Emory University, 2000.

———. *The Invention of the Creek Nation, 1670–1763.* Lincoln: University of Nebraska Press, 2004.

———. "A Miniature Arms Race: The Role of the Flintlock in Initiating Indian Dependency in the Colonial Southeastern United States 1656–1730." Master's thesis, University of Georgia, 1995.

———. "The Mother of Necessity: Carolina, the Creek Indians, and the Making of a New Order in the American Southeast, 1670–1763." In *The Transformation of the Southeastern Indians, 1540–1760,* edited by Robbie Ethridge and Charles Hudson, 79–114. Jackson: University Press of Mississippi, 2002.

Hall, Joseph M. "Making an Indian People: Creek Formation in the Colonial Southeast, 1590–1735." PhD diss., University of Wisconsin, 2001.

———. *Zamumo's Gifts: Indian-European Exchange in the Colonial Southeast.* Philadelphia: University of Pennsylvania Press, 2009.

Hall, Robert L. *An Archaeology of the Soul: North American Indian Belief and Ritual.* Urbana and Chicago: University of Illinois Press, 1997.

———. "Cahokia Identity and Interaction Models of Cahokia Mississippian." In *Cahokia and the Hinterlands,* edited by Thomas E. Emerson and R. Barry Lewis, 3–34. Urbana: University of Illinois Press, 1991.

———. "The Cahokia Site and Its People." In *Hero, Hawk, and Open Hand:*

American Indian Art of the Ancient Midwest and South, edited by Richard F. Townsend, 92–103. New Haven CT: Yale University Press, 2004.

Hally, David J. "'As Caves Beneath the Ground': Making Sense of Aboriginal House Form in the Protohistoric and Historic Southeast." In *Between Contacts and Colonies: Archaeological Perspectives on the Protohistoric Southeast*, edited by Cameron B. Wesson and Mark A. Rees, 90–109. Tuscaloosa: University of Alabama Press, 2002.

———. "The Chiefdom of Coosa." In *The Forgotten Centuries: Indians and Europeans in the American South, 1521–1704*, edited by Charles Hudson and Carmen Chaves Tesser, 227–53. Athens: University of Georgia Press, 1994.

———. "The Nature of Mississippian Regional Systems." In *Light on the Path: The Anthropology and History of the Southeastern Indians*, edited by Thomas H. Pluckhahn and Robbie Ethridge, 26–42. Tuscaloosa: University of Alabama Press, 2006.

———. "An Overview of Lamar Culture." In *Ocmulgee Archaeology 1936–1986*, edited by David J. Halley, 144–74. Athens: University of Georgia Press, 1994.

Hally, David J., and James B. Langford, Jr. *Mississippi Period Archaeology of the Georgia Valley and Ridge Province*. University of Georgia Laboratory of Archaeology Series, report no. 25, Athens, 1988.

Hally, David J., and James L. Rudolph. *Mississippi Period Archaeology of the Georgia Piedmont*. University of Georgia Laboratory of Archaeology Series, report no. 24, Athens, 1986.

Hally, David J., Marvin T. Smith, and James B. Langford, Jr., "The Archaeological Reality of De Soto's Coosa." In *Columbian Consequences*. Vol. 2, *Archaeological and Historical Perspectives on the Spanish Borderlands East*, edited by David Hurst Thomas, 121–38. Washington DC: Smithsonian Institution Press, 1990.

Hanke, Lewis. *The Spanish Struggle for Justice in the Conquest of America*. 1949. Dallas: Southern Methodist University Press, 2002.

Hann, John H. *Apalachee: the Land between the Rivers*. Gainesville: University Press of Florida, 1988.

———. "Florida's Terra Incognita: West Florida's Natives in the Sixteenth and Seventeenth Century." *Florida Anthropologist* 41 (1988): 61–107.

———. *A History of the Timucua Indians and Missions*. Gainesville: University Press of Florida, 1996.

———. *Missions to the Calusa*. Gainesville: University Press of Florida, 1991.

———. *The Native American World beyond Apalachee: West Florida, and the Chattahoochee Valley.* Gainesville: University Press of Florida, 2006.

———. "St. Augustine's Fallout From The Yamasee War." *Florida Historical Quarterly* 68, no. 2 (1989): 180–200.

———. "Translation of the Ecija Voyages of 1605 and 1609 and the González Derrotero of 1609." *Florida Archaeology* 2 (1986): 1–80.

———. "Visitations and Revolts in Florida, 1656–1695." *Florida Archaeology* 7 (1993): 1–296.

Hann, Richard L. "'The Trade Do's Not Flourish as Formerly': The Ecological Origins of the Yamasee War of 1715." *Ethnohistory* 28 (1981): 341–58.

Hanna, Charles A. *The Wilderness Trail, or, the Ventures and Adventures of the Pennsylvania Traders on the Allegheny Path with Some New Annals of the Old West, and the Records of Some Strong Men and Some Bad Ones.* 1911. 2 Vols. New York: AMS Press, 1971.

Hanson, Lee H., Jr. *The Buffalo Site: A Late 17th Century Indian Village Site (46 PU 31) in Putnam County, West Virginia.* West Virginia Geological and Economic Survey Reports of Archaeological Investigations, no. 5, Morgantown, 1975.

———. *The Hardin Village Site.* Lexington: University of Kentucky Press, 1966.

Hart, C. W. M. "A Reconsideration of the Natchez Social Structure." *American Anthropologist,* n.s. 45, no. 3 (1943): 374–86.

Hartshorne, Richard. "The Politico-Geographic Pattern of the World." *Annals of the American Academy of Political and Social Science* 218 (1941): 45–57.

———. "The United States and the 'Shatter Zone' of Europe." In *Compass of the World: A Symposium on Political Geography,* edited by Hans W. Weigert and Vilhjalmur Stefansson, 203–14. New York: Macmillan, 1944.

Havard, Gilles. *The Great Peace of Montreal of 1701 French-Native Diplomacy in the Seventeenth Century.* Translated by P. Aronoff and H. Scott. Montreal: McGill-Queens University Press, 2001.

Hawkins, Benjamin. *Letters of Benjamin Hawkins, 1796–1806.* Collections of the Georgia Historical Society, vol. 9, Savannah, 1916.

———. *A Sketch of the Creek Country in the Years 1798 and 1799.* Collections of the Georgia Historical Society, vol. 3, pt. 1, Savannah 1848.

———. "A Sketch of the Creek Country in the Years 1798 and 1799." In *Letters, Journals, and Writings of Benjamin Hawkins,* edited by C. L. Grant, 285–327. Vol. 1. Savannah: Bee-Hive Press, 1980.

Hayes, Brian. "Natural and Unnatural Disasters." *American Scientist* 93 (2005): 496–99.

Hayward, Hampton D., Caleb Curren, Ned J. Jenkins, and Keith J. Little. "Archaeological Investigations at Stephens Bluff, A Moundville III Site in the Proposed Pafallaya Province." *Journal of Alabama Archaeology* 41, no. 1 (1995): 1–36.

Hazard, Samuel, ed. *Pennsylvania Archives: Selected and Arranged from the Original Documents in the Office of the Secretary of the Commonwealth.* 12 Vols. Philadelphia: Joseph Severns, 1852–56.

———, ed. *The Register of Pennsylvania Devoted to the Preservation of Facts and Documents and Every Other Kind of Useful Information Respecting the State of Pennsylvania.* Vol. 1. Philadelphia: W. F. Geddes, 1828.

Heath, Charles L. "Catawba Militarism: Ethnohistorical and Archaeological Overviews." *North Carolina Archaeology* 53 (2004): 80–120.

Heather, Justin Lee. "Weapons of War in Colonial America: 'The Origins of a National Gun Culture.'" *Journal of Law and Politics* 53 (2003): 53–108.

Heckewelder, John. *History, Manners, and Customs of the Indian Nations.* 1876. New York: Arno, 1971.

Heidenreich, Conrad E. "An Analysis of the 17th Century Map 'Novvelle France.'" *Cartographica* 25, no. 3 (1988): 67–111.

———. "History of the St. Lawrence–Great Lakes Area to AD 1650." In *The Archaeology of Southern Ontario to AD 1650*, edited by C. Ellis and N. Ferris, 475–503. Occasional Publication of the OAS London Chapter, no. 5, 1990.

Henderson, Gwynn A. "Early European Contact in Southern Ohio." In *Ohio Archaeology: An Illustrated Chronicle of Ohio's Ancient American Indian Cultures*, edited by Bradley T. Lepper, 231. Wilmington OH: Orange Frazer, 2005.

Henderson, Gwynn A., Cynthia E. Jobe, and Christopher A. Turnbow. *Indian Occupation and Use in Northeastern and Eastern Kentucky during the Contact Period (1540–1795): An Initial Investigation.* Frankfort: Kentucky Heritage Council, 1986.

Henige, David. *Numbers from Nowhere: the American Indian Contact Population Debate.* Norman: University of Oklahoma Press, 1998.

———. "Primary Source by Primary Source? On the Role of Epidemics in New World Depopulation." *Ethnohistory* 33 (1986): 293–312.

———. "'So Unbelievable It Has To Be True': Inca Garcilaso in Two Worlds." In *The Hernando De Soto Expedition: History, Historiography, and "Discovery" in the Southeast*, edited by Patricia Galloway, 155–77. Lincoln: University of Nebraska Press, 1997.

Hening, William Waller, ed. *The Statutes at Large; Being a Collection of All the Laws of Virginia, from the First Session of the Legislature, in the year 1619*. 1820–23. 13 vols. Charlottesville: University Press of Virginia, 1969.

Henretta, James A. *The Origins of American Capitalism, Collected Essays*. Boston: Northeastern University Press, 1991.

Hensel, Paul R., and Paul F. Diehl. "Testing Empirical Propositions about Shatterbelts." *Political Geography* 13, no. 1 (1994): 33–51.

Hewatt, Alexander. *An Historical Account of the Rise and Progress of the Colonies of South Carolina and Georgia*. 1779. 2 Vols. Spartanburg SC: Reprint Company, 1971.

Hickerson, Daniel A. "Historical Processes, Epidemic Disease, and the Formation of the Hasinai Confederacy." *Ethnohistory* 44, no. 1 (1997): 31–52.

Hill, Mary Cassandra. "Protohistoric Aborigines in West-Central Alabama: Correlations to Early European Contact." In *Bioarchaeology of Native American Adaptation in the Spanish Borderlands*, edited by Brenda J. Baker and Lisa Kealhofer, 17–37. Gainesville: University Press of Florida, 1996.

Hinderaker, Eric. *Elusive Empires: Constructing Colonialism in the Ohio Valley, 1673–1800*. New York: Cambridge University Press, 1997.

Hinderaker, Eric, and Peter C. Mancall. *At the Edge of Empire: The Backcountry in British North America*. Baltimore: Johns Hopkins University Press, 2003.

Hoffman, Bernard G. *Observations on Certain Ancient Tribes of the Northern Appalachian Province*. Smithsonian Institution Bureau of American Ethnology, bulletin 191. Washington DC: Government Printing Office, 1964.

Hoffman, Michael P. "The Kinkead-Mainard Site, 3PU2: A Prehistoric Quapaw Phase Site." *The Arkansas Archeologist* 16–18 (1977): 1–41.

———. "The Protohistoric Period in the Lower and Central Arkansas River Valley in Arkansas." In *The Protohistoric Period in the Mid-South, 1500–1700: Proceedings of the 1983 Mid-South Archaeological Conference*, edited by David H. Dye and Ronald C. Brister, 24–37. Mississippi Department of Archives and History, Archaeological Reports, no. 18, Jackson, 1986.

Hoffman, Paul. "Did Coosa Decline Between 1541 and 1560?" *The Florida Anthropologist*, 50, no. 1 (1997): 25–29.

———. *A New Andalucia and a Way to the Orient: The American Southeast during the Sixteenth Century*. Baton Rouge: Louisiana State University Press, 1990.

Holland, Sharon P., and Tiya Miles, eds. *Crossing Waters, Crossing Worlds: The African Diaspora in Indian Country*. Durham NC: Duke University Press, 2006.

Hollinger, R. Eric. "Residence Patterns and Oneota Cultural Dynamics." In *Oneota Archaeology: Past, Present, and Future*, edited by William Green, 141–74. Office of the State Archaeologist, report no. 20, University of Iowa, Iowa City, 1995.

Hollis, Shirley A. "Contact, Incorporation, and the North American Southeast." *Journal of World Systems Research* 11, no. 1 (2005): 95–130.

Holmes, William F. S. "Hardin Village: a Northern Kentucky Late Fort Ancient Site's Mortuary Patterns and Social Organization." Master's thesis, University of Kentucky, 1994.

House, John H. "Wallace Bottom: A Colonial-Era Archaeological Site in the Menard Locality, Eastern Arkansas." *Southeastern Archaeology* 21 (2002): 257–68.

Howard, James H. *Shawnee! The Ceremonialism of a Native Indian Tribe and Its Cultural Background*. Athens: Ohio University Press, 1981.

———. *The Southeastern Ceremonial Complex and Its Interpretation*. Missouri Archaeological Society, memoir 6, Columbia, 1968.

Hudson, Charles. *The Catawba Nation*. Athens: University of Georgia Press, 1970.

———. "De Soto in Arkansas: A Brief Synopsis." *Arkansas Archeological Society Field Notes* 205 (1985): 3–12.

———. Introduction. In *The Transformation of the Southeastern Indians, 1540–1760*, edited by Robbie Ethridge and Charles Hudson, xxii–xxxix. Jackson: University Press of Mississippi, 2002.

———. *The Juan Pardo Expeditions: Exploration of the Carolinas and Tennessee, 1566–1568*. Washington DC: Smithsonian Institution Press, 1990.

———. *The Juan Pardo Expeditions: Exploration of the Carolinas and Tennessee, 1566–1568*. 2nd ed. Tuscaloosa: University of Alabama Press, 2005.

———. *Knights of Spain, Warriors of the Sun: Hernando de Soto and the South's Ancient Chiefdoms*. Athens: University of Georgia Press, 1997.

———. "Reconstructing the De Soto Route West of the Mississippi: Summary and Comments." In *The Expedition of Hernando De Soto West of the Mississippi, 1541–1543*, edited by Gloria A. Young and Michael P. Hoffman, 143–54. Fayetteville: University of Arkansas Press, 1993.

——— . *The Southeastern Indians.* Knoxville: University of Tennessee Press, 1976.

Hudson, Charles, Robin A. Beck, Jr., Chester DePratter, Robbie Ethridge, and John E. Worth. "On Cofitachequi." *Ethnohistory* 55, no. 3 (2008): 465–90.

Hudson, Charles, and Robbie Ethridge. "The Early Historic Transformation of the Southeastern Indians." In *Cultural Diversity in the U. S. South: Anthropological Contributions to a Region in Transition*, edited by Carole E. Hill and Patricia D. Beaver, 34–50. Athens: University of Georgia Press, 1998.

Hudson, Charles, Marvin T. Smith, and Chester DePratter. "The Hernando de Soto Expedition: From Apalachee to Chiaha." *Southeastern Archaeology* 3 (1984): 64–77.

Hudson, Charles, Marvin T. Smith, David Hally, Richard Polhemus, and Chester B. DePratter. "Coosa: A Chiefdom in the Sixteenth-Century Southeastern United States." *American Antiquity* 50, no. 4 (1985): 723–38.

Hudson, Charles, and Carmen Chaves Tesser, eds. *The Forgotten Centuries: Indians and Europeans in the American South, 1521–1704.* Athens: University of Georgia Press, 1994.

Hudson, Joyce Rockwood. *Apalachee.* Athens: University of Georgia Press, 2002.

Hunt, George T. *The Wars of the Iroquois: A Study in Intertribal Trade Relations.* 1960; reprint Madison: University of Wisconsin Press, 1967.

Hurt, Wesley R. "An Archaeological Survey of the Chattahoochee Valley." Unpublished manuscript, Mound State Monument, Moundville AL, revised 1956 [1947].

Hutchinson, Dale L. *Tatham Mound And the Bioarchaeology of European Contact: Disease And Depopulation in Central Gulf Coast Florida.* Gainesville: University Press of Florida, 2007.

Hutchinson, Dale L., and Jeffrey M. Mitchem. "Correlates of Contact: Epidemic Disease in Archaeological Context." *Historical Archaeology* 35, no. 2 (2001): 58–72.

D'Iberville, Pierre Le Moyne Sieur. *Iberville's Gulf Journals.* Edited and translated by Richebourg Gaillard McWilliams. Tuscaloosa: University of Alabama Press, 1981.

Innes, Stephen. *Creating the Commonwealth: The Economic Culture of Puritan New England.* New York: Norton, 1995.

Jackes, Mary. "The Osteology of the Grimsby Site." Report on file with the author, 1988.

Jackson, Jason Baird. "The Opposite of Powwow: Ignoring and Incorporating the Intertribal War Dance in the Oklahoma Stomp Dance Community." *Plains Anthropologist* 48 (2003): 187–239.

Jacobs, Wilbur. *Wilderness Politics and Indian Gifts: The Northern Colonial Frontier, 1748–1763*. Lincoln: University of Nebraska Press, 1950.

Jemison, E. Grace. *Historic Tales of Tallagega*. Montgomery AL: Paragon, 1959.

Jenkins, Ned J. "Archaeological Investigations in the Gainesville Lake Area of the Tennessee-Tombigbee Waterway." In *Archaeological Investigations of the Gainesville Lake Area of the Tennessee-Tombigbee Waterway*. Vol. 5, *Archaeology of the Gainesville Lake Area: Synthesis*, by Ned Jenkins, 49–149. University of Alabama, Office of Archaeological Research, Report of Investigations, no. 23, Tuscaloosa, 1982.

———. "The Early Origins of the Creeks: The Moundville Connection." Paper presented at the annual meeting of the Southeastern Archaeological Conference, St. Louis, 2004.

———. *Gainesville Lake Area Ceramic Description and Chronology*. Vol. 2, *Archaeological Investigations in the Gainesville Lake Area of the Tennessee-Tombigbee Waterway*. University of Alabama, Office of Archaeological Research, Report of Investigations, no. 12, Tuscaloosa, 1981.

———. "Prehistoric Chronology of the Lower Chattahoochee River Valley: A Preliminary Statement." *Journal of Alabama Archaeology* 24, no. 2 (1978): 73–91.

———. "The Terminal Woodland/Mississippian Transition in West and Central Alabama." *Journal of Alabama Archaeology* 49, no. 1–2 (2003): 1–62.

Jenkins, Ned J., and R. A. Krause. *The Tombigbee Watershed in Southeastern Prehistory*. Tuscaloosa: University of Alabama Press, 1986.

Jenkins, Ned J., and Cyril B. Mann. "An Archaeological Study on the Conecuh Drainage." *The Florida Anthropologist* 38, no. 2, pt. 2 (1985): 136–143.

Jenkins, Ned J., and Catherine C. Meyer. "Ceramics of the Tombigbee-Black Warrior River Valleys." *Journal of Alabama Archaeology* 44, no. 1–2 (1998): 131–87.

Jenkins, Ned J., and Craig T. Sheldon. "Native American Culture Change in Central Alabama 1700 BC-AD 1814." Draft manuscript, Fort Toulouse/Jackson State Historic Site, Alabama Historical Commission, Wetumpka AL, n.d.

Jennings, Francis. *The Ambiguous Iroquois Empire: The Covenant Chain Confederation of Indian Tribes with English Colonies from its Beginnings to the Lancaster Treaty of 1744*. New York: Norton, 1984.

Jeter, Marvin D. Discussant Comments: pts. I and II. In *The Woodland-Mississip-pian Transition: Proceedings of the Twenty-Second Mid-South Archaeological Conference*, edited by Charles H. McNutt, Stephen Williams, and Marvin D. Jeter, 73–76, 182–89. University of Memphis Anthropological Research Center, Occasional Papers, no. 25. Memphis TN: University of Memphis, 2003.

———. "From Prehistory through Protohistory to Ethnohistory in and Near the Northern Lower Mississippi Valley." In *The Transformation of the Southeastern Indians, 1540–1760*, edited by Robbie Ethridge and Charles Hudson, 177–224. Jackson: University Press of Mississippi, 2002.

———. "Late Woodland Chronology and Change in Central Alabama." *Journal of Alabama Archaeology* 23, no. 2 (1977): 112–36.

———. "The Outer Limits of Plaquemine Culture: A View from the Northerly Borderlands." In *Plaquemine Archaeology*, edited by Mark A. Rees and Patrick C. Livingood, 161–95. Tuscaloosa: University of Alabama Press, 2007.

———. "Tunicans West of the Mississippi: A Summary of Early Historic and Archaeological Evidence." In *The Protohistoric Period in the Mid-South. 1500–1700: Proceedings of the 1983 Mid-South Archaeological Conference*, edited by David H. Dye and Ronald C. Brister, 38–63. Mississippi Department of Archives and History, Archaeological Reports, no. 18, Jackson, 1986.

Jeter, Marvin D., Kathleen H. Cande, and John J. Mintz. "Goldsmith Oliver 2 (3PU306): A Protohistoric Archeological Site Near Little Rock, Arkansas." Report submitted to Federal Aviation Administration, Southwest Region, Fort Worth, by Arkansas Archeological Survey, Fayetteville, 1990.

Jeter, Marvin D., Jerome C. Rose, G. Ishmael Williams, Jr., and Anna M. Harmon. *Archeology and Bioarchaeology of the Lower Mississippi Valley and Trans-Mississippi South in Arkansas and Louisiana*. Arkansas Archeological Survey Research Series, no. 37, Fayetteville, 1989.

John, Elizabeth. *Storms Brewed in Other Men's Worlds: The Confrontation of Indians, Spanish, and French in the Southwest, 1540–1795*. 2nd ed. Norman: University of Oklahoma Press, 1996.

Johnson, Jay. "The Chickasaws." In *Indians of the Greater Southeast: Historical Archaeology and Ethnohistory*, edited by Bonnie G. McEwan, 85–121. Gainesville: University Press of Florida, 2000.

Johnson, Jay K., John W. O'Hear, Robbie Ethridge, Brad Lieb, Susan L. Scott, H. Edwin Jackson, and Keith Jacobi. "Measuring Chickasaw Adaptation on the Western Frontier of the Colonial South: A Correlation of Documentary and Archaeological Data." *Southeastern Archaeology* 27, no. 1 (2008): 1–30.

Johnson, Jay K., John W. O'Hear, Robbie Ethridge, Brad Lieb, Susan L. Scott, H. Edwin Jackson, Keith Jacobi, and Donna Courney Rausch. "The Chickasaws: Economics, Politics, and Social Organization in the Early 18th Century." Final report, National Endowment for the Humanities Grant, no. RZ-20620-00, coauthored with Center for Archaeological Research, University of Mississippi, Oxford, 2004.

Johnson, William C. "The Protohistoric Monongahela and the Case for an Iroquois Connection." In *Societies in Eclipse: Archaeology of the Eastern Woodlands Indians, AD 1400–1700*, edited by David S. Brose, C. Wesley Cowan, and Robert C. Mainfort, Jr., 67–82. Washington DC: Smithsonian Institution Press, 2001.

Jones, Calvin B. "Southern Cult Manifestations at the Lake Jackson Site, Leon County, Florida: Salvage Excavations on Mound 3." *Midcontinintal Journal of Archaeology* 7, no. 1 (1982): 3–44.

Jones, David S. *Rationalizing Epidemics: Meanings and Uses of American Indian Mortality since 1600*. Cambridge MA: Harvard University Press, 2004.

———. "Virgin Soils Revisited." *William and Mary Quarterly* 60, no. 4 (2003): 703–42.

Juricek, John T. "The Westo Indians." *Ethnohistory* 11, no. 2 (1964): 134–73.

Kamp, Kathryn A. "Prehistoric Children Working and Playing: A Southwestern Case Study in Learning Ceramics." *Journal of Anthropological Research* 57 (2001): 427–50

Keel, Bennie C. "Salvage Archaeology at the Hardins Site, 31GS29, Gaston County, North Carolina." *Southern Indian Studies* 39 (1990): 1–18.

Keeley, Lawrence. *War before Civilization: The Myth of the Peaceful Savage*. New York: Oxford University Press, 1997.

Kehoe, Alice B. *The Land of Prehistory: A Critical History of American Archaeology*. New York: Routledge, 1998.

———. "Osage Texts and Cahokia Data." In *Ancient Objects and Sacred Realms: Interpretations of Mississippian Iconography*, edited by F. Kent Reilly III and James F. Garber, 246–61. Austin: University of Texas Press, 2007.

———. "'Slaves' and Slave-Raiding on the Northern Plains and Rupert's Land." Paper presented at the annual meeting of the American Society for Ethnohistory, Santa Fe, 2005.

———. "Why Anthropologists Should Abandon the Term 'Chiefdom.'" *American Anthropology Newsletter* 45, no. 4 (2004): 10.

Kelly, P. L. "Escalation of Regional Conflict: Testing the Shatterbelt Concept." *Political Geography Quarterly* 5 (1986): 161–80.

Kelton, Paul. "Avoiding the Smallpox Spirits: Colonial Epidemics and Southeastern Indian Survival." *Ethnohistory* 51, no. 1 (2004): 45–72.

———. *Epidemics and Enslavement: Biological Catastrophe in the Native Southeast, 1492–1715.* Lincoln: University of Nebraska Press, 2007.

———. "The Great Southeastern Smallpox Epidemic, 1696–1700: The Region's First Major Epidemic?" In *The Transformation of the Southeastern Indians, 1540–1760*, edited by Robbie Ethridge and Charles Hudson, 21–38. Jackson: University Press of Mississippi, 2002.

Kenyon, Walter A. *The Grimsby Site A Historic Neutral Cemetery.* Toronto: Royal Ontario Museum, 1982.

Kimball, Geoffrey D. *Koasati Dictionary.* Lincoln: University of Nebraska Press, 1994.

King, Adam. *Etowah: The Political History of a Chiefdom Capital.* Tuscaloosa: University of Alabama Press, 2003.

———. "The Historic Period Transformation of Mississippian Societies." In *Light on the Path: The Anthropology and History of the Southeastern Indians*, edited by Thomas J. Pluckhahn and Robbie Ethridge, 179–95. Tuscaloosa: University of Alabama Press, 2006.

King, Adam, and Maureen S. Meyers, eds. "Frontiers, Backwaters, and Peripheries: Exploring the Edges of the Mississippian World." *Southeastern Archaeology*, Special Thematic Section, 21, no. 2 (2002): 113–226.

Kinietz, Vernon, and Erminie Wheeler-Voegelin, eds. *Shawnese Traditions: C. C. Trowbridge's.* Occasional Contributions from the Museum of Anthropology of the University of Michigan, no. 9. Ann Arbor: University of Michigan Press, 1939.

Kinnaird, Lawrence, ed. and trans. *Spain in the Mississippi Valley, 1765–1794.* Annual Report of the American Historical Association for the Year 1945, vols. 2, 3, and 4. Washington DC: Government Printing Office, 1946–49.

Klingburg, Frank, ed. *Carolina Chronicle: The Papers of Gideon Johnston.* University of California Publications in History. Vol. 35. Berkeley: University of California Press, 1946.

Kniffen, Fred B., Hiram F. Gregory, and George A. Stokes. *The Historic Indian Tribes of Louisiana From 1542 to the Present.* Baton Rouge: Louisiana State University Press, 1987.

Knight, Vernon. J., Jr. "Ceramic Stratigraphy at the Singer-Moye Site, 9sw2." *Journal of Alabama Archaeology* 25 (1979): 138–51.

——. "The Formation of the Creeks." In *The Forgotten Centuries: Indians and Europeans in the American South 1521–1704*, edited by Charles Hudson and Carmen Chaves Tesser, 373–92. Athens: University of Georgia Press, 1994.

——. "The Institutional Organization of Mississippian Religion." *American Antiquity* 51, no. 4 (1986): 675–87.

——. "Ocmulgee Fields Culture and the Historical Development of Creek Ceramics." In *Ocmulgee Archaeology: 1936–1986*, edited by David J. Halley, 181–89. Athens: University of Georgia Press, 1994.

——. "Social Organization and the Evolution of Hierarchy in Southeastern Chiefdoms." *Journal of Anthropological Research* 46, no. 1 (1990): 1–23.

——. *Tukabatchee: Archaeological Investigations at an Historic Creek Town, Elmore County, Alabama, 1984*. University of Alabama, Office of Archaeological Research, Report of Investigations, no. 45, Tuscaloosa, 1985.

Knight, Vernon J., Jr., and Sherée L. Adams, eds. "A Voyage to the Mobile and Tomeh in 1700, with Notes on the Interior of Alabama." *Ethnohistory* 28, no. 2 (1981): 179–94.

Knight, Vernon J., Jr., and Tim S. Mistovitch. *Walter F. George Lake: Archaeological Survey of Fee Owned Lands Alabama and Georgia*. University of Alabama, Office of Archaeological Research, Report of Investigations, no. 42, Tuscaloosa, 1984.

Knight, Vernon J., Jr., and Marvin Smith. "Big Tallassee: A Contribution to Upper Creek Site Archaeology." *Early Georgia* 8, no. 1–2 (1980): 59–74.

Knight, Vernon J., Jr., and Vincas P. Steponaitis, eds. *Archaeology of the Moundville Chiefdom*. Washington DC: Smithsonian Institution Press, 1998.

——. "A New History of Moundville." In *Archaeology of the Moundville Chiefdom*, edited by Vernon James Knight, Jr., and Vincas P. Steponaitis, 1–25. Washington DC: Smithsonian Institution Press, 1998.

Koeppel, Christopher. "Middle Woodland in a 'Shatter Zone': Ceramics from the Ameren Sites in Southern Illinois." Paper presented at the annual meeting of the Society for American Archaeology, Denver, 2002.

Kowalewski, Stephen A. "Coalescent Societies." In *Light on the Path: The Anthropology and History of the Southeastern Indians*, edited by Thomas J. Pluckhahn and Robbie Ethridge, 94–122. Tuscaloosa: University of Alabama Press, 2006.

Kowalewski, Stephen A., and James W. Hatch. "The Sixteenth-Century Expansion of Settlement in the Upper Oconee Watershed, Georgia." *Southeastern Archaeology* 10 (1991): 1–17.

Krause, Richard K. "A History of Great Plains Prehistory." In *Archaeology on the Great Plains*, edited by Raymond W. Wood, 48–86. Lawrence: University of Kansas Press, 1998.

Krauthamer, Barbara. "A Particular Kind of Freedom: Black Women, Kinship, Slavery, and Freedom in the American Southeast." In *Women and Slavery*. Vol. 2, *The Modern Atlantic*, edited by Gwyn Campbell, Susan Miers, and Joseph Miller, 100–27. Athens: Ohio University Press, 2007.

Kroeber, Alfred L. *Cultural and Natural Areas of Native North America*. University of California, Publications in American Archaeology and Ethnography, vol. 38, Berkeley, 1939.

Kuhn, R. D., and R. E. Funk. "Mohawk Interaction Patterns during the Late Sixteenth Century." In *Proceedings of the 1992 People to People Conference*, edited by C. F. Hayes III, C. Bodner, and L. Saunders, 77–84. Rochester Museum and Science Center Research Records, Rochester NY, 1994.

Kupperman, Karen Ordahl. *The Jamestown Project*. New York: Belknap, 2007.

Lafitau, Joseph-François. *Customs of the American Indians Compared with the Customs of Primitive Times*. 2 Vols. Edited and translated by W. L Fenton and E. L. Moore. Publications of the Champlain Society, nos. 48 and 49. Toronto: Champlain Society, 1974 and 1977.

———. *Moeurs des sauvages ameriquains, comparées aux moeurs des premiers temps*. 2 Vols. Paris: Saugrain l'aîne, 1724.

La Harpe, Jean-Batiste Bénard. *Historical Journal of the Settlement of the French in Louisiana*. Edited by Glenn R. Conrad, translated by Virginia Koenig and Joan Cain. Lafayette LA: University of Southwestern Louisiana, 1971.

Lamb, H. H. "Climate History in Northern Europe and Elsewhere" In *Climatic Changes on a Yearly to Millennial Basis: Geological, Historical, and Instrumental Records*, edited by N. A. Morner and W. Karlen, 225–40. Dordrecht, Netherlands: Reidel, 1984.

Lamoreaux, Naomi R. "Rethinking the Transition to Capitalism in the Early American Northeast." *Journal of American History* 90, no. 2 (2003): 1–22.

Langdon, H. H. "Father Joseph de la Roche Daillon Letter of July 18, 1627, Concerning His Time among the Neutral." *KEWA Newsletter of the London Chapter, Ontario Archaeological Society* 81, no. 9 (1981): 2–7.

Langford, James B., and Marvin Smith. "Two Late Lamar Sites Near Rays Corner, Oconee County, Georgia." In *Lamar Archaeology, Mississippian Chiefdoms in the Deep South*, edited by Mark Williams and Gary Shapiro, 104–16. Tuscaloosa: University of Alabama Press, 1990.

Langlois, Gilles-Antoine. *Des villes pour la Louisiane française: théorie et pratique de l'urbanistique coloniale au 18e siécle.* Paris: L'Harmattan, 2003.

Lankford, George. *Looking for Lost Lore: Studies in Folklore Ethnology, and Iconography in Eastern North America.* Tuscaloosa: University of Alabama Press, 2008.

Lapham, Heather. "Glass Beads from the Abbyville Site." In *Abbyville: A Complex of Archaeological Sites in John H. Kerr Reservoir, Halifax County, Virginia,* edited by R. P. Stephen Davis, Jr., and Howard A. MacCord, Sr., 193–206. The Archaeological Society of Virginia, Special Publication, no. 39, Richmond, 2002.

———. *Hunting for Hides: Deerskins, Status, and Cultural Change in the Protohistoric Appalachians.* Tuscaloosa: University of Alabama Press, 2005.

Larsen, Clark Spencer, ed. *Bioarchaeology of Spanish Florida: The Impact of Colonialism.* Gainesville: University Press of Florida, 2001.

Larsen, Clark Spencer, Mark C. Griffin, Dale L. Hutchinson, Vivian E. Noble, Lynette Norr, Robert F. Pastor, Christopher B. Ruff, Katherine F. Russell, Margaret J. Schoeninger, Michael Schultz, Scott W. Simpson, and Mark F. Teaford. "Frontiers of Contact: Bioarchaeology of Spanish Florida." *Journal of World Prehistory* 15, no. 1 (2001): 69–123.

Larsen, Clark Spencer, Christopher B. Ruff, and Mark C. Griffin. "Implications of Changing Biomechanical and Nutritional Environments for Activity and Lifeways in the Eastern Spanish Borderlands." In *Bioarchaeology of Native American Adaptation in the Spanish Borderlands,* edited by Brenda J. Baker and Lisa Kealhofer, 95–125. Gainesville: University Press of Florida, 1996.

Larsen, Clark Spencer, M. J. Schoeninger, D. L. Hutchinson, K. F. Russell, and C. B. Ruff. "Beyond Demographic Collapse: Biological Adaptation and Change in Native Populations of La Florida." In *Columbian Consequences.* Vol. 2, *Archaeological and Historical Perspectives on the Spanish Borderlands East,* edited by David Hurst Thomas, 409–28. Washington DC: Smithsonian Institution Press, 1990.

Larson, Lewis H., Jr. "Functional Considerations of Warfare in the Southeast during the Mississippi Period." *American Antiquity* 37, no. 3 (1972): 383–92.

La Salle, Nicolas de. "The Nicolas de la Salle Journal." In *The La Salle Expedition on the Mississippi River: A Lost Manuscript of Nicolas de La Salle, 1682,* edited by William C. Foster, translated by Johanna L. Warren, 91–126. Austin: Texas State Historical Association, 2003.

———. "Récit de Nicholas de la Salle." In *Découvertes et Établissements des Fraçais dans l'Ouest et dans le Sud de l'Amérique Septentrionale*, edited by Pierre Margry, 545–70. Vol. 1. Paris: D. Jouast, 1876.

Lauber, Almon Wheeler. *Indian Slavery in Colonial Times within the Present Limits of the United States*. 1913. Honolulu: University Press of the Pacific, 2002.

Lavie, Smadar, and Ted Swedenburg, eds. *Displacement, Diaspora, and Geographies of Identity*. Durham NC: Duke University Press, 2001.

Law, Robin. "Warfare on the West African Slave Coast, 1650–1850." In *War in the Tribal Zone: Expanding States and Indigenous Warfare*, edited by R. Brian Ferguson and Neil L. Whitehead, 103–26. 1992. 2nd ed. Santa Fe: School of American Research Press, 1999.

Lawson, John. *A New Voyage to Carolina*. 1709. Edited by H. T. Lefler, with introduction by Hugh Talmadge Lefler. Chapel Hill: University of North Carolina Press, 1968.

Lederer, John. *The Discoveries of John Lederer, in three several Marches from Virginia, and to the West of Carolina, and other parts of the Continent*. 1672. Rochester NY: George P. Humphrey, 1902.

Lehmer, Donald J. *Introduction to Middle Missouri Archaeology*. National Park Service Anthropological Papers, no. 1, Washington DC, 1971.

Le Jau, Francis. *The Carolina Chronicles of Dr. Francis Le Jau, 1706–1717*. Edited by Frank J. Klingberg. Berkeley: University of California Press, 1956.

Lekson, Stephen H. "War in the Southwest, War in the World." *American Antiquity* 67, no. 4 (2002): 607–24.

Lennox, Paul A. *The Hamilton Site: A Late Historic Neutral Town*. National Museum of Man Mercury Series, Archaeological Survey of Canada, paper no. 103, 1981.

Lennox, Paul A., and William R. Fitzgerald. "The Culture History and Archaeology of the Neutral Iroquoians." In *The Archaeology of Southern Ontario to AD 1650*, edited by Chris J. Ellis and Neal Ferris, 405–56. Occasional Publication of the OAS London Chapter, no. 5, 1990.

Le Page Du Pratz, Antoine-Simon. *Histoire de la Louisiane, contenant la découverte de ce vaste pays; sa description géographique; un voyage dans les terres*. 3 Vols. Paris: Lambert, 1758.

———. *The History of Louisiana*. 1774. New Orleans: Pelican, 1947.

Lévi-Strauss, Claude. *The Elementary Structures of Kinship*. Boston: Beacon, 1969.

Lewis, R. B., and Charles Stout. *Mississippian Towns and Sacred Spaces: Searching for an Architectural Grammar*. Tuscaloosa: University of Alabama Press, 1998.

Lewis, Thomas M. N., and Madeline Kneberg. *Hiwassee Island: An Archaeological Account of Four Tennessee Indian Peoples*. Knoxville: University of Tennessee Press, 1970.

Lewis, Thomas M. N., Lynne P. Sullivan, and Madeline D. Lewis. *The Prehistory of the Chickamauga Basin in Tennessee*. 2 Vols. Knoxville: University of Tennessee Press, 1995.

Lieb, Brad. "The Grand Village is Silent: An Archaeological and Ethnohistorical Study of the Natchez Indian Refuge among the Chickasaws in the Eighteenth Century." Master's thesis, University of Alabama, 2005.

Lister, Florence C., and Robert H. Lister. *Chihuahua: Storehouse of Storms*. Albuquerque: University of New Mexico Press, 1966.

Little, Keith J., and Caleb Curren. "The Moundville IV Phase on the Black Warrior River." *Journal of Alabama Archaeology* 18, no. 1 (1995): 55–78.

Littlefield, Daniel F., Jr. *Africans and Creeks from the Colonial Period to the Civil War*. Westport CT: Greenwood, 1979.

Livingood, Patrick. "Recent Discussions in Late Prehistoric Southern Archaeology." *Native South* 1 (2008): 1–27.

Lomax, Derek W. *The Reconquest of Spain*. London: Longman, 1978.

Lopinot, Neal H. "Lifeways: An Archaeobotanical Perspective on the Transition." In *Woodland-Mississippian Transition in the Mid-South: Proceedings of the Twenty-Second Mid-South Archaeological Conference*, edited by Charles H. McNutt, Stephen Williams, and Marvin D. Jeter, 142–48. University of Memphis Anthropological Research Center, Occasional Papers, no. 25. Memphis TN: University of Memphis, 2003.

Lorenz, Karl G. "The Natchez of Southwest Mississippi." In *Indians of the Greater Southeast: Historical Archaeology and Ethnohistory*, edited by Bonnie G. McEwan, 142–77. Gainesville: University Press of Florida, 2000.

———. "Small-Scale Mississippian Community Organization in the Big Black River Valley of Mississippi." *Southeastern Archaeology* 15: 2 (1996): 145–71.

Lupardus, Karen Jacque. "The Language of the Alabama Indians." PhD diss., University of Kansas, 1982.

Lutz, Francis Earle. *Chesterfield: An Old Virginia County.* Richmond: William Byrd Press, 1954.

Lyon, Eugene. *The Enterprise of Florida: Pedro Menéndez de Avilés and the Spanish Conquest of 1565–1568.* Gainesville: University Press of Florida, 1976.

——. *Santa Elena: A Brief History of the Colony, 1566–1587.* South Carolina Institute of Archeology and Anthropology, Research Manuscript Series, no. 193. Columbia: University of South Carolina, 1984.

MacCord, Howard A., Sr. "Summary and Conclusions." In *Abbyville: A Complex of Archaeological Sites in John H. Kerr Reservoir, Halifax County, Virginia,* edited by R. P. Stephen Davis, Jr., and Howard A. MacCord, Sr., 315–24. The Archaeology Society of Virginia Special Publication, no. 39, Richmond, 2002.

MacCormack, Sabine. "Limits of Understanding: Perceptions of Greco-Roman and Amerindian Paganism in Early Modern Europe." In *America in European Consciousness, 1493–1750,* edited by Karen Ordahl Kupperman, 106–14. Chapel Hill: University of North Carolina Press, 1995.

MacNeish, R. S. *Iroquois Pottery Types: A Technique for the Study of Iroquois Prehistory.* National Museum of Canada Bulletin, no. 124, Ottawa, 1952.

Mahan, Alfred Thayer. *The Problem of Asia and Its Effect upon International Policies.* Boston: Little, Brown, 1900.

Malone, Patrick. *The Skulking Way of War: Technology and Tactics among the New England Indians.* Baltimore: Johns Hopkins University Press, 1993.

Mancall, Peter, Joshua Rosenbloom, and Thomas Weiss. "Indians and the Economy of Eighteenth-Century Carolina." In *The Atlantic Economy during the Seventeenth and Eighteenth Centuries: Organization, Operation, Practice, and Personnel,* edited by Peter Coclanis, 297–322. Columbia: University of South Carolina Press, 2005.

Mann, Cyril B., Jr. "Classification of Ceramics from the Lubbub Creek Archaeological Locality." In "Prehistoric Agricultural Communities in West-Central Alabama: Studies of the Material Remains From the Lubbub Creek Archaeological Locality," edited by Christopher S. Peebles, 2–137. Report submitted to the U.S. Army Corps of Engineers, Mobile District, by the University of Michigan, 1983.

Mann, Jason A. "A Reappraisal of the Walnut Creek Phase." Paper presented at the annual meeting of the Southeastern Archaeological Conference, St. Louis, 2004.

Marambaud, Pierre. *William Byrd of Westover 1674–1744.* Charlottesville: University Press of Virginia, 1971.

Marquette, Jacques. "Relation of the Voyages, Discoveries, and Death of Father James Marquette." In *Discovery and Exploration of the Mississippi Valley; with the Original Narratives of Marquette, Allouez, Membrè, Hennepin, and Anastase Douay*, edited by John Gilmary Shea, 1–66. Clinton Hall NY: Redfield, 1852.

Marshall, Richard A. "Lyon's Bluff Site (220K1) Radiocarbon Dated." *Journal of Alabama Archaeology* 23, no. 1 (1977): 53–57.

Martin, Howard N. *Myths and Folktales of the Alabama-Coushatta Indians of Texas*. Austin: Encino, 1982.

Martin, Jack B. "Languages." In *Handbook of North American Indians*. Vol. 14, *Southeast*, edited by Raymond D. Fogelson, 68–86. Washington DC: Smithsonian Institution Press, 2004.

Martin, Joel W. *The Land Looks after Us: A History of Native American Religions*. New York: Oxford University Press, 1999.

———. *Sacred Revolt: The Muskogees' Struggle for a New World*. Boston: Beacon, 1991.

———. "Southeastern Indians and the English Trade in Skins and Slaves." In *The Forgotten Centuries: Indians and Europeans in the American South 1521-1704*, edited by Charles Hudson and Carmen Chaves Tesser, 304–24. Athens: University of Georgia Press, 1994.

Martinez, Francisco. "The Martinez Relation." In *The Juan Pardo Expeditions: Explorations of the Carolinas and Tennessee, 1566-1568*, by Charles Hudson, translated by Paul Hoffman, 317–21. Washington DC: Smithsonian Institution Press, 1990.

Mason, Carol I. "A Reconsideration of Westo-Yuchi Identification." *American Anthropologist*, n.s. 65 (1963): 1342–46.

Mason, Ronald J. "Archaeology and Native North American Oral Traditions." *American Antiquity* 65 (2000): 239–66.

Mauss, Marcel. "Essai sur le don." 1925. Translated by Ian Cunnison as *The Gift: Forms and Functions of Exchange in Archaic Societies*. New York: Norton, 1967.

McCarthy, Cormac. *Blood Meridian, or, the Evening Redness in the West*. New York: Random House, 1985.

McCartney, Martha W. "Cockacoeske, Queen of Pamunkey: Diplomat and Suzeraine." In *Powhatan's Mantle: Indians in the Colonial Southeast*, edited by Peter H. Wood, Gregory A. Waselkov, and M. Thomas Hatley, 173–95. Lincoln: University of Nebraska Press, 1989.

McConnell, M. N. "Peoples 'In Between' The Iroquois and the Ohio Indians, 1720–1768." In *Beyond the Covenant Chain: The Iroquois and Their Neighbors in Indian North America, 1600–1800*, edited by Daniel K. Richter and James H. Merrell, 93–112. University Park: Pennsylvania State University Press, 2003.

McCrady, Edward. *History of South Carolina*. 4 Vols. New York: Macmillan, 1897–1902.

McDowell, William L., Jr., ed. *Colonial Records of South Carolina: Documents Relating to Indian Affairs: May 21, 1750–August 7, 1754*. Columbia: South Carolina Department of Archives and History, 1958.

———, ed. *Journals of the Commissioners of the Indian Trade, September 20, 1710–August 29, 1718*. 1955. Columbia: South Carolina Department of Archives and History, 1992.

McEwan, Bonnie G. "The Apalachee Indians of Northwest Florida." In *Indians of the Greater Southeast: Historical Archaeology and Ethnohistory*, edited by Bonnie G. McEwan, 57–84. Gainesville: University Press of Florida, 2000.

———, ed. *Indians of the Greater Southeast: Historical Archaeology and Ethnohistory*. Gainesville: University Press of Florida, 2000.

———. *The Spanish Missions of La Florida*. Gainesville: University Press of Florida, 1996.

Merrell, James H. *The Indians' New World: The Catawbas from European Contact through the Era of Removal*. Chapel Hill: University of North Carolina Press, 1989.

———. "'Their Very Bones Shall Fight': The Catawba-Iroquois Wars." In *Beyond the Covenant Chain: The Iroquois and Their Neighbors in Indian North America, 1600–1800*, edited by Daniel K. Richter and James H. Merrell, 115–33. University Park: Pennsylvania State University Press, 2003.

Merrens, H. Roy, ed. *The Colonial South Carolina Scene: Contemporary Views, 1697–1774*. Columbia: University of South Carolina Press, 1977.

Mesquida, C. G. and N. I. Wiener. "Human Collective Aggression: A Behavioral Ecology Perspective." *Ethnology and Sociobiology* 17 (1996): 247–62.

———. "Male Age Composition and Severity of Conflicts." *Politics and the Life Sciences* 18, no. 2 (1999): 181–89.

Meyers, Maureen. "Adapting to the Shatter Zone." Paper presented at the annual meeting of the American Society for Ethnohistory, Santa Fe, 2005.

———. "A Site Location Model for Protohistoric Sites on the Savannah River Site, South Carolina." Report submitted to the Savannah River Archaeological Research Plant, 2001.

Milanich, Jerald T. *Florida Indians and the Invasion from Europe*. Gainesville: University Press of Florida, 1995.

——. *Laboring in the Field of the Lords: Spanish Missions and Southeastern Indians*. Gainesville: University Press of Florida, 1999.

——. "The Timucua Indians of Northern Florida and Southern Georgia." In *Indians of the Greater Southeast: Historical Archaeology and Ethnohistory*, edited by Bonnie G. McEwan, 1–25. Gainesville: University Press of Florida, 2000.

Milanich, Jerald T., and Charles Hudson. *Hernando de Soto and the Indians of Florida*. Gainesville: University Press of Florida, 1993.

Miles, Tiya. T*ies That Bind: The Story of an Afro-Cherokee Family in Slavery and Freedom*. Berkeley: University of California Press, 2005.

Miles, Tiya, and Celia E. Naylor-Ojurongbe. "African-Americans in Indian Societies." In *Handbook of North American Indians*. Vol. 14, *Southeast*, edited by Raymond D. Fogelson, 753–59. Washington DC: Smithsonian Institution Press, 2004.

Milfort, Louis LeClerc. *Memoir, or, a Cursory Glance at My Different Travels and My Sojourning in the Creek Nation*. 1802. Edited by John Francis McDermott and translated by Geraldine de Courcy. Chicago: Lakeside, 1956.

Milling, Chapman J. *Red Carolinians*. Chapel Hill: University of North Carolina Press, 1940.

Milner, George R. *The Cahokia Chiefdom: The Archaeology of a Mississippian Society*. Washington DC: Smithsonian Institution Press, 1998.

——. "Epidemic Disease in the Postcontact Southeast: A Reappraisal." *Midcontinental Journal of Archaeology* 5 (1980): 39–56.

——. *The Moundbuilders: Ancient Peoples of Eastern North America*. London: Thames and Hudson, 2004.

——. "Prospects and Problems in Contact-Era Research." In *Bioarchaeology of Native American Adaptation in the Spanish Borderlands*, edited by Brenda J. Baker and Lisa Kealhofer, 198–208. Gainesville: University Press of Florida, 1996.

——. "Warfare in Prehistoric and Early Historic Eastern North America." *Journal of Archaeological Research* 7 (1999): 105–51.

Milner, George R., Eve Anderson, and Virginia G. Smith. "Warfare in Late Prehistoric West-Central Illinois." *American Antiquity* 56 (1991): 581–603.

Minet. "Voyage Made from Canada Inland Going Southward during the Year 1682." In *La Salle, the Mississippi, and the Gulf: Three Primary Documents*,

edited by Robert S. Weddle, translated by Ann Linda Bell, 83–128. College
Station: Texas A&M Press, 1987.

Mistovitch, Tim S., and Vernon James Knight, Jr. *Excavations at Four Sites on
Walter F. George Lake, Alabama and Georgia*. University of Alabama, Office
of Archaeological Report of Investigations, no. 49, Tuscaloosa, 1986.

Mochon, Marion Johnson. "Language History and Prehistory: Mississippian
Lexico-Reconstruction." *American Antiquity* 37 (1972): 478–503.

Moll, Herman. *World Described, or, a New and Correct Sett of Maps*. London:
J. Bowles, 1709–20. http://digitalgallery.nypl.org/nypldigital/dgkeysearchde
tail.cfm?trg=1&strucID=253550&imageID=434918&word=Moll%2C%20
Herman&s=3&notword=&d=&c=&f=4&lWord=&lField=&sScope=&sLeve
l=&sLabel=&total=77&num=0&imgs=12&pNum=&pos=9# (accessed January 15, 2007).

Molto, J. Eldon, and Michael W. Spence, and William A. Fox. "The Van Oordt
Site: A Case Study in Salvage Osteology." *Canadian Journal of Anthropology*
5, no. 2 (1986): 49–61.

Mooney, James. *Historical Sketch of the Cherokee*. 1900. Chicago: Adline, 1975.

———. *Myths of the Cherokee*. Bureau of American Ethnology, Nineteenth Annual
Report. Washington DC: Government Printing Office, 1900.

———. *The Siouan Tribes of the East*. Bureau of American Ethnology, bulletin no.
22. Washington DC: Smithsonian Institution Press, 1894.

Moore, Clarence Bloomfield. "Certain Aboriginal Remains of the Alabama River."
Journal of the Academy of Natural Sciences of Philadelphia 11, no. 3 (1900):
288–347.

Moore, David G. *Catawba Valley Mississippian: Ceramics, Chronology, and Catawba
Indians*. Tuscaloosa: University of Alabama Press, 2002.

Moore, David G., Robin A. Beck, Jr., and Christopher B. Rodning. Afterword.
In *The Juan Pardo Expeditions: Explorations of the Carolinas and Tennessee,
1566–1568*, edited by Charles Hudson, 343–50. 2nd ed. Tuscaloosa: University
of Alabama Press, 2005.

Moore, James, Sr. "An Account of What the Army Did, under the Command of
Col. Moore, in His Expedition Last Winter against the Spaniards and Spanish Indians." *Collections of the South Carolina Historical Society* 2 (1857):
573–76

Morrison, A. J. "The Virginia Indian Trade to 1673." *William and Mary College
Quarterly Historic Magazine* 1, no. 4 (1921): 217–36.

Morse, Dan F. "The Nodena Phase." In *Towns and Temples along the Mississippi*, edited by David H. Dye and Cheryl Anne Cox, 69–97. Tuscaloosa: University of Alabama Press, 1990.

Morse, Dan F., and Phyllis A. Morse. *Archaeology of the Central Mississippi Valley*. New York: Academic Press, 1983.

Morse, Phyllis A. *Parkin: the 1978–1979 Archaeological Investigations of a Cross County, Arkansas Site.* Arkansas Archeological Survey Research Series, no. 13, Fayetteville, 1981.

———. "The Parkin Site and the Parkin Phase." In *Towns and Temples along the Mississippi*, edited by David H. Dye and Cheryl Anne Cox, 118–34. Tuscaloosa: University of Alabama Press.

Mouer, L. Daniel. "The Ocaneechee Connection: Social Networks and Ceramics at the Fall Line in the 16th and 17th Centuries." Manuscript, Virginia Department of Historic Resources, Richmond, 1985.

Muller, Jon. *Mississippian Political Economy*. New York: Plenum, 1997.

———. "Mississippian Specialization and Salt." *American Antiquity* 49 (1984): 489–507.

———. "Prolegomena for the Analysis of the Southeastern Ceremonial Complex." In *Southeastern Ceremonial Complex: Chronology, Content, Context*, edited by Adam King, 15–37. Tuscaloosa: University of Alabama Press, 2007.

———. "The Southern Cult." In *The Southeastern Ceremonial Complex: Artifacts and Analysis*, edited by Patricia K. Galloway, 11–37. Lincoln: University of Nebraska Press, 1989.

Murphy, Carl, and Neal Ferris. "The Late Woodland Western Basin Tradition of Southwestern Ontario." In *The Archaeology of Southern Ontario to AD 1650*, edited by C. Ellis and N. Ferris, 189–278. Occasional Publication of the OAS London Chapter, no. 5, 1990.

Nabokov, Peter. *A Forest of Time: American Indian Ways of History*. New York: Cambridge University Press, 2002.

———. *Where the Lightning Strikes: The Lives of American Indian Sacred Places*. New York: Viking, 2006.

Nagel, Joane. "Constructing Ethnicity: Creating and Recreating Ethnic Identity and Culture." *Social Problems* 41 (1994): 152–76.

Nairne, Thomas. *Nairne's Muskhogean Journals: The 1708 Expedition to the Mississippi River*. Edited by Alexander Moore. Jackson: University of Mississippi Press, 1988.

Namias, June. "Captives." In *The Encyclopedia of North American Indians: Native*

American History, Culture, and Life from Paleo-Indians to the Present, edited by Frederick E. Hoxie, 99–101. Boston: Houghton Mifflin, 1996.

Nance, C. Roger. *The Archaeological Sequence at Durant Bend, Dallas County, Alabama*. Alabama Archaeological Society, Special Publication, no. 2, 1976.

Nassaney, Michael S. "The Bow and Arrow in Eastern North America: A View from Central Arkansas." In *Woodland-Mississippian Transition in the Mid-South: Proceedings of the Twenty-Second Mid-South Archaeological Conference*, edited by Charles H. McNutt, Stephen Williams, and Marvin D. Jeter, 105–8. University of Memphis Anthropological Research Center, Occasional Papers, no. 25. Memphis TN: University of Memphis, 2003.

Nassaney, Michael S., and Kendra Pyle. "The Adoption of the Bow and Arrow in Eastern North America: A View from Central Arkansas." *American Antiquity* 64 (1999): 243–63.

Naylor-Ojurongbe, Celia E. "More at Home with the Indians: African-American Slaves and Freedpeople in the Cherokee Nation, Indian Territory, 1838–1907." PhD diss., Duke University, 2001.

Neilson, Col. Hubert. "Slavery in Old Canada, before and after the Conquest." *Transactions of the Literary and Historical Society of Quebec, Sessions of 1905* 26 (1906): 19–45.

Neitzel, Jill E., ed. *Great Towns and Regional Polities in the Prehistoric American Southwest and Southeast*. Albuquerque: University of New Mexico Press, 1999.

Neitzel, Robert S. *Archeology of the Fatherland Site: The Grand Village of the Natchez*. Mississippi Department of Archives and History, Archaeological Report, no. 28, Jackson, 1997.

Newe, Thomas. "Letters of Thomas Newe from South Carolina (1682)." In *Narratives of Early Carolina, 1650–1708*, edited by Alexander S. Salley, Jr., 177–187. New York: Scribner, 1911.

Newell, Margaret Ellen. *From Dependency to Independence: Economic Revolution in Colonial New England*. Ithaca: Cornell University Press, 1998.

Noble, William C. "The Neutral Indians." In *Essays in Northeastern Anthropology in Memory of Marian E. White*, edited by W. E. Engelbrecht and D. K. Grayson, 152–64. Occasional Publications in Northeastern Anthropology, no. 5. Peterborough, Canada, 1978.

Oatis, Stephen. *A Colonial Complex: South Carolina's Frontiers in the Era of the Yamasee War, 1680–1730*. Lincoln: University of Nebraska Press, 2004.

O'Brien, Greg. *Choctaws in a Revolutionary Age, 1750–1830*. Lincoln: University of Nebraska Press, 2002.

O'Callaghan, Edmund Bailey, ed. *Documents Relative to the Colonial History of the State of New York*. 15 Vols. Albany: Weed, Parsons, 1854–61, 1877–87.

Olafson, Sigfus. "Gabriel Arthur and the Fort Ancient People." *West Virginia Archaeologist* 12 (1960): 32–42.

Oliver, Billy L. "Settlements of the Pee Dee Culture." PhD diss., University of North Carolina, 1992.

Owsley, Frank Lawrence. *Struggle for the Gulf Borderlands: The Creek War and the Battle of New Orleans, 1812–1815*. Gainesville: University Press of Florida, 1981.

Paar, Karen. "Witness to Empire and the Tightening of Military Control: Santa Elena's Second Spanish Occupation, 1577–1587." PhD diss., University of North Carolina, 1999.

Pardo, Juan, "The Pardo Relation." In *The Juan Pardo Expeditions: Exploration of the Carolinas and Tennessee, 1566–1568*, edited by Charles Hudson, translated by Paul Hoffman, 305–16. 2nd ed. Tuscaloosa: University of Alabama Press, 2005.

Parker, Arthur C. *Excavations in an Erie Indian Village and Burial Site at Ripley, Chautauqua Co., New York*. New York State Museum, bulletin 117, archaeology 14, Albany, 1907.

Parry, Jonathan, and Maurice Bloch. Introduction. In *Money and the Morality of Exchange*, edited by Jonathan Parry and Maurice Bloch, 1–32. Cambridge, UK: Cambridge University Press, 1989.

——, eds. *Money and the Morality of Exchange*. Cambridge, UK: Cambridge University Press, 1989.

Pauketat, Timothy R. *Ancient Cahokia and the Mississippians*, Cambridge, UK: Cambridge University Press, 2004.

——. *The Ascent of Chiefs: Cahokia and Mississippian Politics in Native North America*. Tuscaloosa: University of Alabama Press, 1994.

——. *Chiefdoms and Other Archaeological Delusions*. Lanham MD: AltaMira, 2007.

——. "A Fourth-Generation Synthesis of Cahokia and Mississippianization." *Midcontinental Journal of Archaeology* 27 (2002): 149–70.

Pauketat, Timothy R., and A. Barker, eds. *Lords of the Southeast: Social Inequality and the Native Elites of Southeastern North America*. Archeological Papers of the American Anthropological Association, no. 3, Washington DC, 1992.

Pauketat, Timothy R., and Thomas Emerson, eds. *Cahokia: Domination and Ideology in the Mississippian World*. Lincoln: University of Nebraska Press, 1997.

Pavao-Zuckerman, Barnet. "Vertebrate Subsistence in the Mississippian-Historic Transition." *Southeastern Archaeology* 19 (2000): 135–44.

Payne, Claudine, and John F. Scarry. "Town Structure at the Edge of the Mississippian World." In *Mississippian Towns and Sacred Spaces: Searching for an Architectural Grammar*, edited by R. B. Lewis and Charles Stout, 22–48. Tuscaloosa: University of Alabama Press, 1998.

Peebles, Christopher S. "Moundville from 1000 to 1500 AD as Seen from 1840 to 1985 AD." In *Chiefdoms in the Americas*, edited by Robert D. Drennen and Carlos A. Uribe, 21–41. Lanham MD: University Press of America, 1987.

———. "The Rise and Fall of the Mississippian in Western Alabama: The Moundville and Summerville Phases, AD 1000 to 1600." *Mississippi Archaeology* 22 (1987): 1–31.

Pendergast, James F. "The Kakouagoga or Kahkwas: An Iroquoian Nation Destroyed in the Niagara Region." *Proceedings of the American Philosophical Society* 138, no. 1 (1994): 96–143.

———. *The Massawomeck: Raiders and Traders into the Chesapeake Bay in the Seventeenth Century*. Transactions of the American Philosophical Society, vol. 81, pt. 2, Philadelphia, 1991.

Pénicaut, André. *Fleur de Lys and Calumet: Being the Pénicuat Narrative of French Adventure in Louisiana*. Translated and edited by Richebourg Gaillard McWilliams. Baton Rouge: Louisiana State University Press, 1953.

———. *Fleur de Lys and Calumet: Being the Pénicaut Narrative of French Adventure in Louisiana*. Translated and edited by Richebourg Gaillard McWilliams. 1953. Tuscaloosa: University of Alabama Press, 1988.

Perdue, Theda. "Cherokee Relations with the Iroquois in the Eighteenth Century." In *Beyond the Covenant Chain: The Iroquois and Their Neighbors in Indian North America, 1600–1800*, edited by Daniel K. Richter and James H. Merrell, 135–49. University Park: Pennsylvania State University Press, 2003.

———. *Cherokee Women: Gender and Culture Change, 1700–1835*. Lincoln: University of Nebraska Press, 1998.

———. "Race and Culture: Writing the Ethnohistory of the Early South." *Ethnohistory* 51, no. 4 (2004): 701–23.

———. "Slavery." In *The Encyclopedia of North American Indians: Native American History, Culture, and Life from Paleo-Indians to the Present*, edited by Frederick E. Hoxie, 596–98. Boston: Houghton Mifflin, 1996.

―――. *Slavery and the Evolution of Cherokee Society 1540–1866*. Knoxville: University of Tennessee Press, 1979.

Perttula, Timothy K. *The Caddo Nation: Archaeological and Ethnohistoric Perspectives*. Austin: University of Texas Press, 1992.

―――. "Social Changes among the Caddo Indians in the 16th and 17th Centuries." In *Transformation of the Southeastern Indians, 1540–1760*, edited by Robbie Ethridge and Charles Hudson, 246–69. Jackson: University Press of Mississippi, 2002.

Phillips, Philip. *Archaeological Survey in the Lower Yazoo Basin, Mississippi, 1949–1955*. Papers of the Peabody Museum of Archaeology and Ethnology, vol. 60, Cambridge MA, 1970.

Phillips, Philip, James A. Ford, and James B. Griffin. *Archaeological Survey in the Lower Mississippi Alluvial Valley, 1940–1947*. Papers of the Peabody Museum of American Archaeology and Ethnology, vol. 25, Cambridge MA, 1951.

Piker, Joshua. "Crossing Frontiers: Early American and Native American Histories." *Common-Place: A Common Place, An Uncommon Voice* 5 (2005). http://common-place.dreamhost.com/vol-05/no-03/author, accessed July 14, 2007.

―――. *Okfuskee: A Creek Town in Colonial America*. Cambridge MA: Harvard University Press, 2004.

Pluckhahn, Thomas J., Robbie Ethridge, Jerald Milanich, and Marvin Smith. Introduction. In *Light on the Path: The Anthropology and History of the Southeastern Indians*, edited by Thomas J. Pluckhahn and Robbie Ethridge, 1–24, Tuscaloosa: University of Alabama Press, 2006.

Polanyi, Karl. *The Great Transformation: The Political and Economic Origins of Our Time*. Boston: Beacon, 1944.

Pollack, David. *Caborn-Welborn: Constructing a New Society after the Angel Chiefdom Collapse*. Tuscaloosa: University of Alabama Press, 2004.

Poole, Deborah, ed. *Unruly Order: Violence, Power, and Identity in the High Provinces of Southern Peru*. Boulder CO: Westview, 1994.

Poole, Stafford. "War by Fire and Blood: The Church and the Chichimecas, 1585." *The Americas* 22, no. 2 (1965): 115–37.

Power, Susan C. *Early Art of the Southeastern Indians: Feathered Serpents and Winged Beings*. Athens: University of Georgia Press, 2004.

Priestly, Herbert I., ed. and trans. *The Luna Papers: Documents Relating to the Expedition of Don Tritán de Luna y Arellano for the Conquest of La Florida in 1559–1561*. 2 Vols. Deland: The Florida State Historical Society, 1928.

———. *Tristán De Luna: Conquistador of the Old South, A Study in Spanish Strategy.* Glendale CA: Arthur H. Clark, 1936.

Quimby, George I. "Natchez Social Structure as an Instrument of Assimilation." *American Anthropologist*, n.s. 48, no. 1 (1946): 134–37.

Ramenofsky, Ann E. "Historical Science and Contact Period Studies." In *Columbian Consequences*. Vol. 3, *The Spanish Borderlands in Pan-American Perspective*, edited by David Hurst Thomas, 437–52. Washington DC: Smithsonian Institution Press, 1990.

———. *Vectors of Death: The Archaeology of European Contact.* Albuquerque: University of New Mexico Press, 1987.

Ramenofsky, Ann E., and Patricia Galloway. "Disease and the Soto Entrada." In *The Hernando De Soto Expedition: History, Historiography and "Discovery" in the Southeast*, edited by Patricia Galloway, 259–79. Lincoln: University of Nebraska Press, 1997.

Ramsey, William L. "'All and Singular the Slaves': A Demographic Profile of Indian Slavery in Colonial South Carolina." In *Money, Trade, and Power: the Evolution of a Planter Society in Colonial South Carolina*, edited by Jack P. Greene, Rosemary Brana-Shute, and Randy Sparks, 166–86. Columbia: University of South Carolina Press, 2001.

———. "'Heathenish Combination': The Natives of the North American Southeast during the Era of the Yamasee War." PhD diss., Tulane University, 1998.

———. "'Something Cloudy in Their Looks': The Origins of the Yamasee War Reconsidered." *Journal of American History* 90 (2003): 44–75.

Rangel, Rodrigo. "Account of the Northern Conquest and Discovery of Hernando de Soto." In *The De Soto Chronicles: The Expedition of Hernando de Soto to North America in 1539–1543*, edited by Lawrence A. Clayton, Vernon. J. Knight, Jr., and Edward C. Moore, translated by John Worth, 246–306. Vol. 1. Tuscaloosa: University of Alabama Press, 1993.

Rappaport, Roy A. *Pigs for the Ancestors: Ritual in the Ecology of a New Guinea People.* 1968. Long Grove IL: Waveland, 1984.

Rayson, David. "'A Great Matter to Tell': Indians, Europeans, and Africans from the Mississippian Era through the Yamasee War in the North American Southeast, 1550–1720." PhD diss., University of Minnesota, 1996.

Regnier, Amanda R. "A Stylistic Analysis of Burial Urns from the Protohistoric Period in Central Alabama." Master's thesis, University of Alabama, 2001.

———. "A Stylistic Analysis of Burial Urns from the Protohistoric Period in Central Alabama." *Southeastern Archaeology* 25, no. 1 (2006): 121–34.

Reid, John Phillip. *A Law of Blood: the Primitive Law of the Cherokee Nation*. New York: New York University Press, 1970.

Reilly, F. Kent, III, and James F. Garber. *Ancient Objects and Sacred Realms: Interpretations of Mississippian Iconography*. Austin: University of Texas Press, 2007.

Reinhartz, Dennis, and Gerald D. Saxon, eds. *The Mapping of the Entradas into the Greater Southwest*. Norman: University of Oklahoma Press, 1998.

Richter, Daniel K. *The Ordeal of the Longhouse: The Peoples of the Iroquois League in the Era of European Colonization*. Chapel Hill: University of North Carolina Press, 1992.

———. "Ordeals of the Longhouse: The Five Nations in Early American History." In *Beyond the Covenant Chain: The Iroquois and Their Neighbors in Indian North America, 1600–1800*, edited by Daniel K. Richter and James H. Merrell, 11–27. University Park: Pennsylvania State University Press, 2003.

———. "War and Culture: The Iroquois Experience." *William and Mary Quarterly* 40, no. 4 (1983): 528–59.

Riggs, Brett. "Reinterpreting the Chestowee Raid of 1713," manuscript in preparation.

Rights, Douglas L. *The American Indian in North Carolina*. Durham NC: Duke University Press, 1947.

———. "The Trading Path to the Indians." 1931. *Southern Indian Studies* 38 (1989): 49–73.

Ritchie, William Augustus. *A Prehistoric Fortified Village Site at Canandaigua, Ontario County, New York*. Research Records of the Rochester Museum of Arts and Sciences, no. 3, Rochester NY, 1936.

Robbins, Joel, and David Akin. "An Introduction to Melanesian Currencies: Agency, Identity, and Social Reproduction." In *Money and Modernity: State and Local Currencies in Melanesia*, edited by David Akin and Joel Robbins, 1–40. Pittsburgh: University of Pittsburgh Press, 1999.

Robinson, W. Stitt. *Southern Colonial Frontier, 1607–1763*. Albuquerque: University of New Mexico Press, 1979.

Rodning, Christopher B. "Reconstructing the Coalescence of Cherokee Communities in Southern Appalachia." In *The Transformation of the Southeastern Indians, 1540–1760*, edited by Robbie Ethridge and Charles Hudson, 307–46. Jackson: University Press of Mississippi, 2002.

Rogers, J. Daniel. "Chronology and the Demise of Chiefdoms: Eastern Oklahoma in the Sixteenth and Seventeenth Centuries." *Southeastern Archaeology* 25, no. 1 (2006): 20–28.

Romans, Bernard. *A Concise Natural History of East and West Florida, Facsimile Reproduction of the 1775 Edition*. 1775. Florida Facsimile and Reprint Series. Gainesville: University Press of Florida, 1962.

Rose, Jerome. "Mortuary Data and Analysis." In *The Mound 72 Area: Dedicated and Sacred Space in Early Cahokia*, coauthored with Melvin C. Fowler, Barbara Vander Leest, and Steven A. Ahler, 63–82. Illinois State Museum, Reports of Investigations, no. 54, Springfield, 1999.

Rountree, Helen C, ed. *Powhatan Foreign Relations, 1500–1722*. Charlottesville: University Press of Virginia, 1993.

———. *The Powhatan Indians of Virginia: The Traditional Culture*. Norman: University of Oklahoma Press, 1989.

———. "Trouble Coming Southward: Emanations through and from Virginia, 1607–1675." In *The Transformation of the Southeastern Indians, 1540–1760*, edited by Robbie Ethridge and Charles Hudson, 65–78. Jackson: University Press of Mississippi, 2002.

Rountree, Helen C., and Thomas E. Davidson. *Eastern Shore Indians of Virginia and Maryland*. Charlottesville: University Press of Virginia, 1997.

Rowland, Dunbar, and Albert Sanders, eds. and trans. *Mississippi Provincial Archives: French Dominion*. Vols. 1–3. Jackson: Department of Archives and History, 1927–32.

Rowland, Dunbar, A. G. Sanders, and Patricia Galloway, eds. and trans. *Mississippi Provincial Archives, French Dominion*. Vols. 4 and 5. Jackson: Mississippi Department of Archives and History, 1984.

Rudes, Blair A., Thomas J. Blumer, and J. Alan May. "Catawba and Neighboring Groups." In *Handbook of North American Indians*. Vol. 14, *Southeast*, edited by Raymond Fogelson, 301–18. Washington DC: Smithsonian Institution Press, 2004.

Rushforth, Brett. "'A Little Flesh We Offer You': The Origins of Indian Slavery in New France." *William and Mary Quarterly* 60, no. 4 (2003): 777–808.

———. "Slavery, the Fox Wars, and the Limits of Alliance." *William and Mary Quarterly* 63, no. 1 (2006): 53–80.

Russell, Richard J., and Fred B. Kniffen. *Culture Worlds*. New York: Macmillan, 1951.

Sabo, George, III. "The Quapaw Indians of Arkansas, 1673–1803." In *Indians of the Greater Southeast: Historical Archaeology and Ethnohistory*, edited by Bonnie G. McEwan, 178–203. Gainesville: University Press of Florida, 2000.

Sabo, George, III, and Deborah Sabo, eds. *Rock Art in Arkansas*. Arkansas Archeological Survey Popular Series, no. 5, Fayetteville, 2005.

Sabo, George, III, and Leslie Walker. "Mississippian Developments and External Relationships in the Central Arkansas River Valley." Paper presented at the annual meeting of the Southeastern Archaeological Conference, Little Rock, 2006.

Sahlins, Marshall. *Stone Age Economics*. New York: Aldine, 1972.

Sainsbury, W. Noel et al., eds. *Records in the British Public Records Office Relating to South Carolina*. 36 Vols. Columbia: South Carolina Department of History and Archives, 1928–47.

Salley, Alexander S., ed. *Commissions and Instructions from the Lords Proprietors of Carolina to Public Officials of South Carolina, 1685–1715*. Columbia: South Carolina Department of History and Archives, 1916.

——, ed. *Journal of the Commons House of Assembly*. 21 Vols. Columbia: Historical Commission of South Carolina, 1907–49.

——, ed. *Journal of the Grand Council of South Carolina, August 25 1671–June 24, 1680*. Columbia: Historical Commission of South Carolina, 1907.

——, ed. *Narratives of Early Carolina, 1650–1708*. New York: Scribner, 1911.

——, ed. *Records in the British Public Records Office Relating to South Carolina*. 2 vols. Atlanta: Foote and Davis, 1928.

Saunders, Rebecca. "The Guale Indians of the Lower Atlantic Coast: Change and Continuity." In *Indians of the Greater Southeast: Historical Archaeology and Ethnohistory*, edited by Bonnie G. McEwan, 26–56. Gainesville: University Press of Florida, 2000.

——. "Seasonality, Sedentism, Subsistence, and Disease in the Protohistoric: Archaeological versus Ethnohistoric Data along the Lower Atlantic Coast." In *Between Contacts and Colonies: Archaeological Perspectives on the Protohistoric Southeast*, edited by Cameron B. Wesson and Mark A. Rees, 32–48. Tuscaloosa: University of Alabama Press, 2002.

Saunt, Claudio. *Black, White, and Indian: Race and the Unmaking of an American Family*. New York: Oxford University Press, 2005.

——. "History until 1776." In *Handbook of North American Indians*. Vol. 14, *Southeast*, edited by Raymond D. Fogelson, 128–38. Washington DC: Smithsonian Institution Press, 2004.

——. *A New Order of Things: Property, Power, and the Transformation of the Creek Indians, 1733–1816*. Cambridge, UK: Cambridge University Press, 1999.

Saunt, Claudio, Barbara Krauthamer, Tiya Miles, Celia E. Naylor, and Circe Sturm.

"Rethinking Race and Culture in the Early South." *Ethnohistory* 53, no. 2 (2006): 399–405.

Sauvole, Sieur de. *The Journal of Sauvole*. Edited by Prieur Jay Higgenbotham. Mobile: Colonial Books, 1969.

Scarry, John F. "The Apalachee Chiefdom: A Mississippian Society on the Fringe of the Mississippian World." In *The Forgotten Centuries: Indians and Europeans in the American South, 1521–1704*, edited by Charles Hudson and Carmen Chaves Tesser, 327–56. Athens: University of Georgia Press, 1994.

———. "Domestic Life on the Northwest Riverbank at Moundville." In *Archaeology of the Moundville Chiefdom*, edited by Vernon J. Knight, Jr., and Vincas P. Steponaitis, 63–101. Washington DC: Smithsonian Institution Press, 1998.

———. *Excavations on the Northwest Riverbank at Moundville: Investigations of a Moundville I Residential Area*. University of Alabama, Museums Office of Archaeological Services Report of Investigations, no. 72, Tuscaloosa, 1995.

———. "The Late Prehistoric Southeast." In *The Forgotten Centuries: Indians and Europeans in the American South, 1521–1704*, edited by Charles M. Hudson and Carmen Chaves Tesser, 17–35. Athens: University of Georgia Press, 1994.

———, ed. *Political Structure and Change in the Prehistoric Southeastern United States*. Gainesville: University Press of Florida, 1996.

———. "The Rise, Transformation, and Fall of Apalachee: A Case Study of Political Change in a Chiefly Society." In *Lamar Archaeology: Mississippian Chiefdoms of the Deep South*, edited by Mark Williams and Gary Shapiro, 175–86. Tuscaloosa: University of Alabama Press, 1990.

Scarry, John F., and Mintcy D. Maxham. "Elite Actors in the Protohistoric: Elite Identities and Interaction with Europeans in the Apalachee and Powhatan Chiefdoms." In *Between Contacts and Colonies: Archaeological Perspectives on the Protohistoric Southeast*, edited by Cameron B. Wesson and Mark A. Rees, 140–69. Tuscaloosa: University of Alabama Press, 2002.

Scarry, John, and Claudine Payne. "The Chronology of Mound Construction and Use at Lake Jackson." Paper presented at the annual meeting of the Southeastern Archaeological Conference, Little Rock, 2006.

Schaafsma, Curtis F. *Apaches de Navajo: Seventeenth-Century Navajos in the Chama Valley of New Mexico*. Salt Lake City: University of Utah Press, 2002.

Schambach, Frank F. "Mounds, Embankments, and Ceremonialism in the Trans-Mississippi South." In *Mounds, Embankments, and Ceremonialism in the*

Midsouth, edited by Robert C. Mainfort and Richard Walling, 36–43, Arkansas Archeological Survey Research Series, no. 46, Fayetteville, 1996.

Schnell, Frank T. "The Beginnings of the Creeks: Where Did They First 'Sit Down'?" *Early Georgia* 17, no. 1–2 (1989): 24–29.

———. *Late Prehistoric Ceramic Chronologies in the Lower Chattahoochee Valley*. Southeastern Archaeological Conference, bulletin 24 (1981): 21–23.

Schnell, Frank T., Vernon J. Knight, and Gail S. Schnell. *Cemochechobee, Archaeology of a Mississippian Ceremonial Center on the Chattahoochee River*. Gainesville: University Press of Florida, 1981.

Schnell, Frank T., and Newell O. Wright. *Mississippi Period Archaeology of the Georgia Coastal Plain*. University of Georgia Laboratory of Archaeology Series report no. 26, Athens, 1993.

Schoeninger, Margaret J., and Mark R. Schurr. "Human Subsistence at Moundville: The Stable-Isotope Data." In *Archaeology of the Moundville Chiefdom*, edited by Vernon J. Knight, Jr., and Vincas P. Steponaitis, 120–32. Washington DC: Smithsonian Institution Press, 1998.

Schrager, Bradley. "Yamasee Indians and the Challenge of Spanish and English Colonialism in the North American Southeast, 1660–1715." PhD diss., Northwestern University, 2001.

Schroedl, Gerald F. "Cherokee Ethnohistory and Archaeology from 1540 to 1838." In *Indians of the Greater Southeast: Historical Archaeology and Ethnohistory*, edited by Bonnie G. McEwan, 204–41. Gainesville: University Press of Florida, 2000.

Schutz, Noel. "Shawnee Myth in an Ethnographic and Ethnohistorical Perspective." PhD diss., Indiana University, 1974.

Sears, William H. *The Wilbanks Site (9ck5), Georgia*. Bureau of American Ethnology Bulletin 169 (1958): 129–94.

Sempowski, Martha L. "Early Historic Exchange between the Seneca and the Susquehannock." In *The Proceedings of the People to People Conference*, edited by C. F. Hayes III, C. Bodner, and L. Saunders, 51–64. Rochester Museum and Science Center Research Records 23, Rochester NY, 1994.

———. "Fluctuations through Time in the Use of Marine Shell at Seneca Iroquois Sites." In *Proceedings of the 1986 Shell Bead Conference: Selected Papers*, edited by Charles F. Hayes III and Lynn Ceci, 81–96. Rochester Museum and Science Center Research Records No. 20, Rochester NY, 1989.

Sempowski, Martha Lorraine, and L. P. Saunders. *Dutch Hollow and Factory Hollow: The Advent of Dutch Trade among the Senecas*. Charles F. Wray Series in

Seneca Archaeology. Vol. 3. Rochester Museum and Science Center Research, no. 24. Rochester NY, 2001.

Service, Elman R. *Origins of the State and Civilization*. New York: Norton, 1975.

———. *Primitive Social Organization: An Evolutionary Perspective*. New York: Random House, 1971.

Shackelford, Alan G. "On a Crossroads: American Indian Prehistory and History in the Confluence Region." PhD diss., Indiana University, 2004.

Shannon, Thomas R. *An Introduction to the World-System Perspective*. 2nd ed. Boulder CO: Westview, 1996.

Shefveland, Kristalyn. "Hidden in Plain View: Indian Slavery in the Colonial Records of Virginia." Paper presented at the Third Virginia Forum, Fredricksburg VA, 2008.

Sheldon, Craig T. "The Mississippian-Historic Transition in Central Alabama." PhD diss., University of Oregon, 1974.

———, ed. *The Southern and Central Alabama Expeditions of Clarence Bloomfield Moore*. Tuscaloosa: University of Alabama Press, 2001.

Sheldon, Craig T., and Ned J. Jenkins. "Protohistoric Development in Central Alabama." In *The Protohistoric Period in the Mid-South, 1500–1700: Proceedings of the 1983 Mid-South Archaeological Conference*, edited by David H. Dye and Ronald C. Brister, 95–102. Mississippi Department of Archives and History, Archaeological Report, no. 18, Jackson, 1986.

Sheldon, Craig T., Jason A. Mann, and John W. Cottier. "A Late Woodland-Mississippian Culture Contact in Central Alabama." Paper presented at the annual meeting of the Southeastern Archaeological Conference, Charlotte NC, 2001.

Shuck-Hall, Sheri M. *Journey to the West: The Alabama and Coushatta Indians*. Norman: University of Oklahoma Press, 2008.

Silver, Timothy. *New Face on the Countryside: Indians, Colonists, and Slaves in South Atlantic Forests, 1500–1800*. Cambridge, UK: Cambridge University Press, 1990.

Silverblatt, Irene. *Modern Inquisitions: Peru and the Colonial Origins of the Civilized World*. Durham NC: Duke University Press, 2004.

Slotkin, Richard. *The Fatal Environment: The Myth of the Frontier in the Age of Industrialization, 1800–1890*. 1985. Norman: University of Oklahoma Press, 1998.

———. *Regeneration through Violence: The Mythology of the American Frontier, 1600–1860*. 1973. New York: HarperPerennial, 1996.

Smith, Bruce D., ed. *Mississippian Settlement Patterns*. New York: Academic Press, 1978.

Smith, John. *Captain John Smith: A Select Edition of His Writings*. Edited by Karen Ordahl Kupperman. Chapel Hill: University of North Carolina Press, 1988.

Smith, Kevin P. "Patterns in Time and the Tempo of Change: A North Atlantic Perspective on the Evolution of Complex Societies." In *Exploring the Role of Analytical Scale in Archaeological Interpretation*, edited by J. R. Mathieu and R. E. Scott, 83–99. Oxford, UK: Archaeopress, 2004.

Smith, Marvin T. "Aboriginal Depopulation in the Postcontact Southeast." In *The Forgotten Centuries: Indians and Europeans in the American South, 1521–1704*, edited by Charles Hudson and Carmen Chaves Tesser, 257–75. Athens: University of Georgia Press, 1994.

———. "Aboriginal Population Movements in the Early Historic Period Southeast." In *Powhatan's Mantle: Indians in the Colonial Southeast*, edited by Peter H. Wood, Gregory A. Waselkov, and M. Thomas Hatley, 21–43. Lincoln: University of Nebraska Press, 1989.

———. "Aboriginal Population Movements in the Postcontact Southeast." In *The Transformation of the Southeastern Indians, 1540–1760*, edited by Robbie Ethridge and Charles Hudson, 3–21. Jackson: University Press of Mississippi, 2002.

———. *Archaeology of Aboriginal Culture Change in the Interior Southeast: Depopulation during the Early Historic Period*. Gainesville: University Press of Florida, 1987.

———. *Coosa: The Rise and Fall of a Mississippian Chiefdom*. Gainesville: University Press of Florida, 2000.

———. "The Rise and Fall of Coosa." In *Societies in Eclipse: Archaeology of the Eastern Woodlands Indians, AD 1350–1700*, edited by David S. Brose, C. Wesley Cowan, and Robert C. Mainfort, Jr., 143–56. Washington DC: Smithsonian Institution Press, 2001.

Snow, Dean R. *The Iroquois*. Oxford, UK: Blackwell, 1994.

Snow, Dean R., and Kim A. Lamphear. "European Contact and Indian Depopulation in the Northeast: The Timing of the First Epidemics." *Ethnohistory* 35, no. 1 (1988): 15–33.

Snyder, Christina. "Captives of the Dark and Bloody Ground: Identity, Race, and Power in the Contested American South." PhD diss., University of North Carolina, 2007

———. "Conquered Enemies: Adopted King, and Owned People: The Creek

Indians and Their Captives." *Journal of Southern History* 73, no. 2 (2007): 255–88.

Solis, Carlos, and Richard Walling. *Archaeological Investigations at the Yarborough Site (22cl814), Clay County, Mississippi*. University of Alabama, Office of Archaeological Research, Report of Investigations, no. 30, Tuscaloosa, 1982.

Speck, Frank G. "The Catawba Nation and Its Neighbors." *North Carolina Historical Review* 16 (1939): 404–17.

———. "The Delaware Indians as Women: Were the Original Pennsylvanians Politically Emasculated?" *Pennsylvania Magazine of History and Biography* 70, no. 4 (1946): 377–89.

Stahle, David W., Edward R. Cook, Malcolm K. Cleaveland, Matthew D. Therrell, David M. Meko, Henri D. Grissomo-Mayer, Emma Watson, and Brian H. Luckman. "Epic 16th Century Drought over North America." *Eos* 81 (2000): 121–25.

Stanard, William G., and Mary Newton Stanard. *The Colonial Virginia Register*. New York: Munsell, 1902.

Stannard, David E. *American Holocaust: The Conquest of the New World*. New York: Oxford University Press, 1992.

———. "The Consequences of Contact: Toward an Interdisciplinary Theory of Native Responses to Biological and Cultural Invasion." In *Columbian Consequences*. Vol. 3, *The Spanish Borderlands in Pan-American Perspective*, edited by David Hurst Thomas, 519–60. Washington DC: Smithsonian Institution Press, 1990.

———. "Disease and Infertility: A New Look at the Demographic Collapse of Native Populations in the Wake of Western Contact." *Journal of American Studies* 24, no. 3 (1990): 325–50.

Starna, William. "Seventeenth Century Dutch-Indian Trade: A Perspective from Iroquoia." In *A Beautiful and Fruitful Place: Selected Rensselaerswijck Seminar Papers*, edited by Nancy Ann McClure Zeller, 343–50. New York: New Netherlands Publishing, 1991.

Starna, William A., and Ralph Watkins. "Northern Iroquoian Slavery." *Ethnohistory* 38, no. 1 (1991): 34–57.

Steckley, John L. "The Early Map 'Novvelle France': A Linguistic Analysis." *Ontario Archaeology* 51 (1990): 17–29.

Steponaitis, Vincas P. *Ceramics, Chronology, and Community: Patterns at Moundville, a Late Prehistoric Site in Alabama*. New York: Academic Press, 1983.

―――. "Contrasting Patterns of Mississippian Development." In *Chiefdoms: Power, Economy, and Ideology*, edited by Timothy K. Earle, 193–228. Cambridge, UK: Cambridge University Press, 1991.

―――. "Location Theory and Complex Chiefdoms: A Mississippian Example." In *Mississippian Settlement Patterns*, edited by Bruce Smith, 417–53. New York: Academic Press, 1978.

Stewart, John. "Letters from John Stewart to William Dunlop." *South Carolina Historical and Genealogical Magazine* 32 (1931): 1–33, 81–114, 170–74.

Stiggins, George. "A Historical Narration of the Genealogy, Traditions, and Downfall of the Ispocoga or Creek Tribe of Indians." Edited by Theron Nunex, Jr. In *A Creek Source Book*, edited by William C. Sturtevant. New York: Garland, 1987.

Stojanowski, Christopher M. "The Bioarchaeology of Identity in Spanish Colonial Florida: Social and Evolutionary Transformation before, during, and after Demographic Collapse." *American Anthropologist*, n.s. 107, no. 3 (2005): 417–31.

―――. *Biocultural Histories in La Florida: A Bioarchaeological Perspective*. Tuscaloosa: University of Alabama Press, 2005.

―――. "A Population History of Native Groups in Pre- and Postcontact Spanish Florida: Aggregation, Gene Flow, and Genetic Drift on the Southeastern U.S. Atlantic Coast." *American Journal of Physical Anthropology* 123, no. 4 (2004): 316–32.

Stothers, D. M. "Indian Hills (33W04): A Protohistoric Village in the Maumee River Valley of Northwestern Ohio." *Ontario Archaeology* 36 (1981): 47–56.

―――. "The Protohistoric Time Period in the Southwestern Lake Erie Region: European-Derived Trade Material, Population Movement and Cultural Realignment." In *Cultures Before Contact: The Late Prehistory of Ohio and Surrounding Regions*, edited by R. Genheimer, 52–94. Columbus: The Ohio Archaeological Council, 2000.

Stowe, Noel R. "Pensacola Variant and the Bottle Creek Phase." *Florida Anthropologist* 38, no. 2 (1985): 144–49.

Struever, Stuart. "The Hopewell Interaction Sphere in Riverine-Western Great Lakes Culture History." In *Hopewellian Studies*. Vol. 12, edited by Joseph R. Caldwell and Robert L. Hall, 85–106. Springfield: Illinois State Museum Scientific Papers, 1964.

Stubbs, John. "The Chickasaw Contact with the La Salle Expedition in 1682." In *La Salle and His Legacy: Frenchmen and Indians in the Lower Mississippi*

Valley, edited by Patricia K. Galloway, 41–48. Jackson: University Press of Mississippi, 1982.

Sturm, Circe. *Blood Politics: Race, Culture, and Identity in the Cherokee Nation of Oklahoma*. Berkeley: University of California Press, 2002.

Sturtevant, William C. "Turpinambá Chiefdoms?" In *Chiefdoms and Chieftaincy in the Americas*, edited by Elsa M. Redmond, 138–49. Gainesville: University Press of Florida, 1998.

Sugden, John. *Blue Jacket: Warrior of the Shawnees*. Lincoln: University of Nebraska Press, 2000.

——. *Tecumseh: A Life*. New York: Holt, 1998.

Swanton, John R., ed. *Early History of the Creek Indians and Their Neighbors*. 1922. Bureau of American Ethnology, bulletin 73. Gainesville: University Press of Florida, 1998.

——. *Final Report of the United States De Soto Expedition Commission*. 76th Cong., 1st sess., 1939, H. Doc. 71. Washington DC: Smithsonian Institution Press, 1985.

——. "Identity of the Westo Indians." *American Anthropologist*, n.s. 21 (1920): 213–16.

——. *The Indians of the Southeastern United States*. 1946. Grosse Point MI: Scholarly Press, 1969.

——. *Indian Tribes of the Lower Mississippi Valley and Adjacent Coast of the Gulf of Mexico*. Bureau of American Ethnology, bulletin no. 43. Washington DC: Government Printing Office, 1911.

——. *Social Organization and Social Usages of the Creek Confederacy*. Bureau of American Ethnology, 42nd Annual Report, 1924–1925. Washington DC: Government Printing Office, 1928.

——. *Source Material for the Social and Ceremonial Life of the Choctaw Indians*. Bureau of American Ethnology, bulletin 103: Washington DC: Government Printing Office, 1931.

——. "Westo." In *Handbook of the American Indians*, edited by Frederick Webb Hodge, 936. Bureau of American Ethnology, bulletin 30. Washington DC: Smithsonian Institution Press, 1910.

Sylestine, Cora, Heather K. Hardy, and Timothy Montler. *Dictionary of the Alabama Language*. Austin: University of Texas Press, 1993.

Tanner, Helen Hornbeck. *Atlas of Great Lakes Indian History*. Norman: University of Oklahoma Press, 1987.

Taylor, Charles. *Modern Social Imaginaries*. Durham NC: Duke University Press, 2004.

Thomas, David Hurst. *Columbian Consequences*. 3 vols. Washington DC: Smithsonian Institution Press, 1989–91.

———. *Native American Landscapes of St. Catherines Island, Georgia*. 3 vols. Anthropological Papers of the American Museum of Natural History, no. 88, pts. 1–3, New York, 2008.

———. *St. Catherines: An Island in Time*. Athens: University of Georgia Press, 1989.

Thornton, Russell. *American Indian Holocaust and Survival: A Population History since 1492*. Norman: University of Oklahoma Press, 1987.

Thornton, Russell, Tim Miller, and Jonathan Warren. "American Indian Population Recovery Following Smallpox Epidemics." *American Anthropologist*, n.s. 93, no. 1 (1991): 28–45.

Thwaites, Reuben Gold, ed. *The Jesuit Relations and Allied Documents; Travels and Explorations of the Jesuit Missionaries in New France, l610–1791*. 73 vols. Cleveland: Burrows, 1896–1901.

Tonti [Tonty], Henri de. "Extract from a Letter from M. de Tonti to M. d'Iberville, from the Village of the Chacta, February 23, 1702, and Extract from another letter from the same to the same, From the Chacta, March 14, 1702," trans. by Patricia Galloway. In *La Salle and His Legacy: Frenchmen and Indians in the Lower Mississippi Valley*, edited by Patricia K. Galloway, 166–73. Jackson: University Press of Mississippi, 1982.

———. "Memoir by the Sieur De La Tonty." 1693. In *Historical Collections of Louisiana*, edited and trans. by B. F. French. Vol. 1, 52–78. New York: Wiley and Putnam, 1846.

———. "Relation de Henri de Tonty." *Découvertes et établissements des Français dans l'ouest et dans le sud de l'Amérique septentrionale*, edited by Pierre Margry. Vol. 1, 594–99. Paris: D. Jouast, 1876.

Tooker, Elizabeth. "Natchez Social Organization: Fact or Anthropological Folklore?" *Ethnohistory* 10, no. 3 (1963): 359–73.

Tooker, William Wallace. "The Problem of the Rechahecrian Indians of Virginia." *American Anthropologist*, o.s. 11, no. 9 (1898): 261–70.

Townsend, Richard F., ed. *Hero, Hawk, and Open Hand: American Indian Art of the Ancient Midwest and South*. New Haven CT: Yale University Press in association with the Art Institute of Chicago, 2004.

Trigger, Bruce G. *The Children of Aataentsic: A History of the Huron People to 1660*. Montreal: McGill-Queen's University Press, 1987.

———. "Early Iroquoian Contacts with Europeans." In *Handbook of North American Indians*. Vol. 15, *Northeast*, edited by Bruce G. Trigger, 344–56. Washington DC: Smithsonian Institution Press, 1978.

———. *The Huron: Farmers of the North*. New York: Holt, Rinehart and Winston, 1969.

Tuan, Yi-Fu. *Space and Place: The Perspective of Experience*. Minneapolis: University of Minnesota Press, 1977.

Tucker, Sara Jones, comp. *Atlas and Supplement: Indian Villages of the Illinois Country*. 1942. Springfield: Illinois State Museum, 1975.

Turner, E. Randolph. "Protohistoric Native American Interactions in the Virginia Coastal Plain." Paper presented at the annual meeting of the American Society for Ethnohistory, Williamsburg VA, 1988.

———. "Socio-Political Organization with the Powhatan Chiefdoms and the Effects of European Contact, AD 1607–1646." In *Cultures in Contact: The Impact of European Contacts on Native American Cultural Institutions, AD 1000–1800*, edited by William W. Fitzhugh, 208–17. Washington DC: Smithsonian Institution Press, 1985.

Usner, Daniel H., Jr. "American Indians in Colonial New Orleans." In *Powhatan's Mantle: Indians in the Colonial Southeast*, edited by Peter H. Wood, Gregory A. Waselkov, and M. Thomas Hatley, 102–27. Lincoln: University of Nebraska Press, 1989.

———. *American Indians in the Lower Mississippi Valley: Social and Economic Histories*. Lincoln: University of Nebraska Press, 1998.

———. *Indians, Settlers, and Slaves in a Frontier Exchange Economy: The Lower Mississippi Valley before 1783*. Chapel Hill: University of North Carolina Press, 1992.

Vaughan, Alden T., ed. *Early American Indian Documents: Treaties and Laws, 1607–1789*. Vol. 13, *North and South Carolina Treaties, 1654–1756*, edited by W. Stitt Robinson. Bethesda MD: University Publications of America, 2001.

Vehik, Susan C. "Cultural Continuity and Discontinuity in the Southern Prairies and Cross Timbers." In *Plains Indians, AD 500–1500*, edited by Karl H. Schlesier, 239–63. Norman: University of Oklahoma Press, 1995.

———. "Problems and Potential in Plains Indian Demography." In *Plains Indian Historical Demography and Health: Perspectives, Interpretations, and Critiques,* edited by Gregory R. Campbell, 115–25. Plains Anthropologist Memoir, no. 23, Lincoln NE, 1989.

Viau, Roland. *Enfants du néant et mangeurs d'ames: guerre, culture et société en Iroquoisie anciénne.* Montreal: Boréal, 2000.

Vivian, Gordon. *Gran Quivira: Excavations in a 17th-Century Jumano Pueblo.* National Park Service, Archeological Research Series, no. 8, Washington DC, 1964.

Voegelin, C. F., and E. Wheeler-Voegelin. "Shawnee Name Groups." *American Anthropologist*, n.s. 37, no. 4 (1935): 617–35.

Waggoner, May Rush Gwin, ed. *Le Plus Beau Païs du Monde: Completing the Picture of Proprietary Louisiana, 1699–1722.* Lafayette: Center for Louisiana Studies, 2005.

Wallerstein, Immanuel. *The Modern World System.* Vol. 1, *Capitalist Agriculture and the Origins of the European World Economy in the Sixteenth Century.* 1974. New York: Academic Press, 1980.

———. *The Modern World-System.* Vol. 2, *Mercantilism and the Consolidation of the European World Economy, 1600–1750.* 1974. New York: Academic Press, 1980.

———. *The Modern World-System.* Vol. 3, *The Second Era of Great Expansion of the Capitalist World Economy, 1730–1840s.* 1974. New York: Academic Press, 1989.

———. ed. *The Modern World-System in the Longue Durée.* Boulder CO: Paradigm, 2005.

———. *World-Systems Analysis: An Introduction.* Durham NC: Duke University Press, 2005.

Wallert-Pêtre, Hélène. "Learning How to Make the Right Pots: Apprenticeship Strategies and Material Culture, a Case Study in Handmade Pottery from Cameroon." *Journal of Anthropological Research* 57 (2001): 471–93.

Walling, Richard. *Lamar in the Middle Coosa Drainage: The Ogletree Island Site (1Ts238), A Kymulga Phase Farmstead.* Alabama Museum of Natural History, bulletin 15, Tuscaloosa, 1993: 31–48.

Warbuton, Miranda, and Richard M. Begay. "An Exploration of Navajo-Anasazi Relationships." *Ethnohistory* 52 (2005): 533–61.

Ward, H. Trawick, and R. P. Stephen Davis, Jr. "The Impact of Old World Diseases on the Native Inhabitants of the North Carolina Piedmont." *Archaeology of Eastern North America* 19 (1991): 171–81.

———. *Indian Communities on the North Carolina Piedmont AD 1000 to 1700.*

University of North Carolina, Research Laboratories of Anthropology, monograph no. 2, Chapel Hill, 1993.

———. *Time before History: The Archaeology of North Carolina*. Chapel Hill: University of North Carolina Press, 1999.

Warren, Stephen. *The Shawnees and Their Neighbors, 1795–1870*. Urbana: University of Illinois Press, 2005.

Warrick, Gary. "The Precontact Iroquoian Population of Southern Ontario." *Journal of World Prehistory* 14, no. 4 (2000): 415–66.

Warrior, Andy. "Interview with Andy Warrior, December 2006." By Ric Burns. *American Experience: We Shall Remain: A Native History of America*. Episode 2: "Tecumseh's Vision." On file with filmmaker.

Waselkov, Gregory A. *A Conquering Spirit: Fort Mims and the Redstick War of 1813–1814*. Tuscaloosa: University of Alabama Press, 2006.

———. "Historic Creek Indian Responses to European Trade and the Rise of Political Factions." In *Ethnohistory and Archaeology: Approaches to Postcontact Change in the Americas*, edited by J. Daniel Rogers and Samuel M. Wilson, 123–31. New York: Plenum, 1993.

———. "Indian Maps of the Colonial Southeast." In *Powhatan's Mantle: Indians in the Colonial Southeast*, edited by Peter H. Wood, Gregory A. Waselkov, and M. Thomas Hatley, 292–343. Lincoln: University of Nebraska Press, 1989.

———. "The Macon Trading House and Early European-Indian Contact in the Colonial Southeast." In *Ocmulgee Archaeology, 1936–1986*, edited by David J. Hally, 190–96. Athens: University of Georgia Press, 1994.

———. "Seventeenth-Century Trade in the Colonial Southeast." *Southeastern Archaeology* 8 (1989): 117–33.

Waselkov, Gregory A., and Bonnie L. Gums. *Plantation Archaeology at Rivière aux Chiens, ca. 1725–1848*. Report for the Alabama Department of Transportation. University of South Alabama, Center for Archaeological Studies, Archaeological Monograph, no. 7, Mobile, 2000.

Waselkov, Gregory A., and Marvin T. Smith. "Upper Creek Archaeology." In *Indians of the Greater Southeast: Historical Archaeology and Ethnohistory*, edited by Bonnie G. McEwan, 242–64. Gainesville: University Press of Florida, 2000.

Wauchope, Robert. *Archaeological Survey of Northern Georgia*. Society for American Archaeology, memoir 21, Washington DC, 1966.

Wedel, Mildred Mott. "Bénard, Sieur de La Harpe." *Great Plains Journal* 10, no. 2 (1971): 37–70.

Weiner, Annette. *Inalienable Possessions: The Paradox of Keeping-While-Giving.* Berkeley: University of California Press, 1992.

Welch, Paul D. *Archaeology at Shiloh Indian Mounds, 1899–1999.* Tuscaloosa: University of Alabama Press, 2006.

———. "Control over Goods and the Political Stability of the Moundville Chiefdom." In *Political Structure and Change in the Southeastern United States,* edited by John Scarry, 69–91. Gainesville: University Press of Florida, 1996.

———. *Moundville's Economy.* Tuscaloosa: University of Alabama Press, 1991.

———. "The Occupational History of the Bessemer Site." *Southeastern Archaeology* 13 (1994): 1–26.

———. "Outlying Sites within the Moundville Chiefdom." In *Archaeology of the Moundville Chiefdom,* edited by Vernon James Knight, Jr., and Vincas P. Steponaitis, 133–66. Washington DC: Smithsonian Institution Press, 1998.

Wells, John H. *Abbyville: A Complex of Archaeological Sites in the John H. Kerr Reservoir, Halifax County, Virginia.* Archaeological Society of Virginia, Special Publication, no. 39, Richmond, 2002.

Weslager, Clinton. *Dutch Explorers, Traders, and Settlers in the Delaware Valley, 1609–1664.* Philadelphia: University of Pennsylvania Press, 1961.

Wesson, Cameron B. *Households and Hegemony: Early Creek Symbolic Capital, Prestige Goods, and Social Power.* Lincoln: University of Nebraska Press, 2008.

———. "Prestige Goods, Symbolic Capital, and Social Power in the Protohistoric Southeast." In *Between Contacts and Colonies: Archaeological Perspectives on the Protohistoric Southeast,* edited by Cameron B. Wesson and Mark A. Rees, 110–25. Tuscaloosa: University of Alabama Press, 2002.

Wesson, Cameron B., and Mark A. Rees, eds. *Between Contacts and Colonies: Archaeological Perspectives on the Protohistoric Southeast.* Tuscaloosa: University of Alabama Press, 2002.

Wesson, Cameron B., James A. Wall, and David W. Chase. "A Spaghetti Style Gorget from the Jere Shine Site (1Mt6), Montgomery County, Alabama." *Journal of Alabama Archaeology* 47, no. 2 (2001): 132–52.

Wheeler-Voegelin, Erminie. *Ethnohistory of Indian Use and Occupancy in Ohio and Indiana Prior to 1795.* American Indian Ethnohistory: North Central and Northeastern Indians Series. New York: Garland, 1974.

Wheeler-Voegelin, Erminie, and Georg K. Neumann. "Shawnee Pots and Pottery Making." *Pennsylvania Archaeologist* 18, no. 1–2 (1948): 3–12.

Wheeler-Voegelin, Erminie, and Helen Hornbuck Tanner. *Indians of Ohio and*

Indiana Prior to 1795. American Indian Ethnohistory: North Central and Northeastern Indians Series. New York: Garland, 1974.

——. *Mortuary Customs of the Shawnee and Other Eastern Tribes*. Indiana Historical Society, Prehistoric Research Series, vol. 2, no. 4, Indianapolis, 1944.

White, Douglas, George P. Murdock, and Richard Scaglion. "Natchez Class and Rank Reconsidered." *Ethnology* 10, no. 4 (1971): 369–88.

White, Marian E. "Erie." In *Handbook of North American Indians*. Vol. 15, *Northeast*, edited by Bruce Trigger, 412–17. Washington DC: Smithsonian Institution Press, 1978.

——. "Neutral and Wenro." In *Handbook of North American Indians*. Vol. 15, *Northeast*, edited by Bruce G. Trigger, 407–11. Washington DC: Smithsonian Institution Press, 1978.

White, Richard. *The Middle Ground: Indians, Empires, and Republics in the Great Lakes Region, 1650–1815*. Cambridge, UK: Cambridge University Press, 1991.

——. *The Roots of Dependency: Subsistence, Environment, and Social Change among the Choctaws, Pawnees, and Navajos*. Lincoln: University of Nebraska Press, 1983.

Whitehead, Neil. "Tribes Make States and States Make Tribes." In *War in the Tribal Zone: Expanding States and Indigenous Warfare*, edited by R. Brian Ferguson and Neil L. Whitehead, 127–50. 1992. 2nd ed. Santa Fe: School of American Research Press, 1999.

Whittlesey, Dervent S., Charles C. Colby, and Richard Hartshorne. *German Strategy of World Conquest*. New York: Farrar and Rhinehart, 1942.

Widmer, Randolf J. "The Structure of Southeastern Chiefdoms." In *The Forgotten Centuries: Indians and Europeans in the American South, 1521–1704*, edited by Charles Hudson and Carmen Chaves Tesser, 125–55. Athens: University of Georgia Press, 1994.

Williams, Mark, and Gary Shapiro, eds. *Lamar Archaeology: Mississippian Chiefdoms in the Deep South*. Tuscaloosa: University of Alabama Press, 1990.

Williams, Samuel Cole, ed. *Early Travels in the Tennessee Country, 1540–1800*. Johnson City TN: Watauga, 1928.

Williams, Stephen. "The Vacant Quarter and Other Late Events in the Lower Valley." In *Towns and Temples along the Mississippi*, edited by David H. Dye and Cheryl Anne Cox, 170–81. Tuscaloosa: University of Alabama Press, 1990.

Willis, W. S. "Divide and Rule: Red, White, and Black in the Southeast." In *Red*,

White, and Black: Symposium on Indians on the Old South, edited by Charles M. Hudson, 99–115. Athens: University of Georgia Press, 1971.

Wintemberg, William J. *Lawson Prehistoric Village Site, Middlesex County, Ontario.* National Museum of Canada, bulletin 94, Anthropological Series, no. 25, Ottawa, 1939.

Wolf, Eric. *Europe and the People without History.* 1982. Berkeley: University of California Press, 1990.

Wood, Peter H. *Black Majority: Negroes in Colonial South Carolina from 1670 through the Stono Rebellion.* New York: Knopf, 1974.

———. "The Changing Population of the Colonial South: An Overview by Race and Region." In *Powhatan's Mantle: Indians in the Colonial Southeast,* edited by Peter H. Wood, Gregory A. Waselkov, and M. Thomas Hatley, 35–103. Lincoln: University of Nebraska Press, 1989.

Woods, Patricia Dillon. *French-Indian Relations on the Southern Frontier, 1699–1762.* Ann Arbor: UMI Research Press, 1980.

Woodward, Henry. "Woodward's Faithfull Relation of My Westoe Voiage Was Written in December 1674." In *Narratives of Early Carolina, 1650–1708,* edited by Alexander. S. Salley, 125–34. New York: Scribner, 1911.

Woodward, Thomas S. *Reminiscences of the Creek, or Muscogee Indians Contained in Letters to Friends in Georgia and Alabama.* 1859. Tuscaloosa: Alabama Book Store and Birmingham Book Exchange, 1939.

Worth, John E. "Bridging Prehistory and History in the Southeast: Evaluating the Utility of the Acculturation Concept." In *Light on the Path: The Anthropology and History of the Southeastern Indians,* edited by Thomas J. Pluckhahn and Robbie Ethridge, 196–206. Tuscaloosa: University of Alabama Press, 2006.

———. "A History of Southeastern Indians in Cuba, 1513–1823." Paper presented at the annual meeting of the Southeastern Archaeological Conference, St. Louis, 2004.

———. "Late Spanish Military Expeditions in the Interior Southeast, 1597–1628." In *The Forgotten Centuries: Indians and Europeans in the American South, 1521–1704,* edited by Charles Hudson and Carmen Chaves Tesser, 104–22. Athens: University of Georgia Press, 1994.

———. "The Lower Creeks: Origins and Early History." In *Indians of the Greater Southeast: Historical Archaeology and Ethnohistory,* edited by Bonnie G. McEwan, 265–98. Gainesville: University Press of Florida, 2000.

———. "Prelude to Abandonment: The Interior Provinces of Early 17th Century Georgia." *Early Georgia* 21, no. 1 (1993): 25–58.

———. "Spanish Missions and the Persistence of Chiefly Power." In *The Transformation of the Southeastern Indians, 1540–1760*, edited by Robbie Ethridge and Charles Hudson, 39–64. Jackson: University Press of Mississippi, 2002.

———. *The Struggle for the Georgia Coast: An Eighteenth-Century Spanish Retrospective on Guale and Mocama*. Anthropological Papers of the American Museum of Natural History, no. 75, New York, 1995. Tuscaloosa: University of Alabama Press, 2007.

———. *The Timucuan Chiefdoms of Spanish Florida*. 2 Vols. Gainesville: University Press of Florida, 1998.

———. "Yamassee." In *Handbook of North American Indians*. Vol. 14, *Southeast*, edited by Raymond D. Fogelson, 245–53. Washington DC: Smithsonian Institution Press, 2004.

———. "Yamasee Origins and the Development of the Carolina-Florida Frontier." Paper presented at the Fifth Annual Conference of the Omohundro Institute of Early American History and Culture, Austin, 1999.

Wright, Amos J. *Historic Indian Towns in Alabama, 1540–1838*. Tuscaloosa: University of Alabama Press, 2003.

Wright, Gordon K. *The Neutral Indians: A Source Book*. Occasional Papers of the New York State Archaeological Association, no. 4, Rochester, 1963.

Wright, J. Leitch. *Creeks and Seminoles: Destruction and Regeneration of the Muscogulge People*. Lincoln: University of Nebraska Press, 1986.

Wright, Louis B. "William Byrd I and the Slave Trade." *Huntington Library Quarterly* 8 (1945): 379–87.

List of Contributors

ROBIN A. BECK JR. is assistant professor of anthropology at the University of Oklahoma. He is currently codirecting excavations at the Berry site in North Carolina, location of the sixteenth-century Native town of Joara and Juan Pardo's Fort San Juan. He has also worked extensively in the Andes Mountains of Bolivia and Peru. His work has appeared in journals such as *Current Anthropology, American Antiquity, Ethnohistory, Latin American Antiquity*, and *Southeastern Archaeology.*

ERIC E. BOWNE received his PhD from the University of Georgia in 2003. He is the author of *The Westo Indians: Slave Traders of the Early Colonial South* (2005). Bowne is currently working on a book-length guide to late prehistoric Mississippian chiefdoms.

ROBBIE ETHRIDGE is associate professor of anthropology at the University of Mississippi. Her specialties are ethnohistory, cultural anthropology, and environmental anthropology, with a focus on the history of the Southern Indians. She is the author of *Creek Country: The Creek Indians and Their World, 1796–1816* (2003), and she is coeditor of *The Transformation of the Southeastern Indians, 1540–1760* (2002) and *Light on the Path: The Anthropology and History of the Southeastern Indians* (2006). She is also coeditor in chief of *Native South.*

MARY ELIZABETH FITTS is pursuing a PhD in anthropology at the University of North Carolina–Chapel Hill.

WILLIAM (BILL) FOX worked nineteen years as a regional archaeologist in northwestern, north central, and southwestern Ontario and then as senior archaeologist responsible for review of development plans for the Province of Ontario. In 1992 he joined Parks Canada as chief of archaeology for the Prairie and Northern Region and then transferred to the

Western Arctic as CRM manager before moving to a management position at Pacific Rim National Park Reserve on Vancouver Island. He is a research associate of the Canadian Museum of Civilization and continues his active involvement in research and publication on topics related to Native peoples of the Great Lakes region.

PATRICIA GALLOWAY has a BA in French (1966) from Millsaps College and a MA (1968) and PhD (1973) in comparative literature from the University of North Carolina–Chapel Hill, and a PhD in anthropology (2004) also from UNC-CH. She worked as a medieval archaeologist in Europe in the 1970s and then became involved with humanities-oriented computing, which she supported in the Computer Unit of Westfield College of the University of London 1977–79. From 1979 to 2000 she worked at the Mississippi Department of Archives and History, where she was a documentary editor, archaeological editor, historian, museum exhibit developer, and manager of information systems. In 2000 she went to the School of Information, University of Texas–Austin, where she is now associate professor in archival enterprise. Recent publications include *Choctaw Genesis 1500–1700* (1995), *The Hernando de Soto Expedition* (1997), and *Practicing Ethnohistory* (2006), a book of essays. She has also published a book chapter in *Historical Archaeology* (2006) and articles in *American Archivist*, *D-Lib*, and *Ethnohistory*.

CHARLES L. HEATH is a staff archaeologist with the Fort Bragg Cultural Resources Management Program, Fort Bragg, North Carolina, and a PhD candidate in anthropology at the University of North Carolina–Chapel Hill.

NED J. JENKINS is archaeologist for the Alabama Historical Commission, specializing in the prehistory and early history of the American South. In addition to authoring several articles and reports, he is coauthor of *The Tombigbee Watershed in Southeastern Prehistory* (2002).

MATTHEW JENNINGS is assistant professor of history at Macon State College in Macon, Georgia.

MARVIN D. JETER (PhD, Arizona State University, 1977) has been the Arkansas Archeological Survey's station archeologist for southeast Arkansas for most of the time since 1978. He has also worked in Alabama, Arizona, Louisiana, Mississippi, Tennessee, and briefly Illinois. His research emphasizes late prehistoric, protohistoric, and early historic sites in and near the Lower Mississippi Valley (LMV) and the history of archaeology. His publications include the *Choice* award-winning *Edward Palmer's Arkansaw Mounds* (1990), overviews of LMV and regional archaeology, and a number of articles, book chapters, and reviews.

PAUL KELTON is associate professor and chair of the Department of History, University of Kansas. He is the author of *Epidemics and Enslavement: Biological Catastrophe in the Native Southeast, 1492–1715* (2007).

MAUREEN MEYERS is a PhD candidate in the Department of Anthropology at the University of Kentucky. Her dissertation focuses on a frontier Mississippian village in southwestern Virginia.

GEORGE MILNE is assistant professor of early American history at Oakland University. He earned his MA at New York University and his PhD at the University of Oklahoma. He has taught early American and Native American history at the California State University–Los Angeles and the University of Oklahoma.

RANDOLPH NOE (1939–2003) was a probate lawyer and Shawnee descendent from Louisville, Kentucky, who devoted his time away from law to Shawnee history. This abiding passion resulted in a work of critical importance to those interested in Shawnee history: *The Shawnee Indians: An Annotated Bibliography* (2001). He is also the author of *Kentucky Probate Methods* (1976).

SHERI M. SHUCK-HALL is associate professor of history at Christopher Newport University. Her most recent publication is *Journey to the West: The Alabama and Coushatta Indians* (2008), a book-length treatment of the Alabama and Coushatta Indians over three centuries.

STEPHEN WARREN is associate professor of history at Augustana College. He is the author of *The Shawnees and their Neighbors, 1795–1870* (2005), and he has appeared in the documentary film series "We Shall Remain: A Native History of America." He is currently working on a book-length project about place and identity in the Eastern Woodlands during the colonial period.

JOHN WORTH (PhD, University of Florida, 1992) is assistant professor of anthropology at the University of West Florida. His research interests focus on the ethnohistory and archaeology of the Southern Indians during the European colonial era. In addition to numerous articles and chapters, he is also the author of *The Struggle for the Georgia Coast* (1995) and *The Timucuan Chiefdoms of Spanish Florida* (1998).

Index

Charles Town (SC): and disease, 316T; establishment of, 96–97, 257, 298; need for slaves, 282; and slave trade, 147, 257, 258, 315; trade with Yamasees, 284. *See also* Carolina colony; South Carolina colony

Charlevoix, Father, 401, 408

Charlotte Thompson site, 214, 215, 221, 223

Charraw (Sara; Saraw; Cheraw), 140n51, 149, *153*, 154

Cheraw. *See* Charraw

Cherokees: coalescence of, 38, 40, 111; as militaristic slaving society, 35; regulation of Ohio Valley trade, 165–66; and slave trade, 259, 265; Tomahitans, 165–66; trade by, 99; Westos and, 258; and Yamasee War, 327, 328

Chiaha (Olamico), 32, 124, 125, 126

Chicaza (chief), 274

Chicaza (chiefdom), 8, 254, 255, 256, 274

Chichimechos, 96, 298

Chickasawhay, 356

Chickasaws: alliance with English, 337–38; Choctaws and, 335, 337, 340; coalescence of, 38, 39, 40, 111, 315; connection to Sorrels and Summerville IV complexes, 229–31; disease and, 312, *314*, 320–21, 321–22; early contact with Europeans, 336, 337–38; global capitalist economy and, 421; and guns, 341; impact of slave trade on, 356–57; migrations by, 229–30; as militaristic slaving society,

35–36; and slave trade, 258, 320–21, 322, 336, 337–38, 355–56, 379, 394; and Yamasee War, 327

chief. *See micos*

chiefdoms: causes of collapse of, 7; consolidation of, after contact, 40; definition of, 3–4; dynamics of collapse of, 37; as form of government, southward spread of, 368; incompatibility of with European trade system, 40; longevity of in Spanish Florida, 27–28; political structure of, 4; relationships between, 419; as term, 43n5; towns of, 4; types of, 6–7. *See also* cycling of chiefdoms; complex chiefdom; Mississippian world; paramount chiefdom; simple chiefdom

Chigelly, 218, 288

Chipewyans, 31, 375

Chiscas, 33, 35, 297–98, 301

Chitimachas, 360n18, 389

Chiweres, 375–76, 385n63

Choctaw coalescence, 36, 111; cultural commonalities of constituent groups, 340–41; major groups in, 333; nature of, 340; slave raids and, 355–56

Choctaw economy: and deerskin trade, 338, 354, 358, 359, 361n23; European goods in, 354; persistence of Native structures in, 339, 341, 354; trade and, 335, 351. *See also* spheres of exchange in Choctaw economy

Choctaws: ability to resist Chickasaw aggression, 340; ability to resist

lowing, 40; continuities in political organization after, 37, 39–40; Creeks and, 236; Natchez and, 395–96; persistence of Native economies after, 339, 341–42; regional stability before, 7–8; transformation of social and political structures following, 36–42, 60n118. *See also* European exploration

Cool Branch site, 210

Coosa (chief), 8

Coosa (chiefdom): in Chigelly origin stories, 288; collapse of, 9, 12–13, 49n33, 204, 205, 235, 258, 259; Coste and, 254, 256; and Creek coalescence, 32, 235; decline of, 274–75; formation of, 203, 233; history of, 204–5; rise of, 213, 234

Coosada, 261

Coosata King, 326

core region, in world-systems theory, 16–17

cosmology, Mississippian, violence in, 275–77

Coste, 254–55, 256, 258–59, 268n11

Cotachico (emperor of Cofitachequi), 136

Coushatta coalescence: disease and, 256; migration and, 259, 266; slave trade and, 258–59; Soto and, 254–55

Coushattas: clans, 262; and Creek coalescence, 235; cultural ties to Alabamas, 260–61, 262, 270n35; language, 260; Mississippian origins, 254; origin story of, 260,

267; as part of Alabama Nation, 259; towns, 261; variant spellings of, 268n10. *See also* Alabama-Coushattas

Cowetas, 35, 110, 217–18, 221, 234, 258, 265, 288

Creek coalescence, 32, 39, 110, 111, 231–36; Abercrombie phase and, 188–89, 216–18, 219, 234; Alabama River phase and, 224–27; Atasi phase and, 188, 189, 227–28, 235; Big Eddy phase and, 214–16, 219; core population of, 236; Coweta origins, 217–18; Cusseta origins, 217–18; disease and, 315; four foundation towns, 218; Kymulga phase and, 218–19; Lamar Variant and, 205–8, 219, 236; Mississippian predecessors, 198–205, *199, 202,* 287; Moundville Variant and, 188, 208–14, 219, 236; Ocmulgee Fields Variant and, 227–28; primary groups in, 188–89, 200, 235–36; Shine II phase and, 188, 190–91, 205–8, 219; timing of, 237n3; Woodland predecessors of, 195–98, 196T, *197*

Creek Confederacy: alliance with Alabama-Coushattas, 263–64, 265, 267; as coalescent society, 38, 40; disease and, 320–21; English alliance with, 75; English perception of, 271n45; global capitalist economy and, 421; groups under, 110; *métis* leadership in, 62n134; origin of name, 236; origin stories of, 287–90; political organization,

Creek Confederacy (*continued*)
168; and Queen Anne's War, 301;
sense of sacred space in, 168; settlements in Florida, 306; Shawnees
and, 172–73, 174, 177, 184n41,
185n42, 186n46, 235; in Shawnee
mythology, 177; slave raids on
Spanish Florida by, 300–301; and
slave trade, 25, 308, 320–21; trade
agreements by, 41, 300; *talwas* of.
See also Creek coalescence; Lower
Creek coalescence; Upper Creek
coalescence
Crees, 31
Crenay, Baron de, 222
Crenshaw site, 366
Cuba, Natives' flight from Florida to,
296, 303, 304
Culasa, 261
cultural identity of Indians, land and,
163, 167–69, 180n5
cultural imaginary, Choctaws, 340,
354
culture of violence, Spanish, 278
cultures of violence, Native, 272,
275–77, 282
Cusabos, 96
Cussetas, 35, 168, 189, 217–18, 234, 258,
288, 290
cycling of chiefdoms, 7–8, 45n17,
46n18; and ethnic and ceramic
change, 190–91; warfare and, 274.
See also budding; chiefdoms; fissioning

Daillon, Father, 68

Dallas Variant, 204–5, 211, 215, 229,
235, 254
Dead River phase, 195
De Chépart, Captain, 404–5, 407, 409
Deerfoot, 263
deerskin trade. *See* trade, deerskin
Delaware Bay Indians, 31
Delawares, 164, 168, 171, 172, 175, 176
Delgado, Marcos, 223, 226, 230, 261,
262
demographic collapse: and depopulation of Spanish Florida, 28–29,
296, 302, 303–5; and drought in
Lower Mississippi Valley, 372; factors in, 11–12, 47n29; and increased
Iroquoian aggressiveness, 64–65,
74; and Vacant Quarter, 58n91, 367.
See also disease and demographic
collapse; slave trade in Indians,
and demographic collapse; slave
raids; slave raids by Westos; slave
raids on Spanish Florida; slave
trade in Indians
Desnoyers, Madame, 408–10
Dhegiha Siouans: cosmology of, 376,
385n63; migration by, 373, 374, 375,
379; origins of, 373–74, 385n63
diaspora: defined, 250; following
Moundville fissioning, 252–53
disease: and Alabama and Coushatta
coalescence, 256; in Alabama
River phase, 224–26; in Carolina
Piedmont, 119, 129, 134; in
Cofitachequi, 119; epidemics preceding Yamasee War, 312, 322–23;
future directions for research in,
419–20; and increase in Iroquoian

English colonies (*continued*) interference with Native adoption of war captives, 323–28; and linking of Native Americans to world capitalist system, 18, 19, 29; playing of Native groups against each other, 150, 287; provision of guns, 64, 296, 379; responsibility for transformation of lower South, 295; and slave trade, 23, 257, 295, 296, 300, 301, 305–6, 337–38, 339, 355, 379; trade by, 36, 40, 228, 265, 313, 397. *See also* Carolina colony; Charles Town; South Carolina colony

Eno, 154. *See also* Oenock (Eno)

Eries: acquisition of guns by, 71; Beaver Wars and, 105; as coalescent nation, 71, 83; conquest by Iroquois, 70, 85; cultural similarity to Neutrals, 66–67, 71; destruction of, 30, 167; Hurons among, 70; migration by, 105; Neutrals among, 70; in seventeenth century, 66–67; trade by, 105; warfare by, 65, 85; Westos as, 71–72, 82–84, 105, 134, 281. *See also* Richahecrians

Erie-Seneca War (1654–57), 71

Esaws, 111, 122, 144–45, 146, 147, 154, 156–57

ethnic soldiering, of Catawbas, 143, 148–50, 157

Etowah, 5, 193–94, 203, 233

Etowah I complex, *199*

Etowah II complex, *202*

Etowah Variant, 200

European exploration, 336–39; disruption of Native political structures by, 8–9; by English, 135–37; by French, 336–39, 372, 374–75. *See also* contact; Jolliet, Louis; La Salle, Nicholas de; Marquette, Father Jacques; Penicault, Andre; Soto, Hernando de

European settlers: establishment of, 17, 26, 26T, 41, 296; first in U.S. interior, 123; future directions for research on, 421–22; living with Indians, 41; as venture capitalists, 19, 51n52, 421. *See also* Carolina colony; Charles Town; English colonies; French colonies; French colonist; French exploration; Netherlands; Spanish exploration; Spanish Florida; Portugal; Virginia colony

falcons, as motif in art, 273, 293n2

Falls Plantation, 92–94, *93*

fanimingo institutions, 39, 406, 410

Fatherland site, 397

Fire Nation, 65, 68, 69

First Natchez War, 398

fissioning: climatic causes of, 193–95; examples of, 193; of Moundville culture, 190, 193, 195, 213–14, 231, 232, 252–53. *See also* budding

Five Nations. *See* Iroquois Confederacy

Fleet, Henry, 88, 89

Fort Ancient peoples, 68, 88, 164–65, 166, 180n8, 373–74, 384n53

Fort Apalachicola, 228

Fort Rosalie, 399, 404–5, 407, 410

imperialism, Western: and intensi-
fication of intra-Native warfare,
20–26, 55n73; tumultuous impact
on Native societies, 20, 51n53.
See also European exploration;
European settlers
Indian Claims Commission, 182n31
Indian rebellions, in Southwest, 377
Indian Removal Act, 179n1
Indian slave trade. See slave trade in
Indians
Iroquoian groups: conquest of other
nations, 69–70, 85; in early seventeenth century, 66–72; postcontact
intensification of warfare by, 30,
31–32, 63–65, 72–75, 167; precontact warfare by, 30, 63
Iroquois Confederacy: and Beaver
Wars, 84; as cause of domino migration, 374; covenant chain of,
172; defeat of Susquehannocks by,
173; guns and, 65, 69, 85; impact of
disease on, 30; inability of to assimilate conquered nations, 74; as
militaristic slaving society, 29–31;
mourning wars of, 30, 31–32, 72,
73–75, 167; Natives' fear of, 374;
regulation of Ohio Valley trade
by, 166; retreat of, 35; Shawnees
and, 171–72, 175; slave trade and,
25, 72–75, 374–75, 420; trade by,
88, 105; warfare by, 69, 167; Westos
and, 85–86
Ispocoga Nation, 173
Itoyatin, 87

Jackson Lake site, 214, 221, 243n71

Jamestown, 31–32, 33, 257, 277
Jamestown Massacre, 87, 91–92
Jenkins site (1Mt48), 207
Jere Shine site, 203, 205, 207, 220, 223,
239n33, 240n48
Jesuits, retreat from Huronia, 70
Joara (Xualla): collapse of, 132, 133;
cultural tradition of, 128; as
dominant chiefdom, 115, 129, 130;
Lederer in, 132; location of, 116,
122–23; Pardo in, 122–23, 126–27;
rise of, 125; size of, 127–28; Soto in,
120; Westo raids on, 135
Joara Mico, 125, 126–27
Jogues, Father Isaac, 64, 72
Johnson, Nathaniel, 319–20
Johnston, Gideon, 318
Jolliet, Louis, 372, 373, 374
Jones, John, 326
Jones Bluff Complex, 202
Jove, 304

Kadapau, 145–46, 154, 159n18
Kahkwas, 67
Kansas, 373
Kashita, 221. See also Cussetas
Kent phase, 371
Keyauwee, 154
King's Town, 153
Kious, 35
Kiskakon Odawas, 69
Kispokotha division, 169–70, 173–74,
182n29, 184n38, 184n41
Koasati phase, 215, 235
Koasatis, 186n47, 189, 211, 215, 229,
235. See also Coushattas
Kolly, Jean-Daniel, 399

32; characteristics of, 208, 240n49; and Coushatta origin, 254; and Creek coalescence, 188, 208–14, 219, 236; fissioning of, 190, 193, 195, 213–14, 231, 232, 252–53; history of, 208–14; Koasati and, 235; language of, 215; origin of, 251–52; spatial extent, 208, 217

mourning wars: of Iroquois, 30, 31–32, 72, 73–75, 167; of Neutrals, 65, 69; of Westos, 83

Moyano, Hernando, 123, 124, 126

Muklasa (Qulasa), 223, 226, 230. *See also* Miculassa (Moçulixa)

Muklasa site (1Mt10), 207

Mulberry site (38KE12), 118

Musgrove, John, 324, 325

Muskogees, 272, 321

Muspa, 304

Nairne, Thomas: on coalescence, 321; death of, 285–86, 294n48; on disease, 314, 320; measures against French, 360n13; as observer of Native life, 112, 285–86, 303, 406

Naniabas, 334

Nanih Waiya (Choctaw Mother Mound), 334

Nanipacana, 335

Napituca, 8

Napochies, 274–75

Nassaw, 122, 145–46, 148, *153*, 158n11, 161n42

Natchez: Choctaw attacks on, 408; coalescence and, 37–38, 39; contact and, 395–96; and Creek coalescence, 235; destruction of chiefdoms, 38; destruction of Fort Rosalie, 407; diplomacy of, 390, 400–401, 402–4, 409–10; and disease, *314*; enslavement of, 411; French destruction of, 410–11; French taken and enslaved by, 407–9; Grand Village of, 394, 397; guns and, 362n23; human sacrifice at death of Great Sun, 402–4; impact of shatter zone on, 394–95; incorporation of outsiders and refugees by, 389, 390–91, 394, 395, 408, 413n15; isolation from English traders, 36; mythology, 392; political organization, 397, 401; proximity to Choctaws, 335; relations with French, 389–90, 393–94, 395–96, 397–409; religion, 391–92; revolt of 1729, 15, 404–11; slave raids on, 360n18; social structure of, 392–93, 413n12; survival of, 9; trade by, 396–97; tradition of exogamous marriage among, 388–89, 390–91, 392, 393–94, 403, 412; views on French status, 396; women's roles among, 388, 389–91, 400–404, 406–10

Natchezans: Northern, 370–71, 372, 376; Southern, 370

Natchez Paradox, 393

Native economies. *See* economies, Native

Native political systems. *See* political systems, Native

Native religion. *See* religion, Native

Native social structures. *See* social structures, Native

Nau, Father, 72
Nauvasa, 145. *See also* Nassaw
Navajo Nation, 180n5
Necotowance, 92
Needham, James, 95–96
Netherlands: colonization of North America, 17, 26, 26T, 29; and linking of Native Americans to world capitalist system, 18, 19
Neutrals: absorption by Iroquois, 66, 69–70, 85; cultural similarity to Eries, 66–67, 71; dispersion of, 30, 70, 85; migration by, 63; of the Niagra Peninsula, 67; in seventeenth century, 67–70; trade by, 87–88; warfare and, 65, 69, 85; Wenroes and, 84; Westos as, 84, 134
Newe, Thomas, 72, 284
Nicholson, Governor Francis, 145
Nipissings, 68
Nodena phase, 368, 369, 371
Noostee Town, *153*
Northern Natchezans, 370–71, 372, 376
Nustie, 148

Occaneechis: Bacon's Rebellion and, 98, 99; brutality of, 131; destruction of, 137, 154; dominance of Virginia trade, 131; future directions for research on, 420; global capitalist economy and, 421; guns and, 134–35; as militaristic slaving society, 32; raids in Carolina colony, 134–35, *135*; settlement Indians and, 34; trade by, 95, 96–97, 98

Ocheses, 110
Ocmulgee Fields Variant, 227–28, 235, 249n145
Ocmulgees, 110, 289, 321
Ocute, 107, 119
Odawa, 67, 68
Oenock (Eno), 131–32. *See also* Eno
Oheroukouarhronons (People of the Swamp), 68–69, 70, 71
Ohio Valley: displacement of Indians from, 167; first European arrival in, 165; limited access to European goods, 165–66; regulation of trade in, 166; as trade crossroads, 164–65
Ojibwas, 30
Okfuskee, 235
Okmulgee Fields Variant, 235
Olamico (Chiaha), 124, 125, 126
Old Town (Shawnee town), 175
Old Town phase, 371
Oliver phase, 371
Omahas, 373
Omiagarhronnons, 70
Oneidas, 89
Oneotas: Chiwere as, 375–76, 385n63; culture of, 385n63; evidence of warfare in burials of, 366–67; migration by, 375, 384n62, 385n63
Ontwagannhas, 66. *See also* Fire Nation
Opechancanough, 87, 91
Opessa, 175–76
Opoyheatly, 263
orata, 124–25, 126–27. See also *micos*
Order of Santiago, 279
origin stories: of Alabama, 260, 267; of Coushatta, 260, 267; of Creeks,

303–5; devastation caused by, 29, 106–7, 296, 298–99, 300–301, 302–3, 318–19; impact on unallied Indians, 302–3; number captured in, 14; origin of, 297–98; political benefits to English from, 296; in Queen Anne's War, 263–64, 301; Spanish retaliation for, 300; by Yamasees, 285–86, 299–300, 303, 323

slavery, indigenous form of, 21–22, 54n64, 72–75, 281, 378

slaves, African: Choctaw freeing of, from Natchez, 408; Natchez returning of, to French, 410

slaves, Indian: crippling of, in prehistory, 369; demand for, 147, 257, 282, 307; Natchez enslavement, 411; in Spanish colonies, 377–78; uses of, 14, 23, 50n36, 73, 104, 159n16, 257

slaves, white, Natchez enslavement of, 407–9

slave trade in Africans: articulation between Indian slave trade and, 422; displacement of Indian trade by, 99, 306, 379

slave trade in Indians: and Alabamas and Coushattas, 257–59, 263–66, 267; articulation between African slave trade and, 422; and brutalization of Indian cultures, 22–26; capture and marketing of slaves, 13–14; Carolina colony and, 137, 147, 257, 258, 282, 287, 306, 315; and Choctaw spheres of exchange,

356–59; and decline of Native population, 284, 287; devastation caused by, 307–9; differences from precontact slavery, 26; end of, 297, 305–6, 312, 322–23, 328–29; English colonies and, 23, 257, 295, 296, 300, 301, 305–6, 337–38, 339, 355, 379; French colonies and, 339, 360n18, 378–79; groups involved in, 14; Iroquois' lack of participation in, 74–75; and militarization of Indian culture, 21; Native debt incurred from, 306, 323, 326, 328; and Native integration into world capitalist system, 50n42, 295–96, 307; Native motives for participation in, 280–81, 286, 307; Native participation in violence of, 21, 23–24; origin of, 297–98; and rise of militaristic slaving societies, 24–25, 29–34, 82, 147; scholarly downplaying of Native violence in, 23–24, 54n68; and Spanish Florida, 28–29; and spread of disease, 312, *314*, 314–15, 315–16, 318, 320–21; and spread of violence, 281; struggle for control of, in Carolina colony, 106; volume of, 104, 111. *See also* militaristic slaving societies; slave raids

slave trade in Indians, and demographic collapse: among Choctaws, 356; interplay of slaving and disease, 15; number of slaves taken, 14–15; slave raider deaths, 322; in Spanish Florida, 28–29, 296, 302 slave trade in Indians, and political collapse, 9, 50n42, 308; in Carolina Piedmont, 142, 147; impact of militaristic slaving societies and, 24–25, 29–36

smallpox: Alabamas and Coushattas and, 264; in Carolina Piedmont, 134; in Cuba, 304–5. *See also* Great Southeastern Smallpox Epidemic

Smith, John, 19, 86, 277

Snow's Bend site, 216, 255

Soccoro (Hymahi), 116–17

social imaginary, of Choctaws, 340, 354

social structures, Native: continuities between pre- and postcontact worlds, 37, 39–40; transformation of, following collapse of Mississippian world, 36–42, 60n118

Soogela King, 327

Sorrells phase, *206*, 211, 214, 226–27, 229–30

Soto, Hernando de: Choctaws and, 335; disruption of Native political structures by, 8–9, 12, 119, 223–24, 234–35, 256, 258; expedition across Alabama, 214, 215, 219–24, 226, 230–31, 233, 234, 254–56; expedition across Carolina Piedmont, 115, 116–17, 119–21; expedition in Arkansas, 370; military sophistication of, 278; Natchez and, 395; news of arrival of, received in interior, 165; as observer of Native life, 8, 10, 274, 369; and Spanish culture of violence, 278–79; visit

to Cofitachequi, 109; warfare with Indians, 8, 222–24, 234, 255, 277–78, 279–80

South Appalachian Tradition, 201

South Carolina Board of Indian Trade Commissioners, 142, 158n1, 324–25

South Carolina colony: Catawba ethnic soldiering for, 148–50, 157; disease and, 315–18, 316T; kidnapping of Natives by, to settle debt, 327–28; and Queen Anne's War, 301; regulation of Indian trade by, 324–26; and slave trade, 318–19, *319*; trade by, 319–20, 328; Yamasee War and, 327–28. *See also* Carolina colony; Charles Town

Southeastern Ceremonial Complex (SECC), warfare themes in art of, 367

Southern Natchezans, 370

Southwestern Puebloan Indians, shatter zone and, 377–78

Spanish: colonization of North America, 17, 26, 26T, 41; culture of violence of, 278; Indian slavery and, 377–78; and linking of Native Americans to world capitalist system, 18; military sophistication of, 278; naming of Indians by, 369; and trade with Creeks, 228

Spanish exploration. *See* Ayllón, Lucas Vazquez de; Luna, Tristán de; Pardo, Juan; Ponce de León, Juan; Soto, Hernando de

Spanish Florida: conscripted labor system in, 28; depopulation of,

28–29, 296, 302, 303–5; destruction of chiefdoms in, 38; disease and, 12, 28, 296, 320; future directions for research on, 422; Indian slavery and, 377; Native dependence on trade goods, 27; political unrest, 28; resettlement of, by militaristic slaving societies, 296, 306; settlement of, 26–27, 256–57; trade, 56n77; Yamasees as ally of, 107. *See also* missions; slave raids on Spanish Florida

spheres of exchange: in Indian economies, 345–47; and modalities of exchange, 346, 349; and relationships in exchange, 346, 349–50; in Tiv economy, 343–45, 344T. *See also* economies, non-Western

spheres of exchange in Choctaw economy, 348–55, 355T; impact of slave trade in, 356–59; sources of information on, 347–48, 348T. *See also* economies, Native

Stanyarn, John, 326

Starved Rock Shawnees, 169, 171–72, 176

St. Augustine: disease and, 296; English invasion of, 323; establishment of, 27, 256, 280; slave raids and, 296, 302, 303, 304, 319

St. Catherine's Concession, 400, 401

St. Cosme, Jean-François Buisson de, 388–89, 392, 393–94, 396

Stegge, Thomas I, 93

Stegge, Thomas II, 92–95, 99

Stephen's Bluff mound, 216

Stewart, John, 146, 315, 321, 335–36

Stewart Complex, 244nn91–92

Stewart phase, 189, 196T, *206*, 216, 218, 219, 229, 234

Stiggins, George, 173

Stuart's Town, 299, 300

Sualy, 132

Sucah Town, 148, *153*

Sugaree (Suhere Orata), 111, 125–26

Suhere Orata (Sugaree), 111, 125–26

Suheres (Sugarees), 130, 137

Summerville phase, 333

Summerville I phase, 196T, *199*, 208, 211, 231

Summerville II phase, 196T, *202*, 211

Summerville III phase, 196T, *206*, 211

Summerville IV phase, 196T, *206*, 211, 214, 224–26, 229–30

Susquehannocks, 32, 33, 75, 88, 98–99, 105, 173, 420

Taensa, 372, 378

Tagaya, *116*, 125

Taliepacana, 223, 226, 252, *253*, 254, 255, 258, 259

Talimeco, 117–18

Talisi, 220, 233, 234

Tallapoosas, 35, 196T, 265

talwas (towns), in Creek political organization, 168

Tancha, 304

Tanikoua, 372

Taos Pueblo, 180n5

Taposas, 35

Tasattee, 164

Tascalusa (chief), 8, 220, 221–23, 224, 252, 279

on Native societies, 20, 51n53.
See also European exploration;
Mississippian shatter zone
West Jefferson phase, 196T, *197*,
208–9, 212
Westos: adaptability of, 100; and battle of Bloody Run, 81, 86, 90–92;
cannibalism of, 83, 282; culture
of violence of, 282; destruction
of, 34, 75, 96–97, 106, 137, 147,
149, 283–84; early references to,
in Carolinas, 133; as Eries, 71–72,
82–84, 105, 134, 281; global capitalist economy and, 421; groups included in, 84; guns and, 97, 106–7,
108, 112, 134–35, 137, 282, 297,
298; migration by, 86, 90, 374; as
militaristic slaving society, 33–34;
mourning wars of, 83; Native
fear of, 106, 282; as Neutrals, 84,
134; origin of, 82, 99, 105, 281–82;
Richahecrians as, 66, 105; Shawnee
attacks on, 174; trade, 98–99, 137;
trade agreement with Carolina
colony, 97, 106, 108, 137, 282, 299.
See also Richahecrians
Westos and slave trade, 75, 286; experience with indigenous forms of
slavery, 281; impact on Southern
Indians, 81, 104, 106–12; motivations, 25; preeminence of Westos
as slave raiders, 105; raids in
Carolina colony, 107–8, 134–37,
135; raids in Georgia and Florida,
28, 96, 105, 106–7, 111, 298–99, 301;
raids in Virginia, 59n104; raids
on Coushatta ancestors, 258–59;

survival of militaristic slaving societies, 308; trade agreement with
Carolina colony, 97, 106, 108, 137,
282, 299. *See also* slave raids; slave
trade in Indians
Westover Plantation, 95, 102n42
Westo War of 1680, 106, 137, 283–84,
299
Weyane, *153*
Weyapee Town, *153*
White site, 216
White Woman, 392, 407–8, 410–11
Wiggan, Eleazer, 142, 156, 158n1
Wilbanks phase, 201, 233
Wisacky, 132–33
women, European: captured and
enslaved by Indians, 407–9; living
with Indians, 41
women, Indian: authority of, to decide fate of war captives, 323, 324;
as *micos*, 127; public opinion, 340;
role in Choctaw culture, 339, 354;
role in Natchez culture, 388, 389–
90, 400–404, 406–10; as slaves,
386n78; as war captives, 14–15, 22,
54n64, 278, 323
Wood, Abraham, 94, 95, 99, 105, 165
Woodland Period Indians: Creek
predecessors among, 195–98,
196T, *197*; displacement of from
land base, 163–64, 180n5; population fluctuations in, 366; warfare
among, 366
Woodward, Henry: on Choctaws,
335–36; and Creeks, 75, 300; as experienced trader, 19; exploration
of Carolina Piedmont, 135–37;